NATIONAL GEOGRAPHIC

TRAVELER

Mexico

NATIONAL GEOGRAPHIC

TRAVELER
Mexico

Jane Onstott

National Geographic
Washington, D.C.

Contents

How to use this guide 6–7 About the author 8
The regions 53–346 Travelwise 347–90
Index 391–97 Credits 398–99

Page 1: Wooden
mask, Tzintzuntzan
Pages 2–3: Catedral, San
Cristóbal de las Casas
Left: Cactuses, Baja
California

How to use this guide

See back flap for keys to text and map symbols.

The *National Geographic Traveler* brings you the best of Mexico in text, pictures, and maps. Divided into three main sections, the guide begins with an overview of history and culture. Following are 11 regional chapters with featured sites selected by the author for their particular interest. Each chapter opens with its own contents list.

The regions and sites within the regions are arranged geographically. Some regions are further divided into smaller areas. A map introduces each region, highlighting the featured sites. Walks and drives, plotted on their own maps, suggest routes for discovering an area. Features and sidebars give intriguing detail on history, culture, or contemporary life.

The final section, Travelwise, lists essential information for the traveler—pre-trip planning, special events, getting around, emergencies, and a language guide—plus a selection of hotels, restaurants, shops, activities, and entertainment.

To the best of our knowledge, all information is accurate as of the press date. However, it's always advisable to call ahead when possible.

Color coding

282

Each region is color coded for easy reference. Find the region you want on the map on the front flap, and look for the color flash at the top of the pages of the relevant chapter. Information in **Travelwise** is also color coded to each region.

Museo Nacional de Antropología

- 🅜 178 B2
- ✉ Paseo de la Reforma at Gandhi, Bosque de Chapultepec
- ☎ 55/5553-6243
- www.mna.inah.gob.mx
- 🕒 Closed Mon.
- 💲 $$
- 🚇 Metro: Auditorio

Visitor information

Practical information for most sites is given in the side column (see key to symbols on back flap). The map reference gives the page number of the map and grid reference. Other details are address, telephone number, days closed, entrance charge in a range from $ (under $2) to $$$$$ (over $15), and nearest Metro station for sites in Mexico City. Other sites have information in italics and parentheses in the text.

TRAVELWISE

- Color-coded region name
- Town name
- Hotel name & price range
- Address, telephone & fax numbers
- Brief description of hotel
- Hotel facilities & credit card details
- Restaurant name & price range
- Address & telephone number
- Brief description of restaurant
- Restaurant closures & credit card details

CHIAPAS

COMITÁN

🏨 **LOS LAGOS DE MONTEBELLO**
$
BLVD. BELISARIO DOMINGUEZ NORTE 14
TEL/FAX 963/632-1092
Comitán's fanciest hotel is a lovely but slightly faded keepsake of old-fashioned propriety.
🛏 60 ⬛ 💳 AE, MC, V

🍴 **EL GRECO**
$
CUARTA CALLE SUR OTE. 8
TEL 963/632-5173
The set lunch of this second-story restaurant is an absolutely overwhelming array of local victuals.
🕒 Closed D, Sun. 🚫 No credit cards

Hotel & restaurant prices

An explanation of the price bands used in entries is given in the Hotels & Restaurants section (beginning on p. 356).

REGIONAL MAPS

1 A locator map accompanies each regional map and shows the location of that region in the country.
1 Adjacent regions are shown, each with a page reference.

WALKING TOURS

1 An information box gives the starting and ending points, time and length of walk, and places not to be missed along the route.
1 Where two walks are marked on the map, the second route is shown in orange.

DRIVING TOURS

1 An information box provides details including starting and finishing points, time and length of drive, and places not to be missed along the route, or tips on terrain.

NATIONAL GEOGRAPHIC
TRAVELER
Mexico

About the author

Jane Onstott earned a bachelor of arts degree in Spanish language and Hispanic literature from San Diego State University, with a year's study at Spain's Universidad Complutense de Madrid. Since that time she has lived and traveled extensively in Mexico and throughout Latin America. She worked as Director of Communications and Information for the Charles Darwin Research Station in the Galapagos Islands, Ecuador, and as a Spanish-language interpreter and translator in Mexico and the United States. Since 1986 Ms. Onstott has contributed to travel guides covering Mexico, Ecuador, and the United States. A resident of San Diego County for nearly 30 years, she has written chapters on local art, culture, and dining for the book *San Diego Best Places* (Sasquatch Books) and *Insider's Guide to San Diego* (Globe Pequot Press).

History & culture

A Mixtec priest, illustrated in the Nuttall Codex

Mexico today

IN HIS FASCINATING OPUS *THE LABYRINTH OF SOLITUDE*, NOBEL PRIZE-winning poet and essayist Octavio Paz (1914–1998) calls his countrymen defensive, reticent, and remote. Yet most visitors would characterize their Mexican hosts as congenial, helpful people who love a party. This is just one example of Mexico's many contradictions, surprises, and inconsistencies. Moved and motivated by pathos and sentimentality, Mexicans are intense and passionate, yet hide their emotions under a mask of serenity and indifference.

THE LAND

Mexico radiates from its physical and political heart in the highland Valley of Mexico (Valley of Anáhuac), into which more than one fifth of the nation's population crowds. Built from the remains of the ancient Aztec capital, Tenochtitlán, in 1521, Mexico City is surrounded by some of the nation's most fertile farmlands. While at least half of its acreage is arid or semiarid, Mexico produces most of its own food, especially corn, wheat, soybeans, rice, beans, coffee, cacao, fruit, and vegetables.

This geographically diverse country is, nonetheless, dominated by mountains. Marching south from the U.S. border for around 700 miles (1,120 km) are the eastern and western ranges of the Sierra Madre (literally, "mother mountain"): the Sierra Madre Oriental and the Sierra Madre Occidental. In between, the Mexican Plateau cradles a series of lesser ranges and highland valleys, and in the north, the Chihuahua and Sonora Deserts.

Surrounded by the Pacific Ocean and the Sea of Cortés, the Baja California peninsula is equal parts desert and mountain, with eight main mountain ranges, dozens of islands, and a combined coastline of about 3,000 miles (4,800 km). One of the world's longest and most isolated peninsulas, it was linked top to tip by road only in the 1970s.

A mother lode of precious minerals in the Sierra Madre Occidental and Sierra Madre Oriental made these rugged and frequently inhospitable mountains among the first places explored and settled by the Spanish, and minerals are still an important source of revenue. Mexico leads the world in silver mining; copper, lead, zinc, and salt are important commodities. Especially in the central and northwestern forests, mahogany, walnut, rosewood, and other valuable hardwoods are harvested, as are pines for paper and pulp. Despite legislation in 1988 to promote sustainable development, the practice of cattle ranching, slash-and-burn agriculture, and cutting of trees as a domestic fuel source contribute to deforestation, especially in the poorer southern region. Nature-based tourism, although still in its infancy, may be the solution to providing poor communities with viable alternatives to such destructive ecological practices.

Mountaineers are inspired by some of the continent's tallest peaks—including Pico de Orizaba, Iztaccíhuatl, and La Malinche—that cluster around the 19th parallel in the Neo-Volcanic range, at the southern edge of the Sierra Madre Oriental. Like El Nevado de Colima, on the Pacific coast, Popocatépetl volcano is currently active and closed to climbers; villages on its mountainous slopes and in surrounding valleys have been sporadically evacuated.

Mexico's few lowland areas include the Yucatán Peninsula, an unusual limestone shelf of underground rivers and cenotes (sinkholes) jutting into the Caribbean Sea. Extending north and west from the Yucatán along the Gulf of Mexico is a broad expanse of steamy tropical and semitropical lowlands laced by rivers, swamps, and estuaries. Between that and the narrower, longer Pacific littoral, Mexico has 5,320 miles (8,560 km) of coastline.

Along the Pacific coast and into southern Mexico and Guatemala, the Sierra Madre del Sur and Sierra Madre de Chiapas are two mountain ranges whose isolation has preserved the indigenous cultures of its peoples, but at the cost of such basic services

A street mural dwarfs a young girl in Izamal, Yucatán.

as potable water, sewage systems, schools, hospitals, and electricity.

THE PEOPLE

Few countries in the hemisphere have a greater degree of both *mestizaje* (fusion of indigenous and European blood) and indigenous identity. Nearly 30 percent of Mexicans are indigenous, while about twice that number are mestizos. (Some sources put the number of mestizos higher, with fewer indigenous people.) More than 7 million Mexicans speak an indigenous language or dialect, especially Mayan, Mixtec, Náhuatl, Otomí, Purépecha, and Zapotec. Although it cannot be said that whites (9 percent) make up Mexico's rich elite exclusively, it is safe to say that mestizos and Indians comprise the poor—about 40 percent of the population.

In the 16th century, Spanish invaders brought draft animals and the wheel along with Renaissance-era Romanticism and religious zeal. Dozens of independent and unique cultures were eventually conquered and catechized, although pockets of resistance held out until the 20th century. But many native peoples do retain their indigenous identities. Cultural groups such as the Lacandón and the Huichol, who fled to the dense tropical forests and inhospitable mountains, avoided significant contact with mainstream society until well into the 20th century. Even today, the Huichols living in the western Sierra

Mexico City's 120-foot-tall (36.5 m) Monumento a la Independencia, crowned by "the angel," was erected in 1910 to honor the heroes of the War of Independence.

Madre include few Catholic rituals into their spiritual belief system, retaining their traditional gods and ceremonies.

Most indigenous people, though, have blended their ancient gods and customs with saints and religious rites introduced by the

Two travelers chat outside Mexico City's modernistic Hotel Camino Real, which was designed by architect Ricardo Legorreta (b. 1931) and features the works of major artists.

Spanish. Catholicism is practiced—influenced by modern indifference and indigenous dogma—by 88 percent of the population. Around half of the remainder are evangelical Christians, whose form of Christianity sometimes produces conflict with their neighbors. In highland Chiapas, traditional Tzotzil Indians have in recent decades clashed with large populations of villagers who have been converted to evangelical sects. In larger, more mainstream communities, Protestants and Catholics live and work together peacefully.

Fascinating customs and cultures have attracted adventure travelers for centuries. Writer John Lloyd Stephens's (1805–1852) and artist Frederick Catherwood's (1799–1854) published accounts of buried Maya ruins intrigued the Western world in the 19th century. Since then, writers have praised and scoffed, but rarely remained indifferent to Mexico's charms and idiosyncrasies.

MODERN CHALLENGES

Born in the aftermath of the Revolution, the Institutional Revolutionary Party, or PRI (Partido Revolucionario Institucional), was the official government party since 1929. Polls before the 2000 elections showed that people in the most rural areas believed the PRI and the government to be synonymous, and indeed they had every reason to do so. The party won every presidential election, and most governorships, between 1929 and 1994. Beginning in 1978, opposition parties were admitted in the Lower House, or Cámara de Diputados, to promote an illusion of democratic debate, with no chance to effect real change. However, in the 1997 elections, opposition parties actually won more seats in Congress than the PRI. That same year, leftist candidate Cuauhtémoc Cárdenas, of the Democratic Revolutionary Party, the PRD (Partido de la Revolución Democrática), became the first elected mayor of Mexico City.

A series of significant events in the 1990s continued to mobilize the public for political change. Popular presidential candidate Luis Donaldo Colosio was assassinated in 1994. Outgoing president Carlos Salinas de Gortari—credited during his six-year tenure (1988–1994) with a host of economic advances—left behind a trail of scandal and economic chaos, including devaluation of the peso and a bank bailout costing upward of $93 billion. That same year, a guerrilla army calling itself the Zapatista Army for National

Heading back to Tulum, on the coast of the Yucatán Peninsula, with the early morning catch

Liberation, or EZLN (Ejército Zapatista de Liberación Nacional), seized control of several strategic cities in highland Chiapas. Although they quickly retreated to the forest, their Internet postings and media communiqués have drawn world attention to the plight of the nation's disenfranchised peasant populations.

The prudent economic policies of Salinas's successor, Ernesto Zedillo Ponce de León (1994–2000), helped restore the economy, but more surprising were the political reforms started by the Yale-educated economist. Ahead of the 2000 presidential elections, extensive reforms of electoral institutions and a large presence of foreign observers eliminated many of the usual election day "irregularities" and encouraged the electorate to participate. And instead of picking the presumed successor, a traditional practice since the party's formation, the PRI under Zedillo held a nationwide primary election. The result of these ground-breaking reforms was the election of opposition party candidate Vicente Fox Quesada, of the National Action Party, or PAN (Partido de Acción Nacional), in July 2000. Accepting defeat with good grace, PRI candidate Francisco Labastida helped maintain calm and encouraged a peaceful transition to the historic opposition party government.

But the country's now-divided government (none of the three major parties has a majority in Congress, and the constitutional presidency is inherently weak) has hindered positive change during the Fox administration, and the giant from Guanajuato does not control his party as his PRI predecessors have. Campaign promises have remained largely unfulfilled, and most Mexicans are dissatisfied with Fox's performance. Trade with Canada and the United States has doubled since the North American Free Trade Agreement (NAFTA) went into effect in 1994, but expanded industrialization has fouled rivers and created smog and hazardous-waste disposal problems, traffic congestion, and housing challenges, especially in the cities contiguous to the U.S. border, where industrial growth is greatest. Powerful drug cartels fight among themselves and intimidate, kill, and corrupt police and judges who refuse collusion or attempt to restrict their spheres of influence. Tensions among EZLN supporters and the military persist in Chiapas, and the demands of other small but nonetheless significant guerrilla movements must be addressed to ensure future stability.

Despite these and other difficulties it has faced, Mexico has emerged as an important player in the world economy. It has the 14th

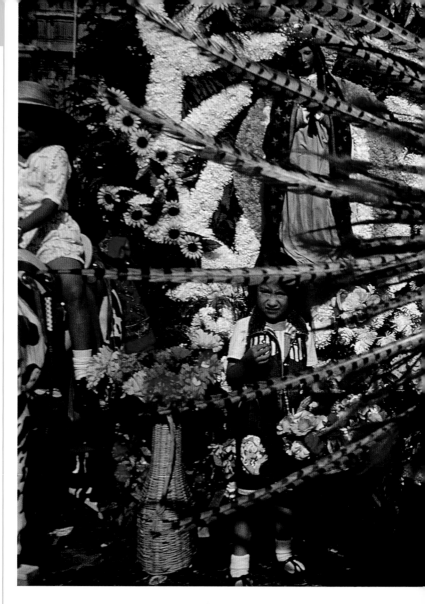

largest gross domestic product in the world, worth some $1,006,000,000,000. Perhaps most important, it has avoided a coup since 1920, longer than any other Latin American nation, and, after years of political demagoguery, is enjoying ever increasing political freedoms.

FESTIVALS & FIESTAS

As a predominantly Catholic country, Mexico celebrates saints' days and other religious holidays with elaborate festivities. Mexicans are great admirers of pyrotechnics and incorporate fireworks whenever possible into their high days and holidays, creating great towers of shooting sparks and rockets that boom throughout the night. They rarely retire early on the night of a fiesta or, for that matter, on the nights preceding it.

Mexico's coastal peoples are especially known for their exuberant fiestas and love of music and dance. The country's most famous Carnaval (pre-Lenten celebration) is held in

Veracruz with masked balls, lavish parades with floats and costumes, and lively all-night street parties. Those of Campeche, Mazatlán, Cozumel, and an increasing number of other communities are also animated, well-attended events. Easter is celebrated with much ceremony; especially moving rituals take place in Oaxaca, San Miguel de Allende, San Luis Potosí, and Taxco. Christmas represents an entire season of family gatherings and special foods, processions, and music.

Celebrating the Festival of the Virgin of Guadalupe, Mexico City

For All Saints' Day and All Souls' Day, families clean and decorate their loved ones' tombs, and in some regions, hold graveside vigils and create lavish home altars in honor of their departed relatives. In Pátzcuaro, Oaxaca, Mérida, and other cities, cultural events and public altars make the family-oriented holiday accessible to visitors. ■

Food & drink

MEXICAN DISHES CAN BE COMPLEX BUT ARE MORE OFTEN SIMPLE AND somewhat subtle. For 5,000 years, corn has reigned as Mexico's most important food, and the plant has religious significance for the Maya, Huichol, and other indigenous groups. Mesoamericans introduced the world to squash (and delicious squash blossoms), beans, chilies, turkey, avocados, tomatoes, sweet potatoes, and chocolate. To this already varied diet the Spanish added wheat (and bread), sugar, rice, and domestic animals: beef and dairy cattle and goats.

With the goats and the dairy cows came cheese. Many varieties are made today, from tangy, crumbly *cotija* to soft, creamy *panela.* Somewhat salty *queso fresco* is crumbled over many savory dishes and served with high-sugar desserts to cut the sweet. From Oaxaca comes *quesillo*, a ball of mild but tangy string cheese. It's used to make *queso fundido*, a delicious cheese fondue served with a stack of flour tortillas and often loaded with mushrooms, chorizo sausage, or strips of mild or hot chilies.

Although tasty homemade flour tortillas typically accompany some dishes, corn tortillas are the traditional staple. Conquistador Hernán Cortés called them maize cakes: flat disks of corn milled with lime and cooked on a hot griddle. Today, neighborhood "factories" produce fresh tortillas throughout the day, although many restaurants and country women make their own. Bread rolls are served in both homes and restaurants, yet to many Mexicans, a traditional meal without tortillas is unthinkable. This said, it's true that the less affluent the family, the more tortillas (in relation to other foods) it probably consumes. For a very poor family, a meal might consist of nothing more than tortillas and salt.

A seemingly endless variety of dishes is prepared with either tortillas or *masa* (finely ground cornmeal). The latter is used to make tamales: dense, rectangular cakes wrapped in corn husks or banana leaves and then steamed. Subtly sweet, plain tamales are served as a light evening meal with coffee or hot chocolate; dessert tamales might surround sweet pineapple chunks; and savory tamales enclose pieces of meat cooked in a chili sauce.

A wide selection of savory snacks is made with tortillas or masa. Although loosely translated as "appetizers," these *antojitos* served at restaurants and from pushcarts are the dishes most foreigners are familiar with. Antojitos also include enchiladas (tortillas smothered in chili sauce) and stuffed tacos and *taquitos,* as well as *chalupas, gorditas,* and *memelas* (griddle-cooked or fried disks of masa topped with crumbled cheese, salsa, onions, and often cilantro).

If each region has its favorite antojitos, each neighborhood has its favorite *taquería.* Specializing in tacos, taquerías range from comfortable restaurants to takeout-only storefronts and bicycle-powered carts. Soft tacos consist of warm tortillas filled with grilled meats and served with a variety of condiments. In a variation, tacos (in this case often called *taquitos*) are rolled around meat or chicken, deep fried, and served with guacamole (avocado sauce) or spicy fresh salsa.

The chili pepper is the tortilla's great companion. From Yucatán's fiery habanero to the relatively mild *chile poblano*, dozens of varieties are used fresh, roasted, or dried. Drying chilies changes both their names and their flavors. For example, the blistering jalapeño when dried produces the distinctive, smoky-tasting *chile chipotle;* the light orange *chile manzano* becomes *chile cascabel.*

Every pepper has a unique flavor. Used blended or chopped, raw or cooked, chilies are combined with onion, garlic, cilantro, and tomatoes (both green and red) to make delicious salsas that accompany almost every meal. Jalapeño and serrano chilies are also served pickled (*en escabeche*), with carrots and onions.

A woman prepares fresh produce for market day in Tlacolula, outside Oaxaca city.

Ground chilies were a key ingredient in *chocolate*, one of the favorite drinks of Aztec royalty. Today, steaming pots of this delicious hot drink are made from bars of bitter chocolate mixed with ground almonds, cinnamon, and sugar. Beaten until frothy, with water or milk, chocolate is a popular accompaniment to a plateful of *pan dulce,*

True tequila is produced only in Jalisco and a few other Mexican states.

or sweet bread. Coffee lovers should try wonderfully aromatic *café de olla,* boiled with cinnamon and *piloncillo* (crude brown sugar). It is definitely more satisfying than the weak *café americano* sold in U.S.-style coffee shops and diners.

Deciding if and when to purchase food from market restaurants, street stands, and itinerant vendors can be difficult. If you strictly avoid all of these, your experience of Mexico will be less than authentic, yet no one wants to risk digestive upset or more serious ailments. There's no guarantee, however, that a prosperous-looking restaurant will be more hygienic than a humble taco stand or a faded

yet well-scrubbed market kitchen. If you decide to go native, head for the most popular stands and check out the vendor and his wares for cleanliness. It's also wise to eat during peak hours, when food is still being freshly prepared and is not left sitting around. Tap water should be strictly avoided. While most vendors do use bottled water in their coffee and other water-based drinks, it's worth investigating if you are in any doubt.

Markets are a great place to mingle with the locals, and are also the place to shop for Mexico's huge variety of tropical and semi-tropical fruits, from which juices and their watered-down counterparts, delicious and refreshing *aguas frescas,* are made. Tourist-oriented restaurants often inexplicably offer only canned or boxed orange, grapefruit, and tomato juices instead of regional favorites such as delightful mango, papaya, guava, and watermelon.

Other popular beverages include *atole* and *horchata.* The former is a thick, filling, slightly sweet drink made of ground rice or cornmeal sweetened with sugar and served warm or at room temperature. The latter is a refreshing cool drink commonly made of filtered rice water, sugar, and cinnamon, sometimes spiked with fresh fruit and almond slivers. Unless the quality of water used is questionable, it's a shame to drink anything out of a can or bottle—with the exception of beer!

Many fine beers are brewed in Mexico. Some are regional, such as Pacífico from Mazatlán, and Montejo and León Negro from the Yucatán; others are seasonal (Noche Buena is sold only around Christmas), but most are fortunately ubiquitous. Baja California's wineries produce wine and brandies of fair to good quality. Cultivated since before the Spanish Conquest, the agave plant produces pulque, a rather gooey, fermented alcoholic beverage—definitely an acquired taste. More palatable are the distilled agave products mescal and tequila (see p. 154).

Mexico is a huge country, and the cuisine varies with the landscape and regional culture. With thousands of miles of coastline, it is known for fresh seafood, and in places such as Cabo San Lucas, at the tip of Baja, chefs have finally gone beyond simple grilling or pan-frying with garlic *(al mojo de ajo)* to add sashimi, sushi, and inspired sauces to their menus. Still, dishes such as *huauchinango a la veracruzana* remain universally popular. Grilled whole with tomato, chili, onion, garlic, parsley, capers, and green olives, Veracruz's version of red snapper is a Mexican standard. Also popular is *ceviche*, any firm, white fish marinated in lime juice and served with fresh chopped onion, chile, tomato, and cilantro. (To make it more hygienic, many cooks briefly boil the fish before "cooking" it in lime.) Depending on the local catch, conch, octopus, or shrimp may be used as well.

Meat is the mainstay of the northern diet, often accompanied by *frijoles charros* (beans cooked with pork rind) and flour tortillas. As well as various types of dried, grilled, and shredded beef, northerners are fond of *cabrito,* or barbecued goat. From the north also come *huevos rancheros* (ranch-style eggs): delicious, sunny-side-up eggs served on a lightly fried corn tortilla and smothered in a mild cooked salsa. This and other breakfast favorites are often accompanied by beans and a basket of fresh tortillas.

Some of the most unusual dishes come from central and southern Mexico. Seven vastly different mole sauces are made in the state of Oaxaca alone. Among the principle ingredients of *mole verde* are pumpkin seeds (*pipián*) and chilies, which produce the green color for which it is named. Fruits and raisins make *mole mancha manteles* bright red: the name means "tablecloth-staining." The classic *mole negro* (black mole, or in Puebla, *mole poblano*) combines such diverse ingredients as stale tortillas, sesame seeds, chilies, chocolate, nuts, peppercorns, and cloves, among about a dozen others. Thought to have been invented by a Puebla nun, this convoluted recipe represents Mexican cuisine at its most complex. Cooks from Tlaxcala, Puebla, and Oaxaca compete to create the most savory adaptation.

The Yucatán Peninsula has its share of unusual and flavorful recipes, especially those from Mérida, where French, Spanish, and Lebanese immigrants have influenced dishes. Locally grown sour oranges are the key to marinated *poc chuc,* savory pork grilled with onions, tomatoes, and garlic. Venison has all but disappeared from menus, but *pollo*

(chicken) and *cochinita* (pork) *pibil* are still seasoned with pungent *achiote* paste, made from the seed of the annatto tree, and cooked in a traditional pit.

Although deer have been hunted nearly to extinction, animals and plants from pre-Hispanic America are still eaten. Worms from the agave fields (*gusanos de maguey)* and

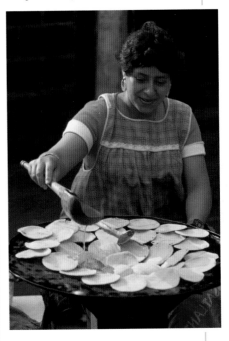

What Hernán Cortés called "maize cakes" are still eaten in many forms.

highly salted and seasoned grasshoppers (*chapulines*) from Oaxaca are fried and sold by the scoop in markets, but also appear in expensive restaurants serving nouvelle Mexican cuisine. Other delicacies include *escamoles* (ant eggs) and *huitlacoche* (black corn fungus), the latter found in crêpes and quesadillas (flour tortillas with melted cheese), as well as in more exotic recipes. With so many unusual foods to try, why settle for a hamburger and soft drink from the inevitable chain restaurant? Right down the road, you might find freshly grilled prickly-pear cactus pads (spines removed) served with a cool glass of cantaloupe juice. ■

History of Mexico

ANCIENT PEOPLES LIVED BY THE RHYTHM OF THE SEASONS, EMPLOYING sun- and moon-based calendars much as we do today, and attuning themselves to a 52-year cycle that may have been respected as far back as the end of the Pleistocene period. Within these circles of time, great civilizations were born and buried, some living in isolation, but most trading and interacting with others from as far off as the Great Plains of the United States and the mountainous spine of Peru. No less fascinating is the history of colonial and modern Mexico, which has blended European and indigenous world views to forge one of the most important developing nations.

EARLY HUMANS

Many scholars agree that some 30,000 or even 40,000 years ago, during the late Pleistocene, humans crossed the Bering Sea from northeastern Asia to North America. Fanning across the continents, family units occupied caves and other available shelters, hunting small game and gathering food.

In the pre-Hispanic era (before the Spanish Conquest), two distinct zones composed the land we now call Mexico. Roughly north of Tampico and the tip of Baja California, extending into today's central United States, were the great, hot deserts and sweeping plains referred to as la Gran Chichimeca. Long after the arrival of European explorers, individual tribes of nomadic hunter-gatherers, collectively referred to as Chichimecas, eked out an existence in this harsh environment. In times of scarcity and drought, they were likely to rain down on the farming villages to the south in a storm of chaos and destruction.

Extending south of la Gran Chichimeca all the way to northern Honduras and El Salvador was a geographic and cultural zone now referred to as Mesoamerica. By the Archaic period (7000–1500 B.C.), many tribes had abandoned the nomadic lifestyle, establishing more sedentary villages. By about 3000 B.C., while still seasonally gathering seeds and fruit, clans had domesticated corn, which they cultivated along with squash, chili peppers, avocados, and a wide variety of other foods. By 1500 B.C., simple agricultural societies existed throughout the region.

Compelling archaeological evidence demonstrates that early Mesoamericans had contact with South American tribes. Seafaring peoples from around Ecuador and Peru brought new and improved varieties of corn, which were successfully crossed with native species. These itinerant traders also introduced fired pottery to the west coast peoples, as well as metallurgy, which was practiced only among the Purépecha (Tarascans) and the Mixtecs (based, respectively, in modern-day Michoacán and Oaxaca). Even the Purépecha language, which is unlike any in North America, has been linked linguistically to Quechua, the language of Peru.

During the early Preclassic, or Formative era (1500 B.C.–A.D. 150), certain societies became sufficiently large and differentiated by class to bring about the construction of impressive public buildings. These required an enormous commitment of man-hours, since neither beasts of burden nor the wheel were available. Among the earliest known examples of this public architecture is a massive artificial plateau, or early pyramid, built around 1350 B.C. at San Lorenzo, in Veracruz.

THE MOTHER CULTURE

The San Lorenzo pyramid was built by the Olmecs, the oldest known civilization in North America. Olmec society was stratified, with an elite class governing nonfarming classes of priests and artisans and a vast plebeian majority. Fertile tropical lowlands with extreme rainfall easily supported slash-and-burn agriculture, and the region's many rivers, lagoons, and estuaries provided an extensive transportation system.

Although there is some early evidence of Olmec culture on the southern Pacific coast, the first great centers were built along the

The smallest of such characteristic Olmec stone "portrait" heads discovered to date weighs 8 tons (8,100 kg).

Gulf, in southern Veracruz and Tabasco. For years the origins of the Olmec language eluded linguists, until clues carved in hieroglyphic writings showed it to be derivative of that of the Mixe-Zoques, whose descendants still inhabit the Pacific coast of Oaxaca and Chiapas states.

San Lorenzo was the first known Olmec city, at its apogee between about 1150 and 900 B.C. Other nearby cities later gained preeminence, including La Venta, Tres Zapotes, and Laguna de los Cerros. At San Lorenzo, rainwater was diverted from the pyramid by drains of basalt. Quarried in the Tuxtla Mountains near Laguna de los Cerros and at other sites, the stone was rolled, dragged, and floated to San Lorenzo in uncanny feats of engineering. Thrones, stelae, and other monumental works of artistry were created, including immense stone heads thought to honor important rulers.

Other forms of art characteristic of the Olmec are its exquisite masks and portable statuettes. Many of these pieces portray deities such as the jaguar and a half-man, half-jaguar being, which may have represented a bridge between the feline god and the ruling dynasty. Jade, greenstone, obsidian, and other materials were imported, as were agricultural products. Olmec exports, including carved symbolic axheads of jade and carved wooden and stone masks and figurines, have been found as far north as Tlatilco, in the Valley of Mexico, and south to the highlands of El Salvador. Although cultural borrowing among highland and Gulf coast cultures was a two-way street, the major artistic, intellectual, and political contributions came from the Olmecs.

As the Olmec culture waned in importance in the tenth century B.C., other cities and citystates emerged in Oaxaca and the highland valleys of central Mexico. Strategically perched above the confluence of three valleys in Oaxaca, Monte Albán prospered from about 500 B.C. At Cuicuilco, south of Mexico City, the round, terraced pyramid built around 400 B.C. (and engulfed by lava from the nearby Xitle volcano some 500 years later) was one of the earliest and most unusual structures of the Preclassic period.

In the Soconusco region of Chiapas, Izapa forms an important link between Olmec and

Maya cultures. This large city peaked in size and artistic achievement between about 300 and 50 B.C., when its inhabitants carved a great number of stelae in a highly narrative, pictorial style similar to those produced in early Maya art. Scattered throughout the region, these monuments demonstrate a devotion to rituals tied to astronomy, agricultural cycles, fertility, and other natural events. Significant similarities between the Maya and the Olmecs include representations of a "Long-Lipped God" (precursor to the Maya rain god Chac, also spelled Chaac) and the use of Long Count (see below) date glyphs. Some experts attribute the latter to the Maya; equally reputable scholars credit the Olmec. The same debate surrounds the earliest hieroglyphic writing system.

CLASSIC CIVILIZATIONS

One of Mexico's earliest and most fascinating civilizations was that of the ancient Maya, who occupied the Yucatán Peninsula, as well as the highlands and lowlands of Chiapas and Central America. (With 3 million people, the Maya today constitute Mexico's largest indigenous population, and many still practice ancient ways.) Maya culture began to blossom just before the Christian era. Its cities produced learned mathematicians as well as artists and architects. With none of the instruments known to the modern world, the Maya achieved great accuracy in astronomy. They had a place-value system of numbers and used several different calendars, including a 365-day solar calendar and a 260-day ritual calendar. The two calendars were meshed to

Battle scenes like those in this ancient fresco at Bonampak helped disprove early theories of Maya pacifism.

produce a 52-year cycle in which each day had prophetic significance. Although other ancient civilizations used these cyclical calendars, only the Olmec and the Maya used the Long Count, a noncyclical calendar. It had a definite start date (by Western reckoning August 11, 3114 B.C.) and was used to record historical events. The Maya also used the most sophisticated system of writing in Mesoamerica: a phonetic script often employing rebuses, or written puns.

The Mayas' exquisite palaces and temples of quarried limestone were faced with brightly painted plaster. Where stone was plentiful, elaborate pictorial and hieroglyphic messages were carved into limestone lintels and stelae. Elsewhere throughout the Maya world, modeled and carved stucco was used to glorify births, marriages, deaths, victories in battle, and other momentous events involving the royal families.

While most Preclassic Maya cities were rather isolated and autonomous, extensive communication characterized the Classic Maya civilizations. "White roads" *(sacbeób),* elevated highways raised up to 15 feet (4.5 m) above the surrounding jungle, gleamed white in the Maya night, possibly to aid couriers who traveled between cities during the cooler hours. These roads, paved with flat stones and stucco, may have served military and religious purposes as well as facilitating commerce and transportation. White roads not only joined one city to another, but also were internal roadways, linking the most important buildings within a city, possibly to help transport icons from temple to temple.

Early on, the Maya established trade with Teotihuacán, in central Mexico, built by a Totonac-speaking people from the Gulf coast. Teotihuacán, in turn, traded as far north as the Oasis America tribes of northern Mexico and the southwestern United States. Like the Maya, the Teotihuacanos were mathematicians and astronomers. Hundreds of years after the demise of the great city of Teotihuacán, Aztec lords made pilgrimages to the ruins to consult with the gods and to bring home relics for their own palaces and altars. According to Aztec legends, the gods gathered there to

Statues of the lesser god Chac Mool, such as this one at Chichén Itzá, have been found from the Yucatán to the central plateau.

Teotihuacán fell into ruin around A.D. 600, when some of its most important buildings appear to have been purposefully burned or dismantled. In Oaxaca, Monte Albán was abandoned around 700, and the decline of the great Maya cities began about a hundred years later. For no obvious reason, ceremonial centers were left by their creators to crumble, often to be reused later by others as places of worship or as burial grounds.

POSTCLASSIC MESOAMERICA

While previously accepted theories held that Classic Maya cities were brought down by peasant revolts, there was actually a relatively smooth and seamless transition to the Postclassic phase between approximately A.D. 900 and 1200. The most important distinction between the Classic and Postclassic eras was the substitution of tribal councils for the kingdoms that had previously ruled. After 1200, monumental art depicting the glories of kings and queens was replaced with more utilitarian public art and architecture.

Another popular misconception regarding the Postclassic era (900–1521) in general is that it was characterized by a breakdown of society and increased warfare. Upon reexamining the evidence, however, most archaeologists agree that warfare and ritual sacrifice continued more or less apace during the period preceding the Spanish Conquest (1521). The clearest example of this is shown in the rise of the Mexica, or Aztecs (see p. 184), an extremely warlike people who sacrificed victims in truly astonishing numbers.

Ritual sacrifice took place throughout Mesoamerica. The standard practice was to rip out the victim's heart with a ceremonial flint knife. Other unfortunates were trussed and rolled down steep pyramids, shot with arrows, or slow roasted on a Divine Hearth. Prior to crop planting, children were sacrificed to appease Tláloc; their frantic cries were thought to please the rain god. In acts of self-sacrifice, nobles bled their arms, tongues, earlobes, and genitals for penitence and purification.

Later played as a spectator sport among traveling teams, pre-Hispanic ball games originated as one-on-one contests of life and death among rival lords. Important captives taken in war were subjected to a ritual ball game in

bring about the current era—the Fifth Sun—sacrificing themselves and in the process creating the sun and the moon. These celestial bodies, honored in two of the largest pyramids in the Western Hemisphere—the Pirámide del Sol and Pirámide de la Luna—would, along with all else in the world, disappear in the inevitable demise of the Fifth Sun, as the previous four worlds had been cataclysmically undone. Mesoamericans expected the world to end and begin anew with each successive era, or "sun." The epoch of the Fifth Sun was expected to be wiped out by earthquakes at the end of one of the 52-year cycles.

which death to the loser assured perpetuation of life and continued success for the winning tribe. The games, played on a rectangular court, had variations, but usually involved using the hips, legs, and arms to pass a small, solid rubber ball through a stone hoop.

Fearing the threat of sacrifice less than a tortuous death during the worst droughts,

The long and triumphant reign of Moctezuma Xocoyotzin (R.1502–1520) was ended by Hernán Cortés.

Chichimec tribes periodically migrated south. The result of one such incursion was the settlement of Tula, north of the Valley of Mexico. The Chichimeca-Tolteca (more commonly called the Toltecs) soon established themselves as people of culture and learning.

For years archaeologists theorized, excavated, and debated to determine whether the Toltecs had, through trade or conquest, come to influence the important Maya site of Chichén Itzá on the Yucatán Peninsula. Conclusive evidence has shown, however, that Tula was actually a trading outpost of Chichén Itzá, and that Maya influence traveled north

to the central plateau as much as, if not more than, it flowed south. The last of the important Chichimec tribes to migrate south were the Aztecs, or Mexica, who wandered from a place they called Aztlán (meaning "place of herons") to found a city in the middle of Lake Texcoco, in the Valley of Mexico, in the late 13th century. In a few hundred years, the Aztecs rose from illiterate nomads from the north to the dominant force in Mesoamerica. With its extensive marketplaces, fine palaces filled with richly dressed lords and ladies, and impressive temples housing a panoply of gods, the city of Tenochtitlán astounded the invading Spaniards. Well-engineered causeways linked the island city to the mainland, and "floating" gardens surrounding the city (see p. 208) provided a ready source of food.

When future conqueror of New Spain Hernán Cortés was two years old, in 1487, up to 80,000 people may have been sacrificed during the dedication of a new temple in Tenochtitlán. Beaten nonstop during the four-day bloodbath, snakeskin drums marked the rise and fall of flint knives as black-painted priests, their long hair matted with blood, ritually sacrificed victims to the war god Huitzilopochtli.

During the reign of Moctezuma Ilhuicamina (Moctezuma I, *R.*1440–1469), Flower Wars were introduced with the purpose of providing rival armies with soldiers for sacrifice. Although the Flower Wars were sham conflicts (a fact the soldiers were not privy to), most of the battles unleashed by the Aztecs were thoroughly real and rarely lost. The Aztecs controlled some 370 cities and had a standing army of 150,000 soldiers, with more in reserve.

One kingdom the Aztecs never conquered was that of the Purépecha, or Tarascans, of Michoacán in the Central Highlands. As one of the few Mesoamerican peoples to use metallurgy, the Purépecha had a definite edge on the battlefield with their bronze weapons. They also differed from other cultured Mesoamerican tribes in religion. Ignoring the rain god Tláloc and other deities so important to their neighbors, the Purépecha worshiped a family of related gods and goddesses linked to creatures of the heavens, Earth, and the underworld.

CONQUEST & EARLY COLONIZATION

Into this world of power, conflict, and beauty burst a new (and in many ways equally violent) enemy: Spain. In the name of Emperor Charles V, Hernán Cortés (1485–1547) and his troops brought the supposed salvation of Christianity and the undeniable curse of serfdom. The Europeans also introduced the wheel, firearms, and beasts of burden, and spread the concept of metallurgy.

An inspired military leader and fervent Catholic, Cortés was driven nearly as much by a love of adventure and a sincere motivation to Christianize the Indians as by a desire for gold and other treasures. Cortés was initially commissioned to explore and chart new lands to the west by the governor of Cuba. Ignoring orders to return to Cuba and relinquish his command, he and his relatively small army were soon involved in skirmishes with native peoples who had been tested and hardened by internal wars and conflicts with the Aztecs. During these early battles the Aztecs' foes and vassals were impressed with the Spaniards' horses and firearms, and other previously unknown accouterments of combat. All of this was reported to Emperor Moctezuma II (*R.*1502–1520), in Tenochtitlán.

The emperor had cause for concern. Ancient prophesy predicted the year 1 Reed, during which Cortés appeared from the east, as the year in which the god-king Quetzalcóatl would return to reclaim his throne, abandoned several centuries before. Wielding booming cannons and commanding strange, armored beasts (horses), Cortés was initially thought to be Quetzalcóatl, and Moctezuma sent gifts of gold, fine garments, and rich food to the Spanish bivouacked on the coast, while simultaneously begging them to return from wherever they came.

Bent on finding the source of the golden treasures and meeting the legendary Aztec leader, Cortés and his most trusted captains scuttled their ships to dispel any thoughts of retreat. They preserved sails and hardware, however, which were used to outfit boats built two years later during a four-month siege that demolished the Aztec capital at Tenochtitlán.

Details of the Spanish battles, alliances, and eventual conquest were recorded by Bernal Díaz, a soldier, who later described them in a fascinating narrative entitled *True History of the Conquest of New Spain*. One detail not overlooked by the sagacious soldier was the importance of the two translators—Jerónimo de Aguilar and la Malinche. The former was a Spanish soldier shipwrecked on a previous expedition and enslaved by the Maya. When

The indigenous culture variously impressed, astonished, and horrified the Spaniard Hernán Cortés.

returned to Cortés, he spoke Mayan and Spanish. A young girl of noble descent, la Malinche had been sold into slavery in Tabasco, and thus spoke Mayan and classical Náhuatl, the Aztec tongue.

La Malinche, baptized and renamed doña Marina by the Spaniards, proved especially helpful to them, with her well-worded translations, grasp of politics, and ability to turn potential foes into allies. Despite horses, cannons, and other military advantages, the Spanish Conquest would not have been possible without the allied strength of Aztec foes: the Tlaxcalans, Totonacs, and, as the end drew near, some of the subject kingdoms that surrounded Tenochtitlán.

Before waging outright war on the Aztecs, a large contingency of Spanish soldiers was entertained for months in the fortified city of Tenochtitlán, almost as captive guests. Emperor Moctezuma wavered between friend and foe as an increasingly indignant retinue of nobles and priests urged him to sacrifice the Spanish to Huitlzilopochtli, god of war. Soon held hostage by his guests and dismissed by his detractors, Moctezuma was killed by his own people during a battle. Afterward, Cortés, la Malinche, and some of the remaining soldiers fled the capital in a daring nighttime exodus.

The last Aztec emperor, Cuauhtémoc (R.1520–1521), was captured and, when he refused to reveal a cache of gold and treasure, was subsequently tortured and hanged. La Ciudad de México, or Mexico City, was raised from the rubble of Tenochtitlán using the forced labor of the conquered people. Favored by fate, his own cunning, and the bravery of his Spanish soldiers, Cortés had crushed the mighty Aztec empire just two years after landing in the New World.

In the chaotic early years of the colony, plebeians who had suffered under the Aztec regime saw one harsh reality replaced with another. And while they would avoid the dreaded sacrificial slab, they were statistically more likely to be worked to death in a mine or dispatched by smallpox, measles, or some other imported disease. Millions of Indians died in the first hundred years of Spanish

Depiction of the Cholula battle (1519), which took place before the conquest of Mexico

domination, possibly more than 90 percent of the indigenous population.

The New World was ruled by a viceregal system. Under the viceroy (answerable only to the king of Spain) were *audiencias* (judicial bodies) in Mexico City and Guadalajara, which controlled a hierarchy of officials, each serving at the whim of his superior. Enormous land grants *(encomiendas)* were awarded to some individuals *(encomendados),* and despite regulations their word was virtually law. Unlike the New England settlers, who drove the indigenous people from their lands (and much later herded them into reservations), Mexico's conquerors interacted with the native

people, depending on Indian labor to work the mines and fields and help run their households.

The conquerors were given girls and women by the tribes they bested in battle, and by the Aztecs who initially treated them as honored guests, producing a caste called mestizos (part European, part Indian). The settlers kept concubines, or less often, took Indian women as legitimate wives.

Unlike the Aztec nobles, who accepted the offspring of their mistresses and raised them in privilege, most Spaniards refused to recognize their bastard children. Consequently, the first generations of mestizos enjoyed no legal status whatsoever. Largely spurned by both Indians and whites, a renegade class was created, with no cultural group and no place within the emerging colony.

Although Indians and mestizos generally suffered ignoble lives, indigenous lords and other lucky individuals who swore fealty to the king were named local strongmen, or caciques, and became bosses ruling over their former dominions. Both caciques and encomendados demanded large amounts of tribute from the peasants, and, whenever possible, usurped Indian lands.

To escape virtual slavery on the encomiendas (and later, on the haciendas that ruled rural Mexico until the 20th century), some Indians fled to the stark deserts or the most inhospitable mountain ranges. Many of those who remained flocked for Catholic baptism, encouraged by the appearance in 1531 of the dark-skinned Virgin of Guadalupe near a shrine to the Indian goddess Tonántzin (see p. 193).

For nearly three centuries of colonial rule, enormous mineral wealth and free or nearly free labor brought great riches to Spain. In the Sierra Madre, gold, silver, iron, zinc, and other minerals also created fabulous personal fortunes. In the wake of the miners, or sometimes leading the way, religious orders established mission churches to convert the natives to Christianity. First to arrive were the Franciscans, who set about catechizing the surrounding areas, followed shortly by the Dominicans, Augustinians, and others. The Jesuits and Franciscans braved the hinterlands of the north and (with the Dominicans) the difficult terrain of Baja California. The Jesuits were expelled from New Spain in 1767 by King

Charles III, who was convinced by rival orders that they were becoming too influential.

INDEPENDENCE

Rich in land and prosperous mines, the Catholic Church was a powerful force in colonial Mexico. Government was weak, and largely controlled by the Church and rich,

Benito Juárez spoke Zapotec before Spanish, and studied for the priesthood before switching to law.

influential families. Despite the wealth and power of some *criollos* (people of Spanish descent born in Mexico), their class did not enjoy all the privileges afforded *peninsulares,* Spaniards born in Spain. Inspired by the American Revolution and the ideals of the Enlightenment—the 18th-century movement rejecting traditional European agendas in favor of more pragmatic approaches to society's problems—dissatisfied criollos and priests bent on social reform began to plot independence in the early 19th century.

Royalist forces learned of a conspiracy in 1810, and the Independence Movement was launched a bit sooner than planned under priest Miguel Hidalgo y Costilla (1753–1811) and intellectuals from Morelia and Querétaro. Not all of Mexico was united in the cause. Isolated Yucatán, for example, had more ties to Europe than to Mexico City. And most peninsulares, having little if anything to gain from independence, remained loyal to Spain.

After initial rebel victories, the Royalists regrouped. The war dragged on with isolated insurgent attacks and little chance of a full-scale success on either side. Also called the "Plan of Three Guarantees" (which were for Mexico to remain Catholic, to be headed by a constitutional monarch, and to guarantee the same rights to those born in the New World as those born in Spain), the Plan de Iguala was signed by Agustín de Iturbide (1783–1824) and rebel leader Vicente Guerrero in 1821. Spain barely opposed losing the colony, and signed the Treaty of Córdoba that same year, through which the conditions set forth in the Plan de Iguala were implemented. According to the agreed-upon covenant, the rich resumed their lives of privilege while the poor remained their chattels. Catholicism continued as the official religion of Mexico.

What followed was a half century of reconstruction and political and economic chaos. Agustín de Iturbide reigned for less than a year as head of the new constitutional monarchy before being forced into exile. After his ousting, a succession of feeble and impoverished governments took turns overthrowing one another. Antonio López de Santa Anna (1794–1876), an energetic general from Veracruz, acted as president on multiple occasions, in between starting and stopping various rebellions throughout the nation. In the countryside, the *campesinos* were ruthlessly exploited as large landholders stole communal lands and the caciques (see p. 31) terrorized anyone who was bold enough to complain.

The weak central government invited foreign intervention. In 1838 the French blockaded the port of Veracruz during the Pastry War, a dispute over damages suffered by a baker and other French nationals during earlier riots in Mexico City. In 1846 the United States declared war on Mexico on trumped-up complaints in order to annex Texas and coveted lands to the west. Landing at Veracruz,

U.S. troops soon captured the Mexican garrison at Chapultepec Castle, Mexico City. As a result of the Mexican-American War (1846–48), the United States gained Texas, New Mexico, Arizona, and Alta California; Mexico lost half of its territory, retaining the Baja California peninsula and lands south of the Río Bravo (called the Rio Grande in the United States).

During the war, fearful whites in the isolated Yucatán Peninsula formed a Maya army, which immediately turned its weapons on the wealthy elite who had so incautiously armed it. Unsophisticated in waging war, the Maya, after launching bloody raids that struck fear into the rich Spanish landholders, succeeded in taking the most important cities and towns of the peninsula. With no desire to rule, they merely wanted revenge and the return of their ancestral lands, and after their few successes simply laid down their weapons and returned to the seasonal planting. But they had not calculated the consequences of their actions. The whites and mestizos reorganized themselves and counterattacked. About half of the Yucatán Maya population was murdered in the ensuing reprisals.

In the ensuing political chaos, Zapotec lawyer Benito Juárez (1806–1872) helped promulgate the Reform Laws, intended primarily to separate Church and state and to reduce the influence of the Church. The ensuing Reform Wars (1858–61) were eventually won by the liberals under Juárez. But empty national coffers forced him to default on international debts, giving France an excuse for invading Mexico and installing (with the approbation of the conservatives) the Austrian Maximilian of Habsburg (1832–1867) as emperor. A short-lived but symbolically important victory against the French invaders was won on May 5, 1862. Young and poorly armed, the defenders routed the French military contingent in a battle that is reenacted each year in Puebla and celebrated throughout the country.

The Second Empire, as it was called, lasted but three short years (1864–67). A just man, Maximilian angered the conservatives by refusing to retract liberal reforms. Still, a foreign king ruling Mexico suited nearly no one, and after French troops were recalled to fight Prussia, the emperor was captured and executed in Querétaro in 1867. President-in-exile Benito Juárez returned to rule the nation for nearly five years before dying of a heart attack in 1872.

Despite his intentions, Juárez's policy of confiscating church property had a disastrous effect on indigenous people. Church lands communally worked by campesino farmers

Porfirio Díaz's dictatorial presidency spanned more than three decades.

were auctioned and snatched up by wealthy hacienda owners. Many indigenous and mestizo campesinos were then forced to work for slave wages on fields they had formerly tilled for their own families.

THE PORFIRIATO

While Juárez is nonetheless lauded as a hero, Porfirio Díaz, who came to power in 1876, is a more controversial figure. Under Díaz, economic and political stability was finally achieved. Construction of an extensive railway system moved goods for national and international consumption, mining and other industries prospered, and foreign investment boomed. A great admirer of European art and architecture, the Oaxaca-born mestizo commissioned luxurious public buildings during his 33-year presidency, which was in reality a thinly veiled dictatorship.

The Porfiriato (era of Porfirio Díaz) revived the economy, restored order out of chaos, and created public works. However, journalistic freedom and political dialogue were strongly repressed, and a national police force, *los rurales,* snuffed out any protest in the countryside. Although an emerging middle class did benefit from a form of trickle-down economics, the peasantry suffered the usual indignities: their lands were illegally confiscated and their people tied to large haciendas by debt-peonage. In a situation that was tantamount to slavery, poor peasants were paid a pittance and bound to the estate on which they worked by debts incurred from purchases such as soap, corn, and coffee from the plantation store. Subsequent generations were held responsible for their forefathers' debts, and so remained trapped by the hacienda system.

REVOLUTION & RECONSTRUCTION

Under the banner of "Effective suffrage, no reelection!", the wealthy, reserved Francisco I. Madero (1873–1913) mobilized the Mexican public against the patriarch Díaz, who was exiled to Europe in 1911. Despite early hopes for a peaceful transition to a more egalitarian system, a lack of consensus on reform agendas soon divided military leaders with wildly disparate goals. Madero's agenda was political reform. In Morelos, south of Mexico City, Emiliano Zapata (1879–1919) fervently demanded the return of stolen communal lands and other agrarian reforms to benefit dispossessed peasants.

Treachery characterized the long and bloody Revolutionary War (1911–17). As president of the republic, Madero was jailed and then assassinated by dissatisfied generals. Zapata was killed in a perfidious ambush arranged by the rival revolutionary (and landowner) Venustiano Carranza (1859–1920). Charismatic (but often unduly violent) military tactician Pancho Villa (1878–1923) was murdered in an ambush several years after the end of fighting.

The Revolution cost approximately two million lives, and many of the victims were unarmed civilians. The conflict dragged on until 1920, when the ideals of the Constitution of 1917 were adopted. The country was economically devastated by years of war. Political unrest reigned, and subsequent transfers of presidential power through nominal elections were accompanied by revolts and instability.

The Constitution promised agrarian reform, but redistribution of land was ignored until General Lázaro Cárdenas del Río (1895–1970) was elected president in 1934. Truly committed to the poor, the mestizo from Michoacán expropriated and redistributed nearly 50 million acres (20 million ha), creating 180,000 *ejidos,* or communal farms. Alarming foreign investors and governments and conservative nationals, Cárdenas's most sweeping reforms were to nationalize the railroads and the oil companies. While encouraging unions and labor organizations, he eliminated the cronies of his predecessor, Plutarco Elías Calles, who had—as tradition dictated—chosen him as successor to the presidency.

It was Calles who enforced previously ignored articles of the new Constitution limiting the power of the Church. When the incensed clergy urged boycotts of church services, enraged Catholics began fighting detractors in grisly street battles. Even after the insurgency, later dubbed the Cristero Revolt , was put down, temples were ransacked and colonial art stolen. The Church's long-standing influence in affairs of state had ended, although most of Mexico's population remained staunchly Catholic.

Supporters of Venustiano Carranza, head of the new government in 1916, pass through the U.S. 6th Infantry's camp near San Antonio, Mexico, on their way to fight Pancho Villa.

TWENTIETH-CENTURY MEXICO
Before 1910, Mexico City was a quiet capital with colonial churches, surrounded by traditional indigenous villages. The Revolution's unrest brought country people to the safety of the capital, where many remained. During World War II, Mexico was launched into the industrial era, and waves of workers relocated to the capital to fill factory jobs. President Miguel Alemán (1946–1952) encouraged development of infrastructure and attracted foreign and national investment in industry.

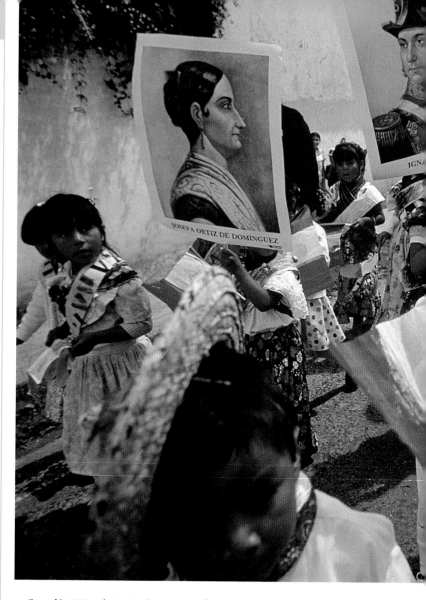

Created in 1929 as the National Revolutionary Party, or PNR, the Institutional Revolutionary Party (PRI) became the official government party, adopting the tricolor of the Mexican flag and ruling with virtual impunity. Internal squabbles and an inability to capitalize on the discontent of campesinos (poor farmers and rural dwellers) and the middle classes rendered the opposition parties totally ineffective, and enabled the PRI to maintain the status quo. From 1929 until 2000, the PRI never lost a presidential election.

World War II brought industrialization to Mexico, after which the country's economy continued to grow. But a population explosion resulted in an ever increasing number of poor, and reforms by Adolfo Ruiz Cortines (1952–1958) and others never truly eased their burden. Heavy investment in petroleum production left the economy vulnerable to fluctuations in the world market for this commodity, and the drop in oil prices in the early

Independence Day parade, San Cristóbal de las Casas

1980s led to recession and huge foreign debt. But although discontent was manifested to one degree or another under various PRI presidencies, the country's system of one-party politics was never seriously challenged.

So Mexicans were stunned, and many jubilant, when in 2000 former Coca-Cola executive and Guanajuato state governor Vicente Fox Quesada was elected president for slightly-right-of-center PAN, the National Action Party.

Political reform has come about slowly, but considering the depth of cronyism and corruption, remarkably peacefully. Despite Mr. Fox's lack of accomplishment, it's been a historic administration. How the voters (discouragingly apathetic in 2003 midterm elections) will vote in 2006 is the subject of intense debate and speculation both within Mexico and around the world. ■

The arts

INFLUENCED BY ITS MULTIETHNIC ROOTS, MEXICAN CULTURE IS AS expressive and varied as the landscape. Spanish baroque architecture quickly mutated to become Mexican baroque, inspired by indigenous themes and a passion for abundance and flamboyance. Folk-dance troupes re-create pre-Hispanic dances in *belle époque* theaters, while in the craggy Sierra Madre, Yaqui men still perform the Deer Dance (*Danza del Venado*) for its original, spiritual purpose. Mestizo culture can be admired in the nation's regional dances, many of which attuned immigrants' instruments and dance steps to an entirely Mexican sensibility.

ARCHITECTURE

Before the Conquest, Mesoamerica's oldest cities and ceremonial centers were laid out much like modern towns. Temples and palaces framed a central plaza, or *zócalo*, in the heart of the town. Along one side was a church; along another the most important public buildings, including the seat of local government. Nearby plazas held open-air markets, and side roads led to businesses and residential neighborhoods. Stone, adobe, and mortar were the main building materials, supplemented by wood and natural fibers such as straw. Important buildings boasted elaborate painted murals and stone carvings; ornamentation and color were important themes.

European tastes and techniques have influenced Mexico's architecture since the 16th century, when the Spanish conquistadors employed indigenous slaves to build palaces and churches from the stones of ruined temples. European images quickly replaced those of the indigenous peoples; paintings of warriors in feathered headdresses disappeared and instead conquerors in helmets stood out on walls and in bold relief on carved stone pillars. Fragments of ancient carvings can, however, still be seen in the walls of churches and city halls from Mexico City to Mérida.

The Spaniards concentrated their construction efforts in populated areas where labor was easy to exploit. Churches and monasteries were among the earliest colonial-era structures, designed in the prevailing European styles. Many of the finest cathedrals were built over several centuries and consist of baroque, Gothic, and plateresque (richly ornamented, suggesting silverware) elements with Mexican influences. Flying buttresses, gargoyles, stained glass, and wooden ceilings carved in the Mudejar style (a blending of Spanish and Arabic artistic elements) were all used in the more ornate cathedrals. In the 17th century, facades were covered with decorative high-relief carvings and multiple religious statues characteristic of the Churrigueresque style (Spanish baroque, named after Spanish architect Benito Churriguera). Moorish-style domes were covered with tiles from Puebla in the 18th century. A flurry of construction in the neoclassical style took place in the late 18th and early 19th centuries, until the War for Independence brought a halt to building.

Some of the first colonial-era residences were monasteries and convents, with cavernous domed-ceiling rooms and elaborately tiled kitchens. European architects and engineers designed palaces for the elite, with multiple patios framed by one- or two-story wings. A similar pattern emerged at haciendas from the Yucatán to Chihuahua. Mexico's colonial-era buildings have survived earthquakes, floods, and gun battles; entire colonial cities, such as San Miguel de Allende, in Guanajuato, are now considered national historic treasures by UNESCO. Massive monasteries have been restored in Querétaro and Oaxaca, and some of the Yucatán Peninsula's finest haciendas now house first-class hotels.

Modern Mexican architecture incorporates design elements introduced by pre-Hispanic, colonial, and Mexican builders. Office towers, government buildings, and resort hotels mimic the pyramids of Teotihuacán and Chichén Itzá; tiles such as those seen covering

A dancer at a Virgin of Guadalupe feast day celebration (December 12) sports an ornate headdress.

17th- and 18th-century buildings in Puebla appear in modern stairways, bathrooms, and kitchens. Craftsmen in Guanajuato have become famous for their *bóvedas,* domed ceilings made entirely of brick.

The first significant skyscraper in Mexico City was designed by Leonardo Zeevaert and erected in 1956 near the frothy art nouveau

Bright colors mark Ricardo Legorreta's Camino Real Hotel, Mexico City.

Palacio de Bellas Artes. The sleek glass Torre Latinoamerica is surrounded by traditional colonial structures, including the exuberantly Churrigueresque Iglesia de San Francisco (1524) and the Casa de los Azulejos, which was built in 1596 and completely covered in handpainted tiles in 1737.

Juxtapositions of old and new styles can be seen in the work of architect Pedro Ramírez Vázquez, who designed the Museo Nacional de Antropología, in Chapultepec Park. With a layout similar to that of an ancient Aztec city, stately buildings face a central patio dominated by an enormous open shelter of carved stone and aluminum. Similar use of natural

and fabricated elements are characteristic of the sleek structures of German-born Mathias Goeritz, who immigrated during the rise of Nazism and taught at both the University of Guadalajara and UNAM, the National Autonomous University, in Mexico City. But far and away the most influential architect of the 20th century was Luis Barragán (1902–1988). His use of clean lines and vivid colors in monumental structures emphasized the importance of the natural elements, including sunlight, in the overall architectural design.

Of the many architects to follow in Barragán's footsteps, one of the most prolific and highly successful is Ricardo Legorreta (1931–). Like that of his friend and predecessor Barragán, Legorreta's innovative style combines massive plain walls painted vivid colors to reflect the movement of light. Collaboration between these two greats produced the Camino Real hotel in Mexico City, with walls and niches painted hot pink, marigold yellow, and deep lavender. This achievement led to many commissions for Legorreta, who is considered one of today's top architects, and who has designed more than a hundred buildings in Mexico and abroad.

The use of brilliant color is, in fact, one of the defining elements of the Mexican aesthetic sense. Plain adobe or stucco structures are painted cobalt blue with marigold trim, lime green, canary yellow, or *rosa mexicano*—a deep pink. Advertisements, public service messages, and campaign slogans in bright colors compete for attention on the facades of homes and businesses, retaining walls, and any other available surface.

ART

Mexico's artistic heritage far predates the European invasion. In 790, Maya artists covered the walls of the Temple of the Paintings at Bonampak, in southeast Chiapas, with murals depicting fierce battles and harmonious tableaux of the royal family. Olmec sculptors carved gigantic round heads in basalt around 1150 B.C., and some of the cave paintings found in Baja California are believed to be 5,000 years old.

But the arrival of Spanish conquistadors drastically changed Mesoamerican art. The Catholic Church became the dominant force in everyday life. Saints and Virgins replaced pantheistic gods and goddesses, and Indian artists were made to paint and sculpt foreign images. European artisans began arriving in New Spain soon after the conquerors, and their indigenous apprentices learned to paint biblical scenes on magnificent *retablos,* the ornate, gilded altarpieces that adorned colonial churches. Sixteenth-century religious art replaced the murals and serpentine sculptures, though Indian artists never completely ignored their origins. Angels drifting through murals sometimes show Maya, Mixtec, and Zapotec features; scrollwork incorporates ancient symbols for wind and fire. The finest Mexican painters were sent to study in Seville and Florence, and Mexican viceregal art retained a primarily Eurocentric tone.

As *criollo* and mestizo artists emerged in the 17th century, Mexican art began to take on a distinct flavor. The dark-skinned Virgin of Guadalupe, who purportedly appeared in 1531 to the Indian convert Juan Diego, was a purely Mexican creation whose image spread throughout the country. Mexicans looked back to indigenous history for inspiration, and painters began portraying scenes depicting Spanish and Aztec warriors in battle.

Mexico's first formal art school, the Real Academia de las Bellas Artes de México, was established in Mexico City in 1731, and European sculptors and painters were commissioned to instruct Mexican artists. Art was superseded by war during the early 19th century as Mexicans battled for independence, though a few of the country's most famous artists and sculptors emerged in the midst of conflict. The portraits of José María Estrada (1830–1862) and landscape paintings of José María Velasco (1840–1912) are cited in particular as evidence of an established Mexican art scene in the 1800s. Velasco is considered the master of 19th-century academic painting; he specialized in landscapes, skillfully depicting the lakes and volcanoes in the Valley of Mexico and the candelabra cactus of Oaxaca. Several of his finest works can be seen at the Museo Nacional de Arte in Mexico City (see p. 190).

The early 20th century was Mexico's belle époque—at least for the wealthy. Under the dictatorship of Porfirio Díaz (see pp. 33–34),

who idolized all things European, Mexicans schooled in European styles and fashions began to celebrate an emerging sense of identity. While still heavily influenced by European training, Mexican artists used their exposure to impressionism, symbolism, and art nouveau styles to embrace Mexican themes. Young artists focused on the iniquities

David Alfaro Siquieros's mural "Torture of Cuauhtémoc" is on display at Mexico City's Palacio de Bellas Artes.

of the dictatorship, and demanded a revitalization of Mexican culture. Gerardo Murillo (1875–1964), one of the most influential painters and intellectuals of the era, protested the European influences in Mexico by changing his surname to Atl, which in the Náhuatl language of the Aztecs means "water." Dr. Atl's work consists mainly of landscape paintings; his view of volcanoes serves as the design for the glass and metal curtain at the Palacio de Bellas Artes (see p. 190).

Many of Mexico's most famous 20th-century artists studied under Dr. Atl, who was as much a spiritual leader as a teacher of art.

He first proposed the idea of covering public buildings with murals by Mexican artists in the early 1900s; the Revolution of 1910 put his plans on hold.

This episode in history solidified the young artists' passion for their country and their desire to create truly Mexican works of art. In 1921, Education Minister José Vasconcelos asked Atl to paint murals (now destroyed) at the Escuela Nacional Preparatoria (National Preparatory School). In 1922, Vasconcelos initiated the muralist movement, which dominated the art scene for nearly 50 years. Atl's students, including Diego Rivera (1886–1957) and José Clemente Orozco (1883–1949), began tracing the entire history of Mexico on the walls of the country's most significant buildings, incorporating pre-Hispanic themes, the Conquest, and the Revolution into massive storyboards.

The muralists quickly became Mexico's most famous artists, and politics their favorite theme. "We repudiate so-called easel-painting," David Alfaro Siquieros (1896–1974) declared in 1922. "Art should no longer be the expression of individual satisfaction, which it is today, but should aim to become a fighting, educative art for all." The most famous muralists painted on canvas as well as walls, but even then they seemed captivated by the tragedies they witnessed or heard about during the Revolution. After training in Europe, painter Francisco Goita (1882–1980) joined Pancho Villa's army as an artistic chronicler of the struggle for freedom and equality. His paintings are gruesome reminders of war.

Architect Juan O'Gorman's "The Independence Mural" combines cultural commentary and superb craftsmanship.

Mexico's 20th-century artists were devoted to the concept of *mexicanidad,* the celebration of their native origins, natural surroundings, and cultural quirks. Much of their work was violent, inflammatory, and highly emotional, but even the most political artists paused from time to time to depict the beauty in their surroundings. Diego Rivera's paintings of tortilla makers and flower sellers portray Mexico's indigenous peoples with beauty and dignity. Rivera's wife, artist Frida Kahlo (1907–1954), known for her anguished self-portraits, often dressed in gorgeous indigenous costumes. The lesser-known painter Antonio M. Ruíz (1895–1964) focused

on scenes of daily life, often filled with humor.

The outside world began appreciating Mexican art with the work of the muralists, who became virtual folk heroes and spokespersons for their country. Orozco, Siquieros, and Rivera all created murals in the United States. Miguel Covarrubias (1904–1957), who contributed to some of Mexico City's most famous murals, worked as an illustrator and cartoonist for the *New Yorker* and *Vanity Fair* in the 1920s and '30s. Rufino Tamayo (1899–1991), one of a small group of painters who preferred to create modern art rather than focus on politics, spent much of his life in New York City.

Today, Mexico has a thriving art scene, as shown by the multitude of galleries and art schools in Mexico City, Oaxaca, San Miguel de Allende, and other centers. Cutting-edge art is displayed at Mexico City's Museo José Luis Cuevas, where a few Picassos and the works of other contemporary artists are displayed with Cuevas's erotic sculptures (see p. 210).

FOLK ART

Weavers, potters, woodcarvers, and glassblowers all feel at home in Mexico, where everyday items are often simple works of art. Early Mesoamerican civilizations created decorated clay water vessels; the Mixtecs crafted fabulous jade and gold pendants and other jewelry—some of the finest in the world at their time. Indigenous artisans quickly learned European techniques after the Conquest, and a new form of folk art emerged from the blend of natural materials, native talents, and foreign influences. Today, popular art is one of Mexico's richest treasures, and craftsmen and women are among its most famous artists.

Mexican folk art is both functional and fanciful, and often reflects patterns and themes handed down for centuries. Weavers in Oaxaca incorporate the highly stylized fret designs from the ruins of Mitla in their woolen rugs. Huichol Indians in Nayarit painstakingly reproduce ancient symbols of lizards, suns, peyote, and stars in beaded ceremonial bowls and in shoulder bags. Enterprising craftsmen and women throughout the country create inexpensive paintings in Day-Glo colors on paper made from the amate tree, used since

pre-Hispanic times to make ledgers and important books.

Religious themes appear in all forms, from painted tin portraits of the Virgin of Guadalupe to handpainted tile groupings of the Stations of the Cross. Nativity scenes, called *nacimientos*, are created from almost any material, from fragile blown glass to

Oaxaca state is rich in crafts, including embroidered clothing, jewelry, and many styles of pottery.

woven straw. The Mexican fascination with all things macabre emerges in multiple forms, from miniature dioramas of skeletons at play to papier-mâché *judases*—garish, larger-than-life-size devils and other characters used in Semana Santa (Holy Week) processions.

Every imaginable material may become art in the hands of a Mexican artisan. In Oaxaca, a whole celebration is devoted to carved radishes. The earth itself has always been a source of inspiration; museums throughout the country are filled with clay vessels and figurines created by the Olmec, Maya, Mixtec, and Aztec cultures. Pottery is one of Mexico's

oldest art forms, and one of its most popular.

Clay is molded and fired into imaginative shapes. The Lancandón Indians in remote Chiapas model red clay into crocodiles and birds; Nahua Indians in Guerrero create water vessels with human shapes. Certain regions are known for their exquisite, fragile pieces. Mata Ortíz pottery, from the Casas Grandes region in Chihuahua, is treasured by knowledgeable collectors, as is the glossy black pottery from San Bartolo Coyotepec, Oaxaca.

The Spanish conquistadors were responsible for some of Mexico's finest ceramics. With very few exceptions, pre-Hispanic potters were unfamiliar with glazing, and the Spaniards imported artisans from their homeland to create fine majolica tiles and tableware. These artists set to work in Puebla, where they created delicate blue-and-white talavera pieces (so named because they resembled the pottery from the town of Talavera de la Reina in Spain). While native artisans added more color, classic talavera designs remained popular, and the majolica technique is still used today to create handpainted vases, dishes, jars, and tiles in the states of Puebla, Tlaxcala, Guanajuato, and Jalisco.

Clay is often the favored medium for musical instruments, toys, dolls, and fantastical figurines. Nearly every early civilization played clay flutes and whistles. Modern artisans let their imaginations soar, creating elaborate scenes of vividly colored miniature figures in ridiculous tableaux. Adam and Eve, the Virgin of Guadalupe, angels, devils, and regular human beings are portrayed in realistic and absurd situations. Some dioramas are as tiny as matchboxes; others as large as a young child. Some of the best painted-clay artists work in Michoacán and Puebla. Potters in Oaxaca make life-size terra-cotta dolls called *muñecas bordadas;* some in Toluca and Puebla specialize in enormous polychromed tree of life figurines stacked with tiny figures and symbols.

Playfulness exerts itself in woodcarving as well. Dragon-like *alejibres* carved from soft wood and painted in almost garish colors started appearing in Oaxaca in the 1980s, along with more lifelike animal characters called *animalitos*. The most elaborate creations now command hundreds of dollars in upscale galleries. Primitive dolls are common among most indigenous groups. The native people of the Sierra Tarahumara fashion small wooden figures wearing traditional white shirts and trousers, while Otomí artisans in Puebla and Hidalgo create sweet-faced cloth dolls wearing the full, lace-edged skirts of their makers.

Wood is frequently employed to create masks, which have been used in religious ceremonies since pre-Hispanic times. The mask makers of Guerrero, Tlaxcala, Morelia, Chiapas, and Oaxaca are especially talented and prolific. Used in folk dances and religious processions, their masks represent saints and demons, poets and politicians, animals and pink-cheeked conquistadors. Some even have realistic glass eyes that open and shut at the tug of a string.

Glass beads were the first gifts and objects of barter of the Spanish, who later introduced glass blowing to native artisans. Exceptional hand-blown glassware and miniatures are today produced in small family workshops as well as large factories, especially in the states of Puebla and Mexico, and around Guadalajara, Jalisco.

Chiapas is home to brilliantly woven and embroidered *huipiles* (blouses) covered with Maya designs. The residents of indigenous villages throughout the state shun modern fashion in favor of woolen ponchos and cotton huipiles covered with vivid embroidered designs. The intricate patterns represent Maya legends and lore. Villagers are identified by their dress, be it the distinctive blue shawls of San Juan Chamula or the beribboned hats worn for special ceremonies in Zinacantán. Villagers in some parts of Oaxaca still wear indigenous dress and create shawls, belts, huipiles, and blouses that are true works of Mexican art.

Religious themes play an important role in Mexican folk art. Many of the masks and costumes used in regional dances represent saints and sinners. Small paintings called ex-votos, often on metal, are used to express gratitude for a religious figure's assistance in solving some problem. Ex-votos first appeared in the late 18th century and picture the devotee in pain or injury praying to a saint or to the Virgin or Jesus Christ. The story of the miracu-

lous cure or resolution to a problem is detailed in script below the scene. A chapel at the Basílica de Nuestra Señora de Guadalupe in Mexico City is filled with ex-votos praising the Mexican saint.

Milagros—small tin (or occasionally silver) charms shaped as various body parts, houses, cows, or cars—are also used as pleas for divine

Skeletons, like this one of papier-mâché, pervade Mexican folk art and feature widely in Day of the Dead celebrations.

intercession. Penitents pin these charms to the robes of statues of favorite saints and pray for relief from pain or the appearance of a cow or a new car. In recent years, some artists have incorporated milagros into jewelry, creating silver chains draped with tiny hearts, legs, and heads.

Mexico's silver tradition began with the Mixtecs: formidable pre-Hispanic metalsmiths whose gold and silver jewelry adorned the ruling elite. During the colonial period, huge quantities of gold and silver were used in the interior decoration of Catholic churches and in religious artifacts. Silver and other precious

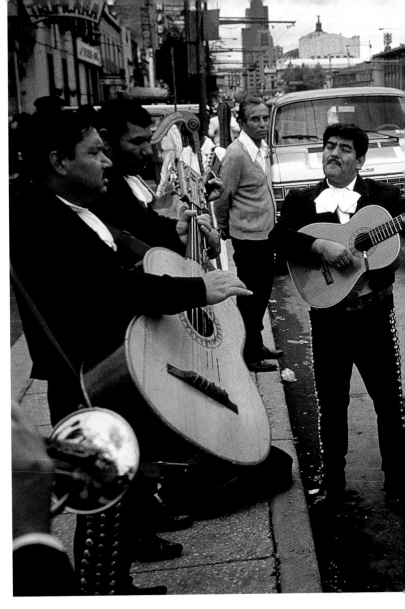

metals are still mined, and modern artisans take inspiration from traditions both old and new to produce jewelry and other handicrafts, mainly of silver. Much of it comes from Taxco, Guerrero—an entire city dedicated to silversmithing.

Printmaking became a popular means of expression in the late 19th century under the hand of José Guadalupe Posada (1852–1913), long considered Mexico's greatest lithographer. Posadas's engravings and etchings in metal and wood were used to print broadsheets distributed by street vendors. His highly detailed etchings depicted crooked politicians with wickedly humorous skeletal bodies and skulls.

A whole genre of broadsheets called *calaveras* (skulls) was created for Day of the Dead celebrations. They satirized everyone and everything with mocking verse and illustrations. Originally created for the masses, Posadas's broadsheets and calaveras caught the attention of artists of the early 20th century.

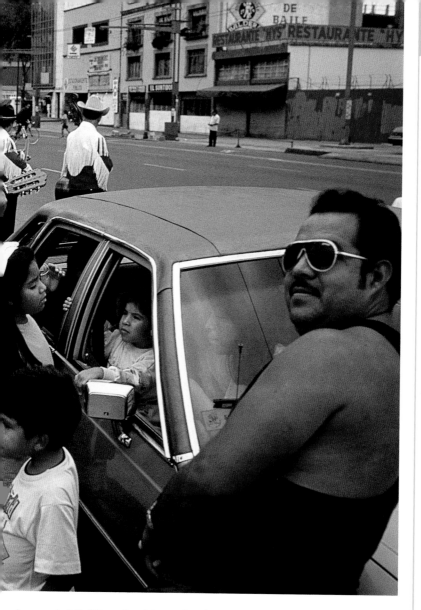

Some nearly deified him as the originator of a truly Mexican art movement. His calaveras certainly provided inspiration to future artists and have become synonymous with modern Day of the Dead celebrations.

Papier-mâché is one of the most popular mediums in Mexican folk art and is used for everything from masks to the ubiquitous *piñatas*. The Linares family of Mexico City is famous for its papier-mâché skeletons, skulls, dragons, and life-size devils. Glamorous

Mariachis in Plaza de Garibaldi, Mexico City

papier-mâché dolls from Guanajuato wear exaggerated makeup and glittery jewelry.

Everything from gold to gourds is used to create art in Mexico. Collectors crave items as simple as a wooden spoon and as intricate as a beaded mask. Certain parts of the country—especially Oaxaca, Chiapas, and Michoacán—are veritable living museums with markets that feel like galleries.

MUSIC

Every Mexican is a musician in his or her soul. As the saying goes, *"También de dolor se canta cuando llorar no se puede."* ("Sorrow also sings, when it runs too deep to cry.")

The most famous and familiar tunes are the *rancheras,* typically played and sung by mariachi musicians with violins, trumpets, and a variety of guitar-like instruments. Some of these songs of lost loves and defeat date back to the Mexican Revolution, when roving musicians carried the ballads of the war-torn northern regions to Mexico City. The *charro* (Mexican cowboy) movies of the 1930s and '40s spread ranchera music throughout the country, and the composer José Alfredo Jiménez added dozens of new songs to the mariachi repertoire.

Until the rise of mariachis and rancheras, most Mexican music was regional, based on indigenous and religious traditions. The advent of radio, film, and television spread mariachi music around the country, until it became a national emblem. The popularity of regional music grew as well, and Mexicans came to appreciate the marimbas of Chiapas and the romantic boleros of composer Agustín Lara, who added the sensual rhythms of Veracruz.

Soulful, passionate ballads are at the core of most of the music played in Mexico. Singers stand out for their ability to evoke all the emotions of even the most common tunes such as "Cielito Lindo" ("Beautiful Little Sky") and "La Paloma" ("The Dove"). Lola Beltrán's passionate singing made her the long-reigning queen of rancheras from the 1950s, while María Félix carried the romantic lyrics of tropical ballads to the sands of Acapulco in the 1940s, captivating the international artsy set with the rhythms of Mexico. Today's balladeers, including Juan Gabriel, Luis Miguel, and Alejandro Fernández, rely on old favorites to enhance their modern repertoires and bring cheers from their fans.

Romance and loss still inspire Mexico's modern musicians, even *rock en español.* Mexico's rock 'n' rollers still love a good heartbreaker but also move forward by combining traditional instruments, electronics, and political themes. Carlos Santana, raised near the border in Tijuana, was the first break-

through artist to bring Mexican influences into the international mainstream. Others have risen to superstardom and garnered fanatical followings both within Mexico and beyond in the process. The pop-rock group Maná and alternative rock band Café Tacuba are well-known outside Mexico, and new sounds are emerging from a burgeoning underground music scene. Versatile and eclectic Oaxaca singer Lila Downs performed several moving songs in the movie *Frida* (2002), one of which was nominated for an Academy Award.

Each part of the country has a particular sound. *Norteño* bands combine accordion, bass, and guitar with polka and ranchera melodies to create a rousing country and western sound popular in the northern regions of Mexico. The lyrics often touch on themes of immigration and national politics. *Cumbia*, salsa, and marimba music, with a tropical beat, bring dancers to their feet in Veracruz, home of the overplayed "La Bamba." The brassy *banda*, or band music, of Sinaloa has a German undertone, which was contributed by immigrants in the 1920s. Familiar and unusual sounds travel the air waves all over the country.

DANCE

Dance in Mexico dates back to Indian cultures and forward beyond "La Macarena." Catholic ritual and indigenous tradition have fused to create dances such as those celebrated during the Easter season by the Yaqui and Maya of Sonora. Deer masks and flowers are elements that remain from an important pre-

Veracruz's famous Carnaval always features a brass band.

Hispanic ritual asking that the deer sacrifice itself for the good of the people. Today, deer-dancers join with others representing Jesus and the Marys to defend the Church from evil men (represented by the Pharisees) in elaborate dances that are held throughout the land.

Ballet folklórico dance groups abound in all parts of the country; some of the finest appear in the most popular tourist destinations. Young children perform in central plazas large and small, and grow up to compete for spots in professional troupes. The reigning favorite is ruled by Amalia Hernández at Mexico City's Palacio de Bellas Artes; watching the theater's Tiffany curtain rise to reveal gorgeously costumed dancers is a necessary ritual for any fan of Mexican dance.

Traditional folkloric dancing began in the 1800s, combining pre-Hispanic, Spanish, and mestizo steps and themes. Regional dances echo the music of immigrants and the rhythms of nature. In San Luis Potosí, dancers perform the *huapango,* a variation of the Spanish fandango. In Veracruz, couples dance the disciplined *danzón,* which originated in Cuba. Even the most famous of all Mexican dances, *el jarabe tapatío* (the Mexican hat dance), originated among mestizos.

The states of Oaxaca, Michoacán, Yucatán, Jalisco, Chiapas, and Veracruz are renowned for their numerous folk dances. In Oaxaca, dancers from throughout the state perform at the annual Guelaguetza, a two-week-long celebration of ethnic heritage held in July. The costumes for dances from Oaxaca and Chiapas are among the most gorgeous imaginable and are works of art that enhance the beauty of the movements and of the wearers. The Dance of the Old Men *(Danza de los Viejitos),* which originated in Michoacán, provides the humorous interlude in performances around the country.

Less familiar dances are performed during religious holidays, especially around Semana Santa (Holy Week). The Cora Indians of Nayarit dance in hallucinogenic agitation for days on end, while the Tarahumara of the Copper Canyon engage in tumultuous, eerie mock battles between soldiers and the Pharisees.

Dancing is part celebration, from birthday parties to formal fiestas. Mexicans of all ages show up at dance halls and clubs to waltz, dance salsa and merengue, or move to the beat of pop or *rock en español.* Mexican discos are typically elegant places where clients dress to impress and dance till dawn.

LITERATURE

Mexico's first books were codices, made of bark paper and animal skin and filled with pictures and symbols. The Maya were particularly prolific and created two of pre-Hispanic Mexico's most important books, along with several codices relating historical events. The *Popol Vuh,* written between 1554 and 1558, is an epic account of supernatural legend and lore, while

Many young men and women practice folk dancing, like those in this University of Guadalajara troupe.

the *Chilam Balam,* written during the 17th and 18th centuries, offers a more realistic account of astronomical observations and historic events. Books in the Náhuatl and Mixtec languages have also remained intact, as have many more stone and stucco carvings relating stories of battle, birth, death, and royal succession.

Although some Spaniards worked to preserve native books and writings, others were equally successful in their post-Conquest campaign to destroy documents they considered works of Satan. One of the most important records of the Conquest itself is *La Historia Verdadera de la Conquista de la Nueva España*

(*True History of the Conquest of New Spain*) by Bernal Díaz del Castillo (ca 1492–1581), a conquistador who later in life related the events of the Conquest with startling clarity.

As might be expected, the ruling Spaniards stuck to European and religious themes in poetry, theater, and literature. The first printing press, which arrived in Mexico in 1537, was used primarily to disseminate information about science, nature, and the country's settlement. A Mexican style of literature began emerging late in the 16th century, as mestizos and *criollos* began drawing on themes of more local significance. The most famous writer of the colonial era was Sor Juana Inés de la Cruz (1651–1695), a nun and prolific poet. Her theme was frequently the plight of the citizens of New Spain, who suffered under Spanish restraints as Mexico's wealth was plundered for the motherland. In one of her most famous poems she wrote:

Señora, I was born in the land of plenty…
to no other land on Earth is Mother Nature
   so generous.
Europe knows this best of all
for this many years, insatiable,
She has bled the abundant veins
of America's rich mines.

Newspapers began to appear in the early 1800s, as did the first novel expressing Mexican sentiments—*El Periquillo Sarniento (The Itching Parrot)*, by José Joaquin Fernández de Lizardi (1776–1827). The printed word was largely used to further political campaigns and social causes in the 19th century, though a few writers created novels with Mexican themes. Francisco I. Madero (who later became Mexico's president) wrote one of the first significant pieces of political nonfiction. His *The Presidential Succession of 1910* was instrumental in the downfall of Porfirio Díaz.

Of all the literature produced in the 20th century, *El Laberinto de la Soledad (The Labyrinto of Solitude)*, published in 1950, stands out as the definitive portrait of the Mexican psyche. Author and Nobel laureate Octavio Paz (1914–1998) attempted to analyze and describe the character of his countrymen and capture the essence of *mexicanidad*. Though controversial, his book is considered a masterpiece, and Paz was revered as the elder statesman of Mexican writers. Carlos Fuentes, author of *La Región Más Transparente (Where the Air Is Clear)* and the *El Gringo Viejo (The Old Gringo)*, is another modern master.

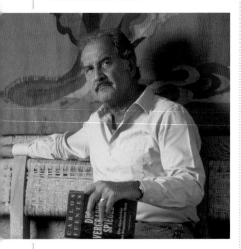

Statesman and author Carlos Fuentes

FILM

Mexico's earliest films helped popularize mariachi music and the lifestyle of the northern Mexico cowboys. Pancho Villa's exploits were a popular theme, as were the trials and tribulations of urban families. They united Mexicans unaccustomed to the music and culture of distant regions, and by the 1930s Mexican film was receiving worldwide attention.

Mexican filmmakers and actors benefited from Hollywood's fascination with Mexico's topography. Many early U.S. Westerns were filmed in northern Mexico, and Hollywood stars frequented the resorts of Acapulco in the 1940s. Dolores del Río (1905–1983), who regularly partied with the Hollywood elite on Caleta Beach, was beginning to gain fame outside Mexico when she caught the eye of the international press at the 1946 Cannes Film Festival. As the star of *María Candelaria* (1944), the hit film directed by Emilio Fernández (1904–1986), Del Río helped popularize Mexican cinema, as did Mario Moreno (1911–1993), better known as Cantinflas, "the Charlie Chaplin of Mexico," and Germán Valdés (also known as Tin Tan). Actress María Félix and actors Jorge Negrete and Pedro Infante were idolized by fans in the forties. Films including *Enamorada* (directed by Fernández) and *Distinto Amanecer* (Julio Bracho) became instant classics. Mexico's most famous director of the 1950s, Luis Buñuel (1900–1983), was a Spaniard who fled his country during the Civil War. His *Los Olvidados* (1950) is another Mexican masterpiece.

In the 1950s and 1960s a flurry of schlock horror films—including Jerry Warren's 1963 *Attack of the Mayan Mummy,* adapted from the 1957 Mexican film *La Momia Azteca*—drew a loyal following. The greatest cult film of all appeared in 1970, when Alejandro Jodorowsky came out with *El Topo,* a violent hodgepodge of surrealism and Western cowboy images. More serious themes emerged in the 1980s. Director Gregory Nava delved into the miseries of illegal immigration in the acclaimed 1983 film *El Norte* (1984). Roberto Rodríguez portrayed modern northern Mexico in his 1993 *El Mariachi* and again in *Desperado* (1995) and *Once Upon a Time in Mexico* (2003).

The most famous film to come out of Mexico in the 1990s was *Like Water for Chocolate (Como Agua Para Chocolate),* the soulful interpretation of Laura Esquivel's best-selling novel. Today, more and more movies, documentaries, and soap operas are being filmed in Mexico. And Mexican filmmakers compete for funding, awards, and attention with their peers around the world, while Mexican actors are gaining fame in their own country and abroad. ∎

An isolated, jagged finger of mountains and desert between the Pacific Ocean and the Sea of Cortés, Baja California was once Mexico's forgotten peninsula. Today it contains the country's fastest-growing tourist destination.

Baja California

Barnacle-encrusted gray whale

Baja California

THOUGH SUPERFICIALLY BARREN AND DESOLATE, THE BAJA CALIFORNIA peninsula has long entranced scientists and adventurers. The author John Steinbeck (1902–1968) explored the coast of Baja around 1940 and wrote in his *The Log from the Sea of Cortez:* "The very air here is miraculous, and outlines of reality change with the moments. A dream hangs over the entire region." A similar feeling inspires a more modern cadre of adventurers, dedicated to exploring every crevice and cove of Baja.

Long and lean, the Baja California peninsula gradually separated from the mainland five million years ago along the San Andreas Fault, bringing with it a series of mountain ranges. At its widest, it stretches just 120 miles (193 km) along the U.S. border. The bulk of Baja's tourists visit the Tijuana–Ensenada corridor or the resorts at Los Cabos, 860 miles (1,300 km) to the south. Between the two lies the Baja of myth and mystery.

At least five indigenous groups were living in Baja when Padre Juan María Salvatierra established the mission church in Loreto in 1697. As missionaries and European adventurers made their way up the peninsula, the native population was decimated by battles or disease. Only about a thousand indigenous people now live in Baja, some following their forefathers' traditions in remote communities.

Baja's two coastlines attract fishermen, surfers, divers, and sailors craving extremes. The Pacific side is renowned for its awesome waves, massive billfish, and migrating whales; the Gulf of California (also called the Sea of Cortez) is a biologist's dream. Here, thousands of species of marine creatures flourish in protected coves and open waters. Nearly every environmental group in the world has an interest in protecting the Gulf of California from commercial fishing and any development that threatens its natural balance. Such concern led to its designation in 2005 as a U.N. World Heritage site.

Despite the harshness of Baja's terrain, its

Baja's desert wilderness offers plenty of solitude for those seeking to get away from it all.

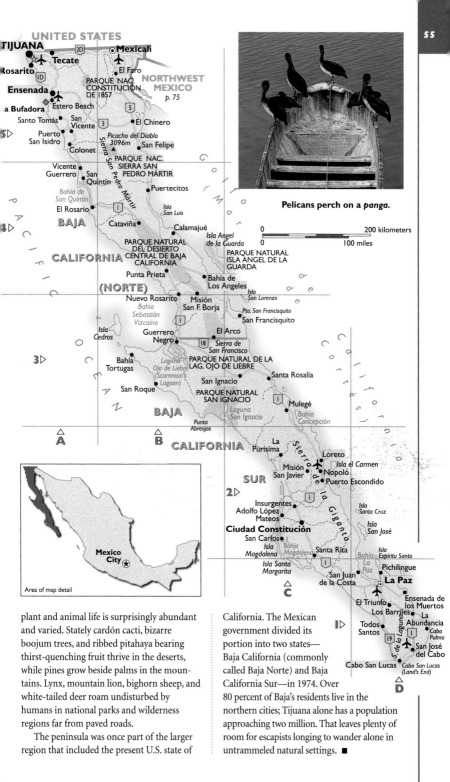

UNITED STATES

TIJUANA

Mexicali

Tecate

Rosarito

El Faro

Ensenada

PARQUE NAC. CONSTITUCIÓN DE 1857

NORTHWEST MEXICO
p. 75

La Bufadora   Estero Beach

Santo Tomás   San Vicente

El Chinero

Puerto San Isidro

Colonet

Picacho del Diablo 3096m   San Felipe

Vicente Guerrero   San Quintín

PARQUE NAC. SIERRA SAN PEDRO MÁRTIR

Bahía de San Quintín

Puertecitos

El Rosario

Isla San Luis

BAJA   Cataviña   Calamajué

Isla Angel de la Guarda

PARQUE NATURAL DEL DESIERTO CENTRAL DE BAJA CALIFORNIA

PARQUE NATURAL ISLA ANGEL DE LA GUARDA

CALIFORNIA

(NORTE)   Punta Prieta

Bahía de Los Angeles

Isla San Lorenzo

Nuevo Rosarito   Misión San F. Borja

Bahía Sebastián Vizcaíno

Pta. San Francisquito

San Francisquito

Isla Cedros   Guerrero Negro

El Arco

Sierra de San Francisco

Bahía Tortugas

Laguna Ojo de Liebre (Scammon's Lagoon)

PARQUE NATURAL DE LA LAG. OJO DE LIEBRE

Santa Rosalía

San Roque

San Ignacio

PARQUE NATURAL SAN IGNACIO

Mulegé

BAJA

Laguna San Ignacio

Bahía Concepción

Punta Abreojos

CALIFORNIA

La Purísima

Loreto

Isla el Carmen

Misión San Javier   Nopoló

Puerto Escondido

SUR

Insurgentes Adolfo López Mateos

Isla Santa Cruz

Ciudad Constitución

Isla San José

San Carlos

Isla Magdalena   Bahía Magdalena   Santa Rita

Bahía Espíritu Santo

Isla Santa Margarita

La Paz   Pichilingue

San Juan de la Costa   La Paz

El Triunfo

Ensenada de los Muertos

Los Barriles   La Abundancia

Todos Santos

Cabo Pulmo

San José del Cabo

Cabo San Lucas   Cabo San Lucas (Land's End)

0   200 kilometers
0   100 miles

Pelicans perch on a *panga*.

Mexico City

Area of map detail

plant and animal life is surprisingly abundant and varied. Stately cardón cacti, bizarre boojum trees, and ribbed pitahaya bearing thirst-quenching fruit thrive in the deserts, while pines grow beside palms in the mountains. Lynx, mountain lion, bighorn sheep, and white-tailed deer roam undisturbed by humans in national parks and wilderness regions far from paved roads.

The peninsula was once part of the larger region that included the present U.S. state of California. The Mexican government divided its portion into two states— Baja California (commonly called Baja Norte) and Baja California Sur—in 1974. Over 80 percent of Baja's residents live in the northern cities; Tijuana alone has a population approaching two million. That leaves plenty of room for escapists longing to wander alone in untrammeled natural settings. ■

Tijuana to Ensenada

Tijuana

⚠ 55 A5

Visitor information

✉ Av. Revolución between Calles 3 and 4

☎ 664/658-2210, 800/310-9687 from the U.S.

www.seetijuana.com

TIJUANA IS MEXICO'S FOURTH LARGEST CITY; ENSENADA IS Baja California's largest port. In between, an ever multiplying number of hotels, businesses, and oceanfront rentals has grown steadily over the past few decades, engulfing once isolated fishing villages and resort hotels alike. But tourism to this region is not new. Since the days of U.S. Prohibition, Tijuana has been attracting day- and night-trippers with its dance halls and discos, raucous bars, and bullfights. South of town, beachfront hotels between Rosarito and Ensenada have long attracted Southern Californians for weekend getaways.

TIJUANA

For some, Tijuana is a shopping destination or a chance to get a glimpse of Mexico while vacationing in Southern California. For

Tijuana's Centro Cultural houses the wonderful Museo de las Californias.

others it's the gateway to adventure farther south. Many tourists see only Tijuana's legendary main street—engaging, overbearing **Avenida Revolución.** The shopping opportunities actually begin at the border, forming an unending corridor of *piñatas,* ceramic Day-Glo piggy banks, and unglazed clay pots. U.S.-style restaurants such as Sanborns and Caesar's (birthplace of the Caesar salad) make the uneasy visitor feel at home.

At Tijuana's two bullrings, sequined bullfighters the equal of any in Mexico divert 1,000-pound (450 kg) bulls with a flourish of

their heavy silk capes. But more palatable to most folks is a visit to **L.A. Cetto winery** *(Av. Cañón Johnson 2108, Col. Hidalgo, tel 664/685-3031, closed Sun., $–$$),* where you can sample a good variety of vintages and tour the facilities.

East of downtown looms the **Centro Cultural Tijuana** *(Paseo de los Héroes at Mina, tel 664/687-9600, $).* Housed in its futuristic-looking, dun-colored dome is the thousand-seat **Omnimax theater** *($).* The adjacent museum has a bookstore, restaurant, and two floors featuring fine arts and anthropology exhibits. The new **Museo de las Californias** *(tel 664/687-9650, closed Mon., $)* displays about 500 pieces that highlight the peninsula's history.

ROSARITO

Just 18 miles (29 km) south of Tijuana lies Rosarito. Today, this fast-growing city heads its own municipality boasting 20 miles (32 km) of coastline with fine beaches. More than 500 shops, stores, and stalls cater to visitors, selling glazed and unglazed pottery, wrought-iron hardware, handcarved wooden furniture, and handicrafts from throughout Mexico. Most shops are along busy **Boulevard Benito Juárez,** a jumble of bars, hotels, and restaurants that is a popular

Rosarito

⚠ 55 A5

Visitor information

✉ Blvd. Juárez 907-14 at Oceana Plaza mall

☎ 661/612-3078

spring-break destination. Just down the coast, **Fox Studios** *(Km. 32.8 Carretera Libre a Ensenada, tel 661/614-9444, 866/369-2252 from the U.S., www.foxploration.com, closed Mon. & Tues., $$$$)* was built as the set for *Titanic,* released in 1997. Since then more movies have been produced there, including *The Weight of Water* and *Pearl Harbor.* Visisitors can explore sets, learn about film production, and enjoy weekend entertainment.

ENSENADA

About 18 miles (29 km) south of Rosarito, Ensenada hugs the northern end of long, well-protected **Bahía de Todos Santos,** discovered by Portuguese explorer Juan Cabrillo in 1542. Ensenada's most important industries are shipping, fishing, agriculture (primarily olives and grapes), and tourism. Proximity to the U.S. border, seafood restaurants, and watersports and fishing make this a favorite weekend getaway. Shopping is concentrated along **Avenida López Mateos,** where folk-art stores and hotels are interspersed with restaurants, bars, and cafés.

Whale-watching excursions leave from the **Sportfishing Pier** *(Blvd. Costero near Av. Macheros)* from December to March. Overnight fishing trips from the pier net bass, bonito, rockfish, and, occasionally, yellowtail. The best fishing is June through September.

South of Ensenada, a natural blowhole called **La Bufadora** shoots up jets of ocean water 80 feet (24 m) high. Below the waterspout, the rocky cove at **Punta Banda** is popular with divers, fishermen, and kayakers. Kayaks are more easily launched at **Estero Beach,** an estuary halfway up the bay with boat ramps, sailboarding, and fishing.

Taste a local vintage at **Bodegas de Santo Tomás** (see p. 386) or one of the wineries tucked into Valle de Guadalupe, about a 30-minute drive east. The largest, **L.A. Cetto** *(Highway 3 Km. 73.5 toward Tecate, tel 646/155-2264),* offers free wine tasting and tours daily 10 to 4; smaller wineries like **Mogor Badan** *(tel 646/177-1484)* and **Monte Xanic** *(tel 646/174-6769)* require an appointment. ∎

One of Tijuana's more picturesque corners

Ensenada
🅰 55 A5
Visitor information
✉ Blvd. Lazaro Cardenas 609-5
☎ 646/178-8588, 800/310-9687 from the U.S.
www.enjoyensenada .com

The towering peaks of Baja's Sierra de la Giganta, near Loreto

Baja Peninsula drive

Until 1974, mostly die-hard naturalists, explorers, and anglers bumped down rutted dirt and sand roads to the tip of the Baja Peninsula. Then the government paved Highway 1, opening Baja to a wider audience. Fortunately, the drive is still arduous enough to discourage crowds. The road meanders from the Pacific to the Gulf of California, passing by and through several mountain ranges. Gravel and dirt side roads lead to rocky coves, sandy beaches, and steep mountain peaks. Some off-road attractions are fairly accessible, while others require high-clearance and four-wheel-drive vehicles, and are reserved for the unique breed of adventurers who claim Baja as their own.

Angeles Verdes (Green Angels, see p. 350) patrol the highway to assist stranded travelers, and local mechanics are extraordinarily ingenious, but drivers should be prepared for heat, potholes, arroyos (watercourses), and wandering cows. Fuel up frequently, and always carry plenty of water, a jack and good spare tire, maps, and spare parts. Forget about speeding past the scenery— many of the crosses at the roadside mark the spot where incautious drivers have died. Instead, take the time to enjoy Baja's extraordinary landscape of cacti, canyons, mesas, and coves.

Hwy. 1 begins just after the San Ysidro border crossing (open 24 hours), connecting San Diego County with **Tijuana** ❶ (see p. 56). Some travelers stop to shop and sightsee in Tijuana; others head south to **Rosarito** (see pp. 56–57) and the shore break at **Cantamar.** Nearby **Puerto Nuevo** (also known as Newport)—once a clutch of friendly lobster shacks—now has three dozen restaurants specializing in lobster, refried beans, rice, and tortillas.

After the frequently congested stretch of Hwy. 1 from Tijuana to Ensenada, the true Baja experience begins. The road descends into the undulating wine country around **Santo Tomás,** then ascends a steep grade and evens out as it passes remote ranches and vineyards at **San Vicente.** Serious agriculture occupies the land around **Colonet, Camalú,** and **Vicente**

Guerrero. Tomato fields run for miles. Side roads lead from Colonet to the formidable peaks of the **Sierra San Pedro Mártir,** far out of sight to the east.

Restaurants (try the local pismo clams), grocery stores, hotels, and beaches make **San Quintín ❷,** 115 miles (185 km) south of Ensenada, a sensible place to break for lunch or the night. Asphalt and dirt streets lead to **Bahía de San Quintín** (79 miles/129 km south of Colonet), where a late 19th-century English wheat-farming venture quickly succumbed to drought. Clamming and bird-watching are popular pursuits here, along with sportfishing.

Some of northern Baja's best beaches lie along the 36-mile (58 km) stretch of Hwy. 1 between San Quintín and **El Rosario,** which has grocery stores and a gas station. South of El Rosario, Hwy. 1 jogs abruptly east to enter Baja's eerie central desert. Most travelers stop to pose beside one of the many towering cardón cacti or wavy branched cirio trees. Some are tempted to camp beside the spooky, flat-topped mesas that would make ideal UFO landing strips. The mesas and low hills give way to fields of enormous boulders around **Cataviña.** A sign indicates the turnoff, 65 miles (105 km) south of Cataviña, to a paved road heading east to **Bahía de Los Angeles** (see p. 73). Later, other signs point to a further turnoff 32 miles (53 km) south at **Nuevo Rosarito,** where high-clearance vehicles can detour 22 miles (35 km) to **Misión San Francisco Borja** (see p. 73).

The next important stop is **Guerrero Negro,** 145 miles (234 km) south of Cataviña, at the Baja California Sur state line. Important as a supply stop but otherwise unexceptional, the bleak, windy town is headquarters for whale-watching expeditions *(Dec.–March; see pp. 68–69).* Nearby **Laguna Ojo de Liebre** (also known as Scammon's Lagoon) is a mating and birthing ground for gray whales and has a large salt-evaporation plant, which produces around a million tons of salt annually.

South of Guerrero Negro the highway cuts inland and up into the mountains for 88 miles (142 km) to **San Ignacio ❸,** a true high-desert oasis (see p. 62). The highway

Sportfishing is big business up and down the length of the Baja Peninsula.

swoops downhill, first touching the Gulf of California at **Santa Rosalía.** Short detours to the south bring you to **Caleta San Lucas,** a mangrove-lined cove with good snorkeling and fishing, and to **Bahía Santa Inés ❹,** where the long, eponymous bay provides great shelling, diving, fishing, and sailboarding.

A riverbed thick with lush palms marks the entrance to **Mulegé** (see p. 63), and it becomes increasingly difficult to keep your eyes on the road. Beautiful **Bahía de la Concepción ❺,** a narrow bay scalloped with coves containing clear, aquamarine water, appears like a glistening mirage. Take a break for a swim at **Coyote, Santispac,** or **Requesón Beaches** and join the campers and kayakers for a cool drink at one of the simple palm-thatched restaurants. The next stop along Hwy. 1 is **Loreto ❻** (see p. 63), 84 miles (136 km) south of Mulegé. **Misión San Javier** (see pp. 73–74), an hour inland up a passable dirt road, may well be Baja's most impressive historic church.

After Loreto, Hwy. 1 climbs into the rusty red **Sierra de la Giganta** in a series of switchbacks and hairpin turns to the Santo

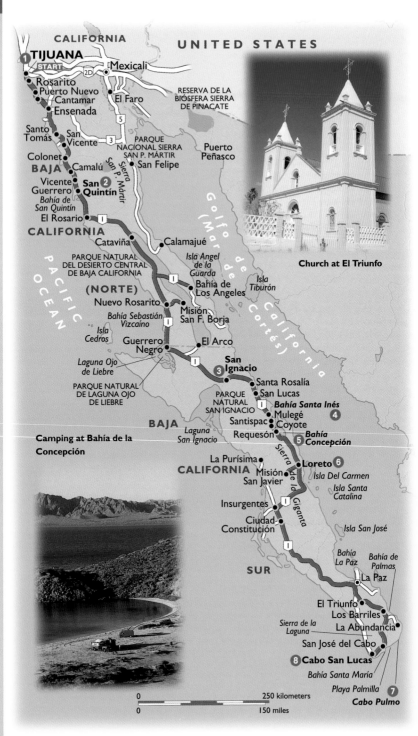

CALIFORNIA

UNITED STATES

1 **TIJUANA**
START
Rosarito
Puerto Nuevo
Cantamar
Ensenada

Mexicali

El Faro

RESERVA DE LA
BIÓSFERA SIERRA
DE PINACATE

Santo
Tomás
Colonet
BAJA
Vicente
Guerrero
*Bahía de
San Quintín*
El Rosario
CALIFORNIA

San
Vicente
Camalú
San 2
Quintín

PARQUE
NACIONAL SIERRA
SAN P. MÁRTIR
San Felipe

Puerto
Peñasco

Church at El Triunfo

Cataviña
Calamajué

PARQUE NATURAL
DEL DESIERTO CENTRAL
DE BAJA CALIFORNIA
(NORTE)

Nuevo Rosarito
*Bahía Sebastián
Vizcaino*
Isla
Cedros
Guerrero
Negro
*Laguna Ojo
de Liebre*

PARQUE NATURAL
DE LAGUNA OJO
DE LIEBRE

*Isla Angel
de la
Guarda*
Bahía de
Los Angeles

*Isla
Tiburón*

Misión
San F. Borja

El Arco

**San
Ignacio** 3

Santa Rosalía
San Lucas
PARQUE
NATURAL
SAN IGNACIO
Santispac
Requesón

Bahía Santa Inés
Mulegé
Coyote
*Bahía
Concepción* 5

BAJA
*Laguna
San Ignacio*

**Camping at Bahía de la
Concepción**

La Purísima
CALIFORNIA
Misión
San Javier

Insurgentes
Ciudad
Constitución

Loreto 6
Isla Del Carmen
*Isla Santa
Catalina*

Isla San José

*Bahía
La Páz*
*Bahía de
Palmas*

SUR

La Paz

El Triunfo
Los Barriles
La Abundancia
San José del Cabo

*Sierra de la
Laguna*

8 **Cabo San Lucas**
Bahía Santa María
Playa Palmilla 7
Cabo Pulmo

0   250 kilometers
0   150 miles

Mulegé, among Baja Sur's greenest oasis, attracts many winter visitors.

Domingo Valley, **Insurgentes,** and **Ciudad Constitución,** Baja Sur's third largest town. Gas up, check the tires, and replenish your water supply here. Wheat, alfalfa, cotton, and corn farms nourished by water from deep wells are the only distractions during the next leg of the journey.

It's almost impossible to keep from speeding through the barren moonscape of dull desert during the 134 miles (216 km) between Constitución and **La Paz.** The road edges **Bahía La Paz** before entering Baja California Sur's busy state capital, a good place to pass the night (see pp. 66–67).

Passing forests of organ and cardón cacti,

- ⛰ See also area map p. 55 A5–D1
- ► Tijuana
- ↔ About 1,125 miles (1,800 km)
- ⊕ 4 days to 2 weeks
- ► Cabo San Lucas

NOT TO BE MISSED

- San Ignacio
- Bahía de la Concepción
- Loreto
- Cabo Pulmo

Hwy. 1 crosses the **Sierra de la Laguna** range south of La Paz and travels through **El Triunfo,** a quirky old mining town. The Gulf of California beckons at **Los Barriles,** the entrance to the fast-growing **East Cape** region. Fish camps and semi-luxurious hotels are tucked away on the beach or the hills above. Sailboarding is very popular at nearby **Bahía de Palmas,** while a detour 11 miles (17 km) south of Los Barriles accesses the East Cape beach road. The pavement ends at La Abundancia. After that, rough travel over washboard roads rewards with sugar-fine beaches dotted with strange rock formations. There's great fishing and reef diving at **Cabo Pulmo** ➐, an underwater preserve.

From Los Barriles, the road swings inland and widens into a four-lane, divided highway near the international airport serving Los Cabos. It passes **San José del Cabo** (see p. 71) and skirts the coast, passing surf spots at **Costa Azul** and **Acapulquito. Playa Palmilla** is particularly recommended for swimming, while **Bahía Santa María** is a perfect snorkeling and diving spot. The journey ends at **Cabo San Lucas** ➑ and Baja California's best-known rock: the natural arch at Land's End (see p. 72). ■

San Ignacio to Loreto

AFTER CROSSING INTO BAJA SUR AT GUERRERO NEGRO,
Highway 1 heads east toward the Sea of Cortez. Ninety sun-baked
miles (145 km) later, the road meets spring-fed San Ignacio. With its
well-preserved mission church poking above the date palms, San
Ignacio offers a glimpse into traditional Baja. Santa Rosalía presents
a 19th-century mining town hardly improved by modern trappings,
while Mulegé and Loreto echo mainland Mexican villages with their
historic missions and plazas, and the Gulf of California adds a rich
and wonderfully wet element to a dry, dusty environment.

San Ignacio
🖾 55 C3
**Visitor
information**
✉ Calle Hidalgo 6
☎ 615/154-0150

The sleepy mountain town of **San
Ignacio** greets the traveler like a
heat-induced mirage. Its Jesuit
founders planted date palms and
orange and fig trees at this desert
oasis, and Dominicans completed
the lava-stone **Iglesia de San
Ignacio de Loyola** adjacent to
the main plaza. Stop in for Sunday
Mass, or visit its small **museum**
(Closed Sun.). San Ignacio serves as
a base for whale-watching excursions to **Laguna San Ignacio**
(see p. 69), and backcountry treks
to prehistoric rock paintings (see
p. 65) in the mountains. Both can
be arranged in town or in advance.

Highway 1 first kisses the gulf
46 miles (74 km) southeast of San
Ignacio at **Santa Rosalía,** established by German copper-mining
entrepreneurs in the late 19th
century, then run by the French.
The cast-iron **Iglesia de Santa
Bárbara** *(Calle Obregón near the
plaza)* was designed by Gustave
Eiffel and shipped in pieces from
France. Arrow-straight streets lined
with wooden houses (built as
homes for miners from India and
China) give Santa Rosalía a
"company town" feel. The mine's
French managers lived on the mesa
north of town, overlooking railroad

tracks and the sea. Check out the view from the restored 19th-century **Hotel Francés** (*Av. 11 de Julio 15 at Jean M. Cousteau, Col. Mesa Francia, tel 615/152-2052*).

Despite its exotic origins, Santa Rosalía is rather unattractive, and most visitors move on after just a short visit. Small hotels serve travelers using the ferry between Santa Rosalía and mainland Guaymas.

Lush **Mulegé,** 38 miles (61 km) south of Santa Rosalía, attracts U.S. and Canadian snowbirds escaping the Northern winter and sports enthusiasts who revel in the town's slow pace, tourist facilities, and green river valley by the sea. Visitors trek into the surrounding mountains to see cave art at **San Borjitas, Trinidad,** or **Piedras Pintas,** or fish, kayak, snorkel, or sailboard along the rocky coast.

Mulegé is centered among orange trees and date palms; small hotels, adventure-tour companies, and restaurants cluster near the plaza. Established in 1705, damaged by a hurricane in 1770, and abandoned in 1828, the town's restored mission church **Santa Rosalía de Mulegé** lies south of the center on Calle Zaragoza. A former prison at the north end of town houses the **Museo de Mulegé** (*Closed Sat., Sun.*), with local memorabilia.

Tucked between the golden sierras and the languid Gulf of California, **Loreto** was once the religious and political center of the peninsula. Its **Misión Nuestra Señora de Loreto** (*Salvatierra at Misioneros*) was built in 1687 and restored in the 1970s. Check out the gilded altar, a statue of the Virgin believed to perform miracles, and the **Museo de las Misiones** (*tel 615/135-0441, closed Mon., $*).

Loreto was Baja's capital for 100 years before a devastating 1829 hurricane. After that the seat of government was moved to La Paz, and Loreto drifted into obscurity. In 1974 the Mexican government pegged the town as a major tourist destination and installed telephones, electricity, paved streets, and an international airport. Neighborhoods rose beside a resort hotel at **Bahía Nopoló;** an 18-hole golf course followed. Nearby **Puerto Escondido** got a new marina and an expanded RV park and hotel.

Today, few planes land at the airport and Loreto retains its provincial air. A handful of hotels and restaurants cater to Loreto's loyal followers and sightseers, who cherish its isolation. Rich feeding grounds around **Isla Coronado,** seahorse-shaped **Isla El Carmen,**

Loreto
◭ 55 C2
Visitor information
✉ Palacio del Municipio, Plaza Cívica
☎ 613/135-0411
www.gotoloreto.com

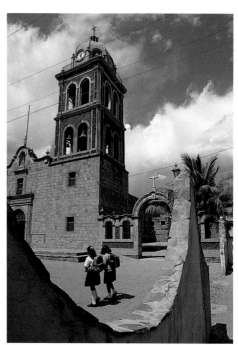

and tiny **Isla Danzante** lure fishermen to schools of dorado, tuna, roosterfish, and billfish, while snorkelers and divers swim with rays and tropical fish, and kayakers paddle around the islands. ∎

Our Lady of Loreto was the first California mission church, built in 1687.

Cave paintings of Baja California

Prehistoric mural paintings are found throughout central Baja California, most at an elevation of more than 1,000 feet (305 m). Some are on exposed rocks, while others crowd the walls and ceilings of caves both small and large. Red and black pigments were most commonly used, in addition to yellow, orange, pink, and white. Some images appear to have been sketched first in white chalk, charcoal, or paint. Favorite subjects were humans and deer (the latter often pierced with arrows), but artists depicted all the creatures that shared their world, including birds, reptiles, rabbits, squids, fish, turtles, whales, and manta rays.

Paintings found within each of the main mountain ranges exhibit a characteristic style. Human figures (*monos*) predominate in the Sierra de Guadalupe near San Ignacio. These are stiff, often bulb-shaped figures with vertical stripes and outstretched arms and legs. In the Sierra de San Borja, large, red figures were painted on huge granite boulders, while to the south, in the Sierra de San Juan and Sierra San Francisco, artists chose the walls and ceilings of caves up to 30 feet (9 m) high as their canvases. Figures from the San Francisco range tend to be red on one half, black on the other, with elaborate head gear.

North and south of this central region, other artistic innovations are seen. Figures in the south tend toward abstraction: Some are filled in with a checkerboard pattern. Northwest of San Borja, paintings tend to be

The walls of Cueva Pintada, Baja California Sur, are covered with depictions of fish, birds, and people (above), while the cave's overhang features huge, polychromatic designs (left).

of a more whimsical nature and employ a broader range of colors, including more pinks and yellows.

But who created these paintings, why, and when? Jesuit priests noted them in the 17th century. The priests' indigenous converts, the Cochimí, attributed the paintings to "giants from the north." Today, experts disagree as to the paintings' provenance, but radiocarbon tests from the Cueva del Ratón site in the San Francisco range date them at nearly 5,000 years old. (Previous estimates had set the newest paintings at 500 to 2,000 years old.) Scholars agree, however, that newer images are superimposed on older ones, indicating that the authors valued the act of creation more than the artistic result.

Several factors determine the quality of surviving paintings, including the rock surface's durability, location, and exposure to the elements. One of the most magnificent and often visited sites is Cueva Pintada, north of San Ignacio in the San Francisco range. Five hundred feet (150 m) of walls and ceilings are covered with paintings of men, women, birds, and sea creatures. How the artist reached the ceiling is not known, but palm trunks or the fibrous skeleton of the cardón cactus may have served as ladders or scaffolding.

UNESCO designated the Sierra de San Francisco and its cave paintings a World Heritage site in 1993, and government and private organizations are collaborating to preserve the sites, involve local communities, and make the art more accessible to visitors. Guided trips can be organized through INAH (the national government research agency) in San Ignacio, next door to the mission (tel 615/154-0222). The best (coolest) time to visit is between November and February. ■

La Paz

DESPITE THE CITY'S FABULOUS LOCATION ON THE GULF OF California and its beautiful nearby beaches, La Paz's character is defined not by tourism but by its busy port and university. This capital city of fewer than 200,000 souls, seated at the bottom of a C-shaped bay, is sophisticated (by Baja standards), with visiting theater and symphonic groups and several worthwhile museums. It's famous for its streaky vermilion sunsets, observed equally well from a solitary, sandy beach on a turquoise inlet or an open-sided restaurant along the bayfront promenade. Nearby are excellent deep-sea fishing and the peninsula's best diving.

The Spanish briefly explored the area in the 16th century, for the most part leaving the cactus-strewn peninsula in peace until the founding of a Jesuit mission in 1720. In a sad irony, the mission was abandoned less than 30 years later, after introduced diseases such as smallpox wiped out almost all of the potential converts. Today a cathedral of the same name, **Nuestra Señora de la Paz,** Our Lady of Peace *(Revolución de 1910 at 5 de Mayo),* occupies the site of the original mission.

The cathedral faces **Plaza Constitución,** which along with the 3-mile (5 km) seawalk, the *malecón,* is one of La Paz's favorite meeting spots. Interesting exhibits on the geology, history, and folk-lore of the region can be found at the **Museo de Antropología** *(Altamirano at 5 de Mayo, tel 612/122-0162, $).* Although the exhibits are labeled in Spanish only, the museum's photographs of the area's natural beauty don't require any translation.

Whale-watching trips in the waters off La Paz can be arranged December through March with the larger hotels and with tour operators in the area.

The best beaches are found to the north of town on the thumb of land that separates La Paz Bay from the Gulf of California. Simple, beachfront restaurants overlook the turquoise bay at **Playa Pichilingue,** near the docks where daily ferries depart for the mainland at Topolobampo and Mazatlán. Lovely **Playa Balandra** has calm water great for swimming or snorkeling (bring your own gear). There are

The pearls

Inspired by tales of fierce, independent women to the west, Spanish conquistador Hernán Cortés led an expedition to the Baja Peninsula, which he presumed to be an island. The Spaniards named it California after an island in Garci Ordónez de Montalvo's popular Spanish novel *Las Sergas de Esplandian (The Exploits of Esplandian),* published in 1510. During his visit, Cortés is said to have obtained some of the area's precious white, pink, and black pearls from the island of Espíritu Santo. By the time author John Steinbeck published his allegorical novel about the misfortunes of a poor oyster-diving family, *The Pearl,* in 1947, La Paz's oysters were history, finished off by a mysterious blight. ∎

La Paz
△ 55 D1
Visitor information
✉ Tourist wharf on Paseo Alvaro Obregón at 16 de Septiembre
☎ 612/124-0103

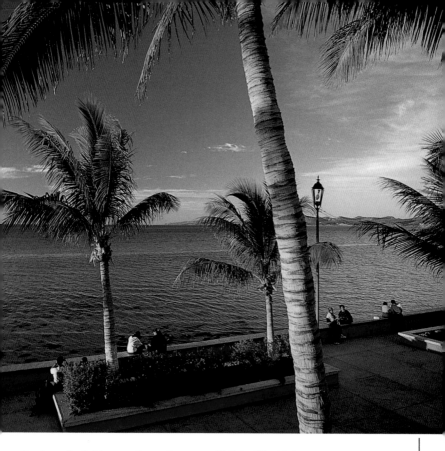

firepits, and primitive camping is allowed. For sustenance, you will have to go a mile or two north to popular **El Tecolote** beach, which has rest rooms, restaurants, and watersports equipment for rent.

Boats are available for rental to travel to **Isla Espíritu Santo,** about 5 miles (8 km) offshore. One of the best dive spots at La Paz, the "Island of the Holy Spirit" offers great visibility almost all year long. Kayakers can explore the coves and inlets off the 14-mile-long (22.5 km) island, and off smaller **La Partida** and **Los Islotes** to the north, both of which have large colonies of sea lions. July through September are the best months to dive with hammerhead sharks and manta

rays near **El Bajo (Marisla) Seamont,** off the north shore of the island.

Gorgeous, more isolated beaches such as **Punta Coyote** and **San Evaristo** are accessible from La Paz via dirt roads, and **La Ventana** and **Ensenada de los Muertos** can be reached as a day-long excursion south of La Paz along Highway 286. You'll pass cactus fields and cattle ranches as you climb into the Sierra de la Laguna. This is soon replaced by rolling hills and farm-lands around **San Juan de los Planes,** where corn, chilies, tomato, and beans are grown. Beyond this small agricultural town, dirt and gravel roads lead to excellent fishing, swimming, and boating beaches. ∎

La Paz's promenade faces calm gulf waters, protected by El Mogote, a long, narrow sandbar.

Whales great & small

Whether literature, movies, television, or actual close encounters have influenced your idea of whales, it's doubtful that these beautiful creatures will leave you indifferent. Orcas, with their large, conical teeth, no-nonsense markings, and the misleading moniker "killer whale," command respect. As the largest mammal on record, the blue whale is nearly mythical—it's difficult to imagine an animal that weighs nearly two tons at birth.

Intelligent and curious, whales are mammals whose ancestors returned to the water millions of years ago, retaining the lungs developed on land but adapting well to aquatic life. Today scientists acknowledge approximately 40 different species. These include baleen whales, which feed on krill (planktonic crustaceans and larvae) and small fish strained through horny plates descending from the upper jaw; and toothed whales, which include orcas, sperm whales, porpoises, and dolphins.

There is no better destination for whale spotting than the Baja California peninsula. Of the ten (some scientists say eleven) surviving baleen whale species, eight are found in the Gulf of California—more than anywhere else on Earth. Visitors may sight the streamlined finback whale, second in size only to the blue. The humpback is often spotted breaching (hauling its gargantuan body completely out of the water) or slapping the surface with a flipper or scalloped tail. Less often seen are Bryde's, minke, sei, and northern right whales. Bottlenose dolphins bodysurf the translucent waves near the shore, while common dolphins perform astounding acrobatics that make

Above: A diving whale shows off its broad, flat fluke.
Left: A gray whale at San Ignacio Lagoon. The whales migrate to Baja from the northern Bering Sea to mate and give birth; they are generally seen January to early April.

How to see the whales

Many reputable tour operators lead excursions of 4 to 14 days; a good number depart from San Diego, California, just across the Mexican border. Cruises focusing on the Pacific Coast (where primarily gray whales are spotted) depart San Diego for Scammon's and San Ignacio Lagoons, and may stop en route at Todos Santos, San Martin, San Benito, or Cedros Islands. Trips to Bahía Magdalena often begin and end in La Paz, Baja California Sur. Land-based excursions charter small planes to camp at San Ignacio or other locations. Inside sheltered lagoons, passengers board pangas to get closer to the marine mammals and their babies. And while fin-back, humpback, blue, and gray whales are seen in the species-rich Gulf of California, whale-watching excursions there are less common. Recommended are: Baja Expeditions, 2625 Garnet Ave., San Diego, CA 92109 (tel 858/581-3311 or 800/843-6967); Natural Habitat Adventures, 2945 Center Green Court, Suite H, Boulder, CO 80301 (tel 800/543-8917); and Searcher Natural History Tours, 2838 Garrison St., San Diego, CA 92106 (tel 619/226-2403). ■

them seem anything but common. Although less gregarious than the humpback, barnacle-encrusted gray whales may approach kayaks or *pangas* (skiffs), allowing thrilled observers the occasional caress.

Gray whales tarry in the protected lagoons of Baja's Pacific Coast; prime breeding grounds include Laguna Ojo de Liebre (also called Scammon's Lagoon) and Laguna San Ignacio, as well as Bahía Magdalena (Mag Bay), the latter protected from the open ocean by a 40-mile-long (64 km) barrier island. Each year an estimated 18,000 to 24,000 gray whales migrate south from summer feeding grounds in the northern Bering Sea. Of these, an unknown number complete the marathon migration to give birth or mate in the relatively warm, shallow, and inviting lagoons and estuaries off the Baja Peninsula. The journey—one of the most ambitious undertaken by any mammal—is an astonishing 5,000 miles (8,045 km). ■

Cabo San Lucas
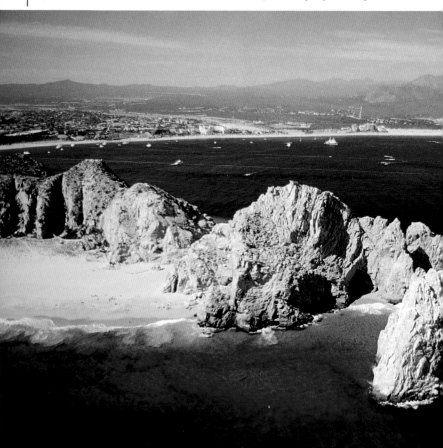
55 D1

Los Cabos

DRAMATIC DESERT SCENERY, BEAUTIFUL BEACHES, AND plenty of action draw visitors to the tip of Baja's narrow peninsula, where the Gulf of California's turquoise waters meet the Pacific Ocean. The deep-sea fishing is world-renowned. In the 1940s, John Wayne, Ernest Hemingway, and others would come in small private planes to hunt and fish, when Cabo San Lucas consisted of a scattering of humble homes opening onto dusty, nameless streets. Today less than three hours from several major U.S. airports, and also easily accessible from La Paz via the transpeninsular highway (completed 1974), Cabo has lost its isolation, but not its desert-by-the-sea allure.

The scenic rock formations at Land's End in Cabo San Lucas mark the southernmost point of the Baja California peninsula.

By the 1960s, a handful of comfortable, seaside hotels had sprung up among the organ cacti and spindly ocotillos. Several decades and many millions of investment dollars later, **Cabo San Lucas** has grown up, although not necessarily matured: at night spots like Squid Roe and

The Giggling Marlin, the mainly American crowd tends to down lots of tequila shooters and dance on the bar. Warm weather, a relaxed atmosphere, and excellent sports facilities lure all types of travelers to the tip of one of the world's longest peninsulas.

Posh resort hotels and a half dozen high-priced golf courses line the 23-mile (37 km) beachfront corridor north of Cabo San Lucas. (To avoid confusion, Cabo San Lucas, San José del Cabo, and the corridor in between have been dubbed "Los Cabos.") Resorts along the corridor have their own beaches and cater to those content to stay put—not a bad idea, since cab rides

in this relatively isolated area begin at around $20. With multiple swimming pools, hot tubs, and restaurants, as well as European-style spas and gym facilities, these vacation spots offer a variety of activities to entertain their guests. If you plan to do much exploring beyond your hotel's swim-up bar, you might consider renting a car.

San José del Cabo was established by the Jesuits in the 18th century. Flowering acacia and Indian laurel trees partially shade the typical Mexican plaza, with its lacy wrought-iron bandstand and matching benches. Fronting the plaza is San José's simple yet winning church, its whitewashed

San José del Cabo

◪ 55 D1

Visitor information

✉ Plaza San Jose, Local 3, Carretera Transpeninsular s/n

☎ 624/142-3310

interior decorated with rather naively drawn gilded accents. Boutiques and restaurants with English-language menus surround the square and line the street into town, but these soon give way to one- and two-story houses and shops geared toward locals. While Cabo San Lucas offers proximity to the marina and boisterous nightlife, San José has a more subdued, more Mexican attitude.

San José's estuary is undergoing changes; it's currently being enveloped by a new marina and other touristic infrastructure. Heading south toward San Lucas,

Painted guitars hanging to dry, some of the local craftwork in Los Cabos

The arch at Land's End, seen here from Playa del Amor, is accessible only by boat.

Costa Azul and Acapulquito Beaches are favored by surfers, while just beyond, **Playa Palmilla** (at the Hotel Palmilla) is the closest recommended swimming beach; **Santa María Bay** is great for diving and snorkeling as well as swimming. Shade umbrellas and snorkel equipment are usually available. **Playa Médano,** on the bay at Cabo San Lucas, is popular for its unlimited watersports. Waverunners, jet skis, catamarans, and banana boats crowd the bay, while overhead, parasailers get a bird's-eye view of Land's End and **El Pedregal,** an exclusive community of American film stars and wealthy retirees. Underneath Cabo's trademark rock arch, **El Arco,** is **Playa del Amor,** a sandy beach accessible by water taxi or inexpensive glass-bottomed boat tour. More secluded beaches can be reached in ATVs or four-wheel-drive vehicles.

The bay's rocky outcrops make for good diving. At a depth of 90 feet (27 m) are the mysterious **sand falls,** a seemingly endless cascade created as the current drags fine sand over an undersea crag and into deeper water. Sportfishing, however, remains Los Cabos' most enduring draw; more marlin and swordfish are caught here than anywhere else in the world. Each October hundreds of serious anglers gather for Bisbee's Black & Blue Marlin Tournament, a three-day event with a purse exceeding $1 million. Although the best billfishing (except for marlin) is generally June through September, the fishing is excellent year-round, for wahoo, tuna, grouper, red snapper, dorado, swordfish, shark, and roosterfish, among others.

A visit to the old mission town of **Todos Santos,** 40 miles (65 km) north of Cabo San Lucas, is a chance to see something outside the tourist zone. Increasingly popular with ex-pats bearing greenbacks, the growing town has a good bookstore and several worthwhile hotels, restaurants, and art galleries. Hikes into the as yet relatively untouched Sierra de la Laguna can be arranged through area hotels or tour operators throughout Los Cabos. ∎

The craggy peaks of the Sierra San Pedro Mártir rise above Bahía de Los Angeles.

More places to visit in Baja California

BAHÍA DE LOS ANGELES

Surrounded by the stark peaks of the eastern San Pedro Mártir mountains, "L.A. Bay" is a beautiful base for fishing, diving, kayaking, and relaxing up and down the Gulf of California, more often referred to as the Sea of Cortez. Offshore, 45-mile-long (72 km) Angel de la Guarda island serves as a barrier for the town's C-shaped bay, which is subject to 22-foot (7 m) tidal surges. To the south is a string of smaller islands, including **Isla Raza,** a sanctuary for seabirds as well as sportsmen and -women. Increasingly popular with all sorts of visitors, the town offers accommodations from rustic camping to **Los Vientos,** with pool, hot tub, and Internet access. The town's small museum, on the west side of the plaza, displays peninsular fauna, marine life, and Indian artifacts. Four-wheel-drive vehicles continue on to **Punta San Francisquito,** 81 miles (131 km) south on isolated Bahía Santa Teresa, where there are rustic cabins, a restaurant, and a fish camp.
⚠ 55 B4

MISIÓN SAN FRANCISCO BORJA

This isolated mission was established by the Jesuits in 1759, farmed by the Franciscans, and completed by the Dominicans. The fine stone church—surrounded by fig, olive, and date orchards—was abandoned in 1818 after disease decimated the local Indian converts. Located 22 miles (35 km) east of Rosarito, near Guerrero Negro (not to be confused with the beach resort north of Ensenada), the active church holds Sunday services. Hire a local to guide you to the area's rock art. Only sturdy vehicles with high clearance should attempt the drive.
⚠ 55 B4

MISIÓN SAN JAVIER

Considered the loveliest and best preserved of all Baja's missions, San Javier, west of Loreto, was the second to be built on the peninsula (between 1699 and 1759). This Moorish-style church, located in a deep valley, contrasts with the thatch-roofed adobe huts found in this region of the Sierra de la Giganta. Admire the stained-glass windows, the 18th-century wooden altar covered in gold leaf, and the statue of St. Francis. High-clearance vehicles can make the rocky, three-hour drive from Loreto in dry weather, but a four-wheel-drive vehicle is best. Hire a guide in Loreto or the town of San Javier to lead you to rock paintings in the region. The town swells with pilgrims around its feast day, December 3, and celebrates the onion harvest, one of its most important crops, August 15. 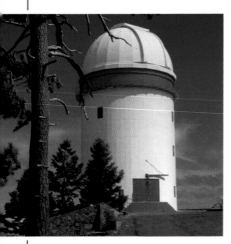 55 C2

PARQUE NACIONAL SIERRA SAN PEDRO MÁRTIR

The granite peaks, high meadows, and fragrant forests of this 49,000-acre (20,000 ha) national park are little visited. Roads are rough and may be closed by winter snows but are accessible to high-clearance vehicles. Fishing, camping, and hiking are permitted. Experienced climbers tackle Picacho del Diablo (Devil's Summit)—the peninsula's highest peak, at 10,154 feet (3,100 m) above sea level. If you prefer to photograph rather than scale the rocky mountain, don't miss the terrific view of the peak from the National Autonomous University of Mexico's observatory, at the end of the park access road. Hikers should take adequate water and supplies, as well as a map and compass; the nation-

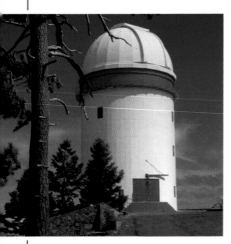

The observatory, Sierra San Pedro Mártir

al park has no facilities and few rangers. 55 B5 ✉ Entrance 47 miles (75 km) off Highway 1 on an unpaved road. Ranger station at Corona de Abajo 💲 $

SAN FELIPE

Until 1951, San Felipe was a sleepy fishing village on the northwestern shore of the Gulf of California, but this resort town of more

than 20,000 now counts tourism as its main source of revenue. It is also the shrimp capital of Baja California. Hugging the northern shore of a wide, relatively shallow natural bay, the relaxed desert town squats in the shadow of Punta San Felipe, a twin-peaked headland nearly 1,000 feet (305 m) high. With less than two inches (5 cm) of rain a year, vegetation is scant, and in summer temperatures may soar to 115°F (46°C). In the winter, U.S. and Canadian snowbirds fill area RV parks and cruise the beach on ATVs. South of town, shrimp boats depart from the marina that also accommodates private craft. Fresh seafood—including a giant *campechana,* a cocktail of shrimp, clams, and octopus—is the main draw of the many casual restaurants along the *malecón,* or seawalk. Extreme tidal fluxes here send beachcombers searching for shells along 12 miles (19 km) of wide, grainy sand beaches south of town, many nearly deserted.
55 B5   **Visitor information** ✉ Calle Manzanillo 300 at Av. Mar de Cortés ☎ 686/577-1155

TECATE

Set in a bowl-shaped valley at 1,690 feet (515 m), Tecate has none of the raucous flavor of most border towns. It thrives on light industry and agriculture, with outlying fields of grain, olives, and grapes. Visitors can tour the **Tecate Brewery** free by appointment *(Av. Dr. Arturo Guerra 70, tel 665/654-9478)* or stroll in the main plaza, **Parque Hidalgo** *(Av. Juárez & Calle Ortíz Rubio).*

On one or two Saturdays per month railway tours *($$$$)* are a good way to see the countryside. They run between Campos, California (in the U.S.), and Tecate. An hour each way, the trip goes through open country and ranchlands. The 1930s train is from the original San Diego & Arizona Railway. In Tecate visitors have free time plus a brewery visit if desired. Reservations must be made through the Internet *(www.sdrm.org).* The city is known for its *pan dulce* (sweet bread) and unglazed pots, planters, and floor tiles. Highway 3 between Tecate and Ensenada winds through low hills past wineries and rustic resorts popular with Mexican families.
55 A5   **Visitor information** ✉ 1305 Callejón Libertad ☎ 665/41095 ■

The geographically diverse region of northwestern Mexico has enormous tracts of high and low desert, more than 1,000 miles (1,600 km) of coast, the world's largest volcanic field, and some of the country's richest farmlands.

Northwest Mexico

Barrel cactus

A Tarahumara man celebrates Easter according to local ritual, in which Christianity is fused with ancient rites.

Northwest Mexico

HARSH YET IMPOSING, MEXICO'S VAST NORTHWEST comprises the states of Sonora, Chihuahua, Durango, and Sinaloa. Seldom visited by tourists, it offers 10,000-foot (3,050 m) peaks clothed in pine-oak forests, North America's first- and third-largest deserts, and a 1,300-mile (2,090 km) coast. Explorers head for the extensive canyon system of Sierra Tarahumara, where it's now relatively easy to organize hiking, horseback riding, or vehicular tours to spectacular waterfalls and lost Jesuit missions.

Roughly following the Gulf of California, the formidable Sierra Madre Occidental runs northwest to southeast. The range's steeper, more dramatic eastern escarpment drops down to Chihuahua's high desert, while to the west, valleys, canyons, and peaks finally give way to the foothills and then the coast. A dozen major rivers drain into the narrow, fertile coastal plain, creating prime farmlands.

In the 16th century, European and *criollo* (Mexican-born Spanish) explorers, adventurers, and Jesuit friars began to infiltrate the harsh northern areas. Along with the elements, they faced the Chichimeca: fierce northern tribes, most of whom even the Aztecs could not conquer. Over the centuries, vast numbers of indigenous peoples, and even entire tribes, succumbed to disease, slavery, deportation, and capital punishment, although sporadic rebellions and wars lasted until the 20th century.

Despite this resistance, the Jesuits founded dozens of mission villages before their expulsion in 1767, while entrepreneurs established incredible mining empires along the western flanks of the Sierra Madre Occidental. Vast ranches supplied the mines, missions, and *presidios* (military posts) with beef, creating immense individual fortunes in the process. Today, ranching is still important, as are forestry, farming, and fishing.

Great distances between sights and a limited tourist infrastructure notwithstanding, the northwest offers an awesome variety of scenery and experiences. Explore the ruins of Oasis America culture at Paquimé (see pp. 82–83) or the surreal moonscapes of silent, solitary Pinacate, with its impossibly wide craters, underground lava tubes, black cinder cones, and shifting sand dunes. Access and services for the Copper Canyon and

Sonora's low-key beach resorts are expanding, and the region's only major beach resort, Mazatlán, is in full swing.

In general, the best time to visit is fall, when soaring summer temperatures have abated, and rain has clothed mountainsides in green and deserts in the fragile blooms of tenacious succulents. ■

◁ 6

Area of map detail

Mexico City

ITED STATES

◁ 5

CIUDAD JUÁREZ

Dunas de Samalayuca

El Barreal

gales
Cananea
Agua Prieta
2
Janos
Lucero
10
Paquimé
Nuevo Casas Grandes
45D
Cumpás
Mata Ortíz
El Sueco
10
Buenaventura
Mazocahui
Gómez Farías
El Pastor
PARQUE NAC. CUMBRES DE MAJALCA
16
mosillo
Sahuaripa
Presa Luis L. León
Llanos de los Caballos Mesteños
◁ 4

Ojinaga

Bravo del Norte

Conchos

Sierra Grande

Casas Grandes

Sonora

Bavispe

Sierra

Presa Plutarco Elías Calles

16
Tonichi
San Nicolás
Cascada Piedra Volada
Chihuahua
tíz
Presa A. Obregón
mas
5D
Cascada de Basaseáchic
PARQUE NAC. CASCADA DE BASASEÁCHIC
Cuauhtémoc
45D
Delicias
Ciudad Obregón
Rosario
PARQUE NAT. BARRANCA DEL COBRE
Creel
Cascada de Cusárare
Ciudad Camargo
Navojoa
Cerocahui
Divisadero
Conchos
La Boquilla del Conchos
Bolsón de Mapimí
Alamos
Urique
Batopilas
Hidalgo del Parral
Jiménez
Yávaros
San Ignacio
El Vergel
49D
Ahome
Choix
Villa Ocampo
Tlahualilo de Zaragoza
◁ 3
Los Mochis
El Fuerte
San Blas
Guadalupe y Calvo
Guanacevi
45
Bermejillo
Topolobampo
Guasave
30
Gómez Palacio
Guamuchil
El Palmito
Pericos
Presa Lázaro Cárdenas
Santiago Papasquiaro
Isla Altamura
15D
Culiacán
DURANGO
Lago de Santiaguillo
40D
Cuencamé
Altata
San Lorenzo
Francisco I. Madero
◁ 2
Durango
El Salto
40
PARQUE NAT. PUERTO DE LOS ANGELES
45
Copala
Mezquital
Mazatlán
Concordia
15
Rosario

C

CHIHUAHUA

Chínipas

Urique

Fuerte

Sinaloa

Presa M. Hidalgo

Presa A.L. Mateos

SINALOA

DURANGO

Ramos

Sextín

Presa La Boquilla

Presa Luis L. León

Nazas

D

Teacapan

NORTHEAST MEXICO   p. 103

0   200 kilometers
0   100 miles

CENTRAL PACIFIC STATES   p. 137

◁ 1

E   F

El Pinacate

LUNAR-LIKE AND OTHERWORLDLY, THE LANDSCAPE OF El Pinacate is as beautiful as it is barren. Huge, craggy craters rise in startling contrast to the flatness of the surrounding desert, and in the western portion of the 1.8-million-acre (728,460 ha) park winds build shifting dunes hundreds of feet high. Geologists and photographers are especially drawn to the rich textures and striking hues of this arid region. NASA was so impressed with Pinacate's extraterrestrial appearance that it sent the crew of *Apollo 14* here to practice working with new moon-landing equipment.

Reserva de la Biósfera Sierra de Pinacate
🗺 76 B6
Visitor information
✉ Highway 8 Km 52
☎ 638/384-9007
(in Puerto Peñasco)

This unique ecosystem in the Gran Desierto de Altar (Mexico's Sonora Desert), designated a UNESCO Man and the Biosphere Reserve in 1993, has the largest concentration of volcanic cones and craters on Earth. Volcanic activity that began three or four million years ago created miles of jagged lava beds so unforgiving that colonial-era wayfarers called it the "Sea of Broken Glass." More than 400 cinder cones (conical mounds formed around a volcanic vent) jut in dramatic waves along the desert floor within a 30-mile-wide (48 km) field. The tallest are raven-colored **Cerro del Pinacate** and **Cerro del Carnegie,** at 4,000 (1,219 m) and 3,700 feet (1,128 m) respectively.

Huge maars, or craters, were probably created when bubbling magma hit groundwater, initiating explosions of steam and blasting rock and lava into the air. One of the most spectacular examples of these black behemoths is **Cráter Elegante,** about 12 miles (19 km) north of the main (east) park entrance. Rising 165 feet (50 m) from the desert floor, the crater's uneven walls are the product of prevailing winds at the time of eruption. Peering over the edge of the mile-wide (1.5 km), 800-foot-deep (245 m) crater inspires nothing short of awe. In addition to the park's ten maars, underground lava tubes and other extraordinary formations provide unlimited opportunities for exploration.

Despite its bleak and desolate first impression, the reserve sustains a variety of plants and animals. Endangered desert bighorn sheep, Sonoran pronghorn antelope, and desert tortoises share the unforgiving desert with the park's namesake, the endemic pinacate beetle. Roadrunners and rattlers are abundant, and more than 550 plant species have been identified. In spring, brief rains encourage white dune evening primroses, yellow desert marigolds, and colorful skeleton weeds to bloom.

Visitors must register at the park's main entrance, 32 miles (51 km) south of the Lukeville, Arizona/Sonoyta border crossing, on Highway 8. There are no facilities at the park; bring your own water and food, and take away all trash. The best time to visit is spring, when temperatures are least extreme and wildflowers most abundant. From late April to September, daytime temperatures may soar to 120°F (49°C); nighttime temperatures in winter can dip below freezing. Sunscreen, sunglasses, water, and a hat are essential. A high-clearance vehicle is advised; four-wheel drive is recommended but not required.

Of the park's two basic campgrounds, **El Tecolote,** 5 miles (8 km) northeast of Elegante, has the best access to hiking trails and the craters. **Cono Rojo,** 14 miles (22 km) northwest of the information center, is a better bet for those wanting to hike up to the volcanic peaks. Backcountry camping is permitted with a few restrictions. ■

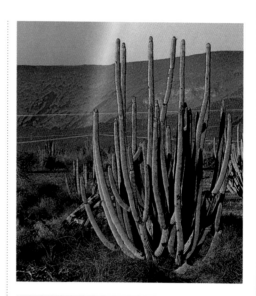

Cactuses

There are about 1,650 species of cactus worldwide, but Mexico has more species and more specimens than any other country. The Sonora, driest and hottest of North America's four deserts, has the greatest diversity of species. Adaptations such as a lack of leaves, shallow wide-ranging roots, and the ability to store water for more than a year allow cactuses to thrive in the uncompromising desert.

Historically, cactuses have provided food, water, building materials, and inspiration for the desert's hardy inhabitants. The Huichol (see p. 13) and other indigenous peoples employ the hallucinogenic peyote cactus to commune with God, seek visions, and heal disease. Prickly pear, saguaro, and organ cactuses provide sweet, juicy, and nutritious fruits. Barrel cactus are a source of emergency water, while other species are burned as fuel or used as living fences. ■

The fruit-bearing organ cactus provides an important food source to desert inhabitants.

Sonora's beaches

DESERT RATS, YOUNG REVELERS FROM NEARBY ARIZONA, and snowbirds (Northerners escaping the winter) have long sought out the solitary, sandy beaches along Sonora's desert coast. Excellent sportfishing, good snorkeling and diving, and proximity to the United States have been among the region's main attractions. Over the past decade, improved tourist infrastructure and the establishment of hotels, marinas, and golf courses have attracted a more demanding clientele, yet at the same time caused disenchantment among fans of the rustic and the remote.

Puerto Peñasco
76 A5
Visitor information
✉ Blvd. Juárez 320 at V. Estrella
☎ 638/383-6122 from the U.S. 800/4SONORA

Backed by cliffs ranging from rust red to gold, simple fishing villages and unpretentious towns from Puerto Peñasco to Guaymas have long provided fresh seafood, cold beer, and a relaxing atmosphere.

Seri men making the crossing to Isla Tiburón, their ancestral homeland and now a protected ecological park

Time-shares, hotels, condos, and private residences are popping up fast, as are restaurants and services geared mainly toward U.S. and Canadian visitors. Spring and fall see fewer tourists and more competitive prices than in the peak winter months.

Just 60 miles (97 km) from the border at Lukeville, Arizona, is **Puerto Peñasco** the first seaside town on Sonora's 600-mile (965 km) coastline. Sandy beaches, rocky coves, and extreme tidal variation attract shell collectors and lovers of long walks. The town was established in the 1920s as a shrimp camp, but long before that British explorers had named the place Rocky Point, a designation still used by most English-speakers today. Overfishing in recent years has significantly reduced the shrimp harvest, once the mainstay of the economy, and tourism is now the most important industry. Building is booming, and there are two full-service marinas with shops, restaurants, hotels, and condos.

CEDO (*Las Conchas neighborhood, tel 638/382-0113, www.cedo intercultural.org*) offers nature walks and talks and slide shows, and has a gift shop. Interested volunteers can help with conservation projects.

South of Puerto Peñasco is **Bahía Kino,** named for Padre Chini (1645–1711), the Italian-born Jesuit priest and adventurer known as Padre Kino. **Kino Viejo,** a simple fishing village, hugs the bay with its fine, sandy beaches, while to the north **Kino Nuevo** is an enclave of Canadian and U.S. vacationers and retirees. Once dominated by RV parks, the 8-mile (13 km) beachfront road that constitutes the town has an increasing number of condos, time-shares, hotels, and private residences. The **Museo de los Seris** (*Blvd.*

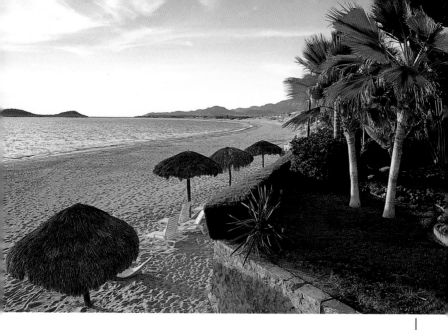

Mar de Cortés at Progreso, closed Mon.–Tues., $) highlights the Seri culture, while the Seri themselves come to town to sell grass baskets, pottery, ironwood statuettes, and necklaces of seashells, seeds, and animal bones. Across the channel from Bahía Kino are **Isla Tiburón** (see p. 84) and tiny **Isla San Esteban,** which have been protected as an ecological reserve since 1963.

The carmine-colored peaks of the **Sierra de Bacochibampo** —including the town's symbol, craggy Tetakawi, or "goat teat hill" —form a magnificent backdrop for **Bahía San Carlos** *(Visitor information, Blvd. Escénico Km. 9.2, tel 622/226-0202),* one of northern Mexico's fastest-growing tourist destinations. Spindly ocotillo cacti with spidery red blooms brighten the surrounding desert in the fall, while snorkelers seek out colorful fish among the rocky outcroppings separating Bahía San Carlos and **Bahía Bacochibampo.** Divers are drawn to the 5,000-foot-deep (1,500 m) **Guaymas Trench,** which attracts an estimated 700 species of marine life. Half- and

full-day fishing boat trips go after yellowtail, sailfish, marlin, and grouper; closer to shore, anglers catch triggerfish and sea bass. The well-protected bay has a full-service marina. A few major resorts line **Playa los Algodones,** on the west end of San Carlos, offering kayaking, jet skiing, and windboarding.

A mountainous peninsula separates San Carlos from more commercial **Guaymas** *(Map ref. 77 C4, visitor information, Malecón Malpica, between Calles 22 & 23, tel 622/222-1751),* about 10 miles (16 km) to the southeast. Bolstered by a significant canning industry and a PEMEX oil refinery, Guaymas is Sonora's main port. Vermilion peaks crouch above its fine natural harbor, crowded with vessels of all shapes and sizes, including oil tankers and shrimp boats. Forecasts of large-scale expansion have produced only a marina and a golf course, and many visitors prefer more vacation-oriented San Carlos. Those who stay in Guaymas are usually seeking a less touristy venue or are boarding the twice-weekly ferry to Santa Rosalía, in Baja California Sur. ■

Sonora's beaches lure U.S. vacationers as well as Mexicans from the scorching interior.

Paquimé

PAQUIMÉ, THE MOST IMPORTANT RUINS IN NORTHERN Mexico, was built by the Oasis America cultural group, who lived in an area extending from northwest Chihuahua and northeast Sonora to the southwestern United States. In its day this commercial center imported turquoise from the north, seashells from the west coast, and copper and obsidian from the Valley of Mexico. Its inhabitants lived in rammed-earth, multiple-story houses similar to the adobes of the Pueblo Indians to the north. Unlike Anasazi-Pueblo villages, however, Paquimé had fixed, interior stairways and an elaborate system of water collection, filtration, distribution, and disposal.

Paquimé

🅰 77 D5

Visitor information

✉ ½ mile (1 km) outside Nuevo Casas Grandes

☎ 636/692-4140

💲 $$

Inhabited since about A.D. 700, this site overlooking the Casas Grandes River began to blossom some time after 1150, reaching its apogee between 1300 and 1450 before being abandoned. Some anthropologists think it was quit earlier, possibly after attacks by Apaches from the north. Five-foot-thick (1.5 m) walls provided insulation from the desert's intense heat and bitter cold.

Aspects of Paquimé's culture show the influence of central Mexico, such as organization of artisans by neighborhood, veneration of the god Quetzalcoatl (Feathered Serpent), and use of ceremonial plazas and I-shaped ball courts.

Today, for the most part, only the first-floor exterior walls and myriad room dividers survive. "We have to restore the crumbling walls at least twice a year," explains Paquimé's director, archaeologist Mercedes Jiménez. "Sun, wind, snow ...everything harms these very fragile structures." Visitors now must enter the site from the back, where the *montículos,* or temple mounds, can still be visited. The **Montículo del Pájaro, Montículo de las Ofrendas,** and **Montículo de los Héroes** are named for birds, offerings, and heroes. **Montículo de la Cruz** is a cross-shaped, raised adobe structure roughly oriented toward the four cardinal points and surrounded by four circular platforms. It was most likely used in agricultural or celestial rituals.

To the south, vestiges of a second floor can be seen at the **Casa del Pozo,** along with partially reconstructed flooring, wooden columns,

Mata Ortíz pottery

Pottery produced in the small village of Juan Mata Ortíz, 12½ miles (20 km) south of Casas Grandes, is exquisite, with extremely thin walls and a soft, bright luster. The techniques originated with Juan Quezada. He spent 15 years experimenting with clay, pigments, and firing techniques before producing his first pots. In 1976, Spencer MacCallum found a few of these unsigned pots in a secondhand shop in New Mexico and traced Quezada to his village. A quarter century later, about half of the town's population makes this internationally collected pottery without the use of a potter's wheel or kiln. While the techniques used are those developed by Quezada, many artisans have devised their own motifs and designs. ∎

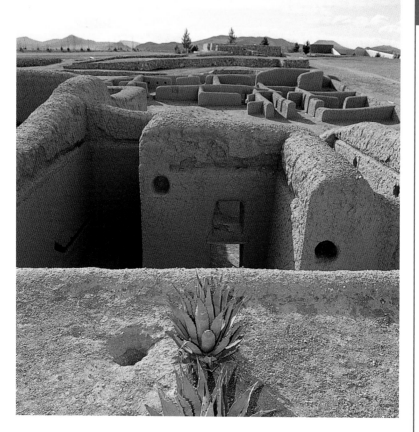

and beams. A stairway leads up to a section of the stone aqueduct that carried water throughout the city. It is not possible to wander the rooms of most of the former dwellings. However, they can still be appreciated from the outside. (The multimedia exhibit in the museum gives a 360-degree, "virtual" tour.)

Beyond the **Casa de los Cráneos** (named for the skulls and human bones found here), more than 90 grave sites were found beneath the **Casa de los Muertos** (House of the Dead). Birds—probably macaws imported from the south—were kept in adobe cages in the adjacent structure, and in the **Casa de la Serpiente;** their feathers were used in ceremonies. South of the Casa de los Muertos is the **Casa de los Pilares**—origi-

nally four to five stories high and today one of the few buildings with walls more than one story tall. To the west, the **Montículo de la Serpiente** is thought to have been dedicated to Quetzalcoatl, revered in central Mexico since the days of Tula (see p. 232).

The **Museo de las Culturas del Norte** (tel 636/692-4140, closed Mon.) highlights the Oasis America culture in general and Paquimé in particular. Examples of the city's pottery are displayed, as are a scale model of the site and artifacts from the mission church built near Casas Grandes in 1660.

Most people visit Paquimé from Nuevo Casas Grandes, 5 miles (8 km) north. This small agricultural town has a few comfortable, if simple, hotels and restaurants. ■

The low, T-shaped doorways of Paquimé's houses—now in ruins—helped deter invaders.

The Seri

Historically, the pantheistic Seri revered the sun and the moon as well the marine turtle, the pelican, and other divine manifestations. However, their lack of totems and monuments led icon-bearing Jesuit priests to consider them godless and to marvel at their unwavering disinclination to convert. The Seri were one of the last indigenous cultures in North America to integrate into European-derived culture and to accept Christianity.

This dancer emulates the deer, revered by the Seri yet also hunted as prey.

They paid a high price for their resistance to mission life and Spanish rule. In 1662, a violent rebellion by a band of Seris was quelled only when every last man and woman had been slain and their children whisked off to the mission. Hanged as cattle rustlers, deported, and decimated by introduced disease, the Seri numbered a mere 150 by the early 20th century. Today, roughly 1,000 individuals speak the native language; most live in the towns of Punta Chueca and El Desemboque, north of Bahía Kino on Sonora's Gulf of California coastline.

Autonomous and proud, the Seri roamed the stark deserts, plains, coasts, and offshore islands long before the arrival of the Spanish. Surviving with the ebb and flow of the seasons, they foraged for food in the Desierto de Altar and fished for shellfish. Their annual marine turtle harvest provided not only a source of food but also a ceremonial link with traditional culture. A long history of storytelling in narrative song is an important part of the Seri heritage; this lyrical recital is passed from generation to generation. Songs are sung in praise of animals that provide food, or to protect them from natural phenomena, including navigating the sometimes treacherous passage to the Isla Tiburón. Deprived of their traditional turtle harvest since 1991,

when a government ban on hunting them and collecting their eggs was put in effect, the Seri struggle to maintain their cultural identity.

Despite pressure to acculturate, the Comcaac, as they call themselves, continue to sing their songs. They support themselves by fishing and by the sale of handicrafts, particularly shell jewelry and carved ironwood statues of lizards, dolphins, and other animals. Working with the Arizona-Sonora Desert Museum in Tucson and a government agency protecting the Gulf of California, the Seri have extensively catalogued natural food and herbs used traditionally as both food and medicine.

ISLA TIBURÓN

Isla Tiburón (Shark Island), ancestral homeland to the Seri, once provided them with refuge from Spanish military expeditions and aggressive cattle ranchers. Mexico's largest island has been protected as an ecological reserve since 1963, but it's owned by the Seri themselves, who also have exclusive fishing rights to el Canal del Infernillo, between the island and mainland. Knowledgeable Seri guides accompany visitors to the biologically diverse island to camp, hike, kayak, and snorkel.

Endangered bighorn sheep roam the island's two mountain ranges, which run north to south, while peregrine falcons, owls, and frigates patrol the skies. Blue-footed boobies show off their powder-blue appendages along lovely, secluded sandy beaches, and red, black, and white mangroves shelter a wide variety of marine fauna. There is good anchorage in the south at Kun Kaak Bay.

Contact the Gobierno de la Comunidad Seri *(Kino Viejo, Sonora, tel 662/242-0590)* for more information. ■

The Seri continue many of their traditional ways. Left, burning bark off sticks used in basketmaking; above, around 1000 Seri speak the native language today; below, a stingray is caught in the waters near Punta Chueca.

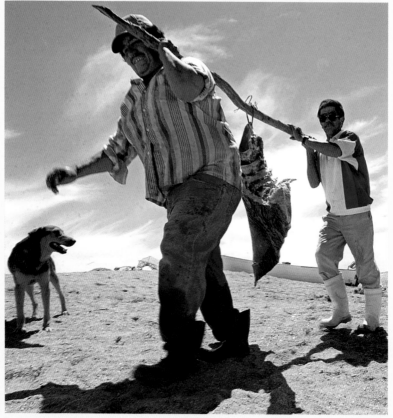

Chihuahua

77 E4

Visitor information

Palacio de Gobierno
Plaza Hidalgo,
Aldama at Guerrero

614/429-3596

Chihuahua

BORN OF A SILVER MINE, BATHED IN THE BLAZING LIGHT of Mexico's huge northern desert, and surrounded by mountains rich in resources, Chihuahua was destined for success. Although today cattle ranching, industry, and timber have replaced mining as the mainstays of the economy, the city continues to prosper and the silver mines still produce. Elegant colonial buildings, precocious Victorian mansions, and self-confident modern sculptures make Chihuahua—despite its disappointing dearth of tiny, big-eyed, namesake dogs—a city to be admired.

Known as the Cradle of the Revolution, Chihuahua looms large in Mexican history. Independence heroes Miguel Hidalgo y Costilla and three of his lieutenants were executed here in 1811. Now the capital of Mexico's largest state, at different times during the French Intervention and the Second Empire (see p. 33) the city served as Benito Juárez's provisional capital. And Pancho Villa—once governor of Chihuahua—based his División del Norte (Northern Division) army here for a number of years during the Mexican Revolution.

Today, although the city's outer limits sprawl, the historic district is attractive and diverse. Remains of an 18th-century aqueduct give portions of the city an old European air. Well-tended gardens surround the wrought-iron bandstand, imported from Paris in 1893, at **Plaza de Armas,** the city's principal square. At one end stands the Churrigueresque **Catedral Metropolitana** (*Libertad at Independencia*), dedicated to St. Francis of Assisi. Indian raids and the expulsion of the Jesuits—who began construction in 1735—delayed the cathedral's completion for nearly a hundred years. Its facade, adorned with statues of the 12 Apostles, is topped by two slender, ocher-colored towers. Inside, note the Venetian chandeliers and the monumental German organ. The late 18th-century main altar of carved limestone is almost obscured by a neoclassic altar of Carrara marble. In the back of the church, the **Museo de Arte Sacro** (*Closed Sat., Sun., $*) has

Northwest Mexico is cattle and sheep country.

17th- and 18th-century religious objects and paintings.

North of the main square, in the **Palacio Federal** *(tel 614/429-3300, ext. 11056, closed Mon., $)*, is the small cell where Padre Hidalgo was imprisoned before his death by firing squad. You can see his Bible, crucifix, and pistol. Across the street stands the stately, three-story **Palacio de Gobierno** *(Plaza Hidalgo, Aldama at Guerrero, tel 614/429-3596)*. Visit the place of his execution, surrounded by murals depicting that event and other episodes in the region's history.

South of the city center, the Revolution and the role of Chihuahua's adoptive son, General Francisco "Pancho" Villa, are detailed at the **Museo Histórico de la Revolución Mexicana** *(Calle 10ª 3014 at Méndez, tel 614/416-2958, closed Mon., $)*. The museum is located within **Quinta Luz,** a mansion named for Villa's legal wife, Luz Corral de Villa. The stately house has original furnishings, as well as photos, documents, firearms, and the black Dodge that

Villa was driving when he was assassinated in 1923. A few blocks north, **Quinta Gameros** *(Paseo Bolívar 401 at Calle 4, tel 614/416-6684, closed Mon., $)* is a wonderfully restored, two-story mansion with a so-so collection of paintings and some elegant art nouveau furnishings.

Several newish museums are worth a look. The **Museo de Arte Contemporánea** at **Casa Redonda** *(Av. Colón at Escudero, Col. Santo Niño, tel 614/414-9061, closed Mon., $)* has, as you might guess, contemporary art. The large-format work of well-known Chihuahua sculptor Sebastián, whose graceful modern metal sculptures are seen throughout Mexico, is reproduced in scale models at **Museo de Sebastián** *(Asv. Juárez at Calle 6, tel 614/410-7506, closed Mon.)* within recently restored **Casa Siglo XIX.**

On Sundays, Chihuahuenses admire the restored buildings of historic **Santa Eulalia,** 15 miles (9 km) southeast of town, or the beauty of Las Grutas Nombre de Dios, en route to the airport. ■

Ornate facade and copper-tiled roof of the cultural center at Quinta Gameros

Sierra Tarahumara
(Copper Canyon)

MEXICANS DELIGHT IN TELLING VISITORS (ESPECIALLY those from the United States) how much bigger and better is the series of canyons collectively known as the Copper Canyon (or more accurately, la Sierra Tarahumara) than the Grand Canyon, in Arizona. And it's true that these dramatic gorges are immense and impressive. Of the six major canyons composing Las Barrancas del Cobre system, four are deeper than the Grand Canyon. In addition to their natural beauty, they are dotted with Jesuit missions, abandoned mines, early 20th-century mansions, and indigenous cave dwellings.

Chihuahua
77 E4
Visitor information
✉ Aldama at Guererro
☎ 614/429-3596

Los Mochis
77 C3
Visitor information
✉ Unidad Administrativa del Gobierno del Estado, at Allende and Ordoñez
☎ 668/815-1090 or 668/815-4970

**Opposite:
Dwarfed by Sierra Madre peaks, a train trundles across one of the Copper Canyon's 37 major bridges.**

LA SIERRA TARAHUMARA

During 10 to 15 million years of the Tertiary era, volcanic activity and shifting tectonic plates created this mountain range, with peaks up to 12,000 feet (3,650 m). Working on surface fissures, time and the action of rain, runoff, and underwater currents carved out the series of deep canyons known collectively as Las Barrancas del Cobre. The hard igneous strata resist erosion, causing dramatic rock formations. Among the six main canyons of the Sierra Tarahumara, depth varies from 4,986 feet (1,520 m) at Barranca Oteros to 6,135 feet (1,870 m) at Barranca Urique. Barranca Sinforosa has the highest elevation, at 8,293 feet (2,528 m) above sea level; Chínipas, at 6,555 feet (1,998 m), is lowest.

Missionaries and miners were the first non-Indians to settle in the pine-scented mountains and deep, scrubby gorges of the Sierra Tarahumara, part of the Sierra Madre Occidental west of Chihuahua. In the 17th and 18th centuries, the Jesuits established simple yet beautiful churches throughout this canyon country—despite drawn-out and widespread local resistance. At the same time, a wealth of copper gave the Copper Canyon (part of Urique Canyon)

and the region its name, and large deposits of gold and silver were discovered in Batopilas.

Forced to labor in the Spaniards' mines and toil on railroads built by Americans and Mexicans, the Indians later lost access to much of their traditionally held lands. Only ten of the 50 indigenous groups living in the Sierra Tarahumara and Chihuahua Desert in the 1600s survives today.

The stalwart Tarahumara (who call themselves Rarámuri, "people who run") number 50,000 to 60,000. Living on a simple diet of corn and beans, they are as rugged as the mountains in which they live. They can run vast distances carrying heavy loads, and team races organized as social events last days. The Rarámuri women dress in a melee of flowered and polka-dotted clothing, with long, flowing skirts, ruffled blouses, and head scarves of contrasting prints. Near tourist areas, they sell sweet-smelling pine baskets, homemade dolls, and simple pottery. Most of the men have traded the traditional white cotton breechcloths (tagoras) and blousey shirts for Western clothing.

The Rarámuri follow traditional migratory patterns, living in caves, along cliffs, or in houses of wood and stone near the canyon's rim in

Chihuahua train station

- ✉ Méndez at Calle 24
- ☎ 614/439-7210, 01-800/122-4373 (toll free within Mexico)
- 💲 \$\$\$\$\$ (one way along the Chihuahua al Pacífico Railway)

Los Mochis train station

- ☎ 668/824-1167

summer months, when temperatures at the canyon bottom may reach 113°F (45°C). The rest of the year, they move to caves or small wooden houses within the canyon. Crops are generally raised 100 feet (300 m) above sea level. Corn is the staple crop, though fruits are also grown.

CHIHUAHUA AL PACÍFICO RAILWAY

Visitors first gained access to this breathtaking canyon world in 1961 with the completion of the Chihuahua al Pacífico Railway. Connecting Chihuahua with Los Mochis on Sinaloa's coast, the narrow-gauge, 415-mile (670 km) line passes 87 tunnels. Of its 37 major bridges, the longest stretches nearly a third of a mile (0.5 km) over a dizzying gorge. To pass the best canyon scenery during daylight hours, travel from west to east and sit on the right side of the train.

Sixty miles (96 km) into the journey, the train begins an impressive ascent, climbing more than 7,500 feet (2,286 m) in just over 150 miles (241 km). Along the way and at the all-too-brief station stops, you'll be rewarded with magnificent canyon views. East of

Creel, the canyons give way to alpine mountains and high valleys backed by tremendous peaks. The train begins a gradual descent through fertile farmland and high meadows to the city of Chihuahua.

To get the most out of your rail adventure, spend one or more nights along the train route. Creel has the most hotels, restaurants, and services and is the most convenient departure point for trips into the canyons. Divisadero has excellent canyon views and several comfortable hotels. At the floor of its eponymous canyon, Batopilas is a long journey from Creel but, once reached, is another good departure point for canyon exploration.

WEST TO EAST

If you start your tour in the west, consider bypassing **Los Mochis** and spending a day in charming **El Fuerte,** 50 miles (80 km) to the east, built as a fort and later used as a major trading post for gold and silver miners. The town still functions as a commercial center for the surrounding farms and ranches. Like nearby Alamos, El Fuerte is an engaging town with cobblestone streets and 18th- and 19th-century

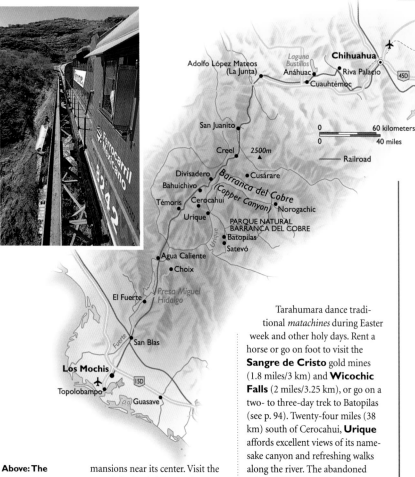

Above: The narrow-gauge 415-mile (670 km) Chihuahua al Pacífico Railway was completed in 1961.

mansions near its center. Visit the 1854 **Iglesia del Sagrado Corazón de Jesús,** the **Palacio Municipal,** and the **Casa de la Cultura,** all on or around the main square, **Plaza de Armas** *(Degollado at Rosales).* The area's lakes are well known for their plentiful largemouth bass.

Lovely **Cerocahui** is tucked in a deep gorge at 5,000 feet (1,525 m) and surrounded by apple orchards (about 10 miles/16 km south of Bahuichivo station). The gateway to the Urique Canyon, this small mountain town was founded by Jesuit priests in 1680. Here, as throughout the sierra, the

Tarahumara dance traditional *matachines* during Easter week and other holy days. Rent a horse or go on foot to visit the **Sangre de Cristo** gold mines (1.8 miles/3 km) and **Wicochic Falls** (2 miles/3.25 km), or go on a two- to three-day trek to Batopilas (see p. 94). Twenty-four miles (38 km) south of Cerocahui, **Urique** affords excellent views of its namesake canyon and refreshing walks along the river. The abandoned mine of **Chiflón,** a 20-minute walk away, is a good place to swim. It's best to hire a local guide when exploring within the canyon.

There are breathtaking views of Urique Canyon from **Divisadero,** where many people choose to spend the night in one of several hotels. There is no actual town, so each hotel provides meals. Arrange a guided tour or horseback riding at **Hotel Divisadero Barrancas** *(tel 614/415-1199).* More magnificent canyon views are seen on a horseback ride to **Wacajipare,** a Tarahumara village about 2½ miles (4 km) into the gorge.

Sierra Tarahumara flora & fauna

The highest mountains of the Sierra Tarahumara, above 8,000 feet (2,440 m), support conifer forests, with Douglas-fir and ponderosa pine. In winter these peaks may be cloaked in snow. Down to 5,900 feet (1,800 m), live oak, juniper, and twisted red *madroño* (strawberry tree) mingle with the still predominant pine, notably the pinyon pine. Between 5,900 and 4,265 feet (1,800 and 1,300 m), the pine-oak forest gives way to the arid tropical deciduous thorn forest, with scrub oak, succulents, mesquite, and some species of cactus. Below 4,265 feet (1,300 m) are the tropical and subtropical riparian forests. Here you will find fan palms next to evergreens, orchids, and wild figs, and, in the humid areas, ceiba, bamboo, and river cane.

About 30 percent of Mexico's mammals can be found in the Sierra Tarahumara, many increasingly rare. A project is currently under way to reintroduce the extremely endangered Mexican wolf. At the higher elevations live black bear, mountain lion, and rattlesnake. Deer, bobcat, coyote, wild boar, white-tail deer, and collared peccary are wide-ranging but elusive and rarely sighted. Most frequently seen are raccoon, skunk, hare, gray fox, squirrel, and bats. Coral snakes and beaded lizards, both poisonous, inhabit the arid tropical thorn forest, while near the canyon bottom live jaguar, jaguarundi, and boa constrictor. Wandering cattle, goats, and pigs upset nature's delicate balance, stripping vegetation traditionally eaten by other species. Throughout the region there are around 50 species of freshwater fish, including catfish, rainbow trout, carp, mullet, and mojarra.

Many species of birds (there are more than 360 in the region) can be seen along the canyon's rim, among them the vermilion flycatcher, black vulture, crested caracara, thick-billed parrot, zone-tailed hawk, and hairy woodpecker. At the canyon's base live the colorful violet-crowned and Lucifer hummingbirds, oriole, tanager, and the magnificent, endangered military macaw. Near rivers look for lilac-crowned parrot and elegant trogan. ∎

Above: The mission church at Satevó, on the canyon floor. Other missions can be found at San Ignacio de Arareko and Cusárare. Above, left: a Yucca plant thrives at an altitude of 8,000 feet near Divisadero.

The train continues to **Creel,** about 36 miles (58 km) from Divisadero and definitely worth a visit. Twenty years ago, there were many horses but few hotels along the packed-earth main street. Today Creel is connected by paved highway to Chihuahua (see pp. 86–87), and visitors benefit from a range of amenities, although the town retains its cowboy charm. Guides, pack animals, horses, and organized tours can be arranged.

A few miles south of Creel, **San Ignacio de Arareko** and its mission church are now accessible by paved road. Outside town, you can rent a rowboat for fishing in **Lago Arareko,** a 100-acre (40 ha) reservoir with woodland campsites and simple cabins. Primitive camping is permitted in surrounding valleys, each named for its unique rock formations: **Valle de los Hongos** (mushrooms), **Las Ranas** (frogs), **Las Chichis** (breasts), and **Bisabírachi** (penises). About 15½ miles (25 km) from Creel, **Cascada de Cusárare** waterfall can be visited on a long day or an overnight camping trip.

About 75 miles (120 km) northwest of Creel, in **Parque Nacional Basaseáchic,** are Mexico's first- and second-highest waterfalls. The 1,486-foot (453 m) **Cascada Piedra Volada** was only recently discovered (at least by outsiders), in 1995. The national park was named for **Cascada Basaseáchic,** best seen during or right after the rainy season (June–October), when the falls plunge 800 feet (243 m) into a

Creel

🅰 77 D4

Visitor information

✉ Casa de las Artesanías, Main Plaza

☎ 635/456-0080

Creel is the jumping-off point for a visit to the Cusárare Waterfall.

rocky pool. Tiny **Batopilas** perches beside a jade-green river of the same name on the canyon's floor. Connected to the world by a paved road only for the last 20 years, the town was originally established in the early 17th century by Spaniards looking for precious metals. These they found in abundance, sometimes as polished silver rocks strewn along the riverbed. Wealth from mining paid for some of the elegant Porfiriato-era mansions that today enliven this remote town. From Batopilas,

hike or ride to the abandoned, fired-brick mission at **Satevó** (4 miles/6.5 km), or take a shorter hike to abandoned **Hacienda San Miguel** or to the stone dam that still supplies the town's aqueduct. Satevó is a "dry" town, gas is expensive, and most restaurants serve just the basics. There are half a dozen simple lodgings. An alternative to the magnificent but hair-raising five-hour, 87-mile (140 km) car or bus trip from Creel is a several-day horse or mule trek from Cerocahui. ■

The stalwart burro

Sure-footed and stoic, the burro doesn't deserve its bad rap. Aside from meaning small donkey, in Mexico the word burro is also used for an idiot, a losing horse, or a drudge. In English, the burro's ancestor, the ass, is also a stupid, stubborn, or perverse person. Despite the negative anthropomorphisms, *campesinos* from Baja to the Yucatán depend on donkeys to carry both themselves and their loads.

Especially useful in rocky, steep terrain, donkeys can carry more weight per pound than horses and survive with less water. They also eat thorny brush, making them well suited to desert and mountain environments. In folklore, the dark cross on their withers is said to be a mark of divine protection bestowed on the species in return for having delivered the Virgin Mary safely to the Holy Land from Egypt. ■

Hidalgo del Parral

The Casa de Alvarado, built in the Italian Renaissance style

SNUGGLED IN AN ISOLATED VALLEY BETWEEN THE foothills of the Sierra Madre and the Chihuahua Desert, Hidalgo del Parral is among the country's richest mining towns. Parral (as it's usually called) produced lead, copper, and silver for more than 350 years before being exhausted in the 1980s. The city also gained fame as the place where Revolutionary hero Pancho Villa was assassinated.

During the 16th and 17th centuries, indigenous slaves worked Parral's mines, suffering huge loss of life due to unsafe conditions and overwork. The miners created altars within the tunnels, frequently dedicated to their patron saint, Nuestra Señora de Fátima. Above ground, the wealthy metal barons built churches and cathedrals, often encrusting columns and walls with crude or refined ore.

The **Parroquia de San José** *(Francisco Moreno at General Benítez)* is decorated with chunks of ore, and its baroque pink quarrystone altarpiece is edged in gold. Built three centuries later, the **Templo de Nuestra Señora de Fátima** overlooks the city near La Prieta mine. It has a plain facade and single bell tower, but its interior walls are also encrusted with silver, gold, copper, and zinc ore.

Parral's mines are played out, but along the city's winding, narrow streets are some lovely mansions. Silver mining peaked in the mid- to late 19th century, and many palatial homes date from that era. The home of the town's founder, mining entrepreneur Pedro Alvarado, restored as **Museo Palacio de Alvarado** *(Lic. Verdad & Riva Palacio, tel 627/522-0290, closed Mon.)*, has a neo-baroque portal and limestone facade carved with human faces and animal figures.

The remodeled **Museo del General Francisco Villa** *(Barreda at Juárez)* displays Revolution-era artifacts and personal effects of Pancho Villa. ∎

Hidalgo del Parral

🗺 77 E3

Visitor information

✉ Miranda at República de Cuba

☎ 627/525-4400

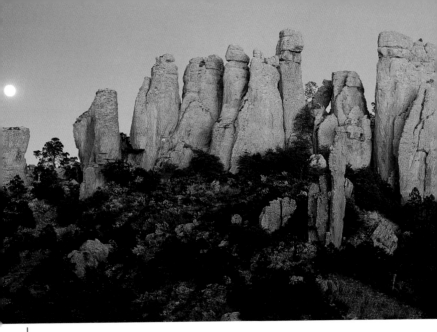

Durango

NESTLED IN THE FERTILE GUADIANA VALLEY, NEAR THE eastern foothills of the Sierra Madre Occidental, the city of Durango is an important agricultural and industrial center. Its colonial past is visible in the well-maintained vintage buildings in the city center—a national historic monument. Friendly people, a mild climate, clean, well-signed streets, and a dearth of tourists make Durango an ideal stop for those seeking a bite of "real" Mexico off the tour-bus trail.

Moonrise over the Sierra de Organos, a popular film set for Hollywood Westerns

Durango
△ 77 E2
Visitor information
✉ Calle Florida 1106
☎ 618/811-2139

Founded in 1563, the city began as an outpost in the wilds of Nueva Vizcaya, New Spain's huge northern province. Both the city and the surrounding region developed slowly, plagued by extreme hostilities between the Spaniards and the Tepehuán and Acaxe Indians. Durango finally flourished in the early 1900s, when the completion of a railroad to Mexico City established it as a shipping center for lumber and minerals from the productive mountains nearby.

The surrounding hills still produce substantial amounts of silver, gold, copper, and iron. One of the world's largest iron ore deposits can be found at **Cerro del Mercado,** just north of the

city. Hundreds of tons of iron ore are transported from this virtual mountain of metal every day.

Durango's historic buildings cluster downtown near the main square, the **Plaza de Armas** (*Av. 20 de Noviembre at Juárez*). On Thursday and Sunday afternoons the state band serenades from the bandstand, which is surrounded by gardens and fountains. The **Catedral,** with its impressive baroque facade, commands the plaza to the north. Locals tell of a young local girl who killed herself after learning of the death of her lover, a French soldier. The girl's ghost is said to hover near sunset in the west bell tower, from which she jumped. Among the cathedral's most precious icons is its gilded *sillería* (row of choir stalls), adorned with bas-relief carvings of saints and apostles.

One block west of Plaza de Armas is the multi-arched **Palacio de Gobierno** (*5 de Febrero between Bruno Martínez & Zaragoza, tel 618/827-0800*). It was built by a Spanish mining tycoon, then seized by the state after the end of colonial rule. Now government headquarters, its interior features colorful murals depicting Durango's history.

Handsome colonial-era houses are sprinkled throughout the historic district. An excellent example of 18th-century Churrigueresque architecture is the **Casa del Conde de Suchil** (*5 de Febrero at Madero, tel 618/813-2601, closed Sun.*), originally the region's mint and now a Banamex bank. The beautiful, neoclassic **Teatro Ricardo Castro** (*Av. 20 de Noviembre at Bruno Martínez, tel 618/811-4694*) hosts opera, orchestra, and dance, and is a film venue.

For an overview of local culture and art, visit the **Museo de las Culturas Populares** (*Juárez 302 Norte & Gabino Barreda, tel 618/825-8827, closed Mon.*), which displays a collection of folk art made by local Mennonites as well as Huichol, Acaxe, and Tepehuán Indians. Modern handiwork, including leather goods and typical wool *sarapes* (blankets), can be found at the **mercado municipal** (*Av. 20 de Noviembre at Pasteur*). The **Museo Regional de Durango** (*Victoria 100 Sur & Aquiles Serdán, tel 618/812-7837, closed Mon., $*), known locally as "El Aguacate," has paintings by colonial master Miguel Cabrera (1695–1768) as well as exhibits on regional history and archaeology. ■

Film sets

Since the 1950s, hundreds of films have been shot on location outside Durango, most of them Westerns. Clear blue skies, a temperate climate, and the absence of power lines and other trappings of modern society make the region well-suited to the role of outdoor film set. *Romancing the Stone* (1984) was filmed here, as were *The Mask of Zorro* (1997) and *Bandits* (2005).

About 8 miles (12 km) north of Durango, Villa del Oeste (*tel 618/810-1212, closed Mon., $*) shimmers like a mirage on the dusty horizon. Built in the 1950s, it was for decades one of Durango's most important sets. When film production dwindled in the 1980s, locals moved in, transforming the scenario into a living, breathing Western town. Other sets to visit in the area include those at Chupaderos, Cañón de los Delgado, and Rancho La Joya (still owned by John Wayne's family). ■

Mazatlán & environs

DESPITE ITS FAMOUS PRE-LENTEN MARDI GRAS
celebration, its world-class billfishing, and some of the tastiest
seafood on the planet, Mazatlán is not one of Mexico's most sought-
after seaside resorts. But admirers of this bayside city of nearly
700,000 couldn't care less if it's spurned by the masses. Fifteen miles
(24 km) of beaches stretch north and south of downtown, and hotel
and restaurant prices are about half of those in Cancún or Los Cabos.

Just 12 miles (19 km) south of the
Tropic of Cancer, Mazatlán enjoys a
semitropical climate. Warm year-
round, it is hottest and steamiest at
the height of the rainy season, in
August and September, but even
then the humidity doesn't compare
to that of resorts farther south.

Most visitors come for the
combination of sand, sun, and
nighttime fun. The **Zona Dorada**
(Golden Zone), north of **Punta
Camarón** (Shrimp Point), has
some of Mazatlán's most popular
beaches. Crowded throughout this
bustling hotel zone are shell and
souvenir shops, sidewalk bars, and
beachfront restaurants. Resort
hotels rent watersports equipment,
and the bay has gentle breakers.
Uniformed vendors stroll the sand,
selling cases of silver jewelry,
striped blankets, Talavera pottery,
and hammocks. Just offshore lie
three islands: **Isla de Pájaros,
Isla de Venados,** and **Isla de
Lobos.** Of the birds, deer, and sea
lions for which they are respectively
named, only the first are in evidence.

The north end of the Golden
Zone (sometimes referred to as "la
Zona Platinum") is home to the
newest resorts, including **El Cid
Mega Resort,** a four-property
hotel and time-share complex with
a marina and 27-hole golf course.
Surfers catch good waves at **Playa
las Brujas** (Witch's Beach), where
thatch-roofed restaurants sell fresh
seafood and host live dance bands
on Sunday afternoons. Walkers

and joggers tend to favor **Playa
Cerritos** (Little Hills Beach)
around the point north of Playa las
Brujas. These and other beaches are
accessible by public buses, taxis,
and *pulmonías* (topless taxis).

South of the Zona Dorada, the
city's long *malecón* (beachfront
promenade) begins at **Playa
Norte.** One block inland is the
Acuario Mazatlán *(111 Av. de
los Deportes, tel 669/981-7815, $$),*
where you can see 150 marine
species in backlit aquariums, as well
as the sea lion, bird, or dive shows.
In addition to gift shops, a snack
bar, a botanical garden, and a small
aviary, there is an extensive
children's playground.

A large statue of a naked fisher-
man and his female companion—
known to the locals as "los Monos
Bichis," or "the Naked Monkeys"—
presides over the south end of the
bay. Fishing boats depart from
Playa los Pinos, where an
informal fish market is held daily
just after dawn. Farther south,
during high tide, young men
dive into the shallow water from
a 45-foot (15 m) platform at
El Mirador.

Walk inland to admire the
streets of historic downtown, its
19th- and 20th-century homes in
various states of repair and
disarray. Many of the one- and two-
story, brick-and-stucco buildings
are painted in bright pastel colors
with white trim, their windows and
doors protected by intricate

Mazatlán

⚔ 77 D2

**Visitor
information**

✉ Carnaval at M.
Escovedo Centro

☎ 669/981-8883

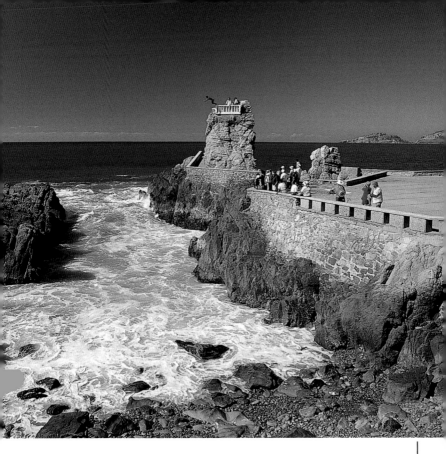

wrought-iron grillwork. The civic and religious heart of the city is **Plaza Revolución** *(Between Calles Flores, Nelson, 21 de Marzo, & Juárez).* Mango and watermelon vendors sit in the shade of tall coconut palms and shiny leafed Indian laurels, while in the cool, dark, subterranean diner underneath the gazebo bandstand, teenagers linger over burgers and soft drinks. On the north side of the square, two distinctive, yellow-tiled spires top the **Catedral.**

A few blocks north of the square is the **Mercado Pino Suárez** *(Juárez & Aquiles Serdán),* a typical market selling clothing and souvenirs, in addition to skinned cow's heads and other victuals. Mazatlán's oldest square, **Plazuela Machado** *(Constitución between*

Frías & Carnaval) is surrounded by sidewalk cafés. The plaza was a gift from Filipino-born Juan Machado, who made a fortune here in commerce and mining in the 1830s and 1840s.

Back at the beach, the road winds south past several lookout points with views of the bay and one of the world's highest lighthouses (500 feet/152 m) at **Cerro de la Crestería,** accessed by a steep, rocky path. From here you will see **Isla de la Piedra** (Stone Island, but really a peninsula), popular with families for weekend picnics. Take a water taxi there and enjoy a walk on the beach and a meal or a cold beer at one of the many seafood shanties. Also here is the new 18-hole **Estrella del Mar golf course** *(tel 669/982-*

Young men in Old Mazatlán imitate the high divers of Acapulco

Colorful Mardi Gras decorations line Mazatlán's downtown parade route.

Carnival

Mazatlán's Carnaval, among the world's most unusual pre-Lenten parties, is also a cultural and family event. The tradition began as friendly battles between 19th-century stevedores, who pelted each other with flour-filled eggshells and recited *comparsas* (rhyming verses mocking their rivals). When rhymes and eggs turned to insults and rocks, town officials replaced the free-for-all with organized parades, regional *tambora* bands (oompah bands with wind and percussion instruments), dance bands, and a reigning queen and king.

Today, tens of thousands of revelers toss confetti instead of flour, and the rhyming tradition continues as a poetry competition. Friday night "Flower Games" consist of a ballet and orchestral and tambora music at the baseball stadium. Saturday night's "Batalla Naval" is a mock naval battle and stirring fireworks display on Olas Altas Bay. ■

3300). Small boats ferry passengers *($)* over from the east side of downtown Mazatlán (save your ticket for the return trip).

Near the base of Cerro de la Cresteria, Mazatlán's sportfishing fleet has a dozen boats eager to help you catch sailfish, marlin, yellowfin tuna, and sea bass. Mazatlán is one of Mexico's premier billfishing destinations—its fishing boats catch and release 12,000 fish each year. Nearby, ferry boats depart for La Paz, in Baja California Sur.

Organized tours are the primary vehicle for visiting the agricultural town of Quelite and the former mining hamlets of Concordia and Copala. The Quelite tour takes visitors to a bakery and tortilla factory, a colorful graveyard, and a rooster farm, after which lunch is served. Just outside **Concordia** (30 miles/48 km from Mazatlán), chunky carved furniture and unglazed ceramic pottery are for sale. In Concordia itself, admire the baroque **Catedral de San Sebastián,** on the main plaza, and take a walk around town before continuing another 15 miles (24 km) to smaller, more isolated **Copala,** winding up into the mountains off Highway 40.

Copala's single street leads to the rustic **Catedral de San José,** where young men sell miniature churches carved from the region's thorny *pochotla* tree. Younger boys offer rides on their tiny donkeys—or a picture of themselves on the sleepy beasts. Visit the church and admire the town's colorful adobe houses dressed in peach and red-violet bougainvillea, organ cacti, and flowering flamboyant trees. Then there's nothing to do except dine in one of the town's three pleasant restaurants before heading back to civilization. Those who want to linger can find rooms to rent in two of the restaurants. ■

Some of the old mansions in Alamos have been converted to inviting bed-and-breakfasts.

More places to visit in Northwest Mexico

ALAMOS

Begun as a mountain mining town, Alamos was among the most lucrative in the 19th century. Yaqui Indian rebellions and the Mexican Revolution eventually put the mines out of business. In the 1940s, crumbling yet still elegant Andalusian-style mansions were discovered and renovated by wealthy foreigners who have created many social clubs and organized activities. During high season you can take a Saturday morning **house and garden tour** *($$$)*. At other times, seek out a guide for a tour of the town *($$$)* at the friendly tourism headquarters.

On the smart **Plaza de Armas** you'll find the modest **Museo Costumbrista de Sonora** *(tel 647/428-0053, closed Mon., Tues., $)*, which highlights Sonora's history, and the **Iglesia de la Purísima Concepción,** a Spanish colonial stone church with a three-tiered bell tower. Locals and tourists promenade around poplar-shaded **Parque Alameda** and shop in the surrounding stores and the municipal market.

For a good view of the town, hike or drive south on Calle Juárez up to **El Mirador** (The Lookout). If you want to go farther afield,

most hotels can arrange visits to abandoned silver mines and Mayo villages (where artisans make traditional wooden masks). Little-visited but nevertheless worthwhile, **Cuchujaqui Ecological Reserve** comprises pine-oak, low deciduous, thorn, and semitropical forests and has more than 200 species of birds, including the endangered spotted owl, pygmy cactus owl, and peregrine falcon. Canyons, dry riverbeds, and riparian environments also attract about a hundred species of migratory birds to the area. This 92,000+-acre ecoreserve bumps right up against Alamos and smaller Aduana ejido. Just east of Alamos, the **Arroyo Cuchujaqui** has a pretty pond for swimming or fishing for large-mouth bass, as does nearby **Presa Adolfo Ruíz Cortines Mocuzarit,** off the Alamos-Navojoa road. The mining town of Aduana—its 17th-century church with a much-venerated statue of the Virgin—is itself worth a visit.

🅰 77 C3 **Visitor information** ✉ Juárez 6 ☎ 647/428-0450

CUAUHTÉMOC

Although established in Chihuahua state since 1921, the Mennonite communities living north and south of Cuauhtémoc still speak their Low German dialect and wear traditional farmer clothing. This large Mennonite group has found peace in Mexico's northern desert, having first fled Europe in search of religious freedom, and later Canada after refusing military service during World War II.

The Mennonites' tidy looking villages, called *campos menonitas,* are numbered, and the woodframe, pitched-roof houses contrast with the typical Mexican towns in the surrounding plains. Day tours out of Chihuahua take you to see their homes. Visit any day but Sunday, which is dedicated to religious services. If you're not up for a full-fledged tour, consider stopping in at the **Museo Menenita** *(Carrertera Cuautémoc—Alvaro Obregón Km. 10.5, tel 625/586-3111, closed Sun., $)* to see photos and implements used by the Mennonites.
🅼 77 D4

CUMBRES DE MAJALCA

About 37 miles (60 km) north of Chihuahua's eponymous capital (the last half on a good dirt road), this 12,000-acre (4,770 ha) park offers accessible hiking and mountain biking, mainly on fire roads. Beginning at 5,250 feet (1,600 m) above sea level, the national park is home to grasslands and pine-oak forests. Rock climbers appreciate the rock formations carved by wind and water erosion. The weather here is generally dry in late winter to early summer. July through September brings afternoon showers (and brilliant cloud formations). Late fall and winter precipitation brings snow to the higher elevations. Primitive camping is permitted, and there are basic cabins too.
Cumbres de Majalca 🅼 77 D4

HERMOSILLO

Four hours south of the U.S. border at Nogales is Hermosillo, Sonora's mid-size state capital, surrounded by golden plains and backed by jagged mountain peaks. It makes a convenient stopping place for travelers headed south. Walk around the battered yet appealing historic district, admiring the **plaza** *(Pino Suárez, P.E. Calles, Yáñez, & Monterrey),* where the neoclassic **Catedral de la Asunción** indulges a few neo-Gothic whims. The crest of the **Cerro de la Campana** affords a fine view of the city; at its base, the **Museo**

Regional de Sonora *(Jesús García at Calle Esteban Sarmiento, tel 662/217-2714, closed Mon., $)* has exhibits on Sonora's history, geology, and anthropology.

South of town, the government-run **Centro Ecológico de Sonora** *(Carretera a Guaymas Km 2.5, tel 662/250-1225, closed Mon., $)* is a center for ecological research and preservation. A 2-mile-long (3 km) path meanders past exhibits of some 300 plant and 240 animal species, many of them endemic to the region. If you come to town in mid-July, join wine-lovers in an annual celebration of the grape harvest at Fiesta de la Vendimia.
🅼 77 C4 **Visitor information** ✉ Edificio Estatal, Calle Comonfort & Paseo del Canal ☎ 662/217-0076 *www.sonoraturismo.gob.mx*

ROSARIO

If you haven't had your fill of former mining towns, visit sun-baked Rosario, whose mines churned out gold and silver for nearly 300 years. Much of the gold seems to have ended up on the baroque altarpiece of **Iglesia de Nuestra Señora del Rosario.** Unlike many of northern Mexico's plain Jesuit mission churches, this 18th-century temple is deliciously baroque. After excessive tunneling of nearby mines caused the original church to sink, it was moved, stone by stone, to its present location on the town square. Rosario is best known among Sinaloans as the birthplace of Mexican mariachi singer and actress Lola Beltrán (1932–1996).
🅼 77 E1

TEACAPÁN

Near Sinaloa's rural southern border, Teacapán and its environs are famous for their plums, shrimp, and mangoes. Cattle ranches and coconut plantations line the 18-mile-long (28 km) peninsula leading to the seaside community. Stop at one of the area's peaceful, white-sand beaches, including **La Tambora, Las Lupitas, Las Cabras,** and **Los Angeles.** Day tours from Mazatlán explore Teacapán's estuaries, where you can see white and pink herons, flamingos, and many other migratory and resident bird species. Within the mangroves is a remarkable pre-Hispanic pyramid of shells accessible only at high tide.
🅼 77 E1 ■

Like the Franciscan missionaries, who produced everything they needed, people from Mexico's arid northeastern states today are hardy and self-sufficient, and are happiest when left alone by the powers-that-be in Mexico City.

Northeast Mexico

Juan Soriano sculpture in Monterrey

Northeast Mexico

AS IN NEIGHBORING TEXAS, THINGS IN NORTHERN MEXICO JUST SEEM *bigger*. Distances in the northeast are certainly vast. This factor, combined with a dearth of mineral wealth (Zacatecas excepted) and the fierceness with which the Chichimec Indians (see p. 28) defended their territory, led to minimal immigration in colonial times. Pirate raids and swampy, mosquito-ridden lagoons made the east coast undesirable as well. However, the late 20th century saw a change in the region's fortune. Monterrey's development of a major brewery, in addition to glass production, cement plants, and iron and steel foundries, has led to its emergence as the nation's leading manufacturing city.

In 1547, the discovery of a rich silver mine in Zacatecas encouraged exploration to the north. But unlike its western counterpart, the Sierra Madre Oriental contained relatively few precious metals. To encourage settlement in the mid-18th century, the Spanish Crown granted resolute individuals huge landhold-ings for sheep and cattle ranches. A wealth of available land and lax Mexican immigration policies led many U.S. citizens to settle the northern Mexican territories; by the time Texas declared itself independent of Mexico in 1836, the ratio of U.S. immigrants to Mexicans living there was four to one.

Below the border at the Río Bravo (known as the Rio Grande in the United States), sheep and cattle ranching continue to contribute to northern Mexico's economy and culture. Meat is the mainstay of the northern diet, usually served with bread rolls or flour tortillas instead of the corn tortillas ubiquitous in central and southern Mexico. Along with *machaca* (dried, shredded beef) and barbecued kid, a favorite meal is *carne a la tampiqueña*—thin, grilled or charbroiled steak accompanied by rice, *frijoles charros* (beans cooked with pork rind and cilantro), grilled green onions, fresh salsa, and avocado.

Mexico's only gypsum dune fields are found in the Area Protegida Pozas de Cuatrociénegas.

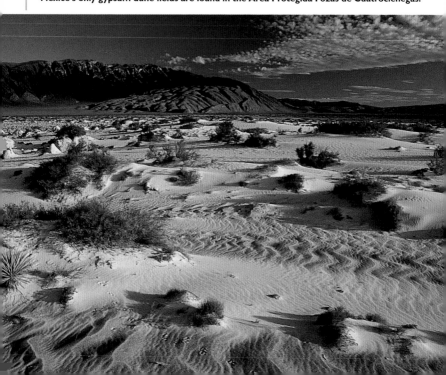

Fishing and shrimping form the base of the coastal economy, although petroleum rules in Tampico. Meanwhile, manufacturing opportunities in border cities and in the Monterrey–Saltillo corridor continue to grow. The inhabitants of inland valleys in the Sierra Madre Oriental practice subsistence agriculture, harvesting apples, prickly pears, nuts, and pine nuts.

Outside the major population centers, northeastern Mexico's wilderness areas invite exploration by adventurous travelers. Appearing like mirages in the scrubby desert are ancient archaeological sites, small towns with gold- and silver-studded churches, and productive vineyards. Despite limited infrastructure, backpacking, canyoneering, and rock climbing are gaining popularity in the rugged and still wild mountain ranges. ■

Area of map detail

Mexico City

Saltillo
🗺 105 B3

Visitor information

✉ Blvd. V. Carranza 3206, Plantabaja Col. Latinoamericana

☎ 844/439-2745

Saltillo

SALTILLO, CAPITAL OF THE STATE OF COAHUILA AND THE oldest city in northeastern Mexico, was founded by Spaniards and Portuguese in 1575 as a strategic station along the Camino Real (Royal Highway). Twenty years later, 87 converted Tlaxcala Indian families from central Mexico voluntarily resettled near the town to help Christianize and pacify anarchistic desert tribes. They brought their weaving traditions, and today the *sarape de Saltillo,* a bright-colored woolen blanket, is a universally recognized Mexican icon.

The refreshingly untouristy city of Saltillo feels both old and modern.

Although the mile-high city sprawls with suburbs and industrial complexes, its historical center is visually appealing, with buildings in a variety of architectural styles. Brick and stucco homes surround the town's open main square, **Plaza de Armas** (*Hidalgo at Juárez*). Wrought-iron benches face inward to the stone-and-bronze central fountain and outward to the pink-stone **Palacio de Gobierno.**

Behind the state government palace is **Plaza de la Nueva Tlaxcala,** a public square whose eye-catching, classic-style statue depicts the city's founders: Spaniards, Tlaxcaltecans, and friars. Three blocks northwest, **Plaza Acuña** (*Aldama between Allende & Flores*) is surrounded by stores, cafés, and the municipal market, where you can shop for leather goods, Saltillo's colorful sarapes, and locally made pottery.

Facing Plaza de Armas is one of northern Mexico's most gorgeous churches, the baroque **Catedral de Santiago de Saltillo** (*tel 844/414-0230*) and adjoining chapel. Built between 1745 and 1800, the base of its Churrigueresque facade is adorned with spiral Solomonic columns covered with fruit and flowers, and its magnificent wooden doors are carved with the images of St. Peter and St. Paul.

West of the cathedral, board the new **Tranvio Turístico** (*Fri.–Sun., $*) at Alameda de Zaragoza park for a guided city tour. You can get off and reboard the trolley four times, or just stay on and enjoy the ride.

On the opposite side of town, the **Museo del Desierto** (*Prol. Pérez Treviño 3745, Parque las Maravillas, tel 844/410-6633, closed Mon., $$*) is a wonderful new steel-and-glass museum covering not only desert plants, animals, geology, paleontology, and ecosystems, but also regional Indian cultures and post-Conquest history. ■

Las Pozas de Cuatro Ciénegas

MANY THINK OF DESERTS AS BARREN, LIFELESS EXPANSES of brown earth and tumbleweeds, but they can be places of surprising beauty, and the Chihuahua Desert has some wonderful surprises. Bubbling out of the desert at Cuatro Ciénegas, hundreds of mineral springs form crystalline pools, lagoons, superficial rivers, and salt marshes lined with sedges and bunchgrass. Wander the adjoining stark-white gypsum dunes on your own, or hire a guide. To see the far-flung pools, you'll need your own transportation.

Cuatro Ciénegas
🗺 105 B4
Visitor information
✉ Zaragoza 10 Norte
☎ 01-800/201-0480
(toll free within Mexico)

Nestled between two spurs of the Sierra Madre Oriental, the **Area Protegida Pozas de Cuatro Ciénegas** (Pools of the Four Marshes Protected Area) forms a rare desert wetland. These grasslands, scrub forest, gypsum dunes, and mineral springs have been protected since 1995. Hundreds of pools—from 1 to 262 feet (30 cm to 80 m) in diameter—are fed by deep subterranean aquifers. Mineral content and the presence of organic materials and algae determine each pool's clarity and color.

Because of its isolation, this unusual desert wetland has a high ratio of endemic fish and reptiles. Of the 16 known fish species, half are found nowhere else. Swimming and snorkeling, permitted in four areas within 6 to 11 miles (10 to 18 km) of the town of Cuatro Ciénegas, are delightful here, especially in the winter, when the water typically reaches 70–82°F (21–28°C).

Mezquites is a slow-flowing river fed by a series of springs, whose depth varies from about 6 inches to 6 feet (15 cm to 1.8 m) along the 2.5-mile-long (4 km) stretch that is open for bathing, kayaking, and canoeing. A natural channel connects two crystal-clear blue pools at **Becerra.** These sites *($)* have *palapa* palm shades and rustic bathrooms. The greenish pool at **Playitas,** used mainly by locals and with no services, is accessed by a dirt road. Primitive camping is allowed.

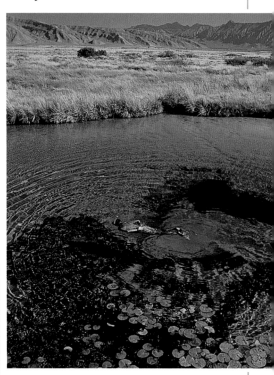

The crystal-clear pool at **Shurince,** which shrinks dramatically in summer, is part of a larger system of interconnected rivers and a lagoon.

Exposed deposits of gypsum from pools such as Shurince are generally blown west, forming sparkling white dunes that tower above the desert floor. Visit the dunes at Becerra springs *($)*, or hire a guide *($$$$$ per group)* at Cuatro Ciénegas's city hall *(municipio)*. ∎

Snorkeling in the mineral pools at Cuatro Ciénegas is especially pleasant in the winter, when water temperatures reach 70–82°F (21–28°C).

Monterrey & environs

SEATED IN A VALLEY AT 1,765 FEET (540 M) ABOVE SEA LEVEL, Monterrey is surrounded by the craggy, abrupt peaks of the Sierra Madre Oriental. Dramatic Cerro de la Silla (Saddle Hill), symbol of the city, lies to the west. A modern, independent-thinking city, Monterrey is the third-largest in Mexico (after Mexico City and Guadalajara). As a leader of industry, it enjoys the nation's highest per capita income and has one of the highest literacy rates.

Monterrey
105 C3
Visitor information
Av. Fundidora 501, Cintermex, Local 82
81/8354-1819, from the U.S. 800/554-5128

Monterrey grew slowly, hindered by fierce Chichimec Indian raids, several serious floods in the 17th and 18th centuries, and the Mexican-American War, when the city was occupied by U.S. troops. Construction of railroad lines in 1881 and tax exemptions for industry under President Porfirio Díaz attracted U.S., French, and British as well as Mexican investors. Construction of the Cervecería Cuauhtémoc brewery in 1890 led to the establishment of a glassworks and a foundry. Today, Monterrey's economy is centered around these industries, as well as cement, steel, beverages, glass, financial services, and automotive products.

In the 1980s, 40 central city blocks separating the state and city government buildings were razed to create the 100-acre (40 ha) **Macroplaza,** or **Gran Plaza** (*Between 5 de Mayo, Av. de la Constitución, Zuazua, & Zaragoza*), a series of green spaces punctuated with fountains and statues. A great place for relaxing and people-watching, this busy, popular park is surrounded by some of Monterrey's early modern buildings, including the steel-and-glass **Condominio Acero building** and the rust red-colored **Faro del Comercio,** a 230-foot (70 m) obelisk designed by Luis Barragán (see p. 40), the father of contemporary Mexican architecture. At the north end of the Macroplaza, at 5 de Mayo, enter the **Palacio de Gobierno** to admire the building's leaded-glass windows honoring heroes of the Revolution, as well as its gleaming parquet floors, crystal chandeliers, and other lovely neoclassic elements.

Extending west from the south end of the narrow park is the **Zona Rosa,** a ten-block pedestrian zone with stores, cafés, juice bars, restaurants, and downtown's nicest hotels. At the southeast corner of the park, the adobe-colored **Museo de Arte Contemporaneo de Monterrey** (*Zuazua at Padre Raymundo Jardón, tel 81/8262-4500, closed Mon., $$*) sports architect Ricardo Legorreta's trademark marigold, purple, and pink accents. The contemporary art museum hosts installation art and other avante garde exhibits (both permanent and changing), and has a restaurant and café. Across the street, the **Catedral de Monterrey** (*Zuazua 1100 Sur, tel 81/340-3752*) has been rebuilt several times owing to fires and floods; its interior was remodeled in the 19th century in the neoclassic style. Worth noting are five murals in the apse, painted in 1942. Near the northeast end of the Macroplaza, the **Museo de Historia Mexicana** (*Dr. Coss 445 Sur, tel 81/8345-9898, closed Mon., $*) provides a fascinating visual history of the nation, with artifacts, religious icons and clothing, scale models, installations, and illustrative maps. Exhibits of popular

Opposite: With an important university and international commerce, today's Monterrey disavows its insouciant founding.

Science and technology are the focus of the Science Museum at Monterrey's Centro Cultural Alfa, enjoyed by kids and adults alike.

art and culture fill the first-floor galleries.

Behind the cathedral, antiques shops, cafés, and bars are cropping up in the restored 19th-century homes of the **barrio antiguo,** an older neighborhood currently in vogue. Within this 15-block area of cobblestone streets and 19th- and early 20th-century houses is one of the city's few remaining examples of secular colonial architecture: **La Casa del Campesino** (*Abasolo between Mina & Naranjo, closed Mon.*). Built in the mid-18th century, it contains later murals describing Mexican history in its chapel. During the barrio's late-November annual festival there are films, exhibitions, and musical performances.

El Obispado (*José Rafael Verger s/n, tel 81/8346-0404, closed Mon., $*) is one of the few things English writer Graham Greene liked about Mexico. He called it "as beautiful as anything out of the Middle Ages." Originally the summer home of one of the last bishops of the viceregal era, this baroque structure houses the **Museo Regional de Nuevo León.** And while Greene's epitaph seems an exaggeration, the building itself—with its sculpted facade and the Chapel to the Virgin of Guadalupe—is more interesting than the period artifacts within.

West of town, the stately, brick-and-ivy **Cervecería Cuauhtémoc** (*Av. Alfonso Reyes 220 Norte, tel 81/8328-5355, closed Sun.*) offers a free guided tour of its brewery (call in advance to arrange an English-language tour) and a sample of the brew in the outdoor beer garden. The adjacent **Salón de la Fama** still documents the history of baseball. *"El beis"* was introduced in the late 19th century by people from the U.S working in Mexico. Before it became established as a Mexican sport, northern Mexican teams played against U.S.

teams, while those in the Yucatán played against Cubans.

El Museo del Vidrio (*Majallanes 517 at Zaragoza, Col. Treviño, tel 81/8863-1000, closed Mon., $*) has, as its name conveys, exhibits of glass, from the lowly beer bottle to the classiest art glass in a variety of formats.

Southwest of the city, on the road to Parque Ecológico Chipinque (see below), the **Centro Cultural Alfa** (*Av. Roberto Garza Sada 1000, tel 81/8303-0002, closed Mon., $$*) houses a planetarium, an Omnimax theater, and a science museum. This modern cultural complex also has a gift shop, a restaurant, and a large mural by Oaxaca artist Rufino Tamayo (see p. 202).

PARQUE NACIONAL CUMBRES DE MONTERREY

Surrounding Monterrey, 619,000-acre (250,500 ha) **Cumbres de Monterrey** actually comprises a series of parks and attractions, each with its own administration and agenda. The park's name refers to the jagged peaks that tower over Monterrey, which lies tucked under a blanket of smog in the valley below. As is the case with many Mexican national parks and reserves, only a small portion is developed for tourism, while the rest serves as a buffer to development, a refuge for wildlife, and in this instance a natural aquifer.

Southwest of Monterrey loom the steely green peaks of **Parque Ecológico Chipinque** (*Carretera a Chipinque Km. 2.5, San Pedro, tel 81/8303-0000, www. chipinque .org.mx, $*), about 12 miles (20 km) from the city center. Chipinque's varied topography includes valleys, canyons, mountain peaks, and pine-oak forests. The mammals most often seen are squirrels, gray foxes, and coati. However, white-tailed deer and black bear are also present,

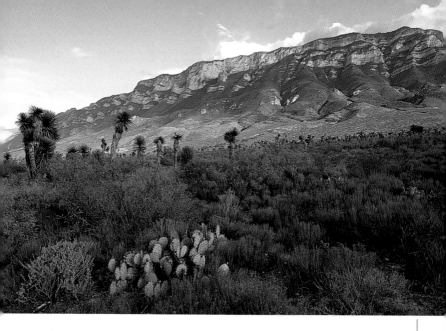

as are at least 120 species of birds and 170 of butterflies. There's camping *($$)* by prior arrangement, or go for the day to hike or mountain bike, take short guided walks from the Visitor Center (reserve several days in advance), or scale one of the park's four peaks (with park guards if you wish). The highest summit is **El Copete de las Águilas** (Eagles' Crest), at 7,410 feet (2,260 m); the most frequently climbed and the symbol of the park is **El "M"** (pronounced EH-may). Both are accessed from a mesa near the entrance to **Hotel Chipinque** *(Meseta Chipinque 1000, tel 81/8173-1777)*, a stone-and-timber lodge with a restaurant overlooking Monterrey and a faux-rustic bar. There are also tennis courts, a swimming pool, gym, sauna, and other facilities.

Rock climbers are attracted to the sheer, 984-foot (300 m) walls of **Cañón de la Huasteca** *(Carretera federal Km. 40.3 south of Santa Catarina, tel 81/8331-6785, $)*, about 12 miles (20 km) west of Monterrey. These canyons once provided local Indians and Spanish settlers with a refuge from Apache raids. In the municipality of Santiago is **Cascadas Cola de Caballo** *(Carr. Cola de Caballo Km. 6 off Hwy. 85, tel 81/347-1599, $)*, an 82-foot (25 m) waterfall named for its resemblance to a horse's tail. A 20- to 30-minute climb from the entrance brings you to the viewpoint; a set of stone steps leads about a third of the way up near the falls, and a dirt path takes you to the summit. Along the last few miles before the park entrance, locals sell wicker furniture, stone carvings, and large ceramic pots.

North of the Cañón de la Huasteca, the **Grutas de García** *(Salida a García, tel 81/347-1533, $$)* is a series of 50-million-year-old caverns filled with stalactites and stalagmites. A winding, illuminated, 4-mile (2.5 km) path and wooden stairs lead through 16 monumental caves, many with 40-foot-tall (12 m) ceilings. Guided tours are given during Semana Santa (Holy Week), on the hour between 9 a.m. and 5 p.m. You can also swim in the outdoor pool or have a meal in the site restaurant. ■

Parque Nacional Cumbres de Monterrey, just outside the city, provides a quick escape for urban residents.

Zacatecas

SURROUNDED BY CRAGGY, ARID MOUNTAINS AND UNUSUAL rock formations, Zacatecas occupies a narrow canyon at 8,900 feet (2,700 m) above sea level. It is chilly during the winter months, when blustery *nortes* (brisk, often cold winds emanating from the north) negate the otherwise warm embrace of mountain chains to both the east and west. Zacatecos are known for their friendly, open demeanor with a hint of cowboy swagger. On weekend evenings, you'll meet them on lively *callejoneadas*, festive musical parties that parade through the smaller streets, often accompanied by a mescal-bearing burro.

Zacatecas
105 B2
Visitor information
Av. Hidalgo 403
492/924-0552
www.zacatecas.gob.mx

Zacatecas ("land where zacate grass grows") gets its Náhuatl Indian name from the grasses that make the surrounding areas ideal ranchlands. The city grew quickly after the discovery of a rich vein of silver at **Cerro de la Bufa** (Wineskin Hill) in 1546, despite uprisings led by the Caxcanes tribe. Financed by the silver barons, the Dominicans, Jesuits, and Augustinians established headquarters here for evangelizing the wild north, leaving a legacy of grand churches and seminaries.

The facade of the **Catedral Basílica Menor** (*South side of Plaza de Armas on Av. Hidalgo, tel 492/922-6211*) is cited as *the* masterpiece of Mexican baroque. Carved of pink sandstone, the church's exterior epitomizes the Churrigueresque style, with almost overpowering ornamentation covering the three-tiered main facade. The interior, sacked during the Reform and again during the Revolution, is nearly naked. On the east side of **Plaza de Armas,** Zacatecas's rather cheerless main square, stands the 17th-century **Palacio de Gobierno** (*Hidalgo 604, tel 492-922-1211*), with murals of local history adorning its interior.

South of the main square, the *beaux-arts* **Mercado González Ortega** (*Hidalgo & Tacuba, tel 492/922-7990*) was converted from a daily market to a shopping mall with several restaurants, losing none of

its splendor during the remodeling. The small **Museo Zacatecano** (*Dr. Hierro 303, tel 492/922-6580, closed Tues., $*) contains naive religious paintings (*retablos*), Huichol art, and 16th- to 18th-century ironwork. Now an auditorium, the nearby **Iglesia de San Agustín** sports a wonderful plateresque facade.

Baroque-style **Templo de Santo Domingo** (*Genaro Codina 227 at Plaza Santo Domingo, tel 492/922-1083*) has a sumptuous interior, with eight Churrigueresque altarpieces; 18th-century paintings decorate the octagonal sacristy. Next door is the **Museo Rafael Coronel** (*Ex-Convento de San Francisco s/n, tel 492/922-8116, closed Wed., $*), with Mexico's largest collection of ceremonial masks (about 5,000). Housed in a 16th-century monastery, the museum also has puppets, pre- Hispanic ceramics, colonial jewelry, and sketches by Coronel's father-in-law, Diego Rivera.

International art dominates the extensive collection in the **Museo Pedro Coronel** (*Av. Fernando Villalpando at Plaza Santo Domingo, tel 492/922-8021, closed Thurs., $*), in a 17th-century Jesuit seminary (that later served as a jail). Check out works by Braque, Dalí, and Chagall, as well as African, Indian, and Asian art. The **Museo de Arte Abstracto Manuel Felguérez** (*Calle Colón at Seminario s/n,*

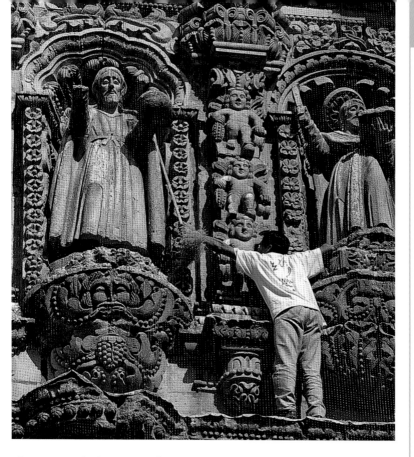

tel 492/924-3705, closed Tues., $) presents the abstract art collection of the museum's namesake in a 19th-century building that was enlarged and remodeled in the 21st century.

Southwest of the town center are several city parks, including **Parque Alameda** *(Villalpando at Av. Torreón)* and **Parque Enrique Estrada** *(González Ortega at Manuel M. Ponce), which* has a fine view of the pink-stone aqueduct that served the city until the early 20th century. West of the park is the **Museo Goitia** *(E. Estrada 102, tel 492/922-0211, closed Mon., $),* with 19th- and 20th-century paintings by half a dozen native Zacatecos.

For a city panorama, drive or hike to **Cerro de la Bufa,** which overlooks the city to the northeast. A museum *(Closed Mon., $),* chapel,

and rotunda commemorate the one-day battle in which Pancho Villa's División del Norte ousted government forces in the Revolutionary War (see p. 34). Alternatively, take the 2,100-foot (640 m) aerial tram, or *teleférico (tel 492/922-5694, $),* from **Cerro del Grillo.** From here you can descend into **"El Edén"** mine *(Antonio Dovali off Av. Torreón, tel 492/922-3002, $),* which for more than 350 years produced silver, gold, copper, zinc, and iron at the cost of many lives. There's a popular disco here after 10:30 p.m. Thurs.–Sat.

Six miles (10 km) southeast of Zacatecas is the **Museo Virreynal de Guadalupe** *(Jardín Juárez Oriente s/n, tel 492/923-2386),* a former Franciscan monastery housing a collection of viceregal religious art. ∎

A worker cleans the almost overpowering baroque facade of the Catedral Basílica Menor.

Ciudad Victoria

⚏ 105 C2

Visitor information

✉ Calle Hidalgo s/n, Gómez Farías

☎ 832/236-2002

Reserva de la Biósfera
El Cielo

EL CIELO (MEANING "THE SKY") STRETCHES BETWEEN TWO spurs of the Sierra Madre Oriental in southwestern Tamaulipas. A dramatic range of elevation (7,218 feet/2,200 m) and a favorable location near the Tropic of Cancer produce vastly distinct ecosystems, including tropical, cloud, pine-oak, and evergreen forests. Designated a biosphere reserve in 1986, the park is a haven for wildlife, while its cloud forest provides a rainwater catchment for the tropical forest and commercial agriculture to the east and southeast.

El Cielo was heavily logged for 30 years from the 1930s, but the lumber companies gave up when rugged topography and a lack of

El Cielo has four distinct ecosystems: tropical rain forest, cloud forest, pine-oak forest, and evergreen forest.

infrastructure proved overwhelming. Today, rustic restaurants and lodgings are available at some of the sparsely populated area's ranches and *ejidos* (community landholdings). Ecotourism, if it takes off, may prove a viable alternative to forestry and a source of much-needed income.

The reserve has a high level of biodiversity. There are 95 species of mammal, including endangered wild cats, white-tailed deer, and black bear. Additionally, there are about 60 species of reptiles and 430 of birds.

About two hours from Ciudad Victoria, natural swimming pools at **El Nacimiento,** the source of **Río Frío,** lures local boys and trav-

elers en route to higher ground. There are several restaurants on the riverbank serving crayfish and fish, and men offer boat trips upriver.

A regular bus service is available as far as **Gómez Farías,** where you'll find a couple of humble but comfortable and charming hostels, guides *($$$$$ per group),* a visitor center, and a few restaurants and stores. If you have a high-clearance vehicle, continue about an hour longer to the tiny hamlet of **Alta Cima,** which hangs above a cloud-forest valley. Hire local guides for day hikes to mountain glens and meadows, and, in season, to waterfalls and streams. You can also arrange for guides and pack animals for longer treks into the reserve. The friendly women at **Restaurant La Fe** prepare simple but filling fare and sell local handicrafts. Adjoining the restaurant are lodgings and a campground. Beyond Alta Cima, a four-wheel-drive vehicle is advisable.

At about 4,590 feet (1,400 m) above sea level, **San José** is tucked into a green valley—the transition zone between cloud and pine-oak forest. From here hike to the **Cueva del Infernillo,** a cave containing a limpid pool. Venturing still farther, you will reach the evergreen forest around **La Gloria,** with more difficult terrain and fewer services, but a more pristine wilderness. ∎

The little explored Sierra del Carmen spills over the U.S.-Mexico border into Big Bend NP.

More places to visit in Northeast Mexico

PARRAS DE LA FUENTE

One of Northeast Mexico's prettiest historic towns, Parras de la Fuente, in Coahuila state, brings a splash of green to the desert. Secular and religious buildings cluster around the center of town; of note are the **Santuario de Guadalupe** (*Viesca & Ocampo*), with its baroque and neoclassic altarpieces, and the 16th-century **Templo de San Ignacio de Loyola** (*Treviño 103 Sur*), with its small museum of old documents, books, and viceregal-era paintings.

At 4,985 feet (1,520 m), the city and surrounding countryside enjoy a pleasant climate well suited to growing figs, dates, pecans, avocados, and grapes. Here you'll find the continent's first winery, built in the late 16th century. Originally the Hacienda de San Lorenzo, and now **Casa Madero** (*Carr. Paila-Parras Km. 18.5, tel 842/422-0111*), it still produces wine and brandy and offers daily tours and tastings 9–5. The harvest is celebrated each August with the week-long Grape and Wine Festival (La Fiesta de la Vendimia).

🗺 105 B3 **Visitor information** ✉ Carretera Parras Paila Km. 3 ☎ 842/422-0259

SIERRA DEL CARMEN & SIERRA LAS MADERAS

Rising out of the forbidding Chihuahua Desert near the Texas border are the rugged mountains of the **Sierra del Carmen,** and to the south, the **Sierra las Maderas.** Desert foothills dotted with bare rock, creosote, opuntia cacti, and mesquite lead up into this virtually uninhabited mountain range. Difficult backcountry hiking accesses dry riverbeds, flower-strewn valleys, grasslands, and, finally, ponderosa woodlands, year-round streams, and peaks over 7,000 feet (2,130 m) above sea level.

Black bear wander in the pinyon-oak forests around **Cañón de la Media Luna** (Half Moon Canyon), where the lovely manzanita bush and the madrone expose shiny white or pinkish wood underneath blistered-looking red bark. Horse trails and old logging roads lead to deep, wooded canyons, home to bobcat, white-tail and mule deer, coyote, and mountain lion. The rugged terrain and lack of infrastructure lead some explorers to book hiking tours out of Texas' Big Bend National Park, just across the border. Others make a base camp at Cañón de la Media Luna, accessed by gravel and dirt roads and on foot from the mining

village of La Cuesta de Malena, off Highway 53.
105 B5

SIERRA DE ORGANOS

Relatively unexplored, this 9.7-square-mile (25 sq km) region of Zacatecas is named for the resemblance of its huge igneous rocks to the branches of the organ cactus. It's perfect for hiking, rock climbing, and mountain biking, but it's a remote destination should you have an emergency. Fantastic canyon views and rock formations have induced cinematographers to film scenes for more than 50 movies here, including *Caveman* (1981). Cabins for up to six people each *($)* at the park entrance offer kitchens, bedrooms, and bathrooms; inquire here about guided horseback expeditions.
105 A2

SOMBRERETE

Sombrerete, in Zacatecas, was once an important producer of lead, tin, mercury,

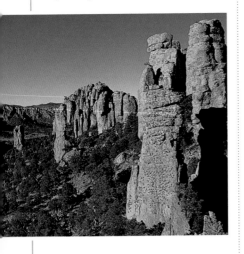

East of Durango, strange and beautiful basalt rock formations characterize the Sierra de Organos.

silver, and gold, and the town has some impressive secular and religious buildings in baroque and neoclassic styles. Visit the 18th-century **Templo de San Francisco,** the **Templo de la Soledad,** and the **Templo de Santo Domingo,** whose main facade is adorned with female caryatid columns. The

town's main fiesta, two weeks beginning February 2, honors the Virgin of Candlemas.
105 A2 **Visitor information** Tel 433/935-1438

TAMPICO

Tampico has merged with Ciudad Madero in the southern extreme of Tamaulipas to form one of Mexico's major seaports and its tenth-largest metropolis. Surrounded on three sides by the Gulf of Mexico, the Pánuco River, and a maze of interconnecting lagoons, this area was fought over by pirates, Spanish settlers, and indigenous tribes throughout the 16th and 17th centuries. Today, late 19th-century and early 20th-century buildings surrounding **Plaza de la Libertad** show French and English influence, while on the waterfront enormous oil refineries, storage facilities, and tankers have replaced the more picturesque structures of former years. Marimba bands entertain on Sunday afternoons in **Plaza de Armas.** In adjacent Ciudad Madero, the **Museo de la Cultura Huasteca** *(Juana Inés de la Cruz at 1 de Mayo, Laguna del Carpintero, tel 833/210-2217, closed Sun., $)* has exhibits on regional history.
105 D1

ZONA ARQUEOLÓGICA LA QUEMADA

About 50 miles (80 km) south of Zacatecas is La Quemada, the ruins of an ancient, unknown culture or cultures, with cylindrical, circular, and rectangular ceremonial structures built of stone, rubblework, and brick. Experts believe they were created by an agricultural group, probably between A.D. 350 and 950. Among the surviving structures is the **Salón de las Columnas** (Room of the Columns), a series of six-foot-tall (1.8 m) brick columns where Huichol Indians today hold private religious ceremonies prior to the spring equinox. The purpose of the building called the **Pirámide Votativa** (Votive Pyramid) is not clear, but the ball court is similar to those used throughout Mesoamerica. Stone and clay roads radiate for over 100 miles (160 km) from the hilltop site, possibly linking northern tribes with more militant peoples to the south. A paved road reaches the site from Highway 54, south of Zacatecas.
105 B2 Tel 492/25085 Closed the three days prior to spring equinox $ ∎

Built by, and often of, silver and gold, the central states embrace both the mighty Sierra Madre and the Bajío lowlands. Their great legacy is baroque and neoclassic edifices and stately plazas paid for by rich mines and successful merchants.

Central Mexico

Pottery design motif

Central Mexico

"ARRIBA, ABAJO, AL CENTRO, AL DENTRO" ("UP, DOWN, TO THE MIDDLE, TO the inside") is a Spanish drinking toast, but it also describes the colonization of Central Mexico. Spurred by the discovery of huge silver deposits in Zacatecas (up), and subsequently Guanajuato (down), Spanish entrepreneurs swarmed "the middle," to extract deposits of mineral wealth from deep within the earth. Guanajuato became a great mining city, while San Luis Potosí (with a shorter-lived silver boom), Aguascalientes, and San Miguel de Allende became important agricultural centers and way stations.

Guanajuato's adobe-lined lanes are steeped in history.

4▷

Luis Moya

3▷ Rincón de Romos

AGUASCALIEN
Aguascalientes ⊙
Calvillo ✈

2▷

△
A

Along with the entrepreneurs came the Catholic Church. In the Sierra Gorda, the Pame tribe were persuaded to give up their nomadic lifestyle and build the missions whose mixture of indigenous and classic ecclesiastic imagery is much admired today. Forty years of warfare against the Guayachicilies around San Luis Potosí, however, proved fruitless in subduing this Chichimec tribe. Peace was achieved only after Franciscan friars convinced Spain to offer palatable terms for peace, including freedom from paying tribute.

Free-thinking clergy were among the instigators of independence from Spain, an idea conceived in Central Mexico. Intellectual and well-spoken, the idiosyncratic priest Miguel Hidalgo y Costilla is considered the father of Mexican independence. Along with Captain Ignacio Allende and others, Padre Hidalgo plotted the Revolution in Querétaro (see p. 136); his famous cry for freedom was rung on the parish bell at Dolores Hidalgo. Both men were quickly captured and executed, losing their lives but unleashing a bloody war.

After independence, mining concerns continued to thrive with an enlarged European market. On the rich plains of the Bajío region, Querétaro merchants amassed great fortunes providing luxury goods and investment capital. Individual fortunes paid for incredible masterpieces of baroque religious and secular architecture, indulging every whim with imported tiles, French furnishings, and goods made locally by talented artisans.

Today the colonial cities of the Mexican heartland merge history, European and mestizo culture, and modernity. Stunning churches and palaces—some now housing hotels, restaurants, and museums—line well-tended plazas, and internationally known musicians perform at Guanajuato's Cervantes

Area of map detail

0   100 kilometers
0   50 miles

Festival (see p. 122) and at San Miguel de Allende's classical and jazz events. Posh colonial-era theaters host the opera and symphony, while *callejoneadas* (roving musical parties) attract students and other less formal types. Throughout the region there are many museums, language schools, and an eclectic range of folk and fine art for sale. ■

Guanajuato

Guanajuato
🗺 119 B2
Visitor information
✉ Plaza de la Paz 14
☎ 473/732-1574
www.guanajuato capital.com

UNLIKE OTHER VENERABLE CITIES THAT RADIATE IN dignified grids from the main plaza, Guanajuato's long, loopy streets intersect at odd angles. Alleys lurch crookedly uphill, decorated with geranium-filled flower boxes and washing hung to dry. A turn in a cobblestone lane may lead to an ancient stairway, a dead end, or one of more than a dozen plazas surrounded by stores, open-air cafés, and rainbow-painted homes. On Fridays and Saturdays *callejoneadas*— moveable parties—snake through town, led by student musicians dressed as Spanish troubadours.

Filled with winding streets and ornate buildings, Guanajuato is one of Mexico's most beautifully preserved colonial cities.

Guanajuato, whose name is derived from a Purépecha Indian word meaning "Hill of Frogs," begins at the bottom of a gorge, sweeping up the surrounding hills in a tapestry of multicolored dwellings. Most sights are located on or just off extended Juárez and Pocitos streets, both of which change names several times as they follow the ancient riverbed. Tunnels underneath the city divert cross-town traffic, easing mid-city congestion.

Once Mexico's most significant mining town, Guanajuato, capital of its namesake state, has a wealth of magnificent churches, museums, theaters, and homes—a successful jumble of rococo, Moorish, neoclassic, baroque, and other

Templo de San Cayetano, Bocamina de Valenciana
28 DE SEPTIEMBRE
PLAZA DE LA ALHÓNDIGA
Museo Regional Alhóndiga de Granaditas
Museo de las Momias, Ex-Hacienda de San Gabriel de Barrera
MENDIZABAL
Museo Casa Diego Rivera
Iglesia de la Casa de Belén
JARDÍN DE LA REFORMA
PLAZA DE SAN ROQUE
PLAZUELA DE SAN FERNANDO
CALZ. DE GUADALUPE
Universidad (Museo de Historia Natural Alfredo Drugés)
Templo de la Compañía de Jesús
AVENIDA
JUÁREZ
Mercado Hidalgo
CARRETERA PANORÁMICA
JUÁREZ
JUAN VALLE
POCITOS
Templo de los Hospitales
Palacio Legislativo
Casa Real de Ensaye
Palacio de Justicia
Museo del Pueblo de Guanajuato
RETANA
San José
Basílica de Nuestra Señora de Guanajuato
PLAZA DEL BARATILLO
PLAZA DE LOS ANGELES
OBREGÓN
PLAZA DE LA PAZ
Palacio Municipal
TRUCO
ALLENDE
JARDÍN DE LA UNIÓN
Callejón del Beso
TÚNEL LOS ÁNGELES
TÚNEL MIGUEL HIDALGO
CALLE ALONSO
San Diego
SOPEÑA
PLAZUELA DE LA CONSTANCIA
Teatro Juárez
PLAZA DR. ROMERO
Monumento al Pípila
CARRETERA PANORÁMICA
Museo Iconográfico del Quijote
POTRERO
TÚNEL SANTA FE

0   200 meters
0   200 yards

styles. An impressive example of Churrigueresque architecture is the **Templo de la Compañía de Jésus** (*Plaza de la Compañía near Hidalgo, tel 473/732-1827*), its fantastic pink-stone facade topped by an elegant neoclassic cupola.

The church originally pertained to the adjacent **Universidad de Guanajuato** (*Lascuráin de Retana 5, tel 473/732-0006*). Established in 1724 as a Jesuit college, the school is now a major university emphasizing the arts and letters. Leafy **Jardín de la Unión,** the city's social hub, occupies the former atrium of the adjacent 18th-century **Templo de San Diego Alcalá.**

Surrounding the park are restaurants, outdoor cafés, a hotel, and **Teatro Juárez** (*Calle de Sopeña s/n, at Jardín de la Unión, tel 473/ 732-0183, closed Mon., $*), whose sober neoclassic facade belies its luscious interior, with both Moorish and art nouveau elements. One long block southeast is the

Museo Iconográfico del Quijote (*Manuel Doblado 1, tel 473/732-6721, closed Mon., $*), where each of the 600 exhibits relates to Spanish author Miguel de Cervantes' Don Quixote or Sancho Panza.

Most of Guanajuato's major sights are found northwest of Jardín de la Unión; many cluster around **Plaza de la Paz** (*Calle de la Paz at Av. Juárez*). Adjacent to the neoclassic green quarrystone **Palacio Legislativo** is the beautiful **Palacio de Justicia** (Supreme Court Building), originally designed by colonial architect Eduardo Tresguerras as the home of Guanajuato's wealthiest mining baron, Count de Rul y Valenciana.

The **Museo del Pueblo de Guanajuato** (*Pocitos 7, tel 473/ 22990, closed Mon., $*) has a varied collection of secular and religious art highlighting 17th- and 18th-century sculpture, paintings, and decorated utilitarian objects. To the east, the bright yellow **Basílica**

Colegiata de Nuestra Señora de Guanajuato houses an eighth-century, polychrome statue of the Virgin on a solid silver pedestal. Thought to be Mexico's oldest Christian icon, it was the gift of King Felipe II of Spain.

Family furnishings and photos, the muralist-painter's sketches and finished canvases, and the work of contemporary artists fill the **Museo Casa Diego Rivera** (*Pocitos 47, tel 473/732-1197, closed Mon., $*), where Rivera was born in 1886.

Soon after its debut as a granary, the **Alhóndiga de Granaditas** was the stage for the first battle in the War of Independence, a rebel success (see p. 32). It was later captured and used as a fortress by Spanish royalists, who hung the severed heads of revolutionary leaders Hidalgo, Allende, Aldama, and Jiménez in cages from its four corners, where they remained until the end of the war. The structure now houses a museum (*Mendizabal 6, tel 473/732-1112, closed Mon., $*), with murals showing topical regional events as well as history, archaeology, and ethnology exhibits. Nearby is the **Mercado Hidalgo** (*Av. Juárez off Mendizabal*), a busy city market. Designed by French architect Gustave Eiffel in 1910, it is an interesting glass and cast-iron structure.

Lovers of the macabre (or the truly tacky) should visit the **Museo de las Momias** (*Explanada del Panteón, tel 473/732-0639, $$*). Within the mummy museum are more than 100 former Guanajuato residents who have been disinterred and displayed in glass cases. A combination of dry atmosphere, unique soil composition, and their descendants' failure to pay cemetery fees permits this ultimate indignity. For a breath of fresh air, continue outside town to the **Ex-Hacienda de San Gabriel de Barrera** (*Carretera Antigua a Marfil Km. 2.5, tel 473/732-0619, $*). Seventeen fabulous gardens, each in a different style, grace this restored hacienda, now a museum with 17th- to 19th-century European art and furnishings.

Perched above the city is the **Templo de San Cayetano,** also known as Templo la Valenciana (*Carretera Dolores Hidalgo Km 2*), built by silver baron the Count of Valenciana. The church's beautifully sculpted facade of pink quarrystone leads to an even more dazzling interior with three gilded altarpieces, respectively plateresque, Churrigueresque, and baroque. The adjacent **Bocamina de Valenciana** (*Carretera Dolores Hidalgo Km. 5, $*) is usually visited as part of a tour. ■

Actors perform the roles of Don Quixote and Sancho Panza at the yearly Cervantes Festival.

Festival Cervantino

Today's internationally known Cervantes Festival had its beginnings in the 1950s, when a university professor encouraged his students to perform *entremeses,* one-act Spanish playlets. The success of these informal outdoor productions led to a more organized, annual event.

Seeking to showcase artists across a wide spectrum of genres, the producers contract traditional, folkloric, and avant-garde theater and music ensembles in addition to Chinese acrobats and other world-class acts. Over the festival's long history, participants have included the Royal Shakespeare Company, the New York Philharmonic Orchestra, and the Black Vampire of Argentina. Today, tens of thousands of spectators attend the two-week event, making advance hotel reservations essential. ■

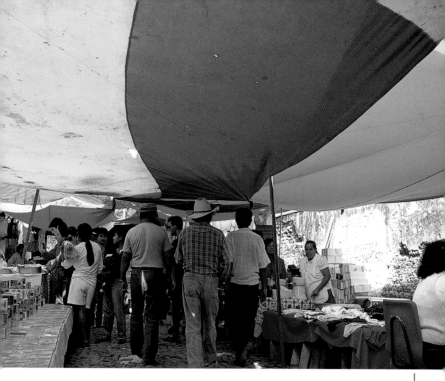

San Miguel de Allende

FEW TOWNS ARE AS SUBTLY ENCHANTING AS SAN MIGUEL. Some places dazzle, others seduce, but San Miguel de Allende most definitely bewitches. Nothing short of magic explains how somewhere so full of foreigners remains so endearingly Mexican. Awash with charming vignettes, this is a painterly town whose steep, cobblestoned streets echo the undulating lines of the surrounding hills. An energetic community of artists produces excellent folk and fine art, in addition to a jazz festival and a classical music concert series.

Originally a mule train stop along the gold and silver highway, San Miguel later prospered as a market village for surrounding haciendas. The Mexican government wisely declared it a national historic monument in 1926, preventing modern-style buildings from destroying its vintage essence. Since then, its simple but pervasive charms have been luring artists, rat-race dropouts, and students of Spanish. The **Instituto Allende** (*Ancha de San Antonio 20, tel 415/152-0190*) offers language courses as well as fine arts; the **Escuela de Bellas Artes** (*Macías 75, tel 415/152-0289*) teaches music, dance, painting, sculpting, and more. Both are located in gracious, two-story, balconied mansions.

Touring the town on foot is most agreeable and mildly aerobic. A good place to begin is the main square, **Plaza Allende** (*Calles Correo, San Francisco, Portal Allende, & Portal Guadalupe*), called "el Jardín" by most people. To *really*

San Miguel de Allende

◪ 119 C2

Visitor information

✉ Southeast corner of Plaza Principal, left of the cathedral

☎ 415/152-6565

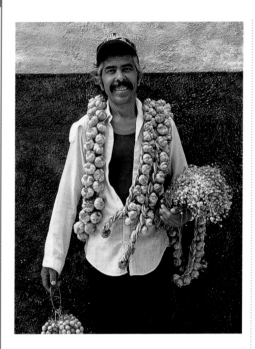

A garlic salesman peddles his wares.

decorative handicrafts imbuing traditional genres—including tinwork, textiles, blown glass, papier-mâché, and jewelry—with design and technical innovations. The city itself seems to fan the artistic flame. For proof of this, look no further than the 19th-century Gothic Revival-style exterior of **La Parroquia de San Miguel Arcángel** (*south side of Plaza Allende*), which untrained local stone cutter Cerefino Gutiérrez is supposed to have designed after looking at postcards of French Gothic cathedrals. The many-steepled church honors the town's patron saint, the Archangel Michael.

San Miguel's other five-star church is the **Oratorio de San Felipe Neri** (*Insurgentes at Loreto*), a few blocks northeast of the main plaza. Multiple domes and towers in different styles top the pink quarry-stone facade. Within, oil paintings detailing the life of Florentine saint Felipe Neri have been attributed to 18th-century Spanish master Miguel Cabrera. In the west transept, the **Santa Casa de Loreto** chapel was commissioned by the Count and Countess de la Canal, whose sculptures flank that of the Virgin Mary. The adjoining **camarín** (dressing room) is an extraordinary, eight-sided baroque alcove with three impressive altarpieces. Other worthwhile 18th-century churches are the **Templo de San Francisco** (*San Francisco at Juárez*) and, just to the east, the **Templo de Nuestra Señora de la Salud.**

For a walk outside town, bring a picnic lunch to the public cacti gardens at **El Charco del Ingenio** (½ *mile/1 km out of town, tel 415/ 154-4715, $*). Outside of San Miguel are many hot water springs that have been channeled to form pools and spas. Most are en route to Dolores Hidalgo; you can get details from the San Miguel tourism department. ■

raise your heart rate, join the annual running of the bulls through the town center the third Saturday of September. As you negotiate the cobblestoned streets and high sidewalks, you'll pass many churches, cozy cafés, and beautiful pastel homes—some well preserved, others deliciously decrepit. To gain entry to some of the town's mansions and lovely gardens, join a Sunday **house and garden tour** (*$$$$$*), organized by the **Biblioteca Pública** (*Insurgentes 25, tel 415/152-0293*). Proceeds go to local charities.

The birthplace of independence hero Ignacio Allende, at what is now the **Museo de la Casa de Ignacio Allende** (*Cuna de Allende 1, tel 415/152-2499, closed Mon., $*), is worth a visit. Wonderful 19th-century architecture with baroque influences is complemented by the museum's display of colonial-era furnishings.

In San Miguel's many stores you will find outstanding utilitarian and

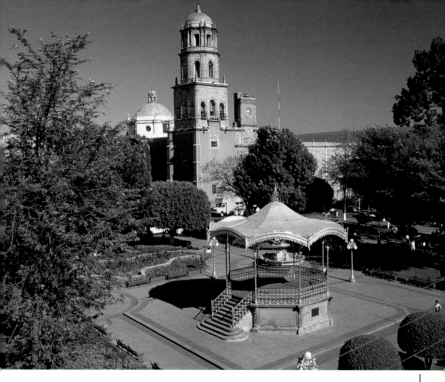

Querétaro & environs

LOCATED IN MEXICO'S FERTILE BAJÍO REGION, QUERÉTARO'S wealth of productive farmland once made it one of New Spain's most important cities. Since it was founded in 1531, the city has figured in important political dramas—from plotting independence from Spain (see p. 32) to signing the disastrous Treaty of Guadalupe Hidalgo, ceding half of the country to the United States in 1848 (see p. 33). Despite Querétaro's status as a major industrial player, its center has baroque churches, historic buildings, and museums well worth exploring.

The Templo de San Francisco (built 1540–50) overlooks Jardín Zenea, Querétaro's pleasant hub.

Plans to throw off colonial rule were nurtured in the **Casa de la Corregidora,** located on the north side of dignified **Plaza de Armas** (*Avs. Pasteur & 5 de Mayo*). In this house Doña Josefa Ortiz de Domínguez, the wife of the Spanish-appointed *corregidor* (mayor), conspired with Miguel Hidalgo, Ignacio Allende, and other intellectuals. *La corregidora* was put under house arrest and later executed. You are welcome to explore the interior courtyards of

the grand home, which now houses state government offices. On the plaza's west flank, admire the baroque facade of the 18th-century **Casa de Ecala,** built of sculpted quarrystone and effusively decorated with Talavera tiles.

The city's hub is congenial **Jardín Zenea** (*Avs. Corregidora, 16 de Septiembre, Juárez, & Madero*), a few blocks to the west, where elderly couples get up to dance when the band strikes up a melodramatic tune. Nearby, the

Querétaro
⚠ 119 C1
Visitor information
✉ Pasteur Norte 4
☎ 442/212-1412

dome of the 16th-century **Templo de San Francisco** is decorated with imported Spanish tiles. Within the adjoining former monastery, the **Museo Regional de Querétaro** *(Corregidora 3 Sur at Madero, tel 442/212-2031, closed Mon., $)* houses furnishings and paintings from the 17th to 19th centuries. A few blocks north, the 19th-century **Teatro de la República** *(Juárez at Calle A. Peralta)* has seen its share of real-life drama. The formal signing of the 1917 Constitution took place here; and Mexico's short-term emperor, Maximilian of Habsburg (see p. 33), was sentenced at the Teatro to die by firing squad in 1867. Today, the neoclassic venue hosts plays and concerts; visitors are welcome to look inside during the day.

The severe early 17th-century facade of the **Iglesia de Santa Clara** *(Madero at Allende, tel 442/212-1777)* belies an extravagant baroque interior. Eduardo Tresguerras (1759–1833), a talented Bajío native, sculpted the adjoining **Fuente de Neptuno** (Neptune Fountain) in 1797. Non-guests can explore the elegant sitting room and bar of the **Casa de la Marquesa** *(Madero 41 at Allende, tel 442/212-0092),* noted for its Mudejar influences and extensive tilework. The **Museo de Arte de Querétaro** *(Allende at Pino Suárez, closed Mon., $)* resides in a fabulous late-baroque building, originally an Augustinian monastery. The museum's extensive collection consists primarily of 16th- to 18th-century paintings from Mexico and Europe. Note the expressions on the faces of the caryatid columns in the monumental inner courtyard.

A Mid-Eastern influence can be seen in the **Iglesia y Convento de Santa Rosa de Viterbo** *(Arteaga at Ezequiel Montes, tel 442/212-1691),* with its Mudejar-style cupola and odd inverted flying buttresses adorned with gargoyles. Inside the church are six baroque altarpieces of gilded wood, a lovely pulpit inlaid with ivory, ebony, and silver, and an 18th-century pipe organ still used today.

After the fall of the Second Empire in 1867 (see p. 33), Maximilian of Habsburg was executed by firing squad on **Cerro de las Campanas** *(Morelos at Tecnológico)* on the city's west side. An **Expiatory Chapel,** built by the Austrian government in 1901, commemorates the site. Near the top of the "Hill of Bells," an enormous statue of Benito Juárez presides over a wonderful view.

Left: The extravagantly tiled flying buttresses of the 17th-century Iglesia de Santa Clara

On the opposite side of the city, monks carry on with their devotions despite the distraction of guided visits to their early 17th-century monastery, the **Convento de la Santa Cruz** *(Independencia at Felipe Luna, Barrio de Santa Cruz, tel 442/212-0235, closed Mon., donation).* A miracle is said to have occurred at this spot during a battle between the Spaniards and the Otomí, the region's original inhabitants. Legend recounts that the Apostle James (Santiago, patron saint of Spain) appeared on a brilliant white horse to urge the Spaniards to victory. (The city is officially called Santiago de Querétaro.) Behind the church is the terminus of a 4,000-foot (1,200 m) aqueduct, built by the Spanish more than 270 years ago.

Less than an hour's drive southeast of Querétaro, **San Juan del Río** *(Visitor information, Av. Juárez at el Templo del Santuario)* is a prosperous market town, known for its baskets, woodcarvings, palm furniture, and semiprecious gems, especially amethysts, Mexican opals, and topaz. Although the countryside between Querétaro and San Juan is productive farm and ranchland, the connecting highway is now lined with factories, and the main reason to visit it is to purchase cut and polished gemstones.

Tequisquiapan, north of San Juan *(Visitor information, Plaza Hidalgo, Andador Independencia 1, tel 427/273-0295),* is smaller and more picturesque. Swimming pools with restaurants and children's play equipment cluster outside town on the road to Ezequiel Montes, where there's also a golf course. Sarapes, wicker baskets, and other local handicrafts are sold at the **Mercado de Artesanías** *(Salvador Carrizal & Ezequiel Montes),* and at stores surrounding the *zócalo,* or main square. The town hosts the yearly Fiesta del Queso y del Vino *(end of May/early June).* Inaugurated in 1976, this popular summer festival crowns a carnival queen and offers the crowds who come food and wine tastings, horse shows, bullfights, and cultural events. ■

Las Misiones de la Sierra Gorda drive

Between 1751 and 1768, five Franciscan missions were built amid the Sierra Gorda, a rugged range heading northeast of Querétaro toward Ciudad Valles, San Luis Potosí. Led by Fray Junípero Serra, Franciscan monks attempted to catechize the Pame (a Chichimec tribe) and encourage them to accept a sedentary life. The unusual mission churches exemplify Mexican baroque style and combine Christian symbols of obvious didactic intent with the sensibilities of the indigenous craftsman.

Young visitors rest on the steps outside Jalpan mission.

The drive along mountain roads is curvy yet beautifully scenic, ascending through a semi-arid landscape to mountain escarpments and valleys peppered with pines.

Jalpan mission ❶ *(tel 429/296-0255)* perches on a bluff 118 miles (190 km) northeast of Querétaro on Hwy. 120. It was the first mission built (1751–58) in this isolated region. On its facade, statues of the Virgin of Guadalupe and the Virgin of Pilar symbolize the equal importance of Mexico and Spain. Near the bottom of the facade, note the double-edged symbolism of the two-headed eagle (a Habsburg icon) devouring a snake (a well-known Aztec icon). Dedicated to the Apostle James, the church has a shell motif, including a shell-inlaid entranceway. The adjacent **Museo Histórico de la Sierra Gorda** *(tel 441/296-0165, closed Mon. and 3–5 p.m.)* has artifacts from the Pame, Chichimec, Purépecha, and monastic cultures.

From Jalpan head northwest on Hwy. 69 toward Río Verde. After about 20 miles (34 km) you will come to **Misión de Concá** ❷ *(tel 01800/029-4240)*, at the entrance to town. Although both the town and adjoining mission are located in Arroyo Seco ("dry riverbed") township, thermal springs abound. The striking

orange-and-red-ocher facade of this church, the smallest in the Sierra Gorda, is notable for detail that mimics the foliage of the semitropical valley in which it sits. The profuse decoration and the rather heavy-handed sculptures show the involvement of indigenous artisans. Crowning the facade is a Trinity, rarely seen in Mexico.

Return to Jalpan and continue on Hwy. 120 for about 12½ miles (20 km) to **Misión de Landa de Matamoros** ❸ *(tel 429/292-5210)*, its elaborate facade resplendent with carved saints tucked within niches. The last mission church to be built, Landa is also the most intact, with a church, cloister, open chapel, atrium, and four *posas*, or corner chapels.

Drive north for 6 miles (10 km). Take a right turn and follow this road for about 10 miles (16 km) to **Misión de Tilaco** ❹ *(tel 427/273-3564)*. As at Jalpan, the sculptures of saints Peter and Paul flank the wide portal. Above, the images of St. Joseph and the Virgin on the second level symbolize familial devotion. Near the top of the facade, a multitude of angels flies up toward a fabulous garden.

Continue another 4 miles (6.5 km) on Hwy. 120 to the left-hand turnoff to **Misión de Tancoyol** ❺ *(tel 429/293-3718)*. Drive about 10 miles (16 km) through the forested valley of Tancoyol (meaning "place of *coyoles*," a regional fruit). This mission's facade is decorated with Franciscan saints and symbols, although two of the interior columns are crowned with a jaguar and a character with Indian features.

Back at Hwy. 120, you can return to Querétaro or make the shorter drive to Ciudad Valles, in the Huasteca region of San Luis Potosí (via Hwy. 85). The second route will take you past **Xilitla** ❻ and the open-air sculptures of Scottish eccentric Edward James (see p. 136).

All of the missions open daily at 7 a.m. and close around sunset; comfortable accommodations can be found in Jalpan and Concá. ■

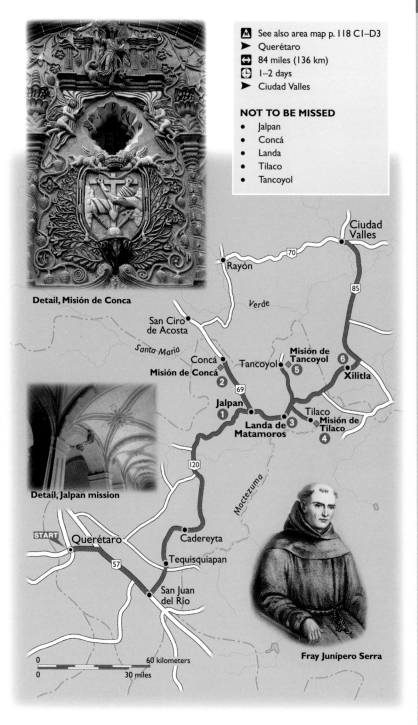

Detail, Misión de Conca

Detail, Jalpan mission

Fray Junípero Serra

LAS MISIONES DE LA SIERRA GORDA DRIVE

⛰ See also area map p. 118 C1–D3
▶ Querétaro
↔ 84 miles (136 km)
🕐 1–2 days
▶ Ciudad Valles

NOT TO BE MISSED
- Jalpan
- Concá
- Landa
- Tilaco
- Tancoyol

Ciudad Valles

Rayón
70
85

Verde

San Ciro
de Acosta

Santa María

Concá
Misión de Concá
2

Tancoyol

Misión de
Tancoyol
5

Misión de
Tancoyol
6
Xilitla

Jalpan
1
69

Landa de
Matamoros

Tilaco
3
Misión de
Tilaco
4

120

Moctezuma

START Querétaro

Cadereyta

Tequisquiapan

57

San Juan
del Río

0   60 kilometers
0   30 miles

San Luis Potosí

A restored historic district warms the now-industrialized state capital.

IN THE MID- AND LATE 16TH CENTURY, THE DISCOVERY OF rich veins of silver in neighboring Zacatecas and Guanajuato flamed the Spanish desire for precious metals. They struck silver at Cerro de San Pedro but established the city of Real San Luis Minas de Potosí (now San Luis Potosí) some 8 miles (5 km) away. The large mineral deposits petered out fairly quickly, but by then San Luis was firmly established as a center of ranching and commerce.

As capital of a huge region encompassing not only today's Nuevo León and Coahuila but also Texas and Louisiana, San Luis Potosí was once the most important city in northern Mexico. Although Monterrey is now the north's industrial leader, San Luis is still a vital and prosperous city, with hundreds of business enterprises.

The city maintains its sense of tradition and, in its historic center, a wealth of colonial and republican-era buildings despite being thoroughly urban. Many are neoclassic, and a number of baroque churches have been remodeled with neoclassic interiors. The busy capital was originally laid out in a grid, each of the seven neighborhoods having its own church and plaza. Surrounding these areas are now skyscrapers, traffic, and all the other components of a large industrial city.

Now home to a million people, San Luis is an engaging city, enjoying a mild climate with little temperature variation throughout the year. Potosinos are proud of their regional cuisine. Specialties include *enchiladas potosinas* (a cornmeal and chili mixture filled with cheese, fried, and garnished with fresh onions) and *tacos Camila* (tortillas filled with cheese, lightly fried, and buried under a medley of vegetables). The city is also known for its chocolates and for *queso de tuna*, a caramelized treat of condensed cactus juice.

Unpretentious restaurants

serving the local fare are found on and around the main square, popular **Plaza de Armas,** also called Jardín Hidalgo *(between Los Bravo, Zaragoza, Othón, & 5 de Mayo).* Upscale cafés and restaurants line Avenida V. Carranza west of **Plaza de los Fundadores.** Also on this busy street is the **Casa de la Cultura** *(Av. V. Carranza 181, tel 444/813-2247, closed Mon., $),* built in the 1920s as an elegant mansion in the English neoclassic style. The cultural center offers literary workshops, concerts, and film festivals, and doubles as a museum housing Mexican and European religious art, regional handicrafts, and pre-Hispanic artifacts.

Several blocks to the east, **Museo de Escultura Federico Silva** *(Alvaro Obregón 80, tel 444/812-3848, closed Tues., $)* displays one of the most important collections of contemporary sculpture in all of Latin America.

North of Plaza de Armas, Calle Hidalgo is closed to traffic for several blocks leading to the municipal market, **Mercado Hidalgo,** making it a pleasant place to walk. South of the plaza, the neoclassic **Caja de Agua** is an unusual monument to public works. Built in 1832, this water storage tank was used by city residents until the 1900s. Water was drawn from one of eight decorated ducts around the reservoir's base. Farther south along Avenida Juárez, 18th-century **Santuario de Guadalupe**

San Luis Potosí
🅰 119 C3
Visitor information
✉ Alvaro Obregón 520, Centro
☎ 444/812-9939

Municipal Tourism office
✉ Palacio Municipal, Jardín Hidalgo
☎ 444/812-2770

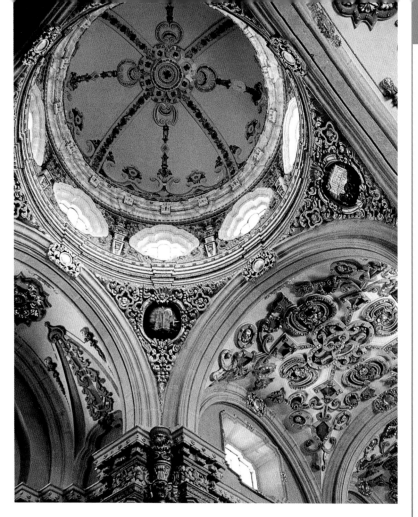

(Calz. de Guadalupe 1005, tel 444/815-0769), built in the shape of the Latin cross, shows a mixture of late-baroque and neoclassic styles. Its high altar has a painting of the Virgin of Guadalupe by Jesús Corral.

On the southwest side of the city, **Parque Tangamanga** *(Diagonal Sur at Av. Himno Nacional, tel 444/817-6322)* has jogging and cycling paths, lakes, mountain-bike trails, swimming pools, barbecue grills, children's play areas, a planetarium, a library, and a museum, and the city's 4,000-seat open-air theater.

About 30 miles (48 km) south of the city lies **Santa María del Río,** a town dedicated to weaving these exquisite shawls of silk (or nowadays, synthetic materials). This region is also known for its hot springs. **Balneario de Lourdes,** 12 miles (20 km) southeast of Santa María along a gravel road, has alkaline waters recommended for liver and kidney troubles, as well as a restaurant and hotel. About 38 miles (61 km) south of the capital, the **Centro Vacacional Gogorrón** has four pools of varying temperatures, and "roman baths"—private pools for up to six people. ■

The Capilla de Aranzazú, within the Museo Regional Potosino, is a chapel unique for its second-story location.

San Luis walk

San Luis Potosí was afforded city status in 1656, but many of its important buildings were constructed in the 18th and 19th centuries. Throughout the historic center are baroque, neoclassic, and Porfiriato structures, built during the presidential era of Porfirio Díaz (1877–1911), who commissioned many buildings in the European style.

Begin your walk at **Plaza de los Fundadores,** at Avs. V. Carranza and D. Carmona. At the northwest corner, visit the late 16th-century **Capilla de Loreto ❶,** its facade graced with a baroque portal. Inside, is one of Mexico's few surviving Jesuit altarpieces. Walk east on Obregón, passing the rectory of the **Universidad Autónoma,** which occupies the former Jesuit monastery.

Continue along the square's east side and turn left on Calle V. Carranza to large, open, traffic-free **Plaza de Armas ❷** *(Jardín Hidalgo),* surrounded by historic buildings and shaded by flamboyant and magnolia trees. Note the sober neoclassic lines of the **Palacio de Gobierno** *(tel 444/812-7470),* which occupies the square's entire west flank. This state government building twice housed the

interim government of Benito Juárez during the French occupation (see p. 33).

Taking a clockwise turn around the square, you will pass the oldest house in the city, the **Casa Virreina,** built in 1736 (but much remodeled). Now an excellent restaurant, it

▶ Capilla de Loreto
⬌ 0.8 mile (1.3 km)
🕓 4 hours
▶ Capilla de Aranzazú

NOT TO BE MISSED
- Templo del Carmen
- Museo Nacional de la Máscara
- Templo de San Francisco
- Capilla de Aranzazú

The city's limestone buildings range from pink and peach to gray and pale yellow.

was once the home of Mexico's only female vicereine, Francisca de la Gandara. On the northeast corner of the square is the 19th-century **Palacio Municipal** *(tel 444/812-5719, closed Sat., Sun.)*.

The imposing **Catedral** ❸ *(tel 444/812-2439)*, one of city's first baroque constructions, dominates the square's southeast corner. Note the Carrara marble statues of the apostles adorning the facade. The church has endured many remodels; inside, its neoclassic altars and Byzantine decorations were added in the 19th century.

A few blocks farther east on Calle Manuel J. Othón is the baroque **Templo del Carmen** ❹ *(tel 444/812-2878)*, its domes covered in multicolored tiles and its Churrigueresque facade nearly as ornate as the cathedral in Zacatecas (see p. 112). Inside are impressive side altars; the main altar, designed by architect Eduardo Tresguerras (1759–1833); and the **camarín de la Virgen,** a baroque chapel whose gold altarpiece is crowned with a giant scallop shell. Within the former convent, el **Museo del Virreinato** *(tel 444/812-5257, closed Mon., $)* shows colonial treasures.

Facing lovely **Plaza del Carmen** on its southeast side is the neoclassic **Teatro de la Paz** *(Villerías 205, tel 444/812-5209, closed*

Mon.), built during the Porfiriato era. Cross Villerías to the French neoclassic building housing the telegraph office and the **Museo Nacional de la Máscara** ❺ *(Villerías 210, tel 444/812-3025, closed Mon., $)*. Originally a private mansion, it now houses hundreds of ceremonial masks from throughout Mexico.

Walk south to Av. Universidad. A right turn brings you to **Plaza de San Francisco,** also known as Jardín Guerrero. Cross the long, rectangular plaza to the pink-stone **Templo de San Francisco** ❻ *(tel 444/812-4646)*, built in the 17th century. Note the Franciscan emblems and saints on the baroque facade. Ask permission to see the lovely Churrigueresque sacristy, with paintings by Miguel Cabrera, Antonio de Torres, and Francisco Martínez. Below the main dome, a ship-shaped crystal chandelier alludes to the evangelical travels of the order's founder, St. Francis of Assisi.

Behind the church, the former Franciscan monastery contains the **Museo Regional Potosino** ❼ *(Plaza de Aranzazú, tel 444/814-3572, closed Mon., $)*, with pre-Hispanic artifacts and colonial-era statues and furnishings. Within the museum, the 18th-century **Capilla de Aranzazú** is a chapel unique for its second-story location and covered atrium. ∎

Real de Catorce

Silver mining, which built Real de Catorce, was never reestablished after the 1910 Revolution.

THIS NEARLY ABANDONED TOWN, ISOLATED AMID THE arid mountains and high desert of the Sierra Madre Oriental, attracts only the most curious or solitary of travelers, as well as pilgrims who come to venerate a miraculous effigy of St. Francis of Assisi. Rarely seen in town, Huichol Indians scour the surrounding hills in search of sacred peyote, a hallucinogenic plant used in mystical rituals throughout the year.

Real de Catorce
119 C4
Visitor information
✉ Constitución 27
☎ 488/887-5071

During its productive years between the late 18th and early 20th centuries, Real de Catorce built impressive private homes for its nearly 40,000 citizens. Many are now crumbling into ruins, while others house modest restaurants, hotels, and businesses.

It doesn't take long to complete the tourist circuit. The simple stone church, the **Parroquia de la Purísima Concepción,** is built in the traditional Latin cross format, with a single sturdy bell tower. Tucked in a side altar, its image of St. Francis of Assisi is said to have miraculous powers, attested by the hundreds of naive ex-votos (paintings giving thanks for blessings received) on display.

Thousands of pilgrims descend on the town each year to celebrate the October 4 holy day associated with the Franciscan Order's founder.

Other structures of note are the stone **palenque,** or cockfighting arena, sometimes used as an amphitheater, and the **bullring** (both from the late 18th century), as well as the dilapidated **Casa de la Moneda,** the former mint. Real de Catorce's clear, starry nights—a consequence of the town's elevation at 9,042 feet (2,756 m) above sea level—are one of its most captivating attractions. For something a little more physical than stargazing, rent a horse through one of the hotels or restaurants and make an excursion outside town. ■

Aguascalientes

THE CAPITAL OF ONE OF MEXICO'S SMALLEST STATES WAS originally conceived as a defensive way station between regional silver mines and Mexico City. Farms and ranches sprang up around it to supply the mining towns, and today the city serves them as a commercial center. North of town lie its namesake hot springs and the San Marcos Winery, where the region's grapes are turned into brandy.

Aguascalientes
🗺 118 A3
Visitor information
✉ Palacio de Gobierno, Plaza de la Patria
☎ 449/915-9504

Aguascalientes is especially popular during Feria Nacional de San Marcos (mid-April to early May), celebrated since the 17th century. It has parades, concerts, fireworks, bull-fights, and livestock expos, with special festivities on the feast day of St. Mark, April 25. Events are at the fairgrounds in the **Jardín San Marcos** and **ExpoPlaza,** connected by pedestrian-only Calle Pani.

With its shade trees, fountains, and surrounding historic buildings, **Plaza de la Patria** is a reminder of the city's colonial past. On the plaza is Aguascalientes' oldest church (1575), the **Catedral Nuestra Señora de la Asunción** *(tel 449/915-1052).* It has endured several renovations, one resulting in its neoclassic facade of pink quarry-stone. Ask to see the 18th-century paintings by Miguel Cabrera. Behind the cathedral el **Museo de Historia Regional** *(V. Carranza 118, tel 449/916-5228, closed Mon., $)* has nine rooms' worth of history. Across the plaza, the lovely **Palacio de Gobierno** *(tel 449/915-1155)* contains murals by Chilean artist Oswaldo Barra Cunningham, a protégé of Diego Rivera.

East of the plaza, the **Museo de Aguascalientes** *(Zaragoza 507, tel 449/915-9043, closed Mon., $)* occupies an early 20th-century palace. See changing contemporary art and the paintings of Aguascalientes native Saturnino Herrán (1887–1918). Across the street, admire the stained-glass windows of the cupola at the **Templo de San Antonio** *(Pedro*

Parga & Zaragoza, tel 449/915-2898).

With temporary exhibits and a permanent collection of young, prize-winning artists, the **Museo de Arte Contemporáneo** *(P. Verdad at Morelos, tel 449/915-7953, closed Mon., $)* is housed in an early 20th-century hacienda near the central plaza. The affiliated **Centro**

El Obraje *(Juan de Montoro 222, tel 449/994-0074, closed Mon., $)* also exhibits modern art.

Local cartoonist and engraver José Guadalupe Posada (1852–1913) created a satirical legacy of political cartoons. See his work at the **Museo José Guadalupe Posada** *(Díaz de León, Jardín del Encino, tel 449/915-4556, closed Mon., $),* a 15-minute walk south of Plaza de la Patria. ∎

Aguascalientes's state government palace (Palacio de Gobierno) resembles many of the government buildings in Spain.

More places to visit in Central Mexico

DOLORES HIDALGO

Mexico's War of Independence officially began in this town, then known as Dolores. On September 15, 1810, Father Miguel Hidalgo y Costilla launched the movement that resulted 11 years later in freedom from Spanish rule (see p. 32). **Casa Hidalgo** *(Morelos 1, tel 418/182-0171, closed Mon., $),* the priest's former home, is now a museum with war artifacts and historic documents. Visit the baroque church, **Nuestra Señora de los Dolores,** on the main plaza, where the priest first sounded the alarm. The town's distinctive tiles can be seen adorning the better hotels and restaurants throughout Mexico; tiles and pottery can be purchased locally. Dolores is also known for its ice cream.

🅰 119 C2 **Visitor information** ☎ 418/182-1164 ✉ 25 miles (40 km) north of San Miguel de Allende; 30 miles (48 km) north of Guanajuato

Lovely gardens and courtyards hide behind Tamuzunchale facades.

LA HUASTECA

Encompassing parts of San Luis Potosí, Veracruz, Tamaulipas, and Hidalgo states, La Huasteca is named for the cultural group that lives in this region of secluded valleys and wild mountains, lakes, forests, and steaming coastal plains. A good base for exploring the region is **Ciudad Valles,** San Luis Potosí's second largest city, near the state's southeast corner. Little visited by tourists, La Huasteca has a variety of natural attractions. Although adventure tourism is still in its infancy, caves await enterprising spelunkers, sheer rock walls tempt climbers, and there are opportunities for rafting, kayaking, hiking, and bird-watching. Cloud-forest conditions prevail in the **Reserva de la Biósfera Abra-Tanchipa,** a 51,890-acre (21,000 ha) biosphere surrounding Ciudad Valles. Abundant rainfall creates lush forests and feeds fabulous waterfalls such as **Tamul, El Salto,** and **Minas Viejas,** where tropical trees sprouting wild orchids surround crystal-clear pools tinged green or blue. Towns such as **Tancanhuitz** and **Tamazunchale**—with large, fairly traditional Huastec populations—can be visited on Sunday market day, to sample local delicacies, buy crafts, and perhaps listen to a *huapango,* regional music accompanied by violins, flute, *jarana* (small guitar), harp, and rhythm instruments.

Ciudad Valles 🅰 119 D3 **Visitor information** ✉ Hidalgo 18, Ciudad Valles ☎ 481/383-2459

XILITLA

Near the Querétaro border and the missions of the Sierra Gorda, Las Pozas is a fantastic garden of sculptures built by surrealist poet Edward James (1907–1986). The wealthy eccentric exchanged Edwardian Britain for peyote-inspired projects in the Mexican highlands. With friend and mentor Plutarco Gastelum and a group of local artisans, the Scot occupied the last 20 years of his life creating an 80-acre (32 ha) dreamscape. About three dozen surrealist concrete structures—some 100 feet (30 m) tall—lose themselves in the equally fascinating tropical forest. At the site are a waterfall and a series of clear pools for bathing. In the nearby town of **Xilitla,** Gastelum built James an equally odd house, now a unique bed-and-breakfast—**Hotel El Castillo** *(tel 489/365-0038).* On Sundays visit Xilitla's open-air market, or take in a church service in the temple, all that remains of the 450-year-old Augustinian monastery.

🅰 119 D2 ✉ Las Pozas: 3 miles (5 km) outside Xilitla ☎ 489/365-0082 🅂 $ ■

Lush and humid, the central Pacific region has a multitude of distinct destinations. There are miles of untrammeled coast, small cities full of understated charm, posh beach resorts, and some of the country's best folk art.

Central Pacific states

A close-up of Huichol Indian yarn art

NORTHWEST
MEXICO
p. 75

NORTHEAST
MEXICO
p. 103

CENTRAL MEXICO
p. 117

0   150 kilometers
0   100 miles

D

Acaponeta

Novillero   Tecuala

Tuxpan

Mexcaltitán   Santiago Ixcuintla

Huejuquilla

Colotlán

Ojuelos de
Jalisco

NAYARIT

Playa
los Corchos   San
Blas   **Tepic**

Bahía
Matonchén

Compostela   Santa María
del Oro

Las Varas   San Pedro
Lagunillas

Encarnación
de Díaz

San Juan
de los Lagos   Lagos
de Moreno

Ixtlán del Río

Jalostotitlán

5▷

4▷

Punta
Mita

Bahía de
Banderas

Puerto
Vallarta

El Tuito

Nuevo
Vallarta

Mascota   **GUADALAJARA**

Ameca

Cocula

Etzatlán

Tequila

Zapopan   Tepatitlán

Tonalá   Arandas

Tlaquepaque   Atotonilco el Alto

Ajijic   Ocotlán

Chapala

La Piedad
de Cabadas

JALISCO

Zacoalco

Lago de
Chapala

Sahuayo

Zamora

Laguna de
Cuitzeo

3▷

Tomatlán

Autlán

Unión de Tula

El Grullo

Sayula

Jacona   Zacapu

4339m
Nevado
de Colima

**Ciudad
Guzmán**

PARQUE NAC. LAGO
DE CAMÉCUARO

Angahuan

Morelia

Zirahuén   Quiroga

**L
Azu**

P. NA
CO.
GARN

Bahía
Chamela

Chamela

Bel-Air Careyes

Barra de Navidad

San Patricio Melaque

Chamela

PARQUE NAC. VOL.
NEVADO DE COLIMA

▲ 3842m

Comala

Colima

Vol. Fuego de Colima

COLIMA

2774m
Vol. Paricutín ▲

PARQUE NAC.
PICO DE TANCITARO

Uruapan   Villa Escalante

Pátzcuaro

Santiago

Manzanillo

Armería

Tepalcatepec

Apatzingán

MICHOACÁ

Puruarán

Nueva Italia   Tiquicheo

PACIFIC

OCEAN

Tecomán

San Juan
de Lima

Coalcomán

Coalcomán
de Matamoros   Aguililla

Arteaga

Presa
del Infiernillo

Huetamo

Balsas

Ciuda
Altamirar

**△
A**   **△
B**

Infiernillo

Balsas

Lázaro
Cárdenas

Bahía de
Petacalco

2▷

Bahía
Bufadero

Playa Azul

Ixtapa

Zihuatanejo   Petatlán

Troncones

**△
C**

GU
E

San Lu
San Pe

Central Pacific states

SHARING A SWATH OF COAST AND THE FOOTHILLS and mountains that rise
abruptly beyond it, central Pacific Mexico has a multitude of distinctly different
destinations. Manzanillo calls itself the "sailfish capital of the world," Puerto Vallarta is a
fast-growing beach resort brimming with art galleries, and Michoacán's undeveloped
coast is the playground of surfers and locals. There are boutique hotels on isolated bays
and beaches, lazy fishing villages on mangrove-lined lagoons, and Acapulco, with its all-
night salsa clubs. Inland are straight-laced Guadalajara, land of mariachis and tequila,
funky Colima, and whitewashed Taxco, looking like a misplaced Mediterranean village.

Indigenous people are not found here in great
numbers. The largest population is the Nahua-
speaking people of Guerrero. In Nayarit,
mountain-dwelling populations of Huichols,
though small in number, maintain their cul-

tural identity and religious practices. Shamans
cure the sick and perform magic rituals, while
everyday citizens are guided by an ancestral
wisdom. Mirroring the Huichols' daily activities are playful, naive-looking figurines that

their ancestors left in the area's unique shaft-tombs (buried at the bottom of vertical passageway) beginning around 250 B.C.

Soon after the fall of Tenochtitlán (see p. 30), the Spanish conquerors fanned out in search of further adventure, bringing to bear the usual influences, including widespread death by disease. The Indians suffered especially violent treatment at the hands of Conquistador Nuño Beltrán de Guzmán. His reign of terror stretched from Sinaloa to Guadalajara: Individuals were branded and sold as slaves, and hundreds of villages burned.

Those Indians who survived disease and injustice literally took to the hills. After de Guzmán was dispatched to a Spanish jail, Bishop Vasco de Quiroga lured the Purépecha back to their villages in today's Michoacán. He built as many hospitals as churches, and schooled indigenous artisans in useful trades.

Today, Michoacán is one of Mexico's leading producers of fine crafts, including copper cookware, wooden furniture, pottery, and elegant lacquerware. The Huichol produce fabulous yarn paintings, masks, and beaded objects for ritual use and for sale to a growing body of collectors. Throughout the region, but especially in Michoacán and Guerrero, ritual masks and elaborate costumes are used during celebrations that incorporate elements of both pre-Hispanic and Catholic ritual. ■

Silver baron don José de la Borda financed the construction of Taxco's Churrigueresque Santa Prisca church in the 1750s.

Tepic & San Blas

Tepic

🗺 138 B4

Visitor information

✉ Av. Mexico at Calzada del Ejército Nacional

☎ 311/214-8071

TEPIC IS THE CAPITAL OF THE SMALL STATE OF NAYARIT, which produces much of the country's tropical fruits and most of its tobacco. In the foothills of the craggy Sierra Madre Occidental at 2,950 feet (900 m) above sea level, the small city is significantly cooler than the coast. About an hour north of Tepic is San Blas, headquarters for birders and beach bums who choose to avoid the fancy resorts. Surrounding this small fishing town are tropical forests, estuaries, and miles of sandy beaches.

TEPIC

Many Huichol men and women still wear traditional clothing.

Tepic is the traditional homeland of the Cora Indians. Along with their close relatives, the Huichol, they fled to the surrounding mountains to escape the cruel

Nuño de Guzmán in the 16th century (see pp. 138–39). Today Tepic is a crossroad of agriculture and commerce, where farmers come to town to buy supplies and sell their produce. Huichol men in white cotton trousers and embroidered tunics sell their handicrafts in front of the large **catedral,** with its neo-Gothic towers. Facing the cathedral across the **plaza principal** (*Av. México Norte at Lerdo Poniente*) is the **Palacio del Municipio,** and surrounding the main square are restaurants and shops. Nearby, the **Museo Casa de los Cuatro Pueblos** (*Hidalgo 60 Oriente, tel 312/212-1705, closed Sun.*) displays clothing and other items from the cultures of its indigenous people and sells indigenous crafts, including leather, musical instruments, carved wood, and Huichol beaded objects and yarn paintings. Housed in a restored 18th-century mansion, the **Museo de Antropología e Historia** (*Av. México 91 Norte at Zapata, tel 311/212-1900, closed Sun., $*) displays pre-Hispanic artifacts, regional folk art, and colonial religious paintings.

South of the main plaza is Tepic's other most important square, **Plaza Constituyentes.** Here is the **Palacio de Gobierno** (*Av. México Sur between Mina & Abasolo*), a

19th-century government building with historic murals on its cupola and interior walls.

Several lovely lakes are within an hour's drive of Tepic. Off the toll road to Guadalajara, a signed road leads to **Santa María del Oro,** where horses and guides can be hired for treks into the nearby mountains. Below the village lies the deep, crystalline crater lake **Laguna Santa María del Oro,** surrounded by verdant hills. You can swim, fish, take a picnic, or a 2¹/₂-hour walk around the lake. Rent kayaks at **Bungalows Koala** *(327/244-0237).* A turnoff just before Santa María leads to **Laguna de Tepeltitic,** shallower than Laguna Santa María but surrounded by lovely forest.

From Tepic, Highway 200 leads to **San Pedro Lagunillas,** another mountain lake.

SAN BLAS

An important port during the colonial era, San Blas is now a laid-back fishing town. There are no fancy hotels here, but a few good restaurants and just enough amenities to entertain a dedicated following. One drawback to a visit is the fierce mosquitoes and *jejenes* (biting gnats, or no-see-ums); bring insect repellent and cover up during the early morning and late afternoon.

San Blas's closest beach is **Playa Borrego.** You can take long walks along the often lonely beach, which terminates in an estuary after about 5 miles (8 km). This beach is infamous for its no-see-ums.

Las Islitas is a lovely stretch of beach punctuated by rocky coves. Lounge in a hammock or play a game of dominoes under a *ramada* (palm-thatch, open-sided structure). Sailboats cruise the bay, which is backed by jungle-clad mountains. Farther round the curve of the bay toward the s mall fishing village of Santa Cruz is **Los Cocos Beach,** shaded by palms.

For many the highlight of their vacation is a boat trip up **Estero San Cristóbal** to **La Tovara** freshwater spring. Herons, egrets, turtles, and other aquatic fauna haunt mazelike canals of mangroves. After an hour-long ride, you'll have an hour to swim in the lovely spring. Have a drink or a bite to eat at the delightful restaurant overlooking the idyllic pool, but come early to beat the groups now bused in from Puerto Vallarta. ∎

San Blas
⚐ 138 B4
Visitor information
✉ Canalizo at Sinaloa, Presidencia Municipal
☎ 323/285-0005

The ruins of the 1773 Contaduría (Counting House) lord over San Blas.

Puerto Vallarta

BAHÍA DE BANDERAS, ON WHICH PUERTO VALLARTA SITS, IS one of the world's biggest bays. Although it had no permanent settlements until the mid-19th century, the bay was charted and used for hundreds of years as a rest stop for pirates, priests, the military, and other sailors. Before a steamy Hollywood romance attracted the world's attention, few travelers had ever seen Puerto Vallarta, an idyllic village with white-sand beaches. It's now a savvy tourist mecca with a string of high-rise hotels marching up and down the bay.

Puerto Vallarta
🅰 138 B4
Visitor information
✉ Juárez at Independencia, Palacio Municipal
☎ 322/223-2500, ext. 131

Puerto Vallarta shot to fame in 1963 during the filming of *Night of the Iguana*.

Puerto Vallarta became an overnight star with the highly publicized romance of Elizabeth Taylor and Richard Burton during the filming of John Huston's *Night of the Iguana* in 1963. (The film starred Burton and Ava Gardner; Taylor tagged along.) And it hasn't stopped growing or attracting vacationers since, the original town having expanded to cover much of 25-mile (40 km) Bahía de Banderas.

The resort specializes in galleries and shops selling fine art and handicrafts, including objects made by the mountain-dwelling and spiritually attuned Huichol. Some galleries focus on the crème de la crème of folk art from the states of Oaxaca, Chiapas, and Michoacán.

The heart of the old city is **Vallarta Vieja,** where buildings are painted white by government decree. Capped in rust-colored roof tiles and draped in bright fuschia-pink bougainvillea, sunlight-dappled houses stagger up palm-covered hills. From there, the **Río Cuale** descends to divide the Old Town into north and south sectors. Pedestrian and automobile bridges both cross the river and access **Isla Río Cuale,** a slip of an island where restaurants, shops, and the small **Museo de Antropología** are surrounded by gardens and brushed with the best breeze in town. Below the Insurgentes Street bridge, a sprawling handicrafts market sells

mainly mass-produced souvenirs.

A few blocks north of the river, **Plaza Principal,** or Plaza de Armas *(Zaragoza, Morelos, Iturbide, & Juárez),* is surrounded by the city hall and the open-air **Los Arcos amphitheater,** which often hosts concerts. The seawalk, or *malecón,* stretches north and south from the main square, itself fronted by bars, shops, and restaurants. The malécon is a great spot at sunset, when the sun glints on a dozen bronze sculptures along its length.

New development lies north of town. First is the **Zona Hotelera,** a mass of high-rise hotels. Most rent water toys along **Playa de Oro,** not quite as attractive since Hurricane Kenna replaced some of its sand with rocks. Farther north is **Marina Vallarta,** an enclave of resort hotels and condos surrounding a 380-slip marina, a popular yacht club, and an 18-hole golf course. Fishing charters and day cruises depart from the **Maritime Terminal.** This development is a favorite among boaters, although its beaches aren't among Vallarta's prettiest.

Farther north still, **Nuevo Vallarta,** at the mouth of the Río Ameca, is actually in the state of Nayarit. Here are a yacht club, condos, marina, and an ever-growing population of resorts, many of them all-inclusives. It is a long way from the action of downtown

Vallarta, but has beautiful beaches and is a good base for exploring Naryarit's small beach towns.

Those who want to be close to the party scene congregate in downtown Vallarta. Near the Río Cuale, **Olas Altas** and **Playa de los Muertos** beaches, just south of Viejo Vallarta, are popular with tourists, locals, and vendors selling mangoes, grilled fish on a stick, sarapes, and most everything else.

The coast highway continues south of downtown, past sandy white beaches scalloped between rocky coves, and hills sprinkled with luxury homes to **Mismaloya,** where *Night of the Iguana* was filmed. Although Hotel Mismaloya has appropriated much of this once pristine cove, it's still a pretty beach with colorful fishing boats in the adjoining lagoon. An inland road leads to **Chino's Paradise** or **El Edén,** inviting small restaurants perched above the Mismaloya River.

From Mismaloya, divers and snorkelers can hire skiffs to **Los Arcos,** a protected underwater park just offshore, or to secluded beaches farther south. Closest is jungle-lined **Boca de Tomatlán,** also accessible by car or bus.

The beaches beyond Boca de Tomatlán are accessible only by boat. Sandy **Playa Las Animas** offers beach toys for rent. **Quimixto** offers good snorkeling. Both have small restaurants. **Yelapa** is a Mexican Shangri-La where thatch-roofed restaurants line the beach. Tour boats descend on these lovely beaches daily, so come early or late to avoid the crowds. ■

Puerto Vallarta's emerald-green hills back up to azure mountains.

La Costalegre

SINCE THE EARLY 1990s, THE 280-MILE (450 KM) STRETCH of idyllic tropical beaches between Puerto Vallarta and Manzanillo has been dubbed La Costalegre. Exclusive resorts have been built on a few of the loveliest beaches. Continued development is inevitable, but for the moment, signed and unsigned roads lead to simple fishing villages, rocky coves that are perfect for fishing or snorkeling, and long bays with modest accommodations. Manzanillo, the Pacific's most important industrial port, manages to combine commercial fishing and shipping with tourism and excellent billfishing.

About 90 miles (145 km) south of Puerto Vallarta, **Bahía Chamela** has several lovely beaches and basic accommodations; camping is permitted. Here also is one of Costalegre's most exclusive resorts. Built in the 1960s (but meticulously maintained), El Careyes is perfect for honeymooners and has a lovely spa. Combining Pacific and Mediterranean styles, the resort is named for the marine turtles that lay their eggs on the beaches of the delightful cove. There's a village and several restaurants at **Playa Perula,** at the bay's southern end. You can fish from the rocks, sit in the shade of beachfront eateries, or hire a skiff to snorkel offshore or see the birds at nearby **Isla Pajarera,** one of half a dozen offshore islands.

Among the Costa Alegre's most exclusive resorts is **Bel-Air Careyes,** built in the 1960s, complete with tennis courts, stables, and polo field. Farther south, **Bahía Tenacatita** is slated for development, but for the moment it's a long stretch of clean white sand fringed by palms. Part of the bay is a coral-covered cove perfect for diving, swimming, and sailboarding, or you can hire a local guide for a bird-watching expedition on a nearby lagoon.

Just before the Colima state line is gorgeous **Bahía de Navidad** (Christmas Bay). At its northern end, **San Patricio Melaque** is a small but growing resort town with a good swimming beach. Crowded around the west end of its long beach is a clutch of thatch-roofed, open-air eateries—a great sunset spot. Many Guadalajara families vacation here on long weekends and holidays, including a week-long celebration for the town's patron, St. Patrick.

You can walk several miles along the sandy beach to **Barra de Navidad,** a sleepy fishing village that recently woke up to larger-scale tourism. Strung out along a sandbar extending into the bay is Barra's white beach. Thatch-roofed restaurants serve up spicy shrimp, fresh fish, and cold beers. The closest beaches are not popular with some swimmers as afternoon breezes attract windsurfers, and winter swells bring surfers. Large areas of mangroves were displaced with the construction of the luxury resorts, marina, and golf course at **Grand Bay Hotel** and **Mesón de Doña Paz.** Birders now mainly stalk their prey through wetlands farther north, around Bahías Tenacatita or Chamela. **Immersion Adventures** (*www.immersion adventures.com*) leads tours there.

Deep-sea fishing charters are available from private operators as well as the local co-op, the **Sociedad Cooperativa de Servicios Turísticos** (*Morelos 1*). Multiple fishing tournaments are

Barra de Navidad
- 🗺 138 B3

Visitor information
- ✉ Jalisco 67
- ☎ 315/355-5100

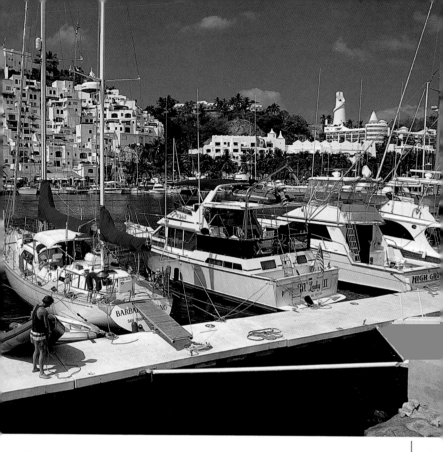

held in January, late May, September, and November. The town honors its patron, St. Anthony of Padua, in the week preceding June 13.

South of Barra de Navidad the highway enters Colima state and passes near, but not along, the coast to **Bahías Manzanillo** and **Santiago.** The bays are divided in two by the Santiago peninsula, a short spit of land on which sits **Las Hadas** resort, opened in 1974 and showcased in the movie *10* (1979). With its brilliant white, "It's a Small World" architecture and air of luxurious comfort, the resort continues to delight travelers. The famous and truly rich, however, have moved on to more exclusive resorts such as **Las Alamandas, El Tamarindo,** and **Hotelito Desconocido,** farther north on the Costalegre proper.

Unlike Ixtapa and Cancún, **Manzanillo** is a real city and a busy port. It is said that ships from the Orient docked here two centuries before the Spanish arrived in Mexico. Instead of a row of restaurants, hotels, and bars such as those in Mazatlán's Golden Zone (see p. 98), Manzanillo's attractions are found here and there along the bay and downtown, located at the far eastern point of the bay. The most pictureque beaches, and those best for swimming are mainly clustered around the peninsula. Despite the industrial flavor, this somewhat unattractive resort does have its admirers: mainly sun-starved Canadians, Mexican families, and deep-sea anglers who come for the big game fish. ■

The marina at Las Hadas, Manzanillo, attracts boaters year-round.

Manzanillo
🅼 138 B3
Visitor information
✉ Blvd. Costera Miguel de la Madrid 875A
☎ 314/333-2264

Plazas and pedestrian malls surround the cathedral in historic Guadalajara.

In & around Guadalajara

GUADALAJARA IS THE MEXICAN'S MEXICO—AN ARCHETYPE of idealized Mexican culture. It's the home town of mariachi music, the romantic ballads performed by large bands of strikingly uniformed musicians playing harps, violins, and soulful trumpets. This is the land of tequila soirees and of plantations of blue agave from which tequila is made. On Sunday afternoons, elegant equestrians known as *charros* perform stylized feats of showmanship far removed from those of any casual cowboy.

Guadalajara

⛰ 138 C4

Visitor information

✉ Morelos 102, Plaza Tapatía

☎ 33/3668-1600

Guadalajara (from the Arabic, meaning "river of stones") was moved several times before a final site was chosen near the west end of the 5,400-foot (1,645 m) Atemajac Valley, 300 miles (480 km) northwest of Mexico City. Several earlier settlements of the same name failed owing to drought and Indian attacks. Once established, the seat of western colonial government soon also became a capital of agriculture and ranching.

As Mexico's second largest city, Guadalajara embraces mainstream, as well as Mexican, culture, with four 18-hole golf courses and three soccer teams, a zoo, a planetarium,

and a large convention center. Many visitors come to shop. Residents from surrounding haciendas and rural communities buy everything from lizard-skin boots and spurs to plows. City folk scour shops and galleries for the region's famous handicrafts: leather clothing, handblown glassware, wood-and-pigskin *(equipal)* furniture, handcrafted and factory tableware, and home accessories of tin, wrought iron, pewter, papier-mâché, and copper.

Many of these modern handicrafts are found in the art-driven satellite villages of Tlaquepaque and Tonalá (see pp. 150–51), which Guadalajara has swallowed, but not digested. In Guadalajara proper, visitors explore the *centro histórico*, a square mile surrounding the cathedral, where historic churches, museums, and shops line pedestrian malls and fountain-filled public squares.

CENTRO HISTÓRICO

Presiding over Guadalajara's historic district is the majestic **catedral** (*Av. 16 de Septiembre between Hidalgo & Morelos, tel 33/3614-5504*), with its yellow-tiled dome and twin spires. Earthquakes and changing fashions have led to many modifications over the years, rendering it Gothic, Moorish, baroque, and neoclassic in style. Its three naves house a dozen side altars; the sacristy is lined with colonial-era paintings.

Plazas surround the cathedral on all sides. To the west is **Plaza Guadalajara,** where free, three-hour city tours depart Saturdays and Sundays at 10 a.m. (*tel 33/3616-3333*) from the **Palacio Municipal,** the municipal palace. Afternoon concerts are held Thursdays and Sundays at the art nouveau bandstand on **Plaza de Armas,** which flanks the cathedral

to the south. Facing this graceful old square is the **Palacio de Gobierno** (*Moreno at Corona, tel 33/3688-1800, closed Sat., Sun.*), a neoclassic government edifice with Churrigueresque decorations. Murals by Jalisco native José Clemente Orozco (1883–1949) embellish the stairwell and the congressional chambers upstairs.

North of the cathedral, the **Rotunda de los Hombres Ilustres** honors Jalisco heroes— primarily writers, painters, and other artists—on a shady plaza of the same name, and horse-drawn carriages await passengers in front of the **Museo Regional de Guadalajara** (*Liceo 60, tel 33/3614-9957, closed Mon., $*). This comprehensive museum occupies the former baroque seminary of San José. Surrounding a typical colonial courtyard are rooms with archaeological and paleontological exhibits, including offerings from area shaft-tombs and a complete mammoth skeleton. Upstairs are colonial paintings, artifacts of West Coast cultures, and other regional history exhibits.

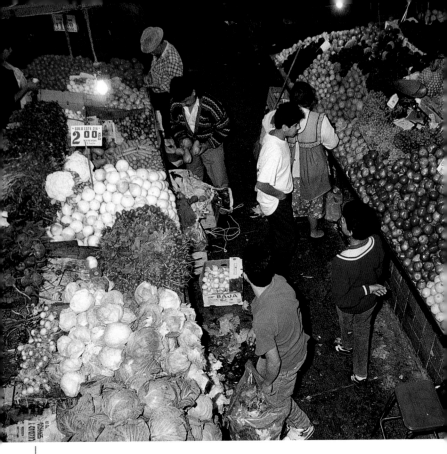

Downtown Guadalajara has many worthy museums. The **Casa Museo López Portillo** (*Liceo 177 at San Felipe, tel 33/3613-2411, closed Mon.*) is a 19th-century home with furnishings typical of an upper-class family (one of this family's sons was the former president of that name). The **Museo Clemente Orozco** (*Av. Aurelio Aceves 27, tel 33/3616-8329, closed Sat., Sun.*) houses personal and professional artifacts of the famous muralist, as well as a huge mural, "Alegoría del Vino" ("The Good Life").

The **Museo de las Artes** (*Juárez 975, tel 33/3134-1664, closed Mon., $*) shows permanent and temporary exhibits of contemporary art. Not far away, **El Museo de las Artes Populares** (*San Felipe 211, tel 33/3614-3891, closed Mon., $*) occupies a classic two-story, 19th-century house restored in the late 20th century. In addition to rooms for temporary exhibits, this has permanent exhibits of Jalisco crafts that are beyond the usual genres. Check out rooms dedicated to *charrería*, music, and cooking implements as well as glass, ceramics, and leather.

Behind the cathedral, **Plaza de la Liberación** is surrounded by imposing government buildings and the neoclassic **Teatro Degollado** (*Degollado s/n at Morelos s/n, tel 33/3614-4773 or 3613-1115, closed Sun.*), inaugurated in 1866 by soprano Angela Peralta. Visit the stunning theater 10 a.m.–1 p.m. to see the interior fresco, illustrating Dante's *Divine Comedy* among other subjects, or better yet, attend a **folk-**

loric show *($$–$$$$)* by the university dance troupe. Nearby, the Ripley's **Museo de la Cera** *(Morelos 217, tel 33/3614-8487, $)* has 120 reasonably lifelike wax figures, including depictions of Madonna (the current one) and a complete mariachi band.

Like Monterrey's Macroplaza (see p. 108), **Plaza Tapatía** was created in the 1980s to incorporate existing churches, government buildings, shops, and public squares into a cohesive entity of green spaces, walkways, sculptures, fountains, and benches. At the east end of the 17-acre (7 ha) public square lies one of Guadalajara's landmarks, the stately **Instituto Cultural Cabañas** *(Cabañas 8, tel 33/3668-1640, closed Mon., $),* a World Heritage site where concerts, film screenings, and performances are held. Originally an orphanage designed by Spanish architect and sculptor Manuel Tolsá, it served this role until the 1970s. Many of José Clemente Orozco's most brilliant murals adorn the walls and ceilings of this neoclassic building, which has hundreds of rooms and several dozen linked patios planted with grapefruit trees. The site museum houses more works by Orozco and hosts temporary exhibits of contemporary art.

Past the modernistic bronze sculpture depicting the Immolation of Quetzalcóatl lies the **Mercado San Juan de Dios** *(Av. J. Mina at Calzada Independencia, tel 33/3618-0506, also known as Mercado Libertad).* A footbridge connects the enormous city market to the church for which it was named. Just beyond is **Plaza de los Mariachis** *(Obregón at Av. J. Mina),* where roving bands in matching silver-studded ensembles serenade song-starved clients at outdoor tables. The plaza (surrounded by bars dedicated to the same endeavors) can be crowded at night, when some visitors might find it intimidating.

Within the city center are several churches of note. **Iglesia de Santa Mónica** *(Santa Mónica 250 at San Felipe, tel 33/3614-6620)* is considered one of Guadalajara's loveliest, its baroque facade graced with a twin portico decorated with Solomonic columns. South of Plaza de Armas, the **Templo de San Francisco** *(Av. 16 de Septiembre 289 at Prisciliano Sánchez, tel 33/3614-4083)* and the **Capilla de Nuestra Señora de Aranzazú** are all that remain of a 16th-century Franciscan monastery. Note the typical Mexican motif—the eagle on the prickly-pear cactus—on the facade of the former, and the gilded Churrigueresque altarpiece inside the latter.

Also south of Plaza de Armas are the **Museo de Arqueología del Occidente de México** *(Calzada Independencia Sur at Av. del Campesino, tel 33/3619-0104, closed Mon., $),* with archaeological exhibits of western cultures, and **Parque Agua Azul** *(Calz. Independencia Sur 973, tel 33/3619-0328, closed Mon., $),* a children's park, which also houses an orchid house, a butterfly pavilion, and an aviary. At the nearby **Lienzo Charro de Jalisco** *(Dr. R. Michel 577, tel 33/3619-3232, $),* families congregate at Sunday noon for that most *tapatío* (native Guadalajaran) of traditions, the colorful *charreada* (rodeo; see p. 154).

ZAPOPAN
About 5 miles (8 km) northwest of central Guadalajara is Zapopan, known throughout Mexico for its diminutive statue of the Virgin of Zapopan. The 10-inch (25 cm) cornpaste statue is said to have cured epidemics and aided the Spanish in battle. After four months of travel between parish churches, the statue is brought back to

Zapopan
138 C4
Visitor information
✉ Av. Vallarta 6503, Plaza Concentro
☎ 33/3110-0754

Zapopan each October 12 during the Romería de la Virgen de Zapopan. Hundreds of thousands fill the streets as the Virgin's entourage heads for the baroque **basílica** (*Hidalgo at Zapata*), begun in 1690. It's a lively party with music and folkloric dances, food vendors, mariachis, men on horseback, and kids in costume.

Next to the church is **Museo de la Arte Huichol,** a government-run shop selling Huichol Indian yarn paintings, beaded masks, and other handicrafts at reasonable prices. Larger than the church itself is the atrium and adjoining **Plaza de las Américas,** surrounded by the flags of North American and Latin American countries.

TLAQUEPAQUE

Once an independent village and now a municipality and suburb of Guadalajara with 600,000 inhabitants, Tlaquepaque is charming if touristy. Its inhabitants have been making pottery since the time of the Spanish incursion; in the Indian dialect, Tlaquepaque means "place on high clay hills." Traditional Tlaquepaque ceramics are fragile earthenware, although today other genres, including more durable stoneware, have been adopted.

The art of glassblowing was introduced in the 19th century, and today hundreds of shops sell miniatures and glassware in addition to pottery, textiles, silver jewelry, tin, wrought iron, high-end furniture, and household accessories. You can watch glassblowers at work at **El Refugio,** on Calle Contreras Medellín. Many shops are themselves works of art, housed in gracious, restored mansions surrounding plant-filled courtyards. Many close for siesta and some all day on Sunday.

But Tlaquepaque has more to

offer than just shopping. This is a fascinating place to walk: There are restaurants, lively cantinas, B&Bs, and several interesting churches.

Pedestrianized Calle Independencia leads to the main square, **Jardín Hidalgo,** and the 18th-century, neoclassic-Byzantine-style **Santuario de Nuestra Señora de la Soledad** (*Prisciliano Sánchez at Morelos*). In the next block, the **Parroquia de San Pedro** (*Guillermo Prieto at Morelos*) was built by the Franciscans in 1813.

Before buying ceramics, take a look at the exhibits of traditional pottery from the Valle de Atemajac and prize-winning contemporary pieces at the **Museo Regional de la Cerámica** (*Independencia 237 at Alfareros, tel 33/3635-5404*), west of the main square. After a day's shopping expedition, relax at **El Parián** (*Between Independencia, Prieto, Morelos, & Madero*), a plaza filled with lively cantinas and open-air restaurants, shops, and strolling mariachis. The town celebrates its annual Feria de San Pedro Tlaquepaque during the last week of June.

TONALÁ

Five miles (8 km) east of Tlaquepaque is Tonalá, a pre-Hispanic regional capital whose Náhuatl name means "place where the sun rises," or "place of the sun." It was also briefly the capital of Nueva Galicia before a dearth of water and other factors forced the settlers to abandon the site. Tonalá produces much of the glass and pottery sold in Tlaquepaque.

On Thursdays and Sundays vendors line the downtown streets in an informal *tianguis* (market) that has taken place since pre-Hispanic times. Throughout the week you'll find shops selling low- and high-fire ceramics, blown glass, pewter, and works of papier-mâché, tin,

---

Tlaquepaque

⚑ 138 C4

Visitor information

✉ Morelos 288

☎ 33/3562-7050

Tonalá

⚑ 138 C4

Visitor information

✉ Av. Hidalgo 21

☎ 33/3284-3092

Opposite: Parroquia de San Pedro church in Tlaquepaque— the charming town makes a refreshing change from congested and urban Guadalajara.

Workers harvest the *piña*, or heart, of the agave plant.

Tequila
🅐 138 C4
**Visitor
information**
✉ José Cuervo 33
☎ 374/742-1756

copper, wood, basketry, and iron. The **Casa de los Artesanos** (*Avenida de los Tonaltecas Sur 140, closed Sat., Sun.*) exhibits fine handicrafts representing the work of more than 50 local artisans.

Handicrafts shops can be found on Avenida de los Tonaltecas and around the **plaza principal** (*Juárez, Pino Suárez, Zapata, & Madero*). Surrounding the square are the Gothic-style **Santuario del Sagrado Corazón** (*Hidalgo at Juárez*) and the **Parroquia de Santiago Apóstol** (*Pino Suárez at Juárez*), one of the oldest temples in the Atemajac Valley. Named for the town's patron saint, the Apostle James, this is the site of festivities in the days preceding July 25, when local men don masks and costumes to perform regional dances.

The **Museo Nacional de la Cerámica** (*Constitución 104 near Hidalgo, tel 33/3683-0494, closed Mon.*) displays ceramic pieces, both modern and ancient, from throughout Mexico. About four blocks away, the **Museo Regional de Tonalá** (*Ramón Corona 73, closed Mon., $*) has rotating fine-

and folk-art exhibits in a traditional adobe, wood-beamed house.

TEQUILA

The pleasant town of Tequila, about 35 miles (56 km) northwest of Guadalajara, sits under an extinct volcano of the same name. Fields of blue agave shimmer in a spiky azure haze around the town. The heart of the agave, or maguey, is used to make tequila in its various forms. Unique not just to Mexico but to the region, true tequila can be made only in Jalisco and four other states (see p. 154).

Larger distilleries such as Sauza and Jose Cuervo give tours, but it's best to arrange ahead of time. Across from the Jose Cuervo factory, on the street of that name, el **Museo Nacional del Tequila** (*tel 33/742-2410, $*) has photos and exhibits of the tequila-making process. For an excursion from Guadalajara, take the Saturday **Tequila Express,** an eight-hour train tour including lunch, mariachis, folkloric dancers, and free tequila! Tickets can be purchased through Guadalajara's Chamber of Commerce (*Av. Vallarta*

4095 at Niño Obrero, tel 3122-7920, $$$$$). Six miles (10 km) south, in **Amatitán**, the **Hacienda San José del Refugio** (tel 33/3942-3900) is a 10,000-acre (4,000 ha) family-run agave plantation of 8 million plants and a distillery producing Herradura tequila, which sets industry standard for efficiency and cleanliness. Tours ($$$) are available daily on the hour between 9 a.m. and noon (call ahead to confirm).

LAGO DE CHAPALA

About 25 miles (40 km) southeast of Guadalajara lies Mexico's largest natural freshwater lake, Lago de Chapala. Its agreeable climate, tree-lined lakefront promenades, and surrounding mountains convinced President Porfirio Díaz to establish a vacation home here. Later discovered by Canadian and U.S. expats, its three principal towns are now home to thousands of foreign residents. Deforestation of the surrounding woods and resulting erosion have sullied the lake, and an explosion of water hyacinths and pollution from the Lerma River contribute to its problems. Rainfall in recent years has at least restored the lake to more or less its original dimensions.

The principal town is **Chapala,** where Mexican families stroll and shop for folk art on weekends. In the early 1920s D. H. Lawrence (1885–1930) penned his first novel, *The Plumed Serpent,* whilst staying in a house on Calle Zaragoza. Restaurants lining the lakeshore serve typical *charales* (fried fish) and tequila accompanied by *sangrita*, a chili, tomato, and orange juice chaser invented here.

Ajijic, about 5 miles (8 km) west of Chapala, is a growing town whose red-tiled adobe houses and narrow cobblestoned streets began attracting artists and writers in the mid-20th century. Galleries and stores sell fine art, handicrafts, and designer clothing. Week-long festivities lead up to the town's patron saint's day, St. Andrew, on November 30, with celebrations at the **Iglesia de San Andrés,** situated on the north side of the town plaza. Smaller villages surround the lake, including **San Juan Cosalá,** with a complex of thermal pools, a restaurant, and accommodations. ■

The Jose Cuervo distillery in the heart of Tequila has been producing the town's namesake product for more than 200 years.

Chapala
🗺 138 C4
Visitor information
✉ Av. Madero 407
☎ 376/765-3141

Tapatío traditions

Guadalajara's contradiction is that the traditions that make it unique are considered prototypically Mexican. In the nostalgic musicals of the 1940s, film stars Pedro Infante and Jorge Negrete personified the Mexican "everyman." When dressed as *charros* in fine felt hats and elegant dress they crooned songs of unrequited love, romance, and machismo. Tequila and charros, mariachis, and generous afternoon siestas are all traditions that both set Guadalajara (and the state of Jalisco) apart and generate a national persona.

A charro demonstrates his roping skills.

White tequila is unaged; *reposado* is aged for at least two months in wooden barrels; and *añejo* is aged at least a year in oak barrels.

If tequila is the unofficial national drink, *charrería* is the official national sport—so decreed by presidential edict in 1933. Charros perform feats of equestrian skill similar to those of a rodeo, but with more finesse and in fancy dress. Teams of six to eight compete in the pan-shaped ring, the *lienzo charro*, performing *suertes* (moves) that range from steer-throwing, bull-roping, and riding to changing horses at a dead run. *La escaramuza charra* is an elaborately choreographed and colorful women's event. Requiring fine mounts, expensive, brocaded outfits, and silver spurs, charrería is a sport for the wealthy.

Another seeming contradiction is that Guadalajara, long Mexico's second largest city, maintains a provincial atmosphere. The typical *tapatío* (Guadalajara native) is traditional, conservative, and Catholic, and like all Mexicans, intensely loyal to his region and family. Native tapatíos—including muralist and painter José Clemente Orozco and writers Juan Rulfo and Agustín Yáñez—are greatly esteemed and their works often quoted.

Guadalajarans are also immensely proud of the national drink, tequila. Made from blue agave, or maguey, a relative of the cactus, true tequila can be distilled only in Jalisco as well as designated areas of Nayarit, Guanajuato, Tamaulipas, and Michoacán.

The better tequilas contain 100 percent blue agave, although only 51 percent is required. The first agave-derived drink was pulque, a mild beer fermented and drunk throughout pre-Hispanic Mesoamerica. The Spaniards took the process further, distilling the fermented brew. When plants are 8 to 12 years old, the heart, or *piña*, weighing up to 120 pounds (55 kg), is extracted, shredded, and cooked for six to eight hours. The resulting *aguamiel* is fermented and twice distilled.

Mariachis add ambience to the *charreada*, as they do at weddings, parties, and sidewalk cafés. The name is thought to be a corruption of the French word *mariage*, meaning "wedding," as the five-piece bands often played at society weddings during the 19th century. Originally featuring two violins, a harp, and *jarana* and *vihuela* (types of guitar), these bands played romantic ballads popular after Mexican independence. Trumpets, now an integral and characteristic part of most mariachi bands, were added only in the 1930s.

All of these traditions can be experienced at the Encuentro Internacional del Mariachi y la Charrería, held each year at the end of August and beginning of September; and in October at the Fiestas de Octubre, a month of art, performances, and music of all kinds. ∎

Right: Mariachi music (above) and feats of horsemanship (below) can be seen at Guadalajara's Encuentro Internacional del Mariachi y la Charrería, held in late summer.

Colima & environs

FOR THOSE WEARY OF FLASHY BEACH RESORTS AND CITIES with countless colonial landmarks, Colima is a delightful retreat. The small state capital is among the safest cities of its size in Mexico, and the downtown area is alive with semitropical greenery. Colimenses take great pride in their city, and this is reflected in the cleanliness of its streets and the courtesy extended to visitors. There are interesting museums, art galleries, live music events, unusual festivals, and magic supply stores, while nearby towns provide a glimpse into the life of a gentler, even less frenetic era.

Founded by the Spanish in 1527, Colima has been repeatedly rocked by earthquakes, leaving few colonial buildings intact. However, the townspeople have taken advantage of their misfortune by transforming whole city blocks into impeccably manicured parks. No fewer than eight elegant green spaces grace the urban center, providing both a feeling of luxuriant openness and a plentiful supply of oxygen.

The city's elevation of 1,800 feet (550 m) above sea level makes it cooler and less humid than the coast, just 28 miles (45 km) away. Most days a welcome breeze blows down from the mountains backing the city, while between July and October, afternoon and early evening rain showers freshen the air. Rain or shine, Thursday and Friday evenings find families and friends at the central plazas enjoying eclectic live music ranging from mariachis and romantic ballads to modern rock.

In the heart of the city are three plazas. **Plaza Principal** *(Reforma between Madero & Hidalgo)* is dominated on the east side by the 18th-century **Catedral Santa Iglesia** *(Reforma 21, tel 312/312-0200)* and the adjacent **Palacio de Gobierno** *(tel 312/312-0431),* whose inner courtyard is decorated with murals depicting Mexican history. Directly behind the cathedral lies the **Jardín**

Quintero, with **Parque Núñez,** an enormous flower garden, four blocks east at the corner of Madero and Juárez. Within walking distance of these plazas are hotels, restaurants and cafés, shops, banks, and a handful of notable museums.

The **Museo Universitario de Culturas Populares** *(Barreda & Gallardo, tel 312/312-6829, closed Mon., $)* has exhibits of popular art, regional textiles, masks, and pre-Hispanic artifacts, including beguiling ceramic figures of short-legged, pot-bellied *tepezcuintle* dogs, once greatly esteemed (and eaten!) by local inhabitants. Its gift shop sells wonderful reproductions of pre-Hispanic pieces. Similar exhibits can be found at the smaller **Museo de Historia de Colima** *(Reforma at 16 de Septiembre, tel 312/312-9228, closed Mon.).* Next door, the **Sala de Exposiciones de la Universidad de Colima** *(tel 312/312-9228, closed Mon.)* presents temporary exhibits of modern art. Perhaps the best permanent collection of fine art can be found in the **Pinacoteca Universidad** *(V. Guerrero 35, tel 312/313-0608, ext. 15, closed Mon.).* The work of local painters is housed in three exquisite mansions linked by courtyards filled with green plants.

One block south of the *plaza*

Colima

🅰 138 C3

Visitor information

✉ Palacio de Gobierno Hidalgo at Reforma

☎ 312/312-4360

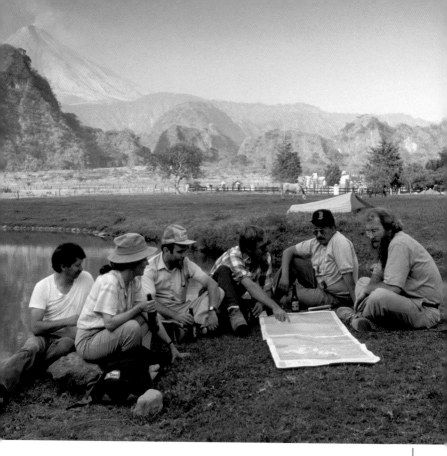

principal, the **Teatro Hidalgo** (*Hidalgo at Morelos*) stands on land given to the city by revolutionary hero Miguel Hidalgo (see p. 32), once a priest in the city. Built between 1871 and 1883, the neo-classic theater hosts concerts, plays, and the occasional opera.

Half a mile (1 km) northeast of the city center, the **Casa de la Cultura** (*Calzada Galván Norte at Ejército Nacional, tel 312/313-0608*) is a modern cultural complex housing a theater, a library, and a video library stocked with classic international and Mexican films. Its most important asset, however, is the **Museo de las Culturas del Occidente** (*tel 312/313-0608, ext. 15, closed Mon., $*). The Museum of Western Cultures has an excellent display of pre-Hispanic ceramic

pottery, including many figures of humans, plus dogs, fish, reptiles, and other animals. One block south, **Parque Piedra Lisa** (*Calzada Galván at Aldama*) is named for its famous smooth stone, a black volcanic rock—the size of a small truck—whose top protrudes from the ground. It is smooth on one side, with steps leading up to the top on the other. Those who slide on it are said to form a lifelong connection with the city and will feel compelled to return to die in Colima.

AROUND COLIMA

North of the capital are several towns well worth visiting. **Comala** is a picture-postcard pueblo of bright white buildings with red-tile roofs 6 miles (10 km) north of

Behind these vulcanologists looms Volcán de Colima, North America's most active volcano.

Here reproduced in red clay, *tepezcuintle* dogs were once greatly esteemed (and eaten) by locals.

Colima. Its number-one attraction is its plaza, with trees shading park benches, a bandstand, and a plain but pretty church. On weekends Colimenses gather in colonnaded restaurant-bars serving local delicacies. Favorite dishes include *sopes* (grilled rounds of *masa* smothered with spicy chicken or pork with onions). During the Fiesta de la Virgin de Guadalupe (December 1–12), vendors sell

locally grown and roasted coffee and hand-carved furniture.

Five minutes outside Comala, by way of the enchanting Camino a Nogueras roadway, is **Hacienda de Nogueras** *(tel 312/315-5380, closed Sun.)*, a former plantation housing a center for anthropological and cultural study. Within the complex is the **Museo Alejandro Rangel** *(tel 312/315-6028, closed Mon.)*, comprising a chapel, locally made furniture, and more of Colima's famous ceramic dogs. A small, attractive restaurant (open sporadically) offers regional specialties such as *pollo en pipian*, chicken in a pumpkin-seed and peanut sauce.

Six miles (10 km) north of Comala, indigenous traditions are maintained in **Suchitlán.** The town is famous for its carved ritual masks, used during Semana Santa (Holy Week) celebrations. Just outside town is a small slope in the road, the **zona mágica,** said to be bewitched. On this slope, stationary vehicles and even water seem to defy gravity and run uphill. The phenomenon remains unexplained.

Fourteen miles (22 km) north of Colima is lovely **Laguna la**

Festivals

There are three large festivals to be enjoyed each year around Colima. The rustic Feria de San Felipe de Jesús is celebrated in the first two weeks of February in Villa de Álvarez, a community 3 miles (5 km) north of the city center. It includes horse parades, bullfights, and regional foods. Taxi drivers dressed in drag parade through town, snatching unsuspecting men from the crowds.

More commercial (and sober) is the Feria de Todos Santos (late October and early November),

which takes place on the enormous fairgrounds just east of Colima. On offer at the event are rides, food, cultural attractions, and regional handicraft exhibits.

During the Fiesta de la Virgin de Guadalupe (December 1–12) downtown Colima is lined with food stalls, live music events are offered nightly, and there are parades and clown shows. Women, children, and babies dressed in regional costume file solemnly in and out of the cathedral, paying homage to the Virgin. ∎

María, a placid green lake surrounded by coffee groves. It offers rowing as well as a rustic hotel and restaurant. Many city-dwellers stop at the **Jacal de San Antonio** en route to the lake. Perched high on a cliff and with incredible views, this restaurant is open on weekends for lunch only.

Just 5 miles (8 km) beyond the lake, twin volcanoes are the main attraction at **Parque Nacional Volcán de Colima.** The park is named not for one but two impos-ing volcanoes just a few miles apart. **Volcán de Colima** (also called Volcán de Fuego, meaning "fire vol-cano") stands 12,989 feet (3,960 m) above sea level, and has erupted nine times in the last four centuries. Activity beginning in January 1999 produced shooting sparks, cascading lava, and other breath-taking pyrotechnical displays clearly visible from Colima. Such activity makes a visit to the volcano and its dormant partner, the **Volcán de Nevado** (meaning "snowy vol-cano"), impossible. If and when the activity subsides, check with the tourist office for maps and tours. ∎

Magic or realism?

C olima has a keen interest in mysticism and a number of shops peddling potions and powders for performing white and black magic. This preoccupa-tion with the spirit world reflects the locals' belief that near Colima exists a portal to another dimension, kept wide open by the active shaman community of Suchitlán (3miles/5 km northeast of Colima). Wizards there are said to transform themselves into animals upon a large stone etched with ancient carvings of female genitalia.

Modern buildings as well as old are reputedly haunted, including a hotel, a hospital, and a café. Ghostly apparitions are taken seriously; some victims report being groped or sexually assaulted by invisible assailants. Although a belief in witches is held throughout Mexico, the exchange of paranormal experi-ences is a pastime particularly enjoyed by Colimenses. ∎

Colima residents enjoy the low-key restaurant-bars of nearby Comala.

Morelia

ORIGINALLY CALLED VALLADOLID AFTER THE SPANISH city, Morelia is the capital of Michoacán state, whose boundaries are roughly those of the former Purépecha (Tarascan) kingdom. Skilled artisans as well as warriors, the Purépecha were never conquered by the Aztecs, nor by the equally bellicose Chichimecs to the north. Established by Spain in 1541, the city grew slowly in the 16th and 17th centuries, and much of its architecture is subdued 18th-century plateresque. Morelia's wide avenues and expansive plazas are American rather than European in character; these, along with its many restored convents and monasteries, give the city a dignified demeanor.

Morelia
138 D3
Visitor information
Nigromante 79, Palacio Clavijero
443/312-8081
www.turismomichoacan.gob.mx

Flanked by two squares, the superb three-nave sandstone **Catedral** (*Av. Madero at Juárez*), built between 1660 and 1744, blends neoclassic elements and a baroque facade whose carved columns and panels create a chiaroscuro effect. The magnificent 4,600-pipe German organ is celebrated each May during the Festival Internacional del Órgano. Locally crafted and characteristic of pre-Hispanic Purépecha art, the cathedral's 16th-century Christ in one of seven lateral chapels is made of a paste of pulverized corn stalks and orchids.

Cater-corner from the cathedral, the **Palacio de Gobierno** (*Av. Madero 63, tel 443/313-0707*) was originally a seminary where radicals José María Morelos (1765–1815) and Melchor Ocampo (1814–1861), both instruments of the independence movement (see p. 32), were schooled. Its stairwell and second floor are covered in 1970s-era murals of regional history by Michoacán artist Alfredo Zalce (1908–2003).

Zalce's work and that of other contemporary artists can be seen at the **Museo de Arte**

Contemporáneo (*Av. Acueducto 18, tel 443/312-5404, closed Mon.*), east of the city center. The restored Porfiriato-era house is within leafy **Bosque Cuauhtémoc.** En route to the park you'll pass the 250-arch **acueducto,** which once supplied fountains throughout the city center with drinkable water.

Bearing straight ahead instead of right past the aqueduct brings you to **Calzada Fray Antonio de San Miguel,** a two-block pedestrian mall connecting to the **Santuario de Nuestra Señora de Guadalupe.** The church's interior received a lavish redecoration in the early 20th century, with molded clay designs combining art nouveau and baroque elements.

Morelia has more than its share of religious buildings, and many today serve secular purposes. Once a Jesuit college, the **Palacio Clavijero** (*Nigromante 79, tel 443/312-8081*) now houses the tourism and other state offices and performance venues; the former church here is a beautiful public library. The **Conservatorio de las Rosas** (*Santiago Tapia 334, tel 443/312-1469, closed Sat., Sun.*), is home to an internationally known boy's choir. The adjoining **Templo de las Rosas** has been totally restored. Once a Carmelite convent, the huge **Casa de la Cultura** (*Av. Morelos Norte 485, tel 443/313-1215, closed Sun.*) hosts classes and cultural events, and houses the Museo de las Máscaras, with more than 100 traditional carved wooden masks.

Showing typical Franciscan restraint, the **Templo y Ex-Convento Franciscano** (*Fray Juan de San Miguel 129 at Humboldt, tel 443/312-2486*) has a simple plateresque facade. Within the old monastery is the government-run folk-art museum and store, the **Casa de las Artesanías.**

A modern reproduction of a pre-Hispanic mask

Born and educated in the city (then called Valladolid), hero of the Independence War (see p. 32) José María Morelos y Pavón has several museums in his honor, including the **Casa Museo de Morelos** (*Av. Morelos Sur 323, tel 443/313-2651, $*), showing personal and war memorabilia. A few blocks away, an eternal flame burns in the backyard of the hero's birthplace, the **Museo Casa Natal de Morelos** (*Corregidora 113, tel 443/312-2793, closed Mon.*); the main house contains a historical library and several Alfredo Zalce murals.

Also worth visiting is the **Mercado de Dulces,** a sweets market behind Palacio Clavijero. Here you will find *ate* (an aspic-like paste made with fruit puree and eaten with soft white cheese), crispy fried *buñuelos* sprinkled with sugar and cinnamon, sweet *empenadas,* and other local treats. The **Museo Regional Michoacano** (*Allende 305, tel 443/312-0407, closed Mon., $*), in an 18th-century palace that once belonged to Emperor Agustín de Iturbide's father-in-law, has paintings and regional artifacts. ■

Pátzcuaro & environs

DROWSING IN THE MOUNTAIN SUNSHINE AT 7,131 FEET (2,170 m) above sea level, Pátzcuaro has long been a center for indigenous culture and folk crafts. After the death of Bishop Vasco de Quiroga (see p. 139) in the mid-16th century, the region's capital was moved from Pátzcuaro to Morelia. Possibly it was the exodus of European power and authority that encouraged native traditions and folk art to flourish. Whether for its native crafts, mountain air, or the almost total lack of modern construction, this lakeside town is probably the most often visited of any in Michoacán state.

Pátzcuaro was the first capital of the Late Postclassic Purépecha kingdom (1200–1521), located in the hilly central part of today's Michoacán. On the southern shores of **Lago de Pátzcuaro,** its inhabitants fished, hunted, and gathered food, and, unlike most Mesoamericans, forged metal tools. Admired as fine craftsmen, they produced brilliant copper utensils, feather work, and *maqueado,* decorated gourds from which the Aztec nobles drank their bitter chocolate. They were excellent warriors as well, resisting absorption into the ever expanding Aztec empire.

The Purépecha were undoubtedly amazed at the total annihilation of their enemy at Tenochtitlán by the Spanish, with their Indian allies and superior weapons. King Tzimtzincha-Tangaxuan II readily accepted the terms of peace set forth by Conquistador Hernán Cortés, swearing fealty to the Spanish Crown, and accepting Christian baptism.

However, the king's fealty made little impression on the brutish conquistador Nuño Beltrán de Guzmán, who as a representative of the colonial governing body, *la real audiencia,* promptly tortured and hanged the Indian sovereign. The persecution, slavery, and torture that de Guzmán inflicted on the local Indians was so excessive—even by 16th-century standards—

that he was finally sent to a Spanish prison for the rest of his life.

After institution of a second, more benevolent audiencia, the task of regaining the natives' trust was given to don Vasco de Quiroga. The Spanish judge was ordained a priest and named bishop on the same day, in 1536. By the time of his death 30 years later, "Tata Vasco" ("Grandpa Vasco") had built as many hospitals and schools as churches, and given numerous towns a craft or vocation to ensure their prosperity.

The tradition of fine craftsmanship continues to this day, and Michoacán has some of Mexico's finest decorative and utilitarian art. Traditional gourd decoration incorporated techniques introduced from Asia. Other arts include weaving, embroidery, metalsmithing, and ceramics, especially tableware.

You can purchase and watch regional crafts being made at the **Casa de los Once Patios** *(Madrigal de las Altas Torres near Lerín),* within a former convent. Another place to view regional crafts is the **Museo de Artes Populares** *(Enseñanza at Alcantarilla, tel 434/342-1029, closed Mon., $),* a pleasing colonial structure that once housed the Colegio de San Nicolás. At the rear is a typical Purépecha wooden dwelling.

Named for its benevolent Spanish benefactor is large **Plaza**

Pátzcuaro
🄰 138 D3
Visitor information
✉ Buenavista 7
☎ 434/342-1214

Vasco de Quiroga *(Portales Hidalgo, Morelos, Matamoros, & Guerrero).* (Street names change at the square.) Different from most Mexican main squares, it is surrounded by houses (now hotels, restaurants, and shops) instead of municipal buildings and churches. One block away is the more intimate Plaza Gertrudis Bocanegra *(Mendoza, Libertad, Iturbe, & La Paz),* named for a heroine of the War of Independence. Facing the plaza on the north side, the **Biblioteca Gertrudis Bocanegra** *(Closed Sun.)* is an unassuming library with an intricate mural of regional history by architect, painter, and muralist Juan O'Gorman (1905–1982).

Pátzcuaro's attraction lies more in popular culture than in ornate churches. The devout regularly visit the **Basílica de Nuestra Señora de la Salud** *(Árciga at Serrato).* Housing the much-petitioned corn-paste Virgin of Health, it is away from the main square, as it was built atop a pre-Hispanic ceremonial site.

Día de los Muertos (Day of the Dead) is a living communion with deceased relatives that is celebrated throughout the region. Because of massive international interest in the festivals of neighboring Janitzio (see "The Lake Region," pp. 164–65), the Pátzcuaro tourism delegation has created a program of cultural events taking place in the week or so surrounding the celebration, October 31 to November 2.

THE LAKE REGION
Many visitors are happy to stroll around Pátzcuaro and make a

Fishing with traditional butterfly nets is now done mainly for tourists.

Once a year, on the Day of the Dead, family graves are cleaned and decorated with candles and flowers.

José María Morelos (see p. 161), with a lookout point in one raised arm ($). Steps from the ferry landing are lined with diminutive souvenir shops and two-table restaurants. Of the lake's five islands, only tiny, less touristy **Yunuén** has accommodations. Rent a room for 2, 4, 8, or 16 people (tel 434/342-4473, $ for a double). Boats leave for all the islands from Pátzcuaro's wharf (10 minutes north of town center, tel 434/342-0681). Boats ($$) depart every 15 minutes or so for Janitzio, on demand for Yunuén and the smaller islands, in which case fewer than four passengers must split the cost of the trip among themselves.

A 55-mile (88 km) road circumvents the lake. On the eastern shore are Ihautzio and **Tzintzuntzan,** two Purépecha towns that shared power with Pátzcuaro before the Spanish Conquest. Tiny Ihuatzio is little visited except for its partially excavated Purépecha ruins. Tzintzuntzan's name means "place of the hummingbirds" in Purépecha, a language related to no other in Mexico. Tzintzuntzan makes for a nice day or half-day excursion from Patzcuaro. Walk along cobbled streets and dirt paths to the lakeshore. The crafts market sells woven straw objects, pottery, and woodcarvings. Across the street, the **pre-Hispanic ceremonial site** (Carr. 15 at entrance to Tzintzuntzan, $) consists of a large rectangular platform supporting five yácatas, stepped pyramids joined to circular structures originally faced with sheets of volcanic stone. The excavated buildings have yielded burial sites, presumably of Purépecha kings. Behind the crafts market is a large religious complex built by the Franciscans. Passing olive trees in the open atrium, you'll come to **Templo de San Francisco,** whose wall decorations and painted wooden ceiling, typical of the area, have

requisite pilgrimage to the pretty but tourist-driven island of Janitzio. But inquisitive souls should consider a trip into the rolling countryside, where many villages and small towns are known for their folk art.

Purépecha religion was based on a family of gods headed by Kurikaweri, lord of the sun and of war, and the earth goddess, Kwerawáperi. In order to convert this pantheistic people, Catholic priests introduced instructive religious plays such as the *pastorela,* a Nativity and Adoration of the Virgin. Today the lake district is known for its many colorful religious celebrations, involving masked and costumed dancers, locally made instruments, and traditional songs. Zirahuén in particular celebrates saints' days and holidays with traditional forms of music and dance.

One of the best-known and most visited islands is **Janitzio,** Lake Pátzcuaro's largest, where evocative Day of the Dead celebrations have been much publicized and massively visited by outsiders. Atop the cone-shaped island is an imposing, block-like statue of Independence War hero been restored. Tzintzuntzan comes alive for Easter week, Day of the Dead, and Christmas pastorelas beginning December 16.

Named for the 16th-century bishop who dedicated his later life to the native population, **Quiroga** was an important crossroad in pre-Cortesian times. Today it's a not-very-picturesque commercial town. A candlelight procession on the first Sunday in July marks the Fiesta de la Preciosa Sangre de Cristo (Festival of Christ's Precious Blood).

Just a mile (1.5 km) beyond Quiroga, **Santa Fe de la Laguna** lives by farming, fishing, and ceramics, specializing in candelabra. The freestanding cross in the atrium of the **Templo de San Nicolás** is typical to Michoacán state. The town celebrates its fiesta on September 14 with fireworks and local dances.

On the far west side of the lake, **Erongarícuaro** lies surrounded by mixed forests, and like other area towns, has chilly winters and warm, rainy summers. A U.S.-owned store makes painted wooden furniture in a huge variety of styles and motifs, including commissioned work.

About 10 miles (16 km) south of Pátzcuaro is **Santa Clara del Cobre,** where artisans produce hand-hammered copper tableware and other decorative . Santa Clara is to copper what Taxco is to silver: a town full of brilliant, hand-crafted metalwork. Well worth a visit is the **Museo Nacional del Cobre** (Morelos 263 at Pino Suárez, tel 434/343-0254, closed Mon., $).

Southwest of Pátzcuaro off Highway 120, **Zirahuén** is a small town on a lake of the same name. Smaller and deeper than Lake Pátzcuaro, Lago Zirahuén is surrounded by pine and oak forests. Known for its music and dance, the town celebrates especially Easter week and the Day of the Holy Cross (May 3). ■

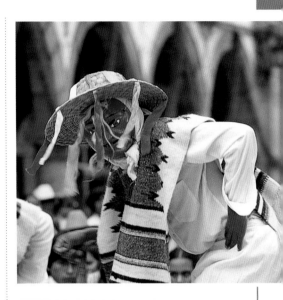

The Dance of the Little Old Men

Regional dances & masks

Indigenous cultures throughout Mexico, but especially in Tlaxcala, Guerrero, and Michoacán, celebrate feast days and festivals with regional dance. Donning masks and sometimes elaborate costumes, the townspeople replay traditional roles that survived the Conquest and, in some cases, were modified by it. Universal themes are the conquest of good over evil and the vanquishing of invaders. Wooden masks representing Spaniards, or "Moors," are painted white, bright pink, or more realistic flesh tones; they are sometimes "two-faced." Tlaxcala masks have glass eyes that open and close when a string is pulled. Animal masks may incorporate horns, whiskers, teeth, claws, and pelts to make them more realistic. Some of the country's most impressive masks are made in the village of Tocuaro, about 6 miles (10 km) west of Pátzcuaro. ■

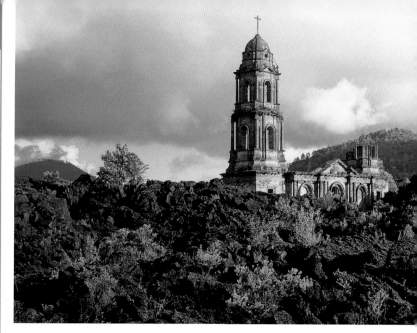

Uruapan
▲ 138 D3
Visitor information
✉ Juan Ayala 16
☎ 452/524-7199

In & around Uruapan

REGARDED BY SOME AS NEIGHBORING PÁTZCUARO'S less popular sister, Uruapan is in fact an interesting colonial city in its own right. Its elevation at 2,000 feet (610 m) below Pátzcuaro gives it a subtropical climate that supports lush vegetation and year-round flowers. In the native Purépecha tongue, Uruapan means "where the flowers bloom." An enchanting national park within the city center, one of the country's largest craft fairs, and a nearby lava-covered ghost town are just three reasons to visit this untouristed market town.

The Purépecha made this region their home centuries before Father Juan de San Miguel arrived from Spain and founded the city in 1533. He built a chapel, market, and school, and founded a hospital, but also instated a feudal system that reduced the Indians to serfs. Under this Spanish *encomienda* system, Uruapan prospered as an important agricultural center. Today the city is renowned as the avocado capital of the world. This fruit can be enjoyed during the week-long Feria del Aguacate (Avocado Fair), held in early November.

The city is laid out in a grid, at the center of which is the **plaza principal.** On the north side of the plaza stands the mudejar and plateresque **La Huatápera** *(Jardín Morelos s/n),* the original hospital erected by Father Juan in the 16th century. Today it houses the **Museo de los 4 Pueblos Indigenas** *(tel 452/524-3434, closed Mon.),* displaying an impressive array of crafts from around the state of Michoacán, including a collection of the beautiful cedar lacquerware for which Uruapan is famous.

Behind La Huatápera, the city's **market** sprawls along Calle Constitución, where the locals sell produce, cheeses, and a variety of crafts, including lacquered trays, gourds, and boxes, and wooden furniture. During Semana Santa (Holy Week), the main square is converted into a huge crafts market. During the event, beautifully carved guitars and violins from nearby Paracho are on sale at super prices.

On either side of La Huatápera, the exteriors of the **Templo de la Inmaculada** and the **Templo de San Francisco** are fine examples of plateresque architecture in local *cantera* (quarrystone). In the neighborhood, two venues connect artisans and culture vultures. **Casa de la Cultura** *(Garcia Ortíz 1, tel 452/524-7613)* hosts workshops, concerts, and expositions. A block from the main square, **Casa Regional del Turista** *(E. Carranza s/n, tel. 452/524-0667)* brings artisans from throughout Michoacán to show off and sell their folk art.

About six long blocks west of the main plaza (a 15-minute walk), at the end of Calle Independencia, lies **Parque Nacional Eduardo Ruíz** *(Calzada Fray Juan de San Miguel s/n, tel 452/524-0197, $).* A model of landscape architecture, this magical park begins at the headwaters of the Río Cupatizio and follows the river for just over half a mile (1 km). Within this limited space are shady stone paths, terraced banks, bridges, waterfalls, and an explosion of flowers. A rainbow is said to form in the mist of the river every day.

More dramatic is a visit to the buried village of **San Juan Parangaricutiro,** where in 1943 the 8,400-foot (2,560 m) **Volcán Paricutín** began its geologically rapid ascent in the middle of a farmer's field. The volcano spewed lava for eight years, and within its relatively short life it forced 4,000 people to evacuate as the lava slowly buried their homes. Today, only the upper facade of the church is visible. To get there, take a bus to **Angahuan** (northwest of Uruapan), where you can rent a horse to San Juan Parangaricutiro or to Volcán Paricutín itself *($$$$$).* Angahuan has a restaurant and rustic accommodations where you can stay if you tarry too long at San Juan Parangaricutiro, 6 miles (10 km) round trip. Sturdy shoes are recommended. ∎

Only the church's upper facade protrudes above the lava that engulfed Parangaricutiro in 1943.

Ixtapa & Zihuatanejo

THEY ARE ALWAYS MENTIONED IN ALPHABETICAL ORDER, but whereas Zihuatanejo (originally Zihautlán, "Place of Women") was a pre-Hispanic settlement and an important port in the early days of the Spanish colony, modern Ixtapa was, about 30 years ago, just a coconut plantation—one of a handful of resorts developed by the Mexican government in the early 1970s. Today the two places are marketed together, pronounced in a single breath that encompasses 15 miles (24 km) of some of the Pacific coast's most scenic beaches.

After a decree in 1561 pronounced Acapulco to be New Spain's only official Pacific port, **Zihuatanejo** diminished in importance. Following centuries of obscurity, the village was connected to the outside world once again by the construction of Highway 200 in the 1960s, and visitors began to trickle in.

Today Zihua's dirt roads have been paved, and folk-art shops and international restaurants lure vacationers from the tree-shaded but sultry streets. Still a working fishing town, it has several elegant boutique hotels right on the sand. Other hotels are tucked up in the foothills, behind the beaches, or in the friendly downtown area. A pedestrian promenade (partially lit at night) connects downtown, which fronts the main beach, **Playa Principal,** to **Playa La Madera,** a pretty and accessible beach popular with picnicking families and groups of young boys.

Taxis are the easiest way to reach **Playa La Ropa** (Clothing Beach), Zihua's lovliest beach, with good restaurants, gentle surf, water sports equipment for rent, and parasailing so you can observe it all from above.

Water taxis from the main dock in Zihuatanejo access **Playa Las Gatas,** protected from the ocean's surge by Punta El Faro headland. Named for once-prevalent nurse sharks (not cats), Las Gatas is a lovely beach that is perfect for snorkeling and swimming. Cafés serve soft drinks and *ceviche,* beer and

snacks, and watersports concessions rent wave runners and other toys.

Located on a shallow, open bay and without the fishing fleet, the beaches at **Ixtapa** are even cleaner than those of Zihuatanejo, but are narrow, slanted at an angle, and largely unprotected from the surf. The hotel zone parallels **Playa del Palmar** for several miles of sandy beaches with access to hotel restaurants and bars and watersports rentals. Across the street are boutiques, pharmacies, and more restaurants. An inexpensive taxi ride between the two towns takes just about 10 minutes.

More isolated beaches can be found at Ixtapa's west end, past the surf spot at **Escolleras** and the Marina Ixtapa, a 620-slip marina and yacht club on a double-pronged cove. Here also is the **Club de Golf Marina Ixtapa** (*tel 755/553-1424.* West of the marina are several more lovely beaches. Beyond Punta Ixtapa, **Playa Quieta** is a tranquil beach with a Club Med hotel. Horses can be rented (*$$$$$*) for early morning or late-afternoon jaunts on the beach at **Playa Linda** (Beautiful Beach).

From Playa Linda pier, water taxis (*$ round-trip*) access popular **Isla Ixtapa,** where you can dive or snorkel, or lounge on the beach or dine at the adjacent restaurants. On the far side of the small island, **Playa Carey** has no facilities and thus offers more solitude.

Ixtapa
🗺 138 D2
Visitor information
✉ Paseo de las Gaviotas 12
☎ 755/553-1570
www.ixtapa-zihuatanejo.org

For those who want to do more than hang out at the beach, fishing co-ops near the pier in Zihuatanejo offer deep-sea fishing for dorado, marlin, yellowfin tuna, roosterfish, sailfish, and mackerel. Yearly tournaments in January and May are gaining popularity.

Snorkel and dive trips can be arranged through several operators, including **Zihuatanejo Scuba Center** (Hotel Paraíso Real, tel 755/554-8156. In addition to the Club de Golf Marina Ixtapa (see p. 168), golfers can play at the 18-hole **Club de Golf Ixtapa Palma Real** (Blvd. Ixtapa s/n, tel 755/553-1163. Regional history and anthropology can be explored at the minuscule **Museo Arqueológico de la Costa Grande** (Plaza Olaf Palme, tel 7/554-7552, closed Sun., $).

About 14 miles (22.5 km) south of Zihuatanejo lies **Barra de Potosí**, a luscious beach backed by rugged mountains. Thatch-roofed restaurants on the beach provide hammocks where you can while away the day. During the dry season, boats tour the adjacent lagoon, where water fowl may be spotted. Half-day tours ($$$$$) are available through Ixtapa or Zihuatanejo tour operators, or you can get there by taxi or city bus. The scenery along the way is lush and beautiful.

About the same distance north of Zihuatanejo is **Troncones,** another area of beautiful beaches where inexpensive and moderately priced hotels and house rentals are cropping up, many owned by Canadian and U.S. citizens. ■

Vacationers relax under individual palm-thatch umbrellas at Isla Ixtapa.

Zihuatanejo
🅜 138 D2
Visitor information
✉ Paseo de Zihuatanejo 21
☎ 755/554-2001

Acapulco

Acapulco
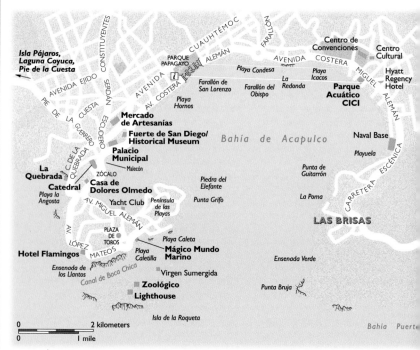 139 E1

**Visitor
information**

✉ Av. Costera Miguel
Alemán 4455 (at
Convention Center)

☎ 744/484-4416

DELICIOUSLY SELF-SATISFIED, THE AGED PORT CITY OF
Acapulco remains a major resort destination for foreign honeymooners and Mexicans cutting loose on annual vacations. Trendy restaurants serve international and haute Mexican cuisine, while friendly
seaside bistros pile on fresh shrimp and Acapulco-style *ceviche*. Still
among the hippest in Mexico, the city's many discos play live and
canned music until the roosters crow in the surrounding hills.

Acapulco's balmy weather ranges
from hot to hotter. Summer rains
(June to October) tend to exacerbate
the heat instead of diminishing it. As
the humidity rises, hotel prices fall,
but the trade-off is high.
Throughout the year, myriad species
of flowering trees produce brilliant
blossoms. Tropical fruits—including
mango, papaya, and watermelon—
appear as fresh drinks or as salads
served with a squeeze of lime and a
sprinkle of powdered chili. On

Thursdays, tradition calls for a late,
leisurely lunch of *pozole*—hominy
soup served with raw onions,
avocado, and oregano.

Although Jet Skis, water skis,
diving and snorkel equipment, and
other water toys are offered by the
hotels crowding Avenida Costera,
this tends to be the most polluted
part of the 4-mile (7 km) bay.
Beaches on or near the points, such
as **Playa Caleta** and **Playa
Puerto Marqués,** are the

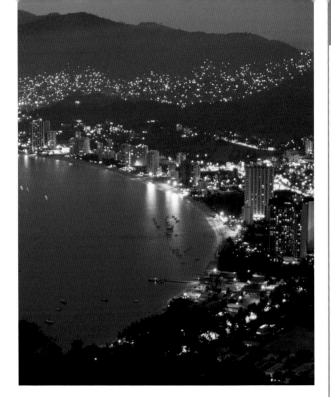

A dazzling view of Acapulco Bay from one of the city's exclusive hilltop neighborhoods

cleanest. If you're hesitant about swimming in murky waters, consider parasailing over the picturesque bay, sportfishing for sailfish or dorado, playing tennis, or golfing at one of the city's six courses.

Acapulco became absolutely hip and happening in the 1960s, when sybaritic Hollywood stars partied in private homes and exclusive restaurants above downtown, before the "scene" marched unequivocally east. Today, nostalgic Acapulqueños stop by for a cocktail at the once-glamorous **Hotel Flamingos** bar, overlooking the surf (and Acapulco's famous sunsets) around **Playitas.** The coast road winds through neighborhoods of older homes, shops, and restaurants to **La Quebrada,** where cliff divers hurtle themselves more than 15 stories into a rocky cove below. Dives (*$*) are usually performed at 1, 7:30, 8:30, 9:30, and 10:30 p.m.

The road continues to twin coves of coarse sand at **Playa Caleta** and **Playa Caletilla,** lined with informal restaurants and water equipment concessions. Separating the two beaches is **Mágico Mundo Marino** *(tel 744/483-9344, $),* a theme park with a sea lion show, water slides, kayak rental, and a restaurant. From Playa Caleta, a ten-minute boat ride *(daily, $$)* or a longer glass-bottom boat tour takes you to hilly **Isla de la Roqueta,** where snorkelers swim about the rocks. During the coolest hours of the day, climb the hill to the **lighthouse** for a view of the sweeping, palm-fringed bay.

From Playa Caleta, Avenida Costera Miguel Alemán (usually simply called "la Costera") curves past the Yacht Club to **downtown Acapulco.** Once the center of tourist attention, it is now left mostly to the locals, who hang out at the laid-back **zócalo.** The cathedral of **Nuestra Señora de** la Soledad, built in the 1930s, combines art deco and Moorish elements with no great success.

At the oceanfront **malecón,** or seawalk, cruise ships disgorge their passengers to haggle at the 350-stall **Mercado de Artesanías** (Velázquez de León near 5 de Mayo), a flea market selling T-shirts, silver jewelry, sandals, and coconut masks. "Booze cruises" ($$$$$) offer afternoon and evening cruises with food, shows, meals, or swimming in addition to drinks.

Constructed in 1615 to protect the Manila galleons from pirates, Acapulco's **Fuerte de San Diego** was destroyed by earthquake in 1776. The fort was rebuilt of stone with a surrounding moat. The **historical museum** (tel 744/482-3828, closed Mon., $) holds permanent exhibits as well as temporary cultural exposi-tions. Don't miss the **Museo de las Máscaras,** with more than 400 of Guerrero state's famous masks as well as less traditional but equally colorful woodcarvings.

Just a few miles northeast of downtown Acapulco is **Sitio Arqueológica Palma Sola** (tel 744/486-1514, daily 8–4, free). English- and Spanish-language signs along the half-mile (800 m) uphill path explain the meaning of the some 18 petroglyphs created by the Yope people who once inhabited the area. (A cab from Parque Papagayo, on Acapulco's main highway, should-n't cost more than $4 one way.)

Locals and visitors fill the thatch-roofed eateries lining **Playa Hornos,** or spread their picnics along the shore. Across the street, flamboyant trees and coconut palms shade children's amusement rides, snack shacks, and dusty soccer fields in the large but neglected **Parque Papagayo.** Animal shows, wave-action pools, waterslides, and swim-ming with dolphins lure visitors across the street to **Parque**

Acuático CICI (Av. Costera Miguel Alemán at Cristóbal Colón, tel 744/484-8210, $$$).

Between placid **Playa Icacos** and the Hyatt Regency hotel (which marks the end of Avenida Costera) lies a less-than-scenic proliferation of hotels, restaurants, drugstores, souvenir shops, discos, and car rentals. Jet-ski, banana-boat, and parasailing concessions line the beach, and drinks and snacks are served under palm-leaf sun shades.

The coast highway's name changes to **Carretera Escénica** as it winds east toward Acapulco's newer developments. Perched high above the ocean on either side of the highway, the exclusive private palaces and hotels of **Las Brisas** are blessed with the ocean breezes for which the suburb was named. From here there are splendid views of the bay, which positively sparkles at night. Many of the resorts on the cliff side of the highway have elevators or steep stairways to semi-private beaches.

Farther east, a number of high-rise hotels lining calm, sandy **Bahía Puerto Marqués** rent water toys, while horses wait for riders at long, wave-beaten **Playa Revolcadero.** Near the airport, you can sip a tropical drink from a seaside cabana at **Barra Vieja,** or take a boat ride around the lagoons of adjoining **Laguna Tres Palos,** a small fishing village.

Twenty-two miles (35 km) northwest of downtown, fresh-water **Laguna Coyuca** is lined with mangroves. Eat at one of the beach shacks, arrange a lagoon tour with a visit to **Isla Pájaros,** or water-ski. The long beach at nearby **Pie de la Cuesta** is a favorite for horseback riding and hammock lounging in simple thatch-roofed restaurants. Both Laguna Coyuca and Pie de la Cuesta are wonderful spots to watch the sun set. ∎

Opposite: Daring cliff divers have impressed onlookers for decades—and have suffered surprisingly few mishaps.

Taxco

DELIGHTFUL SUN-SPLASHED TAXCO WINDS UP AND DOWN narrow, cobblestone streets. U.S. expatriate William Spratling, who started Taxco's first silversmithing workshop, called it the "Florence of Mexico," but physically it's closer to a Mediterranean village. By city ordinance, its white-painted facades crowned with red-tile roofs rise no more than three stories above street level.

Taxco
🅐 139 E2
Visitor information
✉ Avenida de los Plateros 1
☎ 762/622-6616

Most of Taxco's sights are found on or near pretty **Plaza Borda,** where patent-leather grackles voice their urgent calls from the trees. Streets radiate like spokes, surrounded by handsome two- and three-story buildings housing restaurants, silver shops, and homes. Facing the plaza are the **Museo de la Platería** (*Plaza Borda 1, tel 762/622-0658, $*), a small, privately owned silver museum, and the **Centro Cultural Casa Borda** (*Plaza Borda 1, tel 762/622-6634, closed Mon.*), offering art classes, cultural performances, and changing exhibits.

The original Taxco was inhabited by Thalhuica Indians, who paid tribute to their Aztec overlords in gold and silver. After the Conquest, the Spaniards established mines at the site of present-day Taxco (El Nuevo, or New Taxco), relocating workers and engineers from the old city, now known as "Taxco el Viejo." Although silver was mined for centuries and artisans in nearby Iguala were known for their goldsmithing, it was William Spratling (1900–1967) who established the first silver workshop, Las Delicias, in 1931. Today, about 80 percent of the population is involved in silversmithing, and the Ministry of Tourism estimates there are some thousand silver shops, with another thousand vendors selling at the **Saturday market** (*Av. de los Plateros s/n, near the Flecha Roja bus terminal*).

The unequivocal star of this silver city, however, is gold-drenched cross. Sometimes referred to as "the Michelangelo of Mexico," Miguel Cabrera (1695–1768) executed most of the church's paintings.

As you face Santa Prisca, the city's wonderful market—a twisting warren of stalls—is a block to your right. On Thursdays, vendors here and throughout the city sell *pozole*, hominy soup served with a plate of condiments. Other regional foods include *cecina taxqueña* (thin pieces of marinated beef) and barbecued goat. Author John Dos Passos and William Spratling claimed to have invented the lime and tequila concoction "la Berta" at Berta's bar. Still going strong, the cantina claims a secret ingredient—but it's basically tequila, soda, and lime.

A portion of Spratling's collection of pre-Hispanic art is shown at the **Museo Spratling** *(Porfirio Delgado 1, tel 762/622-1660, closed Mon., $)*. Although poorly labeled and displayed, it is worth a look. Of more interest is the nearby **Museo de Arte Virreinal** *(Juan Ruíz de Alarcón 12, tel 762/622-5501, closed Mon., $)*, which houses religious art and liturgical objects. The museum's prized possession is a *túmulo funerario*, a boxlike altar painted with significant scenes from the deceased's life. The beautifully restored 17th-century building has exposed ceiling beams, whitewashed walls, baked earth tiles, and great cityscapes. For an even greater view, climb the steep street behind town to the hilltop **Templo de Guadalupe,** or take the aerial tram from Los Arcos, near the visitor center on Avenida de los Plateros, to **Club de Campo Monte Taxco** *(762/622-1300)*. For a fee, you can play tennis or nine holes of golf here, or swim in the pool. Alternatively, sip a drink at the bar, and enjoy the view—on a clear day you can see Popocatépetl and Iztaccíhuatl. ■

Iglesia de Santa Prisca *(Plaza Borda 1, tel 762/20183)*. The pink quarrystone church is dedicated to obscure, 12th-century Roman martyr Santa Prisca. (After lions in the Roman circus refused to eat her, she was beheaded.) The ornate church was paid for by mining entrepreneur don José de la Borda, who amassed (and gave away) a fortune.

The temple is said to hold 23 tons of gold leaf and, except for the lighting, almost everything is original. The manual, 256-pipe organ—which took six months to bring piece by piece by mule from Veracruz—is still played occasionally during special services. The narrow church's 12 gold and polychrome altarpieces, most of which could use a good cleaning, create a dizzying feeling of excess. Dozens of saints lean out in high relief from the exuberant main altarpiece, dedicated to the Virgin of the Immaculate Conception. The left side chapel was built for the town's indigenous population. Note the unusual crucifix, with the Christ figure's arms above the head, nails in the wrists instead of the hands, and the feet nailed separately to the

More places to visit in the Central Pacific states

LAGOS DE MORENO

Lagos de Moreno is a prosperous place, little visited by foreign tourists. Stately churches of rose-colored limestone and a handful of colonial-era private homes surround its plazas. Located 50 miles (82 km) southeast of Aguascalientes, this small city in the central highlands of Jalisco appears to belong in a more distant era. Visit the baroque **Parroquia de la Asunción,** the parish church *(Hidalgo at the main plaza),* and the sober but elegant **Rinconada de las Capuchinas** *(Miguel Leandro Guerra at Mariano Azuela),* a former convent with a museum and cultural center.

🗺 138 D4 **Visitor information** ✉ Juárez 426 at Francisco González León ☎ 474/741-2124

LOS AZUFRES

About 1.5 hours east of Morelia, near the city of Ciudad Hidalgo, off Highway 15, lies an area of natural hot springs called Los Azufres. Spas offer different levels of service, but most have restaurants, changing rooms, and one or more pools; some have campgrounds and offer massage or other services. For a more natural retreat with few services, head for **Churritaco.** The spring's sulfurous 104°F (40°C) waters are said to benefit the skin.

🗺 138 D3

PARQUE NACIONAL GRUTAS DE CACAHUAMILPA

About 19 miles (30 km) from Taxco is Mexico's largest system of underground caves. Guided tours *(tel 762/622-2274, $$)* leave hourly 10–5, following a 1.2-mile (2 km) lighted path past stalacatites, stalagmites, and rock formations. The entire system comprises about 10 miles (16 km) of tunnels and 20 caves. Minibuses leave from the Taxco bus depot; if you are traveling by car, take the marked turnoff from Highway 55.

🗺 139 E2

SOUTHERN NAYARIT BEACHES

Nayarit State is investing in tourism infrastructure along some 99 miles (160 km) of beaches between San Blas and Nuevo Vallarta. Not far south of San Blas is surfable **Bahía Matanchén,** where there are several pretty beaches near the small town of **Santa Cruz.** Another hour south

is **Playa Chacala** (about a mile from the crossroads of Las Varas). It's rarely crowded (for now), offering just a short string of seafood vendors on the soft white sand. Continuing south, **Rincón de Guayabitos'** long beach is packed on weekends and holidays, its streets loaded with small hotels, grocery stores, and bathing suit shops. **Lo de Marcos** and surrounding beaches **Minitas** and **Los Venados** are nice for fishing. Not 10 miles south, San Francisco is a growing fishing community more often called by its nickname, **San Pancho.** Just beyond on a lovely cove, **Sayulita** is another beach town that's booming. **Punta de Mita,** at the northern tip of Bahía de Banderas, is home to a few high-priced resorts. **El Anclote** is still a fabulous kick-back beach with inexpensive seafood restaurants and surfboard rentals. You can hire boats for fishing, snorkeling, diving, and whale-watching at **Islas Marietas,** offshore. **Cruz de Huanacaxtle** still has a mainly locals feeling, although Canadians and others descend in winter. Burgeoning **Bucerías** is the largest of the lot, with good restaurants and plenty of home rentals and small hotels as well as a beach that heads south nonstop to Nuevo Vallarta.

🗺 138 A4

SANTUARIO DE LA MARIPOSA MONARCA EL ROSARIO

The transvolcanic mountain range in eastern Michoacán is the winter home for the monarch butterfly. The butterflies migrate up to 3,100 miles (5,000 km) from Canada and the Great Lakes. After resting throughout the winter, they mate. The males die; the females prepare for the return journey beginning in early or mid-April.

 El Santuario de la Mariposa el Rosario is the better of two wintering sites open to the public. In a good year the monarchs blanket *oyamel* trees (a type of spruce). Visit late November through March. Park entrance is relatively inexpensive *($$),* but the excursion is more interesting with a knowledgeable guide. Recommended are the state-licensed, English-speaking guides of **Movisa** *(tel 443/312-8723, Morelia)* or **Viajes Maruata** *(tel 443/324-2120),* who lead long day tours from the capital. Call for infomation.

🗺 139 E3 ∎

Despite its urban woes, the nation's capital has a wealth of cultural attractions and a cosmopolitan character. And its history—evident in its art, artifacts, and architecture— is one of the most fascinating in Latin America.

Mexico City

Mexico City architecture reflects old and new.

Mexico City

MEXICO CITY TODAY IS A LOT LIKE THE LITTLE GIRL FROM THE NURSERY rhyme: When she's good, she's very, very good, but when she's bad, she's horrid. To the good, theater, dance, and musical performances—everything from marimba to Mozart—are held in dozens of theaters throughout the city, including three excellent venues on the campus of the National Autonomous University (UNAM). *Mariachi* musicians in matching, silver-studded ensembles croon romantic tunes in historic Plaza de Garibaldi. Upscale boutiques, cutting-edge art galleries, and sidewalk cafés line the main streets in Polanco, la Zona Rosa, la Condesa, Roma, and other diverse neighborhoods.

Flag Day (February 28) is celebrated in the *zócalo*, or central plaza.

Plaza de las **Tres Culturas, Tlatelolco**

La Villa de Guadalupe

MOQUETA

AGENTES NORTE

GUERRERO

Guerrero

VIOLETA

VIOLETA

Revolución

RAYÓN

CENTRO

DE REFORMA

PASEO

REP. DE BRASIL

Palacio de la Inquisición

PLAZA DE GARIBALDI

REP. DE PERÚ

IENTE DE ALVARADO

Museo de San Carlos

Hidalgo

Laboratorio Arte Alameda

Museo Nacional de la Estampa

Museo Franz Mayer

HIDALGO

Bellas Artes

2

LÁZARO CÁRDENAS

Museo Nacional de Arte

Iglesia de Santo Domingo

Capilla de la Expiación

PLAZA SANTO DOMINGO

Antigua Cámera

Ex-Colegio de Cristo

Secretaría de Educación Pública

Templo de la Enseñanza

Ex-Colegio de S. Ildefonso

Museo José Luis Cuevas

Museo Mural Diego Rivera

JUÁREZ

ALAMEDA CENTRAL

Palacio de Bellas Artes

TACUBA

Allende

Palacio Minería

Catedral Metropolitana

Templo Mayor

numento Revolución

Juárez

Palacio Postal

3

4

El Sagrario

Museo S.H.C.P.

Monumento a Cristóbal Colón

5

MADERO

BUCARELI

BALDERAS

LUIS MOYA

Ex-Palacio Iturbide

Gran Hotel

PLAZA DE LA CONSTITUCIÓN (ZÓCALO)

Palacio Nacional

les

EJE CENTRAL

Antigua Casa de los Condes de San Mateo Valparaíso

Zócalo

Suprema Corte de Justicia

△ H

ey's Believe It lot Museum

LUIS CARRANZA

San Juan de Letrán

BOLÍVAR

Palacio de Ayuntamiento

PINO SUÁREZ

Museo de la Ciudad de México

Balderas

Salto del Agua

Isabel la Católica

Pino Suárez

ARCOS DE BELÉN

JOSÉ MARÍA IZAZAGA

DR. RÍO DE LA LOZA

LÁZARO CÁRDENAS

VÉRITZ

BOLÍVAR

Museo Anahuacalli, Jardines Flotantes, Xochimilco

DR. CLAUDIO BERNARD

HÉROES

△ G

AVENIDA CUAUHTÉMOC

NIÑOS

Niños Héroes

△ F

1. Templo de San Juan de Dios
2. Santa Veracruz
3. Iglesia de San Felipe de Jesús
4. Templo de San Francisco de Asís
5. Museo del Calzado el Borceguí

△ E

0		800 meters
0		800 yards

Painter Frida Kahlo's childhood home is now an intriguing museum.

On the down side, several million cars are crowded into the 570-square-mile (1,475 sq km) capital, spewing tons of contaminants into the air each year. At 7,400 feet (2,250 m) above sea level, the megalopolis of some 22 million people is ringed by volcanic mountains that trap the pollution. Visitors must be on the lookout for petty thieves, and there's an established protocol for hailing a legitimate cab.

Despite these considerable dangers and annoyances, el D.F. (short for Distrito Federal, or Federal District) is a fascinating mélange of the hip and the historic. Trendy restaurants in la Condesa serve carpaccio and decaf espresso, while down the street, family-run stands sell tamales and tacos. Mexico City represents the quintessence of the country's *mestizaje,* or blending of Indian and European cultures.

When the Mexica (pronounced meh-SHEE-ka) first wandered into the bowl-shaped Valle de Anáhuac (Valley of Mexico) from the north, they met people of learning: the cultured descendants of the Toltec tribe, with an accurate calendar and elaborate religious rituals (see p. 184). The Mexica, or Aztecs, founded Tenochtitlán on Lake Texcoco and, after rubbing elbows with their civilized neighbors for 200 years, amazed the Spanish conquistadors with their ingenious city of broad avenues lined with brightly painted palaces and temples. After the Conquest, the Spaniards built their new capital, Mexico City, from the ruins of Tenochtitlán and gradually filled in the lake. However, the unstable lakebed has proved a poor foundation, and today scores of 18th- and 19th-century buildings are being restored.

South and southwest of the historic center, the villages of Coyoacán and San Ángel—which predated the Spanish conquest and even the building of Tenochtitlán—have over the years retained their identities. Between the two towns are at least half a dozen captivating plazas surrounded by baroque churches, cobbled streets, and brightly painted homes with flower-filled courtyards. On weekends local artists and antiques dealers sell their wares at agreeably inexpensive prices, while an excellent assortment of the country's handicrafts are sold daily in boutiques and shops.

Xochimilco, one of the southernmost villages on former Lake Texcoco, has produced much of the region's plants and cut flowers since pre-Hispanic times. On Sundays lively groups of friends and families climb aboard *trajineras*—covered punts decorated in plastic flowers—for a leisurely cruise along Mexico City's last remaining system of canals and *chinampas*, or waterborne gardens. ■

Centro Histórico

Mexico's cherished "dark-skinned Virgin" is feted in the zócalo.

VICEREGAL ADMINISTRATIVE OFFICES, PROMINENT homes, cathedrals, and chapels replaced the palaces and temples of the dispossessed Mexica in the nucleus of the new city. Having weathered the centuries and survived the region's intermittent earthquakes, many still fulfill their original purpose; others house bookstores, jewelers, pawnshops, museums, and restaurants. Cosmopolitan and chaotic yet eager to please, downtown D.F. is a synthesis of ancient and modern Mexican culture—and has more churches than you could visit in a month of Sundays.

A good place to begin exploring the city is the 10-acre (4 ha) *zócalo,* or central plaza, built from the rubble of Tenochtitlán. Officially called Plaza de la Constitución, it is the world's second largest square. On the north side of the square, the **Catedral Metropolitana** *(tel 55/5510-0440),* the first cathedral in New Spain, was ordered to be built by Hernán Cortés, but later razed and replaced with the present church, finished in 1813. The dignified baroque facade is dominated by twin 18th-century bell towers.

Inside, worshipers pray at the cathedral's five principal altars and 14 side chapels; much of the exuberant craftsmanship, hidden behind tooled wooden bars, is not apparent upon a casual glance up the nave. Dusky light filters through small stained-glass windows to illuminate the dazzling **Altar de los Reyes,** a gilded wood altarpiece in Churrigueresque style, which took nearly 20 years to complete. Also Churrigueresque is the intricate facade of the adjoining mid-18th-century parish church, **El Sagrario,** covered in an army of carved saints. **La Piedra del**

Centro Histórico
🗺 179 G3
Visitor information
✉ República de Brasil at Moneda
🚇 Metro: Insurgentes

Sol, the 24-ton Aztec "calendar" stone now seen in the Museo Nacional de Antropología (see pp. 198–201), was discovered in El Sagrario's courtyard. The church is closed owing to earthquake damage.

The east side of the zócalo is completely dedicated to the **Palacio Nacional** *(tel 55/5999-2800)*, which displaced Aztec emperor Moctezuma's sumptuous palace. Originally the official residence of the colonial viceroys, the national palace later held the presidential offices, although Benito Juárez was the only president to use this as his official residence. Today, the palace houses various state departments, but for visitors, the draw is 18 years' worth of Diego Rivera murals highlighting Mexican history and culture. To best appreciate the unlabeled murals, hire an English-speaking guide at the foot of the stairwell. Most charge about 50–80 pesos. On the second floor are scenes from pre-Hispanic life at Tenochtitlán, Michoacán, Oaxaca, and Papantla. Smaller panels pay tribute to the rubber tree, corn, cacao, and the agave plant. The last mural on the second floor shows the *mestizaje* of Mexico, the blending of indigenous and Spanish blood and cultures. Cortés is shown as a hideous, syphillitic man; behind him, his mistress, La Malinche (see box, p. 207) holds a green-eyed mestizo baby.

One block south, in the **Suprema Corte de Justicia** *(Pino Suárez 2, tel 55/5522-1500)*, is José Clemente Orozco's mural, "La Justicia" ("Justice"), seen over the main interior staircase. On the south side of the plaza, the tiled exterior of the **Palacio del Ayuntamiento** (Municipal Palace) depicts the coats of arms of Mexico City, Coyoacán, Christopher Columbus, and

Hernán Cortés. The matching structure next door was built in 1935 to accommodate growing Federal District affairs.

Naturally, some of the city's finest architecture stems from its religious past. Built in 1588 as a Jesuit seminary, the **Ex-Colegio de San Ildefonso** *(Justo Sierra 16, tel 55/5702-6378, closed Mon., $$)* was remodeled during the early 18th century but maintains its original baroque and neoclassic facade. Inside, dark orange walls and stone porticos surround a large central patio shaded by giant magnolias. Now owned by the National University, the museum and cultural center hosts events and temporary fine arts exhibits. Don't miss the 80 or more carved cedar choir stalls, rescued from a fire at the St. Augustine monastery, in the ground floor's northwest corner. Each exquisitely rendered chair depicts a different biblical scene. Murals form another part of the museum's permanent collection. Those by José Clemente Orozco along three stories at the building's north end range from somber to cartoony. Diego Rivera's stylized "La Creación" (1922) is tucked away in the Anfiteatro Bolívar on the west side. El Cardenal Restaurant (see p. 369), at the rear of the building, is highly recommended for traditional dishes from throughout the nation.

Nearby, the striking, ultra-baroque interior of the narrow **Templo de la Enseñanza** *(Donceles 102, tel 55/5702-1843, closed Mon.)* is a dazzling display of Spanish colonial wealth. Vacated during the Reform Laws, the late 18th-century convent church was declared a national monument in 1931 and once again functions as a place of worship.

One block north of here, the interior patios of the neoclassic

By night historic downtown, dominated by the Catedral Metropolitana, regains an air of refinement.

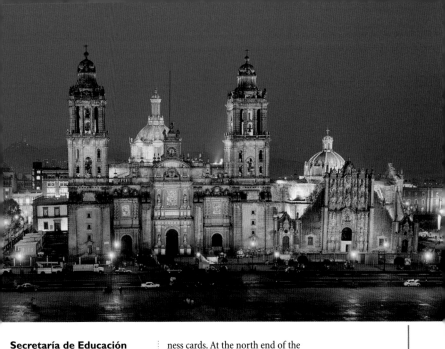

Secretaría de Educación Pública *(Av. República de Argentina 28, tel 55/5328-1000)*, or Ministry of Education, are covered with examples of the Mexican Mural School. Diego Rivera painted nearly 200 panels between 1923 and 1928, notably "La Maestra Rural" ("The Rural Teacher") and "La Liberación del Peón" ("The Peasant's Liberation")—common themes for the socialist painter. The singular "Patriots and Parricides," by Siqueiros, decorates the stairwell near the República de Brasil street entrance.

One of Mexico's oldest squares, the **Plaza Santo Domingo** *(República de Venezuela at Brasil)* shelters the **Portal de los Evangelistas,** a colonnade where *evangelistas* (public scribes) have traditionally performed this function, clacking away on ancient typewriters to complete job applications and "Dear John" letters for the unschooled. A few continue to perform this function, but the area now houses mainly printers who produce wedding invitations, personalized greeting cards, and business cards. At the north end of the plaza, native red *tezontle* (volcanic rock) contrasts with the white-stone Corinthian columns on the facade of the baroque **Iglesia de Santo Domingo** *(tel 55/5529-3906)*. It was built in the early 18th century after floods and earthquakes ruined the first Dominican monastery in New Spain, dated 1527. Inside, note the neoclassic high altar created by Manuel de Tolsá. All that remains of the original structure is the small **Capilla de la Expiación,** or Chapel of Atonement, with its fabulous rococo altarpiece.

The Dominican-led Inquisition was aimed as much at purging political rivals from the colony as in pursuing heretics. A tribunal was established in 1521 in rented buildings surrounding the Plaza de Santo Domingo. The more permanent **Palacio de la Inquisición** *(República de Brasil 33)*, across the street, was not built for another 200 years. It was purchased in 1854 by the National University and is at press time being thoroughly restored. ∎

A brief history of the Mexica

The Mexica, or Aztecs, arrived in the bowl-shaped Valle de Anáhuac (Valley of Mexico) in the late 13th century. They were a poor and barbarous people—with no formal religion, calendar, or system of writing—who wandered south from a place they called Aztlán. Initially reviled and briefly enslaved by more powerful city-states in the valley, the Mexica fled in 1322 to the uninhabited wetlands at the edge of Lake Texcoco, where they founded Tenochtitlán on an island on the lake. Just 50 years later they began their rapid rise to power with a strategic marriage into the royal family of Culhuacán, their former masters.

With the ascent of Itzcóatl to the throne in 1427, there began a systematic conquest and absorption of the established lakeside cities, including Coyoacán, Xochimilco, and Atzcapotzalco—the latter providing access to important freshwater springs at Chapultepec. Through warfare, intimidation, strategic alliances, and a ruthless political agenda, the Mexica extended their domain throughout Mesoamerica. From the time their first king ascended the throne, they began to reinvent their own history and genealogy in a more favorable light, even claiming lineage back to the god-king Quetzalcóatl.

Although governed during its early years by a representative council of elders and speakers, Tenochtitlán soon developed a ruling oligarchy, the *pipiltin*. Most people lived in servitude, subject to laws governing such minutiae as what they ate, drank, and wore. Meanwhile, the extravagant lifestyle of the pipiltin necessitated a constantly expanding empire enriched by plunder and the labor and taxation of subject states. These divergent living standards are reflected in the folk belief of the time that after death nobles were regenerated as gems, beautiful birds, or fluffy white clouds, while commoners became weasels, dung beetles, and skunks.

Few peoples except the Purépecha of Michoacán and some of the fierce Chichimec tribes to the north were able to repel the Mexica war machine. The conquered paid dearly both in tribute and in victims for the sacrificial slab. The Mexica's principle god, Huitzilopochtli (Southern Hummingbird, the god of war), grew in power as the empire grew. Initially an insignificant local deity, the hummingbird demanded human sacrifice on an incredible scale, feasting on hearts and blood from captured warriors, scofflaws, and other unfortunates.

By the time a Spanish expedition under Hernán Cortés arrived on Mexico's east coast in 1519, Tenochtitlán was feared, respected, and hated almost as much by its allies as by its subject states and enemies. Only this far-flung hostility made possible one of history's most amazing conquests (see p. 29). Another important factor was timing. According to legend, Quetzalcóatl had sailed eastwards five centuries before, promising to return in the year One Reed. Cortés's arrival in that very year (a 1:52 probability) convinced the Mexica ruler, Moctezuma, of the god's return. A priest, poet, and philosopher, Moctezuma had been chosen king in 1502 based on his courage in battle, sagacity, and clarity of mind. Ironically, it was his indecision and unwillingness to acknowledge and engage the enemy that led to the downfall of the Mexica empire, and ultimately, to the conquest of Mesoamerica. ∎

Above: Human sacrifice in Mesoamerica
Right above: Moctezuma's historic first meeting with Cortés
Right below: Spanish and Aztec warriors at battle; scene from the Duran Codex

Templo Mayor

UNTIL THE SPANISH CONQUEST, THE TEMPLO MAYOR, OR great pyramid of Tenochtitlán, was the site of coronations, dedications, human sacrifice, and other important civic and religious events. Today, a partial reconstruction of the pyramid allows you to appreciate its building stages, as well as view several surviving rooms and temples. Although the ruins themselves are interesting, it's in the well-designed museum that you'll really get a feel for life in Tenochtitlán. Here, soul-stirring statues of incredible power and pathos are displayed on free-standing pedestals. Jewelry, carved shells, knives used in ritualistic self-sacrifice and human sacrifice, and many other smaller objects are arranged on beds of fine sand in attractive display cases.

Twin temples atop the Templo Mayor pyramid were dedicated to the two most important gods: the southern temple, painted red, housed the war god Huitzilopochtli; to the north was the blue shrine of Tláloc, god of rain and fertility. Still visible on the Tláloc temple are vertical black and white stripes and circles representing rain, eyes, and sky. Before it, a statue of Chac Mool, messenger to the gods, was positioned to receive the hearts of sacrificial victims.

Within the structure, thousands of priests and their acolytes lived and worshiped, accessing apartments and shrines through labyrinthine corridors of polished stone. Each ruler modified or enlarged previous structures; new walls were built out and up, and the intervening space filled with mud and rubble. At the northern extreme of the excavation, note the eagle designs in the **Eagle Warrior room,** the exclusive enclave of the respected military order.

The first four galleries are dedicated to Huitzilopochtli, with themes of war, ritualistic death, and tribute. **Gallery One** has a scale model of the Templo Mayor. In **Gallery Two** you will see votive offerings as well as objects used in sacrifice and self-sacrifice. Among these are the flint knives used to open the chest cavity of sacrificial victims, and needles of filed eagle bones with which the nobles bled their earlobes, genitals, arms, and tongues in penitence and purification rituals. **Gallery Three** houses objects traded or paid in tribute from some of the Mexica's 370 subject towns, including fine gold filigree and turquoise jewelry from Oaxaca, and carved shells from the Caribbean and Pacific coasts.

Large statues, stelae, and the life-size, ceramic standard bearers and eagle warrior statues that guarded Huitzilopochtli's temple form the core of exhibits in **Gallery Four.** Perhaps most impressive is the huge circular stone with relief carving of the moon goddess Coyolxauhqui, whose discovery by city workers in 1978 precipitated the temple's excavation. According to legend, Huitzilopochtli sprang fully armed from the womb of the earth goddess Coatlicue in order to protect her from his 400 siblings, including Coyolxauhqui. (Coatlicue had been impregnated by a feather while sweeping, and her children were outraged over her mysterious and unseemly pregnancy.) Huitzilopochtli beheaded the moon goddess, and the other antagonists fled to the sky, where they became stars. In addition to explaining the demise of the moon each month, this legend undoubtedly helped to establish the fledgling god Huitzilopóchtli during the early days of the kingdom by relating him to the long-venerated earth goddess Coatlicue.

Galleries Five to **Eight** are dedicated to Tláloc. In the first of these is a reproduction of the original wall decoration on the rain god's temple. Also exhibited are figures and images associated with Tláloc, including the frog, eaten by the Mexica as a ritualistic food. **Galleries Six** and **Seven** are dedicated respectively to the area's flora and fauna, and agriculture. The last of the main galleries appropriately describes the end of the Aztec era and the introduction of Christianity and Hispanic rule. Don't miss the last two galleries, near the exit, with fascinating exhibits regarding the cult of death. ■

VISITING THE MUSEUM

Signs are in Spanish, but an excellent English-language audio tour *($$)* is available. Free Spanish-language guided tours are offered Tues.–Fri.; call 5542-4943 for an English-speaking guide.

Life-size eagle warrior statues such as this one guarded Huitzilopochtli's temple.

A walk in & around historic Parque la Alameda

Originally created to be enjoyed by all classes, Alameda Park, its grassy esplanade punctuated with many trees and fountains, became a fenced and elitist park during the long reign of Porfirio Díaz. Today, as intended, it attracts all manner of people and is surrounded by historic churches, museums, and the lovely Palace of Fine Arts. East of the park, the Madero neighborhood, named for Revolution hero Francisco I. Madero (see p. 34), has seen an influx of government funds and private fortunes and extensive restoration of its historic buildings.

Begin your walk at the Sanborns flagship venue in **Casa de los Azulejos ❶** *(Madero 4 at la Condesa, tel 55/5512-1331)*, one of the few nonhotel restaurants open at 7 a.m. This was a popular restaurant during the Mexican Revolution, when it hosted Pancho Villa, Emiliano Zapata, and their troops. The building's exterior is entirely covered in Puebla-style tiles; José Clemente Orozco's intriguing mural "Omnisciencia" (1925) graces the interior stairwell.

Directly across Calle Madero is the **Templo de San Francisco de Asís** *(Madero 7, tel 55/5518-4690)*, originally a Franciscan monastery begun in 1524 under the patronage of Hernán Cortés. Remodeled several times, the surviving Church of St. Francis of Assisi presents an excellent example of Churrigueresque design, especially in the facade and the main altar—the latter destroyed in the previous century but totally reconstructed in the 1940s. Next door is the lovely, 18th-century **Iglesia de San Felipe de Jesús ❷**, dedicated to Felipe de las Casas

Martínez (1572–1597), the first Mexican saint. Its interior is covered in large, extraordinarily beautiful paintings of saints, while the high ceiling gives the small, French neo-Gothic church the illusion of space.

One block east (toward the *zócalo*) on the same side of the street is the **Palacio de Iturbide** *(Madero 17, tel 55/1226-0120, closed Sat., Sun.)*, an 18th-century baroque building

---

- ⓜ See also area map p. 179 F3
- ► Casa de los Azulejos (Sanborns Restaurant)
- ↔ 1.4 miles (2.2 km)
- ⏱ 6 hours
- ► Plaza de la Santa Veracruz

NOT TO BE MISSED
- Palacio de Bellas Artes
- Central Alameda
- Museo Mural Diego Rivera
- Museo Franz Mayer

A Sanborns restaurant now occupies the Casa de los Azulejos (House of Tiles).

of volcanic stone. Now a Banamex bank office, it is open to the public during temporary exhibitions of its fine art collection. Emperor Agustín de Iturbide occupied the luxurious home for a few short years until his exile in 1823.

Turn left at the next corner, Bolívar, and walk two blocks to Calle Tacuba, where a number of colonial buildings, including the Biblioteca del Congreso de la Unión *(Tacuba 27),* have recently received facelifts. Walk east on Tacuba to Calle Mata and the **Plaza Manuel Tolsá 3,** named for the Spanish architect and sculptor (1757–1816) who in 1803 created the **Estatua Ecuestre de Carlos de Borbón.** The statue, which most people call **El Caballito** (referring to the mount rather than the Spanish sovereign), now stands in the center of the plaza.

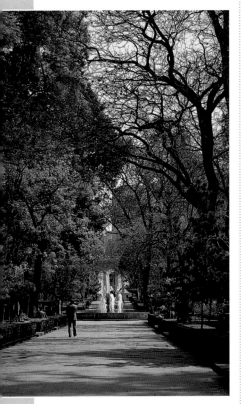

Named for its poplars, Parque la Alameda abounds in ash, pine, and jacaranda trees.

Presiding over the square is the **Museo Nacional de Arte 4** *(Tacuba 8, tel 55/5130-3411, closed Mon., $),* home to a permanent collection of Mexican art with an emphasis on 19th-century paintings. The wrought-iron-and-brass staircase, baroque lamps, and painted ceiling are based on turn-of-the-20th-century European design elements.

Across the street, the **Palacio de Minería** *(Tacuba 5, tel 55/5521-4020, closed Sat., Sun., & university holidays),* also designed by Tolsá, is one of the city's best examples of neoclassic architecture and now houses the Engineering School of the National University (UNAM). Next door, the distinctive, plateresque-style **Palacio de Correos 5** *(Tacuba 1 at Eje Central, tel 5510-2999, closed Sat. afternoon & Sun.),* with its facade of pinkish-yellow quarrystone, was designed by Italian architect Adamo Boari at the beginning of the 20th century. Philatelists and lovers of old books can take the staircase to the third-floor post office library. Major renovations that took place in 1999–2000 have rejuvenated its Moorish, Gothic, Venetian, and Renaissance interior design elements.

Cross busy Eje Central to examine another of Boari's creations, the exquisite **Palacio de Bellas Artes 6** *(Av. Juárez & Eje Central, tel 55/5512-1410, museum closed Mon., $$)* on the east flank of Parque la Alameda. President Porfirio Díaz commissioned the art nouveau-style, Carrara marble palace in 1904, but construction was interrupted by the Revolution. The art deco interior was completed in 1934 by Mexican architect Federico Mariscal. Murals on the second floor include "Mexico Today" (1952) and "Birth of Our Identity" (1953) by Rufino Tamayo. On the third floor are José Orozco's "La Catársis" (1935), David Siqueiros' "New Democracy" (1945), and Diego Rivera's "Man, the Controller of the Universe" (1934), a reproduction of the painting commissioned for the Rockefeller Center and destroyed the following year because of its socialist content. There's no charge to view the art on the first floor or to visit the bookstore, giftshop, or restaurant located there.

From the fine arts palace, head into **Parque la Alameda 7,** created in the early

Talavera tiles accent the dome of San Francisco de Asis, one of the city's earliest monasteries.

17th century. It was expanded in the 1900s to include the former Plaza del Quemadero, where the politically incorrect were burned at the stake during the Inquisition. Numerous monuments and fountains give character to the park. About halfway down Avenida Juárez you'll see the **Juárez Hemiciclo,** a monument of pale Italian marble, Doric columns, and roaring lions honoring statesman and president Benito Juárez. Across Avenida Juárez and a bit west of the monument are a visitor information booth *(Juárez 64 at Revillagigedo, tel 55/5518-1003)* and a 400-room hotel and convention center, currently under construction.

Cross Calle Dr. Mora at the west end of Parque la Alameda. At the rear of the Plaza de la Solidaridad, the **Museo Mural Diego Rivera ❽** *(Colón at Balderas, tel 55/5512-0754, closed Mon., $)* houses Rivera's elaborate 1947 mural "Sueño de una Tarde Dominical en la Alameda" ("Dream of a Sunday Afternoon in the Alameda"), which was moved here after the Hotel del Prado was irreparably damaged in the 1985 earthquake. A schematic identifies the historical and allegorical characters in the mural; there are portraits of Rivera, Frida Kahlo, Sor Juana de la Cruz, the Habsburg emperors, and many

others. Just north of this museum, the **Laboratorio de Arte Alameda** *(Dr. Mora 7, tel 55/5510-2792, closed Mon.)* houses contemporary art, especially that involving electronic media like videos and interactive exhibits.

Reenter Parque la Alameda, walking east. At the metal-roofed bandstand, cross busy Hidalgo (at Trujano) and continue half a block east to **Plaza de la Santa Veracruz,** named for the Church of the True Holy Cross, on the east side of the square. Occupying part of the adjoining former hospital is the **Museo Nacional de la Estampa** *(Hidalgo 39, tel 55/5510-4905, closed Mon., $),* with rotating exhibits from its permanent collection of early lithographs and linoleum prints, as well as visiting print media shows.

On the west side of the square is the baroque Templo San Juan de Dios. Next door, the **Museo Franz Mayer ❾** *(Av. Hidalgo 45, tel 55/5518-2267, closed Mon.)* houses the fabulous applied arts collection of German-born financier Franz Mayer (1882–1975). The galleries surrounding a beautiful central courtyard are full of 16th- to 19th-century Mexican utilitarian and decorative art objects. A separate gallery shows European Renaissance paintings. ■

The new basilica is one of many temples honoring the Virgin at La Villa de Guadalupe.

North of Centro Histórico

NORTH OF THE HISTORIC CENTER, TWO SITES OFFER pre-Cortesian ruins, colonial churches, and a modern 20th-century cathedral. Tlatelolco was a contemporary of Tenochtitlán. Its main pyramid had adjoining temples honoring the gods Tláloc and Huitzilopochtli; they were dismantled by the Spanish to build a church to St. James the Apostle. Farther north, la Villa de Guadalupe honors the Virgin of Guadalupe, whose miraculous appearance on Tepeyac Hill led to the conversion of tens of thousands of natives and eventually to one of Catholicism's most impassioned cults. Both are often included on tours to Teotihuacán, an important archaeological site about an hour to the north (see pp. 228–29).

Tlatelolco
🅰 179 F4
Visitor information
✉ Av. Lázaro Cárdenas at Flores Magón
🚇 Metro: Tlatelolco

TLATELOLCO

Tlatelolco was established in 1338 by a dissident group who left Tenochtitlán to build their own city near the northernmost part of Lake Texcoco. Although allied in matters of mutual security with the Tenochcan kings, Tlatelolco refused to accept their sovereignty but was finally subjugated in 1473 by Axayácatl. An important center for merchants and traders, this city served as the Aztec's most important market—amazing Cortés's visiting troops

with the variety and quality of goods for sale.

Visitors today can see the reconstructed ruins of Tlatelolco, the last stand during the siege that brought down the Aztec empire. As was customary, the **Iglesia de Santiago Tlatelolco,** completed in 1609, was built with stones from the dismantled pyramids. Indian peasant Juan Diego, who witnessed the apparition of the Virgin of Guadalupe in 1531 (see p. 193), was baptized here at the baroque font, with its shell motif characteristic of

St. James the Apostle. To the right of the church, the former Franciscan monastery was the first college to tutor Indians of noble birth, teaching history, philosophy, and Latin.

Mention Tlatelolco to most Mexico City residents, and they'll remember it as the site of a massacre of student demonstrators by government troops just before the 1968 Olympic games. Although there is no official death toll, up to several hundred young demonstrators were gunned down during a political rally. A simple monument on the north side of the temple acknowledges that tragedy.

Don't miss David Alfaro Siqueiros's mural "Cuauhtémoc Against the Myth," combining sculpture with fresco work. It is in the Tecpan building, at the far side of the quadrangle behind the church and monastery, at the site of Cuauhtémoc's former palace.

LA VILLA DE GUADALUPE

Every Mexican schoolchild knows the story of Juan Diego, to whom the Virgin of Guadalupe is said to have appeared on three occasions at Tepeyac Hill. When Bishop de Zumárraga asked the Chichimec Indian for proof of the miracle, the Virgin showered Juan Diego with roses. Returning to the bishop with his precious cargo wrapped in his cloak, Diego found that the roses had disappeared, to be replaced by the image of the Virgin.

An estimated 15 million people make the pilgrimage to Tepeyac each year, many on December 12, the Virgin's feast day. The new, round **Basílica de Nuestra Señora de Guadalupe** (tel 55/5577-6022) was built between 1974 and 1976 to accommodate the faithful. Although unimpressive from the outside, the cavernous structure is imposing inside, with its undulating, wood-slat ceiling,

Pre-Hispanic icons dominate this costume, worn in celebration of the Virgin's feast day.

modern stained-glass windows, floor of polished Mexican onyx, and main altar of Carrara marble. The cloak of Juan Diego, with the Virgin's image clearly visible, is the basilica's most important icon, situated way up high at the back of the church behind the main altar.

An annex of the old basilica houses the **Museo de la Basílica de Guadalupe** (tel 55/5781-6810, $), with religious paintings as well as offerings and ex-votos left over the years by the devout.

Beyond the T-shirt vendors and painted ponies for taking snapshots is the 18th-century **Capilla del Pocito** (tel 55/5577-3844), built at the site of a miraculously appearing spring. This lovely round baroque chapel has a dome of blue and white Talavera tiles and exterior walls of tile, quarrystone, and volcanic rock. Inside, the walls of the tiny chapel are covered with little angel scenes in pastel colors. The holy well for which the temple is named is now dry. At the top of Tepeyac Hill, the **Capilla de las Rosas** denotes the spot of the Virgin's first alleged appearance. ∎

La Villa de Guadalupe
🗺 179 G4
✉ Plaza de las Américas 1
🚇 Metro: La Villa-Basílica

Bosque de Chapultepec, Paseo de la Reforma, & environs

BOSQUE DE CHAPULTEPEC ONCE PROVIDED DRINKING water for the Aztec nation and housed the royal hunting preserves, vacation palaces, and gardens. Today a source of much-needed oxygen, the 2,000-acre (800 ha) park has a zoo and a castle, an elegant restaurant on a swan-dotted lake, and nearly a dozen museums. Bisecting the park and connecting it to the historic center is elegant Paseo de la Reforma, one of the few contributions of the ill-fated Emperor Maximilian (see p. 33).

Bosque de Chapultepec

🅰 178 B2

🚇 Metro: Chapultepec, Auditorio, Constituyentes

The **Monumento a los Niños Héroes** marks the eastern entrance of the park *(Metro: Chapultepec)* and the spot where six young cadets leapt to their deaths rather than surrender to U.S. troops during the Mexican-American War. Here, biking and jogging trails wend their way around monuments, fountains, and most of the park's museums. Lovers embrace beneath the pines, palms, and jacarandas, or converse on wooden park benches. With lots of possibilities for inexpensive family entertainment, the park becomes quite crowded on weekends, especially Sundays, the traditional day for family outings.

The two-story **Museo de Arte Moderno** *(Paseo de la Reforma at Gandhi, tel 55/5211-8729, closed Mon., $)* exhibits the country's most important 20th-century artists, temporary displays, and sculptures of aluminum, stone, bronze, iron, and ceramic in a rambling garden. There is a small but excellent shop and a well-stocked bookstore.

Across the street, the **Museo Rufino Tamayo** *(Paseo de la Reforma at Gandhi, tel 55/5286-6519, closed Mon., $, Metro: Chapultepec)* houses the international contemporary art collection of Oaxaca painter and sculptor Rufino Tamayo (1899–1991), including works by Picasso, Miró, Fernando Botero, Andy Warhol, and others. To the west lies the fabulous **Museo Nacional de Antropología** (see pp. 198–201).

Just beyond the modern art museum is the **Castillo de Chapultepec,** begun in 1785 as a retreat for Spanish viceroys but interrupted by the War of Independence. Perched on a small hill, the building was finished as a military academy and remodeled by Emperor Maximilian of Habsburg and again by president Porfirio Díaz. Since 1939, it has housed the **Museo Nacional de Historia** *(tel 55/5241-3100, closed Mon., $),* whose historical displays and period furnishings are enhanced by murals by Juan O'Gorman, José Clemente Orozco, and David Alfaro Siqueiros. From the castle, walk or board the miniature tram *($)* to the free **Zoológico de Chapultepec** *(tel 55/5553-6263,*

closed Mon., Metro: Auditorio), with a petting zoo and pony rides. Reasonably large, open-air enclosures house about 250 different species, about half of them native to Mexico and a good number endemic. Non-natives include a pair of super-star Chinese pandas.

Midway through the park, west of Avenida López Mateo, are several child-friendly attractions. The **Feria de Chapultepec** *(tel 55/5230-2121, closed Mon., $–$$$, Metro: Constituyentes)*—an amusement park with roller coaster, a rowing lake, a restaurant, and a coffee shop—appeals to both young and old. The interactive **Museo del Papalote** *(Av. Constituyentes*

Right: A modern sculpture and skyscraper dominate the east end of Paseo de la Reforma.

CALZ. OCAMPO
CUAUHTÉMOC
Monumento a Cristóbal Colón, Monumento de Cuauhtémoc
Monumento a la Independencia
Diana de la Cazadora
PASEO DE LA REFORMA
SEVILLA **ZONA ROSA**
Sevilla
AVENIDA CHAPULTEPEC
DURANGO
Museo de Cera, Ripley's Believe It or Not Museum
PARQUE ESPAÑA
PARQUE SAN MARTÍN
AV. NUEVO LEÓN
AV. INSURGENTES

Business is conducted over coffee.

268 at Periférico, tel 55/5237-1700, $$, Metro: Constituyentes) offers dozens of changing, "touch-me" exhibits for kids, such as the bed of nails, bubble room, and broadcasting studio. There's a separate charge for viewing films in the IMAX theater. During February and March, the *Swan Lake* ballet is performed on an island on **Lago Menor;** the rest of the year resident swans abide a less theatrical existence on nearby **Lago Mayor,** interrupted only by people in rented rowboats.

Connecting the park and Avenida Juárez, **Paseo de la Reforma** was once lined with gracious mansions and flowering trees. Today, monumental sculptures decorate the major traffic circles, while busts of Mexico's heroes line both sides of the street. Closest to Parque Chapultepec is **Diana de la Cazadora** *(at Río Misisipi),* a nude bronze statue that was clothed for 25 years from 1942 owing to a burst of civic modesty. The Roman huntress is once again as artist Juan Fernando Olaguíbel

(1896–1971) intended. A graceful, bronzed, winged figure (commonly called *el angel,* or "the angel") sparkles atop a 120-foot-tall (36.5 m) Corinthian column at the **Monumento a la Independencia** *(At Av. Florencia).* The monument was erected in 1910 to honor the heroes of the War of Independence, whose sculptures in Italian marble are found near the base.

A classic bronze statue on a stone pedestal honors the last Mexica emperor, **Cuauhtémoc** *(At Av. Insurgentes).* Its base is carved with scenes of the ruler's capture and subsequent torture by Spanish conquistadors. Four friars surround Christopher Columbus at the **Monumento a Cristóbal Colón** *(At Av. Morelos),* representing the evangelization of the Americas. Just a few blocks southwest of Parque la Alameda, on Avenida Juárez, is the metal, yellow-painted sculpture "Cabeza de Caballo." The modernistic, 90-foot (28 m) piece is the work of

Chihuahua sculptor Sebastián (1948–), who studied at the San Carlos Academy.

NEIGHBORHOODS
North of Chapultepec lies **Polanco,** a mix of well-to-do houses behind high garden walls, businesses in high- and low-rise buildings, hotels, foreign embassies, and restaurants. It was developed in the 1940s when the extensive grounds of **Hacienda de los Morales** (see Restaurants, p. 369) were divided and sold. Chic cafés and restaurants become packed during peak hours, especially along the main thoroughfare, Presidente Mazaryk, and adjacent streets.

The traditional favorite for fine dining and nightlife is the **Zona Rosa,** or Pink Zone, a pie-shaped piece of real estate bordered by Avenida Insurgentes, Paseo de la Reforma, and Chapultepec. The compact neighborhood, now a gay hangout, is a mélange of two-story shops, Internet cafés, strip bars, and boutiques interspersed with high-rise buildings, and is easy to negotiate on foot—especially along the handful of pedestrian-only streets. For some light laughs, visit **Ripley's Believe It or Not Museum** (*Londres 4, Col. Juárez, tel 55/5546-3784, $$*) or the affiliated **Museo de Cera** (*$*), where revolutionaries and rock stars are re-created as life-size wax statues.

Luring shoppers and diners from the Zona Rosa are two neighborhoods to the south: **La Condesa** and **Colonia Roma.** The former is especially known for its hip and trendy restaurants, cafés, and nightspots, many in restored art deco buildings for which this part of the city is known. East of Avenida Insurgentes, the wealthy built lovely homes in Colonia Roma during the first half of the 20th century. The neighborhood declined when residents moved to more fashionable areas such as Lomas de Chapultepec, but is currently experiencing renewed gentrification. ■

Colonial and modern architecture side by side on the Paseo de la Reforma

Museo Nacional de Antropología

Museo Nacional de Antropología
- 178 B2
- Paseo de la Reforma at Gandhi, Bosque de Chapultepec
- 55/5553-6243
- www.mna.inah.gob.mx
- Closed Mon.
- $$
- Metro: Auditorio

THE SPACIOUS NATIONAL ANTHROPOLOGY MUSEUM WAS built in 1964 and received a serious, 13-million-dollar restoration in the late 1990s. This remodel improved lighting, added English-language signage for some exhibits, and provided space for 2,000 new artifacts. Touch-screen computers in most galleries provide a wealth of information, although this is given in Spanish only.

Depiction in gold of the Mixtec sun god

Chihuateotl statue, the Aztec goddess who escorted the sun midday to evening

Opposite: Finds in the Mexica room include the Aztec sun stone.

The remodel did not change the basic structure of the complex of buildings, designed and built by architect Pedro Ramírez Vázquez, and called "one of the most satisfying in modern Mexico" and "an incomparable example of institutional architecture" by author and photographer Hans Beacham in his book *The Architecture of Mexico: Yesterday and Today* (1969). Four large buildings surround a central courtyard, whose open space is nearly half covered by an enormous aluminum canopy supported by a single column faced in carved stone. From the top of the support, an unusual structural element, water splashes down to the patio floor in a refreshing juxtaposition of art, architecture, and precipitation.

In 12 huge exhibition halls surrounding the ground-floor courtyard is Mexico's finest archaeological collection, devoted exclusively to pre-Hispanic civilizations. After breezing through the first three rooms in a sort of crash course in anthropology, visit the remaining rooms in any order, as they are organized according to region. Since the collection is so large, it makes sense to concentrate on the cultures that interest you most. Choose from Preclassic (Valley of Mexico), Teotihuacán, Toltec, Mexica (Aztec), Oaxaca,

Gulf Coast, Maya, Northern Mexico, and Western Mexico. Spectacular and varied archaeological treasures along with photographs, paintings, dioramas, and reproductions of murals and temples create a satisfying portrait of pre-Conquest civilizations. The lack of complete information in English is a drawback for many (resolved to some degree by using the English-language audio tour or by hiring a guide). In most salons, informative video presentations in English and Spanish run consecutively. If you have an interest in pre-Hispanic cultures, one day will probably not be sufficient for studying all the exhibits. Consider dedicating several mornings or afternoons to the museum, visiting other attractions in Parque Chapultepec, or wandering adjacent neighborhoods when the scope and grandeur of the exhibits begin to overwhelm you.

Behind many of the galleries you'll find outdoor patios and gardens sheltering stone sculptures and stelae, reconstructions of houses, and other fascinating, alfresco, large-scale exhibits. In the Maya room, don't miss the full-size reproduction of the royal tomb from the Temple of the Inscriptions at Palenque, Chiapas, and, in the back garden, reproductions of the murals of Bonampak

Oaxaca: People of the south ——

Cultures of the Gulf Coast ——

Villages of the Maya ——

The Northeast ——

The Nahuas ——

and a Chenes-style temple from Hochob, Campeche.

The museum has too many fabulous pieces to name, but you must not fail to see the following: Teotihuacán gallery—reproduction of Tepantitla murals; Toltec gallery—Atlante sculptures and mother-of-pearl-encrusted warrior (both from Tula); Mexica gallery—24-ton sun stone, statue of earth goddess Coatlicue, and the pregnant monkey vessel of polished obsidian (the museum's most costly piece—once stolen but later recovered); Oaxaca gallery—jade bat god mask, Mixtec jewelry, and reproduction of Monte Albán's Tomb 104; Gulf Coast gallery—colossal stone head (Olmec), "adolescent from Tamuin" statue, associated with the corn god; Maya room—carved lintels and stelae from Yaxchilán, clay figurines from Jaina, and Chac Mool from Chichén Itzá.

The ethnology exhibits on the second floor are similarly arranged by region and cultural group. Dioramas and glass-cased exhibits show ceremonial and everyday clothing, as well as masks, pottery, baskets, musical instruments, toys, and all the accouterments of daily life among Mexico's diverse ethnic populations. ■

Above: Coatlicue, the Aztec earth goddess

Left: The Zapotec goddess of 13 snakes

Right: Macuilxochitl, the Aztec god of music and dance, represented here in a tortoiseshell motif

Sierra de Puebla
The Otopans
The Purépecha
Great Nayar
Indigenous communities

Library

Ground Floor

Temporary exhibits
Indigenous cultures of Mexico
Introduction to anthropology
Population of the Americas
Preclassic central plateau

Teotihuacán
The Toltecs
The Mexica
Cultures of Oaxaca
Cultures of Gulf Coast

The Maya
Cultures of the West
Cultures of the North
Nonexhibition areas

The Mexican mural school

Following conquest and colonization, Mexico began to adopt European values and artistic styles. This preoccupation with Old World aesthetics was redoubled during the 34-year reign of Francophile dictator Porfirio Díaz. After Mexico's chaotic Revolution focused attention on land reform and other populist issues, nostalgic Mexicans living abroad spawned an artistic and political movement venerating indigenous people and the working classes. They integrated the intellectualism of Marxism and the romanticism of the Spanish Civil War with a desperate passion for their native Mexico. Many artists participated, but the "Big Three" were Diego Rivera, David Alfaro Siqueiros, and José Clemente Orozco.

The mural movement flourished between 1920 and 1970, especially in the early days under the patronage of prominent philosopher and education minister José Vasconcelos. Although the muralists' radical political views seemingly conflicted with the agenda of the conservative, pro-business administrations of the period, the Mexican government became their patron, and huge public spaces their canvases. The murals' nationalistic content and socialist spirit to some degree substituted for actual revolutionary measures, constituting a sort of political and artistic placebo for the masses. Working within the system, the artists spoke their piece and pursued their art, while the government seemed to support both the arts and radical politics.

Best known outside Mexico is the allegorical work of Diego Rivera (1886–1957). Showing artistic talent from an early age, he entered Mexico City's prestigious San Carlos Academy at the age of ten. After years of experimentation and travel through northern Europe, Paris, and Russia, Rivera developed an unequivocal style. Favoring a palette of deep pastels, he painted rounded, nearly neckless, brown-skinned folk wearing seamless trousers. The simple themes and engaging designs he chose were meant to inspire and educate the common people he almost religiously portrayed in his art. Both Rivera and fellow muralist David Alfaro Siqueiros (1896–1974) were members of the Mexican Communist Party. Siqueiros' work, known for its experimental and innovative technical character, is moody—often violent and chaotic—with strong, bold colors.

The murals of José Clemente Orozco (1883–1949) were influenced by his early work as a caricaturist, although in later years his simple yet stirring style became more expressionistic. The work of all three men centered on social ills and human suffering—especially that of their compatriots.

Less well known than the Big Three, architect and painter Juan O'Gorman (1905–1982), a Coyoacán native, produced realistic murals and paintings in exquisite color and detail. The work of internationally proclaimed Oaxaca impressionist muralist, painter, and sculptor Rufino Tamayo (1899–1991) was taken less seriously at the time because of its lack of direct social commentary. Fermín Revueltas, Alva de la Canal, Fernando Leal, and Miguel Covarrubias are among others who contributed to the wealth of murals in Mexico City. ∎

Viewing the murals

Below is a partial list of places in Mexico City where these masterpieces can be found.

On or near the zócalo: Ex-Colegio de San Ildefonso (see p. 182); Palacio Nacional (see p. 182); Secretaría de Educación Pública (see p. 183); Suprema Corte de Justicia (see p. 182).

La Alameda: Museo Mural Diego Rivera (see p. 191); Palacio de Bellas Artes (see p. 190).

Bosque de Chapultepec: Museo Nacional de Historia (see p. 195).

Universidad Autónoma Nacional de México (UNAM): Biblioteca Central, Estadio Olímpico, and Rectoría (see p. 207). ∎

Right: Father Hidalgo is the centerpiece of this Orozco mural depicting oppression.

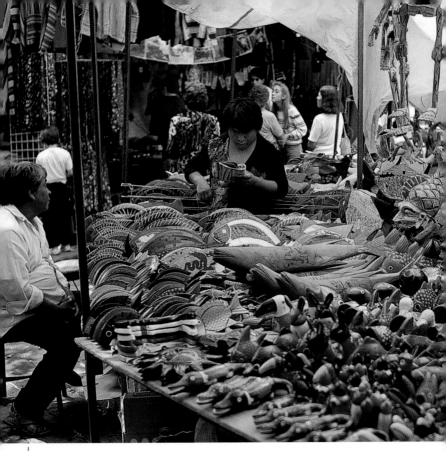

San Ángel
△ 178 D1
Visitor information
✉ Av. Revolución at Madero (Casa de la Cultura)
🚌 Bus: "San Ángel" bus from Insurgentes at Paseo de la Reforma

South of Centro Histórico

MEXICO CITY'S MOST IMPORTANT NORTH–SOUTH AXIS IS 18-mile-long (29 km) Avenida Insurgentes, which skirts the eastern edge of the Zona Rosa. It continues south past the 50-story World Trade Center (formerly the Hotel de México), the Plaza México (the world's largest bullring), and a stunning Diego Rivera mural decorating the curved facade of the Teatro de los Insurgentes. After a few more miles it reaches San Ángel and its neighbor, Coyoacán, two charming towns that have been absorbed by ever growing Mexico City.

SAN ÁNGEL

San Ángel is so pretty that it's been declared a national historic monument. Called Tenanitla before the Conquest, this quiet town of cobblestone streets and colonial- and Republican-era homes is anchored by two pleasing squares, **Plaza de San Jacinto** and, one block away, **Plaza del Convento.** Shoppers and vendors fill the former on Saturdays, when the overflow from the weekly crafts market, **Bazar del Sábado** (*Plaza San Jacinto 44, tel 55/5616-0082*), sets up camp under the pines, cedars, and yucca trees shading the plaza. Also on Plaza de San Jacinto is the simple 17th-century church for which the square is named and the **Casa del Risco** *(Plaza San Jacinto 15, tel 55/5616-2711, closed Mon.)*, an 18th-century residence housing an art museum and cultural center. In the main courtyard, you can't miss the unusual fountain, encrusted with mirrors and shells, as well as European and Mexican ceramic tiles, plates, platters, and cups. Temporary exhibits fill the ground-floor halls, while on the second floor, the permanent collection consists of 15th- to 19th-century European and Mexican paintings. The adjacent library *(Closed Sun.)* has 31,000 volumes related to international law, Mexican history, and criminology.

Just across busy Avenida Revolución, it's a pleasure to prowl around the cloisters and chapels of the **Museo del Carmen** *(Av. Revolución 4, tel 55/5616-2816, closed Mon., $, Metro: Quevedo)*, a museum of primarily religious paintings and artifacts. The former Carmelite monastery, with its magnificent domes of Talavera tiles and exquisite gilded altarpiece in the first-floor chapel, is every bit as interesting as the museum exhibits.

Items of contemporary art from a permanent collection are shown in rotation in the modern, low-ceilinged, glass and aluminum **Museo Carrillo Gil** *(Av. Revolución 1608 at Av. Altavista, tel 55/5550-6284, closed Mon., $)*. In addition to paintings by the Big Three of the Mexican Mural School (see p. 202), there are oils, pen and ink, gouache, and pencil drawings by lesser-known artists.

A short uphill walk along Avenida Altavista brings you to the **Museo Casa Estudio Diego Rivera y Frida Kahlo** *(Diego Rivera 2, tel 55/5550-1518, closed Mon., $, Metro: Quevedo)*, a boxlike modern house

Above: Shoppers browse at one of Mexico City's ubiquitous daily markets.
Above right: Frida Kahlo, who painted dozens of self-portraits, at work on "Portrait of Mrs. Jean Wight" (1931)

Coyoacán
🅐 178 D1
Visitor information
✉ Jardín Hidalgo 1
☎ 55/5659-2256, ext. 181

on steel stilts designed and built by architect and artist Juan O'Gorman. Frida Kahlo and her husband, Diego Rivera, occupied these two houses separated by a catwalk. The first two-story building held Rivera's gallery and, above, his studio. Kahlo both lived and worked in the house behind. The museum has a small collection of the artists' photographs, letters, documents, and personal effects, as well as sketches and paintings by their contemporaries.

COYOACÁN

About 2 miles (3 km) from San Ángel is equally engaging Coyoacán, home to artists and journalists from Mexico and elsewhere, giving it an artistic and intellectual ambience. If you're walking, stop along the way at the **Parque de la Bombilla** *(Av. Insurgentes Sur at La Paz)*, where joggers follow meandering trails under willow, pine, ash, and avocado trees. On weekends kids kick balls and practice tai-chi, and peanut and cotton-candy vendors appear. During the week it's less lively, but you can have space to admire the **Monumento al General Alvaro Obregón,** dedicated to the post-Revolution-era president assassinated in 1928 during the Cristero Revolt (see p. 35). East of the Parque de la Bombilla is the pleasant **Museo Nacional de la Acuarela** *(Salvador Novo 88, tel 55/5554-1801, closed Mon., Metro: Quevedo).* A variety of styles of gouache and watercolors are represented here in a collection donated by watercolorist Alfredo Guati, whose work is also shown.

Calle La Paz intersects with Avenida Francisco Sosa, lined with carefully maintained homes, many of them restored colonials, as well as shops, ice-cream parlors, restaurants, and bars. This is the main street of Coyoacán, a prosperous city when the Mexica first arrived in the Valley of Mexico. It was soon swallowed and digested by the more powerful newcomers. Hernán Cortés also made his headquarters in Coyoacán after the Conquest. The sunny yellow structure mistakenly cited as his home, the **Palacio de Cortés** *(Jardín Hidalgo 1),* houses city government offices and a visitor information booth. Presiding over the opposite side of the square is the **Templo de San Juan Bautista** *(Jardín Hidalgo 8, tel 55/5554-6376).* Constructed in the 16th century, little remains of the original building except the facade and the pilgrim's archway. Inside, its stained-glass windows portraying Franciscan saints illuminate the large, single-nave church and elaborate main altar.

Cafés, restaurants, boutiques, and bookstores surround adjacent **Jardín del Centenario** *(Carrillo Puerto & Centenario),* and, on weekends, vendors, locals, and tourists mill about. As in San Ángel, artists sell oil and acrylic paintings, framed etchings, and other works at reasonable prices.

About five blocks north of the plaza is the **Museo Frida Kahlo** *(Londres 247, tel 55/5554-5999, closed Mon., $$, Metro: Coyoacán).* Self-taught artist Frida Kahlo (1907–1954) was born and died in this cornflower-blue house, which is decorated with items from the popular Mexican culture she embraced. She began to paint during convalescence from a bus accident suffered as a teenager, adopting a deliberately naive style full of Mexican icons and imagery. Her intensely personal canvases, generally smaller-format oil paintings, reflected her constant physical pain and the mental anguish brought on by her inability to conceive and husband Diego Rivera's philandering. Underestimated artistically during her lifetime, this independent woman has become something of a feminist folk hero. In addition to her illustrated diary, love letters, and handpainted body cast are about a dozen of her paintings; the furnishings and decorations form a fabulous folk-art collection. A roomful of colorful clothing was discovered in 2005, and will be catalogued and hopefully added to the collection.

Five more blocks north and east bring you to the **Museo Leon Trotsky** *(Río Churubusco 410, tel 55/5658-8732, closed Mon., $, Metro: Coyoacán).* The house where the exiled Russian revolutionary lived contains his documents and personal effects. A friend of artists Kahlo and Rivera, Trotsky was assassinated (an ice pick through the brain) by Spaniard Ramón Mercader in 1940. The former Communist leader had survived at least one other attempted murder —involving machine guns this time—in which the muralist David Siqueiros, an ardent Stalinist, was allegedly involved.

A storyteller draws a crowd in Coyoacán.

Latin America's largest and oldest university, the **Universidad Autónoma Nacional de México, or UNAM** (*Av. Insurgentes Sur s/n, tel 55/5622-6470, Metro: Copilco or Universidad*), was founded in 1553. Originally occupying different buildings throughout the city, the 800-acre (320 ha) campus was established in the 1950s around the El Pedregal lava fields, south of San Ángel. If you visit the university campus, don't miss Juan O'Gorman's stunning mosaics, which cover all four sides of the Biblioteca Central (Main Library). Nearby, David Alfaro Siqueiros's glass-mosaic mural, "The People for the University, The University for the People," covers the north wall of the Rectoría, or Administration Building, while other dramatic murals cover the south wall and the tower. Directly across Avenida Insurgentes Sur, Diego Rivera's high-relief, natural stone mosaic on the exterior of the **Estadio Olímpico** (Olympic Stadium) depicts ancient and modern sports. ■

La Malinche

In a rust-red, two-story house on the southeast side of Plaza la Conchita, in Coyoacán, Hernán Cortés is said to have installed his interpreter, mistress, and the mother of his son Martín: La Malinche. Called Malintzin in Náhuatl and doña Marina by the Spaniards, the young woman was apparently sold as a slave to noblemen, who gave her, along with others, as a gift to Cortés. For the Spaniards, Malinche proved an invaluable interpreter, adviser, and even military strategist who well understood their enemy. Although her motivations and actions are not really known, this controversial and important historical figure was branded a traitor to the indigenous people. In the modern Mexican lexicon, *"un malinchista"* is a person of questionable patriotism or cultural loyalty. ■

Xochimilco

FAMOUS SINCE PRE-CORTESIAN TIMES FOR ITS FLOWERS, Xochimilco is the last place you can see the remains of the system of canals and artfully engineered garden plots that once threaded Lake Texcoco. This laid-back town (its name means "place of flowers") also has a lovely old cathedral and one of the country's best museums.

Xochimilco
179 G2
Visitor information
✉ Calle del Pino 36, Barrio San Juan
☎ 55/5676-0810

About 15 miles (24 km) southeast of downtown Mexico City, Xochimilco is best known for its *trajineras* (punts) that float the canals, these days sporting mostly artificial flowers. The scene is festive on weekends, when families party and picnic as they wind down from the working week. There are several docks in the main part of town; boats departing from **Embarcadero Celada,** on the west side, tour the **Parque Natural Xochimilco** ecological reserve, created in 1993. You also can tour the reserve's botanical gardens on foot.

The tree-shaded fortified monastery of **San Bernardino de Siena** was built by Franciscans in the late 16th century. It has a plain, sweet, pink facade in the classical style and, inside, a spectacular main altarpiece. Cross the street to the **Mercado,** a great place to take photographs or just admire the local produce, cut flowers, and flowering plants on sale.

No trip would be complete without a visit to the fabulous **Museo Dolores Olmedo Patiño** (*Av. México 5843, tel 55/5555-1016, closed Mon., $$, tren ligero: La Noria*). Numerous drawings and paintings collected by Señora Olmedo include the work of friend and protégé Diego Rivera and colleagues. There are more than 600 pre-Hispanic pieces and a fine collection of Mexican folk art. Have a bite to eat in the glass-walled café, set amidst a garden of cacti and purple-flowered jacarandas. ∎

More places to visit in Mexico City

ANTIGUA CASA DE LOS CONDES DE SAN MATEO VALPARAÍSO

Now housing Banamex offices, this building is one of the city's best examples of 18th-century civic architecture. Note the corner tower with the image of the Virgin of Guadalupe and the family coat of arms on the building's facade. Inside is an unusual double spiral stairway, designed to be used by both servants and their masters without the two groups having to meet. ⓜ 179 G3 ✉ Isabel la Católica 44 at Carranza ☎ 55/5225-6088 🕐 Closed Sat., Sun. 🚇 Metro: Isabel la Católica

CUICUILCO

Located within sight of Xitle volcano, which destroyed the city in about A.D. 300, the Cuicuilco archaeological site is considered the oldest in the Valley of Mexico, dating from the Preclassic era. The most important structure is a rare, circular, four-layered pyramid with an interior altar, discovered in 1922. The *in situ* museum displays photographs of the excavation and artifacts found there, including stelae and the figure of Huehueteotl-Xiuhtecuhtli, the god of fire portrayed as an old man. ⓜ 178 D1 ✉ Av. Insurgentes Sur s/n at Periférico, Col. Ysidro Favela ☎ 55/5606-9758 💲 $ 🚇 Metro: Universidad

EX-COLEGIO DE CRISTO

This slightly scruffy, lopsided 18th-century residence has an interesting collection of caricatures, old engravings, and political cartoons depicting everyone from Fidel Castro and Bill Clinton to Pope John Paul II. ⓜ 179 G3 ✉ Donceles 99 ☎ 55/5704-0459 💲 $ 🚇 Metro: Zócalo

MONUMENTO A LA REVOLUCIÓN

Initiated by president Porfirio Díaz to house legislative offices, this huge art deco building was finished instead as a tribute to the fallen in the Mexican Revolution, which interrupted construction. Inside is the **Museo Nacional de la Revolución,** containing documents, photos, and memorabilia from that war. ⓜ 179 E3 ✉ Plaza de la República, Col. Tabacalera ☎ 55/5546-2115 🕐 Closed Mon. 💲 $ 🚇 Metro: Revolución

Papier-mâché folk art from the Anahuacalli Museum collection

MUSEO ANAHUACALLI

This unusual-looking museum has room to display only 2,000 of its 55,000-piece collection of pre-Hispanic art donated by Diego Rivera. Represented are cultures from Guanajuato (Rivera's home state), the Valley of Mexico, and Teotihuacán, but especially the Pacific states of Colima, Nayarit, and Jalisco. The black volcanic rock and onyx building was designed by Rivera and inspired by pre-Hispanic structures. ⓜ 179 G2 ✉ Calle del Museo 150, Col. San Pablo Tepetlapa ☎ 55/5617-3797 🕐 Closed Mon. 💲 $ 🚇 Metro *(tren ligero)*: Xochipingo

MUSEO DE LA CIUDAD DE MÉXICO

Built of red volcanic stone in the 16th century, this elegant house was redone in the baroque style several hundred years later. It is now a museum of history and culture, offering pre-Hispanic pieces, several rooms of period furnishings, and salons for temporary fine art exhibits. Note the carved wooden doors, imported from the Philippines, and on the courtyard fountain, a *nereda,* or female figure with three tails. Musical performances are held periodically.

🅰 179 G2 ✉ Pino Sears 30 ☎ 55/5522-3640
🕐 Closed Mon. and national holidays 💲 $
🚇 Metro: Zócalo

MUSEO DE SAN CARLOS

Just a few blocks northeast of the Monumento a la Revolución (see p. 209) is this lovely if restrained neoclassic mansion. Diego Rivera and other greats were educated in this former academy of fine arts. Today, its important collection of 15th- to 19th-century European paintings includes Spanish Gothic panels and renaissance, Mannerist, baroque, neoclassic, romantic, and symbolist works.
🅰 179 E3 ✉ Puente del Alvarado 50, Col. Tabacalera ☎ 55/5566-8522 🕐 Closed Tues.
💲 $ 🚇 Metro: Revolución

MUSEO DEL CALZADO EL BORCEGUÍ

Latin America's only museum dedicated solely to shoes has 15,000 exhibits. These include historic shoes (Napoleonic- and Louis XV-era shoes, Chinese slippers, NASA moon boots); folk art representing shoes; and 175 pairs of celebrity shoes, belonging to the likes of Gregory Peck and Pierre Cardin. This fascinating museum is connected to the store of the same name, established in 1895 and specializing in comfortable and orthopedic shoes.
🅰 179 F3 ✉ Bolívar 27, 2nd floor ☎ 55/ 5512-1311 🕐 Closed Sun. 🚇 Metro: Allende

MUSEO JOSÉ LUIS CUEVAS

Painter and sculptor José Luis Cuevas's erotic etchings are rather incongruously housed in the cloister of this 16th-century former convent, a lovely building declared a national monument in 1932. Cuevas's 26-foot-tall (8 m) bronze "La Giganta" dominates the central patio, while smaller statues and paintings line the passageways. On Sundays, the museum often hosts performances of theater, dance, and music.
🅰 179 G3 ✉ Calle Academia 13 ☎ 55/5542-6198 🕐 Closed Mon. 💲 $ 🚇 Metro: Zócalo

MUSEO S.H.C.P.

The first-floor galleries are a bit barren and disappointing, but those on the second floor of this former archbishop's palace are more interesting. These include the "paid-in-kind" collection, acquired through the Mexican system that allows artists to pay income tax in artwork rather than pesos, as well as "hereditary estates" handed down to artists' heirs.
🅰 179 G3 ✉ Antiguo Palacio del Arzobispado, Moneda 4 ☎ 55/5228-1241
💲 $ 🚇 Metro: Zócalo

PLAZA DE GARIBALDI

Five blocks north of the Palacio de Bellas Artes, elegantly uniformed mariachi bands arrive each evening to vie for customers in this famous square. There's no shortage of local color, including taco vendors and pickpockets. Bars and small restaurants facing the plaza run the gamut from cantinas full of maudlin men crooning over a bottle of tequila to live-music dance clubs. It's especially spirited on November 22, the feast day of Santa Cecilia, patron saint of music, with fireworks, folk dancing, food, crafts, and, of course, mariachis.
🅰 179 F4 ✉ Av. Lazaro Cardenas at Honduras 🚇 Metro: Garibaldi

POLIFORUM CULTURAL SIQUEIROS

David Alfaro Siqueiros's "The March of Humanity" covers both exterior and interior surfaces of this 12-sided structure, built specifically for the project. On Saturday and Sunday afternoons, a Spanish-language sound-and-light show enhances the relief and sculptural elements of the unusual mural. (English-speaking groups are accommodated by appointment.) The space doubles as a venue for cultural events.
🅰 178 D1 ✉ Insurgentes Sur 701 at Filadelfia ☎ 55/5536-4520 💲 $ 🚇 Metro: Chilpancingo

SALA DE ARTE PÚBLICO SIQUEIROS

Just before his death, Siqueiros donated his home and its contents to the government, which now displays his finished and unfinished work, including drawings, paintings, sketches, and the mural "Maternity." A second-floor gallery exhibits changing contemporary art.
🅰 178 A2 ✉ Tres Picos 29, Col. Polanco
☎ 55/5545-5952 🕐 Closed Mon. 💲 $
🚇 Metro: Auditorio ■

With its missions and cathedrals, haciendas, archaeological ruins, and markets where Otomí and Náhuatl languages are still spoken, the small central region embodies pre-Cortesian, colonial, and post-Revolutionary Mexico.

Around Mexico City

An amazing baroque interior

Around Mexico City

WITH FEW EXCEPTIONS, THE MAJOR CITIES OF THE CENTRAL PLATEAU, surrounding the Valle de Anáhuac (Valley of Mexico), represent pre-Aztec centers. At the time of the Spanish Conquest they were held in the vicelike grip of the Triple Alliance—Tenochtitlán, Texcoco, and Tlacopan. Cuernavaca was an exclusive spa for the Aztec nobility, and it still attracts the rich and famous, who come on weekends and holidays to their second homes. Priests and nobility made pilgrimages to Teotihuacán, as we do today, to marvel at an ancient culture whose origins remain mired in mystery.

Civilization flourished in the river valleys, plains, and semitropical lowlands surrounding the crescent-shaped Valley of Mexico. So close to the defeated Tenochtitlán and the new capital, Mexico City, the central plateau was promptly carved up by the Spanish Crown. Among the cities Hernán Cortés received from King Carlos V of Spain were Toluca and Cuernavaca, today capitals of México and Morelos states. As a reward for being Spain's indispensable allies during the Aztec campaign and beyond, Tlaxcala enjoyed privileges denied the majority of the conquered peoples.

Unlike the Maya, whose great culture was nearly 500 years past its prime at the time of Spanish Conquest, and the nomadic northern tribes, indigenous culture in the central plateau was in full flower in the 16th century. Skilled indigenous artisans and European craftsmen together produced some of Mexico's most intriguing architecture. Inspired by their desire to convert the natives and glorify God, the Spanish built magnificent cathedrals and far-flung mission churches; Indian craftsmen enthusiastically embraced the baroque style. In Puebla, gilded and

Tepoztlán's isolated valley setting made it a popular retreat in the 1960s and '70s.

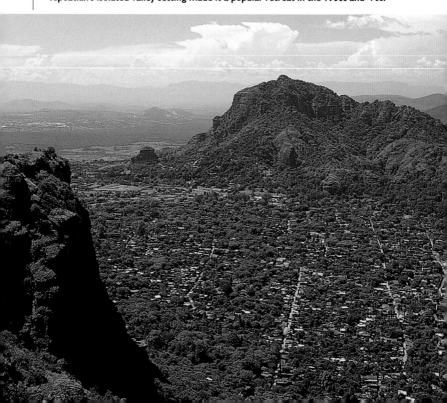

polychrome sculpted plasterwork combined with Talavera tiles adorn myriad churches and private palaces to create an exuberant architecture unique to the state. The monastery murals at Ixmiquilpan, Hidalgo, have unusual native imagery: jaguars, Aztec eagles clutching snakes, and violent battle scenes among native warriors.

Forming a tight circle around Mexico City, the states of Hidalgo, Tlaxcala, Puebla, Morelos, and México are today influenced by their proximity to the capital. Now highly industrialized, the state of México surrounds the Federal District on three sides and has benefited from the accessibility to banks,

transportation, and the powers-that-be. Most of the capital cities of these states are industrialized, yet preserve outstanding churches and secular colonial buildings. ■

Area of map detail

Cuernavaca

🗺 213 B2

Visitor information

✉ Av. Morelos Sur 187, Colonia Las Palmas

☎ 777/314-3872

Cuernavaca

SINCE PRE-HISPANIC TIMES CUERNAVACA (FROM THE Náhuatl name Cuauhnáhuac, meaning "wooded valley") has been much admired. Its temperate climate and generous rainfall make it well suited for growing both agricultural products and ornamental plants. Mexican nobility vacationed here, and Hernán Cortés built himself a palace. For centuries, Cuernavaca has provided a second home for Mexican and international diplomats, politicians, musicians, and other elite. In early April, the Flower Fair beckons with music and garden shows, while outside the city, rivers and more than 40 spas and water parks lure those looking to commune further with nature.

The former palace of Hernán Cortés, built in the 16th century

In spring, Cuernavaca blossoms—even if the *guayaba* trees that gave natives their nickname, *guayabos,* are now few and far between. In the large plaza, people stroll past the plain millennium clock, installed for the year 2000 but already looking half a century old. On the east side, the formidable **Palacio de Cortés** (*Av. Leyva 100, closed Mon.*) has interior murals by Diego Rivera. Inside the palace is the **Museo Cuauhnáhuac** (*tel 777/312-8171, $*), which has displays of colonial art as well as archaeological and historical exhibits.

The **Ex-Convento de la Asunción** (*Av. Morelos at Hidalgo*) has a huge atrium designed to hold many potential Indian converts. Its ornate altar-

pieces were removed in 1959 by reformist priest Sergio Méndez Arce, unveiling wall murals of Mexican San Felipe de Jesús's martyrdom in Japan. Further evidence of the "new Catholicism" is seen in its modern stained-glass windows, a resurrected Christ (instead of a crucifix), and the popular **mariachi mass,** held Sunday mornings at 8.

Not to be missed is the **Museo Robert Brady** (*Nezahualcóyotl 4, tel 777/318-8554, closed Mon., $*), home of the wealthy American collector and expatriate of the same name. Throughout this fabulous house are a thousand pieces of fine and folk art from Mexico and throughout the world, placed in inspired juxtaposition.

Stroll through the landscaped grounds of **Jardín Borda** (*Av. Morelos at Hidalgo, tel 777/318-1050, closed Mon., $*), established by the Taxco mining tycoon José de la Borda. The mansion here later became the summer home of Emperor Maximilian. Visit the site museum (*$*), with exhibits from the French emperor's reign, or listen to music in the garden café during the evening. For more live entertainment, head for the hipper cafés and cantinas around **Plazuela del Zacate** (*Galeana at Hidalgo*). ∎

Xochicalco

Xochicalco

▲ 213 B2

✉ 24 miles (38 km) south of Cuernavaca via Highway 95

☎ 737/374-3090

$ $

FROM ITS PERCH ON A SERIES OF LOW TERRACED HILLS, the "Place of the House of Flowers" archaeological site covers 60 acres (25 ha), most of which are still unexcavated. The fortified city flourished between A.D. 700 and 900, and is considered by some a bridge between the Toltec civilization established in Tula in the tenth century and the Teotihuacán civilization, which disappeared abruptly around A.D. 700. The ruins weren't discovered until the Mexican Revolution, when according to legend, General Emiliano Zapata noticed bullets ricocheting off the grassy hill they were defending. Upon investigation, the "hill" turned out to be a buried pyramid.

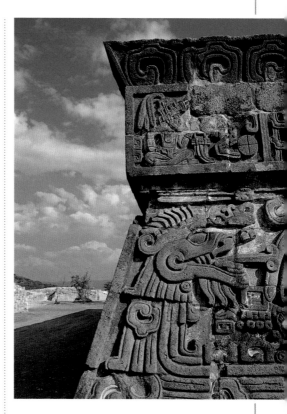

The site spreads down from its high point at the **Plaza Ceremonial.** Facing this sacred square is Xochicalco's most important structure, the **Templo de Quetzalcóatl,** richly adorned in bas-relief carvings of the god. Within the snakes' coils is the repeated figure of a cross-legged personage resembling a Maya priest named 9 Wind, the birth date of Quetzalcóatl. Different types of calendars carved on the pyramid's walls have led to speculation that Zapotec, Maya, and Gulf Coast tribes met together at Xochicalco to discuss astronomy or to synchronize their calendars.

Below, the **Plaza de la Estela de Dos Glifos** (Two Glyph Stelae Square) was a large grassy meeting place with a stele carved with the date 10 Sugarcane 9 Reptile Eye. Still farther down the hill, the I-shaped ball court is considered to be one of the first built on the central plateau and has been influenced by Maya design.

An unusual feature at the site is the underground observatory, where twice a year (May 14–15 and July 28–29), when the sun is at its zenith, a hexagonal shaft of light appears on the floor of the cave. The light enters through a hole bored 26 feet (8 m) through solid rock. There are also the ruins of a cistern for storing water and a *temescal* steam bath.

The site museum (signed in Spanish only) contains many archaeological pieces, including a sun god statue, pottery, and examples of hieroglyphic writings. ■

Carvings of Quetzalcóatl, the Feathered Serpent, cover this temple.

Ruta del Volcán Popocatépetl drive

The Franciscan, Dominicans, and Augustinians divided up the area that now forms tiny Morelos state. Heading clockwise from Cuernavaca lies a necklace of Dominican and Augustinian monasteries established soon after the Conquest. This route through the foothill valleys is especially dramatic in the winter months, when snowcapped Popocatépetl and slumbering Iztaccíhuatl appear, giving the route its nickname, "the Volcano Monasteries."

Murals are used to brighten up the facades of many modern Mexican buildings.

Cuernavaca's **Ex-Convento de la Asunción** ❶ (see p. 214), dedicated to the Virgin of the Assumption, is Franciscan. State and federal grants have funded restoration of many religious paintings, some by renowned colonial artists.

From Cuernavaca, drive about 16 miles (26 km) east on Hwy. 95D to Hwy. 115. Follow Hwy. 115 in the direction of Cuautla to **Tepoztlán** ❷, where you can buy handicrafts and *amate* (bark paper) at the weekend market. In 1550 Dominican friars ousted the god of pulque, Ometochtli, from his temple and used the stones to build the **Convento**

de Nuestra Señora de la Natividad ❸, located on the town's main plaza. Today the town blends Christian and pre-Hispanic rituals, especially during Mardi Gras and the celebration of Our Lady of the Nativity on September 7.

Around the church's plateresque doorway are symbols of the Virgin: the sun, moon, and eight-pointed stars. Dominican symbols include the foliated cross, fleur-de-lis, and torch-bearing dogs. From the cloister, there are views of the seamed hills of the Sierra Tepozteca, where remnants of a pre-Hispanic pyramid, **Tepozteco,** can be reached after an hour's hike.

Continue about 20 miles (32 km) toward Cuautla to **Oaxtepec** ❹ (tel 735/358-0101), once a retreat for the lords of Xochimilco and the Emperor Moctezuma, and now home to one of the state's largest water parks. Some historians call it "Tenochtitlán's granary," as its orchards and fields were an important source of food for the Aztec capital. Oaxtepec's 16th-century **Convento de Santo Domingo** is surrounded by ancient willows, jacarandas, and *amate* and rubber trees. Throughout the adjoining monastery you will see monochrome paintings of Dominican saints.

From Oaxtepec, head north on Hwy. 142 for about 6 miles (10 km) to **Tlayacapan** ❺ ($), whose **Convento de San Juan Bautista** is characterized by its simplicity. The church's pale stone-and-white-stucco facade is crowned with an *espadaña*, a row of small bells in individual arches. Within the refectory museum are a half-dozen wooden, polychrome statues, and within the private chapel there are paintings of Augustinian saints, friars, and the four Evangelists.

Drive east on Hwy. 2 for 6 miles (10 km) past basalt bluffs to the neglected **Convento de Totolapan.** This Augustinian monastery was once virtually covered in paintings. Continue on the same road, which curves south

Detail above doorway, Tepoztlán

Tepozteco

MORELOS

Convento de Nuestra Señora de la Natividad

Tepoztlán

Sierra Tepozteca

PARQUE NACIONAL EL TEPOZTECO

Convento de San Juan Bautista

Yautepec

Tlayacapan

Convento de Totolapan

Oaxtepec

Convento de Santo Domingo

Convento de Atlatlahuacan

Cuautla

Convento de San Juan Bautista

Cuautla

Yecapixtla

Tepoztlán festival fare

to the **Convento de Atlatlahuacan,** about 9 miles (14 km). The former Augustinian monastery is enclosed by a huge, crenelated atrium; the cloister contains earth-tone portrayals of early saints. Dedicated to St. Matthew, the church has a blue nave full of saints and folk altars tucked in candlelit niches.

Continue south on Hwy. 2, turning right onto Hwy. 115 toward Cuautla, and left after about 3½ miles (6 km) onto Hwy. 10 to **Yecapixtla** 6. A slave market during pre-Hispanic times, this town later became a regional Augustinian priory. At the back of the **Convento de San Juan Bautista** stands Cortés's Palace, where the conqueror sometimes stayed. The church's renaissance facade has a rose window and a plateresque portal. Inside,

🅰 See also area map p. 213 B2
▶ Cuernavaca
↔ 80 miles (128 km)
🕐 One day
▶ Cuernavaca

NOT TO BE MISSED
• Tepoztlán
• Tlayacapan
• Yecapixtla

note the Augustinian insignia of the ornate Isabelline pulpit. Head back to Hwy. 115, continue south, and then turn west on Hwy. 160 to return the 39 miles (62 km) to Cuernavaca. ■

In & around Cholula

CHOLULA ("PLACE OF FLIGHT") IS THOUGHT TO HAVE BEEN established by supporters of Quetzalcóatl fleeing religious persecution in Tula. The god-king Quetzalcóatl may have stopped here as well, leaving a cult of devoted followers before sailing east on a raft of snakes, or rising phoenix-like from a self-immolation, according to different legends. Today home to the internationally oriented Universidad de las Américas, Cholula and surrounding villages have some of Mexico's most stunning churches. Forced to abandon the Quetzalcóatl cult by the Spanish, indigenous artisans built inspired churches. Combining pre-Hispanic and European motifs and techniques, they created an eloquent, irrepressible baroque.

**Talavera tiles
cover the facade
of the church at
Acatepec.**

At the dawn of the 16th century, Cholula was a powerful city and an important commercial center under the dominion of the Aztecs. Despite the advice of his Tlaxcala Indian guides, Hernán Cortés stopped here for ten days during his initial march to Tenochtitlán. Upon learning of a plan to slaughter and sacrifice his troops, he ordered a massacre of soldiers and citizens after delivering a speech discouraging idolatry and human sacrifice. The Cholulans' resounding defeat reinforced Cortés's image as an all-seeing superior being.

Within two years the Aztec capital had been conquered, and the Spaniards set about reinventing Cholula, replacing Quetzalcóatl's temples with Christian churches. Abandoned since late Postclassic times, Mesoamerica's largest pyramid, the **Gran Pirámide de Tepanapa** *(Av. Morelos at Calle 6 Norte, $),* was probably just too big to dismantle. The huge structure of sun-dried adobe bricks was constructed in distinct phases over a 1,000-year period (roughly 300 B.C. to A.D. 700).

Unlike other archaeological sites, Tepanapa is accessed exclusively through a 5-mile (8 km) honeycomb of tunnels. Enter on your own, or hire a guide *($$–$$$)* at

the entrance. A small site museum displays period pottery and a cutaway model showing the different layers of the pyramid. Perched on top of the 230-foot (70 m) structure is the **Iglesia de Nuestra Señora de los Remedios.** On a clear day, the late 16th-century church affords a superb view of the city and of Popocatépetl and Iztaccíhuatl volcanoes.

Brightly painted restaurants and shops surround Cholula's large **zócalo**, or main square *(Blvd. Miguel Alemán at Morelos),* some tucked into the arcade on the west side. On the east side lies the entrance to the **Convento San Gabriel** *(Calle 2 Norte s/n),* built by the Franciscans on the site of a pre-Hispanic temple. Inside the monastery is the fascinating **Capilla Real**—modeled after the great mosque of Córdoba, Spain—a maze of columns and colonnades topped by 49 domes. It is currently closed owing to earthquake damage.

Just a few miles south of Cholula are two famous "Indian baroque" churches, unique for their blend of European and native elements. Said to have been designed and executed entirely by native people, the church at **Santa María Tonantzintla** is one of the hemisphere's most astonishing artistic accomplishments. Every inch of the interior is covered in polychrome and gilded, sculpted plaster ornamentation: cherubs (some with Indian faces), flowers, fruit, vines, saints, rosettes, and scrolls. On columns on either side of the main altar, look for mirrors representing respectively wisdom, morality, truth, and humanity.

Less than a mile (1.5 km) farther south is the astonishing **San Francisco Acatepec** church, its fabulous tiled facade a breathtaking barrage of bright yellow, blue-and-white flowered, green, and unglazed brick-red tiles.

Another happy marriage of Old and New World cultures can be found in the town of **Chipilo,** a few miles beyond Acatepec. Many of the townspeople whose great-great-grandparents emigrated from Venice have retained some of their Italian recipes and traditions, including making homemade sausages and dairy products. Today the town is known for its rustic handmade furniture.

Less than 10 miles (16 km) to the northwest of Cholula, **Huejotzingo** is home to an ancient **Convento Franciscano** *(Closed Mon., $)* built between 1529 and 1570. See the cloister, kitchen, and charming chapel, and in the adjoining church admire the beautiful plateresque altar. Huejotzingo is known for its wool *sarapes* (blankets), sold at the outdoor Saturday market, and for its boisterous carnival celebrations. ■

Nuestra Señora de los Remedios church sits upon the Gran Pirámide de Tepanapa, the focal point of the Cholula archaeological site, with Popocatépetl volcano rising beyond.

Popocatépetl & Iztaccíhuatl

Less than 50 miles (80 km) southeast of Mexico City tower active Popocatépetl and its slumbering companion, Iztaccíhuatl. At 17,802 feet (5,426 m) and 17,343 feet (5,286 m) respectively, these geologic giants are the second- and third-highest mountains in Mexico, outpeaked only by Pico de Orizaba, in Veracruz (see p. 244). Popocatépetl has erupted at least 36 times, the last major event being in A.D. 820. It has been the subject of legends and the object of worship since Quetzalcóatl reigned, but it is its recent activity that concerns geologists and the villagers living nearby.

Although Popo and Izta (as they are affectionately called) are both classified as stratovolcanoes, Izta has long been dormant and has no crater. Popo, on the other hand, began to rumble and quake in 1993, with belches and explosions of gas, ash, and rocks. The next year, 25,000 people were evacuated from vulnerable villages when ash and red-hot rocks began to rain down its snowy slopes.

According to legend, Popoca was a poor but valiant youth in love with Mixtli, the lovely daughter of Tizoc, lord of Mexico. Popoca went to battle in hopes of gaining the rank of Caballero Aguila, or Eagle Warrior, thus meriting marriage to the princess. Imagining her beloved's death and her own marriage to the

most ambitious and cruel of her suitors, Mixtli killed herself. Returning triumphant from battle and finding his lover dead, Popoca laid the princess's body atop a high mountain, hoping the snow would revive her. He remained by her side with his smoldering torch, and so the pair gave shape to Popocatépetl (Smoking Mountain) and Iztaccíhuatl (Sleeping Woman).

More than just a fairy tale, Popocatépetl and Iztaccíhuatl figure in modern-day religious ritual. Many villagers consider them to be living beings—simultaneously mountains, humans, and gods. They refer to the pair as "don Gregorio and doña Rosita," who bring rain and fertility to their fields. For the corn-planting season, local rainmakers conduct prayers at sacred sites on both volcanoes, one within a mile (1.6 km) of Popo's crater.

However, Popo is now closed to mountaineers. Still open is the technically more challenging Iztaccíhuatl. Both are accessible from Paso de Cortés, 10½ miles (17 km) off Highway 115. The pass is named for the Spanish conquistador, who is said to have first glimpsed the city of Tenochtitlán from here. ■

Above: Beyond a farmer's cornfields loom Popocatépetl (left) and Iztaccíhuatl.
Right: More than 20 million people live within 50 miles (80 km) of active Popo.

Poblanos demonstrate pride in both city and country during an annual Cinco de Mayo parade.

Puebla

THE CITY OF PUEBLA WAS ESTABLISHED IN 1531 IN A GREEN valley surrounded by three of Mexico's tallest volcanoes—Pico de Orizaba, Popocatépetl, and Iztaccíhuatl. Located within the geologically active "Ring of Fire," the region is periodically rocked by earthquakes; a 1999 quake damaged some of Puebla's precious historic buildings and gorgeous churches, now being restored.

Puebla
213 C2
Visitor information
✉ 5ta Calle Oriente 3
☎ 222/246-2044

Although established as a center of agriculture and trade, Puebla soon diversified to manufacture textiles, glass, and ceramics. To the Moorish-inspired motifs in blue and white imported from Talavera, Spain, indigenous and mestizo craftsmen added earthy reds, oranges, and greens, creating a unique ceramic tradition. Tiles, used in conjunction with effusively carved plasterwork (often painted and gilded) and other baroque ornamentation, created a unique architectural style seen throughout the capital and surrounding towns.

It's not just the architecture of Puebla that overwhelms the senses. Poblano chefs use the huge variety of chilies grown in the region to create many distinctive recipes.

Traditionally prepared around Independence Day, *chiles en nogada* are poblano peppers stuffed with a sweet meat mixture, smothered in walnut cream sauce, and garnished with pomegranate seeds. Prepared using bitter chocolate, nuts, sesame seeds, and chilies, *mole poblano* is a complex sauce served over turkey, chicken, or pork.

The sunny yellow kitchen where mole was allegedly first concocted can be found in the **Ex-Convento de Santa Rosa,** a nunnery confiscated during the Reform and now housing the **Museo de Arte Popular Poblano** (*Calle 14 Poniente at 3 Norte, tel 222/232-9240, closed Mon., $*). The museum showcases folk crafts from throughout the state, including masks and inlaid furniture. In the **Ex-Convento de Santa Mónica,** the Museo de Arte Religioso *(18 Poniente 103, tel 222/232-0178, closed Mon., $,)* shows, in addition to paintings and other more traditional exhibits, an unusual display: the preserved heart of the convent's founder.

Surrounding the shady **Plaza Principal** *(Av. A. Camacho between 2 Sur & 16 de Septiembre)* are many impressive buildings, including the French neoclassic-style **Palacio Municipal** *(Portal Hidalgo 14, tel 222/246-1899)*. At the plaza's northeast corner, the redbrick, sculpted-plaster, and tile facade of the **Casa de los Muñecos** is as fascinating as the colonial paintings within the **Museo Universitario** *(2 Norte 2, tel 222/246-2899, closed Mon., $)*.

Opposite is the impressive **Catedral de la Inmaculada Concepción** *(16 de Septiembre at 4 Oriente, tel 222/232-2316)*, with its severe twin towers and massive interior containing five naves and 14 side chapels. The main altar, by colonial master Manuel Tolsá, is of gold, marble, and smoky onyx.

Behind the cathedral, the **Casa de la Cultura** *(5 Oriente 5, tel 222/232-4647, $)* comprises a theater, art galleries, and a concert hall. Situated inside the House of Culture is the **Biblioteca Palafoxiana,** named for the Bishop Palafox, who donated his large personal library. The collection now numbers more than 40,000 tomes. Another local philanthropist donated the pre-Colombian artifacts, European and American colonial art, and 20th-century Mexican art found at the **Museo Amparo** *(Calle 2 Sur 708 at Av. 9 Oriente, tel 222/246-4646, closed Tues., $)*.

North of the cathedral, the **Iglesia de Santo Domingo** *(5 de Mayo at 4 Poniente, tel*

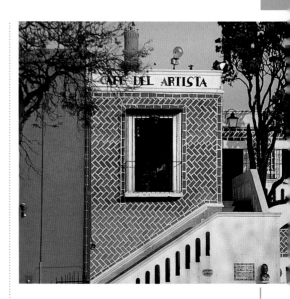

222/242-3643) houses the city's most ornate chapel. Dedicated to Our Lady of the Rosary, the **Capilla del Rosario** is a mind-bending baroque surfeit of decorated gilt plasterwork. A few doors down, the **Museo Bello y Zetina** *(5 de Mayo 409 at 6 Oriente, tel 222/232-4720, closed Mon.)*, the lavishly decorated former home of one of Puebla's wealthy families, is a good example of secular opulence.

The 18th-century **Casa del Alfeñique** *(4 Oriente 416 at 6 Norte, tel 222/241-4296, closed Mon., $)*—named for the similarity of its ornately carved plaster facade to a popular sugar candy of the same name—houses a museum of colonial and pre-Hispanic artifacts. In the same neighborhood, crafts stalls sell *alfeñique* and other typical candies, in addition to factory-made Talavera pottery, at **El Parián** *(2 Oriente & 6 Norte)*, on the old **Plaza San Roque.** You can buy local artwork from workshops at the **Barrio del Artista** *(6 Oriente & 6 Norte)* and **Callejón de los Sapos** *(Calle 4 Sur near Av. 7 Oriente)*, two lively shopping districts. ■

Brickwork as well as decorative tiles embellish Puebla facades.

Tlaxcala & Cacaxtla

Tlaxcala

🅰 213 C2

**Visitor
information**

✉ Av. Juárez 18 at
Lardizábal

☎ 246/465-0900,
ext. 7

MOST PEOPLE VISIT TLAXCALA TO SEE THE FABULOUS PRE-
Hispanic murals at Cacaxtla. But murals aside, Tlaxcala is a lively
and historic town. Surrounding the fountain-filled plaza, patio
restaurants serve regional specialties under the arched colonnade.
Shops sell folk art, including carved wooden canes, striped sarapes,
and colorful carnival masks used throughout the region. Proud of
both its Spanish and indigenous ancestry, the town's motto is
"Heritage of Two Cultures."

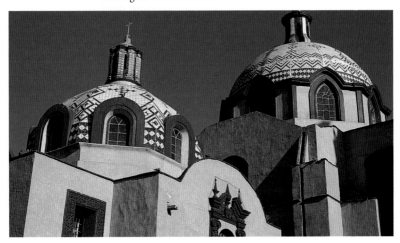

Tlaxcala's colorful
parish church of
San José

Both the tiny state and its
capital city are named for the
Tlaxcaltecans, whose hatred for the
Aztecs made them Hernán Cortés's
trusted Indian allies. Relatively
well treated for their loyalty, the
Tlaxcaltecans voluntarily resettled
in places as far-flung as Santa Fe,
New Mexico, and San Cristóbal de
las Casas, Chiapas, to aid convert-
ing reluctant indigenous groups.

Tlaxcala boasts the first permanent church in New Spain. The
Franciscan monastery **Ex-
convento de la Asunción,** at
Plaza Xicotencatl, was built from
the stones of a pyramid to the rain
god Tláloc. The sacristy holds the
baptismal font where the four lords
of Tlaxcala were baptized before
Cortés marched on Tenochtitlán;
the cloister now houses the **Museo**

Regional de Tlaxcala *(tel
246/462-0262, closed Mon., $)*, with
pre-Hispanic and colonial artifacts
and paintings.

Many of the 16th-century
buildings surrounding **Plaza de la
Constitución** preserve the lower
portions of their original facades,
giving the square a historic uniformity. On the northwest corner, the
Parroquia de San José *(tel
246/462-1106)* has been decorated
in brick and Talavera tiles after several remodels. The brick and rococo
plaster **Palacio de Gobierno**
(tel 246/465-0900) graces the plaza's
north side. Throughout the state
government building's interior,
complex murals describe the city's
indigenous roots and historical
events. The **Museo de Artes y
Tradiciones Populares** *(Emilio*

Sánchez Piedras 1, tel 246/462-2337, closed Mon., $) shows samples of pulque (fermented cactus liquor) and regional weaving and masks, and has demonstrations of how they are made.

On the east side of town, the 18th-century **Basílica de Nuestra Señora de Ocotlán** *(Pocito de Aqua Santa, Carr. a Santa Ana Chiautempan, tel 246/462-1073)* was built at the site of several miraculous appearances of the Virgin Mary within a pine forest *(ocotlán)*. The baroque sanctuary's highly ornate portal and twin bell towers are elaborately carved in white plaster, but even more stunning is the elaborate interior, which took indigenous artist Francisco Tlayotehuanitzin more than 20 years to complete. The octagonal **Camarín de la Virgen** (Virgin's Dressing Room) is completely engulfed in gilded and polychrome angels, saints, flowers, and garlands. At nearby **Capilla del Pocito de Agua Santa** (Chapel of the Holy Spring), pilgrims purchase red-clay vessels for carrying off some of the site's sacred water.

The ruins of a fortified city at **Cacaxtla,** 12 miles (19 km) southwest of Tlaxcala *(tel 246/416-0000, $)*, contain what are arguably Mexico's most important pre-Hispanic murals, discovered only in 1975. Natural pigments mixed with nopal cactus gel were used to paint vivid scenes in blue, red, yellow, black, and white. A combination of Classic lowland Maya painting style and non-Maya hieroglyphics led scholars to believe the murals were painted by Gulf Coast émigrés, the Olmeca-Xicalanca. This group of warrior-merchants flourished between the mid-seventh and tenth centuries, concurring with the demise of nearby Teotihuacán.

A huge structure the size of four football fields contains at least eight layers of construction. Throughout the enormous building, adobe walls, corridors, and open courtyards were covered in stucco and decorated with complex murals. The largest scene, about two thirds intact, depicts warriors dressed as jaguars, apparently in the act of sacrificing rival bird-warriors. Less bellicose murals show images related to trade and fertility.

Most tours to Cacaxtla stop at **Xochitécatl,** a mile (1.6 km) north of Cacaxtla *(Free with Cacaxtla admission)*, where pepper trees sprout on an unusual spiral pyramid of compacted sand covered in stone. Related to fertility, this structure may have been dedicated to the wind god Ehécatl. Both Cacaxtla and Xochitécatl have site museums. ■

Among the best preserved Mesoamerican murals are those at Cacaxtla. This detail shows a nearly life-size "bird-man."

Hidalgo state

THE SILVER AND GOLD MINES IN PACHUCA AND THE surrounding hills, worked since before the Spanish Conquest, have played out and been resuscitated or relocated several times. Yet mining still contributes significantly to the economy, augmented by the manufacture of textiles, cement, and other products. Streets and alleys wind up and down the hilly city, meeting at small plazas that are fronted by contemporary and neoclassic buildings. Like a microcosm of Mexico's heartland, tiny Hidalgo state—in which Pachuca lies—is a patchwork of pulque haciendas, arid plains, working and depleted mines, and 16th-century monasteries.

The old city of Pachuca radiates from the rather severe **Plaza de la Independencia** (Matamoros at Allende), surrounded by an uninspired mix of 20th-century buildings. Dominating the square is the neoclassic **Reloj Monumental,** an imposing clock tower with an eight-bell carillon. Built just prior to the Revolution, its marble statues represent Liberty, the Constitution, Reform, and Independence.

Southeast of the main plaza, the fortress-style **Templo y Ex-Convento de San Francisco** (Arista and Casasola, tel 771/715-2965) began life as a Franciscan church and monastery but has seen many uses over its more than 400-year history, including as stables and a jail. Today it houses the **Centro Cultural de Hidalgo;** the atrium and orchard have been converted to pretty plazas and gardens.

Within the former monastery is the **Teatro de la Ciudad,** built by the Spanish inventor of the "patio system" for amalgamizing silver using quicksilver. Free museums include the small **Museo Regional de Historia** (tel 771/714-3989, closed Mon.) and the **Museo de la Fotografía** (tel 771/714-3653, closed Mon.), with changing exhibits of historic photos from the adjoining **Fototeca Nacional.** The National Photographic Archives offers a reproduction service of its 900,000 images, many from the Mexican Revolution.

Pachuca is located at the northern extreme of the Valley of Mexico, just 56 miles (90 km) northeast of Mexico City. Beyond rises the Sierra Madre Oriental, and en route lies **Mineral Real del Monte,** 7 miles (11 km) northeast on Highway 105, a charming old mining town that has seen ups and downs over the centuries. After a violent miner's strike, the mine was sold to an English consortium, which went bankrupt 25 years later. During its brief tenure, the British firm used miners from Cornwall—who brought soccer and their traditional meat pies, or pasties (called *pastes* in Mexico), a delightful treat now adapted and filled with meat, tuna, potatoes, or sauteed peppers. The tombstones of the English buried in the town graveyard face Britain.

A few miles beyond and off Highway 105 lies **Huasca,** a charming town of cobblestone streets and brightly painted buildings. A smaller road leads from Mineral Real del Monte to the mining town of **Real del Chico** and the adjacent **Parque Nacional El Chico** (tel 771/715-0994), with well-marked hiking and mountain-

Pachuca
🄰 213 B3
Visitor information
✉ Av. Revolución 1300, Col. Periodistas
☎ 771/718-4489 or 771/718-4390

bike trails through pine, oak, and juniper forest. On weekends city-dwellers flee to the 6,670-acre (2,700 ha) park to fish, rock climb, or simply enjoy the mountain air. There are restaurants, paste shops, and a nice hotel; camping is permitted.

About a half-hour away, **Actopan,** 23 miles (37 km) north of Pachuca on Highway 85, celebrates its weekly market each Thursday. Right in the center of town, the **Templo y Convento San Nicolás** (*$*), begun by the Augustinians in 1548, is one of Mexico's most admired buildings. Note the well-proportioned plateresque facade and the barrel vaulting above the **capilla abierta** (open chapel), with its trompe l'oeil coffered ceiling.

Most remarkable, however, are the murals. Many are renditions of illustrations from medieval books vividly painted in blue, brown, ocher, and red. The Apocalypse scenes in the open chapel are among the finest in Mexico. Painted over in layers of whitewash after the Council of Trent—a church edict set forth in the 16th century banning profanity, nudity, and apocalyptic themes in sacred art—they have only recently been uncovered.

Throughout Hidalgo state are over a dozen important former monasteries, built in the 1600s near the largest Náhua and Otomí centers. The Franciscans produced more modest houses of worship in the west, while the Augustinians took the east and built more slowly and lavishly. (See pp. 216–17.) ■

Sunlight warms the pinnacles of El Chico National Park.

Teotihuacán
- 🗺 213 B3
- ✉ 30 miles (48 km) northeast of Mexico City
- ☎ 594/956-0276

Teotihuacán

RISING ABOVE A GOLD, GRASSY PLAIN TO THE NORTHEAST of Mexico City are the ruins of the first true metropolis in the Western Hemisphere. It outlived its contemporary, imperial Rome, and was the greatest city in the Americas until the Mexica (Aztecs) built Tenochtitlán nearly 700 years later. The Mexica elite made frequent pilgrimages to the ruins of Teotihuacán and gave the city its Náhuatl name, meaning "where men become gods."

Scholars today know very little about the people who constructed this magnificent city, or why they abandoned it just a few centuries after it reached its Golden Age, roughly A.D. 200 to 500. Theories include overpopulation, rampant disease, internal power struggles, and rebellion of the masses. Systematic burning of ceremonial buildings points to the purposeful destruction of the city.

At the height of its power, however, fine palaces and temples adorned with bas-relief sculptures and brilliant murals lined **Avenida de los Muertos** (Avenue of the Dead), a broad, straight avenue paved with volcanic stone, set with dazzling mica, and aligned with both the stars and terrestrial landmarks. Its leaders excelled in architecture and astronomy, and had a well-developed religious system. An extensive commercial network extending to the Petén region of Guatemala was probably initiated around the first century A.D.

Today, many of the ceremonial buildings lining Avenue of the Dead have been partially reconstructed, although without their colorful stucco facades. At its southern end stands **La Ciudadela,** the compound of plazas and temples that formed Teotihuacán's administrative and ceremonial center and also the principal secular royal palace for many generations of unknown kings. La Ciudadela is dominated by the **Templo de Quetzalcóatl.**

This temple honored the Plumed Serpent, worshiped as the god of war, water, the dawn, and agriculture. Although the building's lower level was originally entirely covered in fanged serpent sculptures, those on three sides were pulled down not long after its inauguration. The intact west wall is hugely impressive, with rows of stone serpent heads interspersed with images of Tláloc and feathered shells.

At the far extreme of the 2½-mile (4 km) avenue is the **Pirámide de la Luna** (Pyramid of the Moon), a royal funerary monument with tombs dating back to the first century A.D.; the oldest of these may be that of the founder of the royal dynasty. Just over a hundred tall, narrow steps lead to the summit, where you will be rewarded with a view of the arrow-straight Avenue of the Dead, sacred **Cerro Gordo** (Fat Hill) to the north, and lonely plains dotted with prickly-pear cacti and pepper trees. The pyramid has six layers of construction; in contrast, the main structures of the Pyramid of the Sun was built mostly during a single phase.

Smaller, related structures are symmetrically arranged on both sides of the Avenue of the Dead; the most impressive is the **Palacio de Quetzalpapálotl.** Within the building's rooms, open patios, and antechambers are some well-preserved murals. Square stone pillars in the interior patio are

An archaeologist cleans a mural at an apartment in the Teotihuacán barrio of La Ventilla.

decorated with low-relief sculptures of the building's namesake, the Feathered Butterfly, while the temple below it is adorned with a fascinating sequence of quetzals (looking more like parrots), sea shells, and split-tongued Tláloc masks.

Across the avenue, the **Pirámide del Sol** (Pyramid of the Sun), the third largest pyramid in the world, squats like an immense behemoth. Although its base is nearly as broad as that of the Great Pyramid at Giza, at 213 feet (65 m) tall it is less than half the height of the Egyptian pyramid. Underneath the tremendous structure winds a honeycomb of tunnels and caves, which the Aztecs considered the birthplace of the world. Although the four-level, 244-step pyramid has more than twice as many steps as the Pyramid of the Moon, it is slightly easier to climb as the steps are shorter. Thousands of people converge on the structure near dawn each spring equinox hoping to receive a supercharge of celestial energy.

In addition to its ceremonial and commercial functions, 8-square-mile (20 sq km) Teotihuacán was, at its apogee, home to approximately 175,000 people. Neighborhoods of one-story dwellings had shared patios and kitchens, with private apartments for each family. East of the Pyramid of the Sun, several restored apartment complexes with vivid if fractured murals can be visited. The most impressive are those at **Tepantitla**, whose mural depicting the rain god Tláloc in his paradise is re-created at the Museo Nacional de Antropología, in Mexico City (see pp. 198–201).

To get the most out of your visit, spend the preceding night at the Hotel Villas Arqueológicas Teotihuacán (book in advance; see p. 372) within the archaeological zone itself and take advantage of the site's 7 a.m. opening time. Otherwise, take a day trip from Mexico City by limo, bus, or licensed taxi. Near the Ciudadela entrance are a restaurant, a bar, and a warren of souvenir stalls, while the site museum and botanical gardens are located near the Pyramid of the Sun. ∎

While Europe stumbled through the Dark Ages, Teotihuacán's culture shone like a beacon around Mesoamerica.

Tepotzotlán

THE CHURCH AND FORMER SEMINARY AT TEPOTZOTLÁN,
two masterpieces of Mexican baroque overachievement, are reason
enough to visit this town, but also housed within the lavish complex
is perhaps the country's finest colonial art museum. Tepotzotlán
itself, with a population of 50,000 and less than an hour's drive north
of Mexico City, is a breath of fresh air after the congested capital.

Tepotzotlán
🅰 213 B3
**Visitor
information**
✉ Plaza Hidalgo 99
☎ 55/5876-2771

The first evangelists to arrive here
were Franciscans, soon replaced by
the Jesuits at the end of the 16th century. A generous bequest allowed the
order to build the **Seminario de
San Martín,** a seminary for young
indigenous noblemen, the **San
Francisco Javier** novitiate, and
a language school to teach priests
Náhuatl, Otomí, and Mazahua.

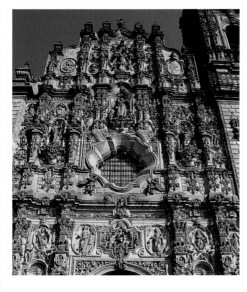

**Carvings of saints,
angels, and floral
and shell motifs
cover San
Francisco Javier's
limestone facade.**

The lovely **Iglesia de San
Francisco Javier** we see today is
the result of an intensive (and
expensive) remodel of the facade,
belfry, and altarpieces almost
immediately after the church was
completed. Imagine the distress of
the priest and generations of
indigenous craftsmen who had
constructed the magnificent edifice

when the Jesuits were suddenly
expelled from New Spain in 1767,
just after its completion.

Not even the complex
Churrigueresque facade of the
church prepares you for its excessive, impressive interior. Within the
church one gilded, intricately
carved altarpiece leads to the next;
there are five on each side in addition to the ebullient main altar
dedicated to St. Francis Xavier.

To the right of the nave are three
fascinating rooms. The **Casa de
Loreto** is a re-creation of the
home of the Virgin Mary, said to
have been miraculously transported
to Loreto, Italy, after the Muslims
invaded the Holy Land. The
Relicario de San José, richly
decorated in paintings and gold,
houses Jesuit relics. Last is the
octagonal **Camarín de la
Virgen,** the dazzling "dressing
room" of carved plaster reserved for
the statue of Our Lady of Loreto.

In the adjoining edifice, the
**Museo Nacional del
Virreinato** (tel 55/5876-2771,
closed Mon., $$) has a fantastic col-
lection of three centuries of colonial
and folk art: paintings, jewelry,
ecclesiastic accouterments, porce-
lain, ivory statuettes, and other trea-
sures. Don't miss the **Capilla
Domestic,** a chapel covered floor
to ceiling in gold leaf and carved
polychrome stucco. More museum
exhibits are located on the second
story; on the lower level are the
kitchen, pantry and cold room, tem-
porary exhibits, and the gift shop. ∎

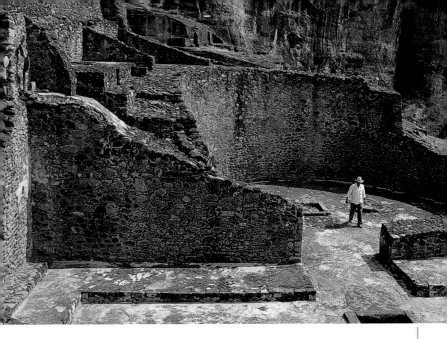

The ruined city of Malinalco was hewn from the living rock.

More places to visit around Mexico City

MONASTERY ROUTES

Two groups of Augustinian monasteries are found in eastern Hidalgo: one in the north, in the rugged Sierra Alta, the other on the dry plains called El Mesquital. Padres set out to convert the Otomí in the sierra in 1537, establishing **Atotonilco el Grande** (today in poor condition) and **Molango,** a rustic mission with a breathtaking valley view. The best of the group is the **Monasterio de los Santos Reyes** in Metztitlán. One of Mexico's finest fortress monasteries, it has the region's only surviving original high altarpiece. There is a wonderful view of the subtropical river valley from the terraced atrium, said to be built on an ancient temple to the moon. The town's name means "moon in the middle."

The plains group consists of **Actopan** (see p. 227), **Epazoyucan,** and **Ixmiquilpan.** Built on a hill associated with the rain god, Tláloc, Epazoyucan is best known for its magnificent 16th-century frescoes. Ixmiquilpan's murals are unique for their many vivid battle scenes and unrestrained indigenous imagery and iconography.

Just outside the ruins at Teotihuacán is **Acolman,** built from the stones of a temple to Quetzalcóatl and noted for its fine plateresque facade.

MALINALCO

Subjugated by the Mexica, or Aztecs, just 50 years before the Spanish Conquest, Malinalco *(Closed Mon., $)* is a ceremonial center carved into living rock. Its **main temple** is entered through the "mouth" of a large fanged serpent. Within is a circular room decorated with relief sculptures of eagle and jaguar motifs; it is believed to have been dedicated to warriors of those cults. It's 426 steps to the few restored buildings, but you're rewarded with a wonderful view over the town. The site is about a mile (1.5 km) from Malinalco ("place of grass blossom."), which is a popular weekend escape from Mexico City. Its **Iglesia del Divino Salvador** is its main attraction; in the adjacent Augustinian monastery are many fine frescoes in its cloister.

🗺 213 B2 **Visitor Infomation**
☎ 714/142-9420

TOLUCA

Toluca is Mexico's highest capital city, at 8,760 feet (2,670 m) above sea level. The city fell to the Aztecs in 1472 and was later presented to Hernán Cortés by King Carlos V. Today, it's a sprawling center of industry, and although its famous **Friday market** (which functions daily) has been relocated near the bus station, there are many museums and things to see centrally. Around the main square are buildings of native volcanic rock, arcaded shops and restaurants, and the **Cosmovitral Jardín Botánico** (*Lerdo de Tejada, Degollado, & Ignacio Rayón, closed Mon., $*), a botanical garden decorated in stained-glass panels. The **Museo José María Velasco** (*Av. Lerdo de Tejada 400, tel 722/213-2814, closed Mon.*) and the adjacent **Museo Felipe Gutiérrez** show the work of these 19th-century painters as well as contemporary artists. The **Centro Cultural Mexiquense** (*Reyes Herdes 302, $*) has a library, a bookstore, a gift shop, a restaurant, and museums of anthropology, modern art, and México state's varied folk art.

Metepec, on the outskirts of Toluca, is famous for its pottery, especially the elaborate

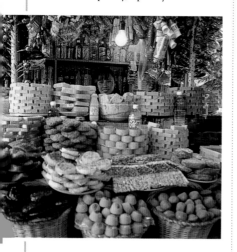

Sweets for sale at the Toluca market

"trees of life," portraying the fall from grace and decorated with Adam and Eve, angels, devils, and saints.

🅰 213 A2 **Visitor information** ✉ Urawa 100 at Paseo Tollocan ☎ 722/219-5190

TULA

Founded by the Spanish around a Franciscan monastery in the early 16th century, Tula was in a previous incarnation the pre-Hispanic capital of the Toltec culture, also called Tollan. Descendants of Chichimeca "barbarians" from the north established Tollan as the center of an important alliance of city-states. King Topoilzin, later associated with the god Quetzalcóatl (who abhorred human sacrifice), was forced to flee around A.D. 987 by enemies devoted to the fierce god Tezcatlipoca, or Smoking Mirror. Under the rule of the latter faction, Tula became a powerful city. It was once thought to have influenced or invaded Chichén Itzá because Chac Mool statues have been found there and because of the similarity of the sites' architectural styles and artifacts (see pp. 338–41). However, Tula is now considered to have been a link along an Itzá trade route stretching north to Paquimé and south to the Yucatán and Central America. At its height between A.D. 900 and 1150, it was destroyed by invaders from the north—most likely by the Chichimec tribes from which it was descended.

The archaeological site is perched on a promontory about a mile (1.5 km) outside of Tula. The excavated portion of the city—one of the largest in Early Postclassic Mesoamerica, covering 5.4 square miles (14 sq km)—consists of several ball courts, pyramids, and temples. The most important building excavated so far is **Pirámide B.** Its temple roof was supported by four tall pillars in the form of Toltec warriors, called Atlantes. (One of the four on site is a replica; the original is at the Museo Nacional de Antropología in Mexico City, see pp. 198–201) Bas-relief sculptures on the outer walls depict coyotes, jaguars, eagles devouring hearts, and composite creatures thought to represent Quetzalcóatl. At the site museum note the statue of Chac Mool, the reclining messenger god brought north from the Yucatán Peninsula.

🅰 213 B3 ☎ 771/718-4489

VALLE DEL BRAVO

About 90 miles (145 km) west of Mexico City, Valle del Bravo is a whitewashed, red-roofed town with popular restaurants and galleries surrounding the main plaza. The town, overlooking **Laguna Avandaro,** an artificial lake with watersports, is visited by wealthy *defeños* (Mexico City residents) escaping the capital on weekends and vacations.

🅰 213 A2 ■

N ot even the tropical heat can dampen the spirit of Mexico's Central Gulf coast inhabitants, whose ancestors conceived Mesoamerica's first true civilization. And the irrepressible jungle still smothers hundreds of archaeological sites.

Central Gulf coast

Jade figurines, found at La Venta, near Villahermosa

Central Gulf coast

RAIN FORESTS, RIVERS, AND RUINS ATTRACT ADVENTUROUS TRAVELERS TO
Tabasco and Veracruz, which form a thin curve of land cupping the Gulf of Mexico.
Geographically impressive, the Central Gulf coast contains vast lowland plains and, in
odd juxtaposition, the country's highest volcanic peak: snowcapped Pico de Orizaba. Its
people are as exuberant as its landscape, famed for their spicy cooking, lively dances, and
sentimental songs.

More than 40 rivers etch the landscape of
Veracruz, creating endless marshy swamps,
which frustrated the Spanish conquistadors in
the 16th century. The state's coastal plains
stretch 424 miles (684 km) along the oil-rich
Bay of Campeche, although its beaches are not
conducive to swimming and sunbathing.
Waterfalls streak the Tuxtla Mountains in the
north, where the Tempoal, Tamesí, and
Panuco Rivers meet, while the Tonalá River
creates a natural border between Veracruz
and Tabasco to the south. In both states, corn,
cacao, tobacco, vanilla, and coffee plantations
cover valleys and plateaus in a lush green
checkerboard that sometimes smothers
the ruins of ancient civilizations.

Though its hot, humid, and
often bug-ridden terrain is far
from welcoming, the gulf
coast has a rich pre-Hispanic
history. Mesoamerica's first

Shady Plaza de Armas is the main square in the coastal city of Veracruz.

known civilization, the Olmecs, flourished in this region between 1200 and 400 B.C. Many remote Olmec sites have been uncovered in Tabasco and Veracruz, but visitors needn't traverse the wilderness to explore ancient cultures. Villahermosa, in Tabasco, has two fine museums showcasing stelae, altars, and sculptures from Mesoamerica's Mother Culture, including giant stone heads and delicately incised ceremonial masks and ax-heads of fine jade.

In Veracruz, the country's second most important archaeology museum displays Olmec artifacts along with those of the Huastec and Totonac cultural groups, whose descendants still live throughout the state. El Tajín, in northern Veracruz, is one of Mexico's most intriguing archaeological sites, depicting what scholars call the "Classic Veracruz" style of art and architecture.

History buffs follow the Ruta de Cortés, an amazing journey of conquest that began with the Spaniard's arrival on the gulf coast in 1519 and ended two years later with the fall of Tenochtitlán. Adventure travelers struggle up steep trails to the summit of Pico de Orizaba, raft the Antigua and Filobobos Rivers, and explore the jungles around Lake Catemaco, while culture buffs are content to wander the port city of Veracruz, haunting the dungeons of San Juan de Ulúa, dancing in the lively Plaza de Armas, or feasting on seafood spiced with chilies and garlic. ■

El Tajín

📍 234 B4

Visitor information

✉ 10 miles (16 km) southwest of Papantla

☎ 28/41-85-00

💲 $

El Tajín

SURROUNDED BY EMERALD-GREEN HILLS, EL TAJÍN MUST have been resplendent at the height of its influence, when stuccoed pyramids painted bright blue and red surrounded the city's great plazas. Although abandoned for around 800 years, the uniformity and density of its construction, the fascinating bas-relief carvings, and the tropical setting still make this a breathtaking site, worth the effort to find.

The ball game served as a ceremonial staging ground of good versus evil, light versus darkness, in order to assure the continued prosperity of the initiating tribe. The 17 ball courts unearthed thus far at El Tajín are ample proof of the importance of sacrifice and

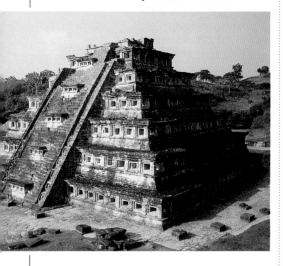

Small plaster figurines may have originally occupied the 365 niches of El Tajín's most outstanding pyramid.

auto-sacrifice (such as bloodletting) in this society.

Archaeologists aren't sure who built this ceremonial and residential city, which was established during the Early Classic period but reached its height toward the end of the Late Classic (A.D. 600–900). A uniformity of design and the repetition of the step-and-fret pattern characterize its architecture. Pyramids were built in the *talud y tablero* style found at Teotihuacán

(see pp. 228–29); in fact, a marked reciprocal influence is seen in these contemporary cities. This distinctive style consists of slanted walls *(taludes)* capped with overhanging vertical panels *(tableros)*. By about A.D. 1200 the site was abandoned, having been burned in an attack—possibly by Chichimecs (see p. 28) to the north.

The site was named by the Totonacs of northern Veracruz, who believe that the 12 ancient ones, or Tajín, live here and cause rain. The jungle-clad city was not discovered until the late 18th century. Restoration is ongoing; to date about 45 of the structures have been restored.

Near the entrance, the **Grupo Plaza del Arroyo** is made up of four stepped pyramids surrounding a large plaza. Beyond are four ball courts consisting of opposing walls on either side of a rectangular court. Although many of El Tajín's ball courts have bas-relief carvings, the most intricate and well-preserved panels are found at the **Juego de Pelota Sur.** Scenes show the god of death witnessing men preparing for war (the ball game), and the final outcome: a ritualistic death to the loser. Central panels on the east and west sides show the god of rain piercing his penis in a ritual self-sacrifice to produce the intoxicating drink pulque.

Just to the north, a large number of buildings are clustered around the magnificent **Pirámide**

de los Nichos, named for its 365 deeply recessed niches, one for each day of the solar calendar. This relatively stocky structure has a single steep stairway on the east side. Hidden within is a duplicate structure, although without the niches. The step-and-fret pattern at the top is repeated on many other structures, including **Edificios 5 and 12,** to the right and left, respectively.

Farther north, the buildings in the group called **Tajín Chico** were most likely the residences of elite citizens. Note the Maya arch on the south side of **Edificio A** and the remnants of murals on **Edificio C,** shaded by a palm-thatch roof. Edificio de las Columnas has carved columns with narrative scenes of rituals practiced by the ruling elite. Three of the columns from the "Building of the Columns" can be found in the modern site museum. Items typical of Classic Veracruz civilization, which predominated along the gulf coast plain, include finely carved ritual objects associated with the ball game: yokes (u-shaped stones, probably replicas of players' belts); *palmas* (objects that hung from the belt); and *hachas,* possibly used as scoring devices.

Adjacent to the museum, gift shop, and restaurant, the **Voladores de Papantla** perform a strange flying ritual for the benefit of visitors. Dressed in elaborate costumes—decorated with sequins, beads, and fringe, and with headdresses encrusted with mirrors and plastic flowers—five Totonac men climb to the top of a hundred-foot (30 m) pole. Inspired by the music of flute and drum performed by their leader, the other four men dive backwards, tied by a rope at the waist that is fastened at its other end to a frame at the top of the pole. With arms outstetched, each "flyer" completes precisely 13 revolutions before landing on the ground. The number of revolutions totals 52, the number of years in an important Mesoamerican religious cycle. The group usually performs at the request of a tour guide, or when enough people congregate. ■

Local men perform a ritualistic flying dance near Papantla's cathedral.

Xalapa

🅰 234 B3

Visitor information

✉ Enrique 14 (Palacio Municipal), north side of Parque Juárez

☎ 228/842-1200, ext. 3109

Xalapa & environs

XALAPA (ALSO SPELLED JALAPA) DESERVES ITS SOBRIQUET, the "Athens of Veracruz," for its culture if not its climate. At 4,680 feet (1,427 m) above sea level, Veracruz's hilly capital city has a bizarre climate of rain, sun, and fog. Once an important stagecoach stop between Mexico City and the port of Veracruz, modern Xalapa is one of the republic's most entertaining capitals. This university town offers art cafés, theater, dance troupes, a fine symphony orchestra, and a world-class anthropology museum. Set on a series of verdant terraces, it is filled with pretty parks and lakes, and the surrounding countryside is famous for its coffee beans and exotic flowers.

Xalapa's heart is **Parque Juárez** *(Enrique between Revolución & Clavijero),* a well-groomed garden overlooking the city but unfortunately surrounded by traffic. On clear mornings, there is a breathtaking view of snowcapped Pico de Orizaba, Mexico's highest mountain at 18,850 feet/5,747 m (see p. 244). Within the urban park, **El Agora** houses an art gallery, theater, and cinema; it's also the place to find out about the city's many cultural performances, including state orchestra and ballet folkloric shows. Across Calle Revolución, the 18th-century **catedral** is remarkable for its unusual sloping nave.

For most, the highlight of a stay in Xalapa is a visit to the **Museo de Antropología** (*Av. Xalapa s/n, tel 228/815-0920, closed Mon., $$*). This modern masterpiece, imitating the city's terraced cityscape, consists of nine staggered platforms surrounded by gardens. The collection is dedicated to Veracruz's three most influential indigenous cultures: the Huastec, Totonac, and Olmec—the latter considered the mother of Mesoamerican culture.

If the kids don't appreciate ancient culture, they may prefer a visit to **Museo Interactivo de Xalapa** (*Av. Murillo Vidal at Cárdenas, tel 228/813-8510, $*), with computers, interactive exhibits, a planetarium, and an IMAX theater (*$*). Closed 2–4 p.m.

Among the thousands of exhibits are massive stone heads carved by the Olmecs, a bone-filled burial ground, carved jaguars, were-jaguars (half-man, half-beast), murals, jade masks, and ritually deformed skulls. An enormous model re-creates the ruins of El Tajín (see pp. 236–37).

Five blocks southeast of Parque Juárez, large, circular **Parque los Berros** is named for the watercress that once grew here. This favorite gathering place of Xalapeños (people from Xalapa) for nearly two centuries is a quiet retreat from the city and has served as a backdrop for the novels of local author Sergio Galindo. Two blocks south, **La Zona de los Lagos** is Xalapa's most popular spot for a Sunday outing; paths meander around a series of lakes surrounded by a wooded canyon. Overlooking the lake at the western entrance to the park is the handsome, 19th-century **Centro Cultural de los Lagos** (*Paseo de los Lagos, tel 228/812-1299*), showing

Veracruz's oldest city, Xalapa, has an interesting mix of colonial and modern buildings.

changing exhibits of arts and crafts.

Venture outside the city to admire the lush countryside. (If you visit between November and March, bring a thick sweater and a raincoat—the light but constant rain known as *chipi-chipi* can be chilling.) The **Jardín Botánico Francisco Javier Clavijero** (*Antigua Carretera a Coatepec Km. 2.5, tel 228/842-1827, $*) is a beautiful botanical garden displaying more than 1,500 varieties of flora found throughout Veracruz state. It features a small arboretum, a large pond with aquatic plants, and a winding, shady path through a riot of greenery.

About 7 miles (12 km) farther south is rural **Coatepec,** famous for its orchids and coffee beans. Visit the **Invernadero María Cristina** (*Miguel Rebolledo 4, tel 228/816-0379*), a greenhouse blooming with orchids. Not far from the city center, hike or take a horseback ride in the 32-acre (13 ha) **Agualegre** (*Río La Marina s/n*), a water park with multiple swimming pools and a water slide for the kids.

Eleven miles (19 km) southwest of Xalapa is the **Cascada de Texolo,** a 132-foot (40 m) waterfall featured in the movie *Romancing the Stone* (1984). To get there, take a taxi to the charming and photogenic small town of **Xico** and then walk about 2 miles (3 km). A set meal is served daily at the site restaurant overlooking the impressive gorge.

Six miles (10 km) east of Xalapa lies **Hacienda Lencero** (*Carretera a Veracruz Km 10, tel 228/812-8500, closed Mon., $*), a 16th-century estate-turned-inn once owned by a Spanish conquistador named Lencero, and later by General Antonio López de Santa Anna (see p. 32). Now a museum of 19th-century furnishings, it has a pretty chapel and extensive gardens surrounded by oaks and other cool-climate trees, plus a small, spring-fed lake. ■

Fuerte de San Juan de Ulúa has been guarding the waters of Veracruz for more than 400 years.

Veracruz

VIBRANT AND VIVACIOUS VERACRUZ IS A BUSY PORT WITH a lively attitude, and visitors are either charmed or repelled by the city's extremes. The climate is hot and sultry, the beaches less than appealing, and the downtown a crowded, cacophonous urban jungle. But those who love Veracruz do so with a passion echoing that of sentimental Jarochos, as city-dwellers are called. They're entranced with the rhythm of marimbas, the scent of salt air, and the whirl of heel-stomping fandango dancers in the main plaza.

Veracruz
🚇 234 C3
Visitor information
✉ Zaragoza at Independencia, Palacio Municipal
☎ 229/932-7593

Prisoners at the **Fuerte de San Juan de Ulúa** (*Av. San Juan de Ulúa s/n, closed Mon., $*) had a less favorable view of the city. Built between 1535 and 1692, the gray-stone fortress served as a defense against pirates and the French and United States naval invasions of Mexico. But the fort is more famous as a brutal dungeon where disease, famine, and flooding awaited those who crossed the dreaded Puente de los Suspiros (Bridge of Sighs) into Ulúa's dank cells. For over three centuries religious and political prisoners were tortured here. In 1915, Venustiano Carranza claimed Ulúa as a presidential residence—surely a deterrent to anyone seeking

that office. The complex is now a museum well worth touring with a knowledgeable guide.

Shipyards and commercial docks line the waterfront east of Ulúa to the pleasant **Paseo del Malecón,** a seaside walkway reminiscent of the *malecón* in Havana. Visiting Cubans feel very much at home in Veracruz, where the *danzón,* a highly disciplined dance that originated in Cuba, is embraced with extraordinary fervor. In the evenings, both professionals and amateurs dance at the city's main square, **Plaza de Armas** (*Avs. Independencia, Zamora, Lerdo, & Zaragoza*).

The crowded plaza, shaded by

laurels, is a natural meeting place for city-dwellers. Musicians and dancers often perform on the plaza's center stage; visitors are welcome to join in the staccato steps of the *jarocho fandango* and the stylized, waltzlike moves of the danzón. Fronting the plaza are the 17th-century **Palacio Municipal** and the 18th-century **Catedral de Nuestra Señora de la Asunción,** topped with a tiled dome. Travelers immune to the noise of the never-ending street scene may want to take a room at one of several colonial-style hotels facing the plaza.

Marimba musicians in crisp, white, pleated shirts play at **Los Portales,** a block-long colonial-era building at the south side of the plaza. Elderly gentlemen sip cups of *lechero,* a frothy mix of coffee and steamed milk, at the wildly popular **Café los Portal** *(Av. Independencia at Zamora, tel 229/931-2759)* and clink their spoons against tall glasses to beckon waiters for refills. This coffee house was once home to **Gran Café de la Parroquia.** After a family feud (conducted with typical jarocho ferocity), la Parroquia moved near the malecón. Visit both places and order a lechero and *bambas* (local sweet rolls).

Several museums highlight the city's tumultuous history. The **Museo de la Ciudad** *(Zaragoza 397 at Esteban Morales, tel 229/989-8873, closed Tues., $)* devotes considerable space to Carnaval, celebrated since the mid-19th century. **Baluarte de Santiago** *(Francisco de Canal at Farías, tel 229/931-1059, closed Mon., $)* is the last remaining section of a series of stone walls and forts that once encircled the city. The **Museo Agustín Lara** *(Blvd. Ruíz Cortines s/n, Boca del Río, tel 229/937-0209, closed Mon., $)* honors one of Mexico's most famous musicians and the composer of

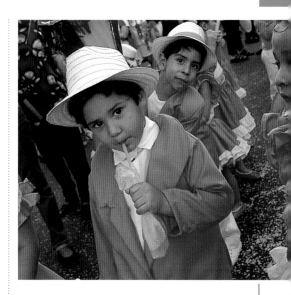

boleros, including "María Bonita" and "Veracruz," which are played over the museum's sound system.

The city's beaches are generally bleak. The best are located south of town at **Playa Mocambo** and **Boca del Río.** Those interested in local sea life might want to avoid swimming altogether in favor of a visit to the **Acuario Veracruz** *(Blvd. Manuel Ávila Camacho at Av. Xicoténcatl, tel 229/932-7984, $$).* A series of galleries displays different marine domains. The doughnut-shaped Main Gallery houses gulf coast species, while in the Freshwater Gallery are specimens from Mexico's lakes, lagoons, rivers, and estuaries. In the Reef Exhibit, seahorses and sea stars, eels, and octopuses cruise outcrops of slow-growing coral.

For a guided visit (via headset, in English or other languages), hop aboard a **Circuito Turístico** *(55/5133-2488 in Mexico City, $$$),* which also serves as transportation to the aquarium, Augustin Lara Museum, beaches, and downtown venues. You can get on and off more than once; board at the post office or any stop. ■

Young and old participate in Veracruz's spirited pre-Lenten Carnaval, the biggest and best in Mexico.

Drive: Arrival of the conquerors

Searching for a route to the East in the early 16th century, Spanish fleets from Cuba encountered instead a fascinating new land. Gifts of gold from friendly Indians were enough to incite future expeditions, and in 1519, 34-year-old Hernán Cortés led a third, historic voyage. Now wary, the Indians came prepared for battle, but the Spaniards' horses and superior weapons made up for their small numbers. Soon joining the Spanish ranks were a shipwrecked Spaniard and an Indian noblewoman who had been sold into slavery by her mother. Speaking Spanish, Mayan, and Náhuatl between them, this pair of interpreters was instrumental in the Spanish success.

Begin the drive in **Quiahuiztlán** ❶, 43 miles (70 km) north of Veracruz. Strategically placed atop Cerro de Bernal and terraced for defensive purposes, it was nonetheless invaded by the Toltecs and then the Aztecs. Quiahuiztlán's Totonac king was the first to make an alliance with Cortés. Today, much of the ruined city remains unexcavated. Most impressive for visitors are several dozen tombs, built in the style of miniature Aztec temples, which have yielded ceramic vessels decorated with geometric and animal motifs. On a clear day, you can see the cove where the Spanish ships anchored.

Head south along Hwy. 180 about 17 miles (27 km) to the ruins of **Cempoala** ❷, a prosperous city that amazed the Spaniards with its gleaming plaster palaces surrounded by gardens and orchards. Anxious to shrug off the yoke of their recently acquired Aztec overlords, this Totonac kingdom also allied with the Spaniards, providing porters and soldiers. The aid of Quiahuiztlán, Cempoala, and the 20-odd related "Hill Tribes" was crucial to Cortés's success in battle. The most important excavated structures include the **Templo Mayor,** constructed of river stones, and the **Templo de las Chimeneas**.

Continue south on Hwy. 180 to **La Antigua** ❸. Landing on the beach on Good Friday, Cortés named the place La Villa Rica de la Vera Cruz (Rich Villa of the True Cross) in honor of the Catholic holiday. Shelters were built and a contingency of soldiers maintained while others marched inland to Tenochtitlán. During the early years of the Conquest, supplies and booty were shipped in and out of the port, providing a vital link to Spain and the Caribbean islands.

When Veracruz was moved to its present location around 1600, this city became "la antigua Veracruz" ("the former Veracruz"), and later simply La Antigua. Visit **La Ermita del Rosario** (Av. Independencia s/n), Mexico's first Catholic chapel, and the **Casa de Cortés,** the ruined Spanish headquarters, draped in vines and sprouting fig trees.

Keep south on the coast highway to the port city of **Veracruz** (see pp. 240–41). After seeing the city, continue to **Boca del Río** ❹, another stop along the conquerors' route. Thirty years ago it was just a simple fishing village at the mouth of the Jamapa River; today it is a busy resort. On weekends, Veracruz families spend long lunches at the lively riverside restaurants, serenaded by local musicians. (The restaurants are open, although less lively, throughout the week.) During June's regional livestock exposition, Boca del Río hosts cock fights, horse races, and other equestrian events.

About 41 miles (66 km) south of Boca del Río is **Alvarado** ❺. Surrounded by water, it faces the sea and is bordered by the huge Laguna de Alvarado, which is fed by several important rivers. This attractive fishing town is known for its lively fandango music, and the celebrations held each Sunday during May for the Fiesta de la Cruz de Mayo. ∎

🗺 See also area map p. 234 C3–C2
➤ Quiahuiztlán
↔ 75 miles (120 km)
🕐 A full day (plus time in Veracruz)
➤ Alvarado

NOT TO BE MISSED
- La Antigua
- Veracruz, Boca del Río
- Alvarado

Palma Sola

START
1 Quiahuiztlán
Lago El Llano
Lago Farallón
Tinajitas

180

Punta Cempoala
Cempoala
Cempoala
2
Actopan

Ursulo Galván
José Cardel
Jalcomulco Samoral
La Antigua
3
Paso de Ovejas

180
140

Santa Fé

VERACRUZ

Mata Loma

Manlio Favio
Altamirano

Soledad de   Jamapa
Doblado

Jamapa

150D   140

Cortés scuttles his fleet, 1518.

0   20 kilometers
0   10 miles

Cempoala

Punta Chivería   Gulf of Mexico

Isla Blanquilla
Isla Anegade de Adentro
Isla Verde   Arrecife
Isla Pájaros   Anegadilla
de Afuera

VERACRUZ   Isla
Santiaguillo

Boca del Río
4   Antón Lizardo   Arrecife
El Cabezo

Paso del Toro
Laguna
Madinga Grande
La Laguna

La Piedra

180

Laguna
Camaronera   Camaronera

Arbolillo
Tlalixcoyan
Laguna de
Blanco   Alvarado   Alvarado
Ignacio   5
de la Llave

Limón
Laguna
Pajarillos

Catedral de Nuestra Señora de la Asunción, Veracruz

Córdoba
🗺 234 B2
Visitor information
✉ Palacio Municipal
☎ 271/712-2531

Orizaba
🗺 234 B2
Visitor information
✉ Av. Colón Poniente 230
☎ 272/726-2222

Córdoba & environs

BOTH CÓRDOBA AND ORIZABA WERE FOUNDED TO protect colonial trade caravans along the Mexico City–Puebla–Veracruz road. They are located in the foothills of the Sierra Madre Oriental, and so are much cooler than the steamy coast and warmer than Xalapa. Geared toward industry and commerce, these two prosperous cities are separated by the luxuriant Metlac River ravine, with miles of hiking trails. From here, intrepid (and experienced) trekkers can assault Mexico's highest peak, Pico de Orizaba, which looms above the luxuriant landscape to the northwest.

For hundreds of years Córdoba thrived on wealth from vast sugar-cane plantations maintained by legions of black slaves. Today the city is relatively large and modern. Historic buildings surround pretty

Symmetrical, snowcapped Citlaltépetl, also called Pico de Orizaba, is the third highest peak in North America.

Parque 21 de Mayo, where the **Iglesia de la Inmaculada Concepción** has a priceless gold altarpiece.

The city's most popular attraction is the **Portal de Zevallos,** a lovely arcade where people meet over locally grown coffee or refreshing mint juleps. A few miles west, **Fortín de las Flores** is famous for its greenhouses and private gardens, best visited during the Fiestas de Mayo, when nursery

tours can be taken. The area between Córdoba and Xalapa offers many opportunities for adventure tourism, including the country's best rivers for white-water rafting (see p. 251).

Though it has a brewery, and cement and textile factories, small, industrial **Orizaba** is nonetheless a pleasant city, retaining some colonial and neoclassic architecture. Facing the main square is the old town hall, an iron building in the art nouveau style purchased from Belgium and reassembled here in 1894. The "new" **Palacio Municipal** *(Av. Colón Poniente 230),* an attractive neo-Gothic building, has a large mural by José Clemente Orozco.

Housed in a lovely colonial structure, the **Museo de Arte del Estado** *(Av. Oriente 4 between Calle Sur 23 & Calle Sur 25, tel 272/724-3200, closed Mon., $)* shows contemporary and older art by foreigners and nationals. The new **Museo de Arqueología** *(Calle Sur 9 at Calle Oriente 4, tel 272/725-4622, closed Sun.)* has 400 pre-Hispanic artifacts and a historical archive.

Dominating all other peaks in Mexico is dormant **Pico de Orizaba,** at 18,855 feet (5,747 m). Its Náhuatl name, Citlaltépetl, means "star mountain." Amateurs can hike the trails along the lower slopes, but only experienced hikers should attempt the summit. ∎

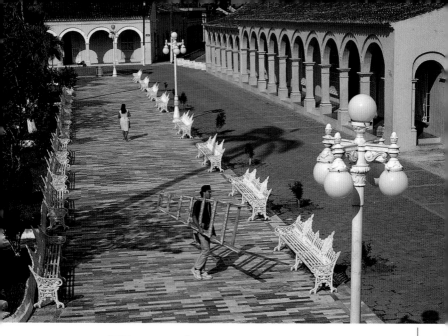

Tlacotalpan

ON THE BANKS OF THE WIDE RÍO PAPALOAPAN IS Tlacotalpan, named a World Heritage site for its beautiful location and well-maintained pre-Revolution buildings. When Mexico was a colony of Spain, this important port and shipyard received schooners and side-wheel steamships that imported European goods and exported tobacco, exotic woods, cotton, and sugarcane.

The town declined in importance with the completion of competing railroad lines and the advent of the Revolution. However, it maintains an air of seductiveness lost in more modern cities. Lining the streets are imposing mansions with ancient red-tile roofs, their Arabesque-style portals brightly painted in Kelly green and cobalt blue, coral, and sunshine yellow, with accents in contrasting colors. Open doorways offer a glimpse of cool patios and ornate front rooms, while the colonnades provide welcome shade.

Visit the **plaza principal,** with its lacy, Mudejar-style bandstand, and the parish church, the **Parroquia de San Cristóbal,** which has beautiful altarpieces of carved wood. The **Museo**

Jarocho Salvador Ferrando (*Manuel M. Alegre 6, closed Mon., $*) exhibits the paintings of the local artist, as well as furnishings and artifacts from the 19th century.

Tlacotalpan vigorously celebrates its patron saint, the Virgen de la Candelaria, from January 31 to February 9. The first three days see musical parades on horseback and El Encuentro de Jaraneros (Meeting of the Revelers), when young and old perform the physically challenging regional dance, the *jarana,* accompanied by harp and guitar. On February 1 there is bull-running and more dancing, while on the saint's feast day, February 2, her icon is serenaded by mariachis during a festive river parade of boats. ∎

Tlacotalpan
🅰 234 C2
Visitor information
✉ Palacio Municipal, Plaza Zaragoza
☎ 288/884-2050

Los Tuxtlas & Catemaco

THE LOS TUXTLAS MOUNTAIN RANGE RISES ABRUPTLY from sea level to about 5,000 feet (1,500 m). One of seven broad geographic zones composing Veracruz state, it is an area of great natural beauty and contains a range of ecosystems, including the continent's northernmost tropical rain forest. However, expanding cattle ranches and farms have dramatically reduced the forests. Tobacco is an important crop, and San Andrés Tuxtla is a cigar-manufacturing center as well as the seat of regional government. Los Tuxtlas' quarries provided the Olmecs the enormous stones from which they carved their famous basalt heads. Today, the region's most visitor-oriented town is Catemaco, in a forested lakeshore setting.

San Andrés Tuxtla
🗺 234 D2
Visitor information
✉ Palacio Municipal, Madero I Altos
☎ 294/947-9300, ext. 606

Catemaco
🗺 234 D2
Visitor information
✉ Palacio Municipal, Av. Carranza
☎ 294/943-0016

Olmec Laguna de los Cerros, at the edge of the Tuxtla Mountains

Santiago Tuxtla, 140 miles (225 km) south of Veracruz, is a commercial hub for the area. While not particularly geared to tourists, it's a pleasant, traditional foothill town with some impressive and photogenic old mansions. Lively equestrian events, some dating back to medieval Spain, are held during July festivities honoring the city's patron saint, the Apostle James. In the main square, **Parque Juárez,** is the **Cabeza de Cobata,** the largest of the colossal Olmec heads found so far and the only one with its eyes closed. The **Museo Regional Tuxteco** (Parque Juárez, tel 294/947-0196, $) exhibits other Olmec artifacts, including some from the **Tres Zapotes** site, 8 miles (13 km) away. One of Mesoamerica's oldest cities, Tres Zapotes was where the first giant Olmec stone head was discovered, in a farmer's field in 1860.

San Andrés Tuxtla, 9 miles (14.5 km) east, took Santiago's place as regional capital in the 19th century. Today it is primarily known as a cigarmaking center with a colorful spring celebration, the Feria de la Primavera, held in May. About 7½ miles (12 km) outside town off the road to Catemaco is **Salto de Eypantla,** a wide, roaring waterfall. At the parking lot, little kids guard your car while their older brothers

lead you down the sometimes slippery slope to a viewing area and a jumble of open-air kitchens. Just a mile or two outside town, **Laguna Encantada,** on the edge of **Los Tuxtlas Biosphere Reserve,** is suitable for birding and swimming and has a humble restaurant. Folks there can guide you to more remote **Poza de la Reina,** an idyllic natural pool, and **Cola del Caballo,** a waterfall resembling a horse's tail. Both are located in the hills above the northeast shore of **Laguna de Catemaco.**

About 7 miles (11 km) east of San Andrés, **Catemaco** hugs the west shore of Mexico's third largest natural lake. The languid town has quite a reputation among Mexicans and foreign visitors for its large number of brujos (witches) and curanderos (healers). Touts whistle at prospective customers as they drive into town, hoping to direct incoming traffic to their patrons' place of business. People throughout Mexico—including the middle and upper classes—consult purveyors of the magic arts to cure ills from lumbago to broken hearts and mal de ojo, the evil eye. Catemaco's notoriety in a country full of such practitioners is due in part to its annual witches' convention, to which the public is not invited.

Perhaps the presence of so many shamans attracted movie moguls to film *Medicine Man* (1992) here. Some location work was done at **Proyecto Ecológico Nanciyaga** *(tel 294/943-0199, www.nanciyaga .com, $),* a privately owned, 100-acre (40 ha) nature preserve on the north shore. You can visit it as part of a short lake tour arranged in Catemaco, but it's more fun to rent one of the minuscule wooden cabins and spend the night. *Temazcal* sweat-lodge ceremonies can be arranged in advance. For no extra charge, you can take a mud bath and rinse off in a crystalline spring. Kayaks and rowboats are available for cruising the lake. Adjacent to Nanciyaga, **La**

Jungla campground is also set in the tropical jungle. These and other natural areas surrounding the lake hide a large number of resident and migratory bird species. ■

Above: The sun sets on Lake Catemaco.

Villahermosa

WITH ITS WILTING TROPICAL HEAT DEFLECTED OFF A cityscape of modern cement, glass, and concrete structures, there's physically not much to recommend Villahermosa, Tabasco's capital. However, those who spend a day or two here usually develop an odd affection for this business-oriented city whose economy is based on petroleum and commerce. There are seafood restaurants, several excellent anthropology museums, and a pedestrian-only zone with a good mix of hotels, cafés, and small museums. And like their neighbors the Veracruzanos, the Tabascans are animated, flirtatious, and friendly.

Founded during Cortés's 1519 exploration, the regional capital was first located at Santa María de la Victoria, named for a minor victory that bore an important result. Defeating a contingency of Tabascan Indians in a skirmish, the Spaniards received a gift of 20 slave women, including La Malinche, who became their invaluable interpreter (see box on p. 207).

Situated on the wide, navigable Grijalva River, the city evolved as a distribution center for rubber, cacao, dyewood, coffee, and bananas. It was later relocated to its present, more easily defended, site and renamed Villahermosa.

Modern Villahermosa sprawls along both banks, and unlike many other Mexican cities, few of the most visited sites are clustered around the main square. Taxis are the easiest way to negotiate the city.

Just a block away from the river, **Parque Benito Juárez** (between *Calles Guerrero & Independencia at Martínez Escobar*), the city's pleasant if unexciting main plaza, is surrounded by the white neoclassic **Palacio de Gobierno** and at the other extreme, the odd-looking **Templo de la Concepción,** a mid-20th-century church with Gothic-style elements.

Behind the state government building, north of the main plaza, lies a pedestrian-friendly zone called the **Zona Luz** or La Zona Remodelada. About eight blocks of urban blight were bulldozed in the 1970s to create a brick-paved zone of art galleries, shops, cafés, and ice-cream stands. Several free museums are worth visiting if you're in the area, including the **Casa Museo Carlos Pellicer** (*Saenz 203, tel 993/314-2170, closed Mon.*), with personal effects of the late Tabascan poet and cultural activist, and the **Museo de Cultura Popular** (*Zaragoza 810, tel 993/314-1117, closed Mon.*). More interesting is the **Museo de Historia de Tabasco** (*Juárez at 27 de Febrero, tel 993/314-2172, closed Mon.*), a museum of the state's history within the **Casa de Azulejos,** an early 20th-century building featuring a tiled facade and eclectic architectural elements.

Southwest of the historic center you will find **CICOM,** a large complex with a popular restaurant, museum, public library, and important theater. The latter, modern **Teatro Esperanza Iris,** was inaugurated in 1981 and named for a well-known Villahermosa singer and actress. The theater hosts the National Ballet as well as concerts, folkloric shows, and other performances.

The important **Museo Regional de Antropología Carlos Pellicer Cámara**

Villahermosa
235 E2
Visitor information
Paseo Tabasco 1504
993/316-2889

(*Carlos Pellicer 511, tel 993/312-6344, closed Mon., $$*) is within the same complex. The anthropology museum gives great attention to the Olmec civilization, which thrived in the Middle Preclassic period (approximately 1200–400 B.C.). On the first floor are galleries for temporary exhibitions and a room for the monumental-size pieces of Maya and Olmec origin. The second floor contains exclusively Olmec and Maya displays, two important cultures that shared a common border around the Tabasco lowlands. Exhibits from these cultures include ceramic and carved stone pieces, such as small jade figurines of mythical were-jaguars—half-human, half-jaguar babies with cleft heads.

The museum tour is best started on the third floor, where maps show the distribution and evolution of civilization throughout Mesoamerica. There are Preclassic pieces from the central plateau and funerary masks, jewelry, and ceramics from Classic-era Teotihuacán. Totonac and Huastec cultures are represented with anthropomorphic and zoomorphic figurines, "smiling face" figures, and wheeled toys. Typical of Classic Veracruz civilization are the axes, yokes, and *palmas*, ritual artifacts inscribed with bas-reliefs that are related to the ball game.

On the west side of town, the **Tabasco 2000** complex has a cultural center, a major shopping mall, a convention center, and a planetarium. Also within this vast complex are the City Hall, or Palacio

Basalt stone heads like this one are now considered monumental portrait-sculptures of Olmec leaders.

Serpentine and colored clay blocks form an unusual jaguar mask mosaic, now on display at La Venta Museum.

Municipal, and the luxurious Camino Real Hotel. The tourist information center is located nearby.

At the south end of the serpentine **Laguna de las Ilusiones** is the al fresco **Parque Museo La Venta** *(Av. Ruíz Cortines at Laguna de las Ilusiones, tel 993/314-1652, closed Mon., $$)*, where more than 30 large Olmec sculptures are set amid lush tropical foliage. Located on a 2-square-mile (5 sq km) island within a coastal swamp near the Tonalá River, **La Venta,** 43 miles (70 km) to the west, rose in importance with the decline of the San Lorenzo settlement, where more colossal heads have been found than anywhere else. San Lorenzo was violently overthrown, and its monuments defaced, around 1200 B.C., after which La Venta apparently reigned as the center of Olmec influence. Now thought to have been a residential as well as ceremonial city, La Venta produced a cone-shaped clay pyramid 110 feet (33 m) tall, the largest of its period in Mexico. Found at the site were a group of 16 small jade figures and an unusual mosaic of serpentine

blocks and ground and colored clays that formed a geometric jaguar mask—now on display at La Venta Museum. When petroleum was first exploited at La Venta, many of these priceless treasures were transferred to this specially designed museum in Villahermosa. (Other artifacts can be found in the Xalapa and Mexico City anthropology museums.)

Hire an English-speaking guide, or take a self-guided tour (exhibits are labeled in English and Spanish). There's also a small zoo *(closed Mon.)*, with spider monkeys, reptiles, and some of the region's larger mammals. A winding path continues past Olmec "altars" (now thought to be thrones), stelae, and jaguar-boys. The huge basalt heads with characteristic full lips and wide noses, wearing what look like football helmets, are considered monumental portrait-sculptures of Olmec leaders.

Ten miles (16 km) east of Villahermosa at Dos Montes is **Yumká** *(tel 993/356-0107, $$)*, a 250-acre (100 ha) park. Two-hour guided tours cover the state's three primary ecological zones: savanna, tropical forest, and lagoons. Visitors can walk through a section of tropical rain forest and across a hanging bridge, and can take a short tram ride through the savanna, ending at a children's playground, restaurant, and gift shop. There is a small additional charge for a boat trip through the lagoon. ■

Adventure tourism

For those seeking an active holiday, Mexico does not disappoint. There are plenty of adventure sports opportunities on offer in out-of-the-way places throughout the country.

Mountain climbers will be inspired by Mexico's "Ring of Fire" volcanic belt, which offers some of the most impressive peaks in the hemisphere, including Pico de Orizaba, the country's highest at 18,855 feet (5,747 m). Iztaccíhuatl provides a challenging yet non-technical climb along many routes, while La Malinche, at 14,636 feet (4,461 m), provides first-timers with a one-day, warm-up ascent.

In Querétaro, rock climbers can scale one of the Americas's largest monoliths, Peñón de Bernal, by different routes of various levels of difficulty. At 8,284 feet (2,525 m) above sea level, the summit perches atop a 157-foot-high (48 m) arête. More accessible are the boxy limestone canyons of Cañón de la Huasteca, between Monterrey and Saltillo in Cumbres de Monterrey National Park. Characterizing the arid, rugged terrain are such sheer cliffs as the 1,000-foot-high (300 m) Torre Diablos and 1,640-foot (500 m) Pico de Independencia. **Aventurismo Guías Profesionales** *(Av. de los Cocuyos 662, Fracc. Acuaducto, Saltillo, Coah., tel/fax 844/417-2469, avgps@terra .com.mx)* leads three-day treks in the area for experienced swimmers and rock climbers. Adventurers hike, swim, rappel, and make jumps into the Matacanes and Hidrofóbia Rivers, accessing little-visited caves and subterranean rivers on long, somewhat strenuous day hikes.

For exuberant, semitropical vegetation visit La Huasteca region, comprising parts of San Luis Potosí, Hidalgo, Tamaulipas, and Veracruz states. This is a land laced with waterfalls, which form grottos and crystalline turquoise pools edged in lacy ferns. Adventure outfitters such as **Eccosports** *(Cerrada de Félix Cuevas 224-B Col. Del Valle, 03100 México D.F., tel 55/5559-3560, e-mail info@eccosports.com.mx)* offer trips combining rock climbing and rappelling with spelunking and rafting.

With its abundant rainfall, lush vegetation, and more than 40 rivers, Veracruz is Mexico's premier rafting destination. One of the most thrilling excursions is a kayak or raft descent of Río Pescados, between Xalapa and Veracruz. Winding through deep canyons dressed in lush semitropical vegetation, the river encompasses 35 class III and IV rapids during a wet, three-hour whitewater trip. The Antigua River (part of the same system) offers class III and IV rapids during the wet season only, roughly July–November. And a few hours north of Xalapa, the Río Filobobos (Class II and III) provides access to the ruins of El Cuajilote and Vega de la Pena (A.D. 200–900), recently discovered within the tropical forest. **Río y Montaña** *(Guillermo González Camarena 500 PB, Santa Fé, México City, tel. 55/5292-5032, www.rioymontana.com)* leads whitewater trips as well as mountain biking, trekking, and climbing in Veracruz, Oaxaca, and elsewhere. ■

More places to visit in the Central Gulf coast

COMALCALCO

The ruined city of Comalcalco lies about 35 miles (56 km) northwest of Villahermosa. Its name means "place of baked clay, or bricks." A lack of suitable local stone meant the builders had to make their temples and pyramids of oven-baked bricks of sand, crushed shells, and clay. Occupied since the first century A.D., this Chontal Maya city (the westernmost of any known Maya site) saw the height of its civilization in the Late Classic period, as did Palenque (see pp. 290–93) and Yaxchilán (see pp. 302–303). Almost two dozen of its nearly 300 structures have been restored, including a ball court, palaces, and temples.

🅰 235 E2   🆂 $

COSTA ESMERALDA

This 13-mile (21 km) stretch of coastline between **Nautla** and **Tecolutla** consists of flat, often lonely sand beaches, bathed by the Gulf's murky waters, lined with palms and interspersed with estuaries. Tecolutla is more geared to visitors, with moderately priced hotels and restaurants serving fresh sea bass, oysters, and *huachinango* (red snapper).

🅰 234 B3

WILD TABASCO

To explore a less-touristy corner of Mexico, head for rural Tabasco, which has rivers, caves, and jungly scenery near the foothills of the Sierra Madre range. Due south of Villahermosa (and en route to Tuxtla Gutiérrez, Chiapas via Highway 195), **Teapa** is a good base for exploration, with two- and three-star hotels. The municipal seat has a picturesque square and several 18th-century Jesuit and Franciscan churches. Just west of town is the **Hotel Ecológico Hacienda Los Azufres** (tel 932/327-5806, www.haciendalosazufres.com.mx), a curative thermal springs with lodgings, meeting rooms, restaurant, and spa treatments. Only a few miles east of Teapa, cave enthusiasts marvel at the eight roomy, lighted caverns of **Grutas de Cocaná,** while serious spelunkers with gear crawl through **La**

Cueva de las Canicas, named for its marble-like calcite deposits.

A bit farther east, the municipality of Tacotalpa offers several ecological reserves. Swim in the natural pool formed by **Agua Blanca** waterfall, in the park of the same name, or explore lighted caves, practice spelunking or rappelling. The reforested, 67-acre (27 ha) **Kolem-Jaá** ecopark (tel 993/314-3696, www.kolemjaa.com.mx) has tent camping, cabins, self-guided trails, and a canopy zip-line as well as mountain biking and other activities, with equipment provided. **Centro Ecoturístico Yu-Balcah** (tel 993/350-0201, www.yubalcah.com.mx, closed Mon.) is a private reserve where you can ride horses, kayak, hike, and rock climb, among other outdoor diversions.

East of Villahermosa, towards Palenque, the **Río Usamacinto** and its tributaries form canyons and waterfalls in the municipality of Tenosique. Near the town of Santo Tomás are the lovely green sinkholes (cenotes) **Ya Ax Ha** and **Aktun Ha.** The county seat, Tenosique is the best base for organizing fishing, rafting, rappelling, and caving expeditions in the region, but don't expect your hosts to speak fluent English. That's part of the adventure.

🅰 235 E2

TUXPAN

Tuxpan, a port city 7 miles (11 km) in from the sea on a river of the same name, has sandy beaches and luxuriant river scenery. Archaeological finds show this site to have been continuously occupied between the Preclassic and Postclassic periods (see pp. 25–28). Locally excavated artifacts preserved in the **Museo de Arqueología** (tel 783/834-6180, cosed Sun.) include pieces found at the ancient Huastec city of Tabuco, across the river. Known for their outgoing personalities, the townspeople celebrate "spring carnival" in May, and, in preparation for the feast day of the patron saint, the Virgin of the Assumption (August 15), a country fair.

🅰 234 B4   **Visitor information**   ✉ Av. Juárez 20   ☎ 783/835-2647, ext. 125 ∎

From Tehuantepec to Tuxtepec, Oaxaca's ethnic groups give the region a distinctly indigenous and idiosyncratic flavor. Many still rely on *curanderos* (healers) and the intervention of saints to cure ills of the flesh and of the spirit.

Oaxaca

Bright wooden devils for sale

Oaxaca

THE STATE OF OAXACA FORMS THE ELBOW OF A GEOGRAPHIC ARM extending south and east to embrace the indigenous heart of Mexico. This is a mountainous land caught in the clutch of the eastern and western Sierra Madre. Dozens of fractured ranges lead to isolated high valleys draped with mist, where tiny hamlets are accessible only on foot or by burro. Farmers goad ox teams up impossible angles to plow their fields, relying on summer storms to water their one or two yearly corn crops. To encourage rain they may pray to ancient gods as well as Catholic saints; despite a deep devotion to the Virgin, many Oaxaqueños observe pre-Christian rituals and believe in the existence of *nahuales,* wizards able to take on different shapes.

Oaxaca counts 570 municipalities, more than any other state. Physical isolation contributes to traditionalism; each village does things its own way. Trique women in mountain villages weave cherry-colored *huipiles* (loose, calf-length dresses) with bright bands of color; near the border with Guerrero, Amuzgo women create brocaded designs for their fine cotton huipiles. During *las velas,* traditional parties in the Isthmus of Tehuantepec, Zapotec women proudly don fancy stiff lace headdresses and petticoats with flowing skirts, and short, brightly embroidered velveteen huipiles.

Of the state's 15 major ethnic groups, the Zapotecs and Mixtecs are the largest, occupying both coastal and mountain regions. Their ancestors built the large ceremonial centers whose ruins dot the central valleys today. Grandest of all, Monte Albán was a contemporary of Teotihuacán, in Central Mexico, reaching its peak of civilization during the Classic period. Its stone-lined ball courts and well-proportioned pyramids overlook Oaxaca, the capital city, which stretches out in the valley below.

The city of Oaxaca is a delightful base for exploring the region. People crowd the *zócalo,* or main plaza, sipping coffee in the outdoor cafés that surround the bandstand where lively marimba bands play. The historic center is peppered with carefully restored architectural treasures, including the sumptuous Santo Domingo church and former monastery, the latter home to Oaxaca's wonderful regional museum. Excursions to magnificent churches and monasteries surrounding the city reveal the extraordinary wealth and aesthetic sensibilities of the Dominican Order in the 16th and 17th centuries.

Oaxaca's 320-mile (515 km) Pacific coast is another important tourist destination. Hotels are popping up along the beautiful bays of Huatulco, one of the smallest of Mexico's planned seaside resorts. Puerto Escondido, a world-famous surf spot, has natural beauty and casual restaurants and hotels. Outside the tourist destinations, fishing villages and inland towns lure adventurous travelers with annual religious festivals and unusual folk art, including masks, pottery, and textiles. ■

Chilies are a staple food and a source of Vitamin C.

Oaxaca

Oaxaca's *zócalo* is active day and night; in the evenings free music and dance events often take place.

IT'S SAID THAT IF YOU SAMPLE *CHAPULINES,* A HIGHLY seasoned local delicacy, you're sure to return one day to Oaxaca. But more of a draw (and less of an acquired taste) than its famous fried grasshoppers is the colonial heart and multiethnic soul of the capital city itself. Baroque churches of locally mined stone glow in the semitropical sunshine; at an elevation of 5,085 feet (1,550 m), Oaxaca enjoys warm weather most of the year, rarely getting too hot or cold. On wrought-iron benches in the main square and adjacent Alameda, people chat, read newspapers, and enjoy the sunshine filtering through the trees, while the state orchestra performs in the shadow of the 16th-century cathedral on lazy Sunday afternoons.

Oaxaca

🗺 254 B3

Visitor information

✉ Av. Juarez 703

☎ 951/516-4828

Only the state of Michoacán gives Oaxaca serious competition in the variety and quality of its folk art. Towns and villages surrounding the capital produce an astonishing variety of items. The Zapotec towns of Teotitlán del Valle and less famous Santa Ana del Valle have been making hand-loomed wool *tapetes* (rugs) for centuries. Other crafts—including smoky black pottery from San Bartolo Coyotepec and carved wood figures from Arrazola—are more recent innovations. These and many more fine handicrafts are sold in upscale shops on and around Calle Alcalá, a pedestrian-only street north of the *zócalo*. If you enjoy bartering and have the time, check the fixed prices in the shops first. You'll find a limited selection of handcrafts (but a big "slice of life") at **Abastos** or **Benito Juárez markets,** along with everything from vice grips to love potions that double as floor polish. Head into the surrounding countryside, to the towns where the items are produced, for some serious bargains and a glimpse of rural life.

While folk art is an important element of Oaxacan culture, the city also has an impressive fine arts and cultural scene. Upcoming and established artists treat regional themes and imagery in contemporary compositions; quite a few excellent galleries are housed in one- and two-story buildings of green, gold, or rose quarrystone. The city hosts an annual international film festival, and free art films are shown weekend nights at **Cinema El Pochote** (*Av. García Vigil 817, tel 951/514-1194*).

Excellent museums also demonstrate the city's commitment to arts and culture. The **Museo de Arte Prehispánico Rufino Tamayo** (*Av. Morelos 503, tel 951/516-4750, closed Tues., $*) displays the private collection of Oaxacan abstract painter, muralist, and sculptor Rufino Tamayo (1899–1991), donated to the state in 1975. About 2,000 pieces representative of pre-Cortesian Mexico are displayed in a restored colonial home in the heart of downtown. The **Museo de Arte Contemporáneo de Oaxaca,** or **MACO** (*Alcalá 202, tel 951/514-2818, closed Tues., $*), is housed in an even more imposing, two-story colonial residence. On the second floor, the permanent collection includes the work of the late Oaxacan naive painter Rodolfo Morales, and of graphic artist Francisco Toledo. Temporary exhibits on the first and second levels show a variety of media.

If the city's 27 historic churches are considered works of art, one of the most cherished is the **Basílica de Nuestra Señora de la Soledad** (*Av. Independencia 107 at Galeana, tel 951/516-7566*), built in the late 17th century to honor Oaxaca's patron saint, Our Lady of Solitude. Oaxacans petition the Virgin for favors, making special pilgrimages culminating on

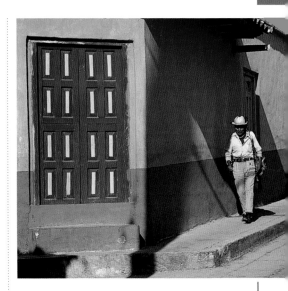

December 18, her feast day. Visit the museum to see gifts left by devotees—from plastic flowers and severed braids to naive ex-votos (pictorial expressions of thanks) painted on wood or tin. The basilica is on the site of a garrison maintained by the Aztecs, who controlled the region in the 15th century.

During this period of Aztec domination, artisans from Tenochtitlán were installed in several neighborhoods, or barrios, each dedicated to a particular craft. Just north of downtown, Xochimilco's centuries-old weaving traditions are still practiced today. Listen for the clacking of enormous looms on Calle Boloños Cacho, east of the pretty parish church, to find weaving workshops where you can purchase custom-made cloth. East of **Parque El Llano** (a city park officially named Parque Juárez), the barrio of Jalatlaco was once a leather-working town. Although few today practice the craft, the quiet cobblestone streets and brightly painted homes and neighborhood restaurants provide a window into Oaxaca's past. ■

Oaxaca's tranquility and year-round mild climate make it a pleasure to visit.

A walk around historic Oaxaca

Oaxaca has a multitude of interesting and historic sites radiating from its lovely main plaza, a tranquil, traffic-free place marking the end of this walking tour. On pedestrian-only Calle Alcalá, shops and restaurants occupy pastel-tinted, two-story buildings erected soon after the city was founded by the Spanish in the 16th century.

The shady and traffic-free zócalo is a peaceful place to sit or stroll.

Begin your walk at the **Arcos de Xochimilco** ❶, south of Calzada Héroes de Chapultepec on García Vigil. The arches of this 18th-century stone aqueduct shrink as the 985-foot (300 m) structure stretches south toward downtown. Individual arches now provide access to modest apartment dwellings. Walk several blocks south along García Vigil to the **Iglesia del Carmen Alto** ❷, where the aqueduct's waters were originally stored. The church hosts a lively fair for the feast day of the Virgin of Carmen (July 16), which initiates the Guelaguetza, an annual festival of dance and music with its roots in pre-Hispanic tradition. Just beyond and across the street from the Church of Carmen Alto is the **Museo Casa de Benito Juárez** ❸ (García Vigil 609, tel 951/516-1860, closed Mon., $), the historic house where Oaxaca's revered statesman lived as a youth in the early 19th century.

Turn left and cross Plazuela del Carmen to Oaxaca's pedestrian-friendly Calle Alcalá and the **Templo y Ex-Convento de Santo Domingo** ❹, home to the **Museo de las Culturas de Oaxaca** (Alcalá at Constitución, tel 951/516-2991, closed Mon., $). Continue east along Plazuela A. Gurrión and Calle Constitución to Calle Reforma. Half a block north on Reforma, stop in at the stamp museum: **Museo de Filatelia de Oaxaca** (Reforma 505, tel 951/516-8028, closed Mon.), an 18th-century building restored in 1998.

Return south along Calle Reforma to the **Ex-Convento de Santa Catalina** (now the Hotel Camino Real), home to the nuns of the Immaculate Conception until the Reform Laws of 1859. Keep south along Reforma, turning right on Morelos and left onto 5 de Mayo. One block south, the belle époque **Teatro Macedonio Alcalá** is a venue for city theater and dance.

Keep south along 5 de Mayo and turn right on Colón. Two blocks west (Colón becomes Las Casas), enter the **Mercado Benito Juárez** ❺, established in 1892. Here you will find locally made blocks of chocolate (for delicious, cinnamon-laced hot cocoa), string cheese (queso oaxaqueños), and piles of fresh vegetables and exotic fruits as well as some clothing and souvenirs. Continue to the **Iglesia San Juan de Díos** ❻ (Aldama at 20 de Noviembre). Although architecturally unimpressive, Oaxaca's first church is dear to its people. The original adobe-and-thatch temple was christened in 1526; the present structure replaced it in the mid-17th century.

A few steps to the east, the **Mercado 20 de Noviembre** was originally a hospital for the adjoining convent. Today it's jammed with informal eateries serving chicken soup, beef stew, and other simple fare. Women sell sweet and savory breads from bins and large wicker baskets at the front of the market.

Exit the market and walk north along Miguel Cabrera to the attractive main plaza, the zócalo (officially called Plaza de la Independencia). At the back of the neoclassic **Palacio de Gobierno** ❼, on the south side of the square, a colorful, two-story mural summarizes Oaxaca history, with the spotlight on native son Benito Juárez. Cross the square to

Outshone by its brightly painted neighbor, a building's facade receives attention.

the 16th-century **Catedral** , on the adjoining plaza, La Alameda. Dedicated to the Assumption of the Virgin Mary, the cathedral has been damaged three times by earthquakes, the most significant in 1714. Its 17th-century pipe organ was completely refurbished in 1991.

The **zócalo** is without a doubt the finest place in the city to rest and refresh yourself. An unannounced remodel in 2005 enraged the citizens, who liked it exactly as it was. Relax on a park bench, or order a meal or a drink at one of the many cafés under the plaza's shady porticos. ■

► Arcos de Xochimilco
↔ 1.6 miles (2.5 km)
🕐 4 to 5 hours
► Zócalo

NOT TO BE MISSED
- Templo y Ex-Convento de Santo Domingo
- Museo de las Culturas de Oaxaca
- Mercado Benito Juárez
- Zócalo

Oaxaca's Dominican monasteries

THE SPIRITUAL CONQUEST OF NEW SPAIN WAS LAUNCHED after the Spanish army under Hernán Cortés literally flattened Tenochtitlán (the site of present-day Mexico City). Franciscan friars were the first ecclesiastics to arrive, establishing themselves throughout populous Central Mexico. A few years later, the Dominicans headed south of Mexico City.

Oaxaca
Ⓜ 254 B3
Visitor information
✉ Av. Juarez 703
☎ 951/516-4828

Frequently criticized for the exorbitant sums spent on their temples, the zealous Dominicans imported skilled designers from Europe. Working with equally talented local craftsmen, priest-architects blended renaissance motifs with Gothic and Mudejar elements of the Spanish plateresque school. Even the thick buttressed walls and stocky towers—intended to help withstand the area's earthquakes—don't detract from the rich embellishment and the high quality of locally quarried stone. The Dominican preoccupation with aesthetics is evident in the unique architectural design, elaborate altarpieces, and fine paintings in a chain of

monasteries stretching from Puebla to Guatemala, many of them in Oaxaca state.

Churches were vandalized after the Reform Laws of 1859 expelled the religious orders. The **Iglesia y Ex-Convento de Santo Domingo,** one of the first and most intoxicating of Oaxaca's church-monasteries, suffered considerable damage during a stint as an army barracks. Today it has been scrupulously refurbished at great expense. The church's narrow *retablo* facade, elaborately carved in four tiers and flanked by two majestic bell towers, is in transitional Renaissance style, with traces of baroque. Inside, bright white stucco honeycombed in gold and polychrome relief extends to vaults, domes, and niches. In fact, every inch of the dazzling interior is covered in high-spirited, Puebla-style decoration. The genealogy of the order's founder, Santo Domingo de Guzmán (ca 1170–1221), spreads seductively if naively in a grapevine motif across the underchoir at the temple's entrance. On the right side of the church, the abundance of scrolls, angels, and arabesques decorating the **Capilla del Rosario** (Rosary Chapel) nearly drowns the saints and apostles portrayed.

The two-story, white limestone cloister of the adjoining monastery is home to the **Museo de las Culturas de Oaxaca** *(Alcalá at Constitución, tel 951/516-2991, closed Mon., $$).* The first floor houses temporary exhibits, an

Oaxaca's Santo Domingo de Guzmán church

20th-century artists & *el tequio*

A Zapotec word translated as "the burden," *el tequio* refers to a person's obligation to contribute to his community, a custom practiced since the days of Monte Albán. Francisco Toledo, a highly successful contemporary painter and graphic artist from Juchitán, in the Isthmus of Tehuantepec, takes this obligation seriously. He has funded or contributed his seemingly limitless energy toward many cultural endeavors in Oaxaca, among them the creation of the Instituto de Artes Gráficos, a wonderful graphics art library and museum, a Braille library, Mexico's first stamp museum, and a papermaking workshop in Vistahermosa, Etla (north of Oaxaca). Fellow artist Rudolfo Morales, who died in 2001, was equally active. Between the two, they formed "los Amigos de Monte Albán," a nonprofit organization working to preserve Monte Albán, and dedicated a good deal of time and money toward the restoration of Oaxaca's priceless Dominican monasteries. ∎

The cloister at the Ex-Convento de Santo Domingo now houses the Museo de las Culturas de Oaxaca.

excellent book shop, and the **Biblioteca Francisco de Burgos,** a library with more than 20,000 historical tomes. Walk up the double baroque staircase to the second floor, its doorways and ceiling richly decorated in the lavish Puebla style. Ten former monastic cells now exhibit artifacts representative of regional culture from prehistoric to post-Revolutionary times; an additional 14 galleries are organized by

cistern

wash house

kitchen garden

novices' latrine

novitiate

main stairway

The narrow, four-tiered facade of Oaxaca's Santo Domingo is in transitional Renaissance style, with traces of baroque.

chapter house

theme, including ceramics, music, and medicine. Gallery 3 houses the invaluable treasures excavated from the tombs at the Zapotec site of Monte Albán (see pp. 264–65), including gold, silver, shell, and jade jewelry. Free tours of the **botanical gardens** are usually given in English *(Tues.–Thurs., 11 a.m. and 4 p.m.; Sat., 4 p.m.)*.

Other important monasteries in the Valley of Oaxaca include **Cuilapan,** which is on the road to **Zaachila** (see p. 271);

Tlacochahuaya, with an outstanding 1620 pipe organ (see p. 266); and the Iglesia del Santo Cristo at **Tlacolula de Matamoros** (see p. 268). In the Mixteca Alta region north of Oaxaca, **Yanhuitlán** was recently restored using many original construction techniques. Of note are its elegant plateresque "door within a door" on the north portal and the stunning main altarpiece containing important 16th-century paintings. Farther on are **Coixtlahuaca,** once the site of a temple to the god Quetzalcóatl; and **Teposcolula,** whose open chapel is said to be the loveliest in Oaxaca. ■

kitchen

cloister (Museo de las Culturas de Oaxaca)

monks' latrine

servants' courtyard

infirmary

church nave

Capilla del Rosario (Rosary Chapel)

facade

Monte Albán

A MILLENNIUM BEFORE THE ARRIVAL OF THE SPANIARDS IN 1521, the Zapotec city now known as Monte Albán was flourishing. Sweet-smelling copal incense wafted from gracefully designed, precisely aligned temples. Architects contrived cisterns to collect rainwater and built a specialized irrigation system. Trade flourished; busy open-air markets sold local goods and imported jade beads, stone implements, metal, minerals, and pigments. Archaeological evidence suggests that trade routes extended as far away as Teotihuacán, north of present-day Mexico City.

Animals were domesticated, deer and other beasts and birds were hunted in the surrounding valleys, and hillsides were terraced and planted with crops and fruit trees. Society was stratified, with warlords, warriors, priests, and bureaucrats among the upper class. Artisans and craftspeople lived and worked in separate districts, according to their craft. There was no central ruler; control was probably shared among families with a common ancestor. As in colonial Oaxaca centuries later, the wealthiest and most influential families lived closest to the central plazas.

Although the Zapotecs were the principal architects of this remarkable city, the original inhabitants may have been Mixe-Zoques from the isthmus, or even relatives of the Olmecs of Veracruz. The Zapotecs (or one of their predecessors) first inhabited the site about 500 B.C., and for reasons unknown abandoned it after around 12 centuries of continuous settlement.

A hundred or more years later, the Mixtecs made the site into an elaborate cemetery. The dead were buried in rectangular and cross-shaped tombs decorated with glyphs, murals, or sculptures, and accompanied by offerings made of ceramic, shell, or precious metals. More than 220 burial sites have been discovered and explored. The most fabulous, **Tumba 7,** yielded more than 500 pieces of gold, amber, and turquoise jewelry, as well as other exquisite articles of jade, silver, crystal, and finely sculpted bone. Most of the artifacts are on display at the Museo de las Culturas de Oaxaca (see p. 258).

Today, several of these tombs are open to visitors, including **Tumba 104,** located on the northwest perimeter of the site. Note the god of corn, Pitao Cozobi, embedded at the top of the facade. Inside are multicolored frescoes showing important people in ceremonial dress. The carved slab in the antechamber originally sealed the tomb.

Aside from the tombs at the north end of the artificial mesa, the place to explore is the **Gran Plaza,** once the heart of the city. At either extreme are the **Platforma Norte** and the **Platforma Sur,** each with stone steps flanked by wide balustrades. Buildings were generally made of irregularly shaped stones cemented with mud, and then covered with facing stones and layers of stucco; newer buildings were superimposed on older ones. **Estructura I,** in the center of the Great Plaza, is a typical Zapotec construction. Single or double scapulary panels at the top of buildings (the latter evident on **Edificio H**) symbolized the sky, or the jaguar's jaw.

The earliest inhabitants built

Monte Albán

◪ 254 B2

✉ 6 miles (10 km) southwest of Oaxaca

☎ 951/516-1215

§ $$

structures of monolithic block walls, some plain, others with elaborate bas-relief sculptures. One of the best-known examples of the latter is the **Galería de los Danzantes,** on the west side of the plaza. It is engraved with large nude male figures depicting slain enemies and the rulers of defeated towns. Their names and those of their towns are inscribed on or alongside their mutilated corpses in Zapotec hieroglyphics. **Estructuras K, L,** and **IV Sur** were among the first constructed. In **Estructura H,** the tomb of five young men yielded one of the greatest Zapotec works of art—a jade mask of the bat god. The skeletons were also adorned with breastplates, necklaces, earflares, pearls, and shells, now in the Museo Nacional de Antropología (see pp. 198–201).

At the plaza's northeast corner, the *juego de pelota,* or ball court, is representative of those in the region. This I-shaped court is flanked on both sides by sloping, stepped walls, and, unlike those in Central Mexico and the Yucatán, shows no evidence of ball hoops.

There's a well-stocked gift shop and bookstore, and a restaurant with an excellent view of the valley. Buses depart on the half-hour from the travel agency at the **Hotel Ribera del Angel** (*Calle Mina 518, five blocks southwest of the zócalo, tel 951/516-6175, $*). There's a surcharge for staying beyond three hours, but this small amount is worthwhile for those who want to examine the site and museum thoroughly. Full tours (*$$$$$*) are another option. ∎

Monte Albán, perched on a hill overlooking three valleys, was among the most advanced cities of its time.

Mitla drive

East of Oaxaca along Hwy. 190 lie four archaeological sites, several 17th-century Dominican monasteries, the world's fattest tree, and Zapotec towns backed by the sun-baked Oaxaca hills. Smoky blue mountains form a persistent backdrop, seemingly rising from the stubby cornfields along either side of the highway.

About 8 miles (13 km) southeast of Oaxaca, the pride of tiny **Santa María el Tule ❶** is its 2,000-year-old *ahuehuete,* or Montezuma cypress tree. Wider than it is tall, the gnarled tree towers above the 17th-century church at its side. Local imagination has found figures in the bark and limbs of the 138-foot-wide (42 m) tree as incongruous as the derrière of Mexican actress and violinist Olga Breesky, the face of Jesus, and a turkey. Behind the church, open-air kitchens serve up local specialties.

Four miles (6.5 km) farther along, turn right toward **Tlacochahuaya ❷,** a small Zapotec village with a picturesque plaza and adobe houses surrounded by stone hills and cornfields. Completed in the early 17th century, the town's Dominican church and monastery perch on the base of the pre-Hispanic temple mound that provided building materials. Covering the interior walls and vaulted ceiling are stylized vignettes of cherubs and flowers rendered in red, gold, blue, and green by indigenous artists. Don't miss the meticulously restored pipe organ, built in 1620, in the choir loft.

Return to the highway and after about a mile (1.5 km), turn right onto a dirt road to **Dainzú** *(tel 951/516-0123, $).* Evidence suggests that this terraced Zapotec city was a contemporary of Monte Albán, and was inhabited some time after 300 B.C. Look for bas-relief carvings of ball players with jaguar faces along the lower section of **Edificio A,** the remains of a step-platform structure.

Another mile (1.5 km) farther along the highway is the turnoff to prosperous **Teotitlán del Valle ❸,** famous for its hand-loomed Zapotec rugs. Purists prefer undyed wool or natural dyes such as the increasingly rare cochineal, a cactus parasite, but most rugs these days are made of wool or synthetic fibers tinted with commercially produced dyes. Some people make a pilgrimage to Teotitlán simply to lunch at **Tlamanalli** *(Av. Juárez 39, tel 951/524-4006, closed Mon. & dinner, $$$),* a Zapotec restaurant of some renown.

	See also area map p. 254
	B3–C2
➤	Oaxaca
⟷	35 miles (56 km)
⏱	All day
➤	Mitla

NOT TO BE MISSED
- Santa María el Tule
- Tlacochahuaya
- Tlacolula
- Mitla

Mural detail from Tlacochahuaya's church

Above: The 2,000-year-old *ahuehuete* tree at Santa María el Tule

Benito Juárez

0   8 kilometers
0   4 miles

Tutla

**Santa María
el Tule** ①

190

**Teotitlán
del Valle** ③

Tlacochahuaya
②

Dainzú

Abasolo

Geometric design, Mitla

OAXACA

Santa Ana
del Valle

Villa Díaz Ordaz

Guelávia
Lambityeco

Tlacolula de Matamoros
④ ⑤

Teitipac

Yagul

Villa de
Mitla   ⑥ ⑦ **Mitla**

190

Matatlán

View over Yagul

MITLA DRIVE

Continue along Hwy. 190 about 5 miles (8 km) to the ruins of **Lambityeco,** an important salt-mining center abandoned about A.D. 750 in favor of Yagul, to the southeast. The interior panels of the altar in the **Casa del Coqui** (Estructura 195) are decorated with figures and symbols of the city's leading lords and ladies. Note the two identical masked figures of Cocijo, god of rain, thunder, and lightning on **Estructura 190;** each holds a water vessel in the right hand and a lightning bolt in the left.

Back on the highway, continue just a mile (1.5 km) to **Tlacolula ④,** where women in distinctive flowered headscarves and plaid skirts preside over the busy Sunday market. A smaller market is held throughout the week. Within the **Iglesia del Santo Cristo,** the town's 17th-century Dominican church is the

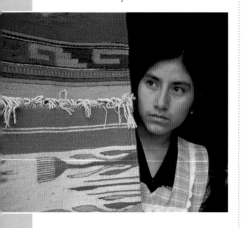

A young rug seller

Capilla del Rosario ⑤, or Rosary Chapel, a stunning example of gilded plasterwork and polychrome relief. Note the fine detail on the wrought iron of the choir grille and pulpit.

Continue southeast along the highway a few miles to **Yagul** (tel 951/516-4828, closed Mon., $), a fortified Zapotec city built on a hilltop for defense. The discovery of more than 30 tombs confirms that this was a residential area; inhabitants were customarily buried underneath the doorway of their homes. The **Palacio de los Seis Patios** may have served as a principal residence.

After another 3 miles (5 km), a short detour off Hwy. 190 takes you to the impressive ruins of **Mitla ⑥** (tel 951/568-0316, $), whose name comes from the Náhuatl word *mictlán,* meaning "land of the dead." The Zapotecs shifted their base of operations to this ceremonial city—and to other centers such as Zaachila, Cuilapan, and Lambityeco—about the time Monte Albán was abandoned (A.D. 700–800). They called the city Lyobaa, meaning "place of rest" or "burial place," and built tombs both above and below ground. As at Monte Albán, Mitla was taken over by the Mixtecs after it was abandoned by the Zapotecs around the 11th century. It was still in use when the Spanish arrived.

The site consists of five groups of buildings once guarded by a fortress on a nearby hill. Of the two that have been excavated, the more exceptional is the **Grupo de las Columnas,** where long masonry halls surround a central plaza. In the first complex, the **Templo de las Columnas** is named for the six enormous pillars that originally supported wooden beams and a large, flat roof. From this structure, enter the **Patio de las Grecas ⑦,** named for the intricate step and fret stone mosaics that adorn its walls. Mitla's almost uniformly geometric decoration reflects the Mixtec influence. As in the Puuc region of the Yucatán, the area's fine limestone made possible such artistic achievement. Unlike those found throughout Mesoamerica at the time, the Mixtec designs lack beasts, gods, and human figures. The narrow rooms surrounding the patio were most likely tombs, and the site itself home to the High Priest of the Zapotec nation and his retinue as well as visiting royalty and soldiers.

The **Grupo de la Iglesia** is what remains of a similar structure disassembled to build the 16th-century **Iglesia de San Pablo Apostol,** named for Mitla's patron saint, the Apostle Paul. Some evidence of this shared heritage can be seen on the stones forming the church's exterior walls. Behind the church, several small structures with decorated lintels and patios are all that remain of the original building. English-language signs explain the Zapotec and Mixtec artifacts displayed at the **Museo de Mitla de Arte Zapoteca** (Av. Juárez 2, tel 951/568-0316, $). ∎

Towns around Oaxaca

Part of the Y-shaped Oaxaca Valley, as seen from the heights of Monte Albán.

SURROUNDING THE CAPITAL, TOWNS LARGE AND SMALL produce the folk art that fills the shops in downtown Oaxaca. Some are prosperous, such as Teotitlán del Valle (see p. 266), whose internationally known weavers have built imposing two-story homes. Others remain poor, with packed dirt streets and fields of corn and alfalfa surrounded by rolling, fawn-colored hills. Zapotec is still spoken in many homes where traditional arts—especially weaving, ceramics, and carving—continue to be practiced.

Although the Spanish conquerors introduced new methods of production, the local people have maintained many of their ancestors' forms and techniques. The Spaniards also restricted metalsmiths to working with nonprecious metals, and craftsmen today produce beautiful work in stamped and molded tin. Symbols such as crosses and saints are juxtaposed with scorpions, birds, frogs, and other traditional icons that emerge from primitive backstrap looms.

Due west of Oaxaca, dusty **Atzompa** squats in the shadow of Monte Albán. It is famous for its green-glazed tableware and unique,

unglazed *muñecas bordadas* "embroidered dolls" designed by the late Teodora Blanca: 2–3-foot (0.75–1 m) female figures, some studded with elephant heads, lizards, and other zoomorphic figures. Artisans along the town's streets will show you their wares if available, but most of the finest work is found at the FONART store (see Shopping, p. 384) or other specialty stores. The scene is quite different in **Arrazola,** where family workshops double as showrooms for colorful *alebrijes,* carved and painted wooden creatures ranging from miniatures to monsters over several feet long.

Oaxaca
🅰 254 B3
Visitor information
✉ Av. Juárez 703
☎ 951/516-4828

Selling bread on the streets of Ocotlán

San Martín Tilcajete, like Arrazola, produces fantastic painted wood figures. Some artisans specialize in devils, others in barroom drunks; the majority make fanciful animals as well. **La Unión Tejalapan** produces wonderfully naive wooden statuettes, including endearing crèches and funky farm animals. Rarely visited by tourists, the town is spread over a series of dry rolling hills, and most artisans sell to shops in Oaxaca.

South of Oaxaca along Highway 175 are several historic towns, including **San Bartolo Coyotepec** (7½ miles/12 km from Oaxaca), famous for its black pottery. Overnight firing of the unglazed pottery in pit kilns produces lustrous patinas from gunmetal gray to sooty black. Shop at the town's co-op, across from the pretty parish church, or wander through town and check the individual artisans' showrooms. Another 7½ miles (12 km) south brings you to **Santo Tomás Jalietza,** where the town's open-air cooperative sells belts, table runners, and other goods made on traditional backstrap looms. The same distance again brings you to **Ocotlán,** known for its fine machetes and knives, the latter sometimes carved with picaresque sayings. The restored Dominican monastery and church on the town plaza are well worth exploring. The former has a wonderful museum showing the unique work of benefactor and local hero, the artist Rudolfo Morales, and of the Aguilar sisters, whos bright ceramic female figures have become Oaxaca icons. Ocotlán is also known for its *mescal minero.*

Wooden carts driven by oxen or horses trundle along the road leading into **Zaachila,** surrounded by the rolling hills of the Zimatlán valley. Early Thursday mornings, locals arrive at the **animal market** on the outskirts of town to barter for shrieking piglets, big-eyed baby burros, and other farm animals. In the town center, the traditional market remains in full swing until mid-afternoon. Visit one of the two pre-Hispanic tombs excavated so far, as well as the appealing 18th-century church dedicated to the Virgin of Juquila.

LA SIERRA NORTE

Oaxaca state promotes "rural tourism," providing access to mountain towns—and the surrounding countryside—with no hotels. This program offers a look at real, rural Oaxaca. Adventurers should set out with open minds, inquisitive hearts, and a Spanish-English dictionary.

About an hour and a half (40 miles/66 km) north of Oaxaca city, **Llano Grande** *(tel 200/125-7541)* is known for the friendliness of its inhabitants and the beauty of the surrounding pine-oak forests. This 19th-century town has magnificent vistas and impressive biodiversity for excellent birdwatching. During Holy Week, Mass is celebrated at **Yaa Tini,** an overlook outside town. This is good mountain biking country; bring your own or rent one in town.

Endemic orchids abound in the cloud forests around **Ixtlán de Juárez** *(tel 955/553-6075),* an area with multiple ecosystems. Within the township of the same name, locals from **Santa Martha Latuvi** *(tel 200/125-7108)* teach visitors about herbal medicines, regionally brewed firewater, and breadmaking. Founded as a mining hacienda, **Santa María Yavesía** *(tel 951/553-6042)* is surrounded by primary forest (great for birding) and offers

lodging with local families, as well as camping. Closer to the capital city of Oaxaca at 6,888 feet (2,100 m) above sea level, the town of **Santa Catarina Lachatao** *(tel 951/514-8271)* has cobblestone streets, red tile roofs, and a 16th-century church.

Guides, meals, and accommodations for these destinations are avail-

Loading straw in Asunción's fields, near Ocotlán

able; call the phone numbers above or the regional tour operator **Sierra Norte** *(tel 951/514-8271, www .sierranorte.org.mx)* for reservations or more information. Bring warm clothing (many towns are more than 9,000 feet/2,700 m above sea level) and comfortable walking shoes. ■

Market towns

These market towns serve local communities, not tourists, but they offer a chance to visit rural Oaxaca and purchase local produce and typical folk art.

Monday Miahuatlán, 62 miles (100 km) south of Oaxaca on Hwy. 175.

Tuesday Ayoquezco, 93 miles (150 km) south of Oaxaca on Hwy. 131; Zimatlán, 15½ miles (25 km) south of Oaxaca off Hwy. 131. Atzompa (see p. 269)

Wednesday San Pedro y San Pablo Etla, 12 miles (19 km) north of Oaxaca off Hwy. 190.

Thursday Zaachila, 9½ miles (15 km) south of Oaxaca on Hwy. 175 West.

Friday Ocotlán 20½ miles (33 km) south of Oaxaca on Hwy. 175 East. San Bartolo Coyotepec (see p. 270)

Saturday Mercado de Abastos, Oaxaca (see p. 256).

Sunday Tlacolula (see p. 268), east of Oaxaca on Hwy. 190. ■

Oaxaca's spectacular festivals

Even the humblest village celebrates its patron saint, sometimes spending the greater part of the annual budget on week-long festivities. Local men lead parades with dissonant yet triumphant trumpets, tubas, and drums; close behind, young beauty queens ride on allegorical floats atop pickup trucks. Shrieking with delight, crowds scatter before *los toros*, reed towers spitting dangerous firecrackers and wielded by zealous young men. Most impressive of all, everyone joins the party.

Radish sculptures made for La Noche de Rábanos (December 23)

Great-grandmas and tiny tots may nod off, but everyone remains until the chill air and the exuberant drunks finally urge families home.

Throughout the state, pre-Cortesian beliefs overlap iconoclastic Christianity to produce rituals as intoxicating as a shot of pure cane liquor. This is literally the case in the eccentric Paso y Credo, a solemn religious procession in which the men of Pinotepa de Don Luis (see p. 274) march from dusk to dawn around the town, taking a ritualistic sip of liquor about every third step. In an Easter-week celebration, the town's men and boys, their bodies painted white with purple icons and slogans, fight a mock battle representing their ancestors' attack on invading Spaniards.

Other traditions, including the Día de los Muertos (Day of the Dead, or All Souls' Day), demonstrate not a clash, but a blending of New and Old World traditions. Near the end of October, villagers and city-dwellers throughout the region begin rejuvenating family graves: weeding, cleaning headstones, painting crosses and crypts. From the evening preceding All Saints' Day (November 1), families begin to entice deceased children—*los angelitos*, or little angels—to the graveside with candles, favorite foods, and (in true Mexican style) loud rockets. As throughout Mexico, Oaxacans relieve gloominess with exuberant partying, and piety is tempered with *picardía*, a mischievous irreverence. Altars—some humble, others lavish—are arranged with traditional sugar-candy skulls embellished with Day-Glo colors, along with yellow-orange *cempasúchil* (marigolds), peanuts, and *pan de muerto* (sweet bread decorated with skulls). These rituals continue through All Souls' Day (November 2) to honor deceased adults.

Even unequivocally Christian celebrations have a unique Oaxaca flavor. On Viernes Santo (Good Friday), purple-robed penitents in long, pointed hoods perform a solemn procession through downtown Oaxaca in El Desfile del Silencio, the Silent Procession. On a more light-hearted occasion, mongrels wearing glasses, cats in glossy capes, birds in beribboned cages, and box turtles in the grubby hands of young owners crowd the courtyard at La Merced church on August 31 for the Blessing of the Animals.

The Christmas season brings nonstop celebrations, including *las calendas,* in which celebrants dance from church to church holding baskets of offerings on their heads. One of Oaxaca's most unusual traditions is La Noche de Rábanos (Radish Night), held December 23. To compete in this classic secular Yule tradition, growers fashion sophisticated tableaux out of carved radishes, toothpicks, and moss.

For more Oaxaca festivals, see "Entertainment & Activities," p. 389. ■

Right, above: Masked revelers enjoy the Carnaval at Tlaxiaco.
Right, below: Zapotec women from the Isthmus of Tehuantepec in party mood

Oaxaca's coast

OAXACA'S COAST ARCS EAST TO WEST, FROM THE BORDER with Guerrero to Chiapas, as if tracing a line along the bottom half of a shallow bowl. Zapotecs and, to a lesser extent, Mixtecs are found up and down the coast; Zoques and Mixes make their home around the isthmus. Chatinos moved into the area around Laguna de Chacahua when the Mixtecs retreated at the arrival of the Spaniards; Zapotec lords fled to the Isthmus of Tehuantepec when the Mixtecs overran the last Zapotec kingdom, Zaachila, in the 14th century. Cultures blend, but in many cases, indigenous peoples speak their own languages and continue many of their great-grandparents' traditions.

Pinotepa Nacional
254 A2

Parque Nacional Lagunas de Chacahua
254 A1

Opposite: One of the state's many beautiful beaches; this one is near Puerto Ángel.

PINOTEPA NACIONAL

The inhabitants of Pinotepa Nacional and the surrounding municipality are characterized as strong, proud, and independent. Most are the descendants of Chatinos, Mixtecs, and blacks—the latter slaves who were shipwrecked and escaped during the early days of the colony. About an hour from the coast, Pinotepa Nacional is not a stop on the tourist trail, but it's an important commercial center. Until well into the 20th century, Pinotepa women wore nothing above the waist except a plain white cotton shawl. Many today still wear striking straight wrap skirts of natually dyed red, purple, and lilac stripes whose pattern varies subtly from one village to the next.

The predominantly Mixtec men throughout the municipality perform elaborate dances at Carnaval, Easter, and major feast days, using masks and story lines passed down over generations. Working around scripts whose meanings have faded with time, dancers don masks of rabbits, dogs, and two-faced Spaniards. **Pinotepa de Don Luis,** 15 miles (24 km) northeast of Pinotepa Nacional, vigorously celebrates both Carnaval and Semana Santa (Holy Week), the former climaxing on the Sunday before Ash Wednesday. There are no tourist accommodations outside Pinotepa Nacional. Visitors may be asked to contribute toward the musicians' refreshments. Be respectful and ask permission before taking photos. Pinotepa Nacional itself has significant Easter celebrations, especially Good Friday and Easter Sunday, celebrated with fireworks, dances, and processions.

PARQUE NACIONAL LAGUNAS DE CHACAHUA

Bird-watchers should check out the coastal lagoons and mangrove swamps of 35,000-acre (14,164 ha) Parque Nacional Lagunas de Chacahua, about halfway between Pinotepa Nacional and Puerto Escondido. Boat tours are especially rewarding during the winter months, when migrating birds arrive. The park entrance is about 17 miles (27 km) along a fairly good dirt road off Highway 200. You can get here on your own via the town of Río Grande (there's a nice beach, Cerro Hermoso, with a simple fish restaurant) or book a tour in Puerto Escondido through **Viajes Dimar** (*Av. Pérez Gasga 905, tel. 954/582-0737, $$$$$*). The same operator runs full-day tours to **Laguna de Manialtepec,** a 10-mile-long (16 km) mangrove lagoon less than 10 miles (16 km) from Puerto Escondido. In the rainy summer

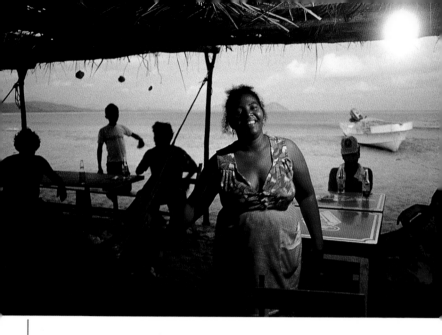

A Chacahua restaurant owner shares a laugh with her customers.

season the Manialtepec River forms an estuary, which birds—including anhinga, parrots, jacanas, and heron—find especially attractive. During the winter you will see the migratory species.

PUERTO ESCONDIDO

Coastal tourism doesn't gain a foothold until Puerto Escondido, connected directly to Oaxaca City by Highway 131 as well as via Pochutla (Highway 175). Surfers were the first to discover this small town, whose name means "hidden port." Until a paved road was completed in the 1970s, they bumped for miles down a bad dirt road to attack some of the world's best waves. Today they can fly in on major airlines for the surf competitions held each August and mid-November, the latter coinciding with the town's *fiesta*, a lively week of cultural events, sportfishing championships, and a beauty pageant. A major festival honoring la Virgen de la Soledad culminates on December 18, when local fishermen take their patron saint on an ocean-going procession that sets out from the main beach.

**Puerto
Escondido**
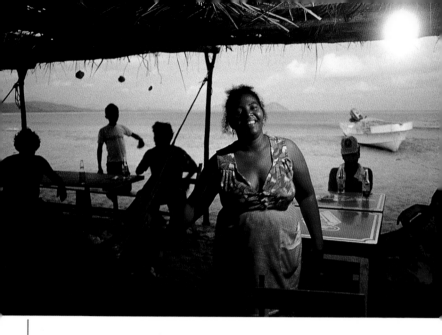 254 B1
**Visitor
information**
✉ Pérez Gasga s/n
(West end of
Adoquín)
☎ 954/582-0175

Puerto Escondido is one of those towns that somehow maintains its identity while catering nonstop to outsiders. The main tourist drag, a four-block-long pedestrian promenade nicknamed **el adoquin** (the paved road), slows down conspicuously only during the hottest hours at midday and sudden downpours. Otherwise, it's pretty much an endless parade. But the mix of foreign and national visitors is nice, the prices are reasonable, and seafood is served from open-air eateries right on the sand. Gangs of barefoot kids play on the palm-studded beach or hawk homemade key chains and seashell trinkets, and by noon the fishermen are disgorging their catch at **Playa Marinero,** the town's most central beach. Some boats transport sunbathers to nearby **Puerto Angelito** and **Playa Carrizalillo,** two secluded coves (also accessible on foot or by taxi) where simple seafood shanties serve up fried fish, *ceviche,* beers, and sodas. Private homes, hotels, and restaurants are starting to crop up on the hills farther west at Carrizalillo and Rinconada neighborhoods;

Bacocho is more established with a few of Puerto Escondido's fancier hotels, discos, condos, and private homes.

East of the main beach, surfers talk shop in palm-thatched, second-story restaurants as they scan **Playa Zicatela** for swells. Sipping a sunset cocktail at one of the many restaurants and bars facing Zicatela Beach, or from the wide green lawn at Hotel Posada Real, at Playa Bacocho, is highly recommended.

For a pre-Hispanic experience, visit **Villas Temazcalli** *(Via Temazcalli 3, tel 954/582-1023).* Throwing aromatic water on hot coals, which are replenished from the outside by a trap door, produces cleansing steam. The traditional-style sweat lodge also offers massage and both personal and ceremonial steam baths on a cliff above Zicatela beach. After you emerge—purified, relaxed, and exfoliated—you can sip a cup of tea and gaze at the ocean below. **Hotel Aldea del Bazar** *(Av. Benito Juárez s/n, Bacocho, tel 954/582-0508),* at Bacocho, also has a temazcalli.

PUERTO ÁNGEL

Once the state's most important port, Puerto Ángel, 51 miles (83 km) southeast of Puerto Escondido, is a sleepy town with a small navy base. Rocky headlands rise on either side of the secluded bay, and basic hotels, restaurants, and homes straggle up the hills and canyons. In 1997 Hurricane Pauline dealt this small community—along with others throughout Oaxaca and Guerrero states—a very nasty smack. Palm-thatched roofs were blown off, homes flooded, and possessions swept away in rivers of mud. But private donations of food, water, and clothing brought relief, and later, self-determined communities cleaned up the mess and affixed new roofs (some people

opted for sturdier but less aesthetic tin roofs), and Puerto Ángel was soon back on track.

There's not much to do except watch the fishermen haul in their catch and explore the area's beaches. If you want to swim close to town, the cleanest beach is **Playa Panteón,** on the west side of the bay; otherwise, hire a fisherman to take you to **Playa la Boquilla,** a quiet beach on a pleasant cove a few minutes away. The most famous beach in the area is **Playa Zipolite,** about 4 miles (6 km) away, where topless sunbathing is accepted. Here and in adjacent **San Agustanillo,** industrious locals have set up informal thatch-roofed restaurants and basic lodgings along the wide, palm-studded, sandy beaches, while the kids peddle *pescadillas* (grilled fish in a flour tortilla), and sodas and beers in buckets of rapidly melting ice. San Agustanillo is popular with body-surfers, and some enterprising local usually has body boards for rent.

For an educational outing visit **El Centro Mexicano de la Tortuga** *(Domicilio Conocido, closed Mon., $),* in nearby Mazunte. Take the obligatory guided tour to see the turtles in large tanks and learn about the conservation of Mexico's seven marine turtle species and several freshwater species. Involving local people in the project provides them with economical alternatives to poaching endangered turtles and their eggs. Until recently, selling turtle meat, oil, and eggs was a viable business venture.

BAHÍAS DE HUATULCO

There's no doubt that Huatulco, about 31 miles (50 km) northeast of Puerto Ángel, has abundant natural beauty and charm. Nine lovely bays with dozens of pellucid coves and lagoons crowd its 21-mile (35 km) coastline. Clear water and

Puerto Ángel
◬   254 B1

Bahías de Huatulco

🗺 254 C1
Visitor information
✉ Hotel Crowne Plaza, Bahía Tangolunda
☎ 958/581-0486
www.hoteleshuatulco.com.mx

plenty of rocky coves make for great snorkeling, and swimming is pleasant year-round. There's no shortage of sunshine or palm trees, and the rugged mountains of the Sierra de Miahuatlán looming just beyond the beach only make the scene more intimate.

Huatulco's coastline first attracted the attention of FONATUR, the Mexican tourism development board, in the 1960s. Construction began in the 1980s, and since then, the once innocent Mixtec fishing village has received a significant makeover. Buildings here are limited to six stories, 70 percent of the development's land has been set aside as an ecological reserve, and mid-range and economical hotels are to be built along with the exclusive five-star resorts. The original plan was scaled back after the economic slump of the mid-1990s: The new plan calls for 1.2 million visitors per year by 2020.

Scenic **Bahía Tangolunda** was the first bay developed and has reached its maximum density of six resorts. Located here are the Quinta Real and Camino Real hotels and the area's only 18-hole golf course *(tel 958/581-0059)*. Concessions rent sailboards, catamarans, and other water toys. You can get PADI dive certification, rent diving gear, or book a snorkel tour through **Action Sports Marina** *(tel 958/581-0055)*. **Playa Consuelo** and **Playa el Arrocito** are small beaches on Tangolunda accessible only by boat.

Bahía Santa Cruz has also been developed, with moderately priced hotels, shops, and several plazas surrounded by cafés. At the southern end of the bay, the underwater preserve at **Playa La Entrega** attracts divers and snorkelers. To the north, tiny **Playa Yerbabuena,** accessible only by boat, is a good place to get away from it all. Sportfishing or bay tours can be arranged at the **Marina Santa Cruz,** through La Sociedad Cooperativa Tangolunda *(tel 958/587-0081)*, or through **Bahías Plus** *(tel 958/587-0216)* or other operators. **Bahía Chahué,** the largest of the bays, has a day spa, a mostly completed marina for private yachts, a beach club, and the largest parking lot ever seen—right out in the middle of nowhere ("If you build it, they will come…"). En route to La Crucecita, Chahué's few hotels, restaurants, and bars are located haphazardly here and there a short walk from the beach.

About a mile (1.5 km) inland from Bahía Chahué, **Crucecita** is a pleasing, custom-built town with

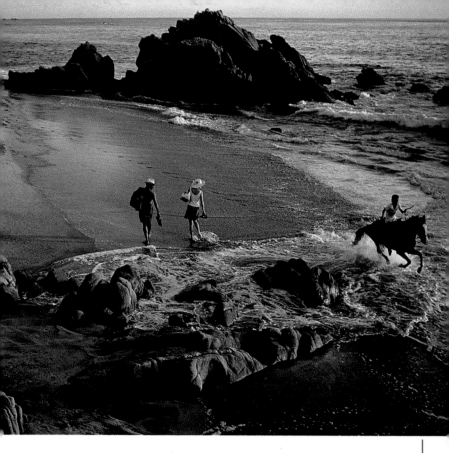

restaurants, a relatively lively night scene, and budget and mid-range hotels within a few blocks of the main square. Other services include banks, a post office, and a market, where the locals shop.

A popular day trip into the lush coastal mountains is a tour of one of the **coffee plantations** established by European immigrants in the 19th century. Tour operators can also arrange day trips to the Centro Mexicano de la Tortuga at Mazunte, Bahía Manialtepec, and Lagunas de Chacahua.

ISTMO DE TEHUANTEPEC

Of the three principal cities in the Isthmus of Tehuantepec, only commerce-oriented **Salina Cruz** is on the water, and touristic accommodations throughout the region are rustic. Neither **Juchitán** nor **Tehuantepec** is terribly scenic—they are sweltering hot and often dusty. Those who visit are inexorably drawn by strength of the culture and the lively, witty people who live here, most descendants of Zapotecs. Travelers often stop off here en route to Chiapas, or to experience *las velas,* exuberant celebrations held throughout the region between April and September—mainly in May. Town life centers around the main plaza and the market, the latter presided over by women in short *huipiles* (boxy blouses) and billowing, ankle-length skirts. In Juchitán, visit **La Casa de la Cultura** (*Jose F. Gómez, one block from the plaza),* which displays 20th-century art and archaeological pieces. ■

Puerto Escondido boasts a string of beaches to suit everyone.

Istmo de Tehuantepec
⚑ 255 D2

More places to visit in Oaxaca

GRUTAS DE SAN SEBASTIÁN

An interesting excursion from Oaxaca is a trip to the underground caves at San Sebastián. Local youths guide you through the 1,300-foot-long (400 m) cave, which has five chambers measuring 65–230 feet (20–70 m) in height. Bring a strong flashlight, and comfortable walking shoes for exploring the cave and the gentle hills of the surrounding countryside. This is a Tourist Yu'u Destination (see below).

▲ 254 B2 **Visitor information** See Oaxaca, p. 256

SAN PEDRO AMUSGOS TO LA MIXTECA ALTA

A few shops selling the finely embroidered *huipiles* (boxy blouses) for which the Amuzgo women are known cluster along Highway 125 as it passes **San Pedro Amusgos,** 32 miles (51 km) north of Pinotepa Nacional (see

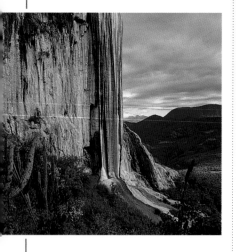

Tourist Yu'u cabins allow you to overnight at such beauty spots as Hierve el Agua.

p. 274). The town celebrates its namesake saint, St. Peter, on June 29 with costumes and a colorful procession, and the Fiesta de la Virgen del Rosario on the first Sunday in October. The two-lane highway winds through the Mixteca Alta region on its way to the capital, passing faded but engaging **Tlaxiaco,** once a strategic Aztec garrison and the site of

one of Oaxaca's first Dominican monasteries. The feast of the Virgin of the Assumption is celebrated the days leading to August 15.

▲ 254 A2–A3 **Visitor information** See Oaxaca, p. 256

SHRINE OF THE VIRGIN OF JUQUILA

Every year hundreds of thousands make a pilgrimage to pray at the shrine of la Virgen Morena de Juquila (the dark-skinned Virgin of Juquila), some coming part or all of the way on foot. The object of adoration is a diminutive statue to which miracles have been attributed. According to legend, when a fire destroyed much of the village, including the house where the icon was kept, the statue was unharmed, its skin darkened. **Santa Catalina Juquila,** a simple town surrounded by mountains, has a fresh, cool climate and plenty of no-frills hotels to accommodate the pilgrims. On the days preceding the saint's day, December 8, there are religious and cultural festivities, including a dawn rosary, processions, and later food, music, dance, and, of course, fireworks.

▲ 254 B2 **Visitor information** See Oaxaca, p. 256

TOURIST YU'U DESTINATIONS

On weekends, especially in hot weather, extended families stake out prime spots under the few shade trees close to the pools. On weekdays, it's not unusual to find yourself alone in the dry, scrubby landscape, where a looping trail leads into the canyon for excellent views of the site's unique mineral formations.

The site has a parking lot, restrooms, and changing facilities. Local women sell *tlayudas* (large, slightly leathery tortillas topped with meat or beans and condiments), bowls of beans, and other simple fare. A half-dozen clean cabins (a few with semi-equipped kitchens, the others with private bathroom) allow folks to spend a night in this star studded spot where the wind whistles down into the canyons. (Double-check with the Oaxaca tourism department to make sure cabins are open.) Buses make the 50-mile (80 km) trip several times a day from the second-class bus station .

■**Visitor information** See Oaxaca, p. 256 ■

Isolated, culturally rich Chiapas offers jungle-draped pyramids and breathtaking scenery. Adopting Christianity early on, the Maya have maintained their own spiritual beliefs, resulting in one of Mexico's most synergistic versions of Catholicism.

Chiapas

Flower motif on the church at San Juan Chamula

Chiapas

TO SPEAK OF CHIAPAS IS TO SPEAK OF THE MAYA, THE LARGEST NATIVE American group north of Peru. About a quarter of Chiapas's people speak an indigenous tongue, and the highland Maya alone have four distinct languages. Owing in large part to centuries of governmental neglect, indigenous communities carry on a traditional way of life. Councils of elders administer rural highland communities, and weavers incorporate thousand-year-old designs in their complicated brocaded *huipiles*. Corn is both literally and figuratively the staff of life; planting and harvesting the grain, and cooking daily tortillas, are activities bound by ritual and blessed with devotion.

The early 16th-century Spanish conquest of Chiapas was particularly swift and brutal. Discouraged by the lack of gold and other riches, the conquerors established San Juan Chamula as a slave market and inflicted other atrocities. Distance from the regulatory *audiencia* (see p. 31) in Mexico City meant little or no meddling in their affairs. Even by the day's standards, treatment of the Indians was beyond harsh, and Bishop Bartolomé de las Casas eventually persuaded the Spanish Crown to revoke many of the Spanish-held land holdings.

Unlike the Aztecs, the Maya at the time of the Conquest were far removed from their Golden Age (A.D. 250–900), when great cities such as Palenque and Yaxchilán flourished. Among the most advanced civilizations of the world at that time, the Classic Maya achieved great heights in mathematics, astronomy, architecture, and the arts.

Today, Chiapas is one of Mexico's most rural states, its economy based on fishing, forestry, and agriculture. Coffee, cotton, bananas, and cacao are among its most important exports, and subsistence agriculture is widely practiced. Mostly mountainous, Chiapas shares a fringe of

Tzotzil men from San Juan Chamula; most locals still dress traditionally.

tropical lowlands with neighboring Tabasco, Campeche, and Guatemala. The state capital and transportation hub, Tuxtla Gutiérrez, lies on a central plain surrounded by plateaus. Little visited by foreign tourists, the Pacific coast is a series of estuaries and fishing villages accessed almost exclusively by rural roads. There's a plan afoot in 2005 to invest millions of dollars to make small Puerto Madero, near the Guatemala border, tourist-ready.

Abundant rain produces waterfalls, lakes, and the *selva lacandona,* one of North America's last remaining rain forests. This endangered land is home to the small Lacandón tribe (for which it is named), who fled Spanish encroachment in their Yucatán homeland. Until a few generations ago, this forest-dwelling people worshiped at the jungle-shrouded ruins of Bonampak. Today, this and

other archaeological sites, only partially rescued from the surrounding jungle, are among the state's most powerful tourist magnets. Its other big draw is San Cristóbal de las Casas, a colonial city whose abundance of traditional culture and indigenous handicrafts attracts droves of visitors despite the area's well-publicized political problems. ■

Area of map detail

Tuxtla Gutiérrez
⚐ 283 B3
Visitor information
✉ Blvd. Belisario Domínguez 950, Edificio Plaza de las Instituciones
☎ 961/602-5074

Chiapa de Corzo
⚐ 283 B3
Visitor information
✉ Av. Domingo Ruiz 1
☎ 961/616-1013

Tuxtla Gutiérrez & environs

TUXTLA MEANS "PLACE OF MANY RABBITS" IN NÁHUATL, and Gutiérrez refers to Joaquín Miguel Gutiérrez, who championed Chiapas's union with Mexico in 1824. This large, hot metropolis replaced San Cristóbal de las Casas as the state capital in 1892 after San Cristóbal sided with the Royalists during the War of Independence. Tuxtla is an important commercial and distribution center for coffee, tobacco, and other locally produced products.

La Pila, the 16th-century redbrick fountain that graces the central square of Chiapa de Corzo

Tuxlta's main thoroughfare is Avenida Central, which divides the sprawling main square, **Plaza Cívica.** Surrounding this central plaza are the post office, modern **Catedral San Marcos,** and several government offices. More attractive is **Parque de la Marimba** (*Av. Central at Calle 8 Poniente*), a shady square where couples dance to live marimba music each evening. If you're not a dancer, look for a coveted folding chair and enjoy the band.

Northeast of the city center, at **Parque Madero,** those who read Spanish can learn about regional archaeology and colonial history in the **Museo Regional de Chiapas** (*Calzada de los Hombres Ilustres, tel 961/613-4479, closed Mon., $*). Also in the park, the **jardín botánico** has labeled tropical plants while the **Centro de Convivencia Infantil** offers miniature golf and other kids' amusements.

Although it is actually a government-run folk-art shop,

the **Casa de las Artesanías** (*Blvd. Belisario Domínguez 2035, tel 961/602-9800, closed Sun.*), northeast of the *zócalo,* seems more like a handicrafts museum with an ethnographic museum at the rear.

The capital's principal attraction is the peaceful, well laid-out **Zoológico Miguel Álvarez del Toro** (*Calzada Cerro Hueco s/n, tel 961/614-4765, closed Mon., $*), about 5 miles (8 km) southeast of downtown. The zoo gives a great overview not just of Chiapas's native animals, which are the only species represented, but also of its plant life. Iguanas, chachalacas (pheasant-like birds), and other harmless creatures roam free, while the more dangerous beasts are kept in expansive enclosures that imitate as much as possible their own habitats. A small museum, store, and restaurant complete the complex.

About half an hour east of Tuxtla Gutiérrez is **Chiapa de Corzo,** a take-off point for boat trips along Cañón del Sumidero (see opposite), but an interesting town in its own right. At the time of the Spanish invasion, the bellicose Chiapaneco tribe dominated the region, having established themselves around 1300. They fought with Maya towns for control of local salt mines and cacao fields, and generally made life so unpleasant that the Maya allied themselves with the Spaniards.

As soon as the Spaniards had dispatched the Chiapanecos for whom the state is named, they

Some people hire a taxi in Tuxtla Gutiérrez for a tour along the rim of Cañón del Sumidero. You can find a restaurant at one of the five lookout points, La Atalaya.

enslaved their former Maya allies. A Spanish settlement established in Chiapa de Corzo in 1528 was soon abandoned for the fresher, mosquito-free climate at what is now San Cristóbal de las Casas.

It's impossible to get lost in Chiapa de Corzo. The main square is crowned by **La Pila,** an octagonal fountain (1562) said to have been inspired by the diadem of Spain's Queen Isabella. Adjacent to the 16th-century **Ex-convento de Santo Domingo,** one block south of the plaza, the **Museo de la Laca** *(Closed Mon.)* shows lacquered gourds made in the town, as well as other lacquered objects from around the world.

One street from Chiapa de Corzo's main plaza, motorboats depart for tours *($$$)* of the impressive **Cañón del Sumidero.** This steep-walled canyon was created millions of years ago by the wild **Río Grijalva,** which was tamed by the construction in 1981 of the **Chicoasen Dam.** Rocky red walls rise as high as 3,280 feet (1,000 m) above the brownish-green river.

Although the canyon is striking, the roar of the boat engine sometimes precludes commentary, and the egrets, kingfishers, crocodiles, and other animals can be hard to spot. Within the canyon the Ixcaret Group has created **Parque Sumidero** *(Av. Independencia s/n, Barro San Miguel, Chiapa de Corzo, tel 961/600-6654. $$$$$),* with hiking, zipline, kayaking, and mountain biking. Most travelers still prefer the standard boat trip. ■

San Cristóbal de las Casas

SURROUNDED BY MAGNIFICENT PINE-COVERED PEAKS, San Cristóbal accepts its beauty with the naiveté of a child. Simple homes in a range of bright colors line cobblestone streets, and even the hordes of foreign backpackers don't diminish the city's cozy, exotic appeal. At 6,890 feet (2,100 m) above sea level, the chilly evenings are perfumed with the smoke from wood-burning stoves and stone fireplaces. The climate is conducive to warm sweaters and jeans, not the bare-as-you-dare ensembles of sweltering Tuxtla Gutiérrez. Visitors en route to Palenque and the lakes at Montebello find themselves postponing travel plans and dreaming of long-term residency.

After an intense but fruitless resistance by the Chiapaneco Indians, the city of Villareal de Chiapa de los Españoles was established in 1528 by Spaniard Diego de Mazariego. It was later renamed San Cristóbal de las Casas in honor of its patron, St. Christopher, and its protector, Dominican monk Bartolomé de las Casas (1474–1566). As the first bishop of Chiapas, de las Casas fought to improve the lives of indigenous men, women, and children under the devastating *encomienda* system, which was tantamount to slavery (see p. 31).

The Spaniards organized the new town in barrios, each with its own church, patron saint, and industry. Today, tradition-minded townspeople still retain neighborhood loyalties, visiting **La Merced** for sweets and wax religious figures, and **Guadalupe** for handmade wooden toys, candles, and leather. The best fireworks are still said to be found in **Santa Lucía.** These neighborhoods are just a few blocks west, east, and southeast of the *zócalo,* respectively.

The **zócalo,** officially Plaza 31 de Marzo, is the physical and social nucleus of the city. It is surrounded by arcaded stores and restored older houses—now banks, bars, hotels, and restaurants. On the west flank is the courtly neoclassic **Palacio**

Municipal, while to the north stands the **Catedral** *(tel 967/678-0665),* built in the 16th century and later remodeled inside and out in the baroque style. Its unusual facade, with stylized floral details, makes a striking background for photos. North and west of the zocalo, two museums have excellent displays of local minerals. The **Museo de Jade** *(Av. 16 de septiembre 16, tel 967/678-2550, $)* has reproductions of pieces valued and traded among many Mesoamerican cultures. El **Museo de Ambar** *(Calle Diego de Mazariegos, adjacent to La Merced, tel 967/678-9716, closed Mon., $)* has the same sort of exhibits and information about this oft-imitated fossil resin.

Two churches perched above the city provide good views and an energizing, if short, uphill walk. The **Templo de Guadalupe** *(End of Real de Guadalupe)* is on the west side. The **Templo de San Cristóbal** *(Hermanos Domínguez at Ignacio Allende)* is higher up and has a better view, but opens only on Sundays and for the feast of the town's patron, St. Christopher.

Solomonic columns and other baroque elements fancify the intricate but soiled facade of the **Templo y Ex-Convento de Santo Domingo** *(Av. Lázaro Cárdenas s/n, tel 967/678-1609).*

San Cristóbal de las Casas
🅼 283 B3
Visitor information
✉ Av. Miguel Hidalgo 2
☎ 9/678-6570

Inside, note the graceful, gilded wood altarpieces and outstanding carved pulpit. Filling the church's extensive open-air atrium is a market of regional crafts. Within the adjacent former monastery, **Sna Jolobil** (see Shopping, p. 385) sells intricate pieces of brocade and other exquisite hand-loomed textiles.

A few blocks north is the living, labyrinthine **mercado municipal** *(Av. General Utrilla at Nicaragua).* The daily market is especially vivid on Saturdays, when Tzeltal and Tzotzil men and women arrive dressed traditionally in brilliant garments, the women's long braids woven with jewel-toned ribbons.

If you want to learn more about native weaving and culture, visit the **Museo Sergio Castro**

(Guadalupe Victoria 38, tel 967/ 678-4289, donation). Art historian Sergio Castro gives nightly lectures and slide shows about local weaving and shows his considerable collection. He speaks Spanish, French, Italian, and English, so call when you hit town to schedule a visit on the appropriate night.

Another home-turned-museum is **Na Bolom** *(Av. Vicente Guerrero 33, tel 967/678-1418, closed Mon., $).* Longtime Chiapas residents Swiss photojournalist Trudy Blom and her husband, Danish archaeologist Franz Blom (both deceased), for decades welcomed students, researchers, and Lacandón Indians into their home. Tours *($$)* provide insight into this unique guesthouse, restaurant, botanical garden, and research library. ■

The colors of the cathedral's facade—red, yellow, white, and black—represent the four directions in the Maya world view. The cross also has pre-Hispanic connotations.

Maya villages around
San Cristóbal

RELIGION, SPIRITUALITY, FAMILY, AND DUTY ARE IMPORTANT to the Maya of Chiapas, and are the threads from which everyday life is woven. Ceremony and custom pervade daily ritual. Society is hierarchical, and village elders still wear the impressive and unusual symbols of their office during ceremonies. Even the elaborate designs woven painstakingly into textiles have significance for both weaver and wearer. Culturally and sometimes physically isolated from mainstream Mexico, the Tzotzil and Tzeltal villages around San Cristóbal maintain ancient traditions as they deal with armed conflict and the interference of well-meaning outsiders.

The Chamula are a large and relatively prosperous group of Tzotzil-speaking people with their municipal seat in **San Juan Chamula,** about 7 miles (11 km) from San Cristóbal. Most women and girls in San Juan wear distinctive, hairy, black-wool wrap skirts held in place by wide cotton belts, and short-sleeved, blue or white blouses lined with decorative trim. Traditional menswear is white cotton trousers and shirt, with a fleecy wool cloak for warmth.

The physical and spiritual center of this traditional town is its enchanting church, dedicated to St. John the Baptist, the Chamulans' most important manifestation of God. The beauty of the church's facade would move all but the most hopeless philistine. An arched doorway—decorated with rows of stylized flowers in sea green, vivid violet, hot pink, gold, and blues—contrasts soulfully with the simple lines of the bright white facade.

The church offers no formal services and has no pews. Seated on the floor amid fragrant pine needles and powerful copal incense, worshipers chant prayers while lighting rows of tiny candles of different colors. Lining the walls are Catholic saints dressed in clothing respectfully woven by the local women. Taking photographs or video recordings inside the church is both strictly forbidden and severely punished with fines and/or jail sentences.

Visitors to town must register at the tourist office, pay a small fee to visit the church, and get a short but stern admonition about church protocol. Visit San Juan Chamula on Sunday if possible, when the church square is filled with vendors, or during a holiday celebration.

About 5 miles (8 km) away, **Zinacantán** is a Tzotzil town whose inhabitants are known for their flowers. Lilies, chrysanthemums, gladioli, and roses grow in their fields and gladden their altars. They can be purchased at the town's small Sunday market,

Left: Carnival celebration in Tenejapa

San Cristóbal de las Casas
🅜 283 B3
Visitor information
✉ Av. Miguel Hidalgo 2
☎ 967/678-6570

although many growers sell them wholesale in the steamy lowlands. Embroidered flowers adorn the women's bright white *huipiles* (blouses) and the thinly striped pink shirts of the men.

Sights in Zinacantán include the **Iglesia de San Lorenzo** *(Isabel la Católica at 5 de Febrero, $)* and the adjacent **Museo Sna Tsotz Levetik,** a traditional building with utilitarian and decorative items.

A half-day guided tour *($$$)* is an excellent way to visit Zinacantán and San Juan Chamula and can be arranged through Na Bolom (see p. 287) or area tour operators. Guides usually visit specific families and arrange weaving demonstrations; they know what can and can't be photographed and have interesting anecdotes. Except for children begging, the indigenous people in Chiapas do not appreciate being photographed. Area tour operators also offer horseback riding tours to San Juan Chamula *($$$)*.

A dramatic ride through the mountains due north of San Cristóbal brings you to **San Pedro Chenalhó,** set in a pretty river valley. As the center for negotiations between government and Zapatista factions, this usually relaxed Tzotzil town has become increasingly suspicious of outsiders. The Sunday market day is still a celebrated rural ritual, however, and reason enough to visit without fear.

Equally rewarding in terms of mountain scenery is a drive to the Tzeltal village of **Tenejapa,** set in a pretty river valley 17 miles (27 km) northeast of San Cristóbal. ■

A colorful Sunday market occupies the plaza in front of San Juan Chamula's church.

Palenque

MORE THAN JUST AN AWESOME ARCHAEOLOGICAL SITE, Palenque has one of the region's last remaining patches of evergreen tropical forest. Epiphyte-draped trees surround graceful pyramids topped with delicate temples, glowing the color of rich cream in the tropical sun. Small rivers crisscross the site, and a series of cascades fills the Queen's Bath, where today's plebeian visitors may now bathe. Trails through unexcavated portions of the 4,400-acre (1,780 ha) reserve lead to parties of squawking parrots and shrieking howler monkeys, where silent Jesus Christ lizards and snakes slink under damp fallen leaves.

Its intense wild setting as well as its harmonious, graceful architecture make Palenque magic. Corbeled vaults permit larger doorways and give the buildings a light, refined appearance enhanced by delicate roofcombs, mansard roofs, and T-shaped windows evocative of the wind god, Ik. Of all the Maya sites, it is among the most elegant, mysterious, and accessible.

Accessibility was the key to Palenque's initial success. Built on a natural terrace overlooking the floodplain of the Río Usumacinta, the city served as the center of trade between the Petén region, the highlands of Chiapas, and the Grijalva Valley. Knowledge and ideas as well as trade goods flowed along the wide Usumacinta, especially during the Late Classic era (A.D. 600–800), when Palenque flourished. Under leaders such as Pakal the Great and his oldest son and successor, Chan Bahlum, Palenque joined Calakmul, Tikal, and Copán as one of the most influential kingdoms of the lowland Maya.

Large panels throughout the city were commissioned to illustrate the royal dynasty and its accomplishments. A dearth of suitable stone in the region explains the use of exquisite bas-relief carvings, in limestone and stucco, in lieu of the stelae favored elsewhere in the Maya world. Many of the carvings were ordered by Chan Bahlum, who traced his lineage back 11 generations, beginning with a mythic ruler nicknamed "Lady Beastie."

Among the most stellar examples are the three elaborate stucco panels within the **Templo de las Inscripciones,** containing about 620 glyphs. Royalty in elaborate feathered headdresses stand on monster masks; each holds a representation of the god K'awil, one of three gods worshiped as mythic ancestors. Access to the temple is now severely limited; get permission to join a 15-minute tour (at 4 p.m.) at the INAH office at the site entrance first thing in the morning.

The monumental structure was commissioned by Chan Bahlum's father, Pakal the Great (or Kan-Hanab-Pakal II), as his royal tomb. Unveiled by Mexican archaeologist Alberto Ruz Lhuillier in 1952 after four seasons of excavation, this is to date Mexico's most elaborate burial site. Sixty-six narrow steps lead deep within the pyramid to the crypt, where portraits of prior sovereigns decorate the walls in stucco relief.

Still bearing traces of red paint, the sarcophagus's 5-ton lid of intricately carved limestone depicts Pakal's descent into the underworld. Near the top, a bird symbolic of the

Palenque
⚠ 283 C4
Visitor information
✉ Calle Francisco Javier Mina at Nicolás Bravo
☎ 916/345-0356

heavens perches on the sacred ceiba tree. The crypt's contents, including Pakal's remains and rings, necklaces, ear spools, and a funerary mask in a mosaic of jade, with eyes of obsidian and shell, are displayed at Mexico City's Museo Nacional de Antropología (see pp. 198–201).

Across the Río Otolum, the **Grupo de la Cruz** (Cross Group) is currently under excavation. In 1998, finds in Temple 19 revealed a previously unknown ruler, Uc-Pakal-Kinich, as well as possible liaisons with rulers at Copán, in present-day Honduras. Surrounding a large plaza, the group takes its name from crosslike images found in the **Templo de la Cruz Foliada.**

Within its sunken courtyard, several sets of carvings depict captured enemy rulers in various poses of submission and mutilation. Depicting not a cross but a holy ceiba tree decorated with corn stalks, the stone panel shows ruler Chan Balum's ascent to power. At the north end of the plaza, five tiers lead to the large **Templo de la Cruz,** which also displays the World Tree motif. Its roofcomb, one of the highest in Palenque, is in excellent condition. Here, panels depicting the royal ancestors emphasize their role as mediators between heaven and Earth. On the west side of the plaza, themes of war and sacrifice dominate the well-preserved **Templo del Sol,** where the face of the jaguar-man god peers from a Maya war shield.

Back across the river, the **Palacio** served the royal family as

Mist envelops the Temple of the Inscriptions. The nine tiers of the 65-foot (20 m) stepped pyramid on which it rests most likely correspond to the nine levels of the Maya underworld.

both ceremonial and living quarters. The complex of vaulted galleries and rooms surrounding interior courtyards was built and added to over many centuries.

On the west steps, glyphs heralding the birth of Pakal the Great are among the site's earliest, while its unusual, four-tiered tower (possibly an observatory) was built just before the city's disintegration.

Northeast of the Palace, divergent paths enter the jungle shade, a welcome respite from the intense tropical sun. After crossing **Río Murciélagos** (Bat River), a right-hand path leads to **Grupo C,** a half-dozen small temples surrounding a central plaza. The left-hand path leads to **Grupo Murciélagos** (Bat Group), a residential complex

To Grupo C,
Grupo
Murciélagos (Bat
Group), & Baño
de la Reina
(Queen's Bath)

Grupo Norte
(North Group)

Templo del Conde
(Temple of the Count)

Juego de pelota
(ball court)

To entrance &
restaurant

Palacio (Palace)

This steep
staircase leads to
a buried tomb
within the Temple
of the Inscriptions

for Maya nobles, and to a series of cascades forming the **Baño de la Reina** (Queen's Bath), a swimming hole today enjoyed by both visitors and locals.

East of the Río Otolum, the four-tiered **Templo del Conde** (Temple of the Count) was named for the 19th-century German eccentric who set up housekeeping here. Nearby is a compact **juego de pelota** (ball court), as well as the **Grupo Norte**, whose plazas and temples were among the last constructed before the city's demise.

A hat, sunscreen, and water will help mitigate the strong sun and steamy heat. Retreat to the restaurant for a meal or cool drink during the hottest hours of the day, or to the air-conditioned **site museum** (*Closed Mon.*), where your ticket stub gains entrance at no additional cost. Excellent exhibits are labeled in English, Spanish, and Tzotzil. Among the museum's collection is the **Palace Tablet,** an intricate stone relief detailing the lineage of Palenque's rulers. Shuttles (*$*) link the ruins and Avenida Juárez, in Palenque town. ■

Templo de la Cruz (Temple of the Cross)

Templo de la Cruz Foliada (Temple of the Foliated Cross)

Templo del Sol (Temple of the Sun)

Río Otolum

Templo de las Inscripciones (Temple of the Inscriptions)

Large stone tablets dot the 4,400-acre (1,780 ha) site.

Drive: Palenque to Parque Nacional Lagunas de Montebello

This route follows the Pan-American Highway (Highway 199) between Chiapas's most famous ruins, Palenque, and Parque Nacional Lagunas de Montebello. The highway climbs out of the tropical jungle to rolling hills and lush temperate valleys around Ocosingo before continuing steeply to the evergreen mountains around San Cristóbal de las Casas. From this endearing colonial city, the route descends slightly in elevation to end at the Guatemalan border. On the way you'll visit major and minor ruins, foamy white waterfalls forming crystalline blue pools, indigenous villages, and prosperous mestizo towns and cities.

An aerial view of the ruins of Toniná

Recommended places to overnight on the way are Palenque, Ocosingo, San Cristóbal de las Casas, and either Comitán de Domínguez or the elegant Parador Santa María, near Chinkultic and the Lagunas de Montebello.

After visiting the ruins at **Palenque** ❶ (see pp. 290–93) drive south along Hwy. 199 for about 14 miles (22 km) to see the 130-foot (40 m) waterfall at **Misol-Ha** ($), most impressive when swollen with late-summer and fall rains. Swim in the pool at the base of the waterfall, or explore the cave behind the falls, which leads to a subterranean pool. The site has restrooms, basic camping facilities, and simple restaurants.

About 25 miles (40 km) to the south, follow a dirt road for several miles to the extraordinary falls of **Agua Azul** ❷ ($).

Surrounded by exuberant tropical vegetation, the river plunges into a rocky gorge, forming hundreds of frothy white falls and, during the dry season, crystal-clear pools that give the site its name: "blue water." Near the parking lot are two main viewpoints plus lots of small restaurants and souvenir stands. Hike down the canyon to bathe in a series of lovely interconnected pools or up past the campground to take advantage of a different view.

Continuing south, the highway curves and climbs past vistas of patchwork fields and farms, abandoning the sometimes oppressive lowlands for the refreshing climate around the Ocosingo Valley, with mixed broadleaf vegetation and many species of birds. Little visited by tourists, **Ocosingo** is a pleasant, fairly prosperous mestizo town.

A detour of about 6 miles (10 km) southeast of Ocosingo on a paved road brings you to the important but little-known ruins at **Toniná** ❸ ($), which flourished at the beginning of the tenth century, around the time Palenque was being abandoned. Here, one of the tallest pyramids of the Maya world rises 230 feet (70 m) above the Grand Plaza, commanding an awesome view of the valley and the mountains to the south. Most likely the city's Mayan name, which means "big house of stones," refers to this massive pyramid.

Construction of this structure took place over more than a thousand years. Successive generations built new palaces and temples; to date, four of the former and ten of the latter have been identified throughout the seven-level pyramid. In 1992, the remarkably

Maya carvings, Toniná

Church at Toniná

Agua Azul

See also area map p. 283
C4–C2

► Palenque
↔ 200 miles (320 km)
⊕ 3 days
► Parque Nacional Lagunas de Montebello

NOT TO BE MISSED
- Palenque
- Agua Azul
- Toniná
- San Cristóbal de las Casas
- Parque Nacional Lagunas de Montebello

well-preserved Mural of the Four Suns was discovered on the sixth level. The 13-foot-long (4 m) stucco painting represents a Maya codex describing the four distinct eras of creation. Crowning the structure are the Temple of the Prisoners and the Temple of the Smoky Mirror. Near the base of the pyramid on the right side lies the sarcophagus of one of the city's last rulers, Tzotz-Choj.

By prior arrangent with Hospedaje y

Restaurante Esmeralda (see Hotels & Restaurants, p. 376) you can take a four-hour horseback riding tour of the luxuriant Ocosingo Valley, or an air excursion via small plane over the same area or to Laguna Miramar (see p. 305) or the ruins at Yaxchilán and Bonampak (see pp. 302–304).

Return to Hwy. 199, and continue west for 70 miles (112 km) along this and Hwy. 190, passing cattle ranches, small farms, and coffee plantations, to **San Cristóbal de las Casas** ❹ (see pp. 286–87). After your visit to this engaging city, return to Hwy. 190 (the Pan-American Highway) and head southeast toward the Guatemalan border.

After about 18 miles (29 km), look for a right-hand road leading to the Tzeltal village of **Amatenango del Valle.** You'll spot the entrance to this unsigned pottery-making town by the characteristic unglazed, burnished clay pots and animal figures in front of homes along the highway. The decorative and utilitarian vessels are fired in the traditional way, under an open-air wood fire. Amatenango's women spend their time building pots instead of weaving, so they must buy the cloth for their *huipiles* (blouses). They embroider the blouses with simple designs in red and yellow.

Continue south another 25 miles (40 km) to **Comitán de Domínguez** ❺ (*Visitor information, Calle Central Benito Juárez 6, Plaza Principal, tel 963/632-0244*), a wonderful small city currently being restored to its colonial splendor with federal grant money. Built by the Spanish as a commercial and transportation hub, the city today serves the same function for Tzeltal Indians and mestizos in outlying ranches.

If you're interested in Mexican history or simply like republican-era edifices and antiques, it's worth a look at the **Casa-Museo Dr. Belisario Domínguez** (*Av. Belisario Domínguez Sur 35, tel 963/632-1300, closed Mon., $*). The medical doctor and Chiapas senator was a Revolution hero

whose frank and unflattering assessment of the Huerta administration led to his assassination in 1913. Dr. Domínguez was born in this gracious house in 1863; preserved here are his instruments, pharmaceuticals, and other medical paraphernalia as well as photographs, documents, and letters that date from the Mexican Revolution.

Other sights of interest in Comitán are the **Catedral Santo Domingo de Guzmán** (*1a Av. Oriente Sur, on the main square*), the **Iglesia San Caralampio** (*2a Calle Norte Oriente at 4a Av. Oriente, tel 963/632-0673*), and the **Museo de Arte Hermila Castellanos** (*Av. Central Sur 51, tel 963/632-2082*), with excellent contemporary Mexican art.

Beyond Comitán, it's less than 10 miles (16 km) to **Tenam Puente** (*closed Mon., $*), a large but unremarkable archaeological site. Built on a strategic hilltop location, this religious center and residential area flourished during the Classic and Early Postclassic periods, after the Maya had abandoned cities such as Palenque.

Continue along the Pan-American Highway, detouring after 10 miles (16 km) onto the road marked "Lagunas de Montebello." Not far down the road, a left-hand dirt road leads to **Chinkultic** ❻ (*$*), a Maya city that was abandoned just a few hundred years after reaching its apogee during the Late Classic period (A.D. 600–900). Not many structures have been restored on this site, but there's an incredible view from the top of the main pyramid—a rather steep climb from the park entrance. Swim in the **cenote azul** (the sinkhole is a bit hard to find; ask the park guard), or visit the ball court, less impressive since its bas-relief sculpture was moved to the Museo Nacional de Antropología in Mexico City (see pp. 198–201).

The last stop of the journey is **Parque Nacional Lagunas de Montebello** ❼ (see pp. 298–99), where more than a dozen lakes of various hues can easily be seen from different viewpoints. ■

For crystalline water, visit Agua Azul in the dry season.

Parque Nacional Lagunas de Montebello

🔼 283 C2

Visitor information

✉ Calle Central Benito Juarez 6, Plaza principal, Comitán

☎ 963/632-4047

Parque Nacional Lagunas de Montebello

LAKES OF DIFFERENT HUES ARE SPRINKLED THROUGHOUT this national park like a handful of translucent marbles flung down by a tempestuous giant. The presence of different kinds and levels of oxides causes the lakes to take on different shades, especially noticeable when the sun is shining brightly. Some glow a deep green, others are emerald, steel gray, greenish-blue, violet, or pale blue. Lagunas de Montebello, Chiapas's only national park, comprises 14,880 acres (6,022 ha) of temperate forest along Mexico's southern border with Guatemala.

One of the park's 50-plus lakes, near the Guatemalan border

Because of weeds growing on the lake bottom and occasional drownings over a period of many years, locals do not recommend swimming in the majority of these lovely lakes. (Bear in mind that

Mexicans are generally not avid swimmers.) However, even they deem a few lakes safe, and others can be toured on log rafts, rowboats, and pedalboats. The most accessible lakes have nearby parking lots and food and soda stands attended by local women eager to prepare you a simple meal or, at the very least, sell you a bag of chips and a drink.

Young local men wait at the park entrance, ready to hop in your car and give you a lake tour for an appropriate tip. Just beyond the entrance gate, the paved road forks. The left-hand road leads to the **Laguna Encantada** (Enchanted Lake); half a dozen lakes can be

appreciated as a slice of water in the distance.

At the far end of the road, hike around large **Laguna Bosque Azul,** take an inexpensive rowboat tour, or rent a pedalboat. Boys offer hour-long horseback excursions in the forest, where you can see native birds, a small cave, and two sinkholes. There is a parking lot and simple restaurant.

To visit the southern lakes, return to the park entrance and take the right fork toward Tziscao, about 7½ miles (12 km) distant. First you will come to large **Laguna de Montebello** (a ten-minute walk down a dirt road), which is recommended for swimming. Park right at the broad lakeshore, where locals rent out their horses and sell snacks.

Continue toward Tziscao. A signed road leads to a cluster of five lovely lakes, **Cinco Lagunas,** which can be viewed from the lookout point. (This group is about a 30-minute walk from the main road.) Farther along the paved road, deep-blue **Lago Pojoj** lies down a steep road. The last of the park's major lakes is **Tziscao,** named for the community along its eastern shore. The **Tziscao Lodge** is at the time of writing still being remodeled, but a new tourist facility has restrooms, a restaurant, and shaded tables. You can swim at the sandy beach or take a rowboat trip around the lake. Motor boats are not permitted on Montebello's lakes.

The lake district is about 30 miles (48 km) southeast of Comitán, where you can pick up a map at the tourist office. The best way to tour the park is by car. If you choose to take a bus or taxi, these can easily be found in Comitán. Buses access both Laguna Bosque Azul and Tziscao, and you can alight at any point in between. ■

The Maya calendar

The Maya and the Aztecs shared the same 260-day ceremonial calendar (*Tzolkin* in Mayan or *Tonalamatl* in Náhuatl), a ritualistic almanac used for astrological prophecies as well as decision-making in daily affairs. Each day was ruled by several lords whose personalities influenced the day, much as the sun, moon, and planets affect daily life according to astrologers. In one of the most significant coincidences in the history of human conflict, Spanish conquistador Hernán Cortés appeared in the very year (1 Reed) of Toltec god-king Quetzalcóatl's prophesied return to power. Convinced of the fulfillment of holy prophecy, the Emperor Moctezuma barely rebelled against his fate (see p. 29).

The Tzolkin, or sacred calendar, was a cyclical calendar of 260 days. As with our days of the week, its 20 named days followed each other in endless succession. Combined with each day was a number from 1 to 13, for a total of 260 days, such as 2 Ahau or 8 Eb. Each day was ruled by the lord of its name and of its number. The number 13 was lucky, so both the 13th day and days paired with the number 13 were often auspicious.

In addition to this sacred calendar, mathematicians devised a 365-day solar calendar, which they knew to be only an approximation of the Earth's solar orbit. This calendar, called the Haab, consisted of 18 periods of 20 days each (totaling 360), plus five unlucky days at the end of the period, called *Uayeb*. The days between the end of one "year" and the beginning of the next were, according to Maya astronomers and priests, extremely unstable and dangerous, as they pertained to neither one year nor the other. The two calendars were then meshed, like two cogs of unequal size, to form the Calendar Round, which permitted a deeper level of both practical and spiritual interpretation. Crops were planted, battles waged, and rulers crowned on the most auspicious dates. The cycle repeated every 52 years.

As these cyclical calendars eventually repeated themselves, they were not useful in recording the date of historical events. For this reason the Maya invented the Long Count, a calendar based on multiples of 20. The most basic unit was a day (called a *kin*, or sun), followed by a *uinal* (20 days), a *tun* (360 days), and so on. Think of it as expressing a date this way: "It happened 5 centuries, 8 decades, 3 years, 2 weeks, and 4 days ago."

Throughout the Classic era, dates carved on thousands of stelae throughout the Maya world precisely recorded birth, death, marriage, ascension to power, and decisive battles, providing today's scientists with many clues about ancient Maya history. According to this manner of reckoning, Creation occurred in the year 0.0.0.0.0., which Maya expert Sir Eric Thompson (1898–1975) interpreted as August 11, 3114 B.C. Most scholars still agree. Its ceremonial date is 4 Ahau 8 Cumku.

Fascinated by mathematics as both a scientific tool and an art, the ancient Maya played endlessly with numbers, had a place-value system of counting, and invented the concept of zero (perhaps adapting an earlier Olmec idea). Using simple observation and their advanced mathematical knowledge, they calculated the orbit of Venus and other planets nearly as precisely as astronomers do today. ∎

The monkey glyph signals "day"; in its hand, the god's head represents six; the skull below stands for ten. The whole thus means 16 days.

Haab (solar calendar)

The Tzolkin and Haab were meshed to form the Calendar Round, which was repeated every 52 years.

Tzolkin (sacred calendar)

named days

The unlucky five-day Uayeb comes at the end of the Haab.

Month glyphs of the Haab

Pop · Uo · Zip · Zotz

Zec · Xul · Yaxkin · Mol

Ch'en · Yax · Zac · Ceh

Mac · Kankin · Muan · Pax

Kayab · Cumku · Uayeb

The numbers

•	• •	• • •	• • • •
1	2	3	4
—	⊡	⊡	⊡
5	6	7	8
9	10	11	12
13	14	15	16
17	18	19	0

The Maya system of counting was based on 20 "digits," literally ten fingers and ten toes. The numbers 0–19 could be written either with head glyphs or using a place-value system based on five. A dot represented 1; a bar, 5; and a seashell or similar glyph, the placeholder 0. These numbers could be written horizontally or vertically. For example, the number 20 would be

Yaxchilán & Bonampak

BOTH YAXCHILÁN AND BONAMPAK FLOURISHED IN THE Late Classic era, united by royal marriage, at times divided by warfare. As it did for other Maya centers in eastern Chiapas, the luxuriant Lacandón rain forest, or *selva lacandona,* supplied their needs, while the wide Usumacinta River and its many tributaries facilitated transportation. Today, these and other protected enclaves form a tiny buffer against deforestation in the threatened Lacandón rain forest and an untouristy destination for lovers of Maya lore.

Yaxchilán
🔺 283 D3

Their jungle location is part of the allure of these two remote archaeological sites. Towering mahogany trees host vines and blossoming epiphytes, creating a home for colorful toucans, parrots, flycatchers, orioles, and tanagers. Vampire bats

The small Lacandón tribe fled to the rain forest during the Spanish colonial period to escape persecution.

hang in the damp chambers of ruined limestone palaces, centipedes creep along moist green walls, mosquitoes suck your blood. Although Yaxchilán is more extensive, and its setting more lush, both sites have a wonderful, wild, "lost in the jungle" feel.

About 118 miles (190 km) southeast of Palenque, **Yaxchilán**

was built on a terrace at a large bend in the Usumacinta River. Howler monkeys roar from the tops of enormous ceiba trees, held sacred by the Maya as the Tree of Life. The humid tropical air seems to have eased the rigid poses of temples, palaces, and stelae, which blend with —but don't completely succumb to—the pervasive rain forest.

Enter the site through Building 19, or **el Laberinto** (the Labyrinth), named for its maze of small rooms. The upper story consists of a central hall annexed by a series of rooms; narrow stairways lead to subterranean chambers. The facade, originally covered in molded and painted stucco, gives way to remnants of roof combs above a wide cornice. This and other vine-draped, gray-green buildings that inspired the name "Place of Green Stones" face the broad, grassy **Gran Plaza.** Among these are a steam room (**Edificio 14**) and an I-shaped **juego de pelota,** or ball court.

Graceful roof combs and upper facades with remnants of beautifully worked figures in stucco and stone are among Yaxchilán's most impressive elements. The large number of intricately carved lintels and stelae tell tales of conquest and ceremonial life: Epigraphers have identified glyphs symbolizing ascension to power, birth dates, and marriage. Among the most impressive lintels are those found on Buildings 12, 16, and 22. Stele 11, moved to the Gran

Plaza from several miles away, is the site's pièce de résistance. The larger figure represents Yaxchilán's most important ruler: Pájaro Jaguar, or Bird Jaguar.

South of the Gran Plaza, stairs lead up to the **Gran Acrópolis,** which commands a fantastic view of the site. Here you will find the well-preserved **Edificio 33,** with its headless sculpture of Pájaro Jaguar, to whom the building is dedicated. The temple's elaborate roof combs are intact, but its fabulous lintel is now at the British Museum in London. Short walks through the jungle bring you to the **Acrópolis Sur** (where **Edificio 40** has traces of original murals) and the **Acrópolis Pequeña,** with excellent bas-relief lintels in **Edificios 42** and **44.**

A less important center under the jurisdiction of Yaxchilán, **Bonampak,** to the south, was established around the year A.D. 600 near the Lacanjá River, a tributary of the Usumacinta. The first outsiders to visit were two Americans working for the United Fruit Company, who in 1946 convinced a

Lacandón Indian to reveal the site of devotional rituals.

The highlight of a visit to Bonampak is the murals of the **Templo de las Pinturas** (Temple of the Paintings). Although the re-creation at Mexico City's Museo Nacional de Antropología (see pp. 198–201) shows the murals with their original, brilliant colors and bold outlines, the fading scenes viewed *in situ* still convey a wondrous force. In the first room, the royal family exults in its heir apparent, while musicians entertain. Above the doorway, the lord of Bonampak, Chaan Muan, is resplendent in embroidered loincloth, jaguar-skin skirt, jade collar, and headdress of quetzal feathers.

Violent battle scenes dominate the second room. A captive kneels in supplication before Chaan Muan, while others are tortured and humiliated. A prisoner of rank slumps in exhaustion on the temple steps. In the third chamber, victory is celebrated with elaborate ritual. Elite women perform a bloodletting of the tongue, while lords in grand costume execute a graceful dance.

Carved lintels, stelae, and vine-draped buildings characterize Yaxchilán.

Bonampak
⬛ 283 D3
Visitor information
✉ Calle Francisco Javier Mina at Nicolás Bravo
 916/345-0356 (Palenque)

Bonampak's powerful murals date from the end of the eighth century A.D.

These murals rank among the finest of Classic Maya art. Attention was paid to expression, foreshortening makes perspective realistic, and each panel is a harmonious triumph of composition. The murals, dated 790, seem to be the last work done at the site. Chaan Muan and his bride from Yaxchilán, Lady Rabbit, may have been the last rulers at Bonampak. No evidence has been found that the baby boy so proudly presented in the temple paintings was ever crowned.

Other temples and palaces on the Gran Plaza and adjoining **Acrópolis** can be explored with the help of a Lacandón Indian guide. Park entrance is free but each visitor must pay for the services of a member of the Lacandón community, who accompanies groups or individuals (*$$$*). Some guides merely take you along without commentary; others relate tales and legends of their forefathers—sometimes strangely interwoven with Bible stories introduced by missionaries during the past century.

Long overland day tours from Palenque visit both sites; a one-hour boat trip from Frontera Corozal (where comfortable tourist accommodations are available) completes the journey to Yaxchilán. Tours in small aircraft can be arranged from Ocosingo, Comitán, and Palenque; most spend one hour at Bonampak and three hours at Yaxchilán. Three- or four-day tours include a visit to Tikal, in the Petén region of Guatemala just across the Usumacinta River.

Some tours tout a long hike to the ruins of Bonampak, which sounds more exciting and adventurous than it really is. Most of the walk is down the paved road, and many hikers complain of sore feet, sunstroke, boredom, or exhaustion. In whatever fashion you arrive, bring mosquito repellent, water, sunscreen, and a wide-brimmed hat, as well as a passport or international identification and tourist card, without which you may not pass military checkpoints. Deadly and territorial fer-de-lance and other poisonous snakes are found here, so watch where you put your hands and feet. ■

Dugout canoes provide convenient transportation in the ever shrinking rain forest.

More places to visit in Chiapas

RESERVA DE LA BIÓSFERA EL TRIUNFO

Located in the Sierra Madre de Chiapas, El Triunfo Biosphere Reserve was established in 1990. Most of its 494,000 acres (200,000 ha) constitute a buffer zone; approximately one fifth of this region of mountains, valleys, and plains has been designated federal land. Pine, mixed, and low tropical forests are home to several species of endangered cats; rare quetzal birds hide in the cloud forest. Permission to enter the reserve must be obtained a week in advance, and visits are advisable only during the dry season *(mid-November–mid-May)*. The park entrance is about 115 miles (184 km) south of Tuxtla Gutiérrez via Angel Albino Corzo. The only accommodations are a rustic lodge, though camping is permitted.
🗺 283 B2 **Visitor information** ☎ 961/611-3891 or 961/611-3975 (CONANP) www.conanp.gob.mx

RESERVA DE LA BIÓSFERA MONTES AZULES

Together with Calakmul Biosphere Reserve and the Petén region of Guatemala, Montes Azules represents the largest remaining virgin rain forest north of the Amazon Basin. The 818,000-acre (331,000 ha) reserve, whose name means "blue mountains," changes significantly in elevation, from near sea level at the Lacantún River, in the south, to around 5,250 feet (1,600 m) in the more mountainous west. The varied topography produces swamps, lakes, rivers, evergreen and tropical rain forest, palm forest, and pine and oak forest. Of the 3,000 plant species, there are 320 species of orchids alone. The best months to visit are January through September.

Services within the park are limited. The town of Emiliano Zapata is working to establish ecotourism and offers lodgings in communal cottages. Guided camping trips of four days or more take you to **Laguna Miramar,** the largest lake in the Lacandón rain forest, with excellent hiking, snorkeling, and canoeing. Trips can be arranged through the **Dana Association,** San Cristóbal *(tel/fax 9/678-0468)*. It is possible to get to Lake Miramar by road (about five hours from Ocosingo) or by small plane, a thrilling 30-minute ride via **Servicios Aereos San Cristóbal** out of Comitán *(tel 963/632-4662)* or Ocosingo *(tel 919/673-0188)*.

Near the park's southern border is **Ara Macao** *(Reforma Agraria, tel 015/2015928),* a government-funded, community-run ecotourism lodge. The comfortable, simple cabins are located on the right bank of the Lacantún River, where you can swim, fish, or explore in a dugout canoe. Local guides lead hikes into the surrounding forest, where there are harpy eagles, hawks, yellow-throated toucans, and the endangered red macaw for which the reserve is named. Its about five hours south of Palenque along federal and state highways to the town of Reforma Agraria; small planes can be chartered in Ocosingo or Comitán.
 283 D3

RESERVA HUITEPEC

On the eastern slope of 8,860-foot (2,700 m) Volcán Huitepec, one of the highest mountains in the Chiapas range, is Huitepec *(Closed Mon., $),* a 335-acre (135 ha) nature reserve.

Oak forest prevails at the lower elevations; higher up are cloud forests cloaked in epiphytes and ferns. Many of the 300-plus plant species have been used for generations by local Maya for medicinal and religious purposes. Trekkers may see foxes, armadillos, flying squirrels, and raccoons, but more easily spotted are some of the reserve's 60 resident bird species. You can wander the forest trails on your own any day of the week or arrange a Tuesday, Thursday, or Saturday guided visit through **Pronatura,** based in San Cristóbal de las Casas *(María Adelina Flores 21, tel 967/678-5000).*
 283 B3

TAPACHULA

Most people visit Tapachula as the gateway to Guatemala, but this is a friendly (if hot and humid) city with several interesting sights in the surrounding countryside. Maya stelae and artifacts can be seen at the **Museo Regional del Soconusco** *(8a Av. Norte 24 entre 1a and 3a Poniente, tel 962/627-0055),* or you can see them *in situ* at the **Izapa** *(Carr. A Talisman s/n, $),* a spread-out archaeological site about 15 minutes outside town. About half a mile (1 km) from the entrance is **Grupo F,** the best restored, with altars and ball court in addition to pyramids and stelae. Northeast of Tapachula and a stone's throw from Guatemala, the town of **Unión Juárez** makes an excellent base for mountain excursions. Bring your bathing suit and take an agreeable alpine walk to the **Cascadas de Muxbal,** where a waterfall tumbling into a narrow gorge forms a pretty pool. Mountaineers can make an overnight assault on 13,400-foot (4,085 m) **Volcán Tacaná.** About 7 miles (11 km) outside town, the working coffee plantation of **Centro Ecoturístico Santo Domingo** *(tel 962/627-0055, $)* was built by early 20th-century German immigrants using imported materials. The chalet-like structure has recently been restored and has a coffee museum and a restaurant serving regional food.
 283 C1   **Visitor information** ✉ Prol. Central Oriente s/n, Plaza Comercial Kamico Local 20   ☎ 962/625-5409 ■

A keel-billed toucan peers from its nest in the rain forest of Montes Azules.

Two-lane highways connect the Yucatán Peninsula's diverse attractions—including lovely beaches and intriguing Maya ruins—like the path on a child's board game. With little exception, the peninsula is as flat as a tortilla.

Yucatán Peninsula

A street scene in convivial Campeche

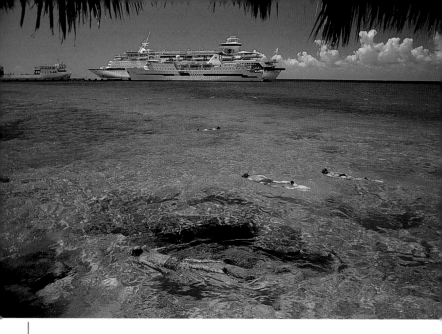

Warm water and the Palancar reef bring cruise ships and solo travelers to Cozumel island.

Yucatán Peninsula

ALONG THE LENGTH OF QUINTANA ROO'S CARIBBEAN COAST, LOVERS HIDE out on sugar-sand beaches, birders stalk their prey among the mangroves, and cruise ships put in at palm-studded harbors used by the Maya a thousand years ago. Throughout the Yucatán Peninsula, rural towns doze in the shadow of whitewashed 16th-century monasteries. Each of the peninsula's three states—Quintana Roo, Campeche, and Yucatán—has scores of archaeological sites shrouded in jungle. Visitors can go deep-sea and fly fishing, snorkel along the world's second largest reef, and dive in underground rivers or in one of thousands of sinkholes. No place in Mexico has so much variety in so compact an area.

The Yucatán Peninsula is a land without lakes or rivers, yet is covered in tropical forests. Rainwater filters through the porous subterranean limestone shelf to create an extensive underground river system. Sinkholes (*cenotes* in Spanish, *dzonot* in Mayan) form when this thin layer of limestone collapses, revealing deep green pools or shallow turquoise lagoons. More than 2,000 have been discovered in the state of Yucatán alone.

Water was sacred to the ancient Maya, who worshiped the rain god Chac. Respected mathematicians, astronomers, and architects, the Maya built fabulous cities during the Classic era (A.D. 250–900). Cosmology, history, celestial events, and community achievements were recorded in the *Chilam Balam*—a living document added to until the 19th century. The Maya also covered stelae and

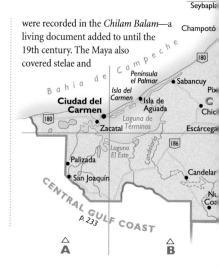

other stone monuments in phonetic hiero-glyphs. Luckily, many survived to be examined, but most of the Maya books were burned by Franciscan monks.

The Yucatán is an amalgam of distinct cultures. It is mainly Maya and Spanish, but waves of Lebanese, French, and other immigrants came as well. Its unique cuisine combines the region's famous citrus fruits, honey, and fiery habanero chilies with saffron, annatto, capers, prunes, and other unusual flavors.

Festivals reflect the diversity too. Hanal Pixan (All Souls' Day) is celebrated in Mérida, Campeche, and throughout the countryside by preparing regional foods and

altars for the dead. Campeche and Cozumel are known for their pre-Lenten carnivals, and upstart Cancún has its jazz festival. ■

Area of map detail

The continued growth of Cancún and other resorts on the Quintana Roo coast is inevitable.

Quintana Roo

Quintana Roo became a state in 1974, shortly after the Mexican government baptized Cancún. It didn't take long for both entities to swell beyond all expectations. The state contains wildly popular vacation destinations, significant Maya ruins, and a coastline that exceeds all superlatives.

The semitropical climate is perfect most times of year, though hurricanes do blow through between September and November. The Caribbean washes white-sand beaches from Cancún to Chetumal, on the border with Belize. Scrubby jungle covers most of the limestone terrain. Subterranean rivers flow through caves and into cenotes, enormous wells of cool, dark water. Tropical fish swim in underwater reserves, while sea turtles lumber ashore on summer nights to lay their eggs.

Cancún attracts most of the state's visitors. Travelers with adventure in mind explore the Riviera Maya—the coastline between Cancún and Tulum. Old-timers bemoan what they call the "Cancúnization" of this area.

The second longest chain of coral reefs in the world runs between Quintana Roo's mainland coast and the islands of Cozumel and Isla Mujeres. Sections of the reefs are littered with wrecked galleons from the 19th century and earlier. The coral they destroyed has grown back; the same can't be said for that crushed by modern cruise ships. Cozumel has become a major cruise port, much to the dismay of marine biologists and scuba divers.

Quintana Roo is suffering growing pains. The southern coast, long the provenance of small dive lodges and private homes, is now called the Costa Maya. The moniker includes the coastline south of Sian Ka'an and inland jungles dotted with restored Maya archaeological sites in both Quintana Roo and Campeche. Majahual, the largest town between Punta Allen and Campeche, has become a cruise port, with ships calling at a modern terminal at Puerto Costa Maya. Development plans include golf courses, resort hotels, and all the trappings of the Riviera Maya. Some of Quintana Roo's most precious attributes have been preserved in nature parks or enhanced in tasteful resorts, but continued growth is inevitable. ∎

Cancún

Cancún
309 F4
Visitor information
✉ Av. Tulum 26 at Coba
☎ 998/884-6531

CANCÚN IS THE NOUVEAU RICHE OF THE RESORT WORLD, lacking culture but rich in real estate. The aquamarine sea laps the shores of the offshore island's northern coast and inland lagoons, while slapping more energetically against the white-sand beaches along the east-facing Caribbean. Sultry days drift into warm evenings, when breezes ruffle coconut palms. Designed in 1970 and developed by government agencies and private investors, Cancún now draws 2.5 million visitors a year. It has the second busiest international airport in Mexico, with direct flights from Europe, South America, and North America.

Cancún lacks the verve of resorts such as Acapulco and Puerto Vallarta, both of which grew rapidly but naturally out of existing villages. But for those with cash to spend, it can still be a wonderful playground. The all-inclusive resorts provide a wide variety of activities.

Most of the larger beachfront hotels rent aquatic equipment, including body boards, snorkeling gear, sailboards, yachts, and personal watercraft, and many offer fishing, diving, and skin-diving tours, party boats, and other such waterborne activities.

Cancún has large shopping malls and boutiques, although fewer open-air markets. Discos rock well into the morning, and restaurants offer international, regional, Mexican, and California cuisine. The city is trying to project a more upscale image with designer shops at Plaza Kukulkán and La Isla. Upscale spa-oriented resort hotels claim beaches away from the all-inclusive action, and Miami-style clubs and restaurants cater to sophisticates. The ¼-mile-wide (0.5 km) island has two 18-hole golf courses at present. One is at the **Hilton Cancún Beach & Golf Resort** (tel 998/881-8016), and the second, the 72-par **Club de Golf Cancún** course (Blvd. Kukulkán Km 6.5, tel 998/883-1230), is in the middle of Nichupté Lagoon. It also has a 13-hole executive course.

Perhaps more exciting for culture lovers are the dozens of well-restored Maya ruins found throughout the peninsula. Therisland also has a 13-hole executive course. Tulum (see p.

320) and Chichén Itzá (see pp. 338–41) are two and three hours' drive, respectively, from Cancún. Rent a car or take a tour to visit these impressive ruins, or to snorkel in sinkholes, dive the peninsula's underground rivers, or visit historic cities such as Valladolid or Mérida in Yucatán state. Cancún is a convenient base for day trips south along the coast and a good point of departure for tours. ■

Parasailing is one of many water-based diversions offered to visitors in Cancún.

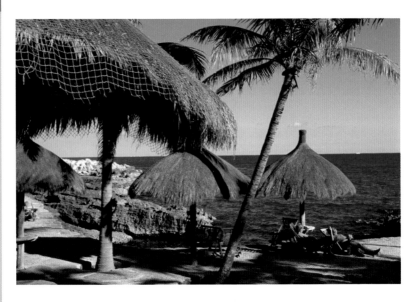

Xcaret Eco Theme park combines the nature, culture, and archaeology of the Riviera Maya.

Riviera Maya drive

You could easily drive from Cancún to Tulum in three hours, but it's better to linger for a couple of days. Dubbed the "Riviera Maya," the coast along Highway 307 is full of diversions. Divers head for spooky cenotes (sinkholes) and caves or sunlit coves teeming with tropical fish; beach bums choose between bikini and beer hangouts or secluded stretches of untrammeled sand; sightseers climb pyramids; shoppers browse through folk-art boutiques; and everyone eats at least one meal of fresh fish a day.

In the 1980s, Hwy. 307 had only two lanes. Pickups and buses lumbered along at a leisurely pace, sharing the asphalt with villagers lopping off roadside branches with machetes for fuel. A few signs pointed the way to campgrounds and small hotels on white-sand beaches. The highway is now four lanes wide, and hulking motor coaches whiz past idle wanderers in VW bugs. Bold entryways announce the presence of theme parks; more modest signs lead the way to special haunts.

Puerto Morelos ❶, 22 miles (36 km) south of Cancún, remains a sandy village with a plain plaza near the waterfront. A coral reef littered with shipwrecks shelters the coastline from surf, but the water close to shore can be grassy and murky. Several luxurious, secluded spa resorts claim patches of jungle and sand north and south of town, while small budget

hotels and dive shops in town cater to travelers seeking something more laid-back. Vehicles bound for Cozumel line up at the ferry dock south of town, and rumors fly of a cruise port or major marina for the town.

🏔   See also area map p. 309 F4–E3
➤   Cancún
↔   80 miles (130 km)
🕐   3 hours to 3 days
➤   Tulum

NOT TO BE MISSED
- Tres Ríos
- Playa del Carmen
- Xcaret
- Paamul
- Tulum

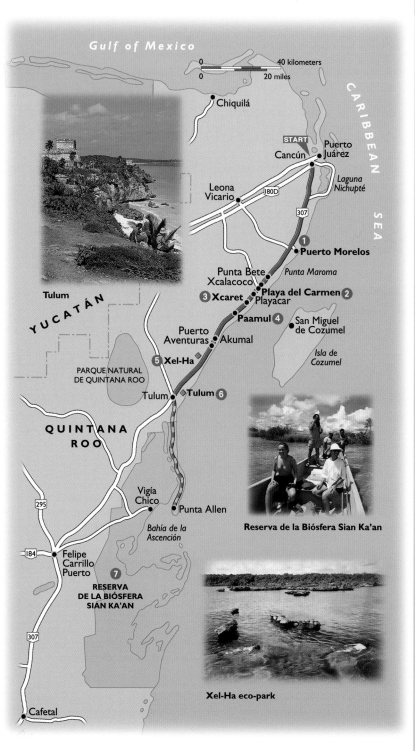

Gulf of Mexico

CARIBBEAN SEA

0   40 kilometers
0   20 miles

Chiquilá

START   Puerto Juárez
Cancún

Leona Vicario
180D
Laguna Nichupté

307

① **Puerto Morelos**

Punta Bete   Punta Maroma
Xcalacoco

③ **Xcaret**   **Playa del Carmen** ②
Playacar

Paamul ④   San Miguel de Cozumel

Puerto Aventuras   Akumal

Isla de Cozumel

⑤ **Xel-Ha**

YUCATÁN

PARQUE NATURAL DE QUINTANA ROO

Tulum   ◆**Tulum** ⑥

QUINTANA ROO

Vigía Chico

295   Punta Allen

Bahía de la Ascención

184

307

Felipe Carrillo Puerto

⑦
RESERVA DE LA BIÓSFERA SIAN KA'AN

Cafetal

Tulum

Reserva de la Biósfera Sian Ka'an

Xel-Ha eco-park

Dirt and paved roads lead from Highway 307 to resorts, nature parks, and secluded hideaway beaches. Maroma, an Orient Express Hotel at **Punta Maroma,** holds sway as an exclusive, luxurious retreat, though the competition is stiff from nearby Ikal del Mar and resorts in the works from Mandarin Oriental and Rosewood. At **Punta Bete,** Capitán Lafitte and a few other small cabaña hotels cater to casual wanderers.

Playa del Carmen ❷, 6 miles (10 km) south of Punta Bete, has long been the main

Thousands of flamingos populate the shores of the Yucatan, including here at Xcaret.

stop between Cancún and Tulum. In just a few decades, it has grown from a small town without telephones into a city of more than 100,000 inhabitants. Banks, supermarkets, auto supply stores, and budget hotels are jumbled together along Av. Juárez, the main entrance to town from Hwy. 307. A steady stream of trucks and taxis continues to the pier, where ferries depart for Cozumel. International restaurants, excellent folk-art shops, and quirky small hotels line Av. 5 and the beach north of town. You can arrange diving, boating, and archaeological tours, or just drowse in a hammock. The south side of town gives way to **Playacar,** a development with an 18-hole golf course and private houses and condos spread about manicured lawns dotted with small Maya ruins. All-inclusive hotels face white-sand beaches in Playacar; some are a long walk from town. Parrots and macaws squawk

from their perches at the aviary at **Xaman-Há** *(tel 984/873-0593, $$$)* in Playacar.

Travelers with time constraints can immerse themselves at **Xcaret ❸** *(tel 984/873-2643, $$$$$),* five minutes south of Playa del Carmen. Spend a full day to get the most out of the steep admission; some activities and rental gear cost extra. You can visit the aviary, museum, botanical garden, and butterfly pavilion, float down an underground river with natural skylights, snorkel in the saltwater lagoon, hike through caves, ride horses, swim with dolphins (expensive and involved), eat at one of five restaurants, and nap on the sand. The evening show is a captivating blend of Maya stories and Mexican folkloric dances.

Once you've passed Xcaret the traffic thins out around **Paamul ❹.** the antithesis of a theme park. Turtles and humans like to burrow into this little haven, the former digging nests in the sand, the latter booking a few nights in a modest hotel. The water is calm, snorkeling

The marine lagoon at Xel-Ha

and diving are satisfactory, and the restaurant serves homemade tacos and fresh fish.

Those who yearn for deluxe amenities head for **Puerto Aventuras,** a planned resort with hotels, condos, a 250-slip marina, and a nine-hole golf course. Stop by the **Museo Pablo Bush Romero,** named for the region's most famous scuba diver. Exhibits cover early scuba gear, the reefs, and booty from shipwrecks. Divers tend to congregate at nearby **Akumal,** where Romero was head-quartered in the 1920s. Hotel cabanas and private homes line the cove here.

Walking through the five-million-year-old caverns and caves at **Aktun Chen** (tel 998/892-0662, www.aktunchen.com, $$$$$) is other-worldly. Guides lead visitors through the jungle, where spider monkeys hang out, to spooky dark caves filled with stalactites and stalagmites. A milky green cenote (sinkhole) seems to glow within one cave. **Xel-Ha** ⑤ (tel 998/ 884-9422, $$$$), the coast's first eco-park, has been revived by the Xcaret team. Mature tropical trees shade pathways leading to an aquamarine cove dotted with the tips of snorkels. Tulum bus tours often stop here. Come early to appreciate it. Scuba divers and snorkelers can explore cool freshwater underground rivers and wells at **Hidden Worlds Cenotes** (tel 984/877-8535, www.hiddenworlds.com.mx). The jungle-shrouded property includes several cenotes and bat caves linked by rough, rutted roads.

The Riviera Maya route ends at **Tulum** ⑥ (see p. 320). Its ruins are famous, but the town remains a quiet settlement. Gas stations, hotels, restaurants, and markets serve those passing through on Hwy. 307, and a narrow road by the sea passes small hotels and campgrounds. This road ends at the **Reserva de la Biósfera Sian Ka'an** ⑦ (see pp. 320–21), a fitting reminder of the Quintana Roo coast as it used to be. ∎

Islands & diving

THE WORLD'S SECOND LONGEST CHAIN OF CORAL REEFS lies just beneath the Caribbean's crystalline surface and stretches from the northern tip of the Yucatán Peninsula to Belize. Oceanographer Jacques Cousteau filmed the reefs in the 1960s; dive organizations now call the chain one of the top three dive spots in the world. Divers can access the reefs from Isla Mujeres, Cancún, and the Quintana Roo coast, but their mecca is Isla de Cozumel.

Cozumel

🗺 309 F3

Visitor information

✉ Calle 2 Norte at Av. 15

☎ 987/872-3132

Cozumel Association of Dive Operators

☎ 987/872-5955, fax 987/872-5966

Isla Mujeres

🗺 309 F4

Visitor information

✉ Av. Rueda Medina 130

☎ 998/877-0307

Opposite: A diver explores Tankah Cenote, one of thousands of sinkholes in the Yucatán.

Maya women once traveled from the mainland to **Cozumel** to honor Ixchel, the goddess of fertility. Today's pilgrims arrive by plane or by ferry from Playa del Carmen, 12 miles (19 km) west, to worship the reefs. Underwater visibility of 80 to 100 feet (23 to 30 m), water temperatures around 80°F (26°C), a 67,133-acre (27,170 ha) marine reserve, and dozens of competent dive operators all enhance Cozumel's reputation.

Divers float along gardens of white, lavender, and pink corals and sponges beside blue angelfish, pink wrasse, yellow butterflyfish, and red grouper, while snorkelers witness similar sights at **Parque Chankanaab** (tel 987/872-2940, $$$), where shallow reefs are home to more than 60 species of fish.

Island life centers around the town of **San Miguel,** where streets are lined with jewelry and souvenir shops geared toward cruise-ship passengers. Walk a few blocks inland to find family-run folk art shops and casual restaurants. The island's oldest hotel, La Playa, houses the **Museo de la Isla Cozumel** (tel 987/872-1475, $), with exhibits on the reefs and local history. The island's longest road curves along the southern tip to the wild windward side where waves and winds batter limestone coves. Turn-offs lead to beach clubs with restaurants and all the water toys you could want. **Mr. Sancho's** (tel 987/876-1629, no admission) offers horseback riding, swimming pools, restaurants, bars, and endless water

activities. **Playa San Francisco** is more laid-back, with hammocks swinging under palms on a quiet beach. Near the southern tip of the island, **Parque Punta Sur** (tel 987/872-2940, $$$$) is a 247-acre (100 ha) nature reserve. The park's attractions include a lighthouse, nautical museum, and long stretches of beach with good snorkeling. Sea turtles nest on windward beaches in summer; biologists usually set up camp at **Punta Morena** to protect the eggs from poachers. The windward coast's first hotel, **Ventanas al Mar,** is an idyllic escape on the site of the biologists' original headquarters. At the end of the coast road a dirt trail leads to a solitary lighthouse at **Punta Celarain** and a few remote partially excavated Maya sites. Local tour companies run four-wheel drive tours to this area.

Inland are the ruins of **San Gervasio** (Carretera Transversal, no phone, $$). This ceremonial center was occupied from A.D. 300 to 1500 and may have contained more than 300 buildings. About a dozen have been restored, including a temple honoring the goddess Ixchel.

Maya women were also drawn to **Isla Mujeres,** where a few scattered ruins honor Ixchel. Divers and escapists favor this 5-mile-long (8 km) limestone shelf just 8 miles (11 km) northeast of Cancún. Black-tip and nurse sharks often doze in 80-foot-deep (24 m) underwater caves. Experts believe a lack of carbon dioxide and overabundance of

oxygen from underwater springs puts the sharks into this somnolent state.

Scattered reefs along the island provide more typical underwater sights; **Coral Scuba Center** (Av. Matamoros 13, tel 998/877-0763) offers trips to the shark caves and **Manchones Reef.** Snorkelers head for **El Garrafón** (Carretera Garrafón, tel 998/849-4950, $$$), an underwater reserve restored in 1999 by the people who created Xcaret (see p. 314). The park's boundaries have grown to encompass the southern tip of the island, now called **Punta Sur** ($). An additional fee is charged for you to visit the lighthouse and Maya ruins at the tip. The waters off Isla's main beach, **Playa Norte,** are more suitable for swimming than snorkeling, and there are several palapa bars, restaurants, and small hotels here. The town consists of a few streets with more restaurants, hotels, and shops; bare feet and bathing suits with cover-ups are acceptable in almost all establishments.

Hacienda Mundaca (Carretera el Garrafón, no phone, $), south of town, dates back to the 19th century. It was built by a Spanish pirate, Fermín Mundaca de Marechaja, who fell in love with an island woman. Parts have been restored, and the grounds contain a small zoo with indigenous animals.

Tour agencies on Isla Mujeres offer bird-watching and snorkeling trips to **Isla Contoy,** 19 miles (30 km) north. Undeveloped and protected as a national wildlife park, the island is home to around a hundred species of birds. Visitors are not allowed to spend the night on the island; dedicated bird-watchers should hire a boat captain to take them to Contoy at dawn, when the birds are most active. ∎

manta ray

lookdown

Above left:
**Blue damsels
on the reef
off Cozumel**
Below:
**El Garrafón
reef, Isla
Mujeres**

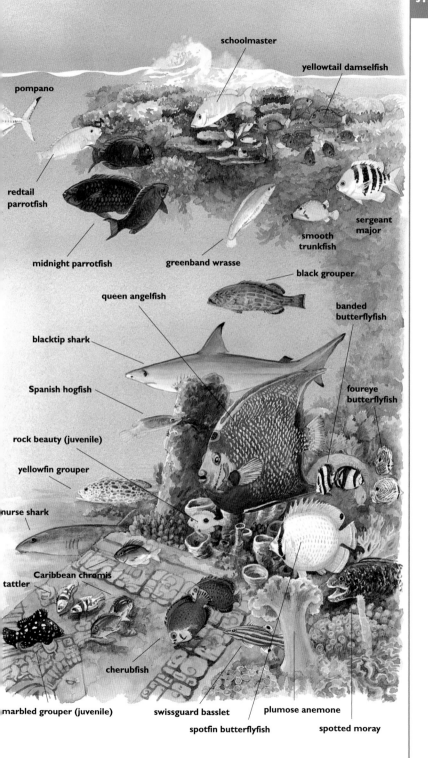

schoolmaster

yellowtail damselfish

pompano

redtail parrotfish

sergeant major

smooth trunkfish

midnight parrotfish

greenband wrasse

black grouper

queen angelfish

banded butterflyfish

blacktip shark

Spanish hogfish

foureye butterflyfish

rock beauty (juvenile)

yellowfin grouper

nurse shark

Caribbean chromis

tattler

cherubfish

marbled grouper (juvenile)

swissguard basslet

plumose anemone

spotfin butterflyfish

spotted moray

Tulum & Sian Ka'an

AN ALABASTER LIMESTONE CASTLE SITS ATOP A GRASSY bluff overlooking the Caribbean Sea at Tulum. Six hundred years ago, Maya sailors relied on beams of light from the castle's windows as they made their way to shore through treacherous reefs. The first Spanish explorers, on the other hand, crashed on the coral; those who survived made their way through a 3,000-foot-long (915 m) wall protecting the small community from invasion by land or sea.

Tulum
🅰 309 E3
☎ 9/883-3671
$ $

Reserva de la Biósfera Sian Ka'an
🅰 309 E2

Sian Ka'an Visitor Center
☎ 998/884-3667
www.ecotravelmexico.com

Detail of the Descending God at Tulum

Tulum may be the most popular archaeological site on the Maya circuit; it's certainly the most accessible. Busloads of tourists arrive every morning from Cancún, just 80 miles (130 km) to the north. It appeared that Tulum would be loved to death, but in 1993 the government built a visitor center away from the site. Visitors walk or take a jitney bus to the ruins and must follow prescribed paths when inspecting the 60 or so buildings. You can no longer climb to the top of **El Castillo,** 40 feet (12 m) above a lawn dotted with restored temples and walls, and only those with a vivid imagination can picture the city in its prime.

Between A.D. 1100 and the Spanish Conquest, Tulum was a trading center, possibly ruled by a wealthy merchant class. Its citizens worshiped the **Descending God,** whose portrait can be seen above the doorway of the temple of the same name. This upside-down god may represent the Bee God, an important deity in a region known for its honey. Paintings in the **Templo de los Frescos** depict Maya gods and goddesses.

The Spanish explorers who survived shipwreck on the reefs below Tulum in 1511 found a busy commercial center whose buildings were painted bright red, blue, yellow, and white. Two of the sailors stayed at Tulum. One, Gonzalo Guerrero, married a Maya woman and fathered the first mestizo children on the peninsula. He helped the Maya fight off Spanish invaders in 1517, but by the end of the century Tulum was a ghost town.

Though Tulum was the only major site right by the sea, the Maya lived and worked all along the Quintana Roo coast. Engineers built an elaborate system of canals dotted with shrines in the mangrove lagoons just south of Tulum. Their work is protected in the 1.3 million-acre (516,110 ha) **Reserva de la Biósfera Sian Ka'an,** 2 miles (3 km) south of Tulum, the last remaining expanse of undeveloped land on the Caribbean coast.

Sian Ka'an encompasses 62 miles (100 km) of beach, two bays, fresh and saltwater lagoons, and the Punta Allen Peninsula. Declared a World Heritage site by UNESCO in 1987, it is home to longtime residents, most of Maya ancestry. The majority live around the community of Punta Allen at the tip of the 22-mile-long (35 km) peninsula and make their living from lobster fishing. Sustainable fishing is allowed in Sian Ka'an; there are even a couple of fishing lodges open to the public.

A dirt road runs the length of the peninsula, passing a ranger station at the park entrance and continuing past idyllic beaches, over small bridges, and through dense, low jungle. The drive can take three hours; bring plenty of fresh water, snacks, and a spare tire. A couple of small hotels and restaurants in Punta Allen fulfill basic needs. The Sian Ka'an Visitor Center has six rustic rooms for overnight stays and an observatory deck. On summer nights, sea turtles drag themselves ashore to lay their eggs on nearby beaches.

Bird-watchers and archaeology buffs enjoy boat tours with **Amigos de Sian Ka'an** *(tel 998/880-6024 in Cancún; www.amigosdesiankaan .org)*, a private nonprofit organization that works closely with park officials. **Eco Colors** *(tel 998/884-3667; www.ecotravelmexico.com)* operates the visitor center and conducts day and night tours through the park's lagoons and canals. More than 350 species of birds have been spotted in the lagoons; fish include snook, tarpon, and bonefish. The boats glide past herons' nests, turtles, and solitary Maya ruins, as guides describe the origins of Sian Ka'an ("birth of the sky" in Mayan). ■

Tulum was a thriving commercial city when the first Spaniards arrived.

More places to visit in Quintana Roo

CHETUMAL
Few visitors make it as far as Chetumal, the capital of Quintana Roo. The peaceful city faces Chetumal Bay, where manatees hide in secret coves and herons fly along the shore. Hotels and restaurants are geared toward business travelers and those crossing into Belize. The excellent **Museo de la Cultura Maya** *(tel 983/832-6838, $$)* is a must-see for archaeology buffs.
309 D1 **Visitor information** ✉ Av. 5, one block from the beach ☎ 983/832-5073

COBÁ
Cobá rises from dense jungle about half an hour's drive from the coast. The archaeological site covers 81 square miles (210 sq km) and may have been the largest city on the peninsula.

Climbing the steep sides of Cobá's tallest pyramid, Nohuch Mul

Only 5 percent of the structures have been restored, and visitors wander through steamy heat to climb 120 steps up the majestic pyramid of **Nohuch Mul.** The frequent squawks of wild parrots and the rare rustling of the branches by squirrel monkeys break the silence. Remains of a ball court, small pyramids, and temples lie at the end of barely cleared trails. Many ornate stelae, carved with life-size depictions of kings and queens and lengthy hieroglyphic texts, stand amid the vegetation. Present-day Maya still burn candles and incense and worship before two or three of these stelae. Carry plenty of water and a map obtained from the rangers at the entrance.

309 E3 ✉ Carretera a Cobá, 30 miles (48 km) west of Tulum $ $

KOHUNLICH
This little-visited Maya site may contain over 200 structures; only 5 have been restored. The most impressive is the **Pirámide de los Mascarones,** where six-foot-tall (2 m) bas-relief masks in stucco from the Early Classic era (ca A.D. 300–450) are said to portray the sun god. Several other restored sites are located in Quintana Roo and Campeche, and the area is popular with adventure travelers and escapists. The site is usually deserted, and there are no facilities. Bring plenty of water.
309 D1 ✉ 42 miles (67 km) west of Chetumal on Hwy. 186 $ $

LAGUNA BACALAR
Fed by freshwater and saltwater streams and springs, Laguna Bacalar, 25 miles (40 km) north of Chetumal, is Mexico's second-largest lake, often called the "Lake of Seven Colors" for its varying shades of green and blue. The shores are lined with vacation homes, *balnearios* (bathing resorts), restaurants, and a few hotels. It's a good base for those wishing to explore remote Maya ruins in the interior.
309 D2

MAJAHUAL AND XCALAK
The 40-mile-long (64 km) **Península Xcalak** is the last undeveloped haven on the coast (except for Sian Ka'an). But the coastline and nearby jungles of southern Quintana Roo (or **Costa Maya**) are slated for development. Cruise ships come to **Puerto Costa Maya,** a terminal north of Majahual, the coast's largest town. Tour buses ply the roads between the coast and Maya archaeological sites in the jungle. A 30-mile-long (48 km) partially paved road runs south of Majahual to the fishing community at Xcalak. Reefs line the coast offshore, but the pièce de résistance is **Banco Chinchorro,** a 24-mile-long (38 km) reef littered with shipwrecks. Boat captains in Xcalak and at the hotels take divers to Chinchorro when the seas are calm. **Costa de Cocos** *(tel 998/831-0110),* a hotel with cabanas on the sand, has a dive shop.
309 E1 ∎

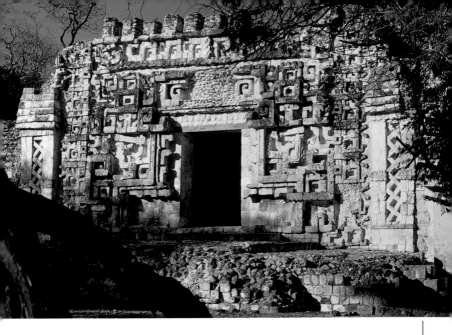

The temples at Hochob have elements of both Río Bec- and Chenes-style architecture.

Campeche

Maya ruins, well signed in English and Spanish, dot the state of Campeche, many with recently installed visitor centers or small bookstores. Calakmul lies buried deep within Mexico's largest remaining rain forest, but Edzná, the best known and most visited pre-Hispanic site, is less than an hour's drive from the visitor-friendly capital city, Campeche. Dozens of other archaeological sites throughout the small state are easily reached along flat, two-lane roads with minimal traffic. Campeche, with its wonderfully restored colonial buildings, makes an excellent base for area excursions.

Campeche may be the country's most languorous capital city. Traffic trundles along slowly within the compact historic district, once enclosed by a hexagonal wall to protect its citizens from pirate attacks. Today, pedestrians stroll the recently refurbished *malecón*, while businessmen discuss oil prices over long lunches at their favorite restaurants. Seafood is the specialty here, and fleets to the south fish for octopus, bay shrimp, and pompano. *Pan de cazón* is not, as its name implies, a bread-based dish, but a filling casserole of shredded thresher shark, tortillas, black beans, and tomato sauce.

Campeche's west-facing beaches along the eponymous bay don't attract many foreign tourists, but wading birds fish in the shallow, warm waters off soft-sand, grass-strewn beaches at pretty Seybaplaya, and small cities such as Champotón attract hunters and sports fishers. Highway 186 heads inland from service-oriented Escárcega to access the ruins at Xpujil, Becán, and Chicanná before continuing east to the Yucatán coast. The most adventurous travelers will want to explore the wild and varied jungles of Calakmul Biosphere Reserve, where hundreds of Maya ruins lie unexcavated.

A road heading north from Xpujil makes it possible to continue to the Chenes-style ruins around Hopelchén, passing en route some of the Maya dwellings still used in the countryside. Round or oval houses of thick adobe walls and high thatch roofs, usually painted white but occasionally plain adobe or a startling sky blue, provide the tradition-minded Maya inhabitants with a cool respite from the impressive peninsular heat. ■

Campeche, with its beautifully restored buildings, is a fabulous city for aimless wandering.

Campeche

THE UNIQUE AND RELATIVELY ISOLATED CITY OF Campeche exudes an aura of swashbuckling romance. Once completely walled to fend off marauding pirates, it retains a quiet, 17th-century elegance unmatched by other colonial cities. There are several interesting museums to explore, but by far the most spectacular attraction is the city itself. An ongoing renovation of downtown facades transforms Campeche into a living museum of colonial and republican-era architecture. Since 1987, hundreds of structures have been restored in delicious tones of pale yellow, earthen brown, celery and dill green, deep gold, and ocher red.

Campeche
🗺 309 C3
Visitor information
✉ Av. Ruíz Cortines s/n, Plaza Moch-Couloh
☎ 981/811-9255

Founded in 1540 by Francisco de Montejo (see p. 333), Campeche gained importance as a port through which gold and silver passed en route to Spain. This wealth did not escape the notice of pirates, who for nearly two centuries besieged the city, sometimes inflicting wholescale massacres. Houses were burned, citizens robbed, women raped; in short, the city was continually sacked.

It was not until 1686 that the Spanish Crown finally took adequate preventive measures. The city was entirely walled, but it was only after twin forts were erected that the pirate attacks finally ceased.

Today, the old city, **Viejo Campeche,** is a compact zone measuring five blocks by nine. Although the walls that once coddled the city in a hexagonal cocoon have largely been destroyed, the seven bastions, or *baluartes,* are mostly intact; those that were demolished have been rebuilt. The two original entrances that once allowed the only access to the city still stand.

The land gate, **Puerta de Tierra** *(Calle 18 opposite Calle 59),* provides a dramatic background for a sound and light show *($$)* featuring dancers and musicians. The schedule varies depending on the season, but there are performances most weekend evenings, and nightly during high season. The sea gate, **Puerta del Mar** *(Calle 8 at Calle 59)*, is now just a large commemorative arch two blocks from the seawall.

Within the compact city center, the neoclassic **Catedral de la Concepción Inmaculada** *(Calle 55 at Calle 10)* incorporates renaissance elements. The pièce de résistance of the rather simple cathedral is the brilliant Holy Sepulcher of carved ebony covered in miniature stamped silver angels and icons tucked in the small, interior museum.

The cathedral stands of the north side of the **plaza principal.** Unlike the main squares in other Mexican cities, Campeche's tranquil park hardly ever seems busy—the majority of townsfolk are found strolling the seaside walkway, the *malecón*, in the evening. The plaza livens up on weekends, however, when the surrounding streets are closed to cars and the symphony orchestra plays in the central bandstand.

Wandering around the city is one of the most pleasant things to do in Campeche. For those who prefer to ride, daily tram tours *($$)* also depart from the main plaza, usually 9–12 and 5–8.

At the outskirts of the historic center is Campeche's spiffy **mercado municipal** *(Av. Circuito Baluartes between Calles 51 & 55)*. Except for fine "Panama-style" hats and some woven goods, Campeche is not known for its crafts, but this organized warren of locally grown produce and other everyday items is nonetheless a fascinating place to shop. The sur-

rounding area is full of shoe stores and other shops.

Located in strategic defensive positions at both ends of the city are Campeche's two historic forts. The completion of imposing **Fuerte San Miguel** *(Av. Escénica s/n)* in 1771 finally put an end to pirate raids. At the south end of the city, this hilltop fort now contains the city's best museum, the **Museo de la Cultura Maya** *(closed Mon, $)*. Housed here are pre-Hispanic artifacts from throughout the state, including quite a few of Jaina island's statuettes portraying people of various stations and professions (see p. 331), and half a dozen spectacular jade funerary masks discovered at Calakmul (see pp. 329).

Northeast of the city center, at **Fuerte San José** *(Av. Francisco Morazan s/n)*, is the **Museo de Armas y Barcos** *(closed Mon., $)*. The Museum of Arms and Boats displays 18th-century weapons, religious art, manuscripts, and model ships. The collection is small, but the view is good.

Several of the bastions that once punctuated the city's hexagonal walls also house small museums. **Baluarte San Carlos** *(Calle 8 at Calle 65, closed Mon.)* houses a simple city museum. The **Museo de las Estelas** *(Closed Mon., $)* of the **Baluarte de la Soledad** *(Calle 8 at Calle 57)*, on the south side of the main plaza, houses a small but worthy collection of carved Maya stelae and artifacts. The exhibit would be much more interesting, however, with some sort of explanation.

Within the thick walls of **Baluarte Santiago** *(Calle 8 at Calle 49, closed Mon., $)* is a small botanical garden, and **Baluarte de San Pedro** *(Calle 51 at Calle 8)* is a shop selling crafts of native design and material. ■

One of two hilltop fortifications that protected the port from pirates

Edzná

 309 C2

✉ 28 miles (45 km)
southeast of
Campeche

$ $

Edzná

EDZNÁ WAS INHABITED BY 400 B.C. AND SERVED AS A regional capital between A.D. 400 and 1000, but its greatest period of influence and monument building corresponds to the Late Classic era (A.D. 600–900). Although not abruptly abandoned as other Mesoamerican cities, its population dwindled slowly after A.D. 1000, finally disappearing at the end of the Postclassic period around 1450. Its appeal lies in the symmetry and monumental character of its structures and in the well-designed layout of the city center.

Located at a crossroads and trade route between the northern Yucatán Peninsula, the southern lowlands, and Ah Kin Pech (today's Campeche city), Edzná shows the influence of several architectural styles. Classic-era carved stelae, many still on site,

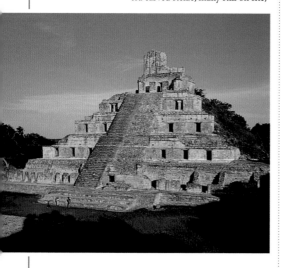

The Templo de los Cinco Pisos, the site's largest structure, was originally faced with stucco and paint.

are common to the southern lowlands, as are roofcombs and corbeled arch roofs. The most telling element of the Puuc style is the complex and symbolic stone mosaics adorning the temple facades.

Unique to Edzná, however, was its vast system of irrigation, constructed between 200 B.C. and A.D. 100 without beasts of burden, metal tools, or the wheel. During the rainy season, when the wide river valley often flooded, water was

collected and redirected to a multitude of reservoirs via canals.

The excavated buildings cluster in the vicinity of the main plaza, **Plaza Principal,** and the adjacent **Gran Acrópolis.** South of the former are the well-restored **juego de pelota** (ball court) and the **Templo Sur.** The temple surmounting this five-level structure appears to be of a different style and was probably added during the Late Classic period.

The site's largest and most impressive building is the **Templo de los Cinco Pisos** (Five-story Temple), located on the Great Acropolis. Sanctuaries on each level are accessed via a central staircase; the tiny temple at the top is crowned by the remnants of a roofcomb. A recently discovered solar phenomenon occurs each year at the planting season (May 1–3) and again at harvest (August 7–9). On these days, the sun enters the normally dark interior to illuminate the face of Itzamná, the sky serpent-creater deity, on a stele within. (The stone remains, but the carving is gone.)

Some of the site's oldest structures have been found on the **Pequeña Acrópolis,** south of the Great Acropolis. Each of the four buildings seated on this raised base faces one of the cardinal directions. West of this acropolis is the **Templo de los Mascarones,** with its modeled plaster masks of the rising and setting sun god on the east and west flanks, respectively. ■

Reserva de la Biósfera Calakmul

THE CALAKMUL BIOSPHERE RESERVE IS MEXICO'S LARGEST remaining tropical forest. This slightly elevated spine on the flat back of the Yucatán Peninsula forms an ecological link between the tropical rain forests of Guatemala's Petén region and the drier, shorter forests to the north. Within the reserve and easily reached by highway are the Maya ruins of Xpujil, Chicanná, and Becán. Meanwhile, Hormiguero, Calakmul, and other remote sites require a bit more effort to reach, but reward the traveler with a true "lost in the jungle" feeling.

Covering more than 1.7 million acres (723,185 ha), Calakmul provides a refuge for nearly a hundred species of mammals, including some of Mexico's endangered felines, such as the puma and jaguar. There are 235 known bird species, including toucans, parrots, macaws, and peninsula natives such as the ocellated turkey.

Despite its protected status, the biosphere is threatened by forestry and colonization. Immigrants from Tabasco, Veracruz, and Chiapas have settled along the fringes in various waves since the 1950s, bringing slash-and-burn agriculture, ranching, and hunting. The nonprofit Pronatura Península de Yucatán, directly involved in park management, works with communities in reforestation and in developing sustainable industries such as handcraft production and rural tourism.

When the municipality of Calakmul was formed in 1996, the town of **Xpujil** became its seat of government. Highway 186 bisects the park at this tiny town, which has a few restaurants and basic hotels, a regional bus service, and a phone, Internet, and fax service. The two-lane highway stretches east and west, connecting Chetumal, the capital of Quintana Roo, with Escárcega—a major

crossroads and regional supply center for Campeche state. Heading north from Xpujil, a paved road leads to Hopelchén,

the Chenes region, and to the state of Yucatán.

Visitors can book tours out of Campeche or hire a guide through the Chicanná Ecovillage Resort (see p. 380), near Xpujil. All of the archaeological sites are open daily 8–5 and charge admission ($).

As they are within a few miles of each other and just off the highway, Chicanná, Becán, and Xpujil can be explored in a day or half day. These sites combine elements of the

The endangered jaguar, one of the mammal species that has its home in Calakmul

Chenes architectural style (most notably their zoomorphic "mask" doorways), prevalent in northern Campeche, with the Río Bec style, typified by twin lateral towers topped by false temples, rounded corners, and false stairways.

Chicanná is a small site whose

Mayan name means "house of the snake's mouth." Occupied during the Late Preclassic period, it reached its peak during the Late Classic, when it may have served as an elite community dependent on nearby Becán.

Brown-and-white pea birds shriek as you cut through a small forest of sapodilla trees to Chicanná's main plaza, around which several ruined buildings are grouped. Typical of the site's Chenes-style structures, the facade of **Estructura II** forms an enormous mask representing the creator god Itzamná. The principal doorway represents the god's open mouth; above it, carved stones depict fangs, nose, and crossed eyes. Along the sides of the building, vertical rows of stone-mosaic Chac masks were once covered in stucco

and bright red pigment. These elements and themes are repeated on many of the site's structures.

Becán, less than a mile (1.5 km) away, served as the capital of the Río Bec area. A long moat built during the earliest days of settlement enclosed the site's largest and tallest buildings and various plazas, an inner city reserved for the elite.

Coiled in front of **Estructura III** are the remains of a round altar representing the feathered serpent god, Kukulcán (called Quetzalcóatl by the Toltecs and others to the north). A dank, dark, bat-lined tunnel penetrates **Estructura VIII,** leading from the building's base on the south side to the east side at the second level. From the top of this pyramid you can see the Temple of the Three Towers at Xpujil, about 5 miles (8 km) to the northeast.

Named for a plant that grows abundantly in the area, **Xpujil** (Cat's Tail), like Chicanná and Becán, flourished in the Late Classic era and combines Chenes and Río Bec architectural styles. Built-in benches such as those found in **Estructuras III** and **IV** suggest the buildings were living quarters.

About 14 miles (23 km) southwest of Xpujil, **Hormiguero** (Ant Hill) was named for the looters' tunnels that researchers found snaking through the site in 1933. Three distinct groups of buildings (North, Central, and South) are surrounded by clusters of dwellings. The Río Bec style predominates, typified by the side towers with rounded corners and false stairways of **Estructura II,** in the South Group. The tropical forests surrounding the ruins are interrupted by pastures, savannas, and marshes. Half-day excursions can be arranged in Xpujil.

Río Bec refers to a group of at least 18 ceremonial structures so spread out that archaeologists are

Left: A stone-carved visage on a Mayan structure in Chicanná **Above:** Becán was once the capital of the Río Bec area, but like other sites nearby remains largely unrestored.

unsure if they belonged to a single community. Hire a guide in Xpujil to take you on a hiking tour to this little-visited site on the Bec River.

Calakmul is located deep within the reserve, 37 miles (60 km) off Highway 186. Troops of monkeys chatter in the trees, and the site has a lovely, lost and alone feel. Since the road was paved in 1993, it's generally quite easy—although slow going on the potholed road— to access the archaeological site.

Discovered in 1931 by U.S. botanist Cyrus Lundell, this extensive city—built on a floodplain and once near a large freshwater lake— is related stylistically to the nearby Petén region of Guatemala. Calakmul was continuously inhabited for more than 1,500 years, from the Middle Preclassic era

(500–300 B.C.) to the Late Postclassic period (A.D. 1200–1521).

The site apparently had several periods of growth and success. For 500 years it was the capital of a kingdom called **Cabeza del Serpiente** (Serpent's Head), uniting such lowland cities as Dos Pilas, Naranjo, and Caracol. After the death of its leader Jaguar Claw and a significant defeat to Tikal in Guatemala, Calakmul appears to have strengthened relations with its northern neighbors of the Río Bec area, and buildings such as **Estructura V** show the influence of the Río Bec style. During this time a great number of stelae were carved and erected. The city declined in importance, and after A.D. 1000 was used almost exclusively as a ceremonial center. ■

Hopelchén, Hochob, & Dzibilnocac

DIRECTLY EAST OF CAMPECHE CITY IS HOPELCHÉN, A small but important town that makes an interesting stop off the tourist trail. Mennonites from surrounding farms come here to sell their homemade cheese and to purchase supplies. Although their young people sometimes rebel, they generally wear traditional farmer clothing and still speak the Low German dialect of their ancestors. South of town are Hochob and Dzibilnocac, two small archaeological sites demonstrating the Chenes-style architecture of the region.

Hopelchén
309 C3

Hochob
309 C2

Dzibilnocac
309 C2

Due north of Xpujil is **Hochob,** 9 miles (14 km) from Dzibalchén off the Dzibalchén–Chencho road. To date, a plaza and four buildings have been excavated, seated on an artificially leveled hill. The giant mask facades of the **Palacio del Este** (East Palace) and **Palacio Principal** (Main Palace), both on Plaza I, provide examples of one of the most important elements of Chenes architecture. The former building has a zoomorphic figure; the latter, the sun god Itzamná, whose squinting eyes appear above the doorway. Chac masks adorn the edges of the Main Palace, and the remains of roofcombs can be seen.

Behind the palace, several cavities in the ground are all that remain of an ancient irrigation system. The false stairways and towers crowned by false temples on **Estructura III,** also on the first plaza, are typical of Río Bec style.

North of Dzibalchén along a paved secondary road, the little-excavated ruins at **Dzibilnocac** are found in the town of Iturbide. Although platforms, pyramid bases, palaces, and vaulted chambers are strewn throughout the site, only one building has been excavated. Combining various architectural elements, the three-story **Templo Palacio** (Estructura I) has the false stairways and temple-topped towers characteristic of the Río Bec style. Well-preserved Chac masks adorn the top temple. The site was a mid-sized ceremonial center between about A.D. 250 and 900, but was inhabited as early as 500 B.C. ∎

A young man from Becal deftly weaves a straw hat.

More places to visit in Campeche

NORTHERN CAMPECHE

Between Campeche city and Yucatán state, Highway 180 passes a series of small towns, each with at least one sight of interest. Sixteenth-century **Hecelchakán,** 37 miles (60 km) north of Campeche, is admired among Campechanos for its *cochinita pibil* (baked pork seasoned with achiote), sold at informal eateries in the main square. **Isla Jaina** (just offshore) is not open to the public, but its famous statuettes can be seen in Hecelchakán's **Museo Arqueológico del Camino Real** *(Closed Mon., $).* About 15 miles (24 km) beyond, it's worth stopping in **Calkiní** to see the cloistered **Clarisa convent church,** with its beautiful carved pulpit and main altarpiece.

Just before the Yucatán border is **Becal,** the birthplace of the famous *jipis,* straw hats varying from very fine, expensive "Panama hats" (a misnomer that annoys Campechanos no end) to colorful, floppy, coarse models to use at the beach. The hats are produced in cellars beneath residents' homes, where humidity keeps the palm fiber supple.
⚊ 309 C3

CAMPECHE'S COAST

Although Campeche is not known for its beaches, a drive down the coast holds a few pleasant surprises. One of the prettiest stretches of beach is found around **Seybaplaya,** an unpretentious fishing town about 20 miles (32 km) south of Campeche. The narrow beach, lined with brightly painted skiffs, heads north about a mile (1.5 km) to **Payucán,** where herons, pelicans, and sandpipers stalk their prey in shallow waters streaked turquoise, gray-green, and blue. Another hour or so south is **Champotón,** the largest town between Campeche and the unattractive, business-oriented oil town of **Isla del Carmen,** farther south. It was in the bay at Champotón, now named **Bahía de la Mala Pelea** (Bay of the Evil Fight) that the Maya soundly defeated the Spaniards for the first time. The unremarkable yet pleasant coastal city of Champotón is a takeoff point for local hunting and fishing expeditions.
⚊ 308 B2

GRUTAS DE XTACUMBILXUNÁN

Near the Yucatán border, the Caves of Xtacumbilxunán are a series of underground limestone chambers with interesting formations. The ancient Maya held these and other caves sacred as a link between this world and the next. If you're driving north from Hopelchén, it is worth the short detour off Highway 261 to visit the caves. After a revamp of the lighting system, the caves are again open—Tues.–Sun., 10.–5. Guided visits only are allowed.
⚊ 309 C3 ■

Yucatán

At the top of the peninsula, pie-shaped Yucatán is the flattest state, with the poorest soil and the least rainfall. Here the tropical forest is low, dense, and scrubby. Hot year round, it is particularly sultry during the rainy months of late summer and fall, when biting bugs are at their worst. December through February is the coolest time of year, when locals dress up in sweaters, while visitors in cotton shirts still manage to break a sweat.

While its beaches are not the white-sand and turquoise-water variety of the Riviera Maya, an isolated coastline offers cheaper prices and an opportunity for discovery. Celestún and Río Lagartos lure bird-watchers, and nearby Isla Holbox is an island haven for escapists. Coastal infrastructure is limited but growing; accommodations outside Merida (with the exception of some stellar five-star boutique hotels) are generally basic. Development of the northern coast was scrapped after Hurrican Isidore, much to the delight of purists and beach bums.

Yucatán's main draw, however, is its Maya ruins. Despite the pressure of busloads of visitors, Chichén Itzá remains among Mexico's top archaeological sites. Strategically placed throughout the large site are Mesoamerica's largest ball court, a sacrificial sinkhole, and stepped pyramids covered in bas-relief carvings.

Yucatán's other antique jewel, Uxmal, is one of a half-dozen excavated sites forming the Puuc Route, a loop of archaeological sites south of Mérida. In the same area of low, rolling hills are unassuming towns with lonesome Franciscan monasteries, orange-scented markets, and loads of appeal for the inquisitive traveler.

Once dedicated to corn and cattle, and later to sugarcane and then sisal fiber, the peninsula's haciendas were sold and subdivided during post-revolutionary land reforms. Today, many have been transformed into luxurious, rural hotels and restaurants. ■

Chichén Itzá is one of the Yucatán's most studied and fascinating sites.

Mérida

A vendor sells fresh local fruit from a stall in Mérida.

THERE IS LITTLE IN MÉRIDA TO REMIND YOU OF ITS PAST AS one of the most important ceremonial cities in the Postclassic Maya world: T'ho (meaning "fifth place"). Some vestiges remain of its days of wealth and European elegance, when *henequen* (sisal) profits paid for elegant Italian furnishings and foreign vacations. Isolated geographically and culturally from the rest of Mexico, Mérida's elite tended to look outside for cultural inspiration. Forged by indigenous labor under the brutal hacienda system, tempered with Maya resilience and sense of self, and enriched by the contributions of immigrants, Mérida is mestizo, but different from anywhere else in Mexico.

Unlike Tenochtitlán, which was felled in a four-month siege (see p. 30), T'ho resisted the invaders for 15 years. The resolute Maya first battled Francisco Montejo (el Adelantado) and later his son, Montejo el Mozo, who finally prevailed in 1542.

Today, Mérida is a city of more than 1.5 million people. Hotels are clustered in historic downtown, with the fanciest highrises along **Prolongación de Paseo Montejo.** Restaurants range from air-conditioned bistros with French menus to fan-cooled terraces and outdoor cafés. Horse-drawn carriages compete with cars, cabs, and diesel-belching buses on the streets downtown. Restored churches and theaters are scattered among modern one- and two-story structures in deep pastel colors— some charming, others crumbling.

Many second- and third-generation buildings surround the city's cultural and civic heart, the **zócalo,** or Plaza Mayor *(between Calles 60 & 62, 61 & 63).* Now a bank, the **Casa de Montejo** *(Calle 63, south side of the plaza)* is one of the city's finest examples of secular plateresque architecture, although only the facade is original. Note the Montejo family crest above the grilled balcony.

Across the plaza to the east, the original church has been incorporated into the **Catedral San Ildefonso** *(Calle 60 at 61),* begun in 1561 and added to over the centuries. Inside, 12 massive columns support the ribbed vaults over the nave of the Spanish Romanesque

Mérida
🅜 309 C4
Visitor information
✉ Teatro Peon Contreras, Calle 60 between Calles 57 & 59
☎ 999/924-9290

interior. Left of the main altar, the **Cristo de las Ampollas** (Christ of the Blisters) is a replica of the original statue, said to have survived an all-night fire with only discoloration and blisters.

Next door, the **Museo de Arte Contemporáneo** *(Calle 60 between Calles 63 & 61-A, tel 999/928-3258, closed Tues., $)* was originally the bishop's residence and now houses temporary exhibits on its second floor. There is a good view of the cathedral from the neo-classic **Palacio del Gobierno** (Government Palace), on the north-east corner of the plaza. Inside, 27 murals painted between 1971 and 1978 depict the disquieting history of regional conquest.

Some Mexican cities are lonely on Sundays, their streets empty except for visitors in search of a meal. Not so Mérida, where every-one seems to stroll the city center, showing off their best clothes. Beginning Saturday evening, the zócalo and adjoining plazas, merci-fully closed to traffic, become venues for free folkloric dance performances, crafts and antiques bazaars, and impromptu street theater. Get a schedule of events at the tourist office, located in a corner of the Italianate **Teatro Peon Contreras** *(Calles 59 & 60)*. If you're in the neighborhood any day before 1 p.m., stop in to admire the theater's frescoes and the early 20th-century marble staircase, restored in the early 1980s. Better still, catch one of the music or dance performances held there. An outdoor café makes for great people watching across the way at convivial **Parque Hidalgo.**

Mérida's sultry climate can be oppressive. The town snaps out of its heat-induced torpor after sundown, when evening breezes ruffle the palms in **Parque Santa Lucía** *(Calles 60 & 55)*. On Thursday evenings at 9 p.m., musicians play

The fancy version of the Yucatecan *huipil* **is the** *terno,* **shown here.**

Dzibilchaltún
⚠ 309 C4
$ $

while young men and women per-form regional dances. On Saturdays after 9 p.m., tourists and locals gath-er in and around El Remate park for **Noche Mexicana** *(Paseo de Montejo & Calle 47)*, an outdoor festival of music, dance, and local crafts. Just up the street is the **Palacio Cantón**—a stately man-sion of Carrara marble, ornate columns, and Italianate *beaux-arts* details—housing the **Museo de Antropología e Historia** *(Calle 43 & Paseo de Montejo, tel 999/923-0469, closed Mon., $)*. Although the Anthropology and History Museum has only a limited number of arti-facts, it's worth the admission price to see the early 20th-century man-sion. The source of some of the museum's artifacts lies 10 miles (16 km) north of Mérida at the Maya city of **Dzibilchaltún.** Most of the sites 8,000 structures are unexcavat-ed, but the lovely jade sinkhole for swimming and the ruined Catholic and Maya buildings make it a worthwhile excursion.

Charming as Mérida is, its buses and cars create significant pollution. The wooded areas, boating lake, children's playgrounds, and small zoo at **Parque Centenario** *(Av. Itzaes between Calles 59 & 65)*, at the city's western boundary, provide a refreshing escape from urban over-load. The **Ermita de Santa Isabel** *(Calles 66 & 77, church closed weekdays)* is another peaceful refuge, with a pre-Hispanic altar and other Maya artifacts in the well-tended gardens. Also known as Our Lady of the Successful Journey, the church was once a stopping place for travel-ers en route to Campeche.

At its founding, Mérida's core was reserved for the elite, sur-rounded by Indian towns and later mixed and mestizo neighborhoods. Each enclave was a world within itself, its social and religious life centered around the parish church.

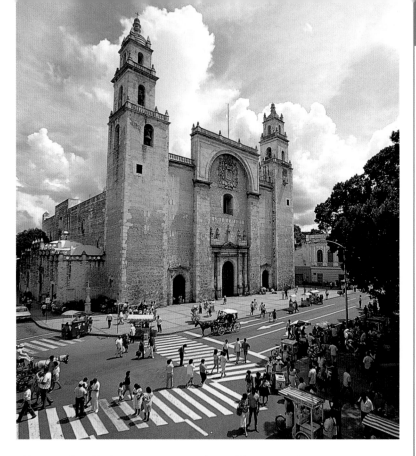

Although swallowed by the city in the 20th century, these barrios still have active churches and lively markets, and make an interesting detour from the main tourist routes.

Visit **Barrio de Santiago,** in the northeast sector, on Tuesday evenings between 8 and 11 p.m., when 1940s-era bands play in the park facing the **Templo de Santiago Apostle** *(Calles 59 & 70)*. Closest to the main plaza is **Barrio San Juan,** with a 16th-century church *(Calles 69 & 62)*. About eight blocks southwest of the main square, the **Barrio de San Cristóbal** welcomed Lebanese and Italian immigrants in the 19th century. Its church *(Calles 50 & 69)* has a sober yet impressive interior decorated with images of the Virgin of Guadalupe (see p. 193).

Northwest of the city center, **La Mejorada** was once separated from San Cristóbal by a hill, demolished during the War of Independence. The lovely old former Franciscan monastery *(Calles 59 & 50)* now houses a school of architecture and the **Museo de la Música** *(Closed Mon.)*.

Mérida makes a logical base for trips throughout the region, as it has a central location and good services. There are casual bed-and-breakfasts and five-star high rises with full amenities, and excellent restaurants serving Yucatecan, Mexican, and international cuisine. There are plenty of shops, too. Choose from Panama-style straw hats, wonderful hammocks, tropical clothing, or the locally made anise and honey liqueur, Xtabentun. ■

Mérida's cathedral—begun in 1561, making it the oldest in mainland America—has a sober, restrained Renaissance facade.

Progreso

Coast & coastal reserves

WHILE QUINTANA ROO ATTRACTS SYBARITES AND SCUBA divers, Yucatán's coast draws slightly more introverted types, such as fishermen and birders. The ever increasing popularity of the Riviera Maya may have encouraged plans for a corridor of resorts between Telchac Puerto and Dzilám de Bravo, but Hurricane Isidore set investors back to square one. Away from the crowds, natural reserves at Celestún and Río Lagartos create a safe haven for domestic and migratory bird species, endangered marine tortoises, and other animal and plant species. And between these two reserves, Maya and mestizo villages languish under the tropical sun.

Like Río Lagartos, Celestún attracts both birds and birders.

With just over 50,000 inhabitants, **Progreso** is a vacation village for Meridians during the hottest summer months. Some travelers find it an interesting port city with a wide, long, sandy beach and water; to others, it's a tumble of cement and stucco buildings without much charm. Calle 19 hugs the coast, lined with seafood restaurants and simple cafés. Progreso's original stone pier has been expanded (twice) and the harbor dredged in a successful effort to lure cruise ships. When they dock here once or twice a week, vendors sell crafts along the malecón.

After strolling on the beach or the boardwalk, you can chill with a book or a beverage, or explore the coast. **Yucalpetén,** about 4 miles (6 km) to the west, attracts many commercial vessels, and a marina for yachts has several sportfishing boats. The aged but picturesque fishing fleet brings home catches of grouper, snapper, and sea bass.

The only significant stretch of beach road in the state is the 50 miles (80 km) between Progreso and Dzilám de Bravo, to the east. A two-lane highway passes salt flats used since pre-Hispanic times, and grassy dunes line the beach, accessed by sandy roads leading off from the highway. Meridians take weekend getaways in tranquil **Chicxulub Puerto,** a fishing village just east of Progreso. Straddling the coast here is the 112-mile-wide (180 km) Chicxulub Crater, created by a meteorite about 65 million years ago and discovered in the 1940s by petroleum geologists. Its impact is thought to have created the peninsula's sinkholes (and possibly polished off the dinosaurs). Other small fishing villages dot the coast, including **San Crisanto** and **Telchac Puerto.**

West of Mérida, **Sisal** was once the state's first important port but lost out to deeper Progreso in the latter part of the 19th century. Although it is a pleasant fishing village today with a nice beach, tourists are often drawn instead to neighboring **Celestún,** 60 miles (90 km) west of Mérida. From here small boats cruise the estuary and mangrove forests of the **Reserva de la Biósfera Ría Celestún** in search of waterfowl, migratory shorebirds, and especially coral-colored flamingo colonies tens of thousands strong. At the edge of the estuary sits Celestún, a quiet town geared for day-trippers from Mérida and backpackers used to rustic accommodations. Three-hour birding tours (most flamingos are sighted between September and March) include a visit to a fresh-water spring (ask for time to swim) and to a forest of petrified trees. Nearby, the ecological reserve **El Palmar** is also beginning to attract nature lovers.

Directly north of Valladolid on the north-central coast is **Reserva de la Biósfera Ría Lagartos,** another wildlife sanctuary. Its long, highly saline estuary attracts white ibis, great white herons, snowy egrets, and flamingos. You can arrange three-hour bird-watching tours (*$$$$$ per boat)* in Valladolid, Mérida, or at Restaurant Isla Contoy (*tel 986/862-0000).* Pelicans roost in the mangroves, and herons stalk fish among their roots. You'll see the flamingo feeding grounds, although the nesting sites are off-limits.

Also great for fishing and relax-ing is **Isla Holbox** (Mayan for "dark hole"), just over the Quintana Roo state line. There are five ferry crossings per day (*$);* at other times private skiffs (*$$$$)* make the trip. Most hotels will arrange fly fishing for snook, tarpin, and bonefish, and ocean fishing for grouper and pampano (*Both $$$$$).* The season is April–July, although ocean fishing continues year round. Other popular pastimes are horseback riding, kayaking, and—from late spring to fall—swimming with whale sharks. ■

As yet undeveloped, the state of Yucatán has miles of solitary beaches.

Chichén Itzá

🔺 309 D3

✉ Highway 180,
72 miles (116 km)
east of Mérida

☎ 999/851-0124

Chichén Itzá

THE MOST ARCHITECTURALLY INTRIGUING AND MAJESTIC
Maya site on the Yucatán Peninsula is Chichén Itzá. Its earliest structures, including an ornate circular observatory, date to the Classic
era (A.D. 250–900) and echo the native Maya architectural details of
the Puuc region south of Mérida. Its famed Castillo was constructed
during the Terminal Classic or Early Postclassic period (A.D. 900–
1200). Scholars once thought this evidence of a Toltec invasion, but
most now agree that the worldly Itzá—successful merchants, who
traveled long distances, often by canoe—in fact influenced the Toltecs
at Tula as they traded with far-flung empires.

**Above: Like the
Europeans of
the day,
Mesoamericans
sometimes
displayed the
severed heads of
their enemies.
Depicted here
is a stone
representation
of this practice,
called a
tzompantli.
Opposite: In the
middleground is
Caracol and, far
beyond, the
temple to
Kukulkán, the
feathered
serpent.**

Unlike the more romantic, vine-shrouded sites of Palenque and
Uxmal, Chichén Itzá has an almost
militaristic appearance. Murals and
stelae (carved stone pillars) depict
warriors, battles, and human
sacrifice, belying the long-held
image of the Maya as a pacifist
people. Over 30 meticulously
reconstructed buildings rise above
artificial platforms, while hundreds
of other structures lie crumbling in
scrubby jungle. The site sprawls
over more than 39 square miles
(100 sq km), of which only about
3½ square miles (9 sq km) may be
visited: Grupo Central, Grupo
Norte, and Old Chichén.

Chichén's oldest structures are
located in the southern part of the
site, an area first settled by the
Maya around A.D. 400. It was

already deserted when the Itzá peoples from the south arrived in the
eighth century and began constructing a major city. Also known
as the Chontal Maya or Putún, the
Itzá were a seafaring people from
what is now Tabasco state. The fact
that they were considered interlopers or at least outsiders is evidenced by the fact that their name
in Mayan means "those who speak
our language badly."

The buildings once thought to
have been Toltec-inspired dominate
the **Grupo Norte,** where
pyramids and temples were constructed atop existing structures
around the tenth century. Over
35,000 people lived in the area in
the 11th century, when Chichén
Itzá was a major religious and
commercial center. But by 1250,
the site was again deserted.

Archaeologists long believed the
Toltec of Tula, 600 miles (965 km)
to the west, conquered the Maya
of Chichén Itzá in the Early
Postclassic period (around A.D. 900)
and imposed their beliefs and
symbols upon their subjects.
However, it is now generally
accepted that the reverse is true:
Chichén Itzá actually influenced
Tula trade, but not conquest.
Turquoise found in Chichén Itzá
was traded from the Oasis America
people of today's southern Arizona,

and gold was imported from as far south as Costa Rica.

The confusion springs from the similarity of carvings, architectural styles, and symbols found at both Chichén Itzá's Grupo Norte and Tula, or Tollan. One of the most significant similarities is the presence of the feathered serpent god, called Kukulcán by the Maya and Quetzalcóatl by the Toltec and other groups. The serpent is particularly important at the **Castillo,** also called Pirámide de Kukulcán, Chichén Itza's most famous structure. Built atop an earlier temple, the pyramidal building has four stairways with a total of 365 steps, corresponding with the number of days in the solar calendar. A square temple at the top is believed to honor Kukulcán.

Thousands of onlookers are drawn to Castillo during the spring and fall equinoxes (normally March 21 and September 21). On these days, the sunlight hits the pyramid in such a way as to create a snake-shaped shadow wriggling down the steps to meet a serpent's head carved at the base. The phenomenon gives testimony to the Maya's incredible skill at mathematics and astronomy.

Chichén Itzá holds many examples of human sacrifice. Near the Castillo is the **Tzompantli,** a platform lined with stone carvings of human skulls. (A similar wall can be found at Tula.) Adjacent to this structure is the **juego de pelota,** or ball court. The traditional ball game had a religious and political significance unknown to most people today. It was a one-on-one game playing a victorious ruler against his defeated enemy—the loser would be sacrificed by being rolled down from the top of the pyramid, his arms and legs bound tightly behind him, to smash on the ground below. The fight was fixed,

of course, so that the conquering ruler could defeat the captive—a symbolic defeat of evil and darkness by light and life, and a reenactment of the creation of the world. In order to ensure his success, the conquering ruler would starve the other player for several weeks before the game and, if he still had too much spirit, break one of his arms or legs before the match. Evidence of this ritual ball game is seen in Mixtec hieroglyphics, Maya codices, and oral reports from eyewitnesses during the early years of the Spanish Conquest.

A dirt trail leads from the ball court to the **Cenote de los Sacrificios,** a deep natural well into which sacrificial victims may have been tossed. Mexican diver Pablo Bush Romero first investigated the well; Jacques Cousteau followed. Both found human skeletons and jade and gold figurines in the murky depths, further demonstrating the Maya belief in human sacrifice.

Back at El Castillo, rows of carved stone pillars called the **Mil Columnas** front the **Templo de los Guerreros** (Temple of the Warriors), where a few bits of murals decorate the walls. More murals of a battle scene line a wall at the nearby **Templo de los Jaguares.** Several statues of the lesser god Chac Mool are scattered around the site; one of the largest sits by this cluster of ruins. The reclining figure holds a flat plate on which human hearts were presented to the gods.

More mysterious and ornate than the newer section, the Grupo Sur is dominated by the **Caracol** (also known as the Observatorio), named for its snail-like shape. Most likely used as an observatory, the Caracol has two levels of stairways and terraces leading to a circular tower with windows facing the four cardinal directions. The Maya were keen astronomers, and studied the cycles of the moon and stars to calculate the passage of time. Their knowledge was particularly important in Yucatán, where crops had to be planted to benefit from the area's limited rainfall.

The Puuc style of architecture is most evident at the **Casa de las Monjas,** whose name, "the Nunnery," was given by the Spanish. Elaborate friezes front the crumbling staircase and window frames at the top of the long structure. Beside the Nunnery, **la Iglesia** (meaning "the Church," another Spanish reference) is also elaborately decorated with ornate carvings of animals and latticework designs. A somewhat overgrown trail leads from the Nunnery to

Chichén Viejo (Old Chichén), where the Itzás let loose their imaginations on structures covered with masks of Chac, bas-reliefs of jaguars and gods, and delicate latticework designs. Some structures are barely visible beneath the ever encroaching jungle brush and vines.

Anyone even remotely fascinated by the Maya should spend at least one night by the ruins. There are several moderately priced hotels and restaurants in the nearby town of **Piste,** but it's worth the splurge to stay closer to the site. Archaeologists who worked here in the early 20th century stayed in cabins at the Hacienda Chichén; both it and the Hotel Mayaland are found by a back entrance to the ruins. ∎

Chac Mool was an intermediary between man and god. Note the plate for receiving sacrifice.

Uxmal & La Ruta Puuc

ONLY IN A LAND AS FLAT AS THE YUCATÁN WOULD SUCH A subtly undulating region be called "hill country." The Mayan word *puuc* describes not only this region, but the Late Classic cities that flourished here and the architectural style that defines them. With few cenotes, or sinkholes, the land could sustain these settlements only after northward-migrating people devised *chultunes* (water tanks), in which to store water for the dry months. They later created hydraulic systems as well. Between A.D. 200 and 1000, more than a hundred settlements prospered throughout the small region in south-central Yucatán and northeast Campeche.

With the demise of the Classic southern lowlands cities such as Tikal, the Puuc flourished between A.D. 800 and 1000 in what Mayanists call the Terminal Classic period. This was a period of intense and uncharacteristic political cooperation among cities, many of which were connected by *sacbés,* or white roads. In classic Mesoamerican fashion, the great religious centers were abandoned after reaching their height of civilization. Theories include over-population, depletion of resources, disease, and increased warfare, but the real reason remains a mystery.

Puuc-style architecture is admired for being among the most harmonious and well-proportioned of the Maya world. It is noted for its stone-mosaic facades, veneer masonry, small relief columns, and hook-nosed Chac masks on the facades and corners of buildings. In a land of uncertain rainfall and no surface rivers, the rain god Chac was an important deity. Walls are often smooth below, while the upper facades are decorated with elaborate geometric shapes. The "false arch," a Maya innovation, reached its most refined at the Palace of the Governor, at Uxmal.

Walled **Uxmal,** 48 miles (78 km) south of Mérida on Highway 261, was a favorite of

19th-century explorer John Lloyd Stephens (see p. 14), who visited several times with traveling companion and artist Frederick Catherwood. Capital of the Puuc region, Uxmal (meaning "thrice built") was founded around A.D. 800 and reached its peak of civilization under Lord Chac, who reigned between about A.D. 900 and 950. Its name refers to three distinct phases of construction. Considered the most lovely of the Puuc cities, it has been extensively restored but, compared to other major sites in Mexico, little studied.

Rising 125 feet (38 m) above the surrounding forest, the **Casa del Adivino** (Pyramid of the Magician) affords a great view of the site and surrounding low forest. The pyramid is also called "House of the Dwarf;" according to legend, it was built in one night by a dwarf hatched from a tiny egg. The tall structure's unusual elliptical base, rounded corners, and harmonious design make it one of the most admired buildings in Mexico—of any age. Steep staircases on either side lead to the temple at its crown, decorated with icons of the planet Venus, the sun, flowers, and serpents. This and other buildings are dramatically lit during nightly narrated sound-and-light shows in English and Spanish.

Uxmal

🔺 309 C3

Just beyond, the **Casa de las Monjas** (The Nunnery) is a quadrangle of four large, low palaces surrounding an open courtyard. Like those at many archaeological sites, the building was named by the Spaniards, who thought its 74 vaulted chambers resembled monastic cells. Covering the palace's upper interior facades are intricate carvings of Chac masks and serpents interspersed with latticework designs. Also within the central group are the **juego de pelota**, or ball court, and the simple **Casa de las Tortugas,** named for the turtles decorating the cornice (much blurred by the passage of time). The more recently restored **Cuadrángulo de los Pájaros** was named for a repeating avian pattern above the doorways.

Cited as one of the most beautiful representations of Puuc-style architecture, the magnificent **Palacio del Gobernador** was built around A.D. 900 on a stepped platform. It seems to have served as both the residence and the administrative center of the ruling elite.

The palace's horizontal plane is, on the east face, interrupted by perhaps the most refined false arches in the Maya world. Its frieze is covered in an intricate geometric mosaic composed of 20,000 carefully cut stones forming Chac masks.

The excellent travertine limestone found in the region was largely responsible for the success of Puuc-style carvings at Uxmal, epitomized in the Governor's Palace. This fine-grained limestone, ranging in color from yellow to red, can be cut into thin plates and polished to a high luster. Only around Mitla, in Oaxaca state, is such a high grade of stone found, and the Mixtecs of Mitla also produced intricate and exacting mosaics.

Just about 13 miles (22 km) to the southeast, **Kabah** was connected by a sacbé to Uxmal. To the east are the greatest number of restored structures, including the impressive **Palacio de los Mascarones** (Palace of the Masks), elaborately decorated with six tiers of Chac masks, each an inlaid stone mosaic. Walk around to

The name Uxmal (meaning "thrice built") refers to the site's three separate phases of construction.

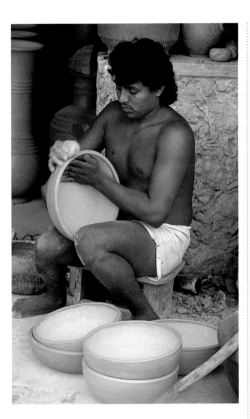

Ticul, known for its pottery, is an unpretentious base for touring the region.

arch, inscribed on the west facade with representations of thatch houses and stylized snakes. One of the best surviving examples of its type, the arch may have served commemorative purposes, or perhaps it was placed at the end of a sacbé.

The highway now loops north toward the caves of Loltún (see p. 346) to the **Ruta de los Conventos,** a series of monasteries built from the beginning of the 16th century for the catechism of the native population. While the churches and adjoining convents have lost much of their glamour, this route returns to Mérida passing typical Maya and mestizo towns. To visit the churches, arrive in the morning or late afternoon, as many are closed between noon and 4 p.m. En route, visit the fruit market in the friendly little town of **Oxcutzcab,** famous for its sweet oranges *(chinas).*

East of Oxcutzcab, **Mayapan** was a late-blooming Maya city that gained importance around the time of Chichén Itzá's demise; some scholars believe Chichén was conquered by Mayapan. Mayapan lacked the excellent craftsmanship and site design of other Puuc cities, and had few important temples and no ball court. The 5-mile-long (8 km) wall, averaging nearly 20 feet (6 m) thick, suggests a fortified city. Its main temple, dedicated to Kukulkán, is a poorly constructed imitation of the Castillo, at Chichén Itzá (see p. 340). Mayapan appears to have been sacked and burned around 1440. With its demise, the Puuc alliance was disbanded and fighting broke out among the region's cities. Soon after, the Spanish conquerors arrived.

The Ruta Puuc can be visited as a rushed day trip out of Mérida or Ticul, or as a more leisurely two-day visit. The latter has the added advantage of an overnight stay at one of several pretty hotels right at the ruins of Uxmal. ∎

the back of the building to see the giant warrior sculptures wearing loincloths and beaded necklaces.

Nearby **Sayil** (meaning "home of leaf-cutter ants") is one of the oldest Puuc cities. The most important structure at this site is the three-story **Gran Palacio,** considered along with the palace of Uxmal to embody classic Puuc architecture. Containing more than 90 rooms, it must have housed the city's ruling elite. **Xlapax,** just a few miles away, is a small site and not much reconstructed. As with Sayil, its palace is decorated with masks of the rain god.

Labná (Old House) is about the same distance farther on. Although inhabited as early as the first century A.D., its most noteworthy construction is the Late Classic ceremonial

The stone buildings at Ek Balam were built more than a thousand years ago.

More places to visit in Yucatán

EK BALAM

Rising to importance during the Terminal Classic era, between A.D. 800 and 1000, Ek Balam, which means "Black Jaguar," was a contemporary of the more well-known site at Uxmal (see pp. 342–343). Today the small set of ruins at Ek Balam is growing increasingly popular with tour groups. The site is both easy to get to, off a two-lane highway approximately halfway between Valladolid and the town of Tizimín, and, as it's quite compact, easy to explore.

Archaeologists aren't sure whether the double ring of walls surrounding the city served a defensive or a more symbolic purpose—perhaps both. Within their crumbled remains are a freestanding arch, ball court, and other buildings constructed in the Chenes style. By far the most impressive building is the Acropolis, which was added to by successive rulers and is known to contain at least one royal tomb. Marvelous, detailed, high-relief carvings of warriors surrounded by detailed iconography are the piece de resistance of this magnificent former palace-cum-mauseleum.

🅰 309 E4 💲 $

GRUTAS DE BALANKANCHÉ

Just a few miles northeast of Chichén Itzá, the Caves of Balankanché were used by the pre-Hispanic Maya for sacred ceremonies. The outer caves were long known to locals, and a sealed chamber with ancient artifacts was discovered in 1959. The pottery shows it was used for religious ceremonies during thousands of years by Preclassic, Classic, and Postclassic civilizations. In the Terminal Classic period, the Maya rain god, Chac, was replaced with Tláloc, worshiped throughout Central Mexico. Many representations of Xipe Totec, god of spring and regeneration, have also been found.

It's awesome to see the urns, some decorated with relief "faces," in situ. Open daily 9–5; guided tours leave on the hour, and it doesn't much matter whether it's in English, Spanish, or French. The caves themselves are the show. Don't forget to tip the guide.
309 D3 $ Tours $$

GRUTAS DE LOLTÚN
Eleven miles (17 km) northeast of Labná along the Ruta Puuc are the Grutas de Loltún, one of the peninsula's most extensive cave systems. The caves were first inhabited by nomadic hunter-gatherers between 9000 and 3000 B.C., who left evidence of their

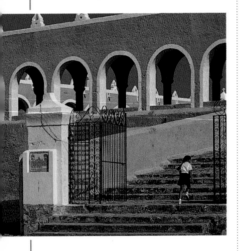

Izamal was a pilgrimage site in the pre-Conquest era.

presence in the form of stone tools. Much later, in the Classic period, the caves were used as a source of water by local inhabitants. Water vessels in both the Mayapan and Chichén Itzá Postclassic ceramic styles have been excavated. The Maya revered five physical features: trees, rocks, mountains, mountain passes, and earth openings—cenotes

and caves, which were considered holy because they presented a transition between the physical and spirit worlds.

Beginning at 9:30 a.m. and leaving approximately every 1.5 hours, guided tours lead through a series of passageways to chambers of various sizes, some with prehistoric paintings or fantastic montages of stalactites and stalagmites. Guides work for tips only, so don't forget the gratuity.
309 C3 $ $$

IZAMAL
Izamal has been an important religious center for millennia. The bustling small town's star attraction is the **Convento de San Antonio de Padua,** built from the stones of a pyramid to the god of the heavens, Itzamná, on which it sits. Light-and-sound shows, in Spanish only, show on Tues., Thurs., and Sat. nights at 8:30. Izamal is a friendly, untouristy town and makes a good base for those who avoid larger cities. Pony traps can be rented on the square for a tour of town, including a stop at the **Pirámide Kinich Kakmó,** all that remains of this once royal Maya city. The huge structure is currently under excavation. The horse-drawn carriages are also useful for visiting artisans shops; drivers know the way to home workshops where hammocks, jewelry, embroidery, and other crafts are offered for sale.
309 D4

VALLADOLID
Although it is the Yucatán's second-largest city, Valladolid has the feel of a small town. In 1847 this colonial-era agricultural center was the scene of the War of the Castes, during which the repressed Maya massacred large numbers of Spanish residents. Worth visiting are the **catedral,** on the *plaza principal*, and the large, 16th-century **Ex-Convento San Bernardino,** three blocks southwest. Outside town, you can visit holy **Cenote Dzitnup,** where light filters through a tiny hole in the ceiling to illuminate the green-blue underground spring or, right at the edge of town, **Cenote Zací.** Valladolid also makes an alternative base for visiting the ruins of Chichén Itzá or the north coast.
309 E3 ■

Travelwise

The Virgin of Guadalupe

TRAVELWISE INFORMATION
PLANNING YOUR TRIP

WHEN TO GO

When you visit depends on what you want to do and see, budget constraints, and your tolerance for wet, hot, or humid weather. Mexico is a large and geographically diverse country, its microclimates dictated by altitude and latitude. June through October is the wettest time, and if you don't mind late-afternoon showers—which in Mexico City clear the air—consider booking your vacation during this low season to avoid the crowds and get cheaper hotel and air rates. Rain may put a damper on beach vacations, however, and late September and October are hurricane season along the Gulf and south/central Pacific coasts (and, less frequently, in Baja). Baja California and the northern deserts are extremely hot in the summer, although diehard fishermen brave the heat for the excellent fishing. Highland cities are hottest March through May, just before the rainy season, while the tropical regions of southern Mexico are hot year round but even hotter, muggier, and more bug-ridden during the rainy season. If you want to avoid both the rainy season and the high season, chose late spring (after Easter) or late fall.

High season is late November (Thanksgiving) to Holy Week (Semana Santa), with especially high hotel rates during Christmas, New Year, and Easter. Mexicans as well as foreigners frequently travel during these holidays, and reservations should be made well in advance.

Those interested in Mexican culture might want to plan their vacation around the country's many colorful fiestas, including the weeks preceding Christmas, Easter, Day of the Dead, pre-Lenten Carnival, and many others. See "Festivals & Fiestas" (pp. 16–17), regional chapters, and "Entertainment & Activities" (pp. 386–89) for specific suggestions. In Mexico, a city or village's saint's day is always cause for celebration. For example, places named San Juan will celebrate on the feast day of St. John, June 24; San Miguel de Allende celebrates its patron, the Archangel Michael, the days preceding September 29. Check with the government tourist office (see individual entries) for more information about specific local festivals.

WHAT TO TAKE

Although Mexicans today are less formal than before, city-dwellers are fashionable and businesspeople dress for success. Except on the more casual coast, Mexican women rarely wear shorts, and men are not seen shirtless except on the beach. Bring lightweight, comfortable clothing for tropical climes, plus a sweater or light jacket. Women should also bring slacks and at least one dressy outfit, men a light sports jacket. Much of Mexico consists of mountains and high plateaus, and while hot during the day can get chilly at night. Comfortable walking shoes are essential for archaeological sites, cobblestone streets, and long walks. A lightweight, long-sleeved shirt prevents mosquito bites, as does an insect repellent containing deet.

As well as the usual—documents and money—take sunscreen, sunglasses, and a hat as the sun is fierce. A small English–Spanish phrasebook is useful. Campers or trekkers should include iodine tablets and filters to purify water if bottled water is unavailable.

ENTRY FORMALITIES

A visa is not necessary for entry into Mexico for citizens of the United States, Canada, the U.K., Ireland, Australia, New Zealand, and much of Western Europe. You will need a tourist card (tarjeta de turista), which can be obtained at embassies, travel agencies, and border crossings; they are also distributed during international flights. Travelers must provide proof of citizenship. For U.S. and Canadian citizens a certified birth certificate (not a copy) is sufficient, along with photo identification; but if you have a passport, bring it. Minors also need a certified birth certificate or passport and a notarized letter of permission from one or both guardians not accompanying the child. U.S. and Canadian citizens can stay up to 180 days with a tourist card.

DRUGS, NARCOTICS, & WEAPONS

To avoid problems, prescription drugs should be brought in their original containers. Drugs such as marijuana and cocaine are illegal, and penalties for drug offenses are strict.

Bringing weapons or ammunition to Mexico is illegal; importing either of these carries huge fines and the possibility of a jail term. Hunters must obtain permits and ID cards to import and transport firearms temporarily; it's best to make arrangements through an authorized wildlife outfitter club, such as a hunting lodge.

PETS

U.S. visitors may bring a dog (or cat) if they provide a pet health certificate signed not more than 72 hours before, and a certificate showing that the animal has been vaccinated against rabies and other contagious diseases.

VACCINATIONS & DISEASE

No inoculations are required for Mexico, but a current tetanus booster is recommended, as is a hepatitis A and/or B inoculation. For travel to rural lowland areas, consider an antimalarial drug or protect yourself against insect bites with a good insect repellent and adequate clothing/ mosquito nets. The Center for Disease Control has a website (www.cdc.gov/travel/camerica.htm) with information about local conditions and health-related issues.

HOW TO GET TO MEXICO

BY AIR

Major airlines serving Mexico from the United States and Canada include: Mexicana, tel 800/531-7921; Aeroméxico, tel 800/237-6639; American, tel 800/443-7300; Continental, tel 800/523-3273; and United, tel 800/241-6522.

Mexico City's Benito Juárez Airport is the connecting hub for flights throughout central and southern Mexico. If your destination is an international airport, your luggage need not pass customs in Mexico City. Confirm arriving and departing flights within 72 hours of flying. In Mexico City, use only official yellow airport taxis, which you prepay within the terminal.

BY BOAT

Many companies offer cruises to Mexico. Ports of call include Ensenada, Cabo San Lucas, Mazatlán, Puerto Vallarta, Manzanillo, Zihuatanejo/Ixtapa, and Acapulco on the west coast. Caribbean cruises berth at Progreso, Cozumel, Cancún, and Playa del Carmen.

BY BUS

From the United States, Greyhound Lines (Tel 800/231-2222) can book travel to most of the major cities in Mexico through agreements with Mexican bus lines.

BY CAR

If you drive into Mexico, buy Mexican auto insurance. Policies issued in the United States do not cover liability within Mexico. Some cover damages, but be sure to check. One-stop insurance offices abound near the busiest border crossings and will issue policies by the day, week, or year. Some also help prepare paperwork for a Temporary Car Importation Permit, which is required when driving beyond the border zone (less than 16 miles/25 km into Mexico, Baja California and Baja California Sur exempt). These can be submitted or filled out at the Mexican customs office, at the border. The fee is about $17; use a major credit card and you'll avoid paying a cash bond (tedious, time-consuming, and costing up to $800) based on the value of the car. If you do not return the vehicle prior to the specified date (up to 180 days) you will suffer large, variable fines and possible impounding of the vehicle. The permit allows multiple reentries during the specified time period. Keep several copies of your permit in different places, as leaving the country without it is problematic.

Also required is proof of ownership of the vehicle, the original vehicle registration or lease contract, proof of Mexican insurance, and a valid driver's license (from your country of origin). You can do the paperwork before reaching the border at a Mexican Consul office.

TRAVELING AROUND MEXICO

BY AIR

Mexicana de Aviación and its subsidiary, Aerocaribe (in the U.S., tel 800/531-7921; toll-free in Mexico, tel 01-800/502-2000; www.aerocaribe.com), Aeroméxico and Aeromar (in the U.S., tel 800/237-6639; toll-free in Mexico, tel 01-800/021-4010), and Aviacsa (Tel 01-800/006-2200, www.aviacsa.com)

are the primary Mexican airlines. Smaller airlines such as Aero California (in the U.S., tel 800-237-6225; in Mexico, tel 01800/685-5500) fly to some three dozen destinations throughout Mexico.

BY BUS

Buses are ubiquitous in Mexico; where there is a road, you'll find a bus to rumble down it. For longer trips, always book first class (primera) or deluxe. These buses have air-conditioning and bathrooms and often show a video en route.

The larger towns have modern bus stations, known as the central camionera or central de autobuses, where tickets can usually be purchased in advance. Only second-class buses may be available to rural areas or tiny hamlets. Some are air conditioned, although rarely efficiently, and they stop whenever a passenger wants to board or descend, lengthening travel time.

It's a good idea to bring snacks, bottled water, and toilet paper. Some long-distance buses stop at restaurants. Check with the tourist information office to make sure the route is safe before booking overnight trips; some routes are discouraged by the U.S. State Department and other foreign government agencies. Robberies, while not exactly frequent, do occur on the most touristed routes, where robbers can be assured of dozens of cameras and other expensive gear. Intercity buses are cheap and frequent, but unpleasantly crowded during rush hours.

BY CAR

Roads vary greatly in Mexico, with the expensive cuota, or toll road, being the best maintained (and safest). The libre, or free roads, are usually fine, although in rainy climates potholes can be a problem. Use extra caution when driving in the countryside, as farm animals may wander onto the road. Don't drive at night, and ask about the condition of roads and the possibility of robberies in each region before you set out. In general, observe speed limits and parking regulations, and watch for speed bumps as you enter and leave towns.

Remember that posted speed limits and distances are in kilometers. The usual speed limit on highways is 100 kph (60 mph); within towns it is 30–40 kph (19–25 mph). Many road signs use symbols, not words, but a few important translations are as follows: *Circulación*, with an arrow, means one-way traffic (very common in towns); *No rebasar* or *No rebase* means no passing; and *Ceda el paso* means yield right of way. On highways, Mexican drivers often use their left-turn signals to indicate that the car behind is free to pass.

BREAKDOWNS

The government-sponsored Angeles Verdes patrol vans have aided stranded travelers since the 1960s. True to their name, the Green Angels (Tel 01-987-8224; 078 from a cell phone— about 70 percent national coverage; from the U.S. or Canada, tel 888/401-3880) are real roadside angels in an emergency, and will change flat tires, provide basic parts and towing services, and suggest competent nearby mechanics. You must pay for parts, gasoline, or other expenses, but service is free (tip them as appropriate).

All gas stations are franchises of the government-owned oil company, PEMEX, and sell three types of fuel: Nova (leaded), Magna Sin (unleaded), and Premium (super unleaded). As a rule of thumb, fill your tank when it's half full or as often as possible when traveling to a remote area. Many stations

are not open at night. It's customary to tip the attendant a few pesos (also to make sure he resets the counter to zero before fueling).

RENTAL CARS

Rental cars are expensive in Mexico, and drop-off rates are high. You'll find substantial savings by booking before your trip and shopping around. Smaller, locally owned companies are sometimes cheaper than international companies such as Hertz, National, and Budget, but their cars may be not be well maintained. Rental companies require you to leave a signed credit-card voucher as a guarantee. Ask whether IVA (value-added tax) is included in the quoted price, what insurance is provided, and what the deductible is. Some credit card companies provide coverage at no extra cost.

For day trips, consider hiring a taxi instead of renting a car. Ask the hotel manager or tourist office for a recommendation, or negotiate with a cabby you find helpful and friendly. The price will be about the same (less if you are a good bargainer) as renting a car, and you won't have to worry about driving in unfamiliar areas or parking. Often you'll also get an informal Spanish lesson or an English-speaking "tour guide" who is happy to tell you all about his native city.

BY FERRY

Auto and passenger ferries connect Baja California Sur and mainland Mexico. Travelers intending to ferry their vehicles from Baja to Sonora or Sinaloa must obtain a Temporary Car Importation Permit (see "How to get to Mexico by car," p. 349), at the international border. The Santa Rosalía ferry serves Guaymas, Sonora (Tel 622/222-0204), twice weekly. The cost for the ten-hour crossing runs about $50 (depending on accommodations) for

passengers; about $225 for vehicles (substantially more for trailers and motorhomes). Several ferries per week connect La Paz (ferry landing at Pichilingue, 10 miles/16 km to the north; ticket office in La Paz at 5 de Mayo 502, tel 612/123-0208) to Topolobampo, Sinaloa (Tel 668/862-1003). Prices for the daily, five-hour La Paz–Mazatlán ferry are about half as much again as for Topolobampo or Guaymas. Reservations are essential, especially during holidays; make them well in advance and reconfirm ten days to two weeks before departure.

On the Caribbean coast, passenger ferries (Tel 987/872-1508) and hydrofoils (Tel 987/872-0588) connect Playa del Carmen to Cozumel, just offshore, on the hour; vehicular ferries depart from nearby Puerto Morelos (Tel 987/872-0950). Passenger ferries are more frequent, inexpensive, comfortable, and hassle-free than the car ferry; you can rent a car, moped, or electric golf cart in Cozumel. Daily passenger ferries connect Puerto Juárez, just north of Cancún, to Isla Mujeres.

BY TRAIN

Other than the exceptional train ride through the Copper Canyon on the Chihuahua al Pacífico Railway (see pp. 88–94) and the Expreso Maya (Tel 999/944-9393, www.expresomaya.com) through the Yucatán Peninsula, train travel is not available.

TRAVELING IN MEXICO CITY

BY CAR

Even if you have driven your own car to Mexico, park it when you get to Mexico City and take radio cabs or the metro; the quagmire of this city's streets is best left to the locals. If you must drive, be aware that a city ordinance to reduce smog dictates which days of the week cars may circulate; this is based on the last number of the car's license plate. Foreigners as well as locals are subject to substantial fines for infractions. For information, check at a gas station, in the newspaper, or with hotel personnel.

BY BUS

Mexico City is well served by a comprehensive yet inexpensive bus service. Routes may or may not be posted at bus stops and may be available at tourist offices. One of the routes most used by tourists connects Chapultepec Park to the Zócalo via Paseo de la Reforma, Avenida Juárez, and Calle Madero. If possible avoid traveling during rush hours, as buses at that time are packed to bursting and traffic can be maddeningly slow. If you must ride on a crowded bus, follow the safety advice given in the Metro section below.

For destinations outside Mexico City, there are four major terminals. Check with the concierge or tourist office before making a long trip to the wrong bus station. Generally, Terminal Central del Norte (Tel 55/5689-9745) serves points north; TAPO (Tel 55/5762-5977), points to the east; Terminal Sur, also known as Tasqueña (Tel 55/5762-5414), points to the south; and Terminal Central Poniente (Tel 55/5271-4519), points to the west.

BY METRO

The subway system in Mexico City is extensive and inexpensive. Beyond the city center, *el tren ligero* is a sometimes aboveground line reaching into suburbs such as Xochimilco. Metro maps are available at most stations and at tourist offices. Most lines operate from 5 or 6 a.m.

to midnight. Weekday rush hours are 6–10 a.m. and 5–8 p.m.; during these hours separate cars are available for women and children to prevent them being squashed against men. While subways can be extremely crowded, negotiating the system can save you from traffic jams on the congested city streets above. Beware of pickpockets and mashers. Hold purses, cameras, and backpacks tightly, and carry currency in a money belt or hidden front pocket.

BY TAXI

Mexico City taxis have received a lot of bad press in the last couple of years, and with good reason. Robbing passengers at gunpoint was the *crime du jour* in around the turn of the century. Using radio cabs instead of roving cabs reduces risk (Tel 55/5271-9146, 55/5271-9058, or 55/5272-6125, or ask your concierge for a recommendation). It's reasonably safe to grab a street cab following these precautions. The cab should be white plus only one color (usually orange or green); license plate number must be painted on the back and side of the car (and be an official taxi plate with colored stripe). Street cabs are usually a fraction of the cost of a radio cab. Both of these types negociate their fee; taxis de sitio are metered.

Taxis are often unmetered and it's best to establish a fare ahead of time. Tipping the driver is not customary. Outside Mexico City, few cab-related robberies have been reported.

BY TRAM

In Coyoacán a narrated tram ride takes tourists on a 50-minute tour (*Tel 55/5559-2433, Mon.–Fri. 10–5; weekends, 11–6, $$*) of the neighborhood's main sights. (English by prior arrangement only.)

PRACTICAL ADVICE

COMMUNICATIONS

MAIL
Although your mail will eventually get to its intended destination, service from Mexico takes from three days to a month to reach the United States. Courier service is available in most cities, but don't count on overnight service; be sure to ask how long the delivery will take. MexiPost is the government-run competition for private couriers such as DHL and FedEx. Some rural Mexicans still rely on the telegraph service, found at (or next door to) post offices, which are generally open Mon.–Fri. 9–6 (although some close at 3), Sat. 9–noon.

TELEPHONE, FAX, E-MAIL, & ADDRESSES
To call or fax Mexico from the United States or Canada, dial 011-52 and then the area code followed by the number. For long-distance calls within Mexico, dial 01, area code, and number. For toll-free calls within Mexico, dial 01-800 and the number.

All towns and cities have seven-digit phone numbers with three-digit LADA (area code), with the exception of Guadalajara, Monterrey, and Mexico City, which have eight-digit numbers and two-digit area codes. This phone system was totally revamped early 2000, and lots of locals and even some printed material still refer to five- or six-digit numbers of old.

Making international calls from Mexico can be expensive. Some public phones are owned by private companies that charge exorbitant rates; if in doubt, dial 0 and ask the operator for international rates before placing a call. (If he or she refuses to tell you, by all means hang up and use a standard public phone.) Most hotels add a high service

PRACTICAL ADVICE

charge for international calls, and not all have direct-dial phones or Internet modems. Many pharmacies and newsstands sell prepaid LADATEL phonecards (20, 50, or 100 pesos) for use with public phones; there are few remaining coin-operated phones. LADATEL phonecards work for calls outside Mexico (make sure to use the 100-peso card). For international calls, dial 00 plus the country code (1 for Canada and the United States; 44 for the United Kingdom).

Most towns have at least one private fax service, which may charge by the minute or by the page. Cities small and large have cybercafés where you can connect to the Internet. Some offices do not have fiberoptic lines, and connections can be slow; try to visit during off-peak hours for a faster connection. Internet cafés generally charge a reasonable $2–4 per hour.

While most street addresses in Mexico have both street name and number, some properties in small towns—or on large boulevards—are labeled simply by street name and "s/n": shorthand for *sin número*, meaning "without number." Whenever possible, a cross street or other reference is added. Properties along highways (*carreteras*) are often addressed simply by their distance in kilometers along the highway in question—for example, "Carr. Transpeninsular Km 19.5." In the case of streets, with the exception of those that are numbered, the designation "Calle" rarely appears in front of the name on maps or in written addresses.

FURTHER READING
Websites & links
The Mexican government tourism website is www.mexico-travel.com. www.mexicodesconocido.com is an excellent information website.

Mexico Online has travel information and breaking news stories: www.mexonline.com. Ecotourism, environmental news, and excellent links concerning the Americas can be found at www.planeta.com.

Reading list
Distant Neighbors, Alan Riding. Knopf publishing Group, New York, 1989.
The Hungry Traveler, Marita Adair. Andrews McMeel Publishing, Kansas City, MO, 1997.
The Labyrinth of Solitude: Life and Thought in Mexico, Octavio Paz. Atlantic Press, Inc., New York, 1982.
The Mexicans: A Personal Portrait of a People, Patrick Oster. HarperCollins, Publishers, New York, 2002.
Mexico: From the Olmecs to the Aztecs, Michael D. Coe. Thames & Hudson Ltd., London, 1994.
The People's Guide to Mexico, Carl Franz and Lorena Havens. John Muir Publications, Santa Fe, NM, 1995.
The Reader's Companion to Mexico, Ed. Alan Ryan. Harcourt Brace & Company, Orlando, FL, 1995.
Travelers' Tales Mexico, Ed. James O'Reilly and Larry Habegger. Travelers' Tales, Inc., San Francisco, 1994.
True History of the Conquest of New Spain, Bernal Díaz. Downtown Book Center, 1995.
Viva Mexico!, Antonio Haas. Librería Británica, 1999.

CONVERSIONS

In general, the metric system is used. Temperatures are in centigrade, distances in kilometers, and so on.

ELECTRICITY

Mexico's electrical system operates on 110 volts AC, with outlets taking two-flat-pin rectangular plugs. Bring adapters for any appliances with three-prong plugs, and a power-surge protector for laptop computers. If a power outage or brownout occurs while you are using your computer, shut it down immediately.

ETIQUETTE & LOCAL CUSTOMS

Mexicans are very polite and very friendly, but not overly casual with strangers. Use the formal address *usted* instead of the informal *tú* when addressing people you don't know, especially in the smaller towns, away from tourist enclaves, and with elders.

When asking directions, be aware that many Mexicans find it embarrassing or impolite to decline to help, even when unsure of the address you are seeking. As they may inadvertently send you in the wrong direction to save face, ask directions often and request landmarks. Also, they rarely give specific street names, although with prompting these may be provided.

It is considered disrespectful to enter churches in skimpy clothing, and to sightsee during church services.

LANGUAGE STUDY

Spanish-language courses are offered by private institutes and those attached to universities throughout Mexico. Some are intensive courses focusing on grammar; others offer cultural classes (for example regional cooking, handcrafts, or archaeology) or *intercambios*, casual one-on-one conversations with a compatible Mexican who wants to practice his or her English and help you with Spanish. Programs generally run from two to four weeks (or more), and students can stay with families or arrange to rent apartments or hotel rooms. Some families rent out rooms to several English-speaking students at a time. Those committed to immersing themselves in the Spanish language should ask for a family that hosts only one student at a time. You can get information, listings, and links to language schools throughout Mexico on www.worldwide.edu.

LIQUOR LAWS

The legal drinking age is 18 years, although identification is rarely checked. The sale of alcohol is prohibited on election days.

MEDIA

NEWSPAPERS & MAGAZINES

Most Mexican reporters rely on stipends from the people or government offices they cover, making impartiality impossible. The newspaper most openly critical of the government is *Reforma;* that and the left-leaning *La Jornada* are the largest circulating nationals. For those who do not read Spanish, larger cities carry the English-language daily *The Herald,* while towns with many English-speaking residents publish their own small weekly or monthly papers. In hotels, airports, and newsstands in larger cities, foreign periodicals such as *Time, Newsweek,* and *U.S. News and World Report* are sold. The Sanborns chain of restaurant/bookstores is a great source of magazines, books, and periodicals about Mexican culture.

TELEVISION & RADIO

Many more Mexicans get their information from radio and television than from newspapers. In addition to two government-run television channels, there are a half-dozen private networks. The largest (and most influential), Televisa, has a line-up of Mexico's universally popular evening soap operas. Cable television is available throughout most of the country; hotels geared to foreign tourists usually have satellite or cable TV.

MONEY MATTERS

The Mexican monetary unit is the peso. Bills come in

denominations of 20, 50, 100, 200, and 500 pesos. Always keep a supply of coins and smaller-denomination bills, especially in non-touristy areas, as change can be hard to come by. U.S. dollars are accepted in border cities and at major resorts, although you almost always get a better deal using pesos. Always keep a supply of small bills for tipping.

Canadians and other foreign travelers will avoid headaches by bringing traveler's checks and cash in U.S. dollars. You can change money at a bank, but a *casa de cambio,* dedicated exclusively to this activity, is usually faster, has longer, more convenient hours, and offers the same or only slightly lower rate. Check exchange rates online at www.oanda.com.

Automatic Teller Machines (ATMs, or *cajeros automáticos*) can be found throughout Mexico, but make sure you have a backup of cash or traveler's checks so you won't be stranded if an ATM is broken or out of money. With ATMs you get an excellent exchange rate, but service charges are $2–12, depending on individual bank policies. Avoid using ATMs at night or in isolated locations. Credit cards also give a good exchange rate. MasterCard, Visa, and, to a lesser extent, American Express are the most commonly accepted, although mainly at tourist-oriented hotels and restaurants.

The value-added tax, called IVA, is ignored by some stores, restaurants, and even hotels; most will add IVA if you ask for a receipt.

NATIONAL HOLIDAYS

Banks, state offices, and many other businesses close on the following holidays. Check ahead before arriving at museums or other tourist destinations. (See also "Festivals & Fiestas",

pp. 16–17, and "Entertainment & Activities," pp. 386–89.)
Jan. 1 New Year's Day (Año Nuevo)
Feb. 5 Constitution Day (Proclamación de la Constitución)
March 21 Benito Juárez Day (Natalicio de Benito Juárez)
May 1 Labor Day (Día del Trabajo)
Sept. 16 Independence Day (Día de la Independencia)
Nov. 20 Revolution Day (Aniversario de la Revolución Mexicana)
Dec. 25 Christmas Day (Navidad)

OPENING TIMES

It is difficult to generalize about opening hours in Mexico, as they vary from region to region. In industrialized areas, government and business offices usually adhere to a 9–5 schedule (but some close at 3 p.m.). In hot climates, however, they may close for two to four hours in the middle of the day, reopening from 4 or 5 until 8 (others do not reopen in the afternoon). Although open until 3 or 5 p.m., banks often exchange money only in the morning. Theaters and museums normally close on Mondays. Standard store hours are 9 until 7 or 8, with a possible siesta break in between. Remember, especially in tropical climates, to assume there will be a siesta break between approximately 2 and 4 or 5 p.m. This even applies to churches.

PHOTOGRAPHY

Black-and-white and slide films are hard to come by, so bring your own. When purchasing film, check the expiration date. Processing is inconsistent, so it's best to take your exposed film home to develop. A lead bag will protect your film from airport X-ray machines. Think twice about photographing people in regional costume; either be very discreet or ask permission. Digital photography is widely used in the larger destinations, where you can usually download photos from your digital camera to a CD if needed.

PLACES OF WORSHIP

About 90 percent of Mexicans are Catholics; in the most historic cities and towns it seems there is a church on every corner. Remember that while these churches may seem like fabulous museums, they remain places of worship. Short shorts and skimpy tops are frowned upon (or forbidden), and men should remove their hats. Avoid sightseeing during Mass.

Tourist offices and hotels can provide a list of the most interesting churches in town, some of which offer mariachi or guitar mass or English-language services. Most cities and towns also have at least one Protestant (often Evangelical) church.

SAFETY

Common sense is your most valuable weapon against crime while traveling in Mexico. Be cautious, but not paranoid. Street crime was uncommon until 1994, when the peso devaluation resulted in increased poverty and hence crime. Leave expensive jewelry at home, and don't flash wads of money or fancy cameras. Most hotels have room safes or a safe in the lobby—use them. Hold onto handbags and daypacks tightly; beware of criminals who might cut the pack open with a razor.

Mexico City unfortunately requires extra caution. Use hotel taxis. When out for a day of sightseeing and in need of a cab, ask the restaurant or shop to call a taxi for you, carry the number of a reliable radio-dispatch company, or as a last option, search for a taxi stand (sitio de taxis). (See also "Traveling in Mexico City by Taxi," p. 351.) For current safety information, contact the U.S. State

Department's website at www.travel.state.gov/mexico.html.

The police in Mexico are underpaid, and graft and corruption are commonplace throughout both government and commercial bureaucracies. Although efforts are being made to eliminate la mordida ("the bite"), this form of small-time bribery continues (see "How to get to Mexico by Car," p. 349).

If you are a victim of a minor crime, consider that the criminal justice system is woefully ineffective, and decide according to your loss (and the hassle involved) the benefit of reporting it to the police. It's worth asking at the tourist office if there's an office to resolve travelers' difficulties such as theft or unsatisfactory service. By all means, if you are the victim of a serious or violent crime, report it to your embassy or nearest consular office at once.

TIME DIFFERENCES

Most of Mexico is on Central Standard Time (CST), one hour less than Eastern Standard Time (EST). Baja California Sur, Sonora, Sinaloa, and Nayarit are on Mountain Standard Time (EST minus two hours); Baja California (Norte) is the only state on Pacific Standard Time (EST minus three hours). Daylight saving time was adopted in 1996.

TIPPING

Most Mexicans tip little if anything in the more humble places, but it's nice to leave ten percent anyway. Fifteen percent is customary for good service in tourist-oriented restaurants; always make sure the service is not included on the bill. Cab drivers are not tipped unless they wait while you shop or sightsee, which obviously requires additional payment. Hotel maids are usually given $1 per day, bellboys $1

per bag. Group tour guides should receive at least $1 per person per half-day; private guides may be tipped 5–10 percent of the tour's price. Gas station and washroom attendants should be given a small gratuity as well.

TOILETS

There is much variation in the toilets you will find in Mexico—some good, some very bad, and many without toilet seats or toilet paper. Try to use the rest room at your hotel or in restaurants, cafés, and bars when you stop for refreshments.

Except in tourist-oriented hotels and restaurants, don't throw toilet paper in the toilet, but in the basket provided. As unappealing as this seems to some, it can avoid serious plumbing problems for the proprietor and a nasty overflow for you.

TRAVELERS WITH DISABILITIES

Mexico has few accommodations for travelers with disabilities, including ramps and wide doorways, although some progress is being made. The newer hotels are usually the best bet, but advance planning is advised. The Society for the Advancement of Travel for the Handicapped (SATH), 347 Fifth Ave., Suite 610, New York, NY 10016; tel 212/447-7284, has a website at www.sath.org with general information and links to other sites.

VISITOR INFORMATION & USEFUL PHONE NUMBERS/WEBSITES

English-speaking operators working for the Ministry of Tourism can provide information about weather, holidays, safety, entry requirements, and other aspects of visiting Mexico, and can recommend hotels and restaurants. From the United States or Canada, dial 800/446-3942. Within Mexico, for general information, legal aid, or other assistance dial 01-800/90392, or in Mexico City, 55/5250-0151 or 55/5250-0123. Website: www .mexico-travel.com.

The U.S. Embassy in Mexico offers assistance to crime victims; dial 55/5080-2000 (24 hours a day). Visitors of other nationalities should call their embassies in the event of an emergency (see below).

Consumer Protection in Mexico City, tel 55/5568-8722.

Mexican Red Cross, tel 065.

The following numbers work throughout Mexico, although not in all towns. For telephone information, call 040; for the police, 060.

EMERGENCIES

EMBASSIES & CONSULATES

The foreign embassies are all based in Mexico City; although many other cities in Mexico have consular offices.

UNITED STATES EMBASSY
Paseo de la Reforma 305, Colonia Cuauhtémoc, 06500, México, D.F., tel 55/5080-2000, www.usembassy-mexico.gov.

CANADIAN EMBASSY
Schiller 529, Polanco 11580, México, D.F., tel 55/5724-7900, www.canada.org.mx.

BRITISH EMBASSY
Río Lerma 71, Col. Cuauhtémoc, 06500 México, D.F., tel 55/5242-8500.
www.britishembassy.gov.uk

HEALTH

The most prevalent health problem experienced by travelers in Mexico is intestinal. Gastrointestinal upset may be caused simply by eating food with a different composition from what you are used to. More serious problems result from drinking unclean water or eating improperly prepared fruit or vegetables. The most common disorder is diarrhea (often called *turista,* or Moctezuma's revenge). Although caution is certainly advised, to stop eating at humble establishments makes for a limiting cultural experience, and fancy resorts are in any case not immune to contagion.

As a general rule, drink bottled beverages, including water, and only ice made from purified water. Eat peeled fruit and vegetables, and avoid raw fish or shellfish. If you do contract turista, drink plenty of clean water and rest for a couple days until the symptoms subside. Beware of over-medicating on antidiarrhea remedies. In worst case scenarios, unclean water can lead to salmonella, hepatitis, typhoid, or other serious diseases. If you have a fever or continued severe diarrhea or headaches, seek the advice of a physician.

Air pollution in Mexico City and Guadalajara is severe (especially December–May) and can cause health problems for small children, the elderly, or those with respiratory problems. High altitude can exacerbate the problem (Mexico City sits at 7,400 feet/2,250 m above sea level and is ringed by mountains that trap the smog). To acclimatize, avoid strenuous

activity, alcohol, and high-fat foods for one or two days.

Local pharmacies dispense advice as well as over-the-counter remedies (and sometimes prescription meds without a prescription); many can direct you to a doctor. The management at your hotel is also a good source for finding a health-care provider. Get information about the vaccines and health risks at the Centers for Disease Control and Prevention's Travelers' Health website: www.cdc.gov/travel.

WHAT TO DO IN A CAR ACCIDENT

Unfortunately, Mexican law prescribes that all parties involved in a vehicular accident resulting in physical harm or material damages be jailed until guilt can be established. For this reason, Mexicans involved in accidents often flee the scene. Obtaining Mexican auto insurance is essential, as it limits liability and, most importantly, it can keep you out of jail (see also "How to get to Mexico by Car," p. 349). Insurers commonly offer day, six-month, and one-year policies for either liability (including medical liability and coverage for passengers, legal aid, bail bond, and towing) or full coverage (above-mentioned services plus theft and collision/property damage).

Baja for Less Mexican insurance (in the U.S., tel 800/258-8600, or try the website www .mexicaninsurance.com) has a convenient program allowing those who drive into Mexico frequently to keep an open insurance account that can be reactivated just prior to a trip by phone or Internet.

HOTELS & RESTAURANTS

While Mexico has some lovely small hotels and plenty of large resorts and business hotels, it doesn't have as many different types of accommodations as some countries. But the major resort destinations and business-oriented cities are represented by world-wide hotel chains, as well as a few Mexican-owned chains. Independently owned hotels run the range of prices, from downright cheap to absolutely upscale. In between are plenty of charming small hotels with prices much more economical than those in the United States, Canada, and Western Europe. The cities most popular with travelers have the greatest range of options.

Restaurants run the gamut from chains such as Sanborns—where kids and other creatures of habit will be comfortable in the plush upholstered booths, with familiar-looking menus—to market stalls and the elegant eateries in exclusive hotels.

PRICES

HOTELS
An indication of the cost of a double room in high season, excluding tax, is given by $ signs.

$$$$$	Over $300
$$$$	$200– $299
$$$	$120–$199
$$	$60–$119
$	Under $60

RESTAURANTS
An indication of the cost of a three-course lunch or dinner without drinks, tax, or tip is given by $ signs.

$$$$$	Over $45
$$$$	$30–$45
$$$	$20–$30
$$	$10–$20
$	Under $10

ACCOMMODATIONS

Hostels are rare in Mexico, but don't despair: inexpensive lodgings are plentiful. Rural areas not usually frequented by tourists may have no formal lodgings; if in doubt ask at the city hall (municipio). In states such as Oaxaca and Chiapas, the government has organized communities in areas of great natural beauty or cultural attractions to provide inexpensive lodgings. Financed by the government, these community-run lodgings are an excellent way to visit otherwise inaccessible parts of the country. Information can be obtained at state or municipal tourist offices, which may also make the reservations via shortwave radio or cell phone.

Campgrounds such as those found in the United States and Canada are few, although RV parks are more plentiful, especially in the Baja Peninsula and the northern Pacific coast, where snowbirds flock. Camping is usually permitted on public property such as beaches; ask permission to camp on ejido (communally owned) lands or private property. B&Bs and guesthouses are also unusual; most are owned and run by foreigners. But connoisseurs of small, intimate hotels will not be disappointed. Cities such as San Cristóbal de las Casas, Oaxaca, and San Miguel de Allende have some one-of-a-kind small hotels. And although many rent for hundreds of

dollars a night, others—equally charming but with fewer amenities—can be had for less than $80.

Resort hotels charge resort prices: You'll pay as much for a Sheraton or Westin hotel in Mexico as in First World countries. Also, prices are usually quoted in dollars, so you'll see no savings as the peso fluctuates. Although you'll pay more at these internationally geared, often high-rise, hotels, you'll almost always get English-speaking staff, concierge service, swimming pools, smoothly running elevators, in-room safes and minibars, cable or satellite TV, and so on. Most beach resorts have at least a few all-inclusive hotels.

Hotels in business-oriented cities such as Mexico City, Guadalajara, Aguascalientes, and Monterrey may offer secretarial services, business centers, meeting rooms, computer modems, and direct-dial phones. The latter two are not as common as you might think, so if these features are important to you, ask before reserving a room. Many business-oriented hotels offer discounts on weekends (sometimes 50 percent or more) or incentives such as buffet breakfasts. Be sure to inquire about different packages, promotions, and discounts.

Rooms should be reserved well in advance at certain times. Beach resorts such as Cabo San Lucas and Cancún fill up during spring break and holidays

(Easter, July and August, and the Christmas season), while hotels in towns with popular celebrations might be booked a year in advance: for example, Taxco's Easter week, Veracruz during Carnaval, or the Christmas season in Oaxaca.

Taxes vary by state. Most charge 15 percent tax, which may be augmented by a 2 percent hotel tax. Others have a 12 percent tax. Many of the more humble establishments either don't charge tax or have included it in the price; make sure you ask in order to compare prices accurately. Unless otherwise stated, the hotels listed have private bathrooms and are open year round. Toll-free numbers listed are for making reservations from the United States and Canada. In very small towns, "domicilio conocido" means "known address," and indicates there are no street names but anyone can point out the establishment.

CREDIT CARDS
AE American Express, DC Diners Club, MC Mastercard, V Visa.

RESTAURANTS

The midday meal is generally eaten between 2 and 5 p.m., although tourists, some office workers, and farmers eat before then. The set meal (called *"el menu del día"* in nicer restaurants and *"comida corrida"* in more humble eateries) is usually a bargain, but often unavailable before 1:30 or 2 p.m. This generally consists of soup, a rice or pasta plate, and an entrée, followed by dessert and coffee or tea. A beverage may also be included; *agua de sabor* is commonly served. These fruit juice and water drinks range from lemonade to watermelon water.

Antojitos roughly translates as appetizers, but they can be filling regional specialties such as *memelas,* tacos, or enchiladas (see p. 18). Dinner is traditionally a very light meal, and although restaurants in tourist areas provide full fare, it's generally much more expensive than a lavish midday meal. In smaller or less touristy towns, and even some of the larger but less cosmopolitan cities, restaurants may close by 7 or 8 p.m. (Note: restaurants listed as "lunch only" are generally open between 1 and 6 p.m.)

While hotel dining rooms and cafés tend to stay open from morning to late at night, some eateries open for lunch and dinner only. They may close between 5 and 6 or 7 p.m., when the dinner hour begins, and some cafés don't open before 9 or 10 a.m. If you want an early breakfast, check opening hours the day before, or stick with hotel restaurants. Check your bill before tipping, as service may be included. Closings for holidays may vary, so it is advisable to phone and reserve a table.
L = lunch
D = dinner

In the following selection, towns are arranged alphabetically under each region heading. Hotels are listed under each location by price, then in alphabetical order, followed by restaurants also by price and alphabetical order.

BAJA CALIFORNIA

BAHÍA DE LOS ANGELES

🏨 LOS VIENTOS SPA & RESORT
$$
CARR. 1, POBLADO LA VENTANA
TEL 664/638-3279
www.losvientosspaandresort.com
You can drive or charter a ten-seater plane to stay at this pretty new beachfront hotel and spa just outside Bahía.
🛏 15 🅿 🏊 💆 🆎 AE, MC, V

CATAVIÑA

🏨 LA PINTA CATAVIÑA
$$
HWY. 1, KM 173, IN CATAVIÑA
TEL 800/336-5454
www.lapintahotels.com
This wonderful hotel and restaurant in the middle of the desert abuts an oasis of palms; prehistoric cave paintings can be seen nearby. There's a courtyard swimming pool, and the brick-domed restaurant serves delicious seafood and international dishes.
🛏 27 🅿 ❄ 🏊 MC, V

ENSENADA

🏨 LAS ROSAS
$$$
CARR. TIJUANA—ENSENADA KM. 105.5
TEL 646/174-4310
FAX 646/175-9059
www.lasrosas.com
An aqua and pink color scheme pervades this romantic yet family-oriented hotel about 10 minutes north of downtown. The inifinity pool overlooks the rocky cove on which the hotel perches. There's jazz or blues most weekends in the bar, good Mexican and international food in the restaurant, and a full-service spa.
🛏 48 🅿 ❄ ❄ 🏊 💆 AE, MC, V

🏨 EL REY SOL
$$
AV. BLANCARTE 130
TEL 646/178-1641, 888/315-2378
FAX 646/174-0005
www.posadaelreysol.com
Comfortable rooms in the three-story, motel-like hotel face the parking area; there's a small pool in the back. But the real star of this show is the 60-year-old, award-winning French restaurant. The extensive menu offers sea bass with cilantro sauce, delicious duck a l'orange, and nearly a dozen traditional canapes and French pastries.
🛏 52 🅿 ❄ ❄ ❄ 🏊 MC, V

🍴 CASAMAR
$$–$$$
BLVD. LÁZARO CARDENAS 987
TEL 646/174-0417
The regional seafood is fresh here, and the calamari comes with a unique oyster sauce. The staff is friendly, and there's a trio on weekend nights. If the downstairs looks discouragingly empty, look upstairs; although it's the smoking section, this is where the sea view is, and the smoke rarely bothers.
❄ AE, MC, V

LA PAZ

🏨 EL ANGEL AZUL B&B
$$–$$$
INDEPENDENCIA 518 AT GUILLERMO PRIETO LA PAZ, 23000
TEL 612/125-5130
www.elangelazul.com
In the heart of downtown, this historic old building, is now a charming B&B surrounded by greenery. Rooms and public areas are awash in color. No smoking in rooms, but you can in the video bar. Breakfast included.
🛏 11 ❄ ❄ ❄ No credit cards

HOTELS & RESTAURANTS

🏨 **LA CONCHA RESORT**
🍴 **$$**
CARRETERRA A PICHILINGUE
KM 5, 23010
TEL 612/121-6344
FAX 612/121-6229
www.laconcha.com
This resort sits right on the sands of beautiful Pichilingue Beach. Smallish, dark rooms overlook the lovely grounds or the Gulf of California. The beach club has an excellent dive shop and watersports equipment rentals. Wonderful international, Mexican, and seafood dishes are served in the poolside restaurant.
ⓘ 151 🅿 🅂 🅂 🏊
🅂 All major cards

🍴 **LA PAZTA**
$$
ALLENDE 35
TEL 612/125-1195
Wonderful, mainly homemade pasta and other Italian dishes are served in this indoor-outdoor trattoria decorated with delightful paintings.
🕒 Closed Tues. D 🅂MC, V

LORETO

🏨 **VILLAS DE LORETO**
$$
SOUTH OF TOWN AT ANTONIO MIJARES AT PLAZA COLONIA ZARAGOZA, 23880
TEL 613/135-0586
FAX 613/135-0355
www.villasdeloreto.com
Rooms with hot showers, comfy beds, and refrigerators overlook the pool and beach at this out-of-the-way inn. RV and tent camping sites are available; smoking is not permitted. Kayaking, diving, and fishing can be arranged at additional cost.
ⓘ 13 🅿 🅂 🅂 🏊
🅂 MC, V

🍴 **PACHAMAMA**
$–$$
CALLE DAVIS 13
TEL 613/135-1655
Delicious Argentine food

(with international and Mexican dishes too) in an informal but cheerful setting typical of laid-back Loreto.
🕒 Closed L. Closed Tues. Closed Sept. 🅂 No credit cards

LOS CABOS

🏨 **CASA DEL MAR BEACH GOLF & SPA RESORT**
🍴 **$$$$$**
CARRETERRA TRANS-PENINSULAR KM 19.5, 23400
TEL 624/145-7700, 888/227-9621
FAX 624/144-0034
www.casadelmarmexico.com
A romantic beach getaway and spa with lovely grounds, several pools and flower gardens, a dusky-cool library/reading room, and lots of services. Hacienda-style rooms in a pleasing palette of golds, rosy pinks, and Mediterranean blues have furnished porches and Jacuzzi tubs overlooking the sea. The classy restaurant, also overlooking the water, serves excellent regional cuisine.
ⓘ 56 🅿 🅂 🅂 🏊
🅂 AE, MC, V

SOMETHING SPECIAL

🏨 **LAS VENTANAS AL PARAÍSO**
Movie stars and moguls hide out at this exclusive, expensive resort along the Los Cabos Corridor. Fireplaces, telescopes, private terraces, and fabulous custom furnishings make guests want to stay put in their rooms. Excellent restaurants, a three-level pool, and hammocks under the palms draw them out.
$$$$$
CARRETERRA TRANS-PENINSULAR KM 19.5, 23400
TEL 624/144-2800, 888/ROSEWOOD
FAX 624/144-2801
www.lasventanas.com
ⓘ 60 🅿 🅂 🏊 🅈
🅂 AE, MC, V

🏨 **MARQUIS LOS CABOS**
🍴 **$$$$$**
CARR. TRANSPENINSULAR KM. 21.5, CORREDOR AT CABO REAL
TEL 624/144-2000, 877/238-9399 IN THE U.S.
FAX 624/144-2001
www.marquisloscabos.com
Sheltered by rocks, the beach at this hacienda-style hotel is safer than most in Los Cabos for swimming. The Cabo Real golf course is just next door; ask about generous golf and spa packages. All of the luxurious suites have ocean views and many amenities.
ⓘ 237 🅿 🅂 🅂 🅂
🏊 🅈 🅂 MC, V

🏨 **CASA NATALIA**
🍴 **$$$$**
BLVD. MIJARES 4, SAN JOSÉ DEL CABO, 23400
TEL 624/142-5100, 888/277-3814
FAX 624/142-5110
www.casanatalia.com
A friendly Luxumborgean and her chef-husband, of Bordeaux, have created this tiny oasis of international chic. Indoors or on the palm-shaded patio restaurant, Mexican ingredients modernize European recipes. Room price includes beach club shuttle and full breakfast; a 22 percent service charge is added.
ⓘ 16 🅿 🅂 🅂 🏊
🅂 AE, MC, V

🏨 **MELIÁ SAN LUCAS**
$$$$
PLAYA EL MÉDANO S/N, CABO SAN LUCAS
TEL 624/143-4444, 800/336-3542
FAX 624/143-0418
Close to the the bay, beach, marina, and Cabo San Lucas's shops, restaurants, and bars, this popular chain hotel has a large pool area often packed with partying vacationers. And the new Nikki Beach Club is a suave hangout.
ⓘ 150 🅂 🅂 🅂 🏊
🅂 AE, MC, V

LOS MILAGROS
$$
MATAMOROS 16, CABO SAN LUCAS
TEL 624/143-4566
FAX 624/143-6005
www.losmilagros.com.mx
The name says it all: This cozy and economical little gem in downtown San Lucas is a miracle in expensive Los Cabos. The inn combines modern and traditional architecture to good effect.
[i] 16 🌊

MULEGÉ

SERENIDAD
$$$
HWY. 2.5 MILES (4 KM) SOUTH OF MULEGÉ, 23900
TEL 615/153-0530
FAX 615/153-0311
www.hotelserenidad.com
E-MAIL serenidad@mulege.com.mx
During Baja's broiling summer (when the billfish really bite), the lovely pool and gardens here offer a respite from the heat. Simple yet serene (as its name implies), this property has its own airstrip and RV park.
[i] 50 🅿 🕐 Closed Sept.
🚭 🅰 🌊 🏦 MC, V

TECATE

SOMETHING SPECIAL

RANCHO LA PUERTA SPA
Since 1940, the Szekely family (and today, more than 250 employees) has been offering guests an ever increasing array of spa treatments and activities: hot riverstone massage, European facials, yoga, meditation, hiking, and loofah-salt glows, to name a few. Stays at the 3,000-acre (1,210 ha) ranch are Saturday to Saturday; first-floor, hacienda-style bungalows decorated with fine Mexican handcrafts are set among luxurious pools, spas, and gardens. Healthful, delicious, vegetarian-oriented meals and round-trip transportation from

the nearby airport at San Diego, California, are included. Reservations required.
$$$$$
HWY. 2, 3 MILES (5 KM) WEST OF TECATE, 21275
TEL 665/654-9155, 800/443-7565; IN U.S. 760/744-4222
FAX 665/654-1108; IN U.S. 760/744-5007
www.rancholapuerta.com
[i] 87 🚭 🅰 🌊 🏦 MC, V

TIJUANA

CAMINO REAL
$$$$
PASEO DE LOS HÉROES 10305, ZONA RÍO 22320
TEL 664/633-4000
FAX 664/633-4001
www.caminoreal.com/tijuana
This high rise retains its fashionable and rather conservative air. The business-oriented property is near the Tijuana Cultural Center and downtown.
[i] 250 🅿 🕐 🚭 🅰 🌊 🔧 🏦 All major cards

CIEN AÑOS
$$$
AV. JOSÉ MARÍA VELASCO 1407
TEL 664/634-3039
Nouveau Mexican cuisine is elegantly presented in this gracious restaurant near the cultural center. Steaks are a specialty, as is *pollo cien años*—chicken and potatoes in a spicy, smoky chili sauce. For dessert, try the guava cheesecake or flan with burnt goat-milk topping. No shorts.
🅿 🕐 Closed Sun. after 8 p.m. 🚭 🏦 All major cards

TODOS SANTOS

HOTEL CALIFORNIA
$$-$$$
JUÁREZ S/N AT MORELOS
TEL 612/145-0525
FAX 612/145-0288
Although there's no a/c, the garden-draped hotel keeps cool via thick walls and the ocean breezes that bless

Todos Santos; rooms have ceiling and floor fans. The bar is a local watering hole. And no, Don Henley never slept here.
[i] 11 🌊 🏦 MC, V

CAFÉ SANTA FE
$$$
CENTENARIO 4
TEL 612/145-0340
The outdoor garden tables of this Italian café are often filled with diners from Los Cabos and La Paz. It's popular for its organic salad greens, homemade pastas, and imported wines.
🕐 Closed Tues., Sept., Oct. 🏦 MC, V

NORTHWEST MEXICO

ALAMOS

HACIENDA DE LOS SANTOS
$$$$
MOLINA 8, 85763
TEL 647/428-0222, 800/525-4800
FAX 647/428-0367
www.haciendadelossantos.com
This antique-studded property has a billiards room, a theater, and its own 19th-century cantina. Individually decorated rooms have wood-burning fireplaces; beds are crisp with fine linens; and the adjacent spa has a full-time masseur and trainer. Children and smoking in rooms are not allowed.
[i] 25 🅿 🚭 🌊 🏦 Most major cards

CHIHUAHUA

HOLIDAY INN HOTEL & SUITES
$$$
ESCUDERO 702, FRACC. SAN FELIPE, 31000
TEL 614/439-0000
FAX 614/414-3313
www.holiday-inn.com/chihuahuamex
Continental breakfast is included in the price of this pretty, all-suites hotel with full

HOTELS & RESTAURANTS

kitchens, located in a residential neighborhood near the city center. The bright white, two-story hotel has a sauna, whirlpool, business services, and lots of room amenities. Includes breakfast.

🏨 74 🅿 ⊠ 🔲 ☎ 🔲 🔲 All major cards

🍴 LA CASA DE LOS MILAGROS
$$

VICTORIA 812, NEAR OCAMPO
TEL 614/437-0693
Sit indoors or out on the courtyard patio of this restored adobe hacienda. Popular with locals and visitors, it offers light Mexican meals, a festive ambience, and live folk music Thurs.–Sun. after 9 p.m.

🔲 Closed L 🔲 🔲 MC, V

DURANGO

🏨 POSADA SAN JORGE 🍴 $

CONSTITUCIÓN 102 SUR
TEL 618/813-3257, 618/812-7490
FAX 618/811-6040
www.hotelposadasanjorge.com
Right around the corner from the cathedral this stately 160-year-old mansion is still a looker. Above the imposing staircase is a mural by local maestro Guillermo Ceniceros; on the first floor are a happening bar and the **Pampas do Brasil** courtyard restaurant, specializing in steaks.

🏨 20 🅿 ⊠ 🔲 MC, V

EL FUERTE

🏨 EL FUERTE LODGE
$$

MONTESCLAROS 37
TEL 698/893-0226
FAX 698/893-1246
www.hotelelfuerte.com.mx
Antiques lean against thick adobe walls and flowering vines hang down from second floor balconies. The restored hacienda is most charming in its welcoming public spaces.

🏨 30 🔲 MC, V

HIDALGO DEL PARRAL

🏨 HOTEL ACOSTA
$

AGUSTÍN BARBACHANO 3
TEL 627/522-0221
FAX 627/522-0657
E-MAIL hotelacosta_2005@
hotmail.com
Parral has mainly simple hotels; one of the nicer ones is this three-story, family-run establishment overlooking the main plaza. The Acosta has no restaurant, but it offers a great view of the cathedral from its rooftop terrace.

🏨 26 🔲 🔲 No credit cards

MAZATLÁN

🏨 PUEBLO BONITO 🍴 $$$

CAMARON SABALO 2121,
ZONA DORADA, 82110
TEL 669/989-8900
FAX 669/914-1723
www.pueblobonito.com
Flamingos pose on the palm-studded grounds of this low-rise, all-suites beachfront hotel. Rooms have equipped kitchens and furnished outdoor patios. Live music and twinkling candlelight complement Italian and Continental cuisine at **Angelo's Restaurant.**

🏨 246 🅿 🔲 🔲 🔲 2 🔲 🔲 AE, MC, V

🏨 PLAYA MAZATLÁN
$$

AV PLAYAS LAS GAVIOTAS,
82110
TEL 800/762-5816, 669/989-0555
FAX 669/914-0366
Mazatlán's original resort hotel is one of the few to resist the timeshare snare. Nicest of the clean-smelling rooms with tiled floors and private terraces are those overlooking the beach.

🏨 425 🅿 🔲 🔲 🔲 3 🔲 🔲 AE, MC, V

🍴 EL CUCHUPETAS
$$

REFORMA 301 AT JESUS
CARRANZA, VILLA UNIÓN
TEL 669/67-04-60
En route to the airport, Isla de Piedra, and excursions into the interior, El Cuchupetas offers fresh, authentic seafood specialties. The large but simple restaurant has flowered oilcloth table-coverings, cement and tile floors, old-time Mazatlán photos, and bilingual menus. Try a *campechana* (octopus, clam, and shrimp cocktail).

🅿 🔲 No credit cards

🍴 HEATHER'S PLACE
$–$$

CAMARÓN SÁBALO ACROSS
FROM OCEANO PALACE
TEL 669/914-2999
For Canadian comfort food (and Mexican dishes), nothing beats Heather's. Come Sundays for turkey and mashed potatoes, Wednesday night for bingo, or any afternoon for a free appetizer during happy hour; 2–5 p.m. Look for live music on weekend evenings, great shrimp and fish plates always.

🅿 🔲 🔲 MC, V

PRICES

HOTELS
An indication of the cost of a double room in high season, excluding tax, is given by $ signs.

$$$$$	Over $300
$$$$	$200– $299
$$$	$120–$199
$$	$60–$119
$	Under $60

RESTAURANTS
An indication of the cost of a three-course lunch or dinner without drinks, tax, or tip is given by $ signs.

$$$$$	Over $45
$$$$	$30–$45
$$$	$20–$30
$$	$10–$20
$	Under $10

PUERTO PEÑASCO

🏨 VIÑA DEL MAR
$$
CALLE IRO. DE JUNIO AT
MALECÓN KINO S/N, COL. EL
PUERTO 83550
TEL 638/383-3600
FAX 638/383-3714
www.vinadelmarhotel.com
There's a beach view from the
restaurant, large pool, and hot
tub. Rooms are simply but
soothingly decorated; suites
have kitchenette or Jacuzzi.
Besides attentive service, they
have a beauty salon with
massage, two bars, and
conference room.
🛈 110 🅿 🚭 🚭 🏊
🚭 MC, V

SAN CARLOS

🏨 HOTEL MARINA TERRA
$$$
TEL 622/225-2020, 888/688-5353
FAX 622/225-2025
www.marinaterra.com
Pastel-decorated rooms are
desert-plain, but there's an
awesome view of sacred
Tetakawi mountain. The busy
marina is a magnet for
boaters; a few minutes away is
a beach club with sports
equipment and volleyball.
🛈 105 🅿 🚭 🚭 🚭
🏊 2 🎽 🚭 Most major
cards

SIERRA TARAHUMARA (COPPER CANYON)

🏨 POSADA MIRADOR
$$$$$
ESTACIÓN POSADA
BARRANCA
TEL 668/818-7046
(IN LOS MOCHIS), 800/896-8196
FAX 668/818-0046
www.mexicoscoppercanyon.com
This log-cabin lodge has a
gorgeous canyon view, and
arranges horse and walking
tours. Rooms have heating,
fireplaces, and balconies, but
no phone or TV. Meals, served
family-style, are included in
the price.
🛈 48 🚭 AE, MC, V

🏨 MISIÓN
$$$$
II MILES (18 KM) FROM
BAHUICHIVO TRAIN STATION,
CEROCAHUI
TEL 668/818-7046
(IN LOS MOCHIS), 800/896-8196
FAX 668/818-0046
www.mexicoscoppercanyon.com
This isolated lodge, a good
base for exploring the Urique
Canyon, books on the
American Plan. A large
fireplace warms the lobby bar;
simply furnished rooms are
surrounded by small gardens
and a vineyard. Generator elec-
tricity is available at intervals.
🛈 38 🚭 AE, MC, V

🏨 COPPER CANYON SIERRA LODGE
About a 15-minute drive from
Creel, this is both the area's
prettiest hotel and the best deal.
Three delicious meals are inluded
in the surprisingly low price, and
served in the lovely dining room
warmed by a stone fireplace.
Rooms near the pine forests and
waterfall of Cusararé are cozy,
each has a fireplace or potbelly
stove. There's no electricity,
which adds to the charm.
$$
DOMICILIO CONOCIDO,
CUSARARÉ
TEL. 800/776-3942 (IN THE U.S.)
www.sierratrail.com
🛈 22 🅿 🚭 No credit
cards

🏨 RIVERSIDE LODGE
$$
DOMICILIO CONOCIDO,
BATOPILAS
TEL. 800/776-3942 (IN THE U.S.)
www.sierratrail.com
A sister property to the
Sierra Lodge, this early-20th-
century hacienda turned hotel
is a lovely base from which to
explore the canyon.
Transportation or a rental
truck can be arranged from
Creel. Credit cards accepted
for prepayment only (MC, V).

No restaurant, but the town
has half a dozen good
restaurants, about the same
number of greasy spoons.
Minimum two-night stay.
🛈 14 🅿 🚭 No credit
cards

🏨 MARGARITAS PLAZA MEXICANA
$
ELFIDO BAUTISA S/N,
CREEL, 33200
TEL/FAX 635/456-0245
You can pay more elsewhere,
but you won't improve much
on this comfortable, friendly
lodging in the center of town
with café tables in the center.
Breakfast and dinner are
included. Both the restaurant
and lodgings are favored by
young, sporty types.
🛈 25 🅿 🚭 no credit
cards

🏨 REAL DE MINAS
$
DONATO GUERRA AT
PABLO OCHOA, BATOPILAS
TEL 649/456-9045
The former manager of
fabulous Riverside Lodge,
borrowed management and
decorating ideas for his own
tiny and tasteful guest lodge in
one of Batopilas's restored
19th-century mansions.
Unfortunately, with no phone,
it's first come, first served.
🛈 8 🅿 🚭 No credit
cards

MONTERREY

🏨 🍽 RADISSON GRAN ANCIRA PLAZA
$$$$
AV. MELCHOR OCAMPO 443
OESTE, 64000
TEL 81/8150-7000, 800/201-7647
FAX 81/8345-1121
Located in the heart of
downtown's pedestrian area
and near the Macroplaza, this
turn-of-the-20th-century
hotel has been designated a
World Heritage site. The

🚭 Nonsmoking 🚭 Air-conditioning 🏊 Indoor/🏊 Outdoor swimming pool 🎽 Health club 🚭 Credit cards **KEY**

HOTELS & RESTAURANTS

open restaurant sits in the impossibly elegant lobby, with its sweeping marble staircase and cathedral ceiling.
(i) 241 P ⬆ Ⓢ Ⓢ ⬛ 🏺 AE, MC, V

🏨 SHERATON AMBASSADOR
$$$$
HIDALGO 310 ORIENTE AT
E. CARRANZA, 64000
TEL 81/8380-7000
FAX 81/8345 1984
www.sheraton.com
A lobby with lots of dark wood is enhanced by the stained-glass ceiling and elegant furnishings in comfortable groupings. Geared toward business travelers, the modern hotel has secretarial services and in-room modems; ask about deals for executive floors and suites.
(i) 240 ⬆ Ⓢ Ⓢ ⬛ 🏺 All major cards

🍽 LUISIANA
$$$$
AV. HIDALGO 530 ORIENTE
TEL 81/3340-3753
Friendly in a clubby, everyone-knows-you sort of way, this downtown restaurant is elegantly decorated and rather dark. It's popular for its typical northern meats—including charbroiled steak and barbecued goat—and other Mexican dishes.
Ⓢ 🏺 All major cards

PARQUE NACIONAL CUMBRES DE MONTERREY

🏨 HOTEL CHIPINQUE
$$
MESETA CHIPINQUE 1000,
GARZA GARCIA, 66297
TEL 81/8173-1777
www.hotelchipinque.com.mx
Perched above Monterrey in the park for which it is named, this comfortable lodge suits those who like nature, racquet sports, and more. At night there's a view of the twinkling cityscape from the restaurant-bar.

(i) 72 P Ⓢ Ⓢ ⬛ 🏺 AE, MC, V

SALTILLO

🏨 CAMINO REAL SALTILLO
$$$
BLVD. LOS FUNDADORES 2000,
25015
TEL 844/430-0000, 800/722-6466
FAX 844/438-0007
This business hotel is east of historic downtown. Locals love **La Buenavista** restaurant—gleaming with polished wood and a stained-glass skylight—for the fine cuts of beef and regional and international food, as well as Sunday brunch at the adjacent **la Huerta** restaurant.
(i) 140 P Ⓢ Ⓢ ⬛ MC, V

🍽 LA CANASTA
$$
BLVD. V. CARRANZA 2485
TEL 844/415-8840
Tile floors, a low wood-beamed ceiling, roaring fireplaces in each large room, and a mix of antique and modern furnishings make La Canasta a Saltillo tradition for long business lunches. The menu features many *antojitos* (appetizers) and other Mexican dishes.
P Ⓢ Ⓢ 🏺 All major cards

TAMPICO

🏨 CAMINO REAL MOTOR HOTEL
$$
AV. HIDALGO 2000, 89140
TEL 833/213-8811
FAX 833/213-9226
Not part of the Camino Real chain, this pretty, low-rise hotel outside Tampico still delights with its tropical landscaping and amenities such as mini-bars and direct-dial phones. The travel agency on site books area fishing trips.
(i) 103 P Ⓢ ⬛ 🏺 All major cards

ZACATECAS

SOMETHING SPECIAL

🏨 QUINTA REAL 🍽 ZACATECAS
This glamorous, wonderfully odd hotel was built in a converted 19th-century bullring. Nonetheless, rooms are airy and comfortable with balconies and either bathtubs or spas. The bar occupies the former bullpens; the elegant restaurant, serving international and regional cuisine, offers fantastic nighttime views of the 18th-century aqueduct.
$$$$
AV. RAYÓN 434, 98000
TEL 492/922-9104, 800/323-7500
FAX 492/922-8440
(i) 47 P ⬆ Ⓢ Ⓢ AE, MC, V

🏨 MESÓN DE JOBITO
$$$
JARDÍN JUÁREZ, 98000
TEL 492/924-1722
FAX 492/924-3500
www.mesondejobito.com
It's a pleasure to be in both the public areas and private rooms of this 19th-century former plantation house and adjoining buildings, though the public areas retain better their sense of history. Service is friendly, and the location off a quiet plaza near the main plaza is another plus.
(i) 60 P Ⓢ AE, MC, V

🍽 LA CUIJA
$$
CENTRO COMERCIAL EL MERCADO, BOTTOM LEVEL
TEL 492/922-8275
A bit of everything is served in this simulated wine cellar: Regional specialties include *pachole* (ground beef and pork in special sauce), the Zacatecas classic, *asado de boda*, grilled meats, and seafood. Music is played Wednesday to Sunday during late-afternoon lunch (2–5 p.m.) and after 9 p.m.
P Ⓢ AE, MC, V

CENTRAL MEXICO

AGUASCALIENTES

🏨 HOTEL QUINTA REAL
🍴 AGUASCALIENTES
$$$$
AV. AGUASCALIENTES SUR 601,
20270
TEL 449/978-5818, 800/323-7500
FAX 449/978-5616
www.quintareal.com
Everything about this
gorgeous hotel whispers
luxury, style, and tradition.
Antique and modern pieces
mix well in pleasing public
spaces of quarrystone and
gleaming marble. Luxurious
rooms with full amenities
overlook the colonial-style
courtyard, a bar with fireplace,
and a formal dining room
serving regional, national, and
international cuisine.
🛏 85 🅿 🚭 🌊 🐾 AE,
MC, V

GUANAJUATO

🏨 LA CASA DE LOS
ESPÍRITUS ALEGRES
$$$
EX-HACIENDA DE TRINIDAD 1,
MARFIL
TEL/FAX 473/733-1013
www.casaspirit.com
Awash in folk art and antiques,
the 16th-century "House of
the Happy Spirits" B&B, several
miles outside Guanajuato, has
individually (and brightly)
decorated rooms, some with
fireplaces. Generous
breakfasts served on a
covered courtyard included.
🛏 8 🅿 🐾 MC, V

🏨 QUINTA LAS ACACIAS
$$$
PASEO DE LA PRESA 168, 36000
TEL 473/731-1517, 888/497-4129
www.quintalasacacias.com
This centrally located, 19th-
century, European-style B&B
has pretty public spaces,
including a library, bar, terraces
shaded by greenery, and a spa
with city view. Luxurious,
individually decorated rooms

have satellite TV, hairdryers,
and cordless phones.
Complete breakfast is included,
and snacks and small meals are
available throughout the day.
🛏 9 🅿 🚭 AE, MC, V

🏨 POSADA SANTA FE
🍴 $$
JARDÍN UNION 12, 36000
TEL 473/732-0084
FAX 473/732-4653
Somewhat dark corridors and
rooms and heavy furnishings
are offset by modest prices
and an unbeatable location on
the city's liveliest square. The
outdoor café-restaurant is a
prime people-watching spot.
🛏 45 🐾 AE, MC, V

🍴 LA HACIENDA DE
MARFIL
$$
ARCOS DE GUADALUPE 3,
MARFIL
TEL 473/733-1148
A wonderful ambience
pervades this small restaurant,
in a restored Mexican colonial
building about 15 minutes
outside Guanajuato. Sample
delightful French dishes such
as rabbit stew in red wine
with mushrooms, or beef fillet
in tamarind sauce.
🅿 🕐 Open 1:30–6 p.m.
Closed Mon. 🚭 AE,
MC, V

🍴 TRUCO 7
$
TRUCO 7
TEL 473/732-8374
Friendly and down-to-earth
describes El Truco, which
hums with conversation. The
steaks, sandwiches, enchiladas,
and other typical Mexican
fare are reasonably good and
the colorful posters, paintings,
and other bric-a-brac make
for a lively atmosphere.
🐾 No credit cards

QUERÉTARO

🏨 LA CASA DE LA
🍴 MARQUESA
$$$$
MADERO 41, 76000

TEL 442/212-0092
FAX 442/212-0098
www.lacasadelamarquesa.com
Tasteful and classy but not
snooty, this hotel in historic
downtown is housed in a
restored 1756 mansion. Suites
are furnished in exquisite
antiques, handpainted tiles,
and plush rugs. The formal
restaurant is offputting to
some, but the nouveau
Mexican and upscale
international dishes lure
others to the elegant tables.
🛏 25 🚭 AE, MC, V

🏨 HOLIDAY INN
QUERÉTARO
$$$
AV. 5 DE FEBRERO 110, 76010
TEL 442/192-0202, 800/465-4329
FAX 442/192-8902
www.holidayinn.com.mx
On Highway 57 near both
downtown and the industrial
zone, this ample three-story
property has modern motel-
like rooms with climate
control, satellite TV, hairdryers,
and other amenities. The large
rectangular pool is great for
swimming laps.
🛏 218 🅿 🍴 🚭 🌊
🐾 AE, MC, V

🏨 MESÓN DE SANTA
🍴 ROSA
$$–$$$
PASTEUR SUR 17, 76000
TEL 442/224-2523
FAX 442/212-5522
www.mesonsantarosa.com
Colonial-style furnishings
reproduce those of the
original, 18th-century inn. The
central location and moderate
price lure repeat customers.
One of the three interior
patios serves as an al fresco
restaurant, dishing up Mexican
favorites with a modern flair,
such as roast kid in pepper
and pulque sauce.
🛏 21 🌊 AE, MC, V

🍴 EL ARCÁNGEL
$$
GUERRERO NORTE 1
TEL 442/212-6542
This warm mansion-turned-

HOTELS & RESTAURANTS

restaurant has lace curtains and small square café tables inside or under a covered patio. Order traditional favorites like squash blossom soup, chicken tacos, or chilies stuffed with cheese and *cuitla-coche*, a corn-fungus delicacy.
🚫 MC, V

SAN LUIS POTOSÍ

🏨 WESTIN SAN LUIS POTOSÍ
$$–$$$
REAL DE LOMAS 1000, 78216
TEL 444/825-0125, 800/937-8461
FAX 444/825-0200
www.westin.com
Located in a residential neighborhood near the historic center, this low rise resembles a palatial hacienda. Inside, however, it is thoroughly modern and equipped with many amenities and business services.
① 123 P 🔁 🚫 🌀 ⬛ 🔲 🚫 AE, MC, V

🏨 PANORAMA
$
CARRANZA 315, 78000
TEL 444/812-1777
FAX 444/812-4591
Businessmen and budget travelers have remained loyal over the years to this older but still respectable property near la Plaza los Fundadores. Enjoy the view from the rooftop bar-restaurant.
① 120 P 🔁 🚫 ⬛ 🚫 AE, MC

🍴 POSADA DEL VIRREY
$$$
JARDÍN HIDALGO 3
TEL 444/812-3280
The converted home of Mexico's first vicereine faces Parque Hidalgo. This popular eatery serves regional specialties on a delightful covered courtyard.
🚫 AE, MC, V

🍴 LA VIRREINA
$$
CARRANZA 839
TEL 444/812-3750

Good food, good service, good everything; some say delightful. Locals and tourists alike flock to this charming restored mansion, smack dab in the historical center, for international and regional favorites.
🚫 Most major cards

SAN MIGUEL DE ALLENDE

🏨 CASA DE SIERRA NEVADA QUINTA REAL
$$$$
HOSPICIO 35, 37700
TEL 415/152-7040, 800/323-7500
FAX 415/152-1436
www.quintareal.com
Several ancient haciendas have been converted as installations for this luxurious hotel. Guest rooms are individually decorated, with lace curtains, antique dressers, and lots of locally made art and handcrafts. If you're not happy with the room you're shown, ask for another. No children under 16.
① 33 P 🚫 ⬛ 🚫 AE, MC, V

🏨 CASA LUNA B&B
$$$
QUEBRADA 117 AT PILA SECA 11
TEL/FAX 415/152-1117
www.casaluna.com
The two converted homes that comprise this friendly B&B are so charming you'll be eager to return at the end of the day, or perhaps you won't leave in the first place. Rock and adobe walls, traditional tile floors, exposed beams, and at least one fireplace in each suite, plus painterly walls everywhere you look.
① 23 🚫 🚫 🚫 MC, V

🏨 CASA CARMEN B&B
$$
TEL/FAX 415/152-0844
Located just one block from the main plaza, this charming B&B has been in business for decades. Rooms surround the

PRICES

HOTELS
An indication of the cost of a double room in high season, excluding tax, is given by $ signs.
$$$$$	Over $300
$$$$	$200– $299
$$$	$120–$199
$$	$60–$119
$	Under $60

RESTAURANTS
An indication of the cost of a three-course lunch or dinner without drinks, tax, or tip is given by $ signs.
$$$$$	Over $45
$$$$	$30–$45
$$$	$20–$30
$$	$10–$20
$	Under $10

beautiful central patio, with requisite fountain. Near the bottom of the $$ category, the price includes breakfast and lunch as well.
① 11 🚫 🚫 Cash only

🍴 MAMA MÍA
$–$$
UMARÁN 8
TEL 415/152-2063
This longtime favorite is still hip and has it all: video bar, live jazz while dining, salsa for dancing, and a good restaurant with Italian and international choices.
🚫 MC, V

CENTRAL PACIFIC STATES

ACAPULCO

🏨 FAIRMONT ACAPULCO PRINCESS
$$$$$
PLAYA REVOLCADERO S/N, 39300
TEL 744/469-1000, 800/441-1414
FAX 744/469-1016
www.fairmont.com/acapulco
Large, airy rooms; immaculate grounds; more than a half dozen restaurants—but what

most draws the crowds are the endless breakfast buffet and the excellent, expensive, sweet-smelling Willow Stream day spa, with myriad treatments. Two 18-hole golf courses.

ⓘ 1,017 🅿 🔁 🚫 🔆 🈂 🛀 🏊 AE, MC, V

🏨 QUINTA REAL
$$$$$
PASEO DE LA QUINTA 6, FRACC. REAL DIAMANTE, 39907
TEL 744/469-1500, 800/323-7040
FAX 744/469-1516
www.quintareal.com
Each of the suites in this refined yet accessible hotel has an ocean view, satellite TV, mini-bar, and other comforts; some have private pools and dining areas. The cream-colored furnishings and decor are "rustic Mexican chic." The property perches on the bluffs with a fabulous view of Acapulco Bay. Take a path or elevator to the swimming pools and beach below. An on-site spa provides massage and various treatments.

ⓘ 66 🅿 🔁 🚫 🔆 🏊 AE, MC, V

🏨 ELCANO
🍴 $$$
AV. COSTERA MIGUEL ALEMAN 75, 39690
TEL 744/435-1500, 877/260-1765
FAX 744/484-2230
www.hotel-elcano.com.mx
A clean, white and cerulean blue theme pervades the smallish, comfortable rooms, breezy public areas, and outdoor **Bambuco** restaurant, which serves fabulous regional favorites with modern touches such as fat shrimp tacos or red snapper grilled with asparagus, shrimp, and clams.

ⓘ 180 🅿 🚫 🔆 🏊 🛀 AE, MC, V

🏨 BOCA CHICA
🍴 $$
PLAYA CALETA S/N, 39390
TEL 744/483-6388, 800/346-3942
FAX 744/483-9513

Guests return not for the plain but adequate rooms, but for the unpretentious. intimate location. The three-story property perches between Caleta Beach and a beautiful cove, great for snorkeling. The restaurant, sushi bar, water sports equipment, and on-site massage are big pluses.

ⓘ 45 🅿 🔆 🏊 AE, MC, V

🍴 BAIKAL
$$$$-$$$$$
CARRETERA ESCÉNICA 16, LA COSTERA
TEL 744/446-6867
Whether or not it's worth all the hype, modern, sleek Baikal is the flavor of the moment. With its awesome view of the bay and fusion menu, it might just stay in vogue for a while.

🕒 No L. Closed Mon., May–Nov. 🏧 Most major cards

🍴 MADEIRAS
$$$$
CARR. ESCÉNICA 33, FRACC. EL GUITARRÓN
TEL 744/446-5636
www.madeiras.com
Sublime international food in a romantic setting with candlelight and quiet music, and open to the breeze overlooking Acapulco Bay. The set menu offers choices of soup or salad, appetizer (such as octopus in vinaigrette), main course, and dessert.

🅿 🕒 Closed L 🏧 MC, V

🍴 EL AMIGO MIGUEL
$-$$
JUÁREZ 31 AT AZUETA, DOWNTOWN
TEL 744/483-6981
This longtime local favorite off the main square in Old Acapulco is served by an energetic young staff. Seafood dishes are traditional and tasty, with no surprises. The original location right on the sand serves equally delicious food.

🏧 MC, V

🍴 LA TORTUGA
$
LOMAS DEL MAR 5-A
TEL 744/484-6985
Low-cost lunch specials, combo plates large enough for two, and excellent *tortas* (breadroll sandwiches) are served in an informal outdoor downtown garden one block off Avenida Costera.

🏧 No credit cards

🍴 100% NATURAL
$
BLVD. COSTERA 200
Enjoy soyburgers, many fruit drinks (or beer or wine), healthful salads, or crispy chicken tacos at this unpretentious little chain restaurant. There are several locations around town. Open from 7–11 p.m.

🕒 B, L, D 🏧 AE, MC, V

BUCERÍAS

🍴 MARK'S
$$-$$$
LÁZARO CÁRDENAS 56, BUCERÍAS
TEL 329/298-0303
Yummy food and a cozy beach 'tude that combines great food with attractive atmosphere and sports on the tube.

🕒 Closed L 🏧 MC, V

COLIMA

🏨 CEBALLOS
$$
PORTAL MEDELLÍN 12, 28000
TEL 312/312-4444
www.hotelceballos.com
Built in the 1880s, this lovingly refurbished edifice has been home to three state governors. Unimaginatively decorated rooms have high ceilings; some have small balconies.

ⓘ 54 🅿 🔆 🏧 MC, V

🍴 LOS NARANJO
$$
BARREDA 34
TEL 312/312-0029
Traditional-minded Colimenses head for this

fan-cooled restaurant near quiet Jardín Quintero. The menu features a long list of traditional Mexican appetizers and many meat dishes, including the *filete especial* for two—steak grilled with green onions, jalapeño peppers, and bacon, served with beans and tortillas.
🅂 No credit cards

🍴 EL CHARCO DE LA HIGUERA
$-$$
JARDÍN DE SAN JOSÉ S/N, BETWEEN 5 DE MAYO AND TORRES QUINTERO
TEL 312/313-0192
A five-minute walk west of downtown, this peaceful outdoor restaurant has a varied menu, offering *tortas* (breadroll sandwiches), chicken, grilled meats, and *pozole* (hominy soup). Guitar music most weekend evenings.
🅂 MC, V

COSTALEGRE

🏨 EL TAMARINDO
$$$$$
MELAQUE–PUERTO VALLARTA HWY. KM 7.5, CIHUATLÁN
TEL 315/351-5032, 888/625-5144
FAX 315/351-5070
www.starwood.com/luxury
Friendly yet exclusive, this resort's wonderfully decorated villas with private plunge pool and outdoor living areas front pretty beaches and an 18-hole golf course. There's a dive shop and lots of outdoor recreation equipment, like bikes and sailboards—but nothing around for miles except beaches and low tropical forest.
🅸 28 villas 🅿 🅂 🅰
🆅 🅂 Most major cards

🏨 HOTELITO DESCONOCIDO
$$$$$
CRUZ DE LORETO, TOMATLÁN
TEL 322/281-4010, 800/851-1143
FAX 322/281-4130
www.hotelito.com
A rustic but thoroughly

pampering retreat away from the world and its woes, the "unknown hotel" is smartly decorated and far from mainstream. You'll have miles of sand as well as an estuary for exploring by bike, horseback, or in a kayak; there's also billiards and a pre-Hispanic steam ritual.
🅸 30 🅿 🅰 🅂 AE, D, MC

🏨 PUNTA SERENA
$$$
TEL 315/351-5427
FAX 315/351-5020
www.puntaserena.com
An adults-only, all-inclusive property on a cliff high above Tenacatita Bay, this boutique hotel offers a variety of spa treatments, ritual steam baths, and nude sunbathing on the semi-private beach far below. Rooms are elegant and comfortable, and the clientele is international.
🅸 24 🅿 🅂 🅂 🅰
🆅 🅂 AE, MC, V

GUADALAJARA

🏨 QUINTA REAL
🍴 GUADALAJARA
$$$$-$$$$$
AV. MÉXICO 2727, 44680
TEL 33/3669-0600, 800/323-7500
FAX 33/3669-0601
www.quintareal.com
Mostly geared toward business travelers, this luxurious property looks colonial but is actually newish, with all the modern conveniences. All of the suites have fireplaces, bathtubs, comfortable furnishings, and locally made handcrafts. Dine on the terrace or indoors on world-class haute cuisine.
🅸 78 🅂 🅂 🅂 🅰
🅂 Most major cards

🏨 DE MENDOZA
$$
V. CARRANZA 16, 44100
TEL 33/3613-4646
FAX 33/3613-7310
www.demendoza.com.mx
A great location, reasonable

rates, a nice swimming pool, and a beautiful lobby enliven this five-story hotel near la Plaza Tapatío. Great city views from the bar, and dancing on weekends.
🅸 110 🅿 🅂 🅂 🅂
🅰 🅂 AE, MC, V

🍴 SANTO COYOTE
$$$
CALLE LERDO DE TEJADO 2379, ZONA MINERVA
TEL 33/3616-6978
Beautiful (albeit almost overwhelming) decor and A-list entrees of nouvelle Mexican and Continental cuisine make this a must-do eaterie with locals as well as visitors.
🅂 MC, V

🍴 EL SACROMONTE
$$-$$$
PEDRO MORENO 1398
TEL 33/3825-5447
Treat all of your senses at Sacromonte, which is particularly known for its excellent service. Icons and candlelit altars provide nighttime ambience in the romantic garden. There are delicious soups (try the blue cheese) and elaborate main dishes, such as duck with deep-fried rose petals.
🅲 Closed Sun. 🅂 MC, V

IXTAPA/ZIHUATANEJO

🏨 LA CASA QUE CANTA
$$$$$
CAMINO ESCÉNICO, PLAYA LA ROPA, ZIHUATANEJO 40880
TEL 755/555-7000, 888/523-5050
FAX 775/554-7900
www.lacasaquecanta.com
Attention to every detail in decor and service makes the Casa que Canta one of Mexico's top hotels. Spacious rooms with ocean views and unusual handpainted furnishings occupy earth-toned buildings on hillside terraces. The beach is a short walk downhill.
🅸 24 🅿 🅂 🅂 🅰 2
🆅 🅂 Most major cards

🏨 BECCOFINO
$$
PLAZA MARINA IXTAPA, VÍA
BLVD IXTAPA S/N, IXTAPA
TEL 755/553-1770
Angelo Pavia, an Italian native,
brings his talents to this
marina restaurant specializing
in northern Italian food. The
wine selection includes
Mexican, Italian, French,
Spanish, and Chilean vintages.
Reserve a table on the lovely
deck overlooking the water.
🏧 AE, MC, V

🏨 COCONUTS
$–$$$
PASAJE AGUSTÍN RAMÍREZ 1
TEL. 755/554-2518
Order appetizers or a yummy
full meal at one of Zihua's
oldest and best restaurants.
Enjoy the modern Continental
cuisine under the stars or on
the open, inside rooms of this
converted old home. There's
live romantic music most
evenings.
🕐 Closed Jun.–Oct. 🏧 AE,
MC, V

🏨 LA SIRENA GORDA
$
PASEO DEL PESCADOR 90,
ZIHUATANEJO
TEL 755/557-2687
A short walk from the town
pier, "The Fat Mermaid" is a
popular and unpretentious
thatch-roofed café serving
traditional seafood cocktails,
ten kinds of seafood tacos
(including "surf and turf"),
soups, and more filling entrees.
Breakfast is recommended.
🕐 Closed Wed. 🏧 No
credit cards

MANZANILLO

🏨 LAS HADAS
$$$$$
AV. DE LOS RISCOS AT VISTA
HERMOSA, 28200
TEL. 314/331-0101, 888/559-4329
FAX 314/331-0121
www.brisas.com.mx
Famous for its capricious
white Moorish architecture,
featured in the movie *10*

(1979), aging Las Hadas finally
got a facelift after being
purchased by the Las Brisas
group. There's an 18-hole golf
course, tennis, and marina. Its
most romantic restaurant,
Legazpi, boasts four-star
service and excellent food.
🛏 220 🅿 🚻 🚭 🌿
🏊 🏋 🏧 Most major
cards

🏨 L'RECIF
$$–$$$
CERRO DEL CENICERO,
CONDOMINIO VIDA DEL MAR,
PENÍNSULA DE JULUAPÁN
TEL 314/335-0900
Always packed with well-
coifed, gray-haired gringos
and the odd (meaning
occasional) Mexican, L'Recif
has a real asset in its primo
position above the crashing
surf. The meandering, dark
road north of Manzanillo
can be a bit unnerving on the
first visit, but surely you'll
come back.
🕐 No L. Closed Easter–Oct.
🏧 MC, V

MORELIA

🏨 VILLA MONTANA
$$$
PATZIMBA 201, 58090
TEL 314/314-0231, 800/525-4800
FAX 314/315-1423
www.villamontana,com
At night, Morelia twinkles in
the distance from the terrace
bar of this lovely oasis of calm.
Cottages dot the terraced
property; landscaped gardens
are peppered with fountains
and sculptures. A spa opened
in spring 2005.
🛏 36 🅿 🏊 🏋 🏧 AE,
MC, V

🏨 FONDA LAS
MERCEDES
$$
LEÓN GUZMÁN 47, 58000
TEL 443/312-6113
In the heart of town, this
delightful eatery is upscale but
cozy, with tables throughout
the covered patio of the
restored colonial building.

Innovative international and
regional dishes include steaks
and *pollo Azteca*—baked
mushroom-stuffed chicken.
🕐 Closed Sun. D 🏧 AE,
MC, V

PÁTZCUARO

🏨 MANSIÓN DE ITURBE
$$
PORTAL MORELOS 59, 61600
TEL 434/342-0368
FAX 434/313-4593
www.mexonline.com/iturbe.htm
Odd but endearing, this
creaky, high-ceilinged hotel
dominates the Plaza de
Quiroga. Some of the walls
and decor have been redone,
lightening the antique feeling;
the restored 17th-century
building is well maintained.
Breakfast is included, and **El
Gaucho** restaurant features
Argentine-style steaks and
live music.
🛏 14 🏧 MC, V

🏨 POSADA DE LA
BASÍLICA
$
ARCIGA 6, 61600
TEL 434/342-1108
FAX 434/342-0659
www.cdctesoros.com
Rooms in this colonial hotel
are simple yet cozy, and the
fireplaces are welcome on
chilly evenings.
🛏 12 🅿 🏧 AE, MC, V

🏨 HOSTERÍA DE SAN
FELIPE
$
AV. LÁZARO CÁRDENAS 321
TEL 434/342-1955
Like almost any tourist venue
in Pátzcuaro, this inn occupies
a charming old building with
exposed ceiling beams and
rock and adobe walls. On
the menu are regional
appetizers (like crunchy dried
chilies stuffed with white
cheese), whitefish, and locally
famous ice cream. If you
don't want to eat alone, stick
to standard Mexican
mealtimes.
🏧 AE, MC, V

PUERTO VALLARTA

🏨 PARADISE VILLAGE
$$$$

PASEO DE LOS COCOTEROS 1,
NUEVO VALLARTA, 63732
TEL. 322/226-6770, 800/995-5714
EXT. 111
FAX 322/226--6752
www.paradisevillage.com

For an all-emcompassing hotel where you needn't even leave the grounds, choose this all-suites property with marina, many water sports, a good (and not expensive) spa, and much more. There's a dance club also, and a shopping center next door; the beach here is pretty, with gentle surf.

🛏 490 suites 🅿 🔁 🆂
🆂 🏊 🍽 🃏 AE, DC, MC, V

🏨 WESTIN RESORT & SPA
$$$$

PASEO DE LA MARINA SUR 205,
MARINA VALLARTA
TEL. 322/226-1100, 800/228-3000
FAX 322/226-1131
www.westinvallarta.com

Of Puerto Vallarta's many fabulous hotels, the Westin is noted for its comfortable, classy rooms with super soft beds, several good restaurants, and the stylish Nikki Beach Club, modeled on the Miami original. There's plenty to keep kids occupied, too. About 15 minutes north of downtown Vallarta.

🛏 280 🅿 🔁 🆂 🆂
🏊 🍽 🃏 AE, DC, MC, V

🏨 DREAMS PUERTO VALLARTA
$$$

PLAYA LAS ESTACAS, CARR.
BARRA NAVIDAD S/N, 48300
TEL 322/221-5000
FAX 322/221-6000
www.camino-real-puerto
-vallarta.com

Formerly the Camino Real, this recently remodeled resort has a dizzying number of activities, and is located on a beautiful, sheltered, sandy beach south of downtown PV. Price includes meals, drinks, and entertainment.

🛏 337 🅿 🔁 🆂 🆂
🏊 3 🍽 🃏 Most major cards

🏨 MOLINA DEL AGUA
$$

AV. IGNACIO L. VALLARTA 130,
COL. E. ZAPATA 48380
TEL 322/222-1907
FAX 322/222-6056
www.molinodeagua.com

There's a youngish Euro vibe around the two large pools, one overlooking the beach. The downtown location is optimum; large trees and other growing things dominate the rambling property. Beachfront rooms enjoy the music of the surf; only some have TVs.

🛏 60 rooms and suites 🅿
🏊 2 🃏 AE, MC, V

SOMETHING SPECIAL

🍽 TRÍO

Tasty, innovative Mediterranean dishes with a Mexican flourish have made this restaurant a favorite with the locals. Dishes include rack of lamb served with mint sauce and ravioli, or red snapper with ratatouille and tiny roast potatoes. The venue is warm and charming, like a favorite friend's well-decorated home.

$$$-$$$$
GUERRERO 264
TEL 322/222-2196
🕐 Closed L 🆂 🃏 AE, MC, V

🍽 EL ARRAYÁN
$$$

CALLE ALLENDE 344,
AT CALLE MIRAMAR
TEL 322/222-7195

Although a relative newcomer, El Arrayan, named for a fruitless tree characteristic of Ole Mexico, serves up very convincing modern versions

---

PRICES

HOTELS

An indication of the cost of a double room in high season, excluding tax, is given by $ signs.

$$$$$	Over $300
$$$$	$200– $299
$$$	$120–$199
$$	$60–$119
$	Under $60

RESTAURANTS

An indication of the cost of a three-course lunch or dinner without drinks, tax, or tip is given by $ signs.

$$$$$	Over $45
$$$$	$30–$45
$$$	$20–$30
$$	$10–$20
$	Under $10

---

of Mexican classics. As appealing as the food is the down-home patio setting, just like Tia Juani's old place.
🕐 Closed L, Tues., Aug.
🃏 MC, V

SAN BLAS

🏨 GARZA CANELA
🍽 $$

PAREDES 106 SUR
TEL 323/285-0112
FAX 323/285-0308
www.garzacanela.com

Run by four sisters, this pretty two-story hotel and its restaurant, **El Delfin,** is a ten-minute walk from the beach and has a pleasant garden.
🛏 50 🅿 🆂 🏊 🃏 AE, MC, V

🏨 MIRAMAR PARAISO
$

KM. 18 CARRETERA COSTERA
SAN BLAS—LAS VARAS, BAHÍA
MATANCHÉN
TEL/FAX 323/254-9030

About 20 minutes from San Blas overlooking the surfing mecca of Matanchén Bay, near the village of Santa Cruz, this former governer's mansion

---

🏨 Hotel 🍽 Restaurant 🛏 No. of bedrooms 🚇 Metro 🅿 Parking 🕐 Closed 🔁 Elevator is a gorgeous digs in serene, simple surroundings. There are camping and RV sites too, as well as a restaurant, bar, and meeting facilities.

🛈 28 🅿 🚫 🌊 🍽️MC, V

🍽️ LA ISLA
$$
CALLE MERCADO AT PAREDES
NO PHONE
A block from the plaza, this seafood restaurant has been around for zillions of years…or so it seems. No wonder: the food is great, and the decorations are quaint, with shells a-go-go. It's a real San Blas institution. Try the flan for dessert.

TAXCO

🏨 POSADA DE LA MISIÓN
$$$
CERRO DE LA MISIÓN 32, 40230
TEL 762/622-0063
FAX 762/622-2198
www.posadamision.com
This colonial-style hotel at the outskirts of town has an open chapel and a pool surrounded by a small garden. Room rates include a buffet breakfast and dinner with a choice of appetizer, main dish, and dessert.

🛈 150 rooms and suites 🅿 🌊 🍽️ AE, MC, V

TEPIC

🏨 FRAY JUNÍPERO SERRA
$
LERDO 23 PONIENTE AT MÉXICO, 63000
TEL 311/212-2525
FAX 311/212-2051
www.frayjunipero.com.mx
Right on the main square, this budget-priced small-businessperson's hotel has well-maintained rooms with satellite TV. Ask for a room on the top floor, which will have a great nighttime view of the church tower, or for one with a bathtub.

🛈 104 🅿 🚫 🍽️ 🍽️AE, MC, V

TLAQUEPAQUE

🏨 QUINTA DON JOSÉ
$$
REFORMA 139, TLAQUEPAQUE
TEL. 33/3635-7522., 866/629-3753
FAX 33/3659-9315
www.quintadonjose.com
A cozy B&B in the heart of Tlaquepaque, its rooms and public areas feature many of the household items you'll shop for in this pretty Guadalajara suburb. English-speaking owners Arturo and Estela Magana are helpful and friendly.

🛈 14 🅿 🚫 🍽️ 🌊 🍽️ AE, MC, V

🍽️ RÍO SAN PEDRO
$–$$
JUÁREZ 300, TLAQUEPAQUE
TEL 33/3659-6136
Eat on the patio or inside this wonderful old house-turned-restaurant in slow-paced Tlaquepaque, away from the bustle of down-town Guadalajara. Chef-owner Mayo and his wife Malena are there to insure good service and excellent Mexican and Continental food. Open from early until late.

🍽️ AE, MC, V

URUAPAN

🏨 HOTEL MANSIÓN DEL CUPATITZIO
$$
CALZADA RODILLA DEL DIABLO 20, LA QUINTA, 60030
TEL 452/523-2100
FAX 452/524-6772
At the edge of Parque Nacional Eduardo Ruiz, this old hotel has the feel of a gracious hacienda, with fine views of the park. Fresh flowers enliven the restaurant's atmosphere, which serves mainly regional and Mexican cuisine.

🛈 57 🅿 🌊 🍽️ 🍽️AE, MC, V

🏨 SHERATON CENTRO HISTÓRICO
$$$–$$$$
JUÁREZ 70, LA ALAMEDA
TEL 55/5130-5300
FAX 55/5130-5255
www.sheratonmexico.com
Brand new in 2003, this Sheraton across from the Alameda park (and near the zócalo and Paseo Reforma) is recommended for its ample rooms, modern business center and meeting rooms, and stunningly sleek architecture and décor. El Cardenal Restaurant is highly recommended for traditional Mexican cuisine.

🛈 457 🅿 🍽️ 🚫 🚫 🍽️ 🍽️Most major cards

🏨 CAMINO REAL MEXICO
$$$
MARIANO ESCOBEDO 700, COL. NUEVA ANZURES, 11590
TEL 55/5263-8888
FAX 55/5263-8889
www.caminoreal.com
Designed by renowned architect Ricardo Legorreta, Mexico City's modernistic low-rise near Chapultepec Park has colorful marigold and hot pink accents and artwork by major artists such as Rufino Tamayo. It's enduringly popular despite the siren's call of newer hotels.

🛈 713 🚇 Chapultepec 🅿 🍽️ 🚫 🚫 🌊 🍽️ 🍽️All major cards

🏨 CONDESA DF
$$$
AV. VERACRUZ 102, COL. LA CONDESA
TEL 55/5241-2600
FAX 55/5241-2640
www.condesaDF.com
Sleek and modern, if not warm and fuzzy, at least reasonably welcoming…the Condesa DF is among Mexico City's hippest hotel. Rooms

HOTELS & RESTAURANTS

stacked around a central courtyard in the 1920s-era building have minamalist furnishings, flat-screen TVs, DVDs, and generally cool decor. (The same owner's equally stylish Habita Hotel is in Colonia Polanco.)

🛏 40 🅿 ⮀ 🛋 🏊 📺 🔲 AE, DC, MC, V

🏨 GRAN MELIÁ MEXICO REFORMA
$$$
PASEO DE LA REFORMA 1, COL. TABACALERA
TEL. 55/5063-1000, 800/336-3542
FAX 55/5128-5028
www.solmelia.com
Mexico City's only hotel presenting live theater, the classy, elegant hotel also has one of the city's best spas. Location is good too, at the west end of Paseo Reforma, near Parque Alameda. Rooms are predictably comfortable, with soothing, classic architectural details and decor in muted colors.

🛏 489 🚇 Hidalgo 🅿 ⮀ 🛋 🏊 🛗 📺 🔲 Most major cards

🏨🍴 PRESIDENTE INTERCONTINENTAL
$$$
CAMPOS ELISEOS 218, COL. POLANCO
TEL. 55/5327-7700
FAX 55/5327-7730
www.intercontinental.com
In addition to an enviable location near Chapultepec Park and next to the Nikko, W, and other swank hotels, this high rise and its half dozen popular bars and restaurants are almost always abuzz with the crème of haute Mexican players—from pop stars to politicos. The 24-hour **Au Pied de Cochon** has wonderful food and reputedly Latin America's largest wine cellar.

🛏 660 🅿 ⮀ 🛋 🛋 📺 🔲 AE, D, MC, V

🏨 PARQUE ENSENADA
$
ALVARO OBREGÓN 13 AT MORELIA, COL. ROMA
TEL. 55/5208-0052
www.hotelensenada.com.mx
A budget hotel in Col. Roma, where regentrification is restoring lovely post-war buildings. There's a diner, laundry, and parking, and two computers for e-mail checking.

🛏 132 🚇 Niños Héroes 🅿 ⮀ 🔲 MC, V

🍴 LA HACIENDA DE LOS MORALES
$$$–$$$$
VÁZQUEZ DE MELLA 525, COL. POLANCO
TEL. 55/5096-3000
Wealthy *defeños* (people from Mexico City) and business executives dine in elegance at this restored 16th-century hacienda on the outskirts of the Polanco neighborhood. Mexican and international fare.

🚇 Polanco (plus a short taxi ride) 🔲 Most major cards

🍴 IZOTE
$$$$$
PRESIDENTE MAZARIK 513, LOCAL 3, POLANCO
TEL. 55/5280-1671
Renowed chef Patricia Quintana produces many innovative nouvelle Mexican dishes at this fine restaurant. Make a meal of the wonderful appetizers, or choose something unusual from the changing menu. In a small strip mall, the milieu is not anything special.

🕓 Closed Sun. D 🔲 AE, MC, V

🍴 CAPICUA
$$–$$$
AV. NUEVO LEÓN 66, LA CONDESA
TEL. 55/5211-5280
Delicious (albeit sometimes salty) Spanish tapas are served in a minimalist restaurant overlooking the street in this browsable

neighborhood. Look for daily lunch specials and a reasonably large wine list.

🔲 MC, V

🍴 FONDA SAN ANGEL
$$–$$$
PLAZA SAN JACINTO, SAN ANGEL
TEL. 55/5550-1641
Open for breakfast as well as lunch and dinner, this casual eatery is a welcome retreat in the south of the city. Eat at a café table facing San Angel's prettiest plaza, or inside in the cool, thick-walled mansion. Call on the head waiter to translate the wide array of choices on the Spanish-language menu. Valet parking.

🔲 AE, MC, V

🍴 GALLOS CENTENTARIO
$$–$$$
REPÚBLICA DE CUBA 79, CENTRO
TEL. 55/5512-1625
This restored old colonial home near Plaza Santo Domingo is as popular with locals as with travelers. The atmosphere is classy, notwithstanding the hundreds of namesake roosters and other items crowding the walls; the mood is festive and the Mexican food is also very good.

🕓 Closed Sun. D 🔲 AE, MC, V

MOSAICO
🍴 **$$–$$$**
MICHOACÁN 10, NEAR AMSTERDAM, COL. LA CONDESA
TEL. 55/5584-3282
A delicious and varied French and Continental menu at reasonable prices means a devoted cadre of repeat customers. The small bistro and adjoining bakery can be packed, due in part to the excellent wine list and charming unpretentious atmosphere.

🕓 Closed Sun. D 🔲 AE, MC, V

⊞ CAFÉ DE TACUBA

$$

TACUBA 28
TEL 55/5518-4950
The third-generation owners
have served tacos, fried
chicken, and their famous
enchiladas in this popular,
festive eatery since 1912; the
matronly waitresses know
their clientele. The restored
mansion is filled with antiques,
paintings, handpainted tiles,
and bric-a-brac.
🚇 Allende Ⓢ AE, MC, V

⊞ SAN FRANCISCO

$$

AMSTERDAM 105 AT LAREDO,
LA CONDESA
TEL 55/5211-2361
Jazz creates a mellow
background at this homey
eatery with whitewashed
brick walls and blond-wood
floors. Choose among the
regional favorites from
throughout diverse Mexico:
pan de cazón (shark layered
with beans, tomato sauce,
and tortillas), squash blossom
soup, and crepes stuffed
with *huitlacoche* (corn fungus).
🕒 Closed Sun. D Ⓢ AE,
MC, V

⊞ SPEZIA

$$

AMSTERDAM 241,
COLONIA LA CONDESA
TEL 55/5564-1367
This Polish restaurant,
featuring delightful roast duck,
borscht, and grilled trout, is
currently very popular with
locals. The courtyard and
indoor setting are elegant, but
diners' dress is studied casual.
🚇 Chilpancingo ⓟ
🕒 Closed Sun. D Ⓢ AE,
MC, V

⊞ VILLA MARÍA

$$

HOMERO 704, COLONIA
POLANCO
TEL 55/5203-0306
www.villamaria.com.mx
Enjoy a frozen margarita
spiked with tamarind juice,
or just savor the rather chic,

lively, crowded-but-not-noisy
ambience and the tacos and
other typical Mexican
favorites. Mariachis are
available for a song.
🚇 Polanco (plus a short taxi
ride) 🕒 Closed Sun. D
Ⓢ AE, MC, V

⊞ CAFÉ LA GLORIA

$–$$

VICENTE SUÁREZ 41,
COL. CONDESA
TEL 55/5511-4180
This hip, casual sidewalk
bistro in the Condesa
neighborhood serves yummy
yet inexpensive international
dishes such as fresh grilled
tuna with ginger butter. Also
wonderful desserts with
espresso, capuccino, or
American-style coffee.
🚇 Chilpancingo Ⓢ MC, V

AROUND
MEXICO CITY

CHOLULA

⊞ LA QUINTA LUNA

$$$

CALLE 3 SUR 702
TEL 222/247-8915
www.laquintaluna.com
Rooms surrounding a central
patio are a refreshing mix of
traditional materials and
modern design. Just a short
walk from city center.
Breakfast included; yummy
traditional and nouveau
Mexican cuisine.
ⓘ 6 Ⓢ MC, V

⊞ VILLAS
ARQUEOLÓGICAS

$$

CALLE 2 PONIENTE 601, 72760
TEL 222/273-7900, 800/258-2633
FAX 222/247-1508
www.clubmed.com
In Mexico, Club Med
properties are found not
just at the sea but at a half-
dozen archaeological sites.
In the shadow of massive
Tepanapa pyramid, this one
has smallish but cozy rooms
and well-maintained grounds.

Breakfast included; meal plans
available.
ⓘ 42 ⓟ 🏊 Ⓢ MC, V

CUERNAVACA

⊞ LAS MAÑANITAS
⊞ $$$$–$$$$$

RICARDO LINARES 107, 62000
TEL 777/314-1466, 888/413-9199
FAX 777/318-3672
www.lasmananitas.com
Beloved for its award-winning
restaurant and as a soothing
retreat from city stress, this
restored hacienda is set on
immaculate grounds with
ponds and fountains. Airy
suites have antique furnishings,
Mexican folk art, and huge
tiled bathrooms; request one
with a fireplace or large
terrace. Innovative regional
cuisine is served overlooking
the garden courtyard.
ⓘ 20 ⓟ 🏊 Ⓢ AE, MC,
V

⊞ LAS ESTACAS

$$

RAYÓN 30, CUERNAVACA
CENTRO, TLALTIZAPÁN (1 HR.
OUTSIDE CUERNAVACA)
TEL 777/312-3817
FAX 777/312-7610
www.lasestacas.com
Throngs of royal palms and
semitropical vegetation shade
this luscious property
surrounding the crystal-clear
Estacas River, used as a
location for shooting Tarzan
TV shows. The many facilities
are open to day-trippers
($$$$$), but it's nicer to
overnight in the dormitory-
style hostel, two-story hotel,
campgrounds, or RV park.
Reservations and
transportation in Cuernavaca,
one hour away.
ⓟ 🏊 Ⓢ MC, V

⊞ CASA GAIA

$$–$$$

BLVD. JUÁREZ 102
TEL 777/312-3656
Dress up for a meal at this
lovely restored mansion.
Try the house salad with
caramelized pears, vinaigrette,

HOTELS & RESTAURANTS

and Roquefort cheese, an appetizer of stuffed Portabello mushrooms, or one of many delicious international dishes. Monday cooking classes; valet parking. Weekend reservations suggested.
🕐 Closed Mon. 🖾 AE, MC, V

EL CHICO NATIONAL PARK

🏨 EL PARAÍSO
🍴 $$–$$$
CARR. PACHUCA–MINERAL DEL CHICO KM. 19
TEL 771/715-5654
FAX 771/715-5659
www.hotelesecoturisticos.com.mx
Within El Chico National Park, this simple hotel offers mountain biking, proximity to hiking trails and to the tiny, picturesque town of Mineral del Chico. The meal plan is suggested, as the international food is truly tasty. Non-guests may dine by previous reservation.
🛏 20 🅿 🖼 🖾 MC, V

METEPEC

🏨 QUINTA DEL REY
$$$
PASEO TOLOCAN ORIENTE KM 5, 52140
TEL 722/211-8777, 888/244-0439
FAX 722/216-7233
Located outside Toluca on the highway to Mexico, this three-story, all-suites property is done up in rustic colonial style.
🛏 42 🅿 🖼 🖼 🖾
🖾 Most major cards

PUEBLA

🏨 CAMINO REAL
🍴 PUEBLA
$$$
CALLE 7 PONIENTE 105, 72000
TEL 222/229-0909, 800/722-6466
FAX 222/232-9251
www.camino-real-puebla.com
One of Mexico's earliest monasteries has been meticulously restored—right

down to the frescoes and fountains—as a gorgeous, centrally located inn. The very refined **El Convento** restaurant is *the* place in Puebla for delicious international fare (dinner only). Make a reservation, dress up, and prepare to splurge.
🛏 83 🅿 🖼 🖼 🖼
🖾 AE, MC, V

🏨 MESÓN SACRISTÍA DE
🍴 LA COMPAÑÍA
$$
CALLE 6 SUR 304 AT CALLEJÓN DE LOS SAPOS, 72000
TEL 222/242-3554
FAX 222/232-4513
www.mesones-sacristia.com
Throughout this two-story boutique hotel antique furnishings and decorative elements are punctuated with more modern regional folk art. Rooms are snug rustic chic, the bar has live music on weekends, and the restaurant serves delicious regional specialties: stuffed chilies, cream of bean soup, and, of course, Puebla's traditional *mole poblano* (a blend of chocolate, nuts, chilies, and more). Includes breakfast.
🛏 9 🅿 🕐 Restaurant closed Sun. D 🖾 AE, MC, V

🍴 FONDA DE SANTA
CLARA
$
AV. 3 PONIENTE 307
TEL 222/242-2659
A welcoming staff complements the generous helpings of delicious regional food at this picturesque, centrally located inn. Select from a range of scrumptious appetizers; for a main dish try the *tinga* (shredded chicken in tomato sauce); then treat yourself to a pastry dessert.
🖾 MC, V

TEOTIHUACÁN

🏨 VILLAS
ARQUEOLÓGICAS
TEOTIHUACÁN
$$

PERIFÉRICO SUR S/N, SAN JUAN TEOTIHUACÁN, 55800
TEL 800/258-2633
FAX 594/956-0244
www.clubmed.com
Perfectly situated at the edge of the archaeological zone, this low-slung, comfortable hotel has small rooms typical of Club Med Arqueológico properties, plus a tennis court.
🛏 40 🅿 🖼 🖼 🖾 AE, MC, V

TLAXCALA

🏨 POSADA SAN
FRANCISCO
$$
PLAZA DE LA CONSTITUCIÓN 17, 90000
TEL 246/462-6022
FAX 246/462-6818
Guest rooms lack the quaint colonial atmosphere of the original mansion, restored to house the bar, lobby, and restaurant. The location in historic downtown, billiards room, tennis court, and large pool are pluses.
🛏 68 🅿 🖼 🖼 🖾 AE, MC, V

🍴 LA CACEROLA
$$
INDEPENDENCIA 9-A
TEL 246/466-1235
Sophisticated versions of
regional cuisine are served
in the two small dining
rooms of this family-style
restored historic property
on Plaza Xicotencatl.
Specialties include myriad
stuffed chilies: try a *chile
relleno en salsa de pulque*
(mild chili in pulque sauce).
🕐 Closed Sun. 🚫 No
credit cards

CENTRAL GULF COAST

CATEMACO

🏨 LA FINCA
$$
CARR. COSTERA 180 KM 147
TEL 294/947-9700
FAX 294/947-9720
www.lafinca.com.mex
Birders love this three-story
lakeshore hotel as it is
surrounded by greenery. Each
room has a balcony, and the
pool has a slide and spa.
🛏 51 🅿 ❄ 🏊
🚫 MC, V

🏨 NANCIYAGA
$
CARR. CATEMACO–COYAME
KM 7 (EAST OF HWY. 180)
TEL/FAX 294/943-0199
For a peaceful and very rustic
retreat, overnight at this New
Age ecological park ($).
Herons wade and crocs snap
just outside the microscopic
lakeside cabins, lit at night by
hurricane lamps. Wander the
jungle, row or kayak on the
lake, then have body mud
treatment and rinse off in the
mineral spring.
🛏 10 cabins 🕐 Closed
Wed. Sept.–Oct. 🚫 No
credit cards

VERACRUZ

🏨 LA DILIGENCIA
$$

INDEPENDENCIA 1115,
CENTRO, 91700
TEL/FAX 229/923-0280
www.granhoteldiligencias.com
From a bar and cigar lounge
to a beauty salon, business
center and Internet service,
this hotel provides most of
the necessary accoutrements.
Recently restored and
revamped, it's situated in the
very heart of old Veracruz.
🛏 121 🅿 ❄ 🚭
🏊 💪 🚫 AE, MC, V

🏨 HOTEL MOCAMBO
$$
CALZADA RUÍZ CORTINES
4000, BOCA DEL RÍO, 94299
TEL 229/922-0200
FAX 229/922-0212
www.hotelmocambo.com.mx
Fabulous and exclusive in the
1930s, this oasis of tropical
calm later faded, but never
lost its charm. The art deco
architecture is now "retro,"
the palm-studded beach still
beckons, and expanded
facilities include sauna, spa,
and massage.
🛏 103 🅿 ❄ 🏊 🏊
💪 🚫 AE, MC, V

🍴 VILLA MARINA
$$$
BLVD. AVILA CAMACHO S/N,
NEAR DESEMBOCADURAS DE
HORACIO DIAZ
TEL 229/935-1034
Open 1 p.m. to 1 a.m.,
Villa Marina has a great
seascape through its large
plate-glass windows, and
serves steaks, regional
dishes, and international
favorites. The specialty,
fresh seafood, is cooked
in many styles; waiters will
help translate the Spanish-
language menu.
❄ 🚫 MC, V

🍴 PARDIÑOS
$$-$$$
ZAMORA 40,
BOCA DEL RÍO
TEL 229/986-0135
Pardiños has been around
forever, and is still popular.
Order Veracruz's signature

dish: whole red snapper
(huachinango) à la
veracruzana—with a sauce
of tomatoes, onions, bell
peppers, and olives—or any
regional seafood dish.
🚫 AE, MC, V

🍴 GRAN CAFÉ DE LA PARROQUIA
$-$$
CALLE 16 DE SEPTIEMBRE AT
MALECÓN
TEL 229/923-2584
A clink of your coffee glass
brings waiters with refills of
steaming java and hot milk in
this legendary Veracruz
coffeehouse near the port.
It's open early (and 'til
midnight), but, as everything
is à la carte, breakfast is
no bargain.
🚫 No credit cards

VILLAHERMOSA

🏨 CENCALI
$$
JUÁREZ AT PASEO TABASCO
S/N, 86040
TEL 993/315-1999
FAX 993/315-6600
www.cencali.com.mx
Two-story Cencali (Náhuatl
for "house on the edge of
the lake") indeed abuts las
Ilusiones Lake; its grounds
are extensive and tropical,
with wandering flamingos.
Small rooms have bathtubs,
hair dryers, safes, and free
airport shuttle. A breakfast
buffet is included in the
price. La Venta museum is
quite close.
🛏 160 🅿 ❄ 🏊
🚫 AE, MC, V

🏨🍴 HYATT REGENCY VILLAHERMOSA
$$
AV. JUÁREZ 106, ZONA
HOTELERA, 86050
TEL 993/310-1234, 800/228-9000
FAX 993/315-1235
www.villahermosa.regency.hyatt
.com
Comfort and class describe
this nine-story business-
oriented property. Soberly

HOTELS & RESTAURANTS

elegant rooms have the usual five-star amenities; public areas include several bars and lounges. **Bouganvillea** restaurant focuses on Mexican specialties and has an awesome Sunday breakfast buffet.

🛏 207 🅿 ⬆ ⬛ ⬛ 🖥 ⬛ Most major cards

🍴 LOS TULIPANES
$$$
CARLOS PELLICER 511
TEL 993/312-9-09
Try some of Tabasco's unusual dishes at "the Tulips," conveniently next to the CICOM (Center for Investigation of Olmec and Maya Cultures) and overlooking the Grijalva River. There's a breakfast buffet (except Monday), after which regional cuisine (try the ugly pelelagarto fish, a large appetizer plate) is served à la carte.

🅿 ⬛ AE, MC, V

🍴 HONG KONG
$
5 DE MAYO 443
TEL 993/312-5996
If you're maxed out on Mexican food, head for this Chinese restaurant in the Zona Luz. It's got all the traditional favorites, including multi-course meals for two or more.

⬛ MC, V

XALAPA

🏨 POSADA COATEPEC
$$
HIDALGO 9, COATEPEC 91500
TEL 228/816-0544
FAX 228/816-0040
www.posadacoatepec.com.mx
This former coffee villa about 4 miles from Xalapa now houses spacious, well-decorated suites with fine wood accents and satellite TV; antiques grace the lovely bar and lobby. Coffee plantation tours can be arranged.

🛏 23 🅿 ⬛ AE, MC, V

🏨 MESÓN DEL ALFÉREZ
$
ZARAGOZA AT SEBASTIÁN CAMACHO 2, 91000
TEL 228/818-6351
FAX 228/818-4703
Diluted washes of bright Mexican colors warm the walls of this restored historic home just behind the government palace. Original materials were preserved whenever possible during the restoration. Continental breakfast included.

🛏 20 🅿 AE, MC, V

🍴 LA ESTANCIA DE LOS TECAJETES
$$
AVILA CAMACHO 90, LOCAL 12, PLAZA TECAJETES
TEL 228/818-0732
With a fine view of the leafy park for which it is named, this downtown restaurant puts its own spin on regional dishes, such as chicken breast stuffed with creamed spinach in mushroom sauce. Music of one genre or another is played most nights after 9 p.m.

🅿 🕐 Closed Sun. D AE, MC, V

🍴 LA CASA DE MAMÁ
$
AVILA CAMACHO 113
TEL 228/817-3144
Decorated in dark tones with antique furniture, this popular restaurant has an impressive international menu including filet mignon and pork loin in Roquefort sauce. Request a table at the back, away from noisy traffic.

⬛ AE, MC, V

OAXACA

BAHÍAS DE HUATULCO

🏨 QUINTA REAL
🍴 HUATULCO
$$$$–$$$$$
PASEO BENITO JUÁREZ 2, BAHÍA TANGOLUNDA, 70989
TEL 958/581-0428, 800/457-4000
FAX 958/581-0429
www.quintareal.com

Characteristic of the chain, this intimate property embodies elegance and comfort. Three levels of suites, designed in understated luxury with cream-colored appointments, have great bay views with all the amenities; some have plunge pools, and there's a shuttle to the beach club with restaurant and pool. Splurge for a special dinner at **Las Cúpulas Restaurant,** serving inspired international cuisine in an elegant setting overlooking the sea.

🛏 54 🅿 ⬛ 🖥 ⬛ AE, MC, V

🏨 CAMINO REAL
🍴 ZAASHILA
$$$$
BLVD. BENITO JUÁREZ 5, 70989
TEL 958/581-0460, 800/722-6466
FAX 958/581-0461
www.camino-zaashila.com
Endless stairs thoughout this graceful, vegetation-drenched beachfront property provide a mildly aerobic vacation. The food is good, the beach is excellent, and the chaises longues are semi-submerged in the free-form pool.

🛏 130 🅿 ⬛ 🖥 ⬛ 🎏 ⬛ Most major cards

🏨 MISIÓN DE LOS
🍴 ARCOS
This intimate Mediterranean-style hotel is in Crucecita, but vans shuttle to its Santa Cruz Bay beach club. Many rooms have balconies; all have classy, low-key decor. The restaurant serves yummy breakfast as well as Mexican and Continental fare, and the gym is a magnet for health-conscious locals. The Internet café serves coffee and desserts.

$
GARDENIA 902, CRUCECITA
TEL 958/587-0165
FAX 958/587-1904
www.misiondelosarcos.com
🛏 14 🅿 ⬛ 🎏 ⬛ AE, MC, V

🏨 **EDÉN COSTA**
🍴 $
CALLE ZAPOTECO S/N,
BAHÍA CHAHUÉ
TEL./FAX 958/587-2480
The main draw here is the excellent and reasonably priced French restaurant, **L'Echalote** ($$–$$$, closed Mon.), which serves some Indochinese dishes as well. The attached hotel, about a five-minute walk from the beach at Chahué, is pleasant; rooms have remote-controlled a/c units and cable TVs.
ℹ️ 11 🚭 ☒ 🏊 ⊗MC, V

🍴 **RESTAURANT DE DOÑA CELIA (AVALOS)**
$$
PLAYA SANTA CRUZ (SOUTH OF PASEO MITLA), BAHÍA SANTA CRUZ
TEL 958/587-0128
At this Huatulco original, you can almost wriggle your toes in the sand as you order a delicious breakfast, lunch, or dinner. Outdoor tables under palm-thatch roofs are blessed by a lovely bay breeze.
⊗ No credit cards

OAXACA

🏨 **CAMINO REAL OAXACA**
$$$$
CALLE 5 DE MAYO 300, 68000
TEL 951/501-6100, 800/722-6466
FAX 951/516-0732
www.caminoreal.com
A converted 16th-century convent on a quiet street in historic downtown, this beautiful property is long on charm. Camino Real Club rooms are larger and offer more amenities. Diners in the colonnaded corridor surrounding a central patio are serenaded by a trio of musicians.
ℹ️ 90 🅿️ 🚭 🏊 ☒ ⊗AE, MC, V

🏨 **HOTEL VICTORIA**
$$
LOMAS DEL FORTIN 1, 68070
TEL 951/515-2633
FAX 951/515-2411
www.hotelvictoria.com.mx
Oaxaca glitters dramatically at night from the gardens and terrace bar of this comfortable hotel above town. Art by local painters of some renown is for sale. Prices for comfortable rooms vary according to size and location. Shuttles are available to downtown.
ℹ️ 150 🅿️ 🚭 🚭 🏊 ⊗AE, MC, V

🏨 **CAZOMALLI**
$
EL SALTO 104 AT ALDAMA, JALATLACO, 68080
TEL/FAX 951/513-3513
www.hotelcazomalli.com
A friendly hotel run by the Pérez Flores family in quiet Jalatlaco neighborhood. Cazomalli has simple but pleasant rooms that surround a central courtyard. Internet service, transportation, and guided tours of the region are available.
ℹ️ 15 ⊗AE, MC, V

🍴 **EL ASADOR VASCO**
$$–$$$
PORTAL DE FLORES 10
TEL 951/514-4755
Ask for a terrace table at this award-winning, second-story, long-time favorite overlooking Oaxaca's busy main plaza. In addition to scrumptious Basque specials are Mexican standards such as the huachinango veracruzano, red snapper in tomato sauce with green olives.
⊗ Most major cards

🍴 **EL NARANJO**
$$
TRUJANO 203
TEL 951/514-1878
A few blocks from the zócalo, this courtyard restaurant has an inspired collection of recipes from throughout Mexico. After an appetizer of marinated goat cheese, try the cold tomato soup with garlic and olive oil, an organic salad, stuffed chilies, or one of the state's seven signature mole dishes.
🕐 Closed Sun. ⊗AE, MC, V

🍴 **LA OLLA**
$–$$
REFORMA 402
TEL 951/516-6668
Very clean and dependable, the centrally located La Olla creates healthful regional, vegetarian, and international dishes. Food is made to order, and a bit slow, but local artwork entertains.
🕐 Closed Mon. ⊗ Most major cards

🍴 **LA ESCONDIDA**
$
CARR. YATARENI KM 7, OFF HWY. TO MITLA
TEL 951/517-6665
Locals flock on weekends and holidays to this smorgasbord of regional cuisine. It's even full midweek, when business-people and tourists come to this outdoor venue 15 minutes from downtown Oaxaca.
🕐 Closed D 🅿️ ⊗AE MC, V

PUERTO ÁNGEL

🏨 **LA BUENA VISTA**
🍴 $
CALLE BUENA COMPAÑÍA, NEAR SECTOR MILITAR NAVAL
TEL/FAX 958/584-3104
Accommodations in sleepy Puerto Ángel are basic, but the "Good View" hotel has screened windows and ceiling fans. At the top of the property, enjoy the breeze as you sample fresh shrimp, fish, or chicken or vegetarian tamales in the open dining room.
ℹ️ 23 🏊 ⊗ No credit cards

HOTELS & RESTAURANTS

PUERTO ESCONDIDO

HOTEL FLOR DE MARÍA
$$
ENTRANCE PLAYA
MARINERO S/N
TEL/FAX 954/582-0536
This is one of the town's favorite restaurants for a night out, and travelers return again and again for nouvelle Continental fare and homemade desserts. Changing nightly specials; closed for lunch. The hotel offers simple rooms across from wonderful Carmen's Bakery, great for coffee, granola, breakfast, and baked goods. No TV.
① 24 🌊 **⊗** MC, V

SANTA FE
$$
CALLE DEL MORO S/N,
ZICATELA BEACH
954/582-0170, 888/649-6407
FAX 954/582-0260
www.hotelsaftafe.com.mx
This is probably Puerto's nicest hotel (it's a serviceable but unimpressive lot), with exhuberant gardens; comfortable rooms and bungalows, and several swimming pools. The Mexican Pipeline here isn't appropriate for most swimmers; the vegetarian restaurant over-looking it is a real winner.
① 70 **P** 🔁 🚫 🚫 🌊 **⊗** AE, MC, V

HOTEL ARCO IRIS
$
CALLE DEL MORRO S/N,
ZICATELA BEACH, 71980
TEL 954/582-1494
FAX 954/582-0432
It's the sum of its parts that makes this bungalow-style hotel worthwhile. Plain rooms have personal patios, tropical landscaping surrounds the pool, and the rooftop video bar and restaurant overlook the town's surfing beach.
① 26 🌊 **⊗** MC, V

TEOTITLÁN DEL VALLE

TLAMANALLI
$$–$$$
AV. JUÁREZ 39
TEL 951/524-4006
Located in the rugmaking town of Teotitlán del Valle, this unpretentiuos, lunch-only, Zapotec restaurant has been featured in *The New York Times* and *Gourmet* magazine. The Mendoza sisters cook squash blossom soup, chicken tamales, turkey in *mole* sauce, and a few pre-Hispanic favorites.
🕒 Closed D, Mon., Eastertime **⊗** No credit cards

CHIAPAS

COMITÁN

LOS LAGOS DE MONTEBELLO
$
BLVD. BELISARIO DOMINGUEZ NORTE 14
TEL/FAX 963/632-1092
Comitán's fanciest hotel is a lovely but slightly faded keepsake of old-fashioned propriety. Everything is spacious, from the ample rooms with high ceilings, to the outdoor pool and the central patio shaded by gnarled Indian laurels and tulip trees.
① 60 🌊 **⊗** AE, MC, V

EL GRECO
$
CUARTA CALLE SUR ORIENTE 8
TEL 963/632-5173
Although its name means "the Greek," the food here is typical *chiapaneco* (Chiapan). The set lunch of this second-story restaurant, four blocks southeast of the main plaza, is an absolutely overwhelming array of local victuals: everything from tripe to tostadas.
🕒 Closed D, Sun. **⊗** No credit cards

PRICES

HOTELS
An indication of the cost of a double room in high season, excluding tax, is given by $ signs.
$$$$$ Over $300
$$$$ $200– $299
$$$ $120–$199
$$ $60–$119
$ Under $60

RESTAURANTS
An indication of the cost of a three-course lunch or dinner without drinks, tax, or tip is given by $ signs.
$$$$$ Over $45
$$$$ $30–$45
$$$ $20–$30
$$ $10–$20
$ Under $10

LAGUNAS DE MONTEBELLO

MUSEO PARADOR SANTA MARÍA
$$–$$$
CARR. A LAGUNAS DE MONTEBELLO KM 22
TEL/FAX 963/632-5116
This Independence-era hacienda—about a 20-minute drive from the lakes—stands by its simple but delicious regional recipes, such as barbecued chicken with rice and *lingua pebre* (beef tongue with fried tomatoes and sherry). Six fabulous rooms are decorated with period antiques from different eras. Restaurant reservations are required.
① 6 **P** **⊗** MC, V

OCOSINGO

HOSPEDAJE Y RESTAURANT ESMERALDA
$
CALLE CENTRAL NTE. 14
TEL/FAX 919/673-0014
www.ranchoesmeralda.net
The former owners of Rancho Esmeralda guesthouse have

opened this pleasant hotel in the heart of Ocosingo, the non-touristy town near the Tonina ruins. Healthful comfort food, with great salads, casseroles, and Mexican dishes, is one of its main draws, and the helpful American owners provide plenty of tips for local travel, and arrange horse riding expeditions.
🛏 4 rooms 🚫 No credit cards

PALENQUE

🏨 CHAN KAH
$$
CARRETERA A LAS RUINAS KM. 3.5
916/345-1134
FAX 916/345-0820
www.chan-kah.com.mx
Each room has large screened windows, comfy furnishings, and a terrace with rocking chairs. The jungly grounds, well-suited for bird-watching, have a stream-fed swimming pool. Free transportation to the nearby archaeological site.
🛏 70 P 🚭 🏊
🅿 MC, V

🏨 CALINDA INN NUTUTÚN
$
CARR. PALENQUE–OCOSINGO KM 3.5, 29960
TEL 916/345-0100
FAX 916/345-0629
Space for camping and a children's playground surround a quick-moving, elbow-shaped river that runs right through the wooded grounds of this hotel, about ten minutes outside Palenque proper. The ample but plain rooms have cable TV.
🛏 67 P 🚭 🚭 🏊
🅿 Most major cards

🏨 MAYA TULIPANES
$
CAÑADA 6, 29960
TEL 916/345-0258
FAX 916/345-1004
Simply furnished rooms have remote-control cable TV and screened windows, the

grounds are pleasant, and the management is friendly. La Cañada is a quiet neighborhood close to downtown Palenque and roadside restaurants.
🛏 48 P 🚭 🏊 🅿 AE, MC, V

🍴 MAYA
$
HIDALGO AT INDEPENDENCIA, CENTRO
TEL 916/345-0042
Legions of loyal fans frequent this plain but popular restaurant at Palenque town's main square. Seafood and regional fare are served under cooling fans; a newer and more charming location in the La Cañada neighborhood (Calle Merle Green s/n, tel 916/345-0216) serves many of the same dependable dishes.
🅿 AE, MC, V

SAN CRISTÓBAL DE LAS CASAS

🏨 PARADOR SAN JUAN DE DIOS
$$–$$$
CALZADA ROBERTA 16, COL. 31 DE MARZO, 29229
TEL/ FAX: 967/678-1167
www.sanjuandios.com
At this boutique hotel in a traditional San Cristóbal neighborhood, all of the individually and eclectically decorated rooms and suites have a fireplace and either Jacuzzi or spa tub. The lovely old republican-era converted home (and mill)—a 20-minute walk from the main plaza—is made of adobe, brick, polished wood, and stone, with traditional red tile roof.
🛏 11 P 🅿 AE, MC, V

🏨 CASA MEXICANA
$$
AV. GENERAL UTRILLA AT CALLE 28 DE AGOSTO, 29200
TEL. 967/678-0698
FAX 967/678-2627
www.hotelcasamexicana.com
Rooms in the newer hotel building are larger and lighter,

but both restored colonial buildings are full of charm. Massage and a few spa services are offered, and there's room service and a contemporary art gallery.
🛏 55 P 🚭 🅿 AE, MC, V

🍴 EL EDÉN
$–$$
CALLE 5 DE FEBRERO NO. 19
TEL 967/678-0085
Hands-down the best food in town, combining the Swiss precision of the husband, the Mexican artistry of his wife, and the personal attention of both. Come for the great steaks and margaritas; all the food is wonderful.
🅿 AE, MC, V

🍴 NA BOLOM
$
AV. VICENTE GUERRERO 33, 29200
TEL/FAX 967/678-1418
Meals are served family-style in the large dining room, and it's a treat to mingle with visiting artists and archaeologists around a shared table. The regional and international recipes are as down-home and wholesome as the setting. Dinner reservations are required for non-guests.
🕑 Closed for L 🅿 MC, V

TUXTLA GUTIERREZ

🏨🍴 CAMINO REAL
$$$
BLVD. DR. BELISARIO DOMÍNGUEZ 1195, 29060
TEL 961/617-7777, 800/722-6466
FAX 961/617-7779
www.caminoreal.com
Not surprisingly, Tuxtla's nicest hotel belongs to the classy Camino Real chain. It's sleek and modern and integrates pool, green spaces, open bars and lounge areas in a pleasing way. The gym offers sauna, steam, hot tub, and

massage. The exceptional 24-hour **Azulejos** café has a heavenly daily breakfast buffet, with many items cooked to order by a platoon of smiling chefs.

🚹 210 🔁 🔲 🖥 🔲
🖪 Most major cards

YUCATÁN PENINSULA

CAMPECHE

🏨 PUERTA CAMPECHE
$$$–$$$$
CALLE 59 NO. 71, 24000
TEL 981/816-7508, 888/625-5144
www.starwoodhotels.com
This lovely member of the Starwood group occupies an entire city block of resuscitated fine old homes. Guest rooms and public areas incorporate both traditional and innovative design elements. Bathrooms, for example, blend bright modern paint and fixtures with original stone walls and tile floors. Beds are luxurious; the small pool is filled from an ancient cistern.
🚹 15 🅿 🔲 🖥 🖪 AE, MC, V

🏨 HOTEL DEL MAR
🍴 $$
AV. RUÍZ CORTINES 51, 24000
TEL 981/811-9191
FAX 981/811-6118
www.hoteldelmar.com.mx
Despite its plain appearance and somewhat bland personality, this low-rise hotel is recommended for its many services (car rental, tour desk, Internet and business services, to name a few) and dining options. It's sandwiched between the boardwalk, perfect for an evening stroll, and the old sea gate leading to the city's heart. **Capitán LaFitte's** is Campeche's most enduring spot for a late-night drink, dinner, or dance.
🚹 146 🅿 🔁 🔲 🖥 🖥 🖪 AE, MC, V

🍴 LA PIGUA
$$
AV. MIGUEL ALEMÁN 197-A
TEL 981/811-3365
A seaside theme prevails at this longstanding favorite near the north end of town. Totally renovated in 2005, it maintains the same seaside theme and decor.
🕒 Closed D 🔲 🖪 MC, V

CANCÚN

🏨 LE MERIDIÉN CANCÚN
🍴 $$$$$
BLVD. KUKULKÁN KM 14, ZONA HOTELERA, 77500
TEL 998/881-2200, 800/543-4300
FAX 998/881-2201
www.lemeridien.com
Public areas and rooms are elegant and restrained, yet the comprehensive European-style spa is warm and inviting. Tasting menus (with optional wines) change monthly at Aioli restaurant.
🚹 213 🅿 🔁 🔲 🖥 🖥 🖪 Most major cards

🏨 HILTON CANCÚN BEACH & GOLF RESORT
$$$–$$$$
BLVD. KUKULKÁN KM 17, ZONA HOTELERA, 77500
TEL 998/881-8000, 800/774-1500
FAX 998/881-8080
www.hiltoncancun.com
This high rise hotel featues tennis courts, an 18-hole golf course, seven outdoor pools, and a comprehensive spa, beauty salon, and health club offering Pilates and yoga. All of the crisply decorated rooms and suites have views of the ocean.
🚹 426 🅿 🔁 🔲 🔲 🖥 7 🖥 🖪 AE, MC, V

🏨 EL REY DEL CARIBE
$$
AV. UXMAL AT NADER, DOWNTOWN, 77500
TEL 998/884-2028
FAX 9998/884-9857
www.reycaribe.com

Rooms with equipped kitchenettes crouch among the overgrown gardens surrounding a smallish pool and solar-heated hot tub downtown. Breakfast included; reiki, massage, and a few other treatments available.
🚹 24 🅿 🔲 🖥
🖪 MC, V

🍴 GLAZZ
$$$–$$$$
BLVD. KUKULKÁN KM 12, LA ISLA SHOPPING CENTER
998/883-1881
Hipster Glazz has several South Beach-style lounges serving champagne cocktails and other yummy drinks. Sushi and inside-out rolls are the stars of the upstairs fusion restaurant.
🅿 🕒 Closed L 🔲 🖪 MC, V

🍴 LA HABICHUELA
$$$–$$$$
CALLE MARGARITAS 25, DOWNTOWN
TEL 998/884-3158
Maya statues, candlelit patios, and splashing fountains create a romantic ambience at this downtown favorite, where couples feast on nouvelle Mexican-Caribbean cuisine such as *cocobichuela*, a curried blend of lobster and shrimp.
🔲 🖪 AE, MC, V

🍴 THAI LOUNGE
$$$–$$$$
BLVD. KUKULKÁN KM 12, LA ISLA SHOPPING CENTER
TEL 998/883-1401
When your Thai waitress tells you the house favorites, it's half the gorgeous menu. Green papaya salad, deep-fried fish, pad Thai—it's all delicious. The trendy bar's huge aquarium has captive dolphins (you might be tempted to "free Willy"). Overlooking the lagoon, it's lovely but quite buggy around sunset; ask for or bring insect repellent.
🅿 🔲 🖪 AE, MC, V

🍴 LA CASA DE LAS MARGARITAS
$$$
BLVD. KUKULKÁN KM 12,
LA ISLA SHOPPING VILLAGE,
ZONA HOTELERA
TEL 998/883-3222
A covered courtyard and second-floor balconies with perky hacienda-style decor. Live music and well-seasoned Mexican dishes.
🅿 🚭 🆎 AE, MC, V

🍴 CASA ROLANDI
$$
PLAZA CARACOL, BLVD.
KUKULCÁN KM 8.5,
ZONA HOTELERA
TEL 9/883-2557
This is another in a small series of inspired restaurants serving Italian Lake District cuisine in an elegant yet unpretentious setting. Recommended are the homemade pastas and the carpaccio. Has a covered patio, bar.
🚭 AE, MC, V

CHICHÉN ITZÁ

🏨🍴 HACIENDA CHICHÉN
$$$
CARR. MÉRIDA–PUERTO
JUÁREZ KM 120
TEL 985/851-0045, 800/624-8451
FAX 999/924-5011
www.haciendachichen.com.mx
The cottages are rustic country elegant, with handwoven bedspreads, wrought-iron bedsteads, and dehumidifiers, but no phones or TV. The ancient chapel is popular with brides and grooms, and the colossal pool beckons even when flecked with leaves from the trees that tower overhead.
🛏 28 🅿 🚭 🆎 All major cards

COBÁ

🏨🍴 VILLAS ARQUEOLÓGICAS COBÁ
$$
NEAR ENTRANCE TO RUINS
TEL 985/858-1527, 800/258-2633
FAX 985/858-1526

Run by Club Med, this simple inn is actually the fanciest place in Cobá. The rooms are a little bit stark, but the open restaurant surrounds a cool swimming pool shaded by deep pink bougainvillea. The hotel hasan excellent library and gift shop.
🅿 🚭 🆎 AE, MC, V

COSTA MAYA

🏨 COSTA DE COCOS
$$
DOMICILIO CONOCIDO,
XCALAK PENINSULA,
OFF CARRETERA 307
TEL 983/831-0110
www.costadecocos.com
Nicely done cabanas on the sand, each with a hammock in front, prove to be a magnet for snorkelers, flyfishers, and divers. The little village of Xcalak is within walking distance.
🛏 14 🆎 AE, MC, V

COZUMEL

🏨 CONDUMEL
$$–$$$
COSTERA NORTE, NORTH OF
BLVD. AEROPUERTO
TEL 987/872-0892
FAX 987/872-0661
This small condo complex is owned by one of the island's top dive-shop operators. Hammocks hang beside the living-room doors that open onto a limestone terrace above blue water. Full kitchens, huge marble bathtubs, and plush mattresses cover all that is needed for a low-key and relaxing vacation.
🛏 10 🚭 MC, V

SOMETHING SPECIAL

🏨🍴 PRESIDENTE INTER-CONTINENTAL COZUMEL
Vivid magenta and cobalt furnishings set against white walls enhance the tropical

feel of the Presidente's rooms; the suites face perfect white beaches. Tropical fish swim close to shore in a crystalline cove beneath El Caribeño restaurant, where guests linger over fresh honeydew or watermelon juice, seafood salads, and other fresh fare. There's a full-service spa onsite, and wonderful meals at dress-up, dinner-only Alfredo di Roma Italian restaurant. Some guests never leave the grounds.
$$$$$
CARR. A CHANKANAAB KM 6.5
TEL 987/872-9500, 800/327-0200
FAX 987/872-9501
www.interconti.com
🛏 253 🚭 🚭 🆎 🆎 AE, MC, V

🍴 GUIDO'S
$$–$$$
RAFAEL MELGAR 23
BETWEEN CALLES 6 AND 8
TEL 987/872-0946
Formerly called Rolandi's, this restaurant (and its vine-drenched, open-air central patio) is a local's retreat and must-do for repeat Cozumel visitors. Wood-fire pizzas, Italian seafood dishes, and homemade bread and calzone all but guarantee a great meal.
🕐 Closed Sun. 🆎 AE, MC, V

🍴 LA CHOZA
$$
R. SALAS 198 Y AV. 10 NORTE
TEL 987/872-0958
Authentic Yucatecan cuisine, served on Mexican crockery under a palm-thatch roof fulfills all dreams of a classic tropical island meal. Superb seafood, stuffed *chile rellenos*, savory marinated pork *cochinita pibil*, and fragrant cinnamon-laced coffee all tempt the senses.
🆎 AE, MC, V

ISLA MUJERES

🏨 VILLA ROLANDI
🍴 GOURMET AND BEACH CLUB
$$$$$
FRACC. LAGUNA MAR KM 7
TEL 998/877-0700
FAX 998/877-0100
www.rolandi.com
Rates at this luxurious all-suites property on a sandy cove include transportation from Cancún, continental breakfast, and lunch or dinner. Suites are fresh and modern, with natural materials and bright colors; all have wide balconies overlooking the beach with umbrella tables and Jacuzzis. Open to the sea breeze, the restaurant has a varied menu of Italian dishes.
🛏 20 🔲 🔲 🏊 🏧 AE, MC, V

IZAMAL

🏨 MANCANCHÉ
$
CALLE 22 NO. 305
BETWEEN CALLES 33 AND 35
TEL 988/954-0287
Of Izamal's few lodgings, this is definitely the most organic. Plants and trees crowd around the eclectically decorated, freestanding rooms, and healthful fare is the rule rather than the exception at the family-style restaurant.
🛏 13 🔲 🔲 🏊 🏧 No credit cards

MÉRIDA

🏨 FIESTA AMERICANA
🍴 MÉRIDA
$$–$$$
COLÓN 451 AT
PASEO MONTEJO, 97000
TEL 999/942-1111, 800/343-7821
FAX 999/942-1122
www.fiestaamericana.com
Probably the prettiest high-rise hotel in Merida, the Fiesta Americana Mérida, in the high-rent district of town on Paseo Montejo, has an elegant lobby above a mini-mall with a bus depot, shops (including Sanborns), and **Los Almendros** restaurant, which specializes in fresh regional food .
🛏 350 🔲 🔲 🔲 🔲 🏊 📺 🏧 AE, DC, MC, V

🏨 CASA DEL BALAM
$$
CALLE 60 NO. 488, 97000
TEL 999/924-8844, 800/624-8451
FAX 999/924-5011
www.yucatanadventure.com.mx
Neither too big nor too small, this centrally located hotel is on a street full of shops, just two blocks from the main square. Eat or drink in the old-fashioned open courtyard, sit in a rocking chair on the covered corridor outside your room, or just enjoy the pleasant rooms that strike a lovely balance between restored colonial and modern.
🛏 51 🔲 🔲 🔲 🏊 🏧 Most major cards

🍴 LA CASA DE FRIDA
$–$$$
CALLE 61 NO. 526
TEL 999/928-2311
Lighter, more modern versions of traditional Mexican meals are making "Frida" as well-known as its namesake. The restored house, offering mainly open patio seating, is decked out in plants, and features plenty of Frida Kahlo images and other paraphernalia of the painter's life.
🔒 Closed Sun., Mon., L 🏧 No credit cards

🍴 LOS ALMENDROS
$–$$
HOTEL FIESTA AMERICANA,
AV. COLÓN 451 AT
PROL. MONTEJO
TEL 999/942-1111
Lunch is the main meal at this well-known restaurant. Famous for its traditional Yucatecan dishes, this location is a more modern setting than the original

downtown restaurant, and popular with local businesspeople. The descriptive menu is a mini-course in Yucatecan cuisine.
🔲 🏧 AE, MC, V

PLAYA DEL CARMEN

🏨 SHANGRI-LA CARIBE
$$–$$$
CALLE 38 BETWEEN AV. 5
AND THE BEACH
TEL 984/873-0611, 800/538-6802
FAX 984/873-0500
www.shangrilacaribe.net
Comfortable and attractive bungalows dot this meandering beachfront property; the nicest ones face the lovely beach. All have twin hammocks on the patio or veranda. Breakfast and dinner are included in the price.
🛏 107 🔲 🔲 🏊 2 🏧 AE, MC, V

🏨 PELÍCANO INN
$$
CALLE 8 S/N
TEL 984/873-0997
Several sand-colored buildings front Playa's most popular beach just one block from the restaurants and shops. The

rooms have tiled floors, cool mint-green and blue fabrics, and blond wood furnishings; the beach restaurant is a popular hangout.
AE, MC, V

YAXCHE
$$–$$$
CALLE 8 BETWEEN AVENIDAS 5 AND 10
984/873-2502
The best Yucatecan food on the coast? That's what some folks say. Order a traditional Maya dish like Tikin Xic (marinated, grilled fish) or one of the chef's inventions, like the Chac Mool (shrimp in a tangerine, chile, and tomato sauce). For dessert there's flaming coffee with ice cream.
MC, V

RIVIERA MAYA

MAROMA RESORT & SPA
$$$$$
HWY. 307 KM 51
TEL 998/872-8200, 866/454-9351
FAX 998/872-8221
www.orient-expresshotels.com
Set amid a 200-acre (80 ha) jungle preserve, Maroma offers privacy, luxury, and decadent pampering. The spa has a New Age bent (crystals and yoga), the restaurant serves sublime seafood and delicious Yucatecan and Caribbean cuisine, and the guest rooms are truly artistic and architectural wonders.
P 🚭 🏊 AE, MC, V

CABAÑAS PAAMUL
$$
CARRETERA 307 KM 85, XPUHA
TEL 984/875-1051
FAX 984/875-1053
www.paamulcabanas.com
The beautiful beach and onsite dive shop are the big draws for these simple cabins without TVs or room

phones. There are campsites and an RV park as well.
🛏 20 P

TULUM

ANA Y JOSÉ HOTEL & SPA
$$–$$$
CARR. CANCUN–TULUM KM 7
TEL 998/887-5470
FAX 998/887-5469
www.anayjose.com
After more than a decade, this simple cabana-style hotel remains one of the best hideaways on the coast. The restaurant is excellent and the rooms are simple yet comfortable. Some don't face the sea, however.
🛏 22 P 🏊 AE, MC, V

UXMAL

VILLAS ARQUEOLÓGICAS UXMAL
$$
CARR. UXMAL KM 76
TEL 997/974-6020, 800/258-2633
FAX 997/976-2040
www.clubmed.com
A friendly, intimate place near the archaeological site. The rooms are comfortable but are less important than the grounds and public spaces, which include a tennis court, pool table, library, and gift shop. None of the guest rooms have TVs. The restaurant serves up a winning combination of local specialties as well as Continental cuisine.
🛏 43 P 🚭 🏊 AE, MC, V

VALLADOLID

EL MESÓN DEL MARQUÉS
$
CALLE 39 NO. 203, 97780
TEL 997/856-2073
FAX 997/856-2280
www.mesondelmarques.com

This converted hacienda has comfortable junior suites with bathtubs. Tour groups flock to the garden patio restaurant, but travelers enjoy the lovely restaurant more for the ambience than for the food.
🛏 90 P 🚭 🏊 AE

XPUJIL

CHICANNÁ ECOVILLAGE RESORT
$$
CARR. ESCÁRCEGA–CHETUMAL KM 144
TEL 981/811-9191
FAX 981/811-1618
www.delmarhotel.com
Comfortable thatch-roofed bungalows painted pastel hues, and each with a patio, wooden tables, and leather chairs, overlook flower gardens. The lodge communicates with civilization via radio (phone and fax lines are in Campeche city), but has direct TV in its library.
🛏 35 P 🏊 AE, MC, V

SHOPPING IN MEXICO

Shopping opportunities and items to buy vary greatly by region. Oaxaca and Chiapas, which have large indigenous populations, produce lovely textiles and simple but excellent pottery, among other items. From the Yucatán come colorful and comfortable string hammocks, fine Panama hats, bright embroidered blouses, and items made of cane and straw.

Mexican handicrafts are not the sole domain of the indigineous artistan. Shops and factories in Guadalajara, Michoacán, and Guanajuato use modern techniques (such as lead-free glazes) in combination with traditional forms and patterns to produce high-quality tableware and a wide variety of household accessories.

Leather goods can be purchased in northern and central Mexico. Leather jackets, belts, briefcases, boots, and shoes are a bargain.

Larger, more cosmopolitan cities have shopping centers that offer a great variety. The Sanborns chain, found throughout the county, sells gifts, music, perfumes and accessories, chocolates and pastries, and books and magazines. Cities known for their handicrafts generally have one or two streets lined with stores and boutiques. Virtually every city, town, and village has either a daily or weekly market; large cities have both. Inquire at the tourist office or hotel which is the most colorful *mercado* (also called *tianguis*) and which is the best for whatever you are seeking.

Market shopping often means you are buying from the producer or his family, and it is a fun way to see the countryside and support local artisans. Try to scout out a few midtown shops first, to be aware of prices and quality. Bartering is expected in marketplaces, although some vendors discourage it. Most, however, will start high, especially with tourists, coming down to half to three quarters of the asking price. It helps to know the value of the item you want to buy.

Markets and small shops generally don't charge tax, and most don't accept credit cards. Outside the tourist areas, some are wary even of traveler's checks. If you're buying large quantities, ask for a receipt to avoid problems with customs in your home country. The larger stores and chains do charge tax, which ranges from 12 to 15 percent Some stores will ship items you buy there as well as items purchased elsewhere. It is illegal to export archaeological artifacts from Mexico; in any case, most pieces offered for sale at archaeological sites are fakes.

The stores, malls, and markets listed below are among the best-known and most established.

BAJA CALIFORNIA

Baja has few native handicrafts. Shops in tourist enclaves—primarily Tijuana, Rosarito, Ensenada, and Los Cabos—import folk art and ceramics from mainland Mexico. The wineries in the north produce decent wines and brandies.

SHOPPING AREAS
Avenida Revolución, between 2nd and 9th Streets, and down Calle 1 to the U.S. border, Tijuana, B.C. A mixed bag of garish statuettes, bright piñatas, leather wallets and purses, silver, onyx chessboards, and more.

HANDICRAFTS
Artesanías la Antigua California, Av. Obregón 220, La Paz, B.C.S., tel 612/125-5230. A medley of handicrafts from throughout the country.
Cartes, at Plaza Bonita, Cabo San Lucas, B.C.S., tel 624/143-1770. A good selection of hand-crafted accessories, along with larger home furnishings.
Tolán, Av. Revolución 1471,

Tijuana, B.C., tel 664/688-3637. Pricey collection of good-quality folk art from throughout Mexico.

MALLS
Plaza Bonita, on the waterfront at Blvd. Marina, Cabo San Lucas, B.C.S. A handful of the nicest gift and curio shops in town.

MARKETS
Mercado Hidalgo, Avs. Sánchez Taboada and Independencia, Tijuana, B.C. Typical Mexican market a short walk from the U.S. border.

NORTHWEST MEXICO

HANDICRAFTS
Casa de las Artesanías de Chihuahua, Av. Juárez 705, Chihuahua, Chih., tel 614/437-1292.
Carries regional crafts including Tarahumara dolls, drums, clay pots, and pine-needle baskets.
Casa de las Artesanías de Chihuahua, west side of main square, Creel, Chih. tel 635/456-0080. A subsidiary of the above store; it also sells regional crafts.
El Nicho Curios, Juárez 15, across from the main square, tel 647/428-0213. Folk art and some treasures ranging from Mexican ex-votos to old jewelry.
Gallery Michael, Camarón Sábalo 19, Mazatlán, Sin., tel 669/916-7816. A floor-to-ceiling collection of well-chosen Mexican crafts, although the inventory has declined in recent years. There's a second shop in the tourist district at Av. de las Garzas 18, tel. 669/916-5511.

MARKETS
Mercado de Artesanías, Victoria 506 and Aldama, Chihuahua, Chih. A block-wide store with jewelry, candy, T-shirts, and regional crafts.
Mercado Central, between Juárez and Serdán, Mazatlán, Sin. This huge market sells produce and other food, along with handicrafts at bargain prices.
Mercado Municipal, between Avs. 20 de Noviembre and 5 de

Febrero and Calles Patoni and Pasteur, Durango, Dgo. *The* place to shop for *sarapes,* leather, and regional sweets.

Stores in the northeast sell such utilitarian products as cowboy boots, saddles, silver belt buckles, leather jackets, fine straw hats, and Saltillo's *sarapes* (bright striped blankets). Industrial Monterrey has shopping malls.

HANDICRAFTS
El Sarape de Saltillo, Hidalgo Sur 305, Saltillo, Coah., tel 844/ 412-4889. Lots of sarapes, as well as ponchos, rugs, leather, silver, copper, and pottery.

LEATHER
Botas Recio, Allende Norte 701, Saltillo, Coah., tel 844/412-1237. Men's shoes, belts, boots, and wallets of exotic leather (such as iguana, sea snake, ostrich, and shark); felt and straw hats.

MALLS & DEPARTMENT STORES
Plaza Fiesta San Agustín, Av. Real de San Agustín at Lázaro Cárdenas, Monterrey, N.L. Monterrey's largest mall, with a Sanborns restaurant/bookstore and a theater.

The central states have a tradition of fine craftsmanship. In Guanajuato state, Dolores Hidalgo is known for handpainted ceramics and tiles; Guanajuato for glassware; and San Miguel de Allende for housewares and folk art. In San Luis Potosí, buy finely woven silk shawls (*rebozos*).

HANDICRAFTS
Artes de Mexico, Calzada Aurora 47 at Dolores Hidalgo exit, San Miguel de Allende, Gto., tel 415/152-0764. This factory outlet specializes in stamped tin, but also sells other housewares.
Casa del Conde, Carr.

Guanajuato–Dolores Hidalgo Km 5, La Valenciana, Guanajuato, Gto., tel 473/732-2550. Imported from elsewhere in Mexico and custom-made housewares of tin, copper, and German silver.
Casa María Luisa, Canal 40, San Miguel de Allende, Gto., tel 415/152-0130. A huge assortment of folk art, carved furniture, and household accessories.

JEWELRY
Joyería David, Calle Zacateros 53, San Miguel de Allende, Gto., tel 415/152-0056. Silver and gold jewelry is made on the premises.

A wide variety of textiles and ceramics are produced in Michoacán and Guerrero. Jalisco, has excellent folk art, and Puerto Vallarta has a large number of shops selling fine art and handicrafts. Silver jewelry is abundant in Taxco, Guerrero.

SHOPPING AREAS
Mercado de Artesanías Turístico, Calle 5 de Mayo, at Paseo del Pescador, Zihuantanejo, Gro. A string of stands selling souvenirs, including ceramics and silver jewelry.
Plaza Los Patios, Blvd. Ixtapa s/n, Ixtapa, Gro. Probably the best of Ixtapa's small commercial centers, with several worthwhile folk-art shops.
Saturday market, Av. De los Plateros s/n, near the Flecha Roja bus terminal, Taxco. Look for the .925 stamp indicating sterling silver.

HANDICRAFTS
Agustín Parra Diseño Barroco, Independencia 158, Tlaquepaque, Jal., tel 333/657-8530. Thirty years' experience building baroque and other period furniture, accessories, frames, and other objects.
Artesanías de Jalisco, Calzadas Independencia Sur and González Gallo, Guadalajara, Jal., tel 3619-4664. Lots of locally made ceramics and blown glass.
Casa de las Artesanías, Ex-

Convento de San Francisco, Fray Juan de San Miguel at Humboldt, Morelia, Mich. Two floors of regional artifacts, each stall selling the craft made in its village.
Casa de los Artesanos, Av. de los Tonaltecas Sur 140, Tonalá, Jal., tel 33/3284-3066. Ceramics, wood, papier-mâché, blown glass, and wrought iron.
Casa de los Once Patios, Pátzcuaro, Mich., see p. 162.
Galería José Bernabe, Hidalgo 83, Tonalá, Jal., tel 3/683-0040. Don José and family continue the 200-year-old technique of *petatillo* (low-fire black and white) ceramics and modern, lead-free, high-fire dishes and crockery.
Plaza de Artesanías, Juárez 145, Tlaquepaque, Jal. A cluster of shops selling regional folk art, blown glass, and pottery.

MALLS & DEPARTMENT STORES
La Gran Plaza, Av. Vallarta 3959, Guadalajara, Jal., tel 3122-3004. A modern complex west of town, with a Sanborns shop/restaurant, cinema, and many stores and restaurants.
Plaza Bahía, Costera M. Alemán 125, Acapulco, Gro., tel 744/485-6939. A large, air-conditioned mall with bowling alley and shops.
Plaza del Sol, Avs. López Mateos Sur and Mariano Otero, Guadalajara, Jal., tel 33/3121-5950. This huge mall has green spaces, a multiplex theater, and a Sanborns in addition to many boutiques and shops.

MARKETS
Mercado Central, Diego Hurtado de Mendoza and Constituyentes, Acapulco, Gro. A bustling, typical market in downtown Acapulco.
Mercado de Dulces, Av. Madero at Gómez Farías, Morelia, Mich. Stalls selling typical sweets of the region.

Fine art galleries are found throughout the city; look in Thursday's *Tiempo Libre* section of *La Jornada* newspaper for show listings. Shopping is particularly pleasant in plein-air weekend markets in Coyoacán and San Ángel. Take extra precautions against pickpockets and muggers in Mexico City; carry no more cash than is needed and leave valuable jewelry and cameras at your hotel. Some advise against carrying ATM cards and credit cards, although this hampers unrestrained shopping.

SHOPPING AREAS
Bazar Sábado, Plaza San Jacinto 11, San Ángel, open Sat. only. Exceptional handicrafts at fair prices within the two-story mansion and outside in the adjacent plaza.
Mercado de Artesanías Insurgentes, Londrés at Amberes, Zona Rosa. A maze of handicrafts in 225 stalls.
Zona Rosa, bounded by Reforma, Niza, Av. Chapultepec, and Florencia. This compact neighborhood has many shops selling jewelry, leather, antiques, and fine art.

FINE ART & ANTIQUES
Jardín del Arte, Plaza Sullivan, Calle Sullivan near Reforma and Insurgentes. Each Saturday more than 100 artists exhibit and sell their paintings and sculptures in this city park.

HANDICRAFTS
Casa Azul, Plaza del Carmen 25, San Angel, tel. 55/5550-3223. A stunning array of art, crafts, and housewares, open daily, in a beautiful blue house.
Centro Artesanal La Ciudadela, Plaza de la Ciudadela at Balderas, tel 5510-1828. More than 300 shops selling crafts from all over Mexico.
FONART, Av. Juárez 89, tel 5521-0171. Folk art and hand-crafted furnishings; stock and selection can be variable.

MALLS & DEPARTMENT STORES
Sanborns, Madero 4, Col. Madero, tel 55/5512-1331. This coffee shop/store sells English-

language periodicals and books as well as perfumes, fresh pastries, chocolates, and gifts. (There are dozens more throughout the city.)

MARKETS
La Lagunilla, Libertad between República de Chile and Allende. Sunday outdoor flea market attracts antiques hunters and coin collectors (including pickpockets).
Mercado Xochimilco, Guerrero between Morelos and 16 de Septiembre, Xochimilco. A pleasant covered market (best on weekends) that is less hectic than those downtown.

AROUND MEXICO CITY

SHOPPING AREAS
La Calle de los Dulces, Puebla, Pue. Shops sell freshly made *camote* (sweet-potato candy) and other regional treats.

HANDICRAFTS
Mercado de Artesanías El Parían, 2 Oriente at 6 Norte, Puebla, Pue. Souvenirs, sweets, textiles, and inexpensive ceramics are sold at a covered outdoor market.
Mercado de Artesanías, *plaza principal,* Tepoztlán, Mor. Local handicrafts and those from central and southern Mexico are sold at a Wednesday and Sunday market in the main square.
Tianguis Sabado y Domingo, Plaza Xicotencatl, Morelos at Independencia, Tlaxcala, Tlax. Weekend folk-art market with typical carved wood, embroidered blouses, masks, and peach and pear liqueurs.

MARKETS
Mercado Cozme del Razo, Hidalgo at Calle 5 Norte, Cholula, Pue. Typical daily market selling handicrafts, fruits, vegetables, and clothing.

CENTRAL GULF COAST

While neither Veracruz nor Tabasco is known for its

handicrafts, both have modern, air-conditioned shopping centers in their capital cities. The region's few typical souvenirs—including items made of vegetable fiber, woven straw fans, and carved gourds—are sold mainly in hotel and museum gift shops.

SHOPPING AREAS
Zona Luz, between Calle 27 de Febrero, Zaragoza, 5 de Mayo and Madero, Villahermosa, Tab. There's nothing special to buy, but the pleasant pedestrian-only zone has pharmacies, ice-cream stores, and clothing boutiques.

MALLS & DEPARTMENT STORES
Plaza Acuario, Blvd. Ávila Camacho s/n, Playón de Hornos, Veracruz, Ver., tel 229/932-8311. Air-conditioned and near the sea, this mall has boutiques and banks but no cinema.
Tabasco 2000, Municipio Libre 7 at Prolongación Paseo Tabasco, Villahermosa, Tab. A cool, marble-lined commercial and shopping center with hotels and restaurants.

OAXACA

This state has a wealth of valuable folk art, and the city of Oaxaca boasts many worthy artists and excellent galleries.

SHOPPING AREAS
(See also box on p. 271.)

Calle Alcalá, between Avs. Independencia and Constitución, Oaxaca. A pedestrian street with many fine shops.

FINE ARTS
La Mano Mágica, M. Alcalá 203, Oaxaca, tel 951/516-4275. Wool rugs from Teotitlán del Valle, oil paintings, and high-end crafts.
Quetzalli, Constitución 104, Oaxaca, tel 951/514-2606. Excellent contemporary paintings by burgeoning and

established artists. There's a café/bar in front.

HANDICRAFTS
Artesanías Chimalli, García Vigil 513-A, Oaxaca, tel 951/514-2101. A small shop with friendly service and quality handicrafts; offers shipping.
Corazón del Pueblo, Alcalá 307, Oaxaca, tel 951/516-7181. A great selection of furnishings and folk art in two stories.
Instituto Oaxaqueño de las Artesanías, Calle Garcia Vigil 809, Oaxaca, tel 951/514-4030. Large inventory of Oaxacan crafts, including black pottery from Coyotepec, leather, straw, textiles, and clothing.
MARO, Av. 5 de Mayo 204, Oaxaca, tel 951/516-0670. Woman's co-op selling regional clothing, herbed mescal, custom-made textiles, and much more.
Mercado de Artesanías, Calle J.P. Garcia near Zaragoza, Oaxaca. Textiles and clothing exclusively are sold here, including embroidered blouses, shawls, and clothing from Tehuantepec.
Milagros Para Ti, Dr Liceaga 107, 951/501-2009, www.milagrosparati.com. A new, expanded location on the Llano Park Calle sells antiques, handcrafts, and shoes from San Miguel de Allende.

MARKETS
Mercado de Abastos, Periférico between Trujano and Minas, Oaxaca. The state's largest market is a labyrinth of stalls selling cooked food, cut flowers, and just about everything else.
Mercado Benito Juárez and Mercado 20 de Noviembre, Oaxaca, see p. 258.

CHIAPAS

The Maya have a long tradition of weaving and brocade, kept alive in some towns by local women's co-ops. You'll also find wool clothing, fabrics, wooden dolls, and lots of other intriguing items, many from Guatemala.

SHOPPING AREAS
Amatenango del Valle, 18 miles (29 km) south of San Cristóbal de las Casas. Many of the humble homes in this town sell lovely unglazed pots and pottery birds.

BOOKS, MAGAZINES & CARDS
La Pared, Av. Miguel Hidalgo 2, San Cristóbal de las Casas, tel 967/678-6367. Mostly used books, in both Spanish and English; also a small display of fine gifts.
Taller Leñateros, Flavio A. Paniagua 54, San Cristóbal de las Casas, tel 967/678-5174. Produces handmade stationery, business cards, and books from 100 percent natural and recycled materials.

HANDICRAFTS
J'pas Joloviletik, Utrilla 43, San Cristóbal de las Casas. Another great co-op with local woven, embroidered, and brocaded textiles and clothing.
Sna Jolobil, Ex-Convento de Santo Domingo, 20 de Noviembre s/n, San Cristóbal de las Casas, tel 9/678-7178. A women's co-op showcasing Maya weaving.

MARKETS
Mercado Municipal, Av. General Utrilla at Nicaragua, San Cristóbal de las Casas. A wonderful warren of candles, copal incense, produce, and hot food; the best market day is Saturday.

YUCATÁN PENINSULA

The Yucatán Peninsula in general has a surprising dearth of folk art (especially in Campeche state). What you will find are high-quality hammocks, fine Panama-style hats, embroidered *huipiles* (sacklike, lightweight women's garments), dresses, blouses, and pleated *guayabera* shirts in sherbet colors for men. The best shopping is in Mérida and Cancún.

BOOKS, MAGAZINES & CARDS
Dante's, Calle 17 No. 138-B at Prolongación Paseo de Montejo, Mérida, Yuc., tel 999/927-7676. A good selection of books, some in English, and a popular coffee shop.
Fama, Av. Tulúm 105, Cancún, Q.R., tel 998/884-6586. Books on the Yucatán Peninsula; a large selection of English-language magazines.

HANDICRAFTS
Arte Maya, Calle 23 No. 301, Ticul, Yuc., tel 997/972-1669. Expensive, museum-quality replicas of Maya archaeological pieces.
El Aguacate, Calle 58 at Calle 63, tel 999/928-6429. Nylon and cotton hammocks in many hues and sizes.

JEWELRY & CLOTHING
Guayaberas Jack, Calle 59 No. 507A, between Calles 60 and 62, 999/928-6002, www.guayaberasjack.com.mx. Excellent selection and service for many styles and colors of men's pleated dress shirts: *guayaberas.* Also some lovely women's dresses and accessories.

MALLS & DEPARTMENT STORES
La Isla Shopping Village, Blvd. Kukulkán Km 12.5, Cancún, Q.R., tel 998/883-5025. A new mall with marina, watersports, water taxi, and 200-plus shops and several wonderful restaurants.
Plaza Kukulkán, Blvd. Kukulkán Km 13, Cancún, Q.R. An upscale mall with a new UltraFemme store for duty-free cosmetics and perfume.

MARKETS
Mercado Municipal, Campeche, Camp, Calle 53 at Baluartes Este. Campeche's main market is one of the Yucatan's cleanest, best organized, and most pleasant for browsing. Surrounded by stores selling shoes and other items.

ENTERTAINMENT & ACTIVITIES

Mexicans are dedicated sports fans. Bullfights are popular, and most large cities have at least one bullring; the fights are generally scheduled to coincide with major holidays or festivals. *Charreadas* (Mexican rodeos) are a specialty of the northern states, Baja California, and Guadalajara (see p. 154), while *fútbol* (soccer) and baseball have a nationwide following. Religious holidays are generally lively affairs with food, dancing, and fireworks. Some are specific to a region or village, others are celebrated throughout the country (see pp. 16–17).

The best known **Carnaval** celebrations take place in Veracruz, Cozumel, Campeche, and Mazatlán but also happen in Guaymas, Sonora; San Juan Chamula, Chiapas; and lots of other towns. Solemn but colorful and engaging celebrations are held during **semana santa,** the week preceding Easter. Cities with especially unusual parades or customs include Oaxaca, Oaxaca; Taxco, Guerrero; Suchitlán, Colima; Real de Catorce and San Luis Potosí, San Luis Potosí; Zacatecas, Zacatecas; Zintzuntzan, Michoacán; and Zinacantán and San Juan Chamula, Chiapas.

Día de Muertos, or Day of the Dead. blends Catholic beliefs with local traditions, creating a pageant that's taken seriously but is a source of merriment and an excuse for family bonding. In the Yucatan, family members create altars to their departed relatives, spruce up family tombs, and make pit-baked tamales to symbolize the link between the living and the dead. Oaxaca state and Michoacán are well known for their rites, and although visitors generally flock to the best known towns (such as Oaxaca, Oax, and Janitzio, Michoacán), lesser known sites have their own rituals.

December 12, **Fiesta de la Virgen de Guadalupe,** is celebrated with Mass, parades, parties, regional music and dance, fireworks, and other festivities, usually for the week before the saint's day. Celebrations take place at the shrines to the Virgen at La Villa de Guadalupe, north of Mexico City; in Tamazunchale, San Luis Potosí; Tuxtla Gutiérrez and San Cristóbal de las Casas, Chiapas; and in other towns.

Following is a listing of Mexico's most important festivals, cultural centers, and activities, by region. Nightclubs and bars mentioned here are only the most interesting or historically important. Check with your hotel concierge or tourist information staff, or the local newspaper listings, for other evening entertainment.

BAJA CALIFORNIA

BARS
Hussong's Cantina, Av. Ruiz 113, Ensenada, B.C., tel 646/178-3210. Popular for over a century.

WINERIES
Bodegas de Santo Tomás, Av. Miramar 666, Ensenada, B.C., tel. 646/174-0836. Tastings ($) are normally at 11, 1, and 3.

BULLFIGHTS
El Toreo, Blvd. Agua Caliente s/n, 2 miles (3 km) east of downtown, Tijuana, B.C., tel 664/686-1510. The season runs from April through Oct.
Plaza Monumental, Av. del Pacífico 1, Fracc. Playas de Tijuana, Tijuana, B.C., tel 664/686-1219, www.bullfights.org. The season runs from May through Sept.

CHARREADAS
Held most weekends May–Sept. Venues vary; call Tijuana Tourism Office, tel 664/658-2210 or 800/310-9687 from the U.S.

CULTURAL CENTERS
Centro Cívico, Social y Cultural, Blvd. Costero at Av. Club Rotario, Ensenada, B.C., tel 6/177-0594. A gallery, museum, and gardens.
Centro Cultural Tijuana, Paseo de los Heroes and Mina, Tijuana, B.C., tel 664/687-9600, www.cecut.gob.mx. History, anthropology, and art museums, theater, gift shop, and restaurant.

FESTIVALS
Fiesta de la Vendemia, Ensenada, B.C., tel 646/178-8588. Wine tastings and cultural events hosted each Aug.
Fiesta de San Javier, Misión San Javier, B.C.S., Dec. 3.

SPORTING EVENTS
Bisbee's Black and Blue Marlin Tournament, Los Cabos, B.C.S., www.bisbees.com. Three days in Oct., with a million-dollar purse.
SCORE Baja 250, 500 and 1000: Grueling off-road desert races in March, May/June, and Oct./ Nov., respectively. www.score-international.com.
The **Newport Beach-Ensenada Sailing Regatta** has been held each April for more than 50 years. www.nosa.org Thousands participate in the **Rosarito-Ensenada 50-Mile Fun Bicycle Ride** held each April and Sept. Call Bicycling West at 858/483-8777 (U.S.) or see www.rosaritoensenada.com.

SPORTFISHING
World-class fishing in Bahía de Los Angeles, Los Cabos, the East Cape, La Paz, Loreto, Mulegé, and San Felipe. On the Pacific, fish in Ensenada and San Quintín Bay.

WATERSPORTS
The sheltered Gulf of California (Sea of Cortez) is preferred for **kayaking,** especially around Bahía de Concepción, Loreto, the East Cape, La Paz, Cabo San Lucas, and many offshore islands. Pacific coast **sailboarding** sites include Punta San Carlos; Punta Abreojos; and San Quintín, Magdalena, Santa Rosaliita, and Almejas bays; on the gulf, try Bahía de Los Angeles, Punta Chivato, Loreto, and the East Cape.

Diving and **snorkeling** are popular off Cabo Pulmo and the sand falls at Cabo San Lucas. **Surfing** is popular but rentals rare. Get surf conditions through the Baja Safari Travel Club (Tel

888/411-2252). Northern Baja's best surfing is during the winter.

Baja Expeditions, 2625 Garnet Ave. San Diego, CA, tel 858/581-3311 or 800/843-6967, www.bajaex.com, is a well-respected company offering island kayaking and scuba diving trips.

WHALE WATCHING
The season is from Jan. through mid-April (see pp. 68–69).

NORTHWEST MEXICO

CULTURAL CENTERS & THEATERS
Centro Cultural de Chihuahua, Ocampo at Aldama, Chihuahua, Chih., tel 614/416-1230. Music, dance, art exhibits.
Teatro Angela Peralta, Carnaval 47, Mazatlán, Sin. Folk dances and cultural events.

FESTIVALS
Navy Day, Puerto Peñasco (Rocky Point) and Guaymas, Son., June 1. Boat parades, mock naval battles, fireworks, beauty contests.
La Feria de la Fundación de Durango and la Feria Agrícola, Durango, Dur., two weeks in mid-July. Consecutive fairs celebrate the city's founding and agriculture and ranching. Music, folk dances, cockfights, horse races, and charreadas.
Fiesta de la Fundación del Pueblo, El Fuerte, Sin. Feast honoring the town's founding, Nov. or early Dec. Carnival rides, foot races, folk dancing.
Ortiz Tirado Music Festival, last two weeks in Jan. Classical music festival in Alamos, Sonora.

SPORTFISHING
Mazatlán, Sin. Sportfishing fleets line the harbor south of town; prices for day charters are similar.

NORTHEAST MEXICO

CULTURAL CENTERS & THEATERS
Centro Cultural Teatro Garcia Carrillo, Allende at Aldama,

Saltillo, Coah. Porfiriato structure hosting concerts and cultural expositions.
Teatro de la Ciudad de Monterrey, Zuazua at Matamoros, Monterrey, N.L., tel 81/343-8974. Large, modern theater.

FESTIVALS
Feria Cultural de Zacatecas, Zac. Cultural programs are planned to coincide with Easter week festivities.
Feria Nacional, Zacatecas, Zac., first two weeks of Sept. Livestock and agriculture exhibitions, bullfights, cultural events.
La Morisma, Zacatecas, Zac., end of Aug. Festival includes a three-day reenactment of a battle between Moors and Christians, plays, and indigenous dancing.
Fiesta de San Isidro Labrador. This holy day, May 15, is celebrated in Jalpán, Querétaro, with fireworks, Mass, music and dance, and a colorful procession.
Fiesta de San Roque. In Querétaro, Qto., the days before Aug. 16 are feted with parades, fireworks, and traditional dances.

FISHING
Freshwater fishing (bass, catfish) in Caballero, Méndez, Vicente Guerrero, and other lakes, surf-casting along the coastal lagoons.

CENTRAL MEXICO

CULTURAL CENTERS & THEATERS
Centro Cultural El Nigromante (or Bellas Artes), Hernandez Macias 75, San Miguel de Allende, Gto., tel 415/152-0289. Arts and crafts classes and cultural events.
Instituto Allende, Ancha de San Antonio 20, San Miguel de Allende, Gto., tel 415/152-0190. Cultural center with galleries, library, and theater; offers Spanish-language and art classes.
Teatro de la Paz, Segunda de Villerías, Jardín del Carmen, San Luis Potosí, S.L.P., tel 444/812-2698. Elegant neoclassic theater.
Teatro Juárez, Calle de Sopena, at Jardín Unión, Guanajuato, Gto.,

tel 473/732-0183. Symphony, opera, and other performances at a lovely Porfiriato-era theater.

FESTIVALS
Feria del Queso y del Vino, Tequisquiapan, Qto., tel 414/273-0295. mid-July. Wine and cheese festival with outdoor theater, folk dancing, concerts, and bullfights.
Feria de San Marcos, Aguascalientes, Ags., tel 449/915-1155, second Saturday of April to first Sunday of May. Mexico's largest and oldest state fair, with cultural events, cockfights, dances, bullfights, and fireworks.
Festival Cervantino, Guanajuato, Gto., tel 473/731-2920, fall. International cultural event; world-class performers.
Fiesta de San Miguel, San Miguel de Allende, Gto., tel 415/152-6565. Traditional dancing, bullfights, fireworks, and concerts culminating at dawn on Sept. 29.

SPELUNKING
Sotano de las Golondrinas, outside the town of Tancanhuitz, east of San Luis Potosí (164 miles/264 km from Ciudad Valle), S.L.P. One of the world's most fascinating spelunking caverns.

CENTRAL PACIFIC STATES

BUTTERFLY MIGRATION
Millions of monarchs winter in Michoacán forest sanctuaries; see p. 176.

CULTURAL CENTERS
Instituto Cultural Cabañas, Guadalajara, Jal., see p. 148.

DANCING & SHOWS
Ballet Folklórico, Teatro Degollado, Calle Degollado between Morelos and Hidalgo, Guadalajara, Jal., tel 33/3616-4991. Regional dances by university troupe Sundays, 10 a.m.
Charreadas, Lienzo Charro de Jalisco, Av. Dr. R. Michel 577, Guadalajara, Jal., tel 33/3619-0315. Mariachi music and superior horsemanship on Sundays, noon.
Espectáculo de la Quebrada, Plazoleta de la Quebrada,

ENTERTAINMENT & ACTIVITIES

Acapulco, Gro., tel 762/483-1400. Cliff divers perform throughout the day, and at night to a dinner, dancing, and music spectacle from La Perla Restaurant at El Mirador.
La Plaza de los Mariachis, Calz. Independencia Sur between Obregón and Mina, Guadalajara, Jal. Mariachis play all night, but most visitors feel safer earlier.
Salon Q, Av. Costera Alemán 3117, Col. Costa Azul, Acapulco, Gro., tel 744/481-0114. Dancing to live salsa and tropical music Wed.–Sun. after 10 p.m.

FESTIVALS

Chapala "carnival," first weekend in March. Unlike the celebration preceding Easter, this event showcases folkloric performances, with food stands.
Encuentro Internacional del Mariachi y la Charrería, Guadalajara, Jal., end Aug./ beginning Sept. A week of charro events and mariachi music.
Feria de la Guitarra, Paracho, Mich., Aug. Competitions, concerts, and display of handcrafted stringed instruments.
Feria de Manzanillo, Colima. April 29–May 1. The town's anniversary is celebrated with dances, music, and rodeos.
Feria de Michoacán, Morelia, Mich., first weeks of May. Typical state fair, with rides, expos, and cultural and music events.
Feria Nacional de la Cerámica. June 15 to July 2. Exhibit, competition, and sale of regionally produced ceramics in Tlaquepaque, Jalisco, just outside Guadalajara. June 29 is also a **Fiesta de San Pedro** (Feast of St. Peter).
Festival Internacional del Organo, Morelia, Mich., tel 443/317-2371, May. International pipe-organ festival held for more than 30 years at the cathedral.
Fiesta de San Antonio Abad, January 17, Taxco, Gro. Pets and domestic animals are dressed in costumes for the priest's blessing at Iglesia de Santa Prisca.
Fiesta de la Virgen de la Salud & La Virgen de la Candelaria in Colima, Colima. Nine days of events culminating Feb. 2, on Candlemas. Other

events—including masked dances —lead up to this date in Suchitlán, Colima, just outside the capital.
Fiestas de Mayo, Puerto Vallarta, Jal., May. A month of art exhibits, music, fireworks, and general merrymaking.
Fiestas de Octubre, Guadalajara, Jal., tel 33/3668-1600, www.fiestasdeoctubre.com.mx, throughout Oct. Mariachis and charreadas, opera, symphony, and arts exhibits.
Fiesta de San Ysidro, Tepic, Nay., several weeks ending May 15. Agricultural fair during which seeds and animals are blessed.
Maundy Thursday, colorful processions are held in Tzintzuntzán, Michoacán.

MEXICO CITY

Tiempo Libre, published in Spanish on Thursdays in the Spanish-language newspaper *Reforma,* lists cultural events and gallery shows, as does the English-language daily *Miami Herald.*

BARS

La Guadalupana, Higuera 14, Coyoacán, tel. 55/5554-6253, is a traditional watering hole with a mainly masculine clientele.
L'Opera, Cinco de Mayo 10 at Mata, tel 55/5512-8959. Historic cantina with period decor, still popular for food and drink.

BULLFIGHTS

Plaza Mexico, Rodin 241 at Holbein, Col. Napoles, tel 5563-3961. Fights takes place Thursday and Sunday at 4:30 p.m. for much of the year in the world's largest bullring. Contact Ticketmaster (Tel 55/5325-9000) or your hotel concierge.

CULTURAL CENTERS & THEATERS

Auditorio Nacional, Paseo de la Reforma 50, Parque de Chapultepec, tel 55/5280-9250. An enormous venue with great acoustics holding mostly music and theater events.
Palacio de Bellas Artes, Av. Juárez and Eje Central, Alameda

Park, tel 55/5521-3633. Folkloric ballets on Wednesday and Sunday evenings and Sunday mornings, as well as symphony, opera, and other performances.
Sala Nezahualcoyotl, Insurgentes Sur 3000, Ciudad Universitaria, tel 55/5622-7112. All types of music and theatrical events. Excellent acoustics.

FESTIVALS

Blessing of the Animals, Cathedral, Jan. 17. Pets and working animals are ceremonially blessed.
Festival Centro Histórico. The three-week cultural festival each April offers a range of musical performances, flamenco ballet, and guided visits to some of the city's lesser-known cultural sites.
Fiesta de la Virgen del Carmen, July 16, is celebrated in San Angel with fireworks, dances, and a traditional fair.

AROUND MEXICO CITY

CULTURAL CENTERS

Centro Cultural de Hidalgo, Arista at Casasola, Pachuca, Hgo., tel 7/111-4150. Houses the City Theater and school of art, museums, gardens, and plazas.

ENTERTAINMENT

Free outdoor band concerts Sunday afternoons, Jardín Juárez, Cuernavaca, Mor.

Flower Fair, Cuernavaca, Mor., Beginning of April. Gardening exhibits and competitions; entertainment.

FESTIVALS

Cinco de Mayo, Puebla, Pue., May 5. Colorful festivities mark this victorious battle against French invaders.
Festival de Nopales, Tlaxcalancingo, Pue., April. Just outside Puebla, Tlaxcalancingo celebrates the prickly-pear cactus with a food fair.
Fiesta de la Asunción, Huamantla, Tlax., Aug. 14. Bull-running through the streets for La Noche que Nadie Duerme (The Night When No One Sleeps).

Fiesta de Hidalgo, Pachucha, Hgo., first two weeks of Oct. Hidalgo state fair.
Fiesta de Tepoztlán, Tepoztlán, Mor., early Sept. Celebration of the Nativity of the Virgin and of the Aztec god Tepoztecatl.

SPAS & WATER PARKS
Morelos state is known for its thermal springs around which water parks (see Las Estacas, p. 371) and resort spas have grown; contact Cuernavaca tourist board (Tel 777/314-3872) for details or www.cuernavaca.gob.mx.

CENTRAL GULF COAST

CULTURE
Folkloric ballet and state orchestral performances are held at El Teatro del Estado, Ignacio de la Llave at Ávila Camacho, Xalapa, Ver., tel 228/817-3110.

FESTIVALS
Carnaval, Veracruz, Ver., week before Lent. Parades and partying begin with the ceremonial Burning of Bad Humor and climax on Shrove Tuesday (Mardi Gras).
Día de la Candelaria, Tlacotalpán, Ver., early Feb. A colorful Candlemas festival with bulls running through the streets and riverboat processions.
Fiesta de Corpus Cristi, Papantla, Ver., movable feast, usually in April. Fireworks, parades, cockfights; traditional dances and performances.
Fiesta de Santiago Apóstle, Santiago Tuxtla, Ver., July 25. Native dances and fiesta in celebration of patron St. James the Apostle.

OAXACA

BOAT TOURS
Santa Cruz Bay, Bahías de Huatulco. Visit the nine bays, disembarking at one or more.

FESTIVALS
Bendición de los Animales, Oaxaca, Aug. 31. The Blessing of pets and farm animals at La Merced church.

Fiesta de las Velas, Isthmus of Tehuantepec, late spring through early fall, primarily in May. Ancient celebrations honoring religious and secular events with lively parties. Contact Oaxaca tourist board for dates.
Guelaguetza, Cerro del Fortín, Oaxaca, generally first two Mondays after July 16. Traditional folk dancing from Oaxaca's seven regions at a hilltop amphitheater.
La Noche de Rábanos, *zócalo*, Oaxaca, Dec. 23. Contestants make tableaux of carved radishes.

FOLK DANCING/DINNER SHOWS
Hotel Camino Real, Oaxaca. Folkloric shows in one of the covered stone patios.

CHIAPAS

CULTURAL CENTERS & THEATERS
Teatro Hermanos Domínguez, Diagonal Hermanos Paniagua s/n, San Cristóbal de las Casas, tel 967/678-3637. Theater hosting music and dance performances.

FESTIVALS
Fiestas de Enero, during two weeks of mid-Jan. Chiapa de Corzo has masked parades, dances, street festivities, mock naval battles, and fireworks.

Celebrations in Zinacantán include la **Fiesta de San Sebastian,** Jan. 20–22; Fridays during Lent; Easter; and Carnaval.

San Juan Chamula has colorful fiestas for Carnaval, Easter, and la Fiesta de San Juan (June 22–24).

TOURS
Visit villages outside San Cristóbal de las Casas on horse tours through area tour operators.

YUCATÁN PENINSULA

CULTURAL CENTERS
Casa de la Cultura, Prol. Av. Yaxchilán SM 25, Cancún, Q.R., tel

998/884-8364, www.casa culturacancun.gob.mx. Sponsors theater, music, conferences, and other activities.
Teatro Peón Contreras, Calle 60 between Calles 57 and 59, Mérida, Yuc., tel 999/924-9290. music and dance performances.

DIVING/SCUBA
Aqua World, Blvd. Kukulcán Km 15.3, Cancún, Q.R., tel 998/848-8327. Full-service aquatic center; game fishing, diving, party boats.
Cozumel Association of Dive Operators, Cozumel, Q.R., tel 9/872-5955. Recommends dive and snorkel guides and operators.

ENTERTAINMENT
Noche Mexicana, Paseo Montejo at Calle 47 and throughout downtown, Mérida, Yuc., Sat. 7:30–11 p.m. Weekly street party including folk dancing, music, crafts, and food.
Sound and light shows, after dark at Chichén Itzá, Uxmal, and the Convento San Antonio de Padua, Izamal, Yuc.; also la Puerta de Tierra, Campeche, Camp.

FESTIVALS
Fiestas del Equinoxio, Templo de Kukulkán, Chichén Itzá, Yuc., first days of spring and fall. At both the spring and fall equinoxes, a serpent-like shadow descends the pyramid to align with the stone snake's head at the bottom.
Festival de Jazz, Cancún, Q.R., late May. A week of jazz performances in various venues.
Festival Internacional de Aves, to the delight of birders, is held each November in and around Mérida for exhibits and lectures, a bird-counting contest, dinners, and of course, birding expeditions
Hanal Pixan, Mérida, Yuc., the days preceding Nov. 2. Traditional food and altars from around the state for Day of the Dead celebrations.
Otoño Cultural, Mérida, Yuc., last week of Oct. through first week of Nov. Autumn Cultural Festival with classical music, dance, and art exhibitions.

LANGUAGE GUIDE

GENERAL
yes; *sí*
no; *no*
please; *por favor*
thank you; *gracias*
you're welcome; *de nada*
hello, hi; *hola*
goodbye; *adiós, hasta luego*
good day; *buenos días*
good afternoon; *buenas tardes*
good evening/goodnight; *buenas noches*
OK; *está bien/de acuerdo*
today; *hoy*
yesterday; *ayer*
tomorrow; *mañana*
Do you speak English?; *¿Habla usted inglés?*
I am from the U.S.; *Soy norteamericano/a*
I don't understand; *No entiendo*
Please speak more slowly; *Hable más despacio, por favor*
What is its/your name?; *¿Cómo se llama?*
My name is...; *Yo me llamo...*
Let's go; *Vamos*
At what time?; *¿A qué horas?*

HELP
I need a doctor/dentist; *Necesito un médico/dentista*
Can you help me?; *¿Me puede ayudar?*
Where is a hospital/clinic?; *¿Dónde hay un hospital/una clínica?*
Help!; *¡Socorro!*

SHOPPING
I'd like...; *Quisiera...*
How much is it?; *¿Cuánto es?*
That's very expensive; *Es muy caro*
Do you take credit cards?; *¿Acepta tarjetas de crédito?*
size; *el talle*
receipt; *el recibo/la nota*
bakery; *la panadería*
bookstore; *la librería*
market; *el mercado/tianguis*
pharmacy; *la farmacia*
shopping mall; *el centro comercial*
supermarket; *el supermercado*

SIGHTSEEING
visitor information; *información turística*
open; *abierto/a*
closed; *cerrado/a*
church; *la iglesia*
cathedral; *la catedral*
country estate; *la hacienda*
museum; *el museo*
tour; *el tour*
town; *el pueblo*
city; *la ciudad*

IN THE HOTEL
Do you have...?; *¿Hay...?*
single room; *una habitación sencilla*
double room; *una habitación doble*
with/without; *con/sin*
bathroom/view; *baño/vista*

IN THE RESTAURANT
menu; *el menú/la carta*
breakfast; *el desayuno*
lunch (main meal); *la comida*
dinner; *la cena*
check; *la cuenta*
takeout; *para llevar*
fixed-price meal; *el menú del día*
a la carte; *a la carta*
vegetarian food; *comida vegetariana*

MENU READER

See also "Food & drink," pp. 18–21.

appetizer; *el antojito*
bread; *el pan*
soup (broth); *la sopa*
soup (cream); *la crema*
salad; *la ensalada*
main course; *el plato principal*
vegetable; *verdura/vegetal*
rice; *(sopa de) arroz*
bean soup; *sopa de frijol*
refried beans; *frijoles refritos*
dessert; *el postre*
spicy; *picante*
beer; *la cerveza*
coffee; *el café*
American-style coffee; *café americano*
Mexican-stye (sweet) coffee; *café de olla*
decaffeinated coffee; *descafeinado*
tea; *el té*
milk; *la leche*
mineral water; *el agua mineral*
ice; *el hielo*
purified water; *el agua purificada*
soft drink; *refresco*
lemonade/orangeade; *limonada/naranjada*
wine; *vino*
apéritif; *aperitivo*
Cheers!; *¡Salud!*
meat; *la carne*
beef; *la carne de res*
pork; *el puerco*
goat; *la cabra/el chivo*
turkey; *el guajolote/pavo*
chicken; *el pollo*
fish; *el pescado*
lobster; *langosta*
octopus; *pulpo*
shrimp; *camarón*
squid; *calamar*

ILLUSTRATIONS CREDITS

Abbreviations for terms appearing below: (t) top; (b) bottom; (l) left; (r) right

Cover: (l), Gettyone/Stone. (c), Images Colour Library. (r), Larry Dunmire. Spine: Gettyone/Stone.
1, Suzanne Murphy-Larronde; 2/3, National Geographic Society/Tomasz Tomaszewski; 4, Robert Holmes Photography; 9, Mireille Vautier; 11, Suzanne Murphy-Larronde; 12/13, Streano/Havens/Trip & Art Directors Photo Library; 14, Suzanne Murphy-Larronde; 15, National Geographic Society/Tomasz Tomaszewski; 16/17, National Geographic Society/Stuart Franklin; 19, Brian McGilloway/Robert Holmes Photography; 20, Rick Strange/AA Photo Library; 21, Nik Wheeler/Corbis UK Ltd.; 23, Suzanne Murphy-Larronde; 24/25, Gianni Dagli Orti/Corbis UK Ltd.; 26/27, Robert Frerck/Gettyone/Stone; 28, AKG- London; 29, Bridgeman Art Library/London; 30/31, Bridgeman Art Library/London; 32, AKG - London; 33, Mireille Vautier; 34/35, Hulton Getty; 36/37, National Geographic Society/ Tomasz Tomaszewski; 39, Isabella Tree/Hutchison Library; 40, Viesti Collection/Trip & Art Directors Photo Library; 41, Tony Morrison/South American Pictures; 42/43, Robert Frerck/Robert Harding Picture Library; 44, Dave G. Houser/Corbis UK Ltd.; 45, Charles & Josette Lenars/Corbis UK Ltd.; 46/47, National Geographic Society/Stuart Franklin; 48/49, Jamie Carstairs; 50/1, Danny Lehman/Corbis UK Ltd.; 52, Sergio Dorantes/Corbis UK Ltd.; 53, James Davis Worldwide; 54, Tom Bean/Gettyone/Stone; 55, David Sanger; 56, Mireille Vautier; 57, Edward Parker/Hutchison Library; 58, Robert Holmes Photography/AA Photo Library; 59, Stuart Wasserman; 60t, James Davis Worldwide; 60b, Lee Foster; 61, Robert Holmes Photography; 62, Robert Holmes Photography/Corbis UK Ltd.; 63, Robert Holmes Photography; 64, David Muench/Corbis UK Ltd.; 65, Robert Frerck/Robert Harding Picture Library; 66/67, Nik Wheeler; 68, Streano/Havens/ Trip & Art Directors Photo Library; 69, Stuart Westmorland/Corbis UK Ltd.; 70/71, Mike Brinson/Getty Images; 71, Richard Cummins/CORBIS; 72, David Sanger; 73, Robert Holmes Photography/ AA Photo Library; 74, Robert Holmes Photography/Corbis UK Ltd.; 75, Mireille Vautier; 76, Robert Cundy/Robert Harding Picture Library; 78, National Geographic Society/Joanna Pinneo; 79, Lee Foster; 80, Patricio Robles Gil/Sierra Madre; 81, Markham Johnson/Robert Holmes Photography; 82, Eleanor S. Morris; 83, Markham Johnson/Robert Holmes Photography; 82, VISOR S.A; 83tl, Patricio Robles Gil/Sierra Madre; 83tr, Patricio Robles Gil/Sierra Madre; 85b, Lynsey Addario/ CORBIS; 86, Robert Francis/South American Pictures; 87, Nik Wheeler; 89, National Geographic Society/Phil Schermeister; 90, National Geographic Society/Joe McNally; 91, Markham Johnson/Robert Holmes Photography; map by National Geographic Maps; 92, MacDuff Everton/CORBIS; 92/93, John Elk III/Elk Photo; 94t, Robert Aberman; 94b, Robert Frerck/ Odyssey/ Chicago/Robert Harding Picture Library; 95, Ernesto Rios/VISOR S.A; 96/97, Robert Frerck/Gettyone/Stone; 98/99, Larry Dunmire; 100, Jan

Butchofsky-Houser/ Corbis UK Ltd.; 101, Kevin Schafer/Corbis UK Ltd.; 103, Robert and Linda Mitchell; 104, National Geographic Society/George Grall; 106, Rick Strange/AA Photo Library; 107, National Geographic Society/George Grall; 109, Adalberto Rios/VISOR S.A; 110, Alex Webb/Magnum Photos; 111, Patricio Robles Gil/Sierra Madre; 113, Robert Francis/South American Pictures; 114, Scott L. Walker; 115, Patricio Robles Gil/ASierra Madre; 116, Robert Frerck/ Odyssey/ Chicago/Robert Harding Picture Library; 117, Suzanne Murphy-Larronde; 118, Isabella Tree/Hutchison Library; 120/121, National Geographic Society/ David Alan Harvey; 122, Eleanor S. Morris; 123, David Sanger; 124, Suzanne Murphy-Larronde; 125, Danny Lehman/Corbis UK Ltd.; 126, Iain Pearson/South American Pictures; 128, VISOR S.A; 129t, Iain Pearson/South American Pictures; 129c, Clotilde Lechuga/VISOR S.A; 129b, Corbis UK Ltd.; 130, Mireille Vautier; 131, Rick Strange/AA Photo Library; 133, Adalberto Rios//VISOR S.A; 134, Stuart Wasserman; 135, Peter Wilson/AA Photo Library; 136, John Bartholomew/Corbis UK Ltd.; 137, Diana Dicker; 139, Brian McGilloway/ Robert Holmes Photography; 140, Danny Lehman/Corbis UK Ltd.; 141, National Geographic Society/Maggie Steber; 142, Danny Lehman/Corbis UK Ltd.; 143, James Davis Worldwide; 144/145, Larry Dunmire; 146, Adina Tovy Amsel/Eye Ubiquitous; 148/149, Rick Strange/AA Photo Library; 151, Jeffrey Greenberg/ Alamy; 152, Suzanne Murphy-Larronde; 153, Royalty Free/CORBIS; 154, Stuart Wasserman; 155t, Danny Lehman/Corbis UK Ltd.; 155b, Suzanne Murphy-Larronde; 156/157, Roger Ressmeyer/Corbis UK Ltd.; 158, Adalberto Rios/Mireille Vautier; 159, Robert and Linda Mitchell; 160, Rick Strange/AA Photo Library; 161, Suzanne Murphy-Larronde; 162/163, National Geographic Society/David Alan Harvey; 164, Isabella Tree/Hutchison Library; 165, Tony Morrison/South American Pictures; 166/167, Robert Frerck/Gettyone/Stone; 168/169, Larry Dunmire; 171, Kelly-Mooney Photography/Corbis UK Ltd.; 173, Philip Enticknap/Travel Library; 174/175, National Geographic Society/ Sisse Brimberg; 177, David Sanger; 179, Chris Sharp/South American Pictures; 180, Picturesque Inc./Trip & Art Directors Photo Library; 181, Mireille Vautier; 182/183, Robert Frerck/Gettyone/Stone; 184, Bridgeman Art Library/London; 185t, Bridgeman Art Library/London; 185b, Bridgeman Art Library/London; 186, Nik Wheeler; 187, Danny Lehman/CORBIS; 189, Rick Strange/AA Photo Library; 190, Guy Marks/Travel Ink; 191, Macduff Everton/Corbis UK Ltd.; 192, David Sanger; 193, Mireille Vautier; 196, Carlos Reyes-Manzo/Andes Press Agency; 197, Rick Strange/AA Photo Library; 198b, Carlos Reyes-Manzo/Andes Press Agency; 199, Robert Aberman; 200c, Carlos Reyes-Manzo/Andes Press Agency; 200bl, Carlos Reyes-Manzo/Andes Press Agency; 200br, Carlos Reyes-Manzo/Andes Press Agency; 203, Kelly-Mooney Photography/Corbis UK Ltd.; 204/205, Carlos Reyes-Manzo/ Andes Press Agency; 205, Bettmann/Corbis UK Ltd.; 207, M Barlow/Trip & Art Directors Photo Library; 208, Nik Wheeler; 209, Rick Strange/AA Photo Library; 211, Robert Frerck/Gettyone/Stone; 212, Clotilde Lechuga/VISOR S.A; 214, Robert Frerck/Odyssey Productions Inc.; 215, Rick Strange/AA Photo Library; 216, Suzanne Murphy-Larronde; 217tr, VISOR S.A;

217bl, Ask Images/Trip & Art Directors Photo Library; 218, Tony Morrison/South American Pictures; 219, National Geographic Society/Sisse Brimberg; 220, Robert Cundy/Robert Harding Picture Library; 221, J Greenberg/ Trip & Art Directors Photo Library; 222, Nik Wheeler/Corbis UK Ltd.; 223, Stuart Wasserman; 224, Iain Pearson/South American Pictures; 225, AKG - London; 226/227, Jonathan Blair/Corbis UK Ltd.; 228, National Geographic Society/Kenneth Garrett; 229, National Geographic Society/Kenneth Garrett; 230, Rick Strange/AA Photo Library; 231, VISOR S.A; 232, VISOR S.A; 233, National Geographic Society/National Museum of Anthropology, Mexico City; 235, Susan Kaye; 236, AM Corporation/Alamy; 237, Diana Dicker; 238/239, Chris Sharp/South American Pictures; 240, Robert Frerck/ Odyssey Productions, Inc.; 241, Jamie Carstairs; 243t, Museo de America, Madrid, Spain/Bridgeman Art Library/ London; 243c, Rick Strange/AA Photo Library; 243b, Dave G. Houser/Corbis UK Ltd.; 244, Edward Parker/Hutchison Library; 245, Mireille Vautier; 246/247, National Geographic Society/Kenneth Garrett; 247, Jamie Carstairs; 248/249, John Elk III/Elk Photo; 250, National Geographic Society/Kenneth Garrett; 253, Suzanne Murphy-Larronde; 255, Kelly-Mooney Photography/Corbis UK Ltd.; 256, Jill Ranford/Ffotograff; 257, R Powers/Trip & Art Directors Photo Library; 258, Cri Rodriguez/VISOR S.A; 259, Isabella Tree/Hutchison Library; 260/261, Robert Frerck/Gettyone/Stone; 262t, Macduff Everton/Corbis UK Ltd.; 262b, Mireille Vautier; 264/265 Michael Macintyre/Hutchison Library; 266, Macduff Everton/Corbis UK Ltd.; 267tl, Edward Parker/Hutchison Library; 267c, Lee Foster; 267b, Steve Watkins/AA Photo Library; 268, Dave G. Houser/Corbis UK Ltd.; 269, Danny Lehman/CORBIS; 270, Mireille Vautier; 271, Mireille Vautier; 272, Mireille Vautier; 273t, David Alan Harvey/ Magnum Photos; 273b, National Geographic Society/David Alan Harvey; 275, Suzanne Murphy-Larronde; 276, David Alan Harvey/Magnum Photos; 278/279, National Geographic Society/ David Alan Harvey; 280, Isabella Tree/ Hutchison Library; 281, Jeremy Horner/ Hutchison Library; 282, Mireille Vautier; 284, Susan Kaye; 285, Rick Strange/AA Photo Library; 286/287, H Elton/Axiom Photographic Agency Ltd; 288, Mireille Vautier; 289, Robert Frerck/Robert Harding Picture Library; 290/291, National Geographic/Kenneth Garrett; 292, Clotilde Lechuga/ VISOR S.A; 293b, Ken McLaren/Trip & Art Directors Photo Library; 294, Danny Lehman/Corbis UK Ltd.; 295tl, Richard Glover/Corbis UK Ltd.; 295tr, Iain Pearson/South American Pictures; 295b, E. Hawkins/Eye Ubiquitous; 296, Isabella Tree/Hutchison Library; 298/299, Danny Lehman/ CORBIS; 300, National Geographic Society/Otis Imboden; 302, Mireille Vautier; 303, Fabienne Fossez/ Ffotograff; 304, Charles & Josette Lenars/Corbis UK Ltd.; 305, Robert Leon; 306, Patricio Robles Gil/Sierra Madre; 307, Adalberto Rios Szalay/VISOR S.A; 308, Larry Dunmire/ The Paradise Library; 310, Danny Lehman/CORBIS; 311, Philip Coblentz/ Getty Images; 312, Susan Kaye; 313t, Susan Kaye; 313c, Larry Dunmire/The Paradise Library; 313b, T Bognar/Trip & Art Directors Photo Library; 314, Alison Wright/Corbis UK Ltd.; 314/315, Rick Strange/AA Photo Library; 317, DDB

Stock Photo; 318t, Caroline Garside/Trip & Art Directors Photo Library; 318b, World Pictures Ltd; 320, Jenny Pate/ Hutchinson Library; 321, Chris Caldicott/ Axiom Photographic Agency Ltd; 322, Picturesque Inc/Trip & Art Directors Photo Library; 323, Robert Frerck/ Gettyone/Stone; 324, John Elk III/Elk Photo; 325, Mireille Vautier; 326, Ask Images/Trip & Art Directors Photo Library; 327, Erwin and Peggy Bauer; 328, Susan Kaye; 328/329, Robert and Linda Mitchell; 330, Richard Bailey/Corbis UK Ltd.; 331, Mireille Vautier; 332, Richard A Cooke III/Gettyone/Stone; 333, Suzanne Murphy-Larronde; 334, Chris Sharp/ South American Pictures; 335, Larry Dunmire/The Paradise Library; 336, Eleanor S. Morris; 337, Macduff Everton/CORBIS UK Ltd.; 338, EJB Hawkins LMPA/Eye Ubiquitous; 339, Larry Dunmire/The Paradise Library; 340/341, Mireille Vautier-Paris; 342/343, Mireille Vautier-Paris; 344, Suzanne Murphy-Larronde; 345, Scott Doggett/ Lonely Planet; 346, Mireille Vautier-Paris; 347, Sergio Dorantes/CORBIS UK Ltd.

The world's largest nonprofit scientific and educational organization, the National Geographic Society was founded in 1888 "for the increase and diffusion of geographic knowledge." Since then it has supported scientific exploration and spread information to its more than nine million members worldwide.

The National Geographic Society educates and inspires millions every day through magazines, books, television programs, videos, maps and atlases, research grants, the National Geography Bee, teacher workshops, and innovative classroom materials.

The Society is supported through membership dues, charitable gifts, and income from the sale of its educational products. Members receive NATIONAL GEOGRAPHIC magazine—the Society's official journal—discounts on Society products, and other benefits.

For more information about the National Geographic Society, its educational programs, publications, or how to support its work, call 1-800-NGS-LINE (647-5463), or write to: National Geographic Society, 1145 17th Street, N.W., Washington, D.C. 20036 U.S.A.
Printed in the U.S.A.

Published by the National Geographic Society
John M. Fahey, Jr., *President and Chief Executive Officer*
Gilbert M. Grosvenor, *Chairman of the Board*
Nina D. Hoffman, *Executive Vice President,*
                President, Books and School Publishing
Kevin Mulroy, *Senior Vice President and Publisher*
Marianne Koszorus, *Design Director*
Kristin Hanneman, *Illustrations Director*
Elizabeth L. Newhouse, *Director of Travel Publishing*
Barbara A. Noe, *Series Editor*
Lawrence M. Porges, *Project Editor*
Cinda Rose, *Art Director*
Carl Mehler, *Director of Maps*
Nicholas P. Rosenbach, *Map Coordinator*
Gary Colbert, *Production Director*
Richard S. Wain, *Production Project Manager*
Jennifer Davis, Judy Klein, Amy Jicha, Amy Jones, Rachel Sweeney, Ruth Thompson, Mapping Specialists, *Contributors to 2006 edition*

First edition: Edited and designed by AA Publishing (a trading name of Automobile Association Developments Limited, whose registered office is Norfolk House, Priestley Road, Basingstoke, Hampshire, England RG24 9NY. Registered number: 1878835).
Rachel Alder & Marilynne Lanng, *Project Managers*
David Austin, *Senior Art Editor*
Sue Gordon, *Senior Editor*
Jo Tapper, *Designer*
Inna Nogeste, *Senior Cartographic Editor*
Cartography by AA Cartographic Production
Richard Firth, *Production Director*
Steve Gilchrist, *Prepress Production Controller*
Picture Research by Debbie Ireland
Cutaway illustrations (pp. 200–201, 262–263, and 292–293) drawn by Maltings Partnership, Derby, England
Coral reef illustration (pp. 318–319) by Ann Winterbotham

Second Edition 2006, ISBN 0-7922-5319-1

Library of Congress Cataloging-in-Publication Data for the first edition:
 Onstott, Jane.
         The National Geographic Traveler : Mexico / Jane Onstott.
     p. cm.
         Includes index.
         ISBN 0-7922-7897-6
         1. Mexico--Guidebooks. 2. Mexico--Description and travel. 3. Mexico--Tours I. Title.
         F1209 .067 2001
         917.204'836--dc21   2001042784

Printed and bound by Cayfosa Quebecor, Barcelona, Spain.
Color separations by Leo Reprographic Ltd., Hong Kong.
Cover separations by L.C. Repro, Aldermaston, U.K.

Visit the society's Web site at http://www.nationalgeographic.com

The information in this book has been carefully checked and to the best of our knowledge is accurate. However, details are subject to change, and the National Geographic Society cannot be responsible for such changes, or for errors or omissions. Assessments of sites, hotels, and restaurants are based on the author's subjective opinions, which do not necessarily reflect the publisher's opinion. The publisher cannot be responsible for any consequences arising from the use of this book.

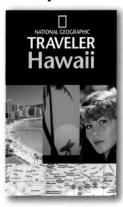